THE INVESTIGATOR'S LEGAL HANDBOOK

Gordon Scott Campbell
B.A., LL.B., B.C.L.
of the British Columbia, Ontario and Nova Scotia Bars

THOMSON
™
CARSWELL

Library and Archives Canada Cataloguing in Publication

Campbell, Gordon Scott
    The investigator's legal handbook / Gordon Scott Campbell.

Includes bibliographical references and index.
ISBN 0-459-24297-0

    1. Criminal investigation—Canada—Handbooks, manuals, etc.
I. Title.

KE9265.C35 2006   363.250971   C2006-904422-8
KF9620.ZA2C35 2006

Composition: Computer Composition of Canada Inc.

One Corporate Plaza   **Customer Relations:**
2075 Kennedy Road   Toronto 1-416-609-3800
Toronto, Ontario   Elsewhere in Canada/U.S. 1-800-387-5164
M1T 3V4   Fax 1-416-298-5082
                              E-mail: carswell.orders@thomson.com
                              Internet: http://www.carswell.com

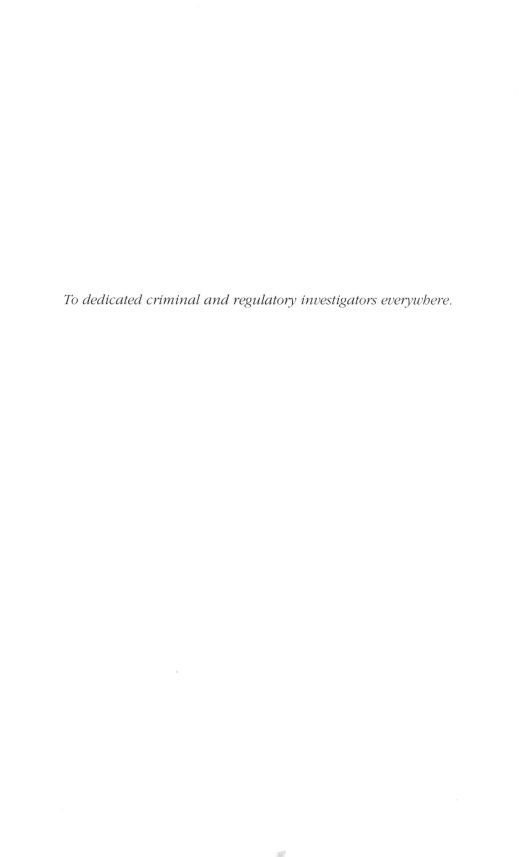

To dedicated criminal and regulatory investigators everywhere.

ACKNOWLEDGMENTS

This book was inspired by the many great conversations I have had over the years with criminal and regulatory investigators in the course of conducting prosecutions, giving legal advice, and providing training in diverse parts of Canada. The knowledge I took away from those conversations has, I hope, led to a work designed to serve the interests of investigators. Among the people I would particularly like to thank for contributing to this book through discussing with me the correct way to think about some of its concepts, reviewing portions of it, working on technical aspects of its publication or generally providing moral support are Kevin Anderson, Joan Barrett, Ivan Bloom, John Brooks, Phyllis DeGioia, Julia Gulej, Patrick Healy, Catherine Leek, Ken Mathies, Andrew Lawetz, David Lepofsky, Eileen Malischewski, Bradley Reitz, Cameron Suggitt, Paul Tinsley, John Vassi Nagy, Keith Veinot and especially Natalie Rowe, Catherine Campbell and George Campbell.

I would be pleased to hear comments from anyone who is reading this book. I can be reached at *gsc@publiclawadvocacy.com*. You may also be interested in the public law resource centre I maintain at *www.publiclawadvocacy.com*.

All the views expressed in this book are mine alone, acting in my personal capacity.

Summary Table of Contents

TABLE OF CONTENTS

DEMYSTIFYING THE LAW AND FOSTERING EFFECTIVE WORKING RELATIONSHIPS

To prevent crime and disorder as an alternative to their repression by military force and by severity of legal punishment.

> Sir Robert Peel, *Principles of Policing*, 1829, quoted in R.J. Marin, *Policing in Canada: Issues for the 21ˢᵗ Century* (Aurora, ON: Canada Law Book, 1979) at 179.

Counsel have a duty to see that all available legal proof of the facts is presented; it should be done firmly and pressed to its legitimate strength, but it also must be done fairly. The role of the prosecutor excludes any notion of winning or losing . . . .

> *R. v. Boucher*, [1955] S.C.R. 16 at 23-24.

In This Chapter

- How this book can help you
- Why this book was written
- The theme of demystification of the law
- The theme of early investigator-prosecutor contact

HOW THIS BOOK CAN HELP YOU

This book provides Canadian criminal and regulatory investigators with enduring legal principles of good investigative practice that lead to sound decisions maximizing positive outcomes at all stages of investigations and prosecutions. Faced with choices like whether to search or not search, charge or not charge, include or not include in the prosecution brief, it is only through sound and well informed decision-making that an investigator will survive the many legal pitfalls awaiting the unwary as a case progresses from first suspicion to exhaustion of the final appeal. I argue in this book that demystification of the law and early investigator-prosecutor contact are the two themes to follow that will best lead to sound decisions being made at every stage of the investigation and prosecution process, which in turn will result in case success.

Demystification of the law is possible through focusing on fundamental legal principles that change little over time, instead of being encumbered by a host of constantly changing court decisions. This book only mentions specific cases to give some context to the principles set out, to help you deal with prosecutors from a position of knowledge, and to illustrate how good or bad case outcomes often result from the applied legal knowledge of the investigators involved. Appropriate early investigator-prosecutor contact derives from understanding how involving prosecutors in your investigations and becoming actively involved at the prosecution stages of a case yourself will make your life easier and your cases more successful. Sometimes demystification of the law will suffice in formulating legally appropriate investigative action, but at other times only formal legal advice will do.

WHY THIS BOOK WAS WRITTEN

As a criminal and constitutional lawyer who has dealt with investigators from local, regional and national police and regulatory agencies during a host of investigations and prosecutions throughout Canada, I have come to realize there will never be enough time or money to complete definitively all the training that is needed for the difficult jobs done by all investigators. Not only is the law just one of the many necessary components of investigator training, but the ever-changing nature of the law makes it one of the most difficult training elements to maintain at an up-to-date level. This book seeks to fill legal knowledge gaps. It can be used collectively by investigators as a ready reference source on the road or in an office, as a training tool in classroom settings by instructors, or individually as a study tool by investigators who want to acquire a lasting understanding of the law as it affects their work.

An overarching goal of this book is to break down compartmentalized thinking that walls off investigations from subsequent prosecutions. While there are sound legal and policy reasons for maintaining a formal distinction between the roles of investigators and prosecutors, in practice investigation and prosecution processes are both part of a seamless continuum where without legally sound investigation there can be no prosecution, and without competent prosecution all investigative efforts are wasted. Lawful investigation leading to sound prosecution results in justice both being done and being perceived by the public to be done. Only through increased involvement of investigators and prosecutors in each other's traditional realms can a better level of mutual understanding develop among them about the challenges each group faces, which is a precondition to greater cooperative effectiveness. Joint initiatives like Integrated Proceeds of Crime and Integrated Market Enforcement units, where investigators and prosecutors are co-located to facilitate a holistic view of complex case investigation and prosecution from the earliest stages of first suspicion, promote such effectiveness.

Knowing the Law

Q&A

Q: If I had wanted to be a lawyer, I would have gone to law school. Why is it my job as an investigator to know so much about the law?

A: Perhaps the best way to think of the distinction between investigators and lawyers when it comes to knowing the law is that it is the job of the investigator to apply the law in its most accepted, non-controversial form, while it is the government lawyer's job to push the envelope on interpreting the law, recommending changes to the law, and acting as an advocate in court to promote a view of the law that favours the public interest. The investigator's challenge lies in discovering the facts using the available law. The lawyer's challenge is to find the law to fit the facts as discovered.

THE THEME OF DEMYSTIFICATION OF THE LAW

The first theme of demystification of the law holds that the law should be an easy to understand tool in the hands of every investigator, not some dusty rare book locked away in a lawyer's office. The process of demystification of the law involves stripping away the clutter. The law is not as complicated as it seems, it is the clutter that gets in the way of understanding. Clutter is created by a proliferation of wordy legislation and even wordier court judgments. There are ways for you to clear away this clutter and focus on the few principles you need to know. Those principles rarely change.

For investigators, three fundamental legal questions must be answered in every case.

1. What law do I need to look at in order to verify compliance or gather evidence of offences?

2. What law covers the possible charges?

3. What law addresses the procedure once charges are laid?

The first and second questions are of the greatest importance, but knowing the answer to the third question lets investigators continue to play a meaningful and proactive post-charge role.

Although I highly recommend that the advice of prosecutors be sought out at the earliest stages of unusual or complex cases, the reality is there will always be many more investigators than prosecutors in Canada. Investigators will be on their own in applying the law to their work at least some of the time, particularly when quick decisions have to be made. Demystification of the law enables you to figure out the answers to those three fundamental questions without being completely dependent on lawyers.

You may not realize what a strong base of legal knowledge you already possess as an investigator. You may already know the offence provisions of the Acts or Regulations you commonly deal with better than the lawyers. You may also have a better grasp of certain basic aspects of the investigative law because of the quick decisions you have to make every day involving that law. It is only for post-charge procedure and evidence law that a prosecutor will likely know significantly more than you do. However, it is still vital for investigators to have some familiarity with this post-charge law; painstakingly collected evidence can be worthless if it does not comply with the rules of courtroom admissibility or a required pretrial notice is forgotten.

Demystification of the law empowers you to take charge of all your investigative functions without being paralyzed by the fear of making a legal error. Reading legislation becomes a useful task if you know that it means what it says. Reading individual cases becomes much less important when you realize that each case is somewhat restricted to its specific facts, may soon be overruled by a higher court or reinterpreted by the same court, and can sometimes be subject to an infinite variety of legal interpretations.

1. Demystifying Changes in the Law

Since it can be difficult even for lawyers to keep up with all the new developments in the law, as an investigator you can't be expected to stay current on the latest legal nuances solely from your own research efforts. You will not be able to embrace demystification of the law if you focus too closely on fact-specific case law details. That is like getting too close to a mosaic where only each individual tile can be seen, making it impossible to appreciate the bigger picture. Demystifying the law requires you to fix long-standing basic legal principles in your mind, together with implementing effective systems of cooperation between investigators and prosecutors that inform you about new and important legal interpretations in a distilled form, rather than forcing yourself to bear the full weight of possibly innumerable, meandering and conflicting case law developments.

Legislation and the common law contain the basic investigative powers and procedures investigators should focus on because they rarely change. The Supreme Court of Canada and provincial appellate courts occasionally come out with significant decisions interpreting those powers and procedures, and sometimes legislators will add new powers or impose new requirements to use old powers. But even when powers and procedures are revised, the new law incrementally builds on the old. Change is not radical. If you know the old principles, the new principles lying beneath the surface of cases and legislation will usually only involve minor alterations to the law.

A completely new Act like the *Youth Criminal Justice Act*, S.C. 2002, c. 1, may initially look radically different from an old Act like the *Young Offenders Act*, R.S.C. 1985, c. Y-1, which dealt with the same subject, but probe deeper and you will usually discover the new Act addresses the same challenges in a different form with certain substantive improvements on the old legislation. The new Act will be part of legal evolution rather than revolution. Sure you will have to adjust your practice when a new Act affecting your work comes into force, but demystification of the law is possible because you will be able to build on your existing legal knowledge base rather than throwing out what you have already learned. Likewise, a new court case may be trumpeted as a total break from the past, but get past the hype and you will see that it relies on cases of decades past to incrementally place a new gloss of interpretation on the law that may be important to know, but can often be distilled down to one sentence like: "give the legal aid 1-800 telephone number when you are advising someone under arrest of rights to counsel."

Dealing with Changes in the Law

Q & A

Q: If the law is always changing, how could I possibly rely on your book? Won't the law have changed shortly after this book was published?

A: This book takes a different approach from only telling you what the law was back on the day the content was finalized. It arms you with a framework of legal principles that will remain solid for a long time to come, together with skills that empower you to find and interpret changes in the law both through your own efforts and by engaging in early investigator-prosecutor contact.

2. Demystifying the *Canadian Charter of Rights and Freedoms*

The only truly radical change to the way the criminal law operates in Canada since it was codified in 1892 happened ninety years later when a new era in Canadian investigations and prosecutions was born on the 1st of July 1982 with the coming into force of the *Canadian Charter of Rights and Freedoms.* You shouldn't be put off from the goal of demystification of the law by the huge impact the *Charter* has had. The intimidating aspect of the *Charter* rests in its consequences, not in its language. Use this book's checklists to ensure you have at least considered the basic principles of the *Charter*, and delve into those principles in more detail within this book's chapters. A broad interpretation of the *Charter* on your part won't paralyze your investigations; it will simply ensure your investigative efforts are not wasted by a court finding a legally risky investigation you ran breached an accused's constitutional rights.

How to Be Sure About What the *Charter* Means

Q & A

Q: It seems that none of the lawyers I speak with can ever agree on what the *Charter* means, so how am I supposed to understand it?

A: The brevity of the *Charter* means it contains many gray areas, but now in its third decade of operation its basic guiding principles have been well established. Stick to those basic principles focusing on the literal language of the *Charter* when you conduct the daily business of law enforcement and you will be able to uphold its values while still getting the job done.

THE THEME OF EARLY INVESTIGATOR-PROSECUTOR CONTACT

The second theme, early investigator-prosecutor contact, is highly beneficial even after the law has been demystified. You will derive the greatest benefit from that contact if you know precisely when contact should occur, and are able to manage contact to your advantage.

1. When to Contact Prosecutors

The growing urgency of investigator-prosecutor contact as a case progresses is illustrated in Figure 1-1, Investigator-Prosecutor Contact Timeline. The necessity of contact increases commensurate with an increase in:

- the stage of investigation; and

- case factual complexity.

The later the stage of the investigative process, and the greater the complexity of the case, the more advisable for you to make a prosecutor aware of the existence of your investigation and seek specific legal advice on how to proceed further. More intrusive investigative techniques will generally be used at later stages of investigation, making investigator-prosecutor contact more urgent. Some investigative techniques like wiretaps will by themselves require mandatory investigator-prosecutor contact because of legislative requirements, but the timeline implicitly takes such mandatory pre-charge contact into account if you presume any wiretap case will fall into the high or very high complexity zones necessitating earlier contact.

When I use the term "prosecutor" in urging early contact, I mean any criminal law advisor. Usually the person giving investigators legal advice will be the same person taking the case to trial, or at least working in the same office as other prosecutors, but the expansion of integrated enforcement teams and new models of delivering legal services to investigative agencies is leading to greater instances of investigators having in-house criminal law advisors who do not prosecute cases. These advisors are, however, usually employed or retained by a provincial or federal attorney general instead of by the investigative agency, and so act somewhat like prosecutors in their independence from investigators. As a case progresses up to the point of mandatory contact, which could be when you seek authorization for an investigative technique requiring prosecutor involvement, submit a case for charge approval, or lay charges, Figure 1-1 illustrates that there will be increasing pressure on investigators to connect with prosecutors for advice.

Fig 1-1 | INVESTIGATOR - PROSECUTOR CONTACT TIMELINE

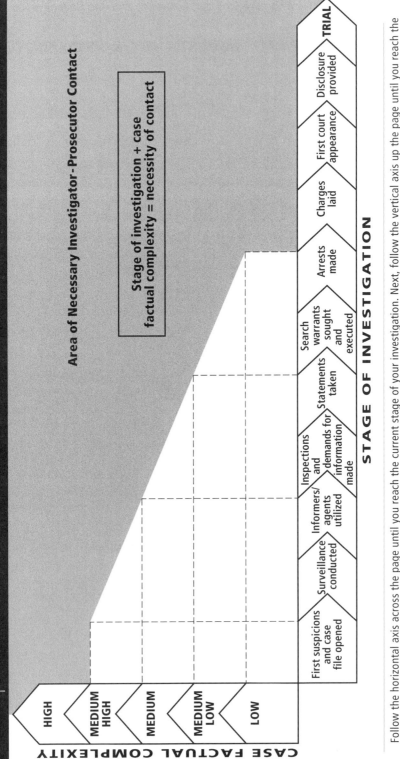

Follow the horizontal axis across the page until you reach the current stage of your investigation. Next, follow the vertical axis up the page until you reach the factual complexity level of your case. Mark the point where the stage of investigation and complexity intersect. The closer the point is to the shaded mandatory contact area, the greater the necessity for investigator-prosecutor contact

2. Managing Investigator-Prosecutor Contact

In order to flourish, any relationship needs to be managed so the parties understand their respective obligations and there are incentives to continue the relationship. The *Memorandum of Understanding Between the Royal Canadian Mounted Police and the Federal Prosecution Service Respecting the Conduct of Criminal Investigations and Prosecutions* (Ottawa, 5 July 2001) (MOU) is representative of agreements where investigators and prosecutors have jointly recognized the merits of early investigator-prosecutor contact. The MOU at para. 3 emphasizes the on-going nature of investigator-prosecutor contact, and the value of investigators and prosecutors assisting each other outside the realm of their respective traditional duties:

> In the exercise of their respective mandates the parties reinforce and respect the independence of each other, while recognizing the need to work together toward common goals. Generally, the RCMP are responsible for the investigation whereas prosecutors are responsible for carrying out the prosecution. Prosecutors can, however, play an important role at the investigative stage as can the RCMP at the prosecution stage.

Because this MOU is publicly available and national in scope, portions of it are referred to throughout this book as examples of the formalized cooperative relations that can be developed by investigators and prosecutors. Other more or less detailed national, regional or local investigator-prosecutor operating arrangements are possible. While establishing early investigator-prosecutor contact does not require anything in writing, written arrangements are a powerful reminder of the balanced nature of mutual obligations in the investigator-prosecutor relationship, and can serve to prevent disagreements from developing into full-blown inter-departmental rows.

It is relatively easy to delineate the traditional realms of investigator and prosecutor responsibilities. In Canada prosecutors don't run investigations, and investigators don't run prosecutions. *R. v. Trang* (2002), 311 A.R. 284, 2002 ABQB 286 at para. 72 succinctly confirmed this point even where a prosecutor was part of an Integrated Proceeds of Crime unit:

> I find that the term "investigative team", which appears in the Department of Justice's *Deskbook* regarding IPOC counsel, is misleading. One has to look at the context of the roles of the members of the IPOC unit to determine what function they fulfill.

> Although Ms. T. . . is described as a member of a team, the evidence is that her role had nothing to do with investigation in terms of conducting surveillance, dealing with informers, monitoring, etc. Rather, the evidence before the Court is that she provided legal advice, obtained judicial orders, and worked with the police in organizing disclosure. To liken this role to that of a junior police officer is to compare apples and oranges.

Even when a "team" approach is taken to developing a case, investigators are the ones who gather the evidence and prosecutors deal with the legal aspects of the case.

It is your responsibility as an investigator to run your case as you see fit. Prosecutors can only offer advice, and may not always be available to do even that. You are the one who ultimately has to make the hard decisions about what to do next during the investigation phase of a case, be it an inquiry into impaired driving or an international drug conspiracy, but carefully managing your relationships with prosecutors will maximize your prospects of effective investigation leading to successful prosecution.

In properly delineating respective investigator-prosecutor responsibilities in a case, you need to avoid "Blame the Other Person Syndrome" (BTOPS). When "bad" case results happen because of development, presentation or consideration difficulties, and they will always happen in an adversarial trial system as exists in Canada and many other common law countries, investigators, prosecutors and the courts may blame each other for perceived shortcomings. This is particularly so where it seems like the accused was up to no good, but either constitutional rights violations during the investigation or the questions witnesses were asked at trial or 1001 other possible deficiencies sunk the case. Better results in future cases are usually possible if investigators and prosecutors take responsibility for deficiencies.

BTOPS is characterized by a lack of introspection, leading to the conclusion that the bad result is always somebody else's fault, and thus someone else's problem to remedy. I have certainly been guilty of it myself on occasion — wrongly figuring that since my presentation of the case was so flawless, either the quality of the investigation or of the judging must be responsible for the adverse result. And I have been blamed on more than one occasion by frustrated investigators who figured that their investigative techniques couldn't possibly be responsible for the result. BTOPS leads to entrenchment of deficient case development practices, with mistakes being repeated over and over. It is through increased investigator-prosecutor cooperation at the earliest stage of a case that BTOPS can be overcome, leading to standards of case investigation and presentation being improved, better acceptance of the evidence by the courts and better case results.

Legal knowledge is best applied during an investigation to keep a case moving forward from left to right along the Figure 1-1 timeline so that a decision can be made on charging. You need to avoid having your case stall because of legal bottlenecks; there are almost always steps that can be taken to unplug those bottlenecks or at least move an investigation in a different direction while legal problems in one area of a case are sorted out. Following the theme of demystification of the law empowers all investigators to personally keep their cases moving over less significant legal hurdles; embracing the theme of early investigator-prosecutor contact will keep those cases moving even when they hit major legal walls.

How Early Should Early Investigator-Prosecutor Contact Take Place?

Q & A

Q: When you advocate early investigator-prosecutor contact, is there such a thing as establishing contact too early?

A: The timing of contact will depend on the purpose of that contact, but the sooner the better is a sound principle to follow. Contact for advice on drafting a warrant obviously needs to take place before you kick in the door of a residence. Contact for advice on drafting charges must occur before those charges are laid. Contact on who will be required witnesses for trial can happen considerably after warrants are executed and charges laid, but still needs to take place a sufficient time prior to trial that any witness can be notified before making conflicting commitments.

For Demystifying the Law and Fostering Effective Working Relationships

KEY POINTS

✓ Demystification of the law involves stripping away the clutter and focusing on a few fundamental legal principles that will change little over time. In every case investigators must answer the questions: what law do I need to look at in order to verify compliance or gather evidence, what law covers the possible charges and what law addresses the procedure once changes are laid.

KEY POINTS

✓ The best demystification of the law practice to follow where the *Charter* is concerned is to do everything reasonably possible to affirm people's rights. Taking a broad interpretation of the *Charter* will not paralyze investigations, but rather will ensure that investigative efforts are not wasted due to courts finding legally risky investigative practices amounted to constitutional violations.

✓ The urgency of early investigator-prosecutor contact increases with a case's factual complexity and the stage of an investigation.

✓ Demystification of the law empowers investigators to keep a case moving over less significant legal hurdles, while early investigator-prosecutor contact can keep a case going even in the face of major legal challenges.

FURTHER READING

Cases

Nelles v. Ontario, [1989] 2 S.C.R. 170. Summarizes prosecutorial powers in the course of discussing what would amount to an improper exercise of those powers: "Among the many powers of a prosecutor are the following: the power to detain in custody, the power to prosecute, the power to negotiate a plea, the power to charge multiple offences, the power of disclosure/non-disclosure of evidence before trial, the power to prefer an indictment, the power to proceed summarily or by indictment, the power to withdraw charges, and the power to appeal" (at 192).

R. v. Boucher, [1955] S.C.R. 16. The seminal case on the role of the prosecutor.

R. v. Campbell, [1999] 2 S.C.R. 956. Discusses the nature of the relationship between prosecutors who give legal advice and the investigators who receive it, and why that advice must be disclosed if investigators rely on it in court to justify their actions.

R. v. Regan, [2002] 1 S.C.R. 297. Explains the rationale for the separation in functions between police and prosecutors.

R. v. Stinchcombe, [1991] 3 S.C.R. 326. Discusses why the initial decision on disclosure relevance is left to the discretion of prosecutors.

Books, Articles, and Reports

D.G. Burrow, *A Practical Guide to Criminal Prosecutions* (Toronto: Carswell, 1992). Intended for beginning prosecutors, this book also gives investigators a good idea about some of the common legal and ethical issues both investigators and prosecutors face.

M. Code, "Crown Counsel's Responsibilities When Advising the Police at the Pre-Charge Stage" (1998) 40 Crim. L.Q. 326.

P. Ceyssens, *Legal Aspects of Policing*, loose-leaf, 2 vols. (Saltspring Island, BC: Earlscourt, 1994). Comprehensive coverage of the civil and administrative law of policing, including the potential civil liability and disciplinary consequences of exceeding criminal and regulatory powers as an investigator.

R.J. Frater, "The Seven Deadly Prosecutorial Sins" (2002) 7 Can. Crim L. Rev. 209. A lively look at what happens when prosecutors get carried away with their jobs and powers, and why they need to be honest, fair and diligent in executing their duties.

Law Reform Commission of Canada, *Working Paper No. 62 — Controlling Criminal Prosecutions: The Attorney General and Crown Prosecutors* (Ottawa: Law Reform Commission of Canada, 1990).

A. Marin, *The Guide to Investigations and Prosecutions: a Critical Analysis of the Modern Legal Obligations Imposed on Investigators and Prosecutors* (Aurora, ON: Canada Law Book, 1995).

A-R. Nadeau & J. Reid, *Annotated Royal Canadian Mounted Police Act and Regulations*, 3rd ed. (Cowansville, Que: Yvon Blais, 2003).

M. Proulx & D. Layton, *Ethics and Canadian Criminal Law* (Toronto: Irwin Law, 2001). Primarily devoted to defence counsel ethics, this work also contains useful material on what prosecutors can and cannot do ethically.

P.C. Stenning, *Appearing for the Crown: A Legal and Historical Review of Criminal Prosecutorial Authority in Canada* (Cowansville, Que: Brown Legal Publications, 1986).

CHAPTER TWO

FINDING AND INTERPRETING THE LAW

To-day there is only one principle or approach, namely, the words of an Act are to be read in their entire context in their grammatical and ordinary sense harmoniously with the scheme of the Act, the object of the Act and the intention of Parliament.

E.A Driedger, *The Construction of Statutes*
(Toronto: Butterworths, 1974) at 67.

In This Chapter

- Basic principles for interpreting any law
- Four tricks of interpretation
- Where to find the law that will help you most
- Interpreting the impact of the *Charter*

BASIC PRINCIPLES FOR INTERPRETING ANY LAW

Crystal balls, Ouija boards, tealeaves — sometimes it may feel like all of them are needed to divine the meaning of a troublesome law, but I will let you in on a little secret: the law means what it says. While there are various legal principles that can be applied to interpreting confusing laws, believe it or not the law generally means no more, or less, than what is written on the page. There is nothing so mystical about the law that only the lawyers have the ability to understand it. The trick is that the law must be read, and reread, every time you intend to rely on it.

Your memory will lie to you, but the law is never more than a book or Internet connection away. To be able to interpret what you are reading, just follow the principles that the words of an Act or Regulation should:

- be given their ordinary, grammatical meaning;

- read harmoniously with the other words and context of the Act or Regulation;

- read consistently with the purpose of the Act or Regulation; and

- read consistently with the intent of legislators who originally brought the Act or Regulation into being.

Check out Figure 2-1, Steps to Interpreting a Law Flow Chart, to see the logical progression interpretation takes. Sometimes you will come up with an acceptable meaning short of following all those steps, while at other times you will wind up at the end of the flow chart still having an unresolved meaning. Remember interpretation is a logical process, with set rules leading to a sensible answer.

First, isolate the words of the Act or Regulation to be interpreted. As statutory provisions interact, like earlier definitions influencing later operative sections, make sure you have isolated all necessary provisions before beginning your interpretation exercise. Next, if you have access to an annotated Act or Regulations, or can type the provision you need to know about into an Internet legal search engine like the one at the Canadian Legal Information Institute (*www.canlii.ca*), you may be able to determine if one leading court case has produced a definitive interpretation. It is most likely that cases will be helpful, but not the last word on the subject.

After checking cases, focus on the text of the Act or Regulation to consider what meaning would be most grammatical. Strive for precision, clarity and common sense. Carefully weigh the nouns, pronouns, adjectives, verbs, adverbs, prepositions and punctuation — they are all there for a reason. Acts and Regulations in more than one authentic language can be interpreted through reconciling a common meaning among them.

An Act or Regulation works as a whole document whose larger context requires considering the purpose of legislation and intent of the drafters. The preamble may say up front exactly what the purpose was meant to be. For example, the *Canadian Environmental Protection Act, 1999*, S.C. 1999, c. 33, contains a very extensive 15-paragraph preamble preceded by the following declaration:

> It is hereby declared that the protection of the environment is essential to the well-being of Canadians and that the primary purpose of this Act is to contribute to sustainable development through pollution prevention.

Fig 2-1 | STEPS TO INTERPRETING A LAW FLOW CHART

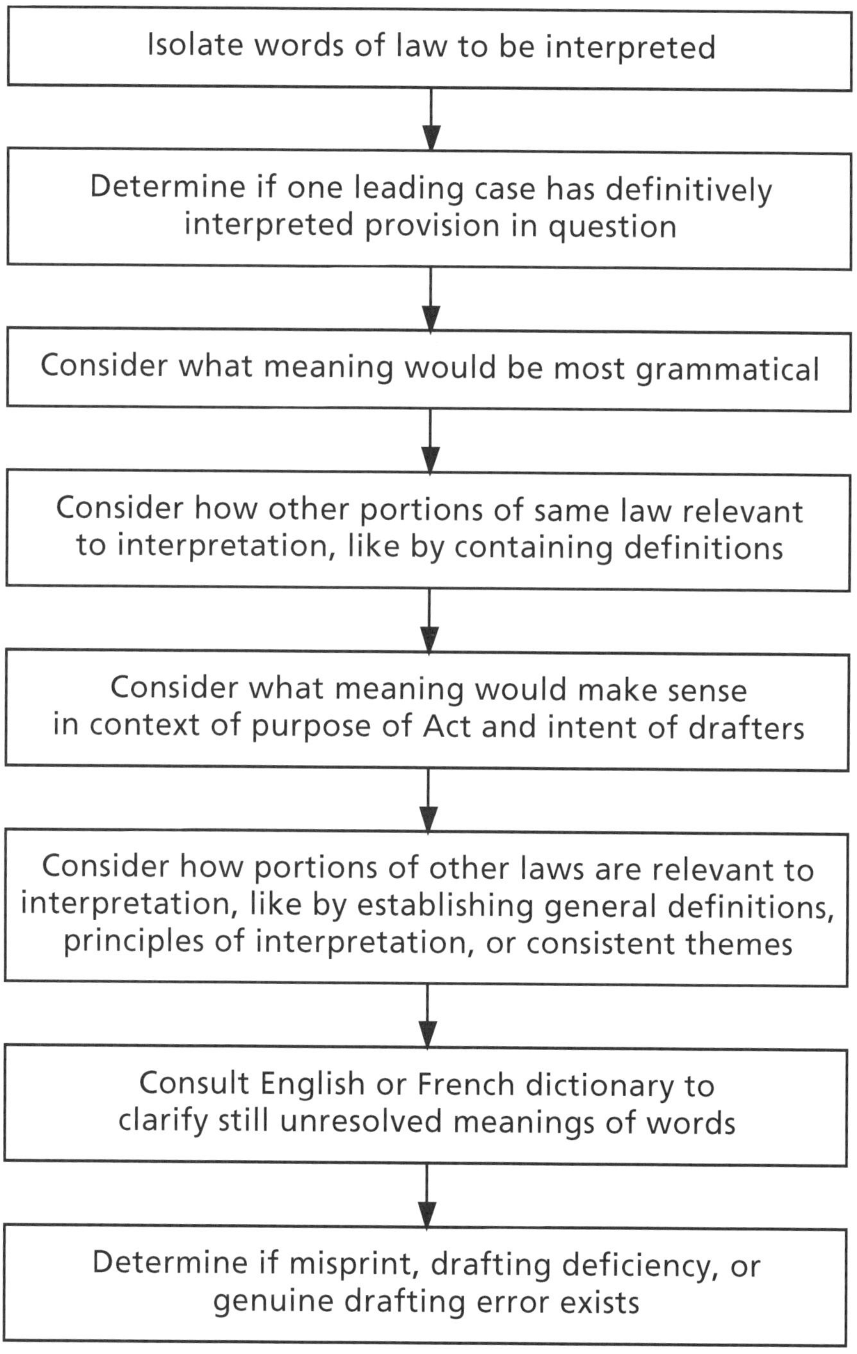

Isolate words of law to be interpreted

↓

Determine if one leading case has definitively interpreted provision in question

↓

Consider what meaning would be most grammatical

↓

Consider how other portions of same law relevant to interpretation, like by containing definitions

↓

Consider what meaning would make sense in context of purpose of Act and intent of drafters

↓

Consider how portions of other laws are relevant to interpretation, like by establishing general definitions, principles of interpretation, or consistent themes

↓

Consult English or French dictionary to clarify still unresolved meanings of words

↓

Determine if misprint, drafting deficiency, or genuine drafting error exists

Because legislators are presumed to have intended something sensible addressing a particular problem when they went to the trouble of passing an Act or Regulation, considering purpose and intent should prevent ambiguous, obscure or manifestly absurd meanings. Acts and Regulations also need to be interpreted in a manner consistent with laws in the same category (like all federal laws relating to the environment), unless a clear intent has been expressed that a newer law supercedes other laws. Portions of laws on any subject passed by the same legislature can be relevant to interpretation by establishing general definitions, principles of interpretation or consistent themes applicable to all Acts and Regulations.

One Legal Interpretation Rule to Remember

Q & A

Q: If, at least to start, I remember only one rule on reading and understanding the law, what should it be?

A: Focus on Driedger's Golden Rule of statutory construction: look at the fundamental purpose of the Act, then apply some common sense and good grammar. There are many other nuances to interpretation, but this rule is a very sound general guide.

FOUR TRICKS OF INTERPRETATION

In interpreting any Act like the *Criminal Code*, there are a few tricks that are helpful to know.

1. Interpretation Trick #1: Look for Definitions Right in the Act or Regulation

If you are trying to figure out the legal meaning of a particular word, check first if it has been explicitly defined at another point in the Act either near the start of the entire Act (around s. 2), the start of a Part (like Part III of the *Criminal Code*) or the start of the section you are interested in (like s. 254 of the *Code*). For example, general terms like "Peace Officer" are defined in s. 2 of the *Criminal Code*, a more precise term like "ammunition" is defined at the beginning of Part III of the *Code* devoted to "Firearms and Other Weapons," and a very precise term like "approved screening device" is defined within s. 254 of the *Code* dealing with the taking of breath or blood samples. A relevant definition may even appear in another more general Act like the *Interpretation Act*, R.S.C. 1985 c. I-21, which defines terms like "Act" and "Regulation."

2. Interpretation Trick #2: Recognize the Difference between "And" and "Or"

Small details can be very important to interpreting Acts or Regulations. There is a vast difference between the words "and" and "or" being used to connect sub-sections of legislation. With "and," both described factors must usually be present in order for the section to be engaged, whereas with "or" either (or both) factors can be present. The significance of a comma (,) or a semi-colon (;) at the end of a sub-section without "and" or "or" immediately following depends on whether "and" or "or" is used later in the same enumeration of conditions. For example, s. 244 of the *Code* says:

> **244.** Every person who, with intent
>
> (a) to wound, maim or disfigure any person,
>
> (b) to endanger the life of any person, or
>
> (c) to prevent the arrest or detention of any person,
>
> discharges a firearm at any person, whether or not that person is the person mentioned in paragraph (a), (b) or (c), is guilty of an indictable offence and liable to imprisonment for a term not exceeding fourteen years and to a minimum punishment of imprisonment for a term of four years.

Here the offence is made out by satisfying *any* of s-ss. (a), (b), or (c) because of the "or" at the end of s-s. 244(b). The comma at the end of s-s. 244(a) acts like another "or" due to the "or" that follows at the end of the next sub-section.

By contrast, look at s-s. 462.38(2) of the *Code*:

> **462.38.** (2) Subject to sections 462.39 to 462.41, where an application is made to a judge under subsection (1), the judge shall, if the judge is satisfied that
>
> (a) any property is, beyond a reasonable doubt, proceeds of crime,
>
> (b) proceedings in respect of a designated offence committed in relation to that property were commenced, and

(c) the accused charged with the offence referred to in paragraph (b) has died or absconded,

order that the property be forfeited to Her Majesty to be disposed of as the Attorney General directs or otherwise dealt with in accordance with the law.

Because of the "and" after s-s. (b), all of s-ss. (a), (b), and (c) must be satisfied to successfully invoke this provision. Here the comma after s-s. 462.38(2)(a) acts like "and," instead of "or," because of the "and" appearing after s-s. 462.38(2)(b). You may find reading a confusing series of provisions aloud, while placing lots of verbal emphasis on the punctuation and connecting words, helps you figure out their meaning.

3. Interpretation Trick #3: Use an English or French Dictionary

A dictionary is a quick and easy way to define words not otherwise defined in an Act or Regulation. A legal dictionary can tell you the way past court cases have defined common words, but a regular dictionary is best for finding the ordinary meaning of a term. Even judges fall back on regular dictionaries in composing their judgments if they can't find another alternative. The Internet has revolutionized dictionary use, with many professional dictionaries now available free on-line and some Web sites facilitate multiple dictionary searches from only typing a single word into one search window.

4. Interpretation Trick #4: Don't Assume the Act or Regulation Was Perfectly Drafted

There may be genuine drafting errors, drafting deficiencies or misprints in the version of the Act or Regulation at which you are looking. If you see a provision that truly and after much thought just doesn't make any sense, check another version of the Act or Regulation to see if the wording is any different; go on-line if you are looking at printed material or get a book if you are looking at an electronic version. It could just be a misprint in the version you are reading, not an error in the authentic Act or Regulation passed by the legislature. The authentic versions of Acts and Regulations are most often the paper copies, but an electronic on-line copy may be more up-to-date and thus have incorporated necessary amendments fixing earlier drafting deficiencies.

If you still see what appears clearly to be an error in an Act or Regulation, like an entire word missing that really has to be there for the legislation to make sense, this could be a genuine drafting error that hopefully will be fixed through later legislative amendment. It may already have been fixed by the time you spot it since even on-line copies of Acts are not entirely up-to-date. If you see what is less clearly an error, but more a deficiency where the facts you are dealing with just aren't covered by the legislation, this may be an intentional omission by a legislature that didn't want to deal with a particular topic. Whether unintentional deficiency or intentional omission, there is not much you can do about laws that don't cover your situation except work around them by getting legal advice to confirm if your interpretation is correct and devise some kind of solution.

Figuring Out the Meaning of the Law

Q&A

Q: Figuring out what the law means isn't really something that we receive training on. How am I supposed to be able to figure it out by myself?

A: Simply read what the law says, then slavishly follow the ordinary meaning of the words unless told otherwise by someone with clearly more legal knowledge than you have. All too often, people needlessly complicate the law by reading in language that doesn't exist, or apply tortuous reasoning in attempts to divine a law's true meaning. Sometimes in making an argument in court lawyers will engage in seemingly bizarre linguistic gymnastics, but as an investigator there is no need for you to get involved in contortions of language. Following the ordinary meaning of words has limitless application: charge drafting is simplified through copying the text of the offence section without adding any kind of fancy additional wording; investigative powers become quite broad when language in an Act can be read as authorizing an action.

WHERE TO FIND THE LAW THAT WILL HELP YOU MOST

In addition to understanding some basic principles of legal interpretation, you also have to know where to find the law to which you are going to apply those new-found, handy interpretive principles. During the first couple of weeks of law school, we were initiated into the fold of legal research through the timeless tradition of the library scavenger hunt. Instead of Easter eggs, we were all sent off hunting in a panicked frenzy for obscure legal references in our labyrinthine library. Fortunately, you don't need even to set foot in a law library anymore to conduct good legal research. The Internet and possibly a couple of books should give you all you need to know. The dramatic way the Internet has transformed access to legal materials since the time I was in law school cannot be overstated. Instead of spending days hunting in airless law libraries like I did, only to find out the volume you need is out for rebinding, virtually all Acts and Regulations in Canada are now available to you in relatively up-to-date versions with only a couple of clicks of a computer mouse.

Learning the Law Step by Step

Q&A

Q: How I am supposed to interpret a law that I don't even know exists?

A: Stick to the basics. It is far better to know a lot about one law, than a little about many laws. First, learn your offences. With the exception of the *Criminal Code*, offence-creating sections make up a very small portion of most Acts. Next, learn some of the basic compliance verification or enforcement powers authorized by the Act you most commonly deal with. Information demand, inspection, search and seizure, and arrest are all key powers you may have. Knowing what legislative authority you have, how far that authority extends, and if judicial authorization is needed to use any of your powers can all be learned just from reading an Act you are appointed under. Don't worry about uncodified "common law" until you have the legislation down cold.

1. Why Focus on Legislative Sources

We are all drowning in case law since electronic reporting started to capture virtually all written and many oral court decisions rendered in every Canadian jurisdiction. The development of legislation is a slow, evolutionary process by comparison. Your compliance verification and enforcement powers are for the most part rooted in legislation, not case law. It is best to leave the interpretation of raw case law to the lawyers, and instead focus on understanding the basics of the legislation governing the offences you most commonly investigate. For many Canadian investigators the *Criminal Code* may be the only Act you ever have to look at, although picking it up is increasingly becoming a weight lifting exercise. Depending on your duties, you might also need to look at other federal or provincial Acts for offences or procedure. Provincial or territorial offence procedure will usually be contained in an Act called something like the "Summary Proceedings Act" or "Offence Act."

I increasingly keep electronic, on-line, free copies of the Acts I most commonly deal with on my computer so I can keyword search them to find those pesky statutory provisions I know are there, but which I can't find in the table of contents or index to any printed version of an Act. The more you work with an Act, the better you will understand its strengths, weaknesses and overall structure. All Acts have an inner beauty to be discovered — really, I am not kidding. When you read an Act you are reading about social history, public opinion, policy development, politics and judicial feedback.

Try to get a sense of an Act's overall structure beyond the two or twenty provisions to which you most commonly refer. It's possible to think about an Act as if it's an art gallery, where the Act's provisions are individual paintings. Some Acts may be composed of entirely new gallery acquisitions, but most Acts will have a collection of both old and new works. How are the paintings arranged on the walls? Which are the old paintings, and which are the new? Which ones perhaps need a bit of cleaning? Which ones are from a realism school, and which are the abstracts? Which ones hold the entire gallery collection together? Focusing on the Act's structure is crucial to demystification of the law, as it lets you navigate around an Act's provisions with ease and continue to understand the common legal threads even if later amendments change the text.

While you do need to stay current with your knowledge of legislative sources, there is no need to lose sleep over amendments to your powers, procedures or offences appearing without any warning. Usually years of problem identification are followed by many months of intra-governmental and sometimes public consultations, succeeded by a few months of draft legislation working its way through the political system. Once passed, new legislation will only come into force on a specified future date.

2. Embracing the Internet Research Revolution

Electronic sources are the future of legal research. Unannotated versions of virtually all federal (*laws.justice.gc.ca*) and provincial (*www.canlii.org*) Acts and Regulations are now on-line. Internet-based commercial research products like WestlaweCarswell LawSource (*www.westlawecarswell.com*) and LexisNexis QuickLaw (*www.lexisnexis.ca*) contain legislation, cases and commentary. Free on-line case law search tools are increasing in number, notably at the Canadian Legal Information Institute (*www.canlii.org*) and the World Legal Information Institute (*www.worldlii.org*).

While the Internet has largely eliminated the tedious paper statute updating process, try to stick with the official site of the Department of Justice or Ministry of the Attorney General responsible for the federal, provincial or territorial legislation with which you are dealing. Those Justice or A.G. sites are more likely to be up-to-date in their legislation offerings than are other sites, with the exception of fee-based sites like WestlaweCarswell. To get the absolutely up-to-date version of an Act if you don't have access to a fee-based site, start with the last official version on the relevant Attorney General's Web site, checking the site's currency date, then jump to recently passed bills on the Web site of the legislature checking for Acts that have come into force since that time. You should be able to spot relevant amending Acts through their names like "An Act to Amend the *Criminal Code* and . . . .", or at least through a full text search of new Acts for references to the Act you are updating. An amending Act will name each section of each Act that has been amended, and spell out the language to be added or deleted.

You may notice that the electronic versions of legislation found on official government Internet sites are often still termed "unofficial." This does not mean that they are any less reliable than printed sources, but reflects a still evolving level of comfort with electronic sources. Their unofficial status will likely only be an issue in the rare situation where you actually have to prove the authenticity of the legislation, in which case the official paper version will almost always prevail.

Notwithstanding the electronic research revolution, law libraries have an enduring value in containing annotated Acts giving short summaries of how provisions have been interpreted by the courts, books with in-depth explanations of the law, and older versions of statutes permitting you to ascertain the state of legislative prohibitions at the time an historic offence was committed. Even small towns throughout Canada have court house or county law association libraries with excellent collections that can usually be used by anyone with permission. Larger law society libraries exist in provincial and territorial capitals. Largest of all are the law school and Supreme Court of Canada libraries, but they are usually only needed for truly esoteric or foreign legal material and inter-library loans may be able to secure their material from a distance.

Dealing with the Deluge of Case Law

Q: Keeping up with legislative amendments is bad enough, but how am I ever supposed to keep up with all those court decisions that seem constantly to be changing the law?

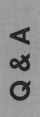

A: Even a specialist lawyer cannot completely keep up with all the decisions Canada's courts issue every day. Reading and understanding the full implications of court decisions is a much more difficult and less certain prospect than reading and understanding legislation. Although important, there might only be a couple of sentences of direct relevance to your work contained in a 50-page Supreme Court of Canada judgment. Either let the lawyers bring important cases to your attention, or take the initiative in approaching them for an interpretation of cases you hear about.

INTERPRETING THE IMPACT OF THE *CHARTER*

Some have said that the advent of the *Canadian Charter of Rights and Freedoms* in 1982 moved us from the trial of the accused to the trial of the investigation, where what is disputed in court is increasingly the legality of investigator conduct rather than the guilt or innocence of the accused. More recently, we may have been moving towards the trial of the prosecution, where the legality of prosecutor conduct is also routinely challenged at trial. While there is understandably some discomfort with the host of changes that have taken place in the law of investigations and prosecutions since 1982, I believe most of the change has been positive and the clock cannot be turned back to pre-1982 times. We all need to avoid nostalgia, be more flexible, and recognize that the changes have made the system fairer but more challenging.

How the evidence was gathered during an investigation is now scrutinized at trial like never before. Relevant and reliable evidence used to be admissible regardless of how it was obtained, as explained in *R. v. Honan* (1912), 26 O.L.R. 484; 20 C.C.C 10 (C.A.) at 16:

> the question is not, by what means was the evidence procured; but is, whether the things proved were evidence . . . the criminal who wields the "jimmy" or the bludgeon, or uses any other criminally unlawful means or methods, has no right to insist upon being met by the law only when in kid gloves or satin slippers; it is still quite permissible to "set a thief to catch a thief."

Compare that to what was said 83 years later in *R. v. Burlingham*, [1995] 2 S.C.R. 206 at 231: "the purpose of this [s-s. 24(2)] test is to oblige law enforcement authorities to respect the exigencies of the *Charter* and to preclude improperly obtained evidence from being admitted to the trial process when it impinges upon the fairness of the trial." Because the *Charter* is now in its third decade of operation, demystification of the law allows you to steer clear of the impermissible investigative action trends in favour of the acceptable action trends. Early investigator-prosecutor contact will assist you in determining precisely where the permissible action line is drawn if your investigation appears to be entering controversial *Charter* territory.

1. A Quick *Charter* Primer Right-by-Right

At only 34 brief sections, the *Charter* is far shorter than most other laws. Its brevity is largely a function of its constitutionally entrenched character. Demystification of the law simply requires you to take the *Charter* at face value, since its provisions for the most part really do mean what they say. You really only have to keep in mind fifteen sections of the *Charter* plus two additional sections of the *Constitution Act, 1982*, of which the *Charter* is a part, together with the other basic legal principles outlined in this book, to ensure your investigations don't run afoul of the *Charter*.

a. *The Reasonable Limits of Section 1*

Section 1 of the *Charter* doesn't create any stand-alone rights, but it provides for important limits on the rights later enumerated:

> **1.** The *Canadian Charter of Rights and Freedoms* guarantees the rights and freedoms set out in it subject only to such reasonable limits prescribed by law as can be demonstrably justified in a free and democratic society.

Section 1 has proved to be the key section of the *Charter* for ensuring investigative practices serving particularly important public purposes can continue to be legally used, even if on their faces they appear to violate *Charter* rights. Examples of practices so saved are random stops for the purposes of checking on impaired driving violations (otherwise found to breach s. 9 arbitrary detention protections) and making an impaired driving breath screening sample demand prior to providing access to counsel (otherwise found to breach s-s. 10(b) rights to counsel). Constitutional lawyers spend a lot of time arguing over s. 1, but investigators needn't worry too much about it. Section 1 operates invisibly behind the rest of the *Charter*, making sure sensible protections are not taken to extremes that paralyze the investigation and prosecution system. The courts will not permit *Charter* rights to interfere with reasonable investigative practices properly authorized by law that are consistent with free and democratic Canadian societal values.

b. *The Fundamental Freedoms of Section 2*

Section 2 of the *Charter* sets out what are referred to as the "fundamental freedoms," presumably because of the great importance to be placed on them:

> **2.** Everyone has the following fundamental freedoms:
>
> (a) freedom of conscience and religion;
>
> (b) freedom of thought, belief, opinion and expression, including freedom of the press and other media of communication;
>
> (c) freedom of peaceful assembly; and
>
> (d) freedom of association.

Of these four freedoms, s-s. 2(b) is likely of greatest concern to investigators because of how it affects investigations into obscenity, child pornography and hate literature, as well as attempts to secure evidence from media outlets. If you think any of your cases might have s. 2 *Charter* implications, early investigator-prosecutor contact is imperative to avoid later costly and possibly futile legal battles.

c. *The Ever Expanding Scope of Section 7*

Section 7 is the *Charter* section whose meaning is perhaps the most difficult to discern just from looking at it:

> **7.** Everyone has the right to life, liberty and security of the person and the right not to be deprived thereof except in accordance with the principles of fundamental justice.

While all Canadians might agree that life, liberty and security are good things to protect, s. 7's general expression of values rather than of concrete rights makes defining its content quite difficult. Section 7 has been the vessel into which the courts have poured investigation and prosecution rights content that doesn't neatly fit elsewhere, like the right to full and timely disclosure. Section 7 rights are not absolute, and may be taken away so long as the deprivation is "in accordance with the principles of fundamental justice" which has been found to be a rule of fairness and natural justice.

d. *The Reasonableness of Section 8*

Section 8 is probably the *Charter* section having the greatest affect on how investigators do their jobs, but may be the most straightforward section for meaning what it says:

> **8.** Everyone has the right to be secure against unreasonable search or seizure.

Section 8 does not offer any general protection from search and seizure, only a protection from "unreasonable" search and seizure. The courts have, after working through thousands upon thousands of s. 8 cases, now offered solid guidance on the scope of s. 8 protection. While s. 8 has imposed a heavier burden to gather grounds and secure prior judicial authorization to engage in investigative actions that previously might not have needed the approval of a judge, legislators have responded to the burden by creating many new investigative tools. Section 8 shouldn't pose any great difficulties so long as investigators understand some basic principles governing when prior judicial authorization is needed, and how to draft documents seeking that approval. Warrantless searches and seizures must proceed under very well accepted legal authority in order not to incur the wrath of the courts who could exclude all evidence so gathered.

e. *The Not Arbitrary Nature of Section 9*

At only eleven words, s. 9 is the shortest *Charter* section of all:

> **9.** Everyone has the right not to be arbitrarily detained or imprisoned.

Section 9 only establishes a protection against arbitrariness, not a blanket protection against all forms of detention or imprisonment. Arrest or detention will *not* be arbitrary so long as a factual basis exists to support the use of the powers relied upon, like observing the commission of an indictable offence by a person to be arrested pursuant to s. 494 of the *Criminal Code*. Recent shocking examples of arbitrariness condemned by the courts include the practice of racial profiling, where an individual is detained for further investigation solely on the basis of his race, not on the basis of reasonable suspicion or reasonable and probable grounds to believe an offence has been committed.

f. *Elaborating on Section 10*

Section 10 *Charter* rights only arise after detention or arrest, instead of applying every time a private citizen interacts with an investigator:

> **10.** Everyone has the right on arrest or detention
>
> > (a) to be informed promptly of the reasons therefor;
> >
> > (b) to retain and instruct counsel without delay and to be informed of that right; and
> >
> > (c) to have the validity of the detention determined by way of *habeas corpus* and to be released if the detention is not lawful.

This is another *Charter* section best understood through a literal interpretation of meaning what it says. The difficulties with s. 10 largely arise from how the courts have interpreted and expanded upon the meaning of s-s. 10(b); only telling a detainee "you have the right to retain and instruct counsel without delay" no longer cuts it.

g. *The Late Engagement of the Wordy Section 11*

Section 11 is the wordiest *Charter* section of all, but is only engaged after charges are laid:

> **11.** Any person charged with an offence has the right
>
> > (a) to be informed without unreasonable delay of the specific offence;
> >
> > (b) to be tried within a reasonable time;
> >
> > (c) not to be compelled to be a witness in proceedings against that person in respect of the offence;
> >
> > (d) to be presumed innocent until proven guilty according to law in a fair and public hearing by an independent and impartial tribunal;
> >
> > (e) not to be denied reasonable bail without just cause;
> >
> > (f) except in the case of an offence under military law tried before a military tribunal, to the benefit of trial by jury where

the maximum punishment for the offence is imprisonment for five years or a more severe punishment;

(g) not to be found guilty on account of any act or omission unless, at the time of the act or omission, it constituted an offence under Canadian or international law or was criminal according to the general principles of law recognized by the community of nations;

(h) if finally acquitted of the offence, not to be tried for it again and, if finally found guilty and punished for the offence, not to be tried or punished for it again; and

(i) if found guilty of the offence and if the punishment for the offence has been varied between the time of commission and the time of sentencing, to the benefit of the lesser punishment.

The solely post-charge engagement of s. 11 is the key to interpreting and managing its myriad provisions. The clock does not start to run on s-s. 11(b) trial delay prior to charges being laid. Self-incrimination protections under s-s. 11(c) only arise after charges have been laid against the person being compelled to be a witness. The presumption of innocence and public hearing obligations of s-s. 11(d) don't apply at the investigative stage because criminal jeopardy has not been triggered through the laying of a charge. Sub-sections 11(e) through (i) also codify important rights afforded to an accused, but tend to mean what they clearly say; of most concern to investigators among those sub-sections is likely s-s. 11(e) which generally affirms reasonable bail as a right, not a privilege, unless the prosecution can justify deprivation of that right.

h. *The Sentencing Limits of Section 12*

Section 12 of the *Charter* is more a matter for prosecutors rather than investigators:

12. Everyone has the right not to be subjected to any cruel and unusual treatment or punishment.

Because of the primary role played by investigators in choosing charges to be laid, and the assistance they provide in formulating sentencing recommendations, investigators do need to understand there are constitutional limits on how far Canada's system of criminal and regulatory sanctions can go.

Proportionality must exist between the seriousness of the offence and severity of sanction. Thus *R. v. Morrissey*, [2000] 2 S.C.R. 90 at para. 54, upheld Parliament's imposition of a mandatory four-year minimum sentence for use of a firearm while committing certain serious offences on the basis that firearms offences are inherently serious:

> Extra vigilance is necessary with guns, and while society would expect people to take precautions on their own, unfortunately people do not always do so. Consequently, Parliament has sent an extra message to such people: failure to be careful will attract severe criminal penalties. The sentence represents society's denunciation, having regard to the gravity of the crime; it provides retributive justice to the family of the victim and the community in general; and it serves a general deterrent function to prevent others from acting so recklessly in the future.

By contrast, *R. v. Smith*, [1987] 1 S.C.R. 1045, struck down Parliament's imposition of a mandatory seven-year minimum sentence for importing narcotics by focusing on the hypothetical importation of one marihuana cigarette leading to the minimum sentence:

> the offence of importing enacted by s. 5(1) of the *Narcotic Control Act* covers numerous substances of varying degrees of dangerousness and totally disregards the quantity of the drug imported. The purpose of a given importation, such as whether it is for personal consumption or for trafficking, and the existence or nonexistence of previous convictions for offences of a similar nature or gravity are disregarded as irrelevant. Thus, the law is such that it is inevitable that, in some cases, a verdict of guilt will lead to the imposition of a term of imprisonment which will be grossly disproportionate.

i. *The Immunities of Section 13*

Section 13 of the *Charter* constitutionally entrenches in a simplified and automatic form already existing statutory protections again self-incrimination:

> **13.** A witness who testifies in any proceedings has the right not to have any incriminating evidence so given used to incriminate that witness in any other proceedings, except in a prosecution for perjury or for the giving of contradictory evidence.

Interpreting s. 13 has caused the courts difficulty because in Canada a non-accused witness has no right to refuse to testify or answer questions because of self-incrimination concerns, only the protection that those answers will not later be used against the witness giving them. This principle is enshrined in s. 5 of the *Canada Evidence Act*, R.S.C. 1985, c. C-5:

> **5.** (1) No witness shall be excused from answering any question on the ground that the answer to the question may tend to criminate him, or may tend to establish his liability to a civil proceeding at the instance of the Crown or of any person.
>
> (2) Where with respect to any question a witness objects to answer on the ground that his answer may tend to criminate him, or may tend to establish his liability to a civil proceeding at the instance of the Crown or of any person, and if but for this Act, or the Act of any provincial legislature, the witness would therefore have been excused from answering the question, then although the witness is by reason of this Act or the provincial Act compelled to answer, the answer so given shall not be used or admissible in evidence against him in any criminal trial or other criminal proceeding against him thereafter taking place, other than a prosecution for perjury in the giving of that evidence or for the giving of contradictory evidence.

Disputes over whether self-incrimination protection only covers the words uttered by a witness (known as "use immunity"), or extends to evidence subsequently discovered as a result of those words (known as "derivative use immunity") means investigators should think twice before planning to compel a person to testify about offences for which that person also might be charged in separate proceedings. Whenever immunity is a potential case issue, the earliest of investigator-prosecutor contact is called for.

i.   *The Challenges of Implementing Section 14*

Section 14 *Charter* rights to an interpreter have not proved terribly controversial:

> **14.** A party or witness in any proceedings who does not understand or speak the language in which the proceedings are conducted or who is deaf has the right to the assistance of an interpreter.

Implementation of those rights can, however, be challenging. You may encounter difficulties with interpreters who do not have a complete command of the language or dialect spoken by witnesses or accused, interpreters who summarize rather than simultaneously translate everything said in court, and even interpreters from small linguistic communities who are personally connected to the accused or other witnesses in a case. Early investigator-prosecutor contact is required to sort out anticipated interpretation or translation issues.

k. *The Future of Section 15*

Section 15 *Charter* equality guarantees are rarely invoked (at least not successfully) in the course of investigations and prosecutions, but the open-ended nature of those rights, which have been very important in the civil context, means that equality arguments in the criminal courts could become more common in the future:

> **15.** (1)Every individual is equal before and under the law and has the right to the equal protection and equal benefit of the law without discrimination and, in particular, without discrimination based on race, national or ethnic origin, colour, religion, sex, age or mental or physical disability.
>
> (2) Subsection (1) does not preclude any law, program or activity that has as its object the amelioration of conditions of disadvantaged individuals or groups including those that are disadvantaged because of race, national or ethnic origin, colour, religion, sex, age or mental or physical disability.

Even now, markedly different treatment of similarly situated individuals through the operation of a law or investigator conduct could lead to a successful s. 15 claim, perhaps as a result of a discriminatory practice like racial profiling.

l. *Will Sections 25, 27 and 28 Ever Become Investigation or Prosecution Factors?*

Sections 25, 27, and 28 of the *Charter* have to date not been substantially dealt with by the courts in the investigations or prosecutions context, but future interpretation of these sections could be significant for investigations or prosecutions found to be inconsistent with aboriginal, multicultural or sexual equality values in Canada:

> **25.** The guarantee in this Charter of certain rights and freedoms shall not be construed so as to abrogate or derogate from any aboriginal treaty or other rights or freedoms that pertain to the aboriginal peoples of Canada including

(a) any rights or freedoms that have been recognized by the Royal Proclamation of October 7, 1763; and

(b) any rights or freedoms that now exist by way of land claims agreements or may be so acquired.

. . .

27. This Charter shall be interpreted in a manner consistent with the preservation and enhancement of the multicultural heritage of Canadians.

28. Notwithstanding anything in this Charter, the rights and freedoms referred to in it are guaranteed equally to male and female persons.

It is worth keeping on eye on Supreme Court of Canada decisions of the next few years to see if ss. 25, 27 or 28 become factors in investigations or prosecutions.

m. *The Applicability of Section 32*

Section 32 of the *Charter* is another one of those sections that literally means what it says:

32. (1) This Charter applies

(a) to the Parliament and government of Canada in respect of all matters within the authority of Parliament including all matters relating to the Yukon Territory and Northwest Territories; and

(b) to the legislature and government of each province in respect of all matters within the authority of the legislature of each province.

The courts have had to resolve who or what is a part of "government" subject to the *Charter*, as opposed to those in the private sphere who are principally accountable under provincial human rights codes or the common law for their actions. The actions of all investigators employed by or acting under the direction of a state entity are covered by the *Charter*, including informers who become state agents, but private citizens or security guards who collect evidence are generally not subject to the *Charter* if they do so without state direction.

n. *The Long Reach of Section 35*

Although s. 35 of the *Constitution Act, 1982* is not part of the *Charter*, its guarantees may affect outcomes and resources required to pursue investigations and prosecutions, particularly those involving hunting, fishing or gathering offences:

> **35.** (1) The existing aboriginal and treaty rights of the aboriginal peoples of Canada are hereby recognized and affirmed.
>
> (2) In this Act, "aboriginal peoples of Canada" includes the Indian, Inuit and Métis peoples of Canada.
>
> (3) For greater certainty, in subsection (1) "treaty rights" includes rights that now exist by way of land claims agreements or may be so acquired.
>
> (4) Notwithstanding any other provision of this Act, the aboriginal and treaty rights referred to in subsection (1) are guaranteed equally to male and female persons.

While negotiation and civil litigation are the primary means for resolution of aboriginal rights issues, it seems inevitable that some aboriginal law issues will continue to arise in the criminal courts either as test cases or defences to routine charges. Several of the cases I was involved in when working as an environmental prosecutor involved claims of aboriginal or treaty rights, some of whose results had very significant impacts like *R. v. Marshall*, [1999] 3 S.C.R. 456; 3 S.C.R. 533, which clarified the scope of activities that could be pursued under certain 18th century aboriginal treaties of peace and friendship.

Charter law is currently much more certain than aboriginal law. Investigators need to take aboriginal and treaty rights claims seriously, treat the rights alleged and the people who advance them with respect, and contact a prosecutor as soon as any aboriginal or treaty rights claim is mentioned. Aboriginal or treaty rights claim greatly complicate disclosure and trial procedures.

Getting the Job Done in the Age of the *Charter*

Q: How am I supposed to continue doing my job in the face of paranoia over my every action possibly leading to a *Charter* remedy?

A: You can't over intellectualize your every action from a *Charter* analysis perspective and still be an effective investigator. Following the theme of demystification of the law will give you a few basic principles that if followed should avoid *Charter* breaches in the vast majority of cases, while early investigator-prosecutor contact will enable you to get advice about those few doubtful situations where demystification of the law still leaves you mystified.

2. Understanding *Charter* Legal Risks According to Type of Remedy

a. *Working Towards Protecting the Right, Not Towards Surviving the Remedy*

Sections 24 of the *Charter* and 51 of the *Constitution Act, 1982* are arguably the most important of all constitutional provisions applicable to investigations and prosecutions, since it is cold comfort for an accused to have a right if there is no remedy through which it can be enforced. The courts have offered guidance on the tests to be used for determining whether a constitutional remedy should be granted, but the application of those tests gives considerable discretion to the trial judge. There are principally three types of constitutional remedy in Canada:

- a s. 52 *Constitution Act, 1982* remedy striking down or modifying legislation inconsistent with the constitution that "is, to the extent of the inconsistency, of no force or effect";

- a s-s. 24(2) *Charter* remedy excluding evidence "where the admission of it in the proceedings would bring the administration of justice into disrepute";

- a s-s. 24(1) *Charter* remedy that is "just and appropriate in the circumstances."

While the legality of actions under the *Charter* can now be predicted with some certainty, the remedies that may flow from *Charter* contraventions cannot be so accurately anticipated. Sometimes evidence will be excluded from trial, and at other times it won't. Occasionally the greater remedy of a stay of proceedings will be granted, but usually other lesser remedies will be ordered. Because of the unpredictability of remedies, each and every investigator needs to work towards protecting the right, not towards surviving the remedy.

b. *The Constitutional Invalidity Remedy*

Investigators are entitled to assume that the legislation they are given to work with is constitutionally valid. Being told later that an offence or power to investigate an offence was indeed unconstitutional due to the "no force or effect" remedy even though it had been relied upon for years by investigators across Canada can come as quite a shock, but it is best to leave the constitutionality of legislation to the lawyers to worry about. They can spend years arguing through multiple trials and appeals before a final judgment rules definitively on constitutionality. Sometimes there may be a temporary jurisdictional patchwork of constitutional validity as a case winds its way through the appeal process, with what is constitutional in one province being unconstitutional in another until the Supreme Court of Canada finally decides the issue. However, if legislation is struck down or modified by the courts, investigators do need a way to find out about it, quickly spread the word and adapt their practices to the new law.

c. *The Evidence Exclusion Remedy*

Of greater concern to investigators is the "evidence exclusion" remedy; it is the actions of investigators that are usually cited by the courts in support of the necessity of evidence exclusion. The test for s-s. 24(2) *Charter* exclusion was established in *R. v. Collins*, [1987] 1 S.C.R. 265, and summarized in *R. v. Law*, [2002] 1 S.C.R. 227 at para. 33:

> In *Collins* . . . this Court grouped the circumstances to be considered under s. 24(2) into three categories: (1) the effect of admitting the evidence on the fairness of the subsequent trial, (2) the seriousness of the police's conduct, and (3) the effects of excluding the evidence on the administration of justice.

The Supreme Court of Canada and lower courts have laboured at great length to elaborate on the three basic exclusion factors, but there remains an inherent subjectiveness in assessing fairness, seriousness and effects that makes exclusion results very difficult to predict. Sub-section 24(2) is in theory an inclusionary rather than exclusionary rule as the burden is still on the accused to demonstrate why evidence should be excluded, even after a *Charter* breach has been established. Exclusion is not automatic upon a rights breach being found connected to evidence gathered. However, certain types of *Charter* breaches, particularly those that can be termed self-conscriptive in the way evidence was gathered like through omitting rights to counsel prior to a statement being made while an accused is detained, in practice render this an exclusionary rule at least some of the time.

d. *The Open-Ended Remedy*

The "just and appropriate in the circumstances" s-s. 24(1) *Charter* remedy could arise from the actions of investigators, prosecutors or systemic justice issues. The open-ended nature of the s-s. 24(1) remedy means the types of remedies that can be awarded are only limited by the creativity of counsel and the courts. The stay of proceedings is commonly sought under s-s. 24(1) since it will more surely than any other remedy terminate proceedings, but as noted in *R. v. O'Connor*, [1995] 4 S.C.R. 411 at paras. 68-69, it is not a remedy that should be commonly granted:

> I would think that the remedy of a judicial stay of proceedings would be appropriate under s. 24(1) only in the clearest of cases.
>
> . . .
>
> Remedies less drastic than a stay of proceedings are of course available under s. 24(1) in situations where the "clearest of cases" threshold is not met . . . In this respect the *Charter* regime is more flexible than the common law doctrine of abuse of process. . . . It is important to recognize that the *Charter* has now put into judges' hands a scalpel instead of an axe—a tool that may fashion, more carefully than ever, solutions taking into account the sometimes complementary and sometimes opposing concerns of fairness to the individual, societal interests, and the integrity of the judicial system.

R. v. Power, [1994] 1 S.C.R. 601 at 616, suggested one of the situations where a stay of proceedings would be justified was: "Where there is conspicuous evidence of improper motives or of bad faith or of an act so wrong that it violates the conscience of the community."

Alternatives to the stay of proceedings under s-s. 24(1) depend on the *Charter* section breached and the circumstances surrounding that breach. Some possibilities are:

- adjournment for the purpose of review by accused of newly disclosed material;

- adjournment for the purpose of accused subpoenaing additional witnesses;

- accused able to recall witnesses for examination or cross-examination;

- declaration of a mistrial;

- consideration in favour of accused on sentencing;

- court costs to accused;

- damages to accused.

Investigators can provide considerable assistance in a prosecution by coming up with creative remedies to *Charter* breaches, which prosecutors could then suggest to the court, short of remedies that will make a conviction impossible. The goal is at least to avoid a stay of proceedings by giving the court some viable alternatives.

e. *The Underlying Theory of* Charter *Remedy Choice*

Charter remedies will not always be solely compensatory in nature through seeking to put the victim of the rights violation back in the same position occupied before the violation took place. Compensation as the sole goal of *Charter* remedies would be problematic because of the difficulties in measuring just how much damage was suffered and determining what type of remedy would best address that damage. Usually the loss suffered from a *Charter* breach will not be an economic one, so the simple payment of monetary damages cannot begin to address that loss. Some *Charter* remedies like the stay of proceeding may primarily have a deterrence goal — to deter those who breached the accused's *Charter* rights from doing so again — the theory being if cases involving *Charter* breaches are not allowed to proceed to conviction, those involved in breaches will stop violations so convictions can once again be obtained. Maintaining the integrity of the system is another type of *Charter* remedy goal that may favour the stay of proceedings. With the integrity of the system at stake, even if a rights violation does not affect the fairness of an accused's trial a court may conclude a stay of proceedings or other remedy is justified in order to make it perfectly clear the court will not condone illegal conduct on the part of investigators or others working as part of "the system."

3. Understanding Civil Liability Consequences of *Charter* Breaches

Poor investigative practices can also lead to bad outcomes at later civil proceedings brought by accused or victims. Civil consequences will usually be for non-*Charter* reasons, but cases like *Jane Doe v. Metropolitan Toronto (Municipality) Commissioners of Police* (1998), 39 O.R. (3d) 487 (Ont. Ct. Jus. (Gen. Div.)) at paras. 175-76 & 184, have confirmed investigators do face possible civil liability for breach of *Charter* rights:

> the plaintiff has established that the defendants had a legal duty to warn her of the danger she faced; that they adopted a policy not to warn her because of a stereotypical discriminatory belief that as a woman she and others like her would become hysterical and panic and scare off an attacker, among others.

> A man in similar circumstances, implicit from Det. Sgt. C. . .'s comment, would have been warned and therefor had the opportunity to choose whether to expose himself to danger in order to help catch the attacker.

> . . .

> I am satisfied on the facts of this case that the plaintiff's damages are the same in respect of the two basis upon which her action is founded i.e. negligence and breach of *Charter* rights.

Doing everything you can to uphold the rights of both accused and victims will mitigate or eliminate successful civil claims against investigators acting in the normal course of execution of their duties.

4. Ensuring Investigative Actions Are Taken in Good Faith

Occasionally, even if investigators are diligent in watching that their actions are in accordance with the *Charter*, *Charter* violations will still occur. A small written error might be introduced during the drafting of a search warrant; an investigator might become distracted by some other event and delay giving a detainee his rights to counsel; pages may stick together in a photocopier resulting in a few pages of investigator notes being omitted from a disclosure package. When a remedy is later being considered by a court for these kinds of legal deficiencies, whether investigators were acting in good faith can count for a lot. While many of the legal implications of the *Charter* may not always be within the control of investigators, being well informed about the *Charter's* requirements and doing the utmost to abide by them are fully within investigator control and could weigh heavily in any court assessment of investigator good faith.

a. *The Value of Good Faith*

Mixed signals have been sent by the courts concerning the value of good faith. Where breaches leading to self-incrimination are involved, good faith may not count for much. But the courts have given investigators considerable credit for acting in good faith where they could not have possibly known the law they were operating under would later be interpreted in a way that disapproved of their actions, as in *R. v. Wong*, [1990] 3 S.C.R. 36 at 59:

> the police acted in good faith. . . . the *Charter* breach stemmed from an entirely reasonable misunderstanding of the law by the police officers. . .the bulk of the police investigation in this case was completed before this court released its decision in *Hunter* v. *Southam Inc.* . . . and well before electronic surveillance was held to constitute a search . . . it can in fairness be said that the police in conducting themselves as they did acted in accordance with what they had good reason to believe was the law, and before they had had a reasonable opportunity to assess the consequences of the *Charter* on their established practices.

The courts have not been so forgiving where good faith claims by investigators are not reasonable, as in *R. v. Kokesch*, [1990] 3 S.C.R. 3 at 33:

> I do not wish to be understood as imposing upon the police a burden of instant interpretation of court decisions. The question of the length of time after a judgment that ought to be permitted to pass before knowledge of its content is attributed to the police for the purposes of assessing good faith is an interesting one, but it does not arise on these facts. The police here had the benefit of slightly more than 12 years to study *Eccles*, slightly less than six years to consider *Colet*, and slightly more than two years to digest the constitutional warrant requirement set out in *Hunter*. Any doubt they may have had about their ability to trespass in the absence of specific statutory authority to do so was manifestly unreasonable, and cannot, as a matter of law, be relied upon as good faith . . ..

b. *Staying Current with Legal Developments*

Because good faith does appear to have value so long as investigators have been duly diligent in learning and applying the law, there is a strong incentive to stay current on all recent legal developments. Staying current will minimize a court's propensity to impose a *Charter* remedy for investigative actions investigators could not reasonably have known were breaches of the *Charter*, as explained in *R. v. Evans*, [1996] 1 S.C.R. 8 at para. 30:

> I would not characterize the violation of s. 8 in the present case as particularly grave. The good faith of the police in the present case cannot be questioned: the trial judge expressly found that the police were aware of this Court's decision in *Kokesch* and felt that their actions in approaching the Evans' front door were consistent with that decision. As a result, although the initial "olfactory" search of the Evans' home has now been found to have been constitutionally impermissible, the police were unaware that the search was beyond their investigatory powers. The subsequent search of the Evans' home was undertaken in reliance on a warrant. Although I have found that the warrant was invalid, the police (who at all times believed that they were acting in an appropriate manner), had no reason to doubt the validity of the warrant at the time that the search of the Evans' home was conducted.

There are a variety of institutional steps that investigative agencies can take to ensure their members are always found by the courts to be in constitutional good faith in pursuing their duties.

c. *Addressing Investigative Good Faith through Investigator Training*

Charter training standards for investigators can be viewed from two levels. At the higher level, training would prevent any *Charter* breaches from occurring in the first place. This is obviously the ideal situation, but achieving absolute *Charter* compliance in Canada's ever-shifting constitutional landscape is not a realistic goal. Instantaneous transmission, understanding and application of new jurisprudence by members of investigative agencies is unlikely, and even with instantaneous application there remain the ostensibly valid laws that are only declared unconstitutional long after investigators have taken actions only later challenged at trial. The Supreme Court of Canada does not, in any case, appear to hold investigators to such a high standard, except in connection with self-incriminatory breaches. Therefore on the lower level, adequate training to ensure good faith findings will simply ensure objectively reasonable compliance with the *Charter*.

Four aspects of investigator training, dealing with learning, reinforcement, testing and monitoring, can address the goal of investigative good faith:

- the provision of objectively sufficient initial training in basic *Charter* concepts and how to apply them;

- the provision of continuing education in such concepts that addresses all significant new law in as timely a fashion as is objectively reasonable;

- ensuring those who are provided training have absorbed the material and are able to apply it at an objectively reasonable level;

- ensuring those who have been trained do in fact apply the material at an objectively reasonable level.

One-time training without follow-up and monitoring arguably is not sufficient.

The courts have not required perfection when assessing the conduct of investigative agencies and their members in the context of the *Charter*, but an objectively reasonable and knowledgeable standard of conduct is to be expected in the absence of which a host of *Charter* remedies may ensue. Canadian jurisprudence, although not unanimous on the point, indicates good faith will be a significant factor weighing against engagement of the full panoply of *Charter* remedies when an objectively reasonable standard of conduct can be made out. Investigative good faith won't cancel out *Charter* breaches, or eliminate all remedies, but it can greatly lessen their impact. I would therefore urge all investigators to consider how their understanding and application of the law can be enhanced to the point at which good faith findings will always be made by the courts.

For Finding and Interpreting the Law

KEY POINTS

✓ A provision of a law should be given its ordinary and grammatical meaning, read harmoniously with the other words of the law, consistent with the purpose of the law and the intent of the legislators who enacted it.

✓ Focus on legislative sources to avoid drowning in case law. The Internet is now your most useful source of up-to-date law, but supplement it with printed annotated copies of the most common Acts you enforce that will explain the meaning of legislation in plain language and give summaries of the most important cases. In addition, keep handy one or two books covering investigative powers, evidence admissibility, and court procedure.

KEY POINTS

✓ Because of the unpredictability of constitutional remedies, all investigators need to work towards protecting the right, not towards surviving the remedy. *Charter* remedies may seek to compensate those affected by the breach of rights, deter future commission of similar rights breaches, or protect the overall integrity of the justice system, and can have consequences for investigators in civil as well as criminal proceedings.

✓ Adequate initial and continuing investigator legal training, and the monitoring of how that training is applied in the field, will maximize findings of investigator constitutional good faith and minimize the award of remedies for actions investigators could not have reasonably known would breach the *Charter*. The courts do not require investigators to conduct legally perfect investigations, but the law does require an objectively reasonable standard of applied legal knowledge.

FURTHER READING

Cases

Application under s. 83.28 of the Criminal Code (Re), [2004] 2 S.C.R. 248. Deals with interpreting the law in accordance with the Constitution: "legislation is enacted to comply with constitutional norms . . . where two readings of a provision are equally plausible, the interpretation which accords with *Charter* values should be adopted" (at para. 35).

Bell ExpressVu Limited Partnership v. Rex, [2002] 2 S.C.R. 559. Contains a comprehensive review of the principles of statutory interpretation: "The preferred approach recognizes the important role that context must inevitably play when a court construes the written words of a statute: . . . 'words, like people, take their colour from their surroundings'" (at para. 27).

R. v. Ulybel Enterprises Ltd., [2001] 2 S.C.R. 867. Applies principles of statutory construction to interpreting regulatory legislation, and reaffirms support for the quotation starting this chapter: "This famous passage from Driedger 'best encapsulates' our Court's preferred approach to statutory interpretation . . . . Driedger's passage has been cited with approval by our Court on frequent occasions in many different interpretive settings which need not be mentioned here" (at para. 29).

Books and Articles

1. *Statutory Construction Books*

A good statutory construction book doesn't go out of date, but newer books are equally worth considering.

P.-A. Coté, *The Interpretation of Legislation in Canada*, 3d ed. (Toronto: Carswell, 2003). The leading statutory construction work in French, now translated into English.

E.A. Driedger, *On Construction of Statues*, 2nd ed. (Toronto: Butterworths, 1982). The standard, definitive, and surprisingly concise book to which the Supreme Court of Canada keeps referring.

R. Sullivan, *Sullivan and Driedger on Construction of Statutes*, 4th ed. (Toronto: LexisNexis Butterworths, 2002). A more voluminous later edition of the Driedger book with extensive new case law, but the basic principles of interpretation remain much the same.

R. Sullivan, *Statutory Interpretation* (Concord, ON: Irwin Law, 1998). A more concise version of her Driedger book.

2. *Annotated Criminal Codes*

Unannotated *Criminal Codes* are more portable and less expensive, but having at least one copy of an annotated *Code* in each detachment of investigators is well worth the moderate increase in size and price, and it will usually include a few other related annotated Acts like the *Controlled Drugs and Substances Act.*

E.L. Greenspan & M. Rosenberg, *Martin's Annual Criminal Code, 2006 Edition* (Aurora, ON: Canada Law Book, 2005). One of the two most commonly used annotated *Codes.*

G. P. Rodrigues, ed., *Crankshaw's Criminal Code of Canada*, 9 vols., loose-leaf (Toronto: Carswell, 1993). A nine-volume supplemented loose-leaf *Code* that adds legislative history and academic commentary to the usual case annotations.

P. Schneider & A. Dubois, *Bilingual Criminal Code and Related Legislation, Quebec Annotations* (Toronto: CCH, 2003). Because not all Quebec lower court decisions are translated into English, those working outside of Quebec may not become aware of useful cases interpreting the *Code* and related statutes that emanate from Canada's second most populous province. This book provides summaries of those Quebec cases, and a bilingual text of the *Code* useful for making comparisons between the English and French meanings of the text.

D. Watt & M. Fuerst, *The 2006 Annotated Treemear's Criminal Code* (Toronto: Carswell, 2005). The other of the two most commonly used annotated *Codes.* As a prosecutor I usually preferred to use the Treemear's *Code* over the Martin's *Code* because of what I found to be more relevant case commentary to my practice, but which one you like is a matter of personal preference.

3. *Annotated Regulatory Acts*

This is only a small sampling of the annotated Acts out there.

E.L. Greenspan & M. Rosenberg, *Martin's Related Criminal Statutes, 2005-2006 Edition* (Aurora, ON: Canada Law Book, 2005).

R. Libman, *The 2005-2006 Annotated Contraventions Act* (Toronto: Carswell, 2005).

R.S. Nozick, *The 2006 Annotated Competition Act* (Toronto: Carswell, 2005).

R.W. Pound, ed., *Stikeman Income Tax Act Annotated*, 39th ed. (Toronto: Carswell, 2006).

M.D. Segal, *The 2005 Annotated Ontario Highway Traffic Act* (Toronto: Carswell, 2005).

M.D. Segal & R. Libman, *The 2005 Annotated Ontario Provincial Offences Act* (Toronto: Carswell, 2005).

R.M. Synder, *The 2006 Annotated Canada Labour Code* (Toronto: Carswell, 2005).

4. *Legal Research and Citation Guides*

Although written primarily for lawyers, legal research and citation guides can be of great use to investigators by explaining how to find legislation, cases and other material. They also explain what the cryptic notations after cases mean, like that (1999), 81 D.L.R. 356 (Ont. C.A.) means you will find the case in the 81st volume of the Dominion Law Reports at page 356, and it was decided in 1999 by the Ontario Court of Appeal.

J.R. Castel & O.K. Latchman, *The Practical Guide to Canadian Legal Research*, 2nd ed. (Toronto: Carswell, 1996).

M. Fitzgerald, *Legal Problem Solving: Reasoning, Research and Writing*, 3rd ed. (Markham, ON: LexisNexis Butterworths, 2003).

M.J. Iosipescu and P. Whitehead, *Legal Writing and Research Manual*, 6th ed. (Markham, ON: LexisNexis Butterworths, 2004).

D.R. MacEllven et al., *Legal Research Handbook*, 5th ed. (Markham, ON: LexisNexis Butterworths, 2003).

McGill Law Journal, *Canadian Guide to Uniform Legal Citation*, 5th ed. (Toronto: Carswell, 2002).

T. Tjaden, *Legal Research and Writing* (Toronto: Irwin Law, 2001).

J.A. Yogis et al., *Legal Writing and Research Manual*, 5th ed. (Aurora, ON: Canada Law Book, 2000).

A. Zivanovic, *Guide to Electronic Legal Research*, 2nd ed. (Aurora, ON: Canada Law Book, 2002).

5. Charter *Sources*

An immense amount has been written about the *Charter*; here I only offer a very selective reading list.

J.M. Arbour, "The Protection of Aboriginal Rights within a Human Rights Regime: In Search of an Analytical Framework for Section 25 of the *Canadian Charter of Rights and Freedoms*" (2003) 21 Sup. Ct. L. Rev. (2d) 3.

S. Boucher & K.D. Landa, *Understanding Section 8: Search, Seizure and the Canadian Constitution* (Toronto: Irwin Law, 2005).

J. Cameron, ed., *The Charter's Impact on the Criminal Justice System* (Toronto: Carswell, 1996). A collection of essays plus a quite interesting summary of roundtable comments made by a group of criminal law judges, lawyers and academics.

G.S. Campbell, "Language, Equality and the *Charter*: From First to Third Generation Rights and Beyond" (1994) 4 N.J.C.L. 29.

S.A. Cohen, "The Paradoxical Nature of Privacy in the Context of Criminal Law and the *Canadian Charter of Rights and Freedoms*" (2002) 7 Can. Crim. L. Rev. 125.

P. Hogg, *Constitutional Law of Canada*, loose-leaf (Toronto: Carswell, 1992). The standard Canadian constitutional law text.

K. Jull, "Remedies for Non-Compliance with Investigative Procedures: A Theoretical Overview" (1985) 17 Ottawa L. Rev. 525.

S. Penney, "Taking Deterrence Seriously: Excluding Unconstitutionally Obtained Evidence under Section 24(2) of the *Charter*" (2004) 49 McGill L.J. 105.

K. Roach, *Constitutional Remedies in Canada*, loose-leaf (Aurora, ON: Canada Law Book, 1994). A useful work that focuses on remedies rather than rights.

CHAPTER THREE

THE IMPORTANCE OF NOTE-TAKING

The Committee recommends that the Attorney General request that the Solicitor General issue a statement to all police officers emphasizing the importance of taking careful, accurate, and contemporaneous notes during their investigations. (The statement should emphasize that disclosure requirements after Stinchcombe cannot be thwarted by making less accurate or less comprehensive notes.)

The Committee recommends that, upon request, copies of relevant original notes should be disclosed, subject to editing or non-disclosure where the public interest requires it, including where necessary, to protect confidential informants, the existence of ongoing investigations, and the integrity of police investigative techniques.

> *Report of the Attorney General's Advisory Committee on Charge Screening, Disclosure and Resolution Discussions* (Toronto: Queen's Printer, 1993) at 150-151.

In This Chapter

- How to freeze moments in time
- The rise of the note-taking obsession
- Answering qualifying questions for the use of notes
- Adopting effective note-taking procedures
- Giving effective testimony from your notes

HOW TO FREEZE MOMENTS IN TIME

Notes freeze moments in time. Sometimes those moments will be thawed out at later dates. At other times they will remain frozen forever, a testament to how investigators passed a few minutes or days of their lives. The closer in time to actual events that notes are made, the fresher those events will be when taken out of the note deep-freeze. The more complete the recounting of events originally recorded in the notes, the better the factual product to emerge from the freezer. The spottier and more haphazard the notes, the greater the risk that only frost encrusted factual fragments will be available for defrosting.

Although I am a big fan of video recording as an extremely accurate tool of evidence preservation, it is not a substitute for good note-taking practices. Video recording does a better job than notes at flash freezing what appears in front of the camera, but is inferior in capturing context, what happened before and after the recording, and what was happening immediately outside of the video camera frame. Video recording particularly cannot see into the mind of anyone appearing in a recording, and cannot record opinions unless they are expressly stated, whereas notes reflect the inner mental workings of the note-taker, and can capture opinions and beliefs like belief in reasonable and probable grounds. Demystification of the law tells you not to be paranoid while taking notes for fear you will somehow make a mistake, but early investigator-prosecutor contact is required when problems with notes arise to ensure any resulting disclosure and trial delay difficulties do not compromise case viability.

THE RISE OF THE NOTE-TAKING OBSESSION

It is ironic that written jottings, which are only supposed to serve as an aid to an investigator's direct recollection of events, have now taken on a preeminently important life of their own. The now common practice of disclosure of original notes, instead of just providing a will-say or can-say document, contributed to this note-taking obsession, as did increased questioning of the credibility of investigators. But the frequent discovery that there were relevant facts, however minor in importance, in original notes that did not make it into the formal case summaries provided to the prosecution and eventually disclosed to the defence justified calls for notebook disclosure.

Not only will good note-taking immeasurably assist your recollection months or years after events took place, it will also serve to bolster your overall credibility with the court as in *R. v. Wallace*, 2005 CarswellOnt 207;

2005 CanLII 1088 (S.C.) at para. 99: "Officers P. . . and S. . . impressed me as conscientious, diligent and capable officers whose note taking was careful and meticulous." It will be difficult to question the accuracy of your recollection if everything was recorded in writing at the time it happened. Courts are increasingly questioning whether events or statements happened the way investigators claim they did if no contemporaneous notes were made of them.

Without notes, recalling a fact such as what the weather was like on a particular day nine months ago would seem to require incredible powers of recollection. It certainly is possible to have an accurate recollection without notes, but you must ask yourself whether a court will believe your memory is accurate. We are not yet at the stage where a witness is forbidden from testifying to a fact that was not noted down close to the time events transpired, however a recent trend in the case law holds that there needs to be an explanation of why a significant fact was not noted but is nonetheless being advanced at trial through investigator testimony as in *R. v. Burrows*, 2004 ONCJ 357 at para. 38:

> Police, routinely, note significant events in their memo books. It serves as an aide memoir. It assists in refreshing memory. It adds confidence to the evidence which is often given months and months later. With respect to this police officer, it cannot be acceptable to say: I didn't note it down because I would remember it. Not when it comes to important details. It is necessary for the officer to note down, somewhere, significant observations.

There the court acquitted the accused, finding that the officer's testimony alone, without having made any contemporaneous notes on the key evidentiary point of the basis for a breath sample demand, was insufficient proof that a sample had been properly obtained.

Where notes are well constructed, courts will accept them for all manner of facts as in *R. v. Husulak*, (2004) 248 Sask. R. 66; 2004 SKPC 60 at fn 19:

> The officers' watches were not synchronized. The Court accepts Cst. P. . .'s notations as to timing of events . . . because he was the primary investigator and his note-taking was detailed, specific and consistent. Hence, the Court found it to be reliable and trustworthy.

Once you have good note-taking systems in place, they should operate smoothly without much tinkering on your part, and will greatly enhance the prospects of case success.

Are Notes Replacing Testimony?

Q & A

Q: If field notes are now so important, why doesn't the prosecutor just file them as exhibits at the start of every case so the court knows up front what is, and is not, in those notes?

A: Every document is lifeless at trial without a witness to breathe life into it from having created the document, or having some knowledge of it like through seizing it from the accused's possession. First-hand testimony about original events is still better evidence than notes about those events — the testimony may have more detail, the testimony will be under oath, and cross-examination of the testimony is possible. Notes remain a supplement to testimony, not a replacement, unless the facts stated in the notes are the best evidence available.

ANSWERING QUALIFYING QUESTIONS FOR THE USE OF NOTES

Prosecutors will ask you five questions either at the start of your testimony or when you first ask to refer to your notes in order to "qualify" them as accurate for the purposes of refreshing your memory:

Q: Did you personally make any notes of the events you are here to give testimony about?

Q: Did you make the notes contemporaneous with or soon after the events they describe?

Q: Have you made any additions or deletions to the notes since the time you made them?

Q: Do you still have an independent recollection of those events?

Q: Do you require your notes for the purpose of refreshing your memory?

As an investigator, you need to answer yes to each of these questions in order to be able to refer to your notes when giving testimony at trial. Before the trial judge rules on whether you can make reference to the notes, defence counsel will have an opportunity to cross-examine you on their "qualification" that will involve targeting weaknesses like whether you were really the one who created the notes, whether some notes were made long after the events they record, whether improper changes have since been made to those notes, and whether you still have even an inkling about what really happened during one part of one day many months ago.

It is rare for notes not to be qualified, but it does happen. More common is that your testimony is given little weight because of problems concerning where the original information in the notes came from, how much time passed between your involvement in complex events and the time you made notes of those events, that portions of the notes appear to have been later inexplicably altered, or that you have only the most hazy of independent recollections left of events that transpired long in the past. All these problems are avoidable by following good note-taking practices.

1. Why Personally Make Notes

Just because notes are in your handwriting does not prove you personally made them. Checking precise details like times against the notes of other investigators is good practice, but copying another investigator's notebook word for word does not qualify as note-taking since you aren't recording what you personally observed or overheard. Even an investigator only acting as a witness to a statement needs to take reasonable notes of the circumstances surrounding the statement, instead of completely relying on the notes of the investigator directing the statement as happened in *R. v. Barrett* (1993), 64 O.A.C. 99 at paras. 16-17:

> the note-taking practices of the hold-up squad officers left much to be desired. Sgt. V . . . of the hold-up squad testified that he attended with his partner, Sgt. H. . ., to interview the appellant. Sgt. H. . . did all of the questioning and, while doing so, he recorded, in his notebook, every question and every answer provided by the appellant. Meanwhile, Sgt. V. . . was merely a witness to this interview. He took no active part and made no contemporaneous notes of it, although he had his notebook with him in the interview room. His testimony was assisted by reference to entries in his notebook which he made after the interview was over. He made these notes by reading Sgt. H. . .'s notebook and, since he agreed with the content, he initialed Sgt. H. . .'s notebook and copied H. . .'s notes into his own book. When asked in cross-examination why he did not take his own independent notes while the interview was being conducted, he replied: "That's not the way we conduct our investigations". It is not for me to tell the hold-up squad how to proceed for investigative purposes, but in so far as there are evidentiary consequences to those practices, I can say that they are unsatisfactory. Whenever possible, every officer in attendance at the interview who will want to refer to his or her notes as a memory aid for the purpose of giving evidence should take contemporaneous, independent notes. I would not expect as complete

> notes from the person conducting the interview and it is surprising
> here to find that those are the only notes and that they purport to
> be verbatim.

Here it would have been easy for the witness to the interview to at least record details of interview time and place, the accused's demeanour, and other circumstances relevant to voluntariness and the *Charter*. It should have been the witnessing investigator who did most of the note-taking — any questioning investigator would understandably have trouble taking verbatim notes of all questions and answers while at the same time carrying on a conversation with the witness. Because the statement notes had been made by the questioning investigators, the court had a hard time believing they were verbatim; poor note-taking practices cast doubt on all the investigators' testimony.

Even being in an undercover situation where you are not able to make notes as events happen does not eliminate your obligation to personally make notes, but a court will likely give you some leeway to make those notes later in the day. Occasionally having others make notes for you will be okay, like when you radio in observations to a central note-taker who records your words, but you must review those notes close to the time the events took place to ensure their accuracy and thus be able to later rely on them at trial. Being completely reliant on others for the entire content of your notes means you cannot honesty answer yes to the question of whether you "personally" made notes of the events about which you are to testify.

2. Why Make Contemporaneous Notes

Because precise details of any event usually become more difficult to remember as time passes, details must be noted down at the time those details happen or extremely soon thereafter. Times, statements and numbers will likely have to be noted at least on rough notes at the same time they are observed or overheard for a recollection to be believably accurate. More general observations like weather conditions or who attended a meeting might be recorded later the same day, but an investigator should definitely not go off shift without having completed at least basic notes, other than in exceptional circumstances like when an injury is suffered on duty.

Inability to confirm that notes were made contemporaneously with the events being testified to may render investigator testimony highly suspect as in *R. v. McKennon*, 2004 CarswellOnt 5237 (Sup. Ct. Jus.) at paras. 22-24:

Traffic stops are generally low visibility interactions between the state and the citizen and scrutiny by the courts is critical to curb abuses of power such as they might exist. We have come to expect accurate and honest evidence from police officers testifying about traffic stops in order to understand whether lawful authority was constitutionally exercised.

The note-taking of the three police witnesses in this case is entirely unsatisfactory. The defence submitted that the officers collaborated in some measure in writing their notes. The witnesses denied this. None made contemporaneous notes, although here at trial . . . [they] initially claimed they had in part. Why contemporaneous notes were not made was not answered by the witnesses. Contemporaneity promotes accuracy and a fulsome independent account even if jot or rough notes are subsequently posted up to a more polished narrative or summary.

The officers could not provide times as to when each made notes on February 21, 2003. Any note writing appears to have transpired after discussions with the C.I.B. officers who did not testify in this trial.

Recognize that the making of your notes is itself a significant event, and confirm that time in your notebook as well.

3. Why Track Additions or Deletions to Notes

There is no rule prohibiting investigators from making additions or deletions to notes after the time they were originally made. Accuracy in note-taking means that if, after completing your notes you realize you forgot to include an important detail or a note is incorrect, you have an obligation to correct the error. Any additions or deletions that you make to your notes must be tracked so a court can be satisfied you personally made your notes in a sufficiently contemporaneous manner. Minor note discrepancies between investigators are understandable because of differences in human perception and should not have a significant impact on credibility. Major note discrepancies must be reconciled before coming to trial by investigators collectively studying all available records to determine whose notes are correct, and then making clearly flagged additions or deletions to the incorrect notes.

In making additions or deletions, four factors need to be indicated next to a new or struck-out notation:

1. new text is indicated as a later addition;

2. deleted text is still visible to show what was originally included in error;

3. the date of the addition or deletion;

4. your initials indicating you personally made the addition or deletion.

Electronic notes may require some creative reformatting to ensure these factors are included. From those four factors, prosecution and defence counsel will be able to examine and cross-examine on the circumstances surrounding why information was originally left out or entered in error, and a trial court should be able to get a picture of the credibility of additions or deletions. Your credibility as a witness may be severely compromised if it only comes out after much cross-examination that you did make changes to your notes weeks after originally preparing them, perhaps because you were worried they were too different from notes of other investigators also working the case.

So long as you are prepared at trial for the inevitable questions targeting how any of your testimony can be believed if you made an error in your notes that you later corrected and disclosed prior to trial, your credibility will be preserved. Successfully dealing with cross-examination on additions or deletions to notes could go as follows:

Q: So, are there other portions of your notes where you made additions or deletions?

A: No, just the one place I have already indicated.

Q: How can you be sure about that?

A: Because every time I make an addition or deletion, I clearly mark it as such, indicate the date it was made, and initial the change. You can see that is what I did for the one notation change I already testified about.

Q: Is it possible you made a change, and forgot to put the date and your initials?

A: No.

Q: Well, the one change you made is a pretty major change, wouldn't you agree?

A: I believed the accuracy of the fact was important enough to the case that I needed to change my notes.

Q: Well, if you got that one major thing wrong, how can we have any confidence that any other part of your notes is not also wrong?

A: I carefully made my notes immediately after the events in question. Although I had originally identified one of the persons arrested as David Blair because that was the name he had given me, I later established through fingerprint checks that his real identity was David Roundtree. When I was informed of this fact by the investigator in charge of the case, I decided to note his true identity in my notebook next to the name he had originally given me. I believe it is because of my focus on details that the error was caught in the first place, and I am now certain all my notes are accurate.

4. Why Maintain a Recollection of Events Independent from Your Notes

Your notes are not a replacement for an independent recollection of the events to which you are testifying. They can be used during your testimony only for the purpose of refreshing your memory. Notes that assist your memory represent a "present memory revived" (revived by the prompting of the notes). If you truly have no recollection of the events recorded in your notes, your notes might be tendered into evidence as a "past recollection recorded" (recorded in the notes). However, even if your notes are found to be admissible as a past recollection recorded, they might not be given the same weight by the court as would your oral testimony. Credibility of notes alone is difficult to test through cross-examination, and bare words on a page can be a cold and lifeless way to tell a story unless a very skilled writer crafted them.

R. v. Fliss, [2002] 1 S.C.R. 535 at para. 63, sets out the four criteria that must be met for notes of an event to be admissible as a past recollection recorded:

- the recollection was recorded in a reliable way;

- the recollection was sufficiently fresh at the time it was recorded to be probably accurate;

- the recollection can now be said to have represented the knowledge of the witness making the notes at the time it was recorded; and

- the original notes must be tendered if available.

Investigators faced with a past recollection recorded situation still need to be able to authenticate the notes, testify their note-taking methods were reliable, and describe what those methods were.

I once had a prosecution witness who not only denied knowledge of the drug trafficking observations he had recorded in his notebook, but couldn't say he had made the notes at the time of the events, and denied ever seeing the transaction — even though his notes said he saw it, and his partner had laid charges as a result of those observations. The case was beyond hope, far past the point where I could have attempted to admit the notes as a past recollection recorded. I discontinued the calling of further evidence, which shortly after was followed by an acquittal. This result need not have happened if the witness had reviewed his notes prior to trial, and discussed any difficulties with me or another prosecutor before getting on the witness stand. With advance warning, alternative modes of refreshing a witness' memory or securing additional witnesses can be explored.

The law does not insist that every precise detail be remembered independently after looking at notes. You have some wiggle room in what constitutes present memory revived, where you can read precise details like licence plate numbers right out of your notebook and still call those details a present memory. But for general facts, reading large passages of your notes out loud word for word on the witness stand will only demonstrate to the court that you don't have the independent recollection necessary to give testimony refreshed by the notes.

5. Why You Must Require Your Notes to Refresh Your Memory

The purpose of referring to your notes while testifying is to refresh your independent recollection of events. If your memory is so good that it doesn't require refreshing, then you will not be permitted to look at your notes. Occasionally I have run across witnesses who, in the course of my trying to qualify their notes, answer the qualifying questions with "yes" except for the last "do you require your notes for the purpose of refreshing you memory?" where I get an emphatic "no!" These witnesses make the mistake of thinking that toughing it out without their notes will bolster their credibility.

I don't believe avoiding any reference to notes ever improves credibility beyond the point of the careful witness who only takes the occasional quick glance at notes. Saying you don't at all need your notes to refresh your memory is a very risky strategy, because there is a good chance defence counsel can prove you wrong by cross-examining you on some small note detail that you have not perfectly memorized. Then instead of being someone who reasonably enough concedes the odd note check will help your memory, you will be someone who had an answer proven wrong. The court will start to wonder where else your answers might have been wrong.

How Independent Does a Recollection Need to Be?

Q&A

Q: These notes qualifying questions seem pretty artificial to me. My recall of the details really depends on how remarkable the case was, and how long ago I dealt with it. How can I honestly say I have an independent recollection of events, and only require my notes to refresh my memory, in routine cases like the hundreds of impaired driving check stops I conduct throughout the year?

A: You do need to have some recollection of events you are testifying about to affirmatively answer the notes qualifying questions, but you don't need to independently remember every single detail since your notes can "refresh" your memory. Your memory might not extend past recalling dealing with the accused, some of your basic conversation and observations, and that you ultimately laid a charge because the accused failed a blood-alcohol test. Your notes can prompt you for details like the date and time of stop, exact conversations and observations, exact readings, exact rights and cautions provided, and exact outcome of your investigation. If you truly don't remember anything about the case, and don't even recall ever seeing the accused before, you need to say so because your notes definitely won't be refreshing your memory.

ADOPTING EFFECTIVE NOTE-TAKING PROCEDURES

1. Why Follow a Particular Format and System of Note-Taking

The law does not care how you personally make your notes, just that those notes get made in a way having circumstantial guarantees of reliability. Most investigators still use small field notebooks to write in because they are very portable and simple to use. Notes can be made in them as events are happening, in any environmental conditions — a pencil can even be used in rainy or cold conditions where ink will not work. Their only limitation is that they tend to fill up fairly quickly; investigators must have a reliable way of storing past notebooks so they can be easily retrieved for future cases.

Investigation notes made in larger notebooks or on notepads are equally acceptable from a legal perspective, and may be more practical in complex cases where an investigator is coordinating activities at a search site or examining commercial crime. I would still suggest maintaining a field notebook unless a larger notebook or notepad will be carried at all times when on duty — you never know when some useful fact might be seen or overheard, and thus need to be written down. I caution against using notepads because of the tendency of their individual sheets to get out of order, or become scattered among a vast arrays of different files; if you choose to use them, a very well organized file folder system will be necessary to keep track of your notes.

Electronic note-taking through typing entries into a computer is increasingly being resorted to. I do not believe it is yet a complete substitute for handwritten field notes because of challenges in making contemporaneous electronic notes, but every investigator carrying a mini-computer where notes could be instantly made just like in current field notebooks would represent an immeasurable advance in the justice system. Preparing the prosecution brief and disclosure package would only involve an automatic download of information. Most electronic note-taking currently seems to be going on back at investigator offices, many hours after relevant events have happened, which will require rough notes made on paper to get times and other precise details right.

Whatever note-taking format is used, it needs to be consistent and a system to keep track of the notes must be in place. Inconsistent formats lacking a tracking system combined with increasing case scope and complexity can lead to disclosure debacles as happened in *R. v. Trang*, 2002 ABQB 744 at para. 134:

> Staff Sgt. N. . . . created handwritten notes from about February 12, 1999 until around April 19, 1999. He was aware of the importance of note-taking. He chose to stop using this method of note-taking and to rely mainly on the laptop notes which the investigators had started using around February 25, 1999, and the various draft affidavits, "resort to" memoranda (request for approval to monitor additional numbers which he prepared), police occurrence reports (R2s and R1s) and some handwritten notes on foolscap. As the file developed, it became more and more difficult to keep up with the handwritten note-taking, for example when he was involved in drafting Affidavit 1635 as well as reviewing calls. His initial good intentions were eroded by the amount of work that he had to do. He found taking handwritten notes was onerous and redundant; the laptop was available and most of the investigative steps that he was taking were in relation to "resort to's," and those notes were

kept directly on the "resort to" document. In some instances regarding incidents or particular investigative efforts, he made notes on foolscap, and the notes were removed from the tablet and put in a file folder. He did not keep notes about where he was keeping his notes, nor did he keep an inventory of the documents that were ultimately found in the six boxes in the fall of 2001. He did not generally keep notes or a log of what other investigators would report to him during the course of the investigation. Sometimes he would jot down notes before adding the information to the Affidavits; he did not believe he had kept these types of notes. Other times, he typed the information from investigators directly into the draft. On cross-examination, Staff Sgt. N. . . acknowledged that individual examples of handwritten notes which he had taken were not onerous.

A hardbound notebook with sequential dated entries or effective note-taking software used consistently could have avoided the situation in *Trang* where box after box of undisclosed potentially relevant material continually emerged into the blinding spotlight of court scrutiny.

2. Why Notes Must Be Legible

Legibility is an absolute necessity if investigator notes are to be included in the prosecution brief and disclosure package. Printing (or typing) notes is best. Before passing your case notes on to whomever will prepare the prosecution brief, you need to assess whether your style of note writing or the quality of note photocopying render any of your notes illegible. When acting as the investigator-in-charge of a case, you need to assess the entire prosecution brief for legibility before it leaves your hands. If any notes are incomprehensible, a typed copy should be prepared by the investigator who originally made them. Dealing proactively with legibility issues will save you lots of grief down the road when the prosecution or defence might demand legible copies at the last minute.

There may be times when you think notes are legible, but the defence or prosecution disagrees. The time you will waste arguing with them over whether or not the notes are illegible could be greater than the time it will take you to produce a typed copy. Ignoring prosecution or defence requests for legible notes risks the result of *R. v. Bidyk*, 2003 SKPC 124 at paras. 55-56:

> I find that the notes are not sufficiently legible so as to compare them with the officer's report included in the disclosure. Nor are they sufficiently legible to understand their content. The Crown

conveyed the request for a typed copy to the Officer without protest or comment. Indeed the Crown has not refused to provide the notes; rather the Officer has refused and no reason was given for the refusal. There is no dispute but that the Defence is entitled to an officer's notes. That being the case it is reasonable that where the notes are illegible that the defence receive a typed or legible copy of these notes. As counsel is entitled to an officer's notes as a matter of disclosure prior to trial, it follows that the Defence cannot be required to wait until the officer is on the witness stand before the notes are deciphered. I do not consider a request for a typed copy of the officer's notes to be onerous provided it is not insisted upon at the outset but rather is requested only once Counsel has received a copy and has first attempted to read the notes without success. This decision addresses police officer's notes, only. It will be up to another court on another occasion to decide whether transcription would be required of other documents included in Crown disclosure. Clearly the arresting officer has a significant role as both witness and investigator.

The notes of an arresting officer on charges of impaired driving and driving while over .08 are clearly important to preparation for the Defence. Refusal to provide this disclosure in this case is a breach of s.7 of the *Charter*.

Those reviewing the prosecution brief or disclosure package should not feel like they are playing a game of Scrabble, endlessly having to arrange and rearrange hazy letters on a page in an attempt to make out legible words. Instead of a double word score, illegibility may lead to a stay of proceedings.

3. Why Include the Details in Your Notes

Making sure all relevant details are included in your notes both guarantees you won't later forget important bits of what happened, and proves to the court that what you are testifying about really did happen. Some necessary details for your notes might include:

- the times of *all* relevant events;
- the means by which you made your observations, including technical specifications of mechanical or electronic aids like binoculars so that claiming to see a specific denomination of money change hands from 50 metres does not strain credulity;

- physical descriptions that rely not just on skin colour and clothing, and instead try to fix on unique identifying features that will enable in-court identification of accused months or years later;

- statements (and questions) recorded as close to word-for-word as possible, regardless of how insignificant a statement might seem at the time it is made;

- the factual basis supporting your use of investigative powers;

- reasons for stopping any person or vehicle;

- the basis for arresting any person;

- the basis for searching any person or place;

- the basis for taking any other action against a person that requires a legal threshold be crossed, like administering a roadside breath screening test;

- lists of what, from where and from whom items were seized; and

- what was done with any item after it was seized.

The Visual Observations Checklist, at the end of this chapter, will help you review the details of your surveillance notes for completeness shortly after you make them. Granted there is more to investigator note-taking than just recording observations, but this is an area where detail really counts and lends itself to a checklist format. You may also find the Reasonable and Probable Grounds (RPG) Threshold Checklist, at the end of Chapter 8, and the Detention, Arrest and Statement Rights to Counsel and Caution Checklist, at the end of chapter 12, of additional help in reviewing note-taking completeness.

4. Why Seek Clarity in Note-Taking

Since the primary purpose of notes is to refresh memory, they need not be constructed in overly artful sentences and paragraphs. Point form may sometimes suffice, as may abbreviations, but notes that rely on too many abbreviations run a risk of confusing others as happened in *R. v. Drake*, 2001 CarswellNfld 376 (Prov. Ct.) at para. 35:

> But Cst. F. . .'s evidence is confusing for me. That is partly because of the shorthand method he employed when making the notes and some inconsistencies in his testimony. Earlier in these reasons, when discussing Cst. F. . .'s use of the "Q", "BD" and "PC" refer-

ences, I used them myself partly to be true to the way his evidence was related and partly to convey the effect his testimony had for me. I am at a loss, without the benefit of continuing references to the pre-printed forms and Cst. F. . .'s "additions" to them, to keep the references clear in my mind. I do have less difficulty with the BD references than the Q references, for obvious reasons, but the constant use of initials, takes away from the clarity of the matter. It strikes me that the phrases "Roadside Demand", "Breathalyzer Demand", "Right to Counsel", and "Police Caution" are relatively simple and could easily be incorporated in the note-taking process and would certainly avoid the confusion that a proliferation of initials tends to wreak.

Field notes that cannot be deciphered by the prosecution, defence, court or even your own colleagues because of lack of clarity and excessive use of abbreviations may need to be redone for the purpose of the prosecution brief and disclosure package. A complete will-say or can-say as discussed below may avoid redoing notes in some situations, but the most efficient way to prepare notes is to make them clear the first time round.

Clarity in field note-taking may sound like a dubious proposition, but there are a few things you can do to maximize the chances of your notes being understood by others:

- print, don't write;

- use a black or blue ballpoint pen to minimize ink run, and enhance character darkness for later photocopying;

- use a lined notebook to keep notes straight and spaced apart;

- use a notebook with a hardcover to maximize durability, and minimize the chances of notes being destroyed if subjected to extreme abuse;

- clearly indicate places in notes where a statement or seizure of an item has been recorded by using a mark like "*" to catch later readers' attention;

- write in a style you are comfortable with so when you rely on the notes to give testimony they will speak to you in the same way you will speak to the court;

- err on the side of leaving too much white space in the notebook, not so little that reading the notes is a difficult chore and there is no room to later make corrections;

- draw carefully labeled diagrams right in the notebook when they better describe events than words alone;

- staple scrap pieces of rough notes right into the notebook next to the entries that expand on them; and

- try not to include confidential informer identifying information that will later necessitate a black marker scavenger hunt through all your notebooks in the hope of finding and deleting all such references prior to defence disclosure being made.

Most investigative agencies will have detailed note-taking policies that expand on the basic points mentioned here.

5. Why Attempt to Preserve Rough Notes

Rough notes jot down visual observations as they happen. They are made on anything from proper pads of paper to the sides of cigarette packages. There is nothing wrong with investigators making rough notes; the sooner notes are made, the easier it is to demonstrate in court that details in the notes were accurately recorded. Preserving rough notes where possible, perhaps by stapling them into a notebook, allows later demonstration that they were faithfully transcribed, and perhaps expanded on, into the formal notes of an investigator.

There is not yet any definitive requirement to preserve all rough notes, but courts have been moving in that direction as in *R. v. Satkunananthan* (2001), 143 O.A.C. 1 at paras. 71 & 80:

> every officer who took rough notes during surveillance destroyed them. The officers explained that in 1993 it was not standard practice to keep rough notes made during surveillance. Although the officers were not advised to shred their notes, there was no policy prohibiting the destruction of notes. One officer, S. . ., testified that the procedures governing preservation of notes had changed greatly as a result of court decisions and the Martin Report
>
> . . .
>
> The importance of preserving original notes is undoubtedly understood differently today than at the time of this investigation and similar actions by police officers could well constitute "unacceptable negligence" in a different context. However, in the circumstances of this case, where the sparse rough notes and the surveillance report were fully transcribed in notebooks that were pre-

served and disclosed to the defence, it was open to the trial judge
to find that the surveillance officers had complied with their duty
to preserve evidence.

An explanation by investigators at trial of how and why rough notes were dealt with in a particular way goes a long way towards addressing concerns of improper destruction.

If it is not possible to preserve rough notes, extra care must be taken to perfectly transcribe and *not* improve on their content. Improper improving isn't just changing the substantive content, like changing your initial rough note of green eyes to what you confirm later are brown eyes, but also includes changing the language used, usually because of a misguided intent to make it more acceptable to the court. Don't change notes like "fat ass" to "large rear." The first characterization appears more credible to a court, if that is how you would describe the observation on the street. Accurately transcribe profanity — the judge's ears won't break to later hear it.

6. Why Protect Privileged Information

No privileged information should remain in the notes you pass on to the prosecutor through the prosecution brief. Privileged information that you might need to record somewhere could fall under informer privilege, as discussed in Chapter 4, as well as solicitor-client or public interest privilege, as dealt with in Chapter 9. Privilege will be breached if a prosecution brief containing privileged information is copied and sent out as part of the disclosure package. Either copy your notes, black out the privileged information on the copy, and then recopy the blacked-out pages, or better yet don't include privileged information in your notes in the first place — record it in a special secure file in your office.

If you do hold back privileged information, prepare confidential instructions for the prosecutor identifying that a privilege issue exists, specifying the class of information to be protected, and explaining the reason for protection. For example, you could say something like: "the exact location from which surveillance on the target was conducted cannot be revealed as it is important to protect it for use in future investigations, and its disclosure would endanger the safety of a member of the public who allowed us to use that location." It is only if the potential privilege issue is properly explained to the prosecutor in advance of trial that the best information protection can be sought.

7. Why Follow Agency Note-Taking Policies

Many investigative agencies have formal note-taking policies addressing how notes are made, in what format, the deadline for completion, by whom and who holds a property interest in those notes. Those policies tend to be legally sound; it is compliance with them that causes difficulties. *R. v. Hutchens*, 1998 CarswellOnt 4033 (Ont. C.J. (Prov. Div.)) at paras. 26-27, found police note-taking policies to be well developed, with extensive note-taking instructions preprinted in each memo book:

> intended to result in the Memorandum Book being a contemporary record of all of the time in the officer's work day, including the lunch break. They are the culmination of the Police Services Board's policy and procedure directives and rules as provided for in the *Police Services Act* . . . The only exception to the mandatory rule of keeping contemporaneous notes are in specific exceptions granted by the Chief of Police in specific special circumstances such as drug investigations when an officer is working undercover.

But serious disclosure problems arose from failures to follow policy, as noted at para. 29:

> the failure by the officers to follow standard police note taking procedures and their consistent failure to take adequate notes concealed the origins of the investigation, the initial involvements of Constables R. . ., T. . . and M. . ., and the circumstances of key witness interviews and the police acquisition of crucial documents. These "missing notes" and this missing "paper trail" were the subject of defence requests for disclosure, documented above, and the ultimate reason for the delay in this matter coming to trial.

The court found at para. 61 that "Policy and Procedures with respect to contemporaneous note taking . . . are being ignored," summarizing at paras. 130-131 a few of the problems:

> In this application I have learned that the police did not initially record their interview with the princip[al] complainants and witnesses, and did not keep track of the initial manner and time of the reception of documents. One of those initially interviewed, without any notes taken, Mr. Bowler, is now dead. I have learned that T. . . and R. . . obtained bank records and other material without disclosing to the defence how it was obtained.
>
> When confronted with these irregularities in the Pre-Trial process, the police stalled, or dissembled, or simply refused to follow up

> until the defence threatened to commence this application. R. . . is
> now retired and doesn't know where his notes are.

The court found the accused's ability to make full answer and defence had
been so impaired by note-taking deficiencies to justify a stay of proceedings.
Investigators who are lax in following applicable agency note-taking policies will lead a court to wonder what other investigative policies may have
had corners cut during the building of the case. Note-taking practices really set the tone for an entire investigation.

8. Why Prepare Will-Says and Can-Says

Even though field notes are now disclosed, there is still value in having
a brief one paragraph summary of each investigator's evidence present in
both the prosecution brief and disclosure package as a "will-say" or "can-
say." Without that summary, it can be impossible for either the prosecution
or defence to figure out prior to trial the precise roles investigators played
in a case. After all, field notes are supposed to be for your own use, not part
of a formal presentation. Incomprehensible notes can even lead to a failure
of the entire case if anticipated evidence is misunderstood so necessary
investigators are left off the required witness list, or are not asked necessary
questions when on the stand.

A will-say or can-say, interchangeable terms for the same documents
depending on where you work in Canada, ideally is prepared for each and
every witness, not just for civilians who don't have notes. Usually the lead
investigator prepares them based on information contained in the investigative file, they are checked for accuracy with the witnesses if necessary, and
differ from formal witness statements in that they are summaries, *not* verbatim statements, of the evidence each witness *can* or *will* provide. Each can-
say or will-say is contained on a separate page, states the witness' name,
place of employment, role in the investigation, and summary of evidence.
Figure 3-1 provides a Sample Can-Say/Will-Say Statement for a witness who
has only very minor involvement in a case. These documents may initially
create slightly more work than just photocopying investigator notes, but
save work in the long run by eliminating the frequent need to recopy notes
into a more legible form or respond to endless pretrial inquiries or trial
questioning by the prosecution and defence about an investigator's role.

Fig 3-1

SAMPLE WITNESS CAN-SAY/WILL-SAY STATEMENT

Case name: R. v. Howard Smith and Melvin Jones

Witness name: P/C Priscilla Boudreau

Organization: Royal Canadian Mounted Police - Manitoba Drug Task Force

Role in Investigation: Security officer for search of 123 Maple St., Winnipeg, MB

Summary of evidence that can be given:

On 8 May 2005 at 10 p.m., I attended at 123 Maple St. in Winnipeg with other members of the Manitoba Drug Task Force to assist in the execution of a search warrant. I acted solely as a security officer, and did not seize anything, take any statements, nor do I have any other evidence to provide.

A can-say/will-say is not a substitute for good detailed field notes, nor should it simply repeat what is in those notes. It is a very brief summary of how a particular witness is relevant to the case. It assists both the prosecutor and the defence in assessing if, how, and where the witness fits into the case puzzle. Here P/C Boudreau might have attended briefings leading up to the execution of the warrant, or had other peripheral involvement in the case which is mentioned in her notebook, but which does not appear in the can-say/will-say because it is not material evidence.

Will-Says and Can-Says Versus Notes

Q&A

Q: We used to provide will-says to the prosecutor's office for disclosure to the defence, but then defence counsel started demanding copies of all our notes. Since the notes are more complete than the will-says ever were, we've stopped providing will-says. Why should we go to all the trouble of providing both notes and will-says?

A: At the time notes are made by investigators, it is usually impossible to know what details in those notes will be relevant to a trial, and whether a prosecution will ever ensue. The primary purpose of making notes is to later refresh the note-taker's memory about the details of a case, not to provide a concise synopsis of relevant witness evidence for an upcoming trial. Will-says or can-says are provided for the very different purpose of telling the prosecutor and defence in summary form what relevant evidence a particular witness has to offer.

GIVING EFFECTIVE TESTIMONY FROM YOUR NOTES

1. Why Testimony Inconsistent with Notes Hurts Credibility

Notes are there to refresh your memory, so use them to do so. Occasional note checks will not hurt credibility, but even minor discrepancies from those notes in your oral testimony can undermine an otherwise sound case. Those who are truly the most skilled as witnesses review their notes and resolve note discrepancies before trial, take the briefest of glances at notes, can quickly turn up any page of notes containing a detail relevant to an answer, and never read those notes out loud in court unless requested to do so by the prosecution, defence or court.

Consistency between notes and testimony means more than merely avoiding express contradictions. Glaring omissions from notes that later become key parts of oral testimony also qualify as inconsistencies. You are not restricted to only giving testimony about what is in your notes, but the onus may be on you to justify why you left out something that becomes an important element of your trial testimony.

In *R. v. Carlson*, 2003 BCSC 593 at paras. 46-53 an officer's testimony appeared to both expressly contradict and include significant details omitted from her notes:

> On the evidence, I am satisfied, on a balance of probabilities, that Constable G... stopped the accused's vehicle not because she observed an unsecured licence plate and wished to check the vehi-

cle's registration and insurance documents, but pursuant to a criminal investigation. I reach that conclusion for the following reasons.

First, the Constable agreed on cross-examination that the complainant had indicated that the residence could possibly be a drug house, and her evidence regarding her initial dispatch to the location was that persons claiming to be police officers investigating drug offences had been there. Thus, she had been observing the residence at 12166 101A Avenue as a place possibly connected to drugs.

Second, her notes indicate that she checked the licence plates on all of the vehicles at the house, including the van, at the same time while she was parked in the cul-de-sac. I do not accept her evidence that she checked the number on the van later, after she had stopped it, and then went back and wrote the information into a space she left in her notes. Her testimony seemed evasive and was unconvincing in this regard.

Third, there was no reference in her notes to a licence plate, to insurance or to any possible *Motor Vehicle Act* infraction, nor was there such reference in her discussion with Mr. Carlson or in her Report to Crown Counsel. I recognize, as Crown counsel pointed out, that police officers are not uniform in their note-taking practices and that sometimes they only record what they need to as an aide-memoire. However, the fact that the notes do not confirm Constable G. . .'s version of events is a factor that I take into account. Fourth, no ticket was issued with respect to a dangling licence plate or any other *Motor Vehicle Act* offence.

. . .

Here the officer did not assert that the detention was pursuant to a criminal investigation, but instead testified that her reason for stopping Mr. Carlson was to check the vehicle's insurance and registration documents. The Crown did not argue that there was articulable cause to stop the vehicle pursuant to a criminal investigation. Such an argument would have been wholly inconsistent with Constable G. . .'s testimony.

Therefore, having rejected her evidence, I find that the detention was unlawful.

To save this case, the officer involved should have made more complete field notes, included any missing details as identified additions for the prosecution brief and disclosure package, and dealt with note deficiencies pointed out to her during her testimony in a very direct way rather than coming across as "evasive and unconvincing."

Consistency Through Preparation

Q&A

Q: How am I supposed to testify in a perfectly consistent way with my notes if I am not supposed to read my notes as I testify?

A: Consistency is achieved through advance preparation, rather than reading as you testify. Read over your notes before the trial. Sort out any inconsistencies between your memory and the notes at that point. During the trial after qualifying your notes it is acceptable to read your notes for precise details like a licence plate number you would not be expected to memorize.

2. Why Stick to "Dids" Rather than "Would Haves"

Investigators need to consistently follow a reliable system of detailed note-taking so they can later testify in court about how they took their notes and what they "did" do in a particular case, rather than what they "would have" done because it was their standard practice. A "did" guarantees testimonial reliability. A "would have" is ambiguous, prone to exceptions, and does not inspire confidence in the accuracy of the note-taker.

R. v. Pilarinos, 2002 BCSC 798 at paras. 17-19, illustrates the trial credibility problems an investigator will struggle with if she cannot demonstrate what practice she consistently followed in taking notes:

> I find from the evidence that she had no real recollection of how she took her notes in this case. She repeatedly said "I would have". Even when she was asked not to respond in that manner, she continued. She was obliged to fall back on the practice she usually kept when taking notes. She recalled making notes on a napkin which she later destroyed. She recalled going to the washroom in the restaurant and dictating on a tape-recorder. She also telephoned one of her team-mates, who she no longer recalled, and told that person a narrative, which he or she wrote down and returned to her. She could not say for certain that the conversation she heard was in the right chronology.
>
> Thus, some of her record is from information she gave to another person, who wrote it down, and then gave it back to her. None of the tape-recordings she made were kept or transcribed verbatim. She was not clear when she made her notes. She prepared an

appendix afterwards which she said "would have been" sourced from her tape-recorder, her handwritten notes on the napkin and possibly information from a phone call. She said when she does receive information from her team mates she attempts to match it against her recollection of the conversation.

In cross-examination, Constable C. . . testified that she wrote down everything she could hear down onto the paper napkin and then transcribed it into her notes. Minutes later she said that she did not write down everything she heard on the napkin and said that she ran out of room on the napkin. Then she said she was unable to continue writing because there were people walking around.

This investigator's scattered testimony about note-taking practices led the court to exclude her evidence because it could not be said her notes were made in a reliable way, or that she knew them to be true at the time they were made, plus the original notes had been destroyed by the time of trial.

Saying it was your usual practice to do something is not credible evidence you actually did it in a specific case, as pointed out in *R. v. Mahar*, 2004 BCPC 28 at paras. 8 & 13:

The sergeant acknowledged that he was a veteran police officer with many years experience, and had been involved in many impaired driving investigations. The sergeant also acknowledged that he recognized that he was dealing with a care and control case, and it was, and I quote, "his practice" to attempt to start any vehicle in like circumstances. He has no note of doing so in this case. However, he says the keys were in the ignition, and that he leaned into the vehicle and started it up.

. . .

I find that [the] Sergeant . . . was mistaken about the location of the keys. They were not in the ignition. I am not persuaded that, while it may have been his practice to start a vehicle in such a care and control type of investigation, that he did so in this instance. In fact, I find the vehicle was not operable due to the lack of fuel.

Even a usual practice needs to be noted down at the time the practice is resorted to if it may become important in proof of a case. Clear, contemporaneous and complete notes are the goal.

On the Importance of Note-Taking

KEY POINTS

✓ If a fact is not in your notes, it might not be accepted by the courts unless it is of the most general nature. An investigator may need to offer an adequate explanation for why a significant fact was not noted, but is nonetheless being advanced at trial as the truth. When notes are well constructed, courts will accepts them for all manner of facts and they will enhance your credibility as a witness.

✓ Notes must be qualified as being made personally, contemporaneously with events in question, with any subsequent additions or deletions clearly identified, and the person relying on them must have an independent recollection of events in order for them to be used to refresh memory in court.

✓ Disclosure obligations require a consistent format of clear, complete, legible note-taking, with a system to track all notes taken by all investigators. Details that need to be recorded include times, means of observations, physical descriptions, statements, factual bases for use of investigative powers, lists of what, from where and whom items were seized, and what was done with items after their seizure.

✓ Preferably preserve or at least faithfully transcribe rough notes. Black out all potentially privileged information from investigator notes before they are included in the prosecution brief or disclosure package, and flag any confidential Crown instructions and the general nature of deletions. Preparing will-say or can-say statements is still important even where personal notes are being disclosed.

✓ The witnesses most skilled at delivering testimony resolve note discrepancies before trial, only glance at and can quickly navigate around notes, and stick to "dids" rather than "would haves" when recounting their actions in a case.

Use this checklist to review field notes for completeness, or to record observations directly.

A   CONDITIONS OF OBSERVATIONS

❏ Location observations taken from: _____

   ❏ Investigators present at observation post: _____

❏ Location being observed: _____

❏ Names of observation target(s): _____

❏ Time observations conducted: _____

❏ Weather: _____

❏ Visibility: _____

❏ Artificial lighting: _____

❏ Distance to target(s): _____

❏ Height above/below target(s): _____

❏ Obstructions in line of sight: _____

❏ Mechanical aids used to observe: _____

❏ Electronic aids used to observe: _____

❏ Observations recorded:

   ❏ In notebooks by _____

   ❏ On audio recording by _____

   ❏ In photos by _____

   ❏ On video by _____

B   WHAT WAS OBSERVED

Target #1 ❏ physical appearance: _____

              _____

              ❏ description of clothing: _____

              _____

              ❏ description of physical mannerisms: _____

              _____

              ❏ description of vehicle/residence including plate number and address:

              _____

              ❏ identified by name as: _____

              _____

Target #2 ❏ physical appearance: _____

              _____

❑ description of clothing:_____

❑ description of physical mannerisms:_____

❑ description of vehicle/residence including plate number and address:
_____

❑ identified by name as:_____

Target #3 ❑ physical appearance:_____

❑ description of clothing: _____

❑ description of physical mannerisms:_____

❑ description of vehicle/residence including plate number and address:
_____

❑ identified by name as: _____

Activity observed:

❑ target #___ speaking with target #___

❑ target #___ handing object to target #___

❑ target #___ entering/leaving premises/vehicle with target #___

❑ target #___ doing_____with target #___

Other observations:_____
_____
_____
_____
_____
_____
_____
_____
_____

FURTHER READING

Cases

R. v. Carosella, [1997] 1 S.C.R. 80. Deliberate destruction of relevant notes taken by a third-party may result in a stay of proceedings being imposed by the trial court.

R. v. Fliss, [2002] 1 S.C.R. 535. Sets out criteria for notes to be admitted as a past recollection recorded.

R. v. La, [1997] 2 S.C.R. 680. Lost notes could entitle an accused to a stay of proceedings, but a remedy depends on the relevance of the notes and the circumstances of the loss, including whether an alternative source of similar information is available and the degree of negligence leading to the loss.

R. v. Satkunananthan (2001), 143 O.A.C. 1. It is acceptable to transcribe rough notes into more complete final notes that are supplemented by the notes of a central note-taker.

Books

G. Araco, *Principles of Law Enforcement Report Writing*, 2nd ed. (Toronto: Thomson, 2004).

R.L. Bintliff, *How to Write Effective Law Enforcement Reports* (Englewood Cliffs, N.J.: Prentice Hall, 1991).

K. Jakob, *A Guide to Police Writing*, 3rd ed. (Toronto: Carswell, 2002).

K. Rogers-Rupp, *Police Writing: A Guide to the Essentials* (Upper Saddle River, NJ: Pearson/Prentice Hall, 2005).

CHAPTER FOUR

THE USE AND PROTECTION OF INFORMERS

Informer privilege is an ancient and hallowed protection which plays a vital role in law enforcement.

R. v. Leipert, [1997] 1 S.C.R. 281 at para. 9.

In This Chapter

- The value and challenges of informers
- Carefully guarding informer privilege
- Distinguishing investigation informers from charge informers
- How offering inducements to informers affects credibility
- Dealing with assistance and immunity agreements
- Limitations on prosecutor involvement with informers
- The who and how of avoiding entrapment

The relationship between informers and their handlers is a very human one, but an invisible legal web binds them together. Information flows through the web from informer to investigator, and tangible or intangible compensation sometimes flows back from investigator to informer. Some strands of the web might be made up of vague rumours, others of authenticated documents or covertly made recordings. Some strands could be small amounts of cash, others wide-ranging grants of immunity. Although these strands each exert some force in holding the relationship together, informer privilege is the substance that really makes the entire web strong. It is extremely difficult for outsiders to cut through the privilege that suffuses the web, but an informer can voluntarily choose to break free from it.

THE VALUE AND CHALLENGES OF INFORMERS

Sometimes referred to as human sources, and also called agents when they are acting at the direction of investigators, informers play a variety of vital roles in criminal and regulatory investigations. While you may hear "informers" also called "informants," the term "informant" is used by academic researchers like anthropologists to refer to people who provide information that assists their research, so it is best if investigators stick to using "informer." Some informers are useful only for developing initial leads, others contribute information to search warrant applications, and the best of them establish reasonable and probable grounds to lay charges. Investigators handling informers face many challenges in protecting informer safety through maintaining privilege, not impairing informer credibility through improperly offered inducements to cooperate, and maintaining case integrity by avoiding actions taken by themselves or their agents amounting to entrapment.

Courts have repeatedly stressed the value of informers and the risks they take, as in *R. v. Scott*, [1990] 3 S.C.R. 979 at 994:

> The value of informers to police investigations has long been recognized. As long as crimes have been committed, certainly as long as they have been prosecuted, informers have played an important role in their investigation. It may well be true that some informers act for compensation or for self-serving purposes. Whatever their motives, the position of informers is always precarious and their role is fraught with danger.

The ancient and hallowed protection informer privilege offers to those who provide information to investigators permits the shielding of informer identity from disclosure in most cases, but there are important exceptions to this protective rule that every investigator needs to know.

My experience with informers and their information has led me to expect the unexpected, and develop contingency plans. There is always an unpredictable element in whether an informer will tell investigators only what they want to hear, will disappear prior to trial, or will recant earlier statements when it comes time to testify at trial. Canadian law enforcement agencies each have distinct policies on when and how human sources can be employed, but there are legal requirements common to all informer situations which make demystification of the law possible. The Informer

Checklist, at the end of this chapter, will help you confirm whether you have considered the most important of those requirements. Where the informer-investigator relationship is more complex, early investigator-prosecutor contact will pay great dividends.

CAREFULLY GUARDING INFORMER PRIVILEGE

Any information potentially leading to informer identity being revealed must not be disclosed to the defence and cannot be spoken of in court testimony without the informer having waived privilege. A detail as small as the location from where police observations were conducted could trigger informer privilege if a private citizen made her residence available. *R. v. Leipert*, [1997] 1 S.C.R. 281 at para. 14, emphasized that "informer privilege is of such importance that it cannot be balanced against other interests. Once established, neither the police nor the court possesses discretion to abridge it." There are three key rules to remember about this privilege.

1. Informer Privilege Rule #1: The Privilege Effectively Belongs to the Informer

In theory informer privilege belongs to the Crown, but the Crown cannot waive the privilege without consent of the informer, so in a sense the privilege also belongs to the informer. The inadvertent disclosure of an informer's identity could lead to the informer being harmed or a civil suit brought against those who made such a disclosure. Risks of accidental informer privilege waiver must be guarded against, as noted in *R. v. Leipert*, [1997] 1 S.C.R. 281 at para. 16:

> The fact that the privilege also belongs to the informer raises special concerns in the case of anonymous informants, like those who provide telephone tips to Crime Stoppers. Since the informer whom the privilege is designed to protect and his or her circumstances are unknown, it is often difficult to predict with certainty what information might allow the accused to identify the informer. A detail as innocuous as the time of the telephone call may be sufficient to permit identification. In such circumstances, courts must exercise great care not to unwittingly deprive informers of the privilege which the law accords to them.

Once informer privilege is compromised, it is too late to get the cat back in the bag.

If there has been an inadvertent breach of privilege it might still be possible to negotiate a privilege waiver agreement with an informer, but an informer in that unenviable position should receive independent legal advice. Without waiver, continuing to protect some semblance of privilege could result in an untimely but necessary termination of a prosecution. That is the price that sometimes must be paid for informer information.

2. Informer Privilege Rule #2: The "Innocence at Stake" Exception Takes Precedence

The "innocence at stake" exception to informer privilege can be invoked if the accused demonstrates to a court that there will not be a fair trial without knowing the identity or other details connected to an informer. As *R. v. Scott*, [1990] 3 S.C.R. 979 at para. 37, put it: "In our system the right of an individual accused to establish his or her innocence by raising a reasonable doubt as to guilt has always remained paramount." An accused must follow the procedure set out in *R. v. Leipert*, [1997] 1 S.C.R. 281 at para. 33:

> When an accused seeks disclosure of privileged informer information on the basis of the "innocence at stake" exception, the following procedure will apply. First, the accused must show some basis to conclude that without the disclosure sought his or her innocence is at stake. If such a basis is shown, the court may then review the information to determine whether, in fact, the information is necessary to prove the accused's innocence. If the court concludes that disclosure is necessary, the court should only reveal as much information as is essential to allow proof of innocence. Before disclosing the information to the accused, the Crown should be given the option of staying the proceedings. If the Crown chooses to proceed, disclosure of the information essential to establish innocence may be provided to the accused.

Prosecutor and investigator cooperation is required to probe whether there is a valid foundation to any exception claim, ascertain how much privileged information might satisfy defence disclosure demands, and discuss the situation with the informer to determine willingness to waive privilege over the necessary amount of information.

There are primarily three situations where the innocence at stake exception can be successfully invoked:

- where the informer is a material witness to the crime being prosecuted;

- where the informer is acting as an "agent" of the state; or

- where allegations of *Charter* infringement lead to informer identity disclosure being necessary to establish the basis for valid state investigative actions.

Before proceeding too far with any investigation, a determination must be made of whether informer identity, because of the role an informer is playing in a case, will ultimately need to be exposed as part of trial disclosure. An informer who is also an agent has to understand that giving testimony in court may be necessary. If an informer-agent is not willing to testify with revealed identity, then that informer's use in the case needs to be discontinued and other avenues of investigation pursued. The entire investigation may have to be discontinued if an informer-agent who will not waive privilege has already played a pivotal role in gathering evidence.

Declining to Answer Because of Informer Privilege

Q&A

Q: What should I do if I am on the witness stand, and am asked a question by defence counsel that requires an answer that could reveal the identity of an informer, but the prosecutor does not object to the question?

A: The prosecutor will usually not be as well versed in the facts of the case as the investigators who gathered the evidence, and therefore may not realize the expected answer will compromise informer identity. It is up to you as a witness to decline to answer the question, based on informer privilege, and to clearly state why this answer would tend to reveal identity. If the prosecutor then suggests you answer the question anyway, but you are *sure* an answer would compromise the informer, you should continue to refuse to answer. While technically you cannot speak privately to the prosecutor when under oath as a witness, the court may grant leave for you to do so to sort out the situation so that you can explain the facts to the prosecutor and the prosecutor can explain the law to you. If you both still disagree over whether the question should be answered, you should ask for time to seek independent legal counsel.

3. Informer Privilege Rule #3: Agents Are Informers But Informers Are Not Always Agents

Not all informers are agents of the state, regardless of whether or not they are paid for their information, but all agents are informers. Agents are therefore still able to rely on informer privilege, except to the extent that identity information must be disclosed to ensure the accused receives a fair trial. Knowing when an informer becomes an agent is vital to considering what guarantees of confidentiality can be offered to someone who assists an investigation. If the informer takes an active part in the investigation beyond merely providing information, like through introducing a narcotics investigator to a dealer, then the informer may be an agent. But if the informer only passes on information, like that there are drugs in a particular apartment, without express direction from a law enforcement agency to gather that information, then there will likely be no agent status.

A "But For State Direction" test applies in determining whether an informer is also an agent according to *R. v. Broyles*, [1991] 3 S.C.R. 595 at 608:

> In some cases, it will be clear that the person . . . was an agent of the state. For example, if the statements were made to a police officer or to a prison official, whether in uniform or in plainclothes, there could be no question that the statements were made to an agent of the state. In other cases, it will be less clear. Where the statements are made to an informer . . . it may be arguable whether or not the coercive power of the state was brought to bear on the suspect in obtaining the statement from him or her.

> In determining whether or not the informer is a state agent, it is appropriate to focus on the effect of the relationship between the informer and the authorities on the particular exchange or contact with the accused . . . A relationship between the informer and the authorities which develops after the statement is made, or which in no way affects the exchange between the informer and the accused, will not make the informer a state agent for the purposes of the exchange in question. Only if the relationship between the informer and the state is such that the exchange between the informer and the accused is materially different from what it would have been had there been no such relationship should the informer be considered a state agent for the purposes of the exchange. I would accordingly adopt the following simple test: would the exchange between the accused and the informer have taken place, in the form and manner in which it did take place, but for the intervention of the state or its agents?

Ask yourself anytime you are faced with an informer or agent dilemma, would the information, transaction or event involving the informer have happened "But For State Direction?" If the answer is yes, then you may not have an agent. If the answer is no, then there likely is an agent relationship.

The agent versus informer distinction can be a very fine one. The general principle is that informers who are material witnesses or *agent provocateurs* are effectively agents for the purpose of identity disclosure. The disclosure is necessary under the "innocence at stake" exception so that the accused can adequately test the prosecution's case during the trial. Figure 4-1, Just an Informer or Also an Agent Determination Flow Chart, provides guidance on the kinds of questions you should ask yourself and prosecutors in determining early in a case whether a private party involved in the investigation is solely an informer, or might also be regarded by the courts as an agent whose identity will have to be disclosed to the defence.

The Proper Use of the Terms Agent and Informer

Q: If I don't know if a source is an agent or an informer, how should I refer to that source in my notes?

A: Agents are still informers, although informers are not always agents. It is fair to initially refer to a source as an informer, even if technically the source is playing a role that might later be characterized as an agent, but the prosecution brief and disclosure should clarify agent status. Don't, however, fall into the habit of referring to every source in your notes simply as a "reliable confidential informer" without specifying why you believe the source to be reliable and confidentiality needs to be protected.

DISTINGUISHING INVESTIGATION INFORMERS FROM CHARGE INFORMERS

Investigation informers advance an investigation through providing information that assists with the discovery of admissible evidence, but don't directly provide that admissible evidence because they won't or can't testify about it at trial, and sometimes because their information doesn't amount to much more than rumour. Anonymous source information and known source information without waiver of privilege both fall into the investigation informer category. A "basic investigation informer" may only point your inquiries in the right direction, while an "advanced investigation informer" whose information is reasonably credible can be extremely useful to establishing the reasonable and probable grounds needed to secure authorization for a warrant or electronic surveillance. Investigation informer identify can be well protected in these circumstances because the guilt or innocence of an accused is not at issue in a warrant, though you do need to explain in

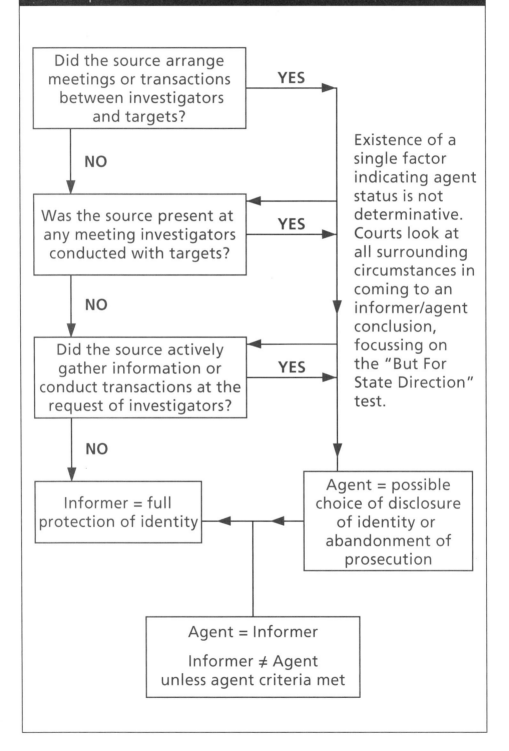

Fig 4-1 | JUST AN INFORMER OR ALSO AN AGENT DETERMINATION FLOW CHART

Did the source arrange meetings or transactions between investigators and targets?

YES

NO

Was the source present at any meeting investigators conducted with targets?

YES

NO

Did the source actively gather information or conduct transactions at the request of investigators?

YES

NO

Existence of a single factor indicating agent status is not determinative. Courts look at all surrounding circumstances in coming to an informer/agent conclusion, focussing on the "But For State Direction" test.

Informer = full protection of identity

Agent = possible choice of disclosure of identity or abandonment of prosecution

Agent = Informer

Informer ≠ Agent unless agent criteria met

the supporting affidavit the basis for why the source should be believed without giving away so much detail as to effectively reveal identity. In contrast to investigation informers, "charge informers" provide potentially admissible trial evidence because of their willingness to testify and the substantial credibility of their evidence.

I had one case where money and delayed deportation were strong enough motivators for an investigation informer to help police set up all sorts of undercover drug buys, but the prospect of imminent deportation after trial hardly encouraged him to be a reliable charge informer. When it came time for him to testify he was nowhere to be found, even though he had been waiting in court earlier that day. Following the early investigator-prosecutor contact theme in that case would preferably have permitted a proactive, joint pre-charge, or at least pretrial, assessment of whether the informer would be as dependable a charge informer as he had been an investigation informer.

Compelling a Source to Testify

Q&A

Q: What should I do if an informer agrees to testify, and has been subpoenaed, but then does not show for the trial? I don't want to burn the informer for future cases, but the prosecutor is talking about seeking a material witness warrant because this is a key witness needed to prove the case.

A: You and the prosecutor must discuss three things: how important is the witness to the present case, how important is the witness to future cases, and how likely will the witness still be truthful and forthcoming in giving testimony if brought in on a warrant? If the witness has already agreed to waive informer privilege, then it is ultimately the prosecutor's call on whether to attempt to compel testimony, but your knowledge of the informer's personality is vital in making an informed decision about a material witness warrant.

HOW OFFERING INDUCEMENTS TO INFORMERS AFFECTS CREDIBILITY

If the flow of information from informer to investigator is purely one-way (informer to investigator, not investigator to informer), then there is little cause for concern over inducements affecting informer credibility. If an informer is receiving something in return, that consideration needs to be disclosed along with the relevant informer information at the investigation stage in an information to obtain a search warrant or wiretap, and at the trial stage as part of disclosure. The *Report of the Kaufman Commission on Proceedings Involving Guy Paul Morin* (Toronto: Queen's Printer, 1998) commented in Recommendation 47 on what could amount to disclosable informer consideration:

> 3. Any offers or promises made by police, corrections authorities, Crown counsel, or a witness protection program to the informer or person associated with the informer in consideration for the information in the present case.
>
> 4. Any benefit given to the informer, members of the informer's family or any other person associated with the informer, or any benefits sought by such persons, as consideration for their co-operation with authorities, including but not limited to those kinds of benefits already listed in the Crown Policy Manual.
>
> 5. As noted earlier, any arrangements providing for a benefit (as set out above) should, absent exceptional circumstances, be reduced to writing and signed and/or be recorded on videotape. Such arrangements should be approved by a Director of Crown Operations or the In-Custody Informer Committee and disclosed to the defence prior to receiving the testimony of the witness (or earlier, in accordance with *Stinchcombe*).

Courts will review the context in which any consideration was offered in order to determine its affect on informer credibility.

The greater the value of the consideration, the greater the incentive the informer has to tell investigators what they want to hear regardless of what the truth might be. But a mere incentive to lie does not inevitably lead to the conclusion that a lie is being told, as noted in *R. v. Vetrovec*, [1982] 1 S.C.R. 811 at 821:

> Wigmore argued that the influence of the promise of immunity must depend on the nature of the charge and the personality of the accomplice. Even in cases where a promise of immunity is offered, it should not always be assumed that the accomplice cannot be trusted. "[C]redibility is a matter of elusive variety," Wigmore said, "and it is impossible and anachronistic to determine in advance that, with or without promise, a given man's story must be distrusted."

While investigators have control over inducements like money that form part of "assistance agreements" not involving charge consideration, any charge inducements like staying outstanding charges or immunity from future charges are effectively part of "immunity agreements" and can only be provided by senior prosecutors.

DEALING WITH ASSISTANCE AND IMMUNITY AGREEMENTS

1. How to Draft Assistance and Immunity Agreements

Assistance agreements can take various oral or written forms, depending on the type and level of assistance and consideration being traded. Immunity agreements must always be in writing, signed by an appropriate prosecutor and the informer. Demystifying the law means investigators shouldn't be afraid to negotiate either assistance or (with the help of prosecutors) immunity agreements. Early investigator-prosecutor contact will ensure agreement terms represent defensible joint efforts.

Like any legal contract, a good assistance or immunity agreement strives to cover all angles so no one is later surprised by the consequences. Both types of agreement need to address the same basic points:

- the names of the parties (usually the informer and the appropriate Attorney General);

- the names of all persons who will directly benefit from the agreement;

- what information or other assistance the informer will provide concerning which people, activities, places, and dates;

- whether through a waiver of privilege the informer will be required to provide truthful testimony at trial consistent with information the informer previously provided;

- what the informer will be provided in return: money, charge or sentencing consideration, protection, or something else within the power of the state to grant; and

- what will amount to and be the consequences of a breach of the agreement by either party.

Immunity agreements also need to address a number of additional points:

- the conduct and offences for which immunity is being provided;

- agreement limitations, like not extending to crimes other than those specified in the agreement;

- the form of immunity, like staying particular charges or undertaking not to prosecute charges yet to be laid.

Courts are willing to give a lot of leeway in how the wording of assistance or immunity agreements is structured, so long as that wording does not amount to an inducement to commit perjury as noted in *R. v. Dikah* (1994), 18 O.R. (3d) 302 (C.A.), at paras. 45-46, affd. *R. v. Dikah*, [1994] 3 S.C.R. 1020:

> Paragraph 7 of the agreement with Agent 21 merely makes explicit what would otherwise be assumed, that is, that the result of the agent's efforts would be considered in deciding his compensation. The value of paragraph 7 is that it makes that term readily ascertainable and capable of full exploration at trial before the trier of fact. I see great merit in committing a compensation agreement with an agent to writing so that there can be no doubt at trial as to the terms of the agent's employment. The impact of those terms on the agent's reliability as a witness can then be fully considered by the trier of fact.

> . . . . Agent 21's compensation was in no way related to any testimony he might give at trial. He was paid in full long before he testified. In *Xenos*, the witness was to be paid a certain amount of money if he testified in a certain manner. This arrangement may well be "a direct invitation to perjury and the fabrication of evidence" . . . in that the promise of payment may induce the witness to testify in a certain manner regardless of the truth of that testimony. Nothing in the agreement with Agent 21 made his compensation dependent on the content of his evidence, or the result of the trial.

In this example, the agent's credibility was not adversely affected by the financial reward received because he fully received that reward before giving testimony, and the terms of the reward had been clearly spelled out in writing so the court was fully able to asses the impact of the agreement. Payment after testimony could have an adverse affect on credibility, but would be most objectionable if payment was linked to results of the case. The ideal situation supporting credibility occurs where an informer testifies without any explicit promise of reward.

2. A Deal Is a Deal

Neither the prosecution nor the beneficiary of the assistance or immunity agreement can easily back out of a concluded deal so long as the other party upholds its side of the bargain. Severe consequences should result if either side breaches the agreement. For the informer, the consequences of breach might be commencement of criminal proceedings that had been agreed to be held in abeyance. *R. v. Crneck* (1980), 30 O.R. (2d) 1 (H.C.J.) at 10, suggests the prosecution also needs to be held accountable for breach of an immunity agreement:

> With respect to the first part of the argument relating to the bringing of the administration of justice into disrepute by withdrawing from an agreement arrived at after serious consideration, it seems to me there is considerable merit in the proposition. During the course of argument, the hypothetical case was discussed of a promise of a grant of immunity to "A", who, along with "B", was alleged to have committed a crime. "A" assists the Crown and testifies against "B", who in the result is convicted. The Crown then turns around and prosecutes "A" for the same crime, contrary to the terms of the agreement. Would that conduct be regarded, not only by lawyers but by the community at large, as unconscionable?

The court implied the answer was "yes," and that a stay of proceedings for abuse of process should be entered by the court in such a case. Because it is tough to back out of a deal, investigators and prosecutors have to make sure they get the deal they really need covering all possible contingencies arising from unexpected developments in the relationship between the state and the informer.

3. Why Investigators Cannot Grant Immunity

It is the Attorney General as the chief law officer of the Crown or a delegated official who are the only ones capable of granting immunity, *not* the investigators. This principle applies even at the stage of a case where charges have not yet been laid. In the case of most *Criminal Code* or provincial offence prosecutions, it will be the Attorney General of the province who must grant the immunity. In the case of all other federal Acts and in the three Territories it will usually be the Attorney General of Canada.

Because of the split jurisdiction on immunity between two or more Attorneys General, it can be difficult to secure a grant of immunity against all offences an informer may have committed. "Immunity baths" that immunize someone against all offences that person has ever committed do, in any case, make for very bad public policy. Negotiated immunity for prior drug deals or tax evasion must not unintentionally grant immunity for past murders. Immunity is time and act specific, and needs to be reflected as such in an immunity agreement.

If an informer is interested in immunity, investigators need to have three questions answered at an early stage of their dealings with that informer.

- What offences is immunity desired for?

- What is the date range for the commission of those offences?

- In what territorial jurisdictions were those offences committed?

Without knowing the details of "what," "when" and "where," it is impossible to secure immunity without risk of an immunity bath.

Promises of Immunity

Q & A

Q: I already promised one of my informers immunity from being charged for anything he does in helping out an investigation into a fraudulent passport ring. We didn't go into detail on what the immunity covered, but I figured he couldn't get into much trouble, and really I was just speaking for myself with respect to charges. Yesterday that informer was arrested by another agency while at a meeting with targets from my case, and has been charged with possession of a prohibited weapon and possession of cocaine. Since those charges have nothing to do with my investigation, I assume the immunity agreement would not apply. In any case, I just found out I don't have the authority as an investigator to offer immunity. Is there a problem here?

A: Regrettably there is a significant problem. Even though you did not have the authority to offer immunity, you were acting as an agent of the state at the time you made the promises, so all of the state could be bound. Any prosecution might be found by a court to be abusive, given what you promised. A situation like yours would have to be sorted out at the highest investigative agency and prosecution service management levels to determine what approach should be taken in court.

4. Factors Used in Deciding If Immunity Should Be Granted

Deciding whether or not immunity should be offered to someone involves determining whether the public interest will be better served by a grant of immunity than it is by the pursuit of a prosecution, taking into account factors like:

- whether the information provided relates to a serious offence or the prosecution serves an important public purpose — immunity will rarely be granted in cases of minor offences;

- whether the informer's cooperation or testimony is truthful, candid, and would be credible in court;

- whether the case could not proceed without the informer's testimony;

- whether the information is available from another source not requiring a grant of immunity;

- the role the person seeking immunity played in the offences — it's usually not in the public interest to give immunity to a high level criminal figure only for the purpose of convicting minor figures;

- the strength of the prosecution's case against the informer — a weaker case against an informer may be more compatible with a grant of immunity, as it is less likely the informer would be convicted if a prosecution were to proceed;

- previous grants of immunity to the informer — persons should not be given a licence to commit crime through regular grants of immunity;

- if the informer came forward to reveal the crime before investigators had detected it; a large-scale fraud scheme where one of the individuals involved comes forward to reveal the scheme favours a grant of immunity to that person.

Investigators who believe an immunity agreement will best advance the investigation of a case must be prepared to sell prosecutors on the idea by addressing the foregoing factors in a written justification for immunity, prepare a preliminary draft immunity agreement, and propose a face-to-face meeting with prosecutors to answer questions probing potential pitfalls of an immunity deal.

5. Choosing between Testimonial and Transactional Immunity

There are primarily two forms of immunity: testimonial and transactional. Testimonial immunity protects a witness from having things said to investigators later used against that witness in court. The two levels of testimonial immunity are "use immunity" and "derivative use immunity." Use immunity is relatively easy to operate and protects things said from later being directly used against the person who said them. Derivative use immunity is fraught with difficulties over what evidence can later be admissible against a witness as obtained through independent investigation, and what evidence is immunized by being obtained through derivative use of the information originally provided by the witness.

The cases of Oliver North and John Poindexter are two famous examples from the United States of the perils of prosecutions being pursued even with independent evidence when use and derivative use immunity have been granted. North and Poindexter were prosecuted and convicted for their roles in the Iran-Contra arms for hostages affair, but their convictions were later overturned by appellate courts that held it was impossible to determine the effect North and Poindexter's immunized compelled testimony at televised hearings before Congress had on witnesses who testified at their later criminal trials. A decision needs to be made early in any case involving informers on whether immunity is to be offered not only from testimonial use or derivative use, but also whether complete transactional immunity from certain types of charges is appropriate.

Transactional immunity is a far simpler thing to manage than immunity from use or derivative use of testimony. Transactional immunity offers immunity to a particular person from prosecution for specific acts committed at a certain place and time based on evidence obtained from *any* source, and unlike the other two forms of immunity is not directly or indirectly tied to the contents of what the statement maker says to investigators. By stipulating the immunized transactions, different transactions committed around the same time, but only coming to light after the grant of immunity, may still be prosecuted. Transactional immunity avoids endless debates over where evidence came from when it is sought to be admitted during a prosecution against a person who has received some kind of derivative evidence immunity grant. Transactional immunity advocates that a choice be made over whether an informer is a legitimate prosecution target for all crimes by walling off offences that can be prosecuted from those that cannot. If investigators do not wish uncertain limitations placed on potential charges that can be laid against a person, then they should consider abandoning plans to use that person as an informer benefiting from some kind of immunity guarantee. You can't always have your cake, and eat it too.

6. Maintaining Informer Credibility After an Assistance or Immunity Agreement

If you do get the go ahead to proceed with an assistance or immunity agreement, what matters most is how negotiations with an informer are approached, not whether it is the informer or investigators who first bring up the subject of assistance or immunity. To be able to assess whether the potential informer has anything of value to offer, the usual process followed is for investigators to take an initial "induced" statement from the informer, which will be inadmissible in court. Although the understanding among all parties is that it will be inadmissible, the statement should still be video — or at least audio — recorded so that those involved in making the final decision on immunity can later review and assess the information given. Once it has been determined the informer's information is worth negotiating over, details about exactly what is required to do a deal can be discussed and other "voluntary" recordings take place where the informer is interviewed to secure admissible evidence.

The ideal situation drawing out informer information without promising anything up front is illustrated in *R. v. Brown*, 2000 MBQB 25 at paras. 11-13:

> In her initial communication with the informer, she advised that if he were willing to talk, they would have to hear everything he had to say before any assessments could be made. It is clear from this testimony that the informer was seeking something in return, but it is equally apparent that K. . . was not directing the informer to do anything by way of eliciting further information. Sergeant K. . ., an experienced police officer, was aware of the problems with jailhouse informants and, in particular, the danger in creating a state agency relationship with such informants. She testified that in all their dealings, they made no promises, nor were any directions, advice, encouragement or the like given to him to do anything.
>
> She made arrangements to pick up the informer the next day and indicated she did not want any details, but wanted him to make a statement, which she referred to as a "KGB statement". The informer already had a statement from . . . Brown prior to contacting the R.C.M.P. and, accordingly, the statement was obtained without any direction or elicitation on the part of K. . . or anyone else.
>
> . . . She testified she made no offers to help the informer, and did not give him any instructions on interrogation or how to approach Brown or any matters pertaining to questioning him regarding the Lac du Bonnet homicide.

Video recording informer debriefing sessions will guard against an informer later changing his or her story.

Video recording informer statements will also protect against accusations that informer information was intentionally or unintentionally first planted in the informer's mind by the investigators themselves through the use of leading questions like: "what can you tell us about Josephine Smith's involvement in a bank robbery on 14 September, 2001?" Here the question presumes there was involvement, and even gives a precise date. Better to start with only asking for information about a named person, and then adding a few details if the name alone elicits no response. The job of the interviewing investigators is to collect information, not provide it. Figure 12-1 suggests a Video Statement Taking Room Set-Up and a Video Statement Checklist appears at the end of Chapter 12.

Investigator Duty Where Inconsistencies in Informer Testimony

Q & A

Q: What should I do in a case where an informer is testifying in court, and everything appears to be going well with the testimony the informer is giving, in that it's very favourable to the prosecution, except that it differs significantly from a statement the informer previously gave to me?

A: You have a duty to bring the statement discrepancies and potential perjury to the prosecutor's attention. The prosecutor will likely put the prior inconsistent statement to the witness, and provide an opportunity to correct current testimony. If the witness insists the current story is correct and the prior statement inaccurate, the prosecutor will have to explore the discrepancies with the witness, including possibly cross-examining on the prior inconsistent statement. The prosecutor must decide if it's wise to continue with the prosecution if the informer has become unreliable.

7. Ensuring Voluntariness of Agreements with Informers

For any complex assistance agreement, and *always* for immunity agreements, the informer requires independent legal advice on the obligations, benefits and overall drafting of the agreement to avoid later accusations that he didn't know to what he was agreeing. Both the agreement and the assistance provided through it might be invalid without informed consent, as in *R. v. Bégin*, (2002) 6 C.R. (6th) 360 (Que. C.A.) at para. 17:

> The appellant was arrested by . . . homicide investigators on March 3, 1996. Upon his arrest, the appellant asserted his right of silence and declined to give a statement. He asked to see his Carcajou handlers and sought their intervention. They told him that one of his options was to seek an "informer's contract", and mentioned the names of two notorious criminals who, having done so, were rewarded with leniency and favourable conditions of detention. The appellant chose to pursue that option and asked to sign the

mentioned contract immediately. His Carcajou handlers replied that he would first have to confess. *Only then did he agree to do so.*

In that case there was an impermissibly strong incentive to tell investigators what they wanted to hear because the promise of an assistance and immunity agreement was predicated on the accused first confessing to particular crimes; the court held the statements so obtained to be involuntary and thus inadmissible. That result could have been avoided if investigators had involved a lawyer acting for the accused in their discussions. If after repeated investigator urging and offers to pay for the cost an informer refuses to seek out a lawyer, investigator-informer agreement negotiations could proceed but the refusal should be well documented.

LIMITATIONS ON PROSECUTOR INVOLVEMENT WITH INFORMERS

An in-person meeting is the best way for a prosecutor to assess the courtroom credibility of any informer who will be giving trial testimony, but prosecutors must avoid inadvertently becoming witnesses in their own cases because of their interaction with informers or other witnesses. Prosecutors will be no good to you in court as prosecutors if they become witnesses. Even if they do not ask any questions, by attending interviews during the initial evidence gathering phase of an investigation prosecutors might become witnesses to what was said or not said, and to the voluntariness of the statements.

R. v. Regan, [2002] 1 S.C.R. 297 at para. 64, ultimately found prosecutors interviewing victims at the pre-charge stages of a case to be acceptable practice for assessing credibility if adequate safeguards are in place. However, the long history of litigation over the many prosecutor interviews done in that case demonstrates the great care that must be taken when prosecutors meet civilian witnesses:

> The question before this Court is whether the Crown's objectivity is necessarily compromised if Crown counsel conduct pre-charge interviews of witnesses without the single, express intention of screening out charges before they are laid. In essence, this Court has been asked to consider whether, at law, Crown prosecutors must be prevented from engaging in wide-ranging pre-charge interviews in order to maintain their essential function as "Ministers of Justice". First, it is my view that different provinces have answered this question differently, and that the trial judge erred in his evaluation of the standard practice across the country on this

> issue. Furthermore, while the police tasks of investigation and charge-laying must remain distinct and independent from the Crown role of prosecution, I do not think it is the role of this Court to make a pronouncement on the details of the practice of *how* that separation must be maintained.

Regan found that there is some flexibility concerning what can permissibly happen at prosecutor meetings with civilian witnesses, but that all such meetings must be treated with great caution, particularly those in which new evidence might emerge.

Investigators should have completed the evidence gathering stage of a case, and have conducted their own informer credibility assessment, including reconciling inconsistencies between informer and other case information, before proceeding with an informer-prosecutor meeting. If any notes are taken at the eventual informer-prosecutor meeting, it should be an investigator and not the prosecutor who takes them. Taking notes places the investigator in the best position to later give any necessary testimony about what took place in the meeting, further guarding against the prosecutor becoming a witness.

THE WHO AND HOW OF AVOIDING ENTRAPMENT

Sometimes informers who also qualify as agents are used to arrange criminal activity with investigative targets. If employed correctly, agents can be very effective at gathering evidence which would otherwise not be detected by normal investigative means. If employed incorrectly, the actions of agents can lead to allegations of entrapment, be an abuse of process, and result in a judicial stay of proceedings for all charges. If it is illegal for an investigator to do something, then it is likewise illegal for an agent to do the same thing at the direction of an investigator, even if the investigator did not specify how the agent should do the thing.

Entrapment can arise both where investigators or their agents actually induce the commission of an offence, and where they merely offer an opportunity to commit one. Even simply offering an opportunity to commit an offence is only permissible after investigators have reasonable suspicion a person is already engaged in criminal activity, or pursuant to a *bona fide* investigation in a targeted area. To put it another way, random virtue testing is not allowed, nor is coercion to commit an offence. Although entrapment arguments are not limited to cases involving informers, entrapment is dealt with in this chapter because informers acting as agents are so frequently involved in situations that the courts find amount to entrapment.

In figuring out what is permissible investigation, and what is forbidden entrapment, an investigator has to primarily consider two questions.

- Who can be approached as a target?

- How far can an approach go in encouraging the target to participate in a crime?

Any information received from an informer, even if untested, could be the basis for reasonable suspicion, so long as investigators have some belief in the reliability of the source. An anonymous Crime Stoppers tip, without further investigation or corroborating evidence, will not constitute reasonable and probable grounds, but could constitute reasonable suspicion depending on how detailed it is. It is highly unlikely an informer who only provides reasonable suspicion to target a general area would ever be subject to identity disclosure through the "innocence at stake" exception.

Once a legitimate target has been chosen, investigators cannot go beyond "providing an opportunity" to engage in illegal activity to that target. In deciding whether conduct passes beyond providing an opportunity into the realm of entrapment, *R. v. Mack*, [1988] 2 S.C.R. 903 at 904-905, suggested looking at ten factors:

- the type of crime and the availability of other investigative techniques for its detection;

- whether an average person in the accused's position would be induced into committing a crime;

- the persistence and number of attempts made by investigators before the target agreed to commit the offence;

- the type of inducement used, including deceit, fraud, trickery or reward;

- whether investigators merely became involved in on-going criminal activity, or originated the offence;

- whether investigators exploited human emotions like compassion, sympathy and friendship;

- whether investigators exploited a vulnerability of the target like a mental handicap or substance addiction;

- how involved the investigators were in the offence, as compared to the target;

- the use of threats, implied or express;

- whether the conduct of investigators undermines other constitutional values.

In short, according to *R. v. Mack*, [1988] 2 S.C.R. 903 at 976, entrapment occurs when investigators or their agents "engage in a conduct which offends basic values of the community." This is a fair play rule. This does not mean honest play. Undercover investigators and their agents can lie to targets, but there are certain tactics that simply are not fair to use against people, tactics that would compel them to commit offences they would not otherwise commit if those tactics were not employed.

Liability for Entrapment

Q & A

Q: What if my paid agent arranges a deal with a target for me, and to encourage the deal the agent makes a veiled threat to the target without my knowledge. If the target still seems to voluntarily participate in the deal when I meet with him, why should I as an investigator be held responsible for the agent's conduct when an entrapment argument is later made to a trial court?

A: If the agent sets up deals at your request, then the agent is effectively part of the state, regardless of whether the agent is even paid by you. The agent therefore has to play by the rules. But each case is factually specific, so if the agent did make a threat it will not necessarily be fatal to your case if all other factors indicate the target was keen to voluntarily participate in the deal, and there was no other abusive conduct. Try to be aware of everything the agent does and says to a target, since the agent saying or doing something can be like an investigator doing or saying the same thing. If it is abusive for an investigator to do it, then it is abusive for an agent to do it, and it may amount to entrapment.

For the Use and Protection of Informers

KEY POINTS

✓ Courts place a very high value on the protection of informers and will shield their identities by maintaining informer privilege. An informer must consent to any waiver of informer privilege. The "innocence at stake" exception to informer privilege may require a choice between revealing informer identify with the consent of the informer, or discontinuing proceedings.

✓ Whether an informer is also an agent of the state affects the degree of confidentiality that can be guaranteed to the informer. The "But For State Direction" test applies to determining whether an informer is also an agent — would the information, transaction, or event have happened without the state having directed the informer in a particular course of action?

KEY POINTS

✓ Information from a "basic investigation informer" may just point the investigation in the right direction. An "advanced investigation informer" may support a search warrant or authorization for electronic surveillance if credible, compelling and corroborated information is provided, but an explanation of the basis for belief in the informer is required. A "charge informer" whose information is used as the basis for laying charges must be especially credible and willing to testify at trial.

✓ Consideration given in exchange for information or testimony can affect the credibility of an informer and must be fully disclosed. The greater the value of the consideration, the greater the incentive to tell investigators what they want to hear instead of telling the truth.

✓ Investigators can make assistance agreements either orally or in writing, but only prosecutors are able to conclude immunity agreements, which must always be in writing. Both types of agreements must clearly set out what is being provided by the state, what is expected in return, and the consequences of agreement non-compliance. The informer must give free and informed consent to any agreement. If some form of immunity is to be part of an agreement, remember transactional immunity is far simpler to manage than use or derivative use testimonial immunity. Consider whether the public interest would be better served by a grant of transactional immunity than it would by pursuit of a prosecution against the beneficiary of the immunity.

✓ Random virtue testing or coercion to commit offences can amount to entrapment, and must be guarded against through careful investigation practices and control over informer-agents acting at the direction of investigators.

Informer identifying code: _____

Investigation identifier:_____

Lead investigator:_____

Detachment:_____

Tel:_____ Fax: _____

Cell:_____ E-mail: _____

A   INFORMER IDENTITY PROTECTION

❏ Identity of informer known

❏ Informer completely anonymous

  ❏ CrimeStoppers tip

❏ All material in prosecution brief and disclosure package
  vetted to ensure no informer-identifying information present

❏ Informer acted as agent

❏ Informer advised about existence of informer privilege

  ❏ Informer willing to waive informer privilege

  ❏ Informer has obtained independent legal advice on informer privilege

  ❏ Informer has executed a written waiver of informer privilege

  ❏ Informer prepared to testify in court

❏ Witness protection program requested by informer

  ❏ Informer approved as suitable for witness protection program

  ❏ Informer entered into witness protection program

B   INFORMER RELIABILITY

Motivation of informer for providing information:

  ❏ money

  ❏ consideration on potential charges

  ❏ consideration on charges already laid

  ❏ consideration on sentencing

  ❏ other: _____

Informer's powers of observation and recall: ❏ excellent ❏ good ❏ fair ❏ poor

❏ Informer provided prior assistance:____previous times over a total period of
                          ____days/months/years

❏ Accuracy of past information provided: ❏ excellent ❏ good ❏ fair ❏ poor

Results of information previously provided by informer:

❏ discovery of evidence **x**____

❏ arrests **x** ____

❏ convictions **x** ____

❏ no effect

❏ Informer has criminal record for: _____

_____

❏ dishonesty or affront to justice offences

❏ dated record

❏ Informer information corroborated in present case by:

❏ other informers **x** ____

❏ investigators, e.g. through observations

❏ physical evidence:_____

❏ Investigators intend to use informer in future investigations

❏ Assistance agreement concluded with informer

❏ consideration given: _____

❏ Immunity agreement requested by informer

❏ Immunity agreement concluded with informer

❏ Immunity agreement authorized by Attorney General(s)_____

_____

❏ Immunity for current charges:_____

❏ Immunity for past charges:_____

❏ Immunity for conduct during investigation period: _____

❏ Other comments on informer: _____

_____

_____

_____

_____

_____

_____

_____

_____

FURTHER READING

Cases

R. v. Barnes, [1991] 1 S.C.R. 449. Demonstrates how entrapment may be avoided where no reasonable suspicion exists against a person because of a *bona fide* inquiry presenting the opportunity to sell drugs in a problem drug area.

R. v. Durette, [1994] 1 S.C.R. 469. Represents a practical application of the balance that must be struck between protecting informer identity and providing disclosure so full answer and defence to charges can be made. The burden is on the prosecution to justify the non-disclosure of relevant information.

R. v. Garofoli, [1990] 2 S.C.R. 1421. Establishes that indicia of reliability for an informer's tip must be given in order for it to constitute reasonable and probable grounds to search.

R. v. Leipert, [1997] 1 S.C.R. 281. Defines the scope of informer privilege.

R. v. Mack, [1988] 2 S.C.R. 903. Defines what constitutes entrapment.

R. v. Scott, [1990] 3 S.C.R. 979. Establishes that a stay of proceedings is permissible to protect informer identity.

Books and Reports

E.G. Ewaschuk, *Criminal Pleadings and Practice in Canada*, loose-leaf (Aurora, ON: Canada Law Book, 1997). See particularly Chapter 12:6297 ("Criminal Conduct By State Agent") and Chapter 16:14040 ("Informant Privilege").

Federal Prosecution Service Deskbook, loose-leaf (Ottawa: Justice Canada, 2000). See particularly Chapter 35 "Immunity Agreements" [on-line: *canada.justice.gc.ca/en/dept/pub/fps/fpd/*].

Law Reform Commission of Canada, *Working Paper No. 64 — Immunity From Prosecution* (Ottawa: Law Reform Commission of Canada, 1992).

L.E. Lawler, *Police Informer Privilege* (Ottawa: Law Reform Commission of Canada, 1984).

CHAPTER FIVE

THE BOUNDARIES OF REGULATORY INSPECTIONS, INFORMATION DEMANDS AND INQUIRIES

The principle against self-incrimination was never intended to assist individuals in committing regulatory offences.

R. v. Fitzptrick, [1995] 4 S.C.R. 154 at para. 48.

In This Chapter

- Understanding regulatory and criminal universe differences
- How predominant purpose controls regulatory powers
- The scope and limits of inspection powers
- The scope and limits of demands for information
- The scope and limits of inquiries
- Ensuring proper appointment of regulatory investigators
- The special position of military investigators
- When it makes sense to exercise restraint in the use of regulatory powers of intrusion and compulsion

UNDERSTANDING REGULATORY AND CRIMINAL UNIVERSE DIFFERENCES

Science fiction and fantasy writers sometimes spin out tales of parallel universes, where similar people at similar points in human evolution live out very different lives because of one or two crucial historic, scientific or environmental differences. The basic premise of those stories involves the separate universes occasionally overlapping, resulting in people who slip from one universe into another being compelled to cope with changes in their lives that a parallel universe imposes. Well, there are in fact two parallel universes all investigators must learn to live within: a criminal universe and a larger and more rapidly expanding regulatory universe.

In the zone where the criminal and regulatory universes share a border, investigators must adapt to a different legal environment each time they cross the frontier. Some investigators will even live out the entirety of their careers with one foot in each universe. To navigate around these universes, every investigator must be able to distinguish regulatory from criminal offences, understand the flexible *Charter* standards rationale for the array of intrusive regulatory compliance verification powers exercisable only in the regulatory universe, and know when a shift in predominant purpose will restrict use of those powers. Figure 5-1 shows a Map of the Regulatory and Criminal Universes that illustrates their distinctions and interactions.

1. The Fundamental Character of Each Universe

The dominant distinction between the regulatory and criminal universes, as defined by what amounts to an offence in each universe, was explained in *R. v. Wholesale Travel*, [1991] 3 S.C.R. 154 at 216 & 218-219:

> The common law has long acknowledged a distinction between truly criminal conduct and conduct, otherwise lawful, which is prohibited in the public interest. Earlier, the designations *mala in se* and *mala prohibita* were utilized; today, prohibited acts are generally classified as either crimes or regulatory offences.

> . . .

> It has always been thought that there is a rational basis for distinguishing between crimes and regulatory offences. Acts or actions are criminal when they constitute conduct that is, in itself, so abhorrent to the basic values of human society that it ought to be

Fig 5-1 MAP OF THE REGULATORY AND CRIMINAL UNIVERSES

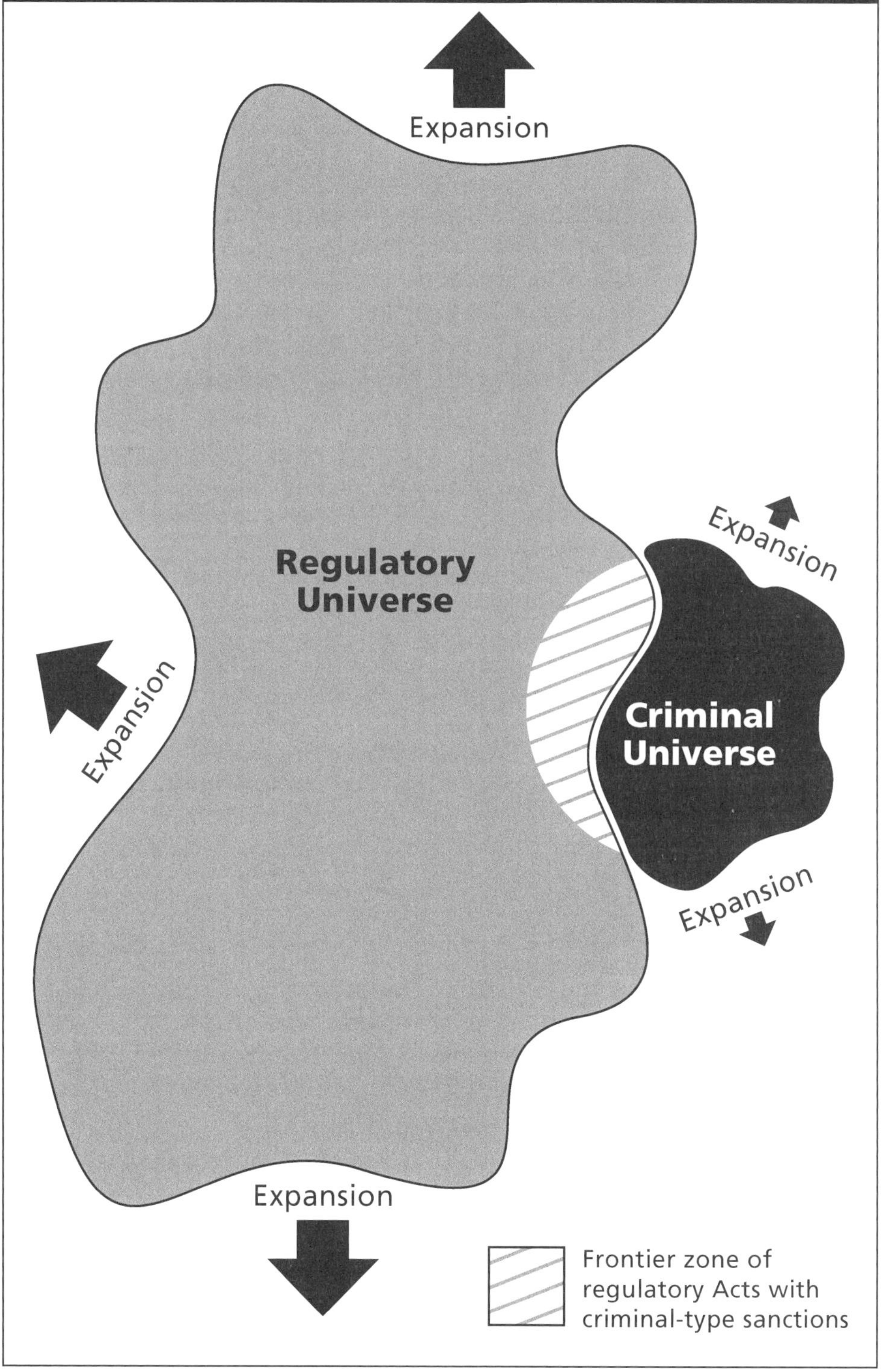

Expansion

Expansion

Regulatory Universe

Expansion

Criminal Universe

Expansion

Expansion

Frontier zone of regulatory Acts with criminal-type sanctions

prohibited completely. Murder, sexual assault, fraud, robbery and theft are all so repugnant to society that they are universally recognized as crimes. At the same time, some conduct is prohibited, not because it is inherently wrongful, but because unregulated activity would result in dangerous conditions being imposed upon members of society, especially those who are particularly vulnerable.

The objective of regulatory legislation is to protect the public or broad segments of the public (such as employees, consumers and motorists, to name but a few) from the potentially adverse effects of otherwise lawful activity. Regulatory legislation involves a shift of emphasis from the protection of individual interests and the deterrence and punishment of acts involving moral fault to the protection of public and societal interests. While criminal offences are usually designed to condemn and punish past, inherently wrongful conduct, regulatory measures are generally directed to the prevention of future harm through the enforcement of minimum standards of conduct and care.

The different goals of the regulatory and criminal universes lead to each universe taking a different approach to the way it protects privacy interests, in the standards that must be met for proof of an offence, in the stigma associated with investigation, prosecution, and conviction for offences, as well as in the severity of punishment imposed for those offences.

2. Categorizing Offences as Regulatory or Criminal

Don't be confused by the different ways the term "criminal" is sometimes used. Occasionally the courts will refer to the penal provisions of a regulatory Act as "criminal" because those regulatory offences fall in a frontier zone close to the boundary between the criminal and regulatory universes in terms of severity. This does not mean that the standards of the criminal universe apply to verifying compliance with that Act. For example *R. v. Jarvis*, [2002] 3 S.C.R. 757 at paras. 57, 59-60, & 62, said of s. 239 *Income Tax Act*, R.S.C. 1985, c. 1 (5th Supp.), tax evasion offences:

the presence in the ITA of s. 239 does nothing to alter the regulatory or administrative nature of the inspection and requirement powers

. . .

It is plain that the s. 239 offences are no trifling matter as this provision bears at least the *formal* hallmarks of criminal legislation, namely, prohibitions coupled with penalties .... They may be prosecuted upon indictment, and conviction can carry up to five years' incarceration. It is because of these factors that the penal sanctions in s. 239 are, in certain contexts, referred to as "criminal".

That is not to say, however, that they are "purely" or "quintessentially" criminal *for Charter purposes.*

. . .

In sum, the ITA is a regulatory statute, but non-compliance with its mandatory provisions can in some cases lead to criminal charges being laid.

The legal principles governing compliance verification and enforcement of tax evasion offences including applicable *Charter* standards remain very much regulatory in nature.

Courts have been quite receptive to arguments that even the punitive provisions of Acts establishing regulatory schemes are part of the regulatory universe, like in *R. v. Wilcox* (2001), 192 N.S.R. (2d) 159; 2001 NSCA 45 at paras. 108-109:

The essence of criminal law is moral blameworthiness; the essence of regulation is that those engaging in regulated activities maintain a certain minimum standard of care .... Criminal offences reinforce crucial social values, the violation of which merits disapprobation and punishment .... Regulatory offences, by contrast, are not primarily concerned with values, but with results ....

Applying these considerations, the *Fisheries Act* is clearly regulatory in nature. The alleged offences in issue here are . . . far removed from the typical concerns of the criminal law .... The enforcement and penal provisions are ancillary to the Act's regulatory purpose. The conduct in issue does not give rise to the sort of moral disapprobation or stigma associated with true criminal offences.

The best demystification of the law principle that you can be guided by in going about your investigative duties is to assume all federal and provincial Acts and the offences they create, other than the *Criminal Code* and the *Controlled Drugs and Substances Act*, inhabit the regulatory universe — unless you are informed otherwise.

The huge and rapidly expanding spectrum of acts or omissions that can constitute a regulatory offence means that all investigators will be increasingly dragged into dealing with regulatory matters. A now very out of date estimate of regulatory offence expansion was provided in *R. v. Wholesale Travel*, [1991] 3 S.C.R. 154 at 221:

> Some indication of the prevalence of regulatory offences in Canada is provided by a 1974 estimate by the Law Reform Commission of Canada. The commission estimated that there were, at that time, approximately 20,000 regulatory offences in an average province, plus an additional 20,000 regulatory offences at the federal level. By 1983, the commission's estimate of the federal total had reached 97,000. There is every reason to believe that the number of public welfare offences at both levels of government has continued to increase.
>
> Statistics such as these make it obvious that government policy in Canada is pursued principally through regulation. It is through regulatory legislation that the community seeks to implement its larger objectives and to govern itself and the conduct of its members. The ability of the government effectively to regulate potentially harmful conduct must be maintained.

A five-fold increase in only nine years, with more than two decades having passed since the last estimate, means there are now a phenomenal number of regulatory offences out there. The numbers of criminal offences pale by comparison.

3. The Rationale for More Intrusive Regulatory Powers

Because there is no direct and immediate victim to report a regulatory offence like tax evasion to the authorities, the victim being the public at large, the courts have found wide-ranging powers of inspection, information demand and inquiry to be justified in implementing regulatory regimes that serve the public good. The rights of the individual to privacy are balanced with the rights of society to expect regulations will be obeyed, as explained in *Comité Paritaire v. Potash*, [1994] 2 S.C.R. 406 at 419 & 421:

> The federal and provincial legislatures have, in a number of statutes, included powers of inspection . . . . These statutes deal with areas as diverse as health, safety, the environment, taxation and labour. The common thread is found in their underlying purpose: harmonizing social relations by requiring observance of standards reflecting the sometimes delicate balance between individual rights and the interests of society. Inspection — or the threat of it — especially if it is done without notice, is a practical means of encouraging such observance.

. . .

> The underlying purpose of inspection is to ensure that a regulatory statute is being complied with. It is often accompanied by an information aspect designed to promote the interests of those on whose behalf the statute was enacted. The exercise of powers of inspection does not carry with it the stigmas normally associated with criminal investigations and their consequences are less draconian. While regulatory statutes incidentally provide for offences, they are enacted primarily to encourage compliance. It may be that in the course of inspections those responsible for enforcing a statute will uncover facts that point to a violation, but this possibility does not alter the underlying purpose behind the exercise of the powers of inspection. The same is true when the enforcement is prompted by a complaint. Such a situation is obviously at variance with the routine nature of an inspection. However, a complaint system is often provided for by the legislature itself as it is a practical means not only of checking whether contraventions of the legislation have occurred but also of deterring them.

Over the years I have observed a tendency among regulatory investigators to be overly conservative when it comes to exercising the regulatory compliance verification powers available to them, due at least in part to misplaced beliefs that much more restrictive criminal law protections from self-incrimination and unreasonable search and seizure apply throughout the regulatory context. Legislators accepted that powers of regulatory intrusion and compulsion would be needed, which is why they provided them to you, so you need to embrace them if your terms of appointment and case facts permit their use.

R. v. McKinlay Transport Ltd., [1990] 1 S.C.R. 627 at 648, summarized the rationale for *not* needing reasonable and probable grounds (RPG) of an offence to utilize regulatory compliance verification powers:

> the Minister of National Revenue must be given broad powers in supervising this regulatory scheme to audit taxpayers' returns and inspect all records which may be relevant to the preparation of these returns. The Minister must be capable of exercising these powers whether or not he has reasonable grounds for believing that a particular taxpayer has breached the Act. Often it will be impossible to determine from the face of the return whether any impropriety has occurred in its preparation. A spot check or a system of random monitoring may be the only way in which the integrity of the tax system can be maintained. . . . The need for random monitoring is incompatible with the requirement . . . that the person seeking authorization for a search or seizure have reason-

able and probable grounds, established under oath, to believe that
an offence has been committed.

Developing RPG of a particular offence is simply not the overall goal of regulatory compliance verification.

4. Preconditions on the Use of Regulatory Compliance Verification Powers

Inspection, demand and inquiry powers go by different names, and may or may not exist within a particular federal, provincial or territorial Act, so you might have to hunt around to discover their existence. A chart of a Comparison of Statutory Powers of Inspection, Information Demand, Inquiry and Search appears at Figure 5-2 illustrating the basic advantages, limitations and applicability of each of those four principal types of information-gathering power. Before using any regulatory power, investigators not only need to be certain they are operating in compliance verification mode within the regulatory universe, but also that all statutory preconditions have been met.

Preconditions generally fall into two classes: those that anchor regulatory powers in the regulatory universe, and those that through tying regulatory powers to purpose, place and people ensure that only a limited class of people and places are legitimate targets. While most preconditions are set out in each Act, some have been created or modified by the courts. For inquiries and dwelling place inspections, an Act may stipulate that certain preconditions have to be established to a judicial officer by evidence under oath. Together, the preconditions ensure regulatory investigators cannot run amok by intruding into the life of every Canadian on the mere chance such a person may not be complying with an obscure regulation. Notably absent from the list of preconditions is RPG of an offence.

The six principal preconditions to the use of regulatory compliance verification powers are:

1. explicit authorization by the regulatory Act whose compliance is being verified;

2. proper investigator appointment to enforce the regulatory Act;

3. the predominant purpose of the inspection or information demand (but not inquiries, which are currently exempt from this condition) is ensuring compliance with the Act, not the gathering of evidence for a prosecution;

Fig 5-2

COMPARISON OF STATUTORY POWERS OF INSPECTION, INFORMATION DEMAND, INQUIRY AND SEARCH

	INSPECTION	INFORMATION DEMAND	INQUIRY	SEARCH
Can be conducted prior to (and occasionally after) reasonable and probable grounds of an offence	X	X	X	
Usually requires reasonable and probable grounds of an offence				X
Generally requires a written judicial prior authorization for use of power			X	X
Investigators may directly look for and examine documents or other things	X			X
Investigators may seize things	Usually can only take copies	Things provided in response to a demand	Subpoena *duces tecum* may allow documents to be retained	Only if seizure power present
May compel answers to written questions		X		
May compel answers to oral questions		X	X	
May compel answers under oath			X	

This chart gives a general idea of which powers an investigator should consider when seeking particular forms of information. This comparison holds true for many inspection, information demand, inquiry and search situations, but legal nuances and differences in legislation authorizing these powers requires the separate consideration of each set of case facts as they arise. Investigators pursuing purely criminal investigations will generally be limited only to powers of search.

4. reasonable grounds to believe the target location is subject to regulation by the Act;

5. reasonable grounds to believe the target location contains something subject to regulation by the Act; and

6. reasonable grounds to believe a person against whom powers are to be exercised is subject to regulation by the Act, or is an employee of an organization or found in a location subject to such regulation.

Thus reasonable grounds *are* required to believe in a particular set of facts before the use of regulatory powers is possible, it is only RPG of an offence that are not needed. Where all of these preconditions are met, information that can only be dreamed about by criminal investigators may be gathered through intrusive and compelled means in pursuit of regulatory objectives.

The Regulatory/Criminal Distinction

Q&A

Q: This whole regulatory versus criminal distinction sounds very artificial to me. Some offences claimed to be regulatory, like tax evasion, can lead to five years in jail, while other so-called criminal offences like assault may wind up with a $100 fine being imposed. How is it really possible to make sense of the distinction?

A: It is true that the regulatory/criminal distinction is mainly of a theoretical legal nature, but it has important practical consequences for investigators. It enables the courts and legislators to justify the use of intrusive and coercive information gathering powers for regulatory matters, even when serious punishments can occasionally follow from answers to those inquiries. As law, like most things in life, is about balance, the regulatory/criminal distinction balances privacy protections in personal life with the public interest of being able to check if people are complying with government regulations largely imposed on them because of their voluntary participation in a regulated activity.

HOW PREDOMINANT PURPOSE CONTROLS REGULATORY POWERS

1. Following the Predominant Purpose Compass

Even if you are sure an Act inhabits the regulatory universe, you may not be able to utilize its compliance verification powers if your predominant purpose is to collect evidence for a prosecution rather than simply verify compliance with the Act. *R. v. Jarvis*, [2002] 3 S.C.R. 757 at para. 88, explained why the predominant purpose of any regulatory inspection or information demand is so important:

> In our view, where the predominant purpose of a particular inquiry is the determination of penal liability, CCRA officials must relinquish the authority to use the inspection and requirement powers . . . . In essence, officials "cross the Rubicon" when the inquiry in question engages the adversarial relationship between the taxpayer and the state. There is no clear formula that can answer whether or not this is the case. Rather, to determine whether the predominant purpose of the inquiry in question is the determination of penal liability, one must look to all factors that bear upon the nature of that inquiry.

Keep notes of what your purpose is, and the reasons for the purpose, so you can later explain that purpose at trial.

British Columbia (Securities Commission) v. Branch, [1995] 2 S.C.R. 3, found at para. 7 that the predominant purpose test strikes a balance:

> the crucial question is whether the predominant purpose for seeking the evidence is to obtain incriminating evidence against the person . . . or rather some legitimate public purpose. This test strikes the appropriate balance between the interests of the state in obtaining the evidence for a valid public purpose on the one hand, and the right to silence of the person compelled to testify on the other.

The use of the term "predominant" is significant, because it means a legitimate background, incidental or subsidiary purpose could still be the gathering of evidence for a prosecution should compliance verification turn up an offence.

I would like to tell you demystification of the law allows a short pithy maxim to be applied to predominant purpose so you can always know when you are on the right side of the law, but sadly that is not the case. This is an area where early investigator-prosecutor contact is needed to stay current with legal developments. Regulatory investigators cannot fear the use of intrusion and compulsion powers in the face of some legal uncertainty; those powers were created because regulatory compliance is so difficult to verify without using them. Boldly use intrusion and compulsion powers where you can justify a regulatory compliance verification predominant purpose, but keep close control over that verification so you can quickly back off should you sense a shift in purpose caused by a factor like RPG of an offence. A purpose shift may be a little tremor, rather than a major earthquake.

2. Indicators of Predominant Purpose

Factors indicating predominant purpose can be revealed through various questions.

- Do RPG of an offence exist?

- Is the conduct of investigators more consistent with regulatory compliance verification or gathering evidence of an offence?

- Where one regulatory agency branch primarily handles compliance verification, and another branch mainly deals with evidence gathering, which branch is dealing with the case?

- Is the information being collected relevant to compliance verification in general, or only to the prosecution of offences?

RPG is probably the best marker to watch when assessing whether your case is about to undergo a shift in predominant purpose — like a weathervane to tell which way the predominant purpose winds are blowing — through an event like the discovery of damning evidence of non-compliance during an inspection, or a damning admission made in response to an information demand. But as noted in *R. v. Jarvis*, [2002] 3 S.C.R. 757 at para. 89, RPG is not solely determinative of the issue:

> To begin with, the mere existence of reasonable grounds that an offence may have occurred is by itself insufficient to support the conclusion that the predominant purpose of an inquiry is the determination of penal liability. Even where reasonable grounds to suspect an offence exist, it will not always be true that the predominant purpose of an inquiry is the determination of penal liability. In this regard, courts must guard against creating procedural shackles on regulatory officials; it would be undesirable to "force the regulatory hand" by removing the possibility of seeking the lesser administrative penalties on every occasion in which reasonable grounds existed of more culpable conduct . . . In most cases, if all ingredients of an offence are reasonably thought to have occurred, it is likely that the investigation function is triggered.

Certainly suspicion alone does not trigger a predominant purpose shift, as *R. v. Jarvis*, [2002] 3 S.C.R. 757 at para. 90, recognized: "On what evidence could investigators ever obtain a search warrant if the whiff of suspicion were enough to freeze . . . fact-finding?" While the laying of charges is an external indicator of RPG that strongly indicates a predominant purpose shift, the truest measure of predominant purpose may be internal indicators like early investigator memos identifying that the goal of all actions against a target was to see if enough evidence could be gathered to lay charges.

A contextual approach to predominant purpose means purpose could shift at earlier or later points in case development depending on the class of regulation, like earlier in a tax than an environmental context, as in *R. v. Bagnell* (2004), 224 N.S.R. (2d) 20; 2004 NSPC 29 at paras. 15, 19, 40, & 42, where no adversarial relationship was found to have arisen to prevent on-going inspections for environmental contraventions until *after* the point when charges were laid:

> At the inception of the process, when he made the various applications, there is no sense in which he could be said to stand in an adversarial relationship to the State, even though they may have had different interests in regard to the property. As matters developed over the summer and fall of 2002, the relationship acquired a more adversarial character, but not until November of 2002 did the permission-seeking process come to an end with the formal rejection letter by DOEL.
>
> . . .
>
> Where the entry of a state agent is for the purpose of conducting a simple examination of a natural feature of the property, or some potential environmental insult to it, this is a particular context within which courts should not readily declare a warrantless search to be unreasonable. In *Wilcox* Cromwell, J.A. notes that in questioning whether the *Charter* has been infringed, one cannot always establish clear lines which divide regulatory inspections from criminal investigations. When he says citing the Supreme Court of Canada in *Wholesale Travel* that "what is important are not labels but the values at stake in the particular context", I think he calls upon courts to consider such things as the importance of tidal ponds to ecosystems such as the Bras d'Or Lakes, and the legitimate state interest in saving these from destruction.
>
> . . .
>
> Even absent an application for regulatory approval of some sort, where fishery officers or other agencies take an interest in activity occurring on private property which might reasonably involve damage or destruction of habitat, or some other environmental insult, an inspection/search conducted bona fides, performed reasonably, with the minimum amount of intrusion, may not be unreasonable, even in the absence of a warrant and consent. However, where the Defendant here has made an application for regulatory

approval concerning the very activity in question any resulting search is even more obviously reasonable. Accordingly I find no violation of the Defendant's s.8 *Charter* Right.

. . .

I do think however, that a line was crossed when, subsequent to laying charges, the Fishery Officer entered the property without warrant and without permission. By then the Defendant's application was formally rejected. There is no sense in which the approval-seeking process was still open. DFO thereafter was in a pointedly antagonistic relationship with Mr. Bagnell. It appears it was simply gathering more evidence to bolster the pending prosecution. Under principle set out in *Jarvis*, I rule inadmissible evidence obtained by entry after November 18, 2002.

There a variety of contextual factors, including minimally intrusive inspections conducted during an administrative approval review process for an important public purpose, dictated a late shift in predominant purpose notwithstanding strong suspicion of an offence.

3. The Predominant Purpose Test as a Check on Pretext Inspections

Predominant purpose keeps pretext inspections in check. A regulatory highway-traffic vehicle stop to inspect registration, insurance documents, and the safety condition of a vehicle would amount to an impermissible pretext inspection if the predominant purpose of the inspection was a search for drugs possibly leading to criminal charges. Defence counsel and the courts are sufficiently savvy and skeptical of regulatory inspections that turn up evidence of serious criminal offences that investigators involved in such situations will have to demonstrate the utmost good faith and proper purpose at trial in the face of extensive cross-examination to ensure evidence admissibility.

4. Dealing with Parallel Regulatory Compliance Initiatives and Criminal Investigations

Another challenge of verifying regulatory compliance is dealing with the interface between different regulatory compliance initiatives and criminal investigations. The combinations and permutations are virtually endless:

- two information gathering actions taken under the same regulatory Act, but covering different date ranges;

- two information gathering actions taken under different regulatory Acts, covering the same date range;

- two information gathering actions, one taken under a regulatory Act and one proceeding under a criminal Act.

So long as different investigators are conducting separate inquiries at different times and not sharing information, predominant purpose interaction will not be an issue. But increasingly investigative agencies with different mandates are cooperating either on an informal basis or as part of formal joint task forces. From a practical perspective, such cooperation makes infinitely good sense. From a legal perspective, such cooperation can pose major challenges.

R. v. Jarvis, [2002] 3 S.C.R. 757 at paras. 95-97, addressed situations where investigators with a predominant compliance verification purpose pass information on to those with a prosecution purpose, or where two groups of investigators conduct parallel investigations — one having a regulatory and the other a criminal purpose:

> It follows that there is nothing preventing auditors from passing to investigators their files containing validly obtained audit materials. That is, there is no principle of use immunity that prevents the investigators, in the exercise of their investigative function, from making use of evidence obtained through the proper exercise of the CCRA's audit function. Nor, in respect of validly obtained audit information, is there any principle of derivative use immunity . . . . If a particular piece of evidence comes to light as a result of the information validly contained in the auditor's file, then investigators may make use of it.
>
> . . .
>
> The predominant purpose test does not thereby prevent . . . parallel criminal investigations and administrative audits. The fact that the CCRA is investigating a taxpayer's penal liability, does not preclude the possibility of a simultaneous investigation, the predominant purpose of which is a determination of the same taxpayer's tax liability. However, if an investigation into penal liability is subsequently commenced, the investigators can avail themselves of that information obtained pursuant to the audit powers prior to the commencement of the criminal investigation, but not with respect to information obtained pursuant to such powers subsequent to

> the commencement of the investigation into penal liability. This is
> no less true where the investigations into penal liability and tax lia-
> bility are in respect of the same tax period.

If you run up against parallel information gathering actions, be prepared to
preserve your purity of purpose. Don't let a compliance verification purpose
be contaminated by an appearance of working on behalf of an evidence
gathering investigation. Once your compliance verification inquiries are
complete, there may be legal avenues through which the results can be
passed to others with a prosecution purpose.

5. Why the Predominant Purpose Test Doesn't Apply to Inquiries

Inquires are treated differently from inspections and information
demands with respect to the point at which they can no longer be pursued.
Del Zotto v. Canada, [1999] 1 S.C.R. 3, established an inquiry can be used
even when the predominant purpose is to build a case for prosecution. *R.
v. Jarvis*, [2002] 3 S.C.R. 757, in establishing the predominant purpose test
for inspections and information demands did not overrule *Del Zotto* v.
Canada, [1999] 1 S.C.R. 3, and in fact cited *Del Zotto* with approval. The best
explanation for why predominant purpose governs inspections and information demands, and not inquiries, is that an inquiry is largely a judicially
supervised process. To take the s. 231.4 *Income Tax Act* inquiry as an example, a judicially appointed hearing officer will be present to control procedural fairness, immediate recourse is available to a superior court to rule on
refusals to answer questions, and the target and witnesses can be represented by counsel. None of these protections are available for inspections or
information demands, which are exercised largely at the discretion of investigators.

Inquiries can also be distinguished from inspections and information
demands by their typical use against third-parties. There is ultimately no
protection in Canada against incrimination, only a protection against self-
incrimination, thus so long as inquiries are gathering information from third-
party witnesses they have a low risk of running afoul of the *Charter*. Calling
the target of an investigation at an inquiry is a whole other matter where the
predominant purpose test might apply. This is admittedly a complex area of
the law where early investigator-prosecutor contact is mandatory in setting
up any kind of inquiry.

Monitoring On-Going Compliance

Q: I am a labour inspector. If we can no longer inspect a business because we have reasonable and probable grounds to believe the business owner has committed labour offences and our predominant purpose in making inquires is to collect evidence of those offences, how can we monitor on-going compliance and protect workers from new offences?

A: An evidence gathering predominant purpose does not stop you from monitoring on-going compliance, it only stops you from using powers of intrusion and compulsion without prior judicial authorization. This means that the date range that your predominant purpose targets for evidence collection is off-limits to further inspection of documents, but future dates where you have a predominant purpose of regulatory compliance verification can still be subject to inspection. Likewise, if you or others also enforce a class of regulatory legislation like environmental laws that is different from the labour laws where your predominant purpose is evidence collection, then you can continue to inspect under those other Acts for any date range.

THE SCOPE AND LIMITS OF INSPECTION POWERS

1. The Six Questions Whose Answers Define the Limits of Inspection Powers

Regulatory inspection powers are wide-ranging with respect to which locations may be entered and which items may be examined. The most significant limitation on them is the requirement that reasonable belief exist that the place and items inspected contain information relevant to the administration or enforcement of the Act under which the inspection takes place. Each Act authorizing an inspection power will have its own clearly stated limits on who and what can be inspected, plus where, when, why and how an inspection may take place.

These six questions defining the limits of inspection power can be answered by using demystification of the law techniques involving reading the statutory language authorizing the power. For example, consider how s. 231.1 of the *Income Tax Act* answers those questions:

> **231.1.** (1) An authorized person may, at all reasonable times, for any purpose related to the administration or enforcement of this Act,

(a) inspect, audit or examine the books and records of a taxpayer and any document of the taxpayer or of any other person that relates or may relate to the information that is or should be in the books or records of the taxpayer or to any amount payable by the taxpayer under this Act, and

(b) examine property in an inventory of a taxpayer and any property or process of, or matter relating to, the taxpayer or any other person, an examination of which may assist the authorized person in determining the accuracy of the inventory of the taxpayer or in ascertaining the information that is or should be in the books or records of the taxpayer or any amount payable by the taxpayer under this Act.

and for those purposes the authorized person may

(c) subject to subsection 231.1(2), enter into any premises or place where any business is carried on, any property is kept, anything is done in connection with any business or any books or records are or should be kept, and

(d) require the owner or manager of the property or business and any other person on the premises or place to give the authorized person all reasonable assistance and to answer all proper questions relating to the administration or enforcement of this Act and, for that purpose, require the owner or manager to attend at the premises or place with the authorized person.

(2) Where any premises or place referred to in paragraph 231.1(1)(c) is a dwelling-house, an authorized person may not enter that dwelling-house without the consent of the occupant except under the authority of a warrant under subsection 231.1(3).

The statutory text reveals the limits of *Income Tax Act* inspection power to be:

- who = "a taxpayer or any other person";
- why = "for any purpose related to the administration or enforcement" of the Act;
- when = "any reasonable time";
- where = "enter into any premises or place where any business is carried on or property is kept . . .";

- what = "book and records . . . and any document that relates or may relate to the information that is or should be in the books or records of the taxpayer or to any amount payable by the taxpayer under this Act" plus "property in an inventory . . . any property, or process, or matter . . . an examination of which might determine the accuracy . . . .";

- how = "inspect, audit or examine" plus "require the owner or manager or any person on the premises . . . to give all reasonable assistance . . . and to answer all questions . . . ."

Those answers show the *Income Tax Act* contains especially broad inspection powers, largely due to the pervasive nature of its regulation throughout Canada. Investigators need to be able to answer those six questions before using inspection powers, and make notes of how any inspection they conduct is consistent with those answers so inspection can later be justified in court if challenged.

2. Even Targeted Inspections Are Not Searches in Disguise

Don't be confused by arguments that inspections are searches in disguise. Canadian courts know the difference, although defence counsel may at times cross-examine investigators, trying to get them to admit what they were conducting was really a search. Look at *R. v. Fleming*, (2003) 104 C.R.R. (2d) 75 (Nfld. & L. Prov. Ct.) at para. 44:

> Notwithstanding the submissions of the Accused that an "inspection" is an euphemism for a search, the Courts in this Province have found a distinction between a search and an inspection, and have in fact upheld similar legislative provisions. The distinction between an inspection and a search is to be found in the *purpose* for which it is carried out. An inspection is a means of ensuring compliance with legislation, while a search is a means of gathering evidence of non-compliance with legislation. Clearly, there will be times when an inspection may well segue into a search.

Try to keep straight in your head when you are verifying compliance, as opposed to when you are gathering evidence of non-compliance; this can be a very fine distinction to make.

3. Understanding the Limitations on Dwelling Place Inspections

a. *Why Dwelling Places Are Different*

The courts have consistently assigned dwelling places among the highest expectations of privacy, but *Comité Paritaire v. Potash*, [1994] 2 S.C.R. 406 at 424, confirmed it is perfectly fair to exercise intrusive inspection powers even there: "Depending on the nature of the industry, it is possible that certain inspections may take place at the home of the employer, when it coincides with their workplace. That possibility does not, however, make the inspection powers less reasonable." Anything from illegal fish, to toxic chemicals, to labour violations might be hidden in a dwelling place.

Most Acts treat dwelling places as an exception to their general regulatory inspection powers, with an inspection of a dwelling place in most cases only being possible upon consent being given by the occupant, or with an "inspection warrant" issued under a provision likes. 218 of the *Canadian Environmental Protection Act, 1999*, S.C. 1999, c. 33:

> **218.** (2) An enforcement officer may not enter a private dwelling-place or any part of a place that is designed to be used and is being used as a permanent or temporary private dwelling-place except
>
> (a) with the consent of the occupant of the place; or
>
> (b) under the authority of a warrant issued under subsection (3).
>
> (3) Where on *ex parte* application a justice is satisfied by information on oath that
>
> (a) the conditions for entry described in subsection (1) exist in relation to a private dwelling-place,
>
> (b) entry to the dwelling-place is necessary for any purpose relating to the administration of this Act, and
>
> (c) entry to the dwelling-place has been refused or there are reasonable grounds for believing that entry will be refused,
>
> the justice may issue a warrant authorizing the enforcement officer named in it to conduct an inspection of the dwelling-place subject to any conditions that may be specified in the warrant, and author-

izing any other person named therein to accompany the enforcement officer and exercise any power specified in the warrant.

An inspection warrant application is made to a judge or justice, supported
by an affidavit setting out facts that justify its issuance including why there
are reasonable grounds to believe there is in a particular place anything subject to regulation by the Act in question, just like in a search warrant application. Inspection warrants most notably diverge from regular search and
seizure warrants in their requirement for facts supporting why entry will be
refused or has actually been refused.

b. *How to Deal with the Requirement for Informed Consent to Enter Dwelling Places*

A circular precondition problem can arise: without grounds to believe
consent will be refused no dwelling place inspection warrant will be available, but there is no ability to seek a warrant if consent has been granted,
even if doubts exist over whether it was informed consent. In one of my
cases the trial judge held that while an accused had indeed consented to an
inspection of his residence, and so an inspection warrant could *not* have
been obtained, informed consent had not been given thus the results of the
inspection and subsequent search with a warrant were inadmissible at trial.
While "informed consent" is a difficult enough concept to get a handle on
within the criminal law realm, there is much less guidance available for the
regulatory realm.

The informational standard for regulatory dwelling place inspection consent could be as onerous as in cases of criminal investigation, or be subject
to lesser *Charter* standards. At a minimum, someone in control of the
dwelling place should be informed of the Act being relied upon, given a
brief summary of the factual basis for the inspection, and told in a general
way about the items for which you will be looking. It would be best to also
advise that there is no obligation to consent, consent can be withdrawn at
any time, and explain the potential consequences of inspection. The decision to consent would likely be subject to the same standards of voluntariness as other statements made to persons in authority: be the product of a
functioning mind, and not be made under duress or as a result of threats,
promises, or trickery that would shock the community.

Seeking consent to enter a dwelling place has the drawback of losing
the element of surprise if consent is refused. Investigators could alternately
attempt to go straight for an inspection warrant by setting out in the information to obtain the reasonable grounds they have to believe that *informed*

consent will not be granted because of what investigators understand to be the high standards that must be met. Even if such a warrant application is refused and investigators wind up having to seek consent, they will be able to demonstrate the utmost good faith at trial. While the "if in doubt, get a warrant" maxim applies here as much as anywhere because of the degree of privacy intrusion, don't let dwelling place inspection warrant requirements put you off doing very proactive inspections in places with lessened expectations of privacy.

The Contradiction of Inspection Warrants

Q: Isn't an "inspection warrant" a contradiction in terms? I understood that either you do an inspection, or you get a warrant, but you don't do both at the same time.

A: No, it isn't a contradiction since you are still conducting a regulatory inspection, but you need prior judicial authorization to do so. An inspection warrant looks and acts like a search warrant in many respects, except reasonable and probable grounds of an offence are not required and the predominant purpose of the inspection is regulatory compliance verification.

c. *What Constitutes a Dwelling Place*

Dwelling places are not limited to buildings, and can include vehicles, vessels or even aircraft, but to constitute a dwelling place a space generally needs to be:

- designed to be a dwelling place, thus a sleeping bag on the floor of a restaurant kitchen would not qualify; and

- actually be used as a dwelling place, so a house completely converted to office space would also not qualify.

However, the law doesn't restrict the definition to a traditional residence and includes dwelling places which are:

- permanent or temporary, so a dwelling place need not be a full-time residence and could be a place only lived in while working, like a cabin with bunks on a fishing vessel;

- mixed use, so a house where part of the basement is used as office space would still constitute a dwelling place — but if there was a separate outside entrance to the office that clients regularly entered through the office space might be inspected independently from the dwelling.

Because of the way they limit inspection powers, courts will not unreasonably stretch dwelling place boundaries. In *R. v. Fleming*, (2003) 104 C.R.R. (2d) 75 (Nfld. & L. Prov. Ct.) at paras. 51-52, the court rejected the argument that inspection powers were improperly employed against an outbuilding used for a business that was near the residence of the business owner:

> Notwithstanding the suggestion that the stage in question is part of the "curtilage" of Flemming's house, an unheated fishing stage which extends from shore on land near one's home out over the public waters of a harbour is not an extension of that home, and calling it an extension of the home does not attach it to the home, or cloak it with the rights that a person enjoys in relation to his or her home. The stage in this case is not attached to Flemming's dwelling house, nor is it even on the same parcel of land as his house. Instead, it is across the road from his house, on a wharf extending out into the waters of Lamaline Harbour. It is a building used by Flemming to mend nets and store equipment used in the fishing industry. There is a spectrum of expectation of privacy, extending from vessels at one end of the spectrum, where there is little expectation of privacy, all the way up to the highest level of privacy enjoyed in a dwelling house . . . this Court finds that there is little expectation of privacy in a stage.

All investigators need to be aware of dwelling place inspection limitations, but they should not unduly hamper most regulatory compliance verification.

THE SCOPE AND LIMITS OF DEMANDS FOR INFORMATION

Sometimes used as a preliminary step to, in conjunction with, or after an inspection, demands for information are authorized under many regulatory statutes and enable investigators to compel persons falling under the regulation of an Act to answer questions relevant to the administration or enforcement of that Act. Information demands are more powerful than inspections in not requiring investigators to have any prior knowledge about where to look for relevant information, but are less powerful in needing to rely on the cooperation and truthfulness of those from whom they demand information. Demand powers take a greater variety of forms than do inspection powers: under some Acts demands can only take the form of question-

ing during site inspections, while in other Acts they are free-standing powers authorizing the delivering of written or oral demands by a variety of
means. The most important difference between regulatory inspection and
information demand powers is that the search warrant is a judicially authorizeable alternative to the inspection power, whereas the information
demand has no real post-predominant purpose shift alternative — unless an
inquiry power is available, or investigators can wait for a preliminary inquiry
subpoena to take effect on a non-target. Information demands should therefore be used at the earliest stages of regulatory compliance verification
before any shift in purpose has occurred that might forbid further compulsion power use.

1. Misperceptions about the Protection against Self-Incrimination

Information demands made on persons who might eventually be
charged with an offence are not somehow unfair, as explained in *R. v.
Fitzpatrick*, [1995] 4 S.C.R. 154 at paras. 30 & 42:

> In this regulatory environment, we must be careful to avoid auto-
> matically applying rules that have been developed respecting self-
> incrimination in the criminal sphere.
>
> . . .
>
> Just because the information may later be *used* in an adversarial
> proceeding, when the state seeks to enforce the restrictions neces-
> sary to accomplish its regulatory objectives, does not mean that the
> state is guilty of coercing the individual to incriminate himself.

Information demands can only be made when operating well within the
confines of the regulatory universe, and not in areas of overlap with the
criminal universe where compliance verification has transformed into gathering evidence for a prosecution.

2. Using Information Demands as Tools to Pin Down Answers

Although the target of an information demand in theory has no real
choice about providing information, and may face significant penalties for
non-cooperation, in practice a person can simply say the information sought

does not exist, has been destroyed, or its whereabouts is unknown. The best use of information demands could be in pinning people down to one story that cannot be changed years later at trial to suit whatever explanation is then offered as a defence. If a demand is to be used effectively, *very* detailed questions must be asked so all the facts a witness admits to knowing are established at an early stage. Comprehensive information demand interviews can take hours to complete.

By using a script of common questions prepared in advance to be asked of everyone during information demand interviews, you might eventually detect contradictory answers that can be further explored and get closer to the truth than if you did not ask consistent questions of every witness. A script of questions should not, however, restrict improvised follow-up questions — the script is only there to ensure nothing is missed. I had one case where regulatory investigators were instructed by their supervisor to only ask the exact same eight questions when interviewing each witness. Not surprisingly, they didn't find out very much since some witnesses gave one-sentence answers, some didn't understand the questions, and some had no knowledge relevant to those questions but might have had other relevant knowledge if only different questions had been asked. That supervisor got it half right in believing there was value in consistent questioning, but incorrectly concluded it was somehow unfair to pursue wide-ranging follow-up questions that drag details from short answers, clarify details from evasive or confusing answers, and head into promising unexplored territory.

3. The Forms That Information Demands and Their Responses Can Take

If the Act you are operating under is silent on what form an information demand can take, it is usually safe to assume both oral and written demands are possible. Using written information demands might be more efficient from a use of resources perspective, but can be less effective at getting helpful answers. The target of a written demand will have considerable time to craft a response, and investigator follow-up to a written demand response could require entirely new demands with further delays. By contrast, oral demands can take the form of a conversation, but it may later be more difficult to prove exactly what information was demanded if a person fails to comply with an oral demand — video or at least audio recording all oral demands and responses is highly advisable.

Whether investigators can specify the particular form of response to an information demand depends on the wording of the Act relied upon. Compare any information demand power you are wondering about to the language of the power considered in *Tower v. Minister of National Revenue*, 2003 FCA 307 at para. 20, which found that s-s. 231.2(1) of the *Income Tax Act* could indeed require information to be provided in a particular form:

> **231.2.**(1) Notwithstanding any other provision of this Act, the Minister may, subject to subsection (2), for any purpose related to the administration or enforcement of this Act, including the collection of any amount payable under this Act by any person, by notice served personally or by registered or certified mail, require that any person provide, within such reasonable time as is stipulated in the notice,
>
> > (a) any information or additional information, including a return of income or a supplementary return; or
> >
> > (b) any document.

After examining the wording of s. 231.2 the court concluded:

> Paragraph 231.2(1)(a), when properly interpreted, empowers the Minister to compel a taxpayer to provide "information", meaning knowledge or facts. In order to exercise this power, the Minister must be able to ask questions to elicit the knowledge, facts or figures. The words "return of income or supplementary return" in paragraph (a) does not detract from this interpretation as the preceding word "including" means that the phrase is not exhaustive of the meaning of "information." These words enable the Minister not only to get the information regarding a taxpayer's income, but also to specify the form in which this information must be provided, i.e. a tax return containing prescribed information rather than in a letter. In my view, the Minister is therefore able to compel production of documents and records under paragraph 231.2(1)(b) and ask questions to elicit knowledge or facts under paragraph 231.2(1)(a).

It must be remembered, however, that the *Income Tax Act* has a broader reach than most pieces of regulatory legislation.

You may be disappointed in the level of detail provided in a response to an information demand if you are expecting elaborate spreadsheets to be prepared and instead only receive a brief telephone call giving a few figures. The best way to get a particular form of response is to very carefully phrase the demand. At the very least the form of a response needs to be intelligible to investigators, otherwise it will not be in compliance with the demand.

4. Reasonable Time Limits for Compliance with Information Demands

The amount of time that is reasonable to comply with an information demand will be directly proportionate to the onerousness of the demand requirements. If it is an oral demand for information likely within the personal knowledge of the demand target, then immediate compliance might be required. Where a written demand poses a complex series of questions, or seeks extensive documents, several weeks might be a reasonable time frame for a response. In prosecutions for failure to comply with a demand, the courts have been critical of investigators who have provided only a few days to comply with demands that require carefully crafted responses. Sometime between 30 and 90 days is probably a reasonable time to give for compliance with most information demands, other than brief oral demands made during the course of an inspection.

Because of the on-going need to monitor regulatory compliance, a new demand with a new deadline can be issued for exactly the same information even when an earlier deadline to comply with a demand has expired and failure to respond has been punished. A further refusal to comply can lead to yet another prosecution as happened in *R. v. Grimwood*, [1987] 2 S.C.R. 755 at para. 3:

> Further demands by the Minister create fresh time periods within which the taxpayer is required to comply and fresh offences for non-compliance within those time periods for which he may be prosecuted. Any other interpretation would have the effect of frustrating what is essentially a self-assessment system of taxation.

The courts fully support the use of information demands as part of legitimate regulatory compliance verification, and such demands cannot simply be ignored. But if wide ranging verbal questioning of witnesses is what investigators think would best verify regulatory compliance, then a formal "inquiry" could be a more effective tool.

THE SCOPE AND LIMITS OF INQUIRIES

1. How Inquiries Are Different

An inquiry can be convened under a few regulatory Acts like the *Income Tax Act* and the *Competition Act*, R.S.C. 1985, c. C-34, and will result in witnesses being compelled to attend at a particular location to answer questions under oath and possibly produce documents. The information gathered from the inquiry can then be used as the basis for further regulatory investigation, to obtain search warrants, or to lay charges. The inquiry power differs from an information demand in its formality, the "under oath" nature of its questioning, its ability to refer question refusals to a court for contempt sanctions, and its preparation of a report at the end of the taking of evidence.

The person appointed to preside over an inquiry may be known by different names like a "hearing officer" under the *Income Tax Act* or "presiding officer" under the *Competition Act*. This officer makes rulings on procedural points arising in the course of the inquiry, like whether a question should be answered, but will not make any definitive findings like guilt or innocence. Application must usually be made to a judge of a superior court to enforce orders of the hearing officer. An inquiry will also have a person appointed to direct the course of government questioning, who for the *Income Tax Act* is known as the "inquiry officer" or for the *Competition Act* is the "Commissioner of Competition." A written report of the evidence is prepared at the end of an inquiry to be forwarded to the responsible Minister, who can then decide to proceed with further compliance verification steps, lay charges, or terminate proceedings.

Regulatory compliance verification inquiries are distinct from public inquires like the *Commission of Inquiry into the Sponsorship Program and Advertising Activities* (the Gomery Inquiry) established under Part I of the *Inquiries Act*, R.S.C. 1985 c. I-11. The purpose of public inquiries is still fact finding, but their primary aim is usually to discover the truth rather than whether regulatory universe laws have been broken. Because of their different goals, public inquiries are not surprisingly held in public while regulatory compliance verification inquiries will usually be held behind closed doors to protect the privacy of witnesses and targets.

2. Inquiry Powers in Action

Section 231.4 of the *Income Tax Act* provides a good example of an inquiry power in a regulatory Act:

231.4 (1) The Minister may, for any purpose related to the administration or enforcement of this Act, authorize any person, whether or not the person is an officer of the Canada Revenue Agency, to make such inquiry as the person may deem necessary with reference to anything relating to the administration or enforcement of this Act.

(2) Where the Minister, pursuant to subsection (1), authorizes a person to make an inquiry, the Minister shall forthwith apply to the Tax Court of Canada for an order appointing a hearing officer before whom the inquiry will be held.

(3) For the purposes of an inquiry authorized under subsection (1), a hearing officer appointed under subsection (2) in relation thereto has all the powers conferred on a commissioner by sections 4 and 5 of the *Inquiries Act* and that may be conferred on a commissioner under section 11 thereof.

(4) A hearing officer appointed under subsection (2) in relation to an inquiry shall exercise the powers conferred on a commissioner by section 4 of the *Inquiries Act* in relation to such persons as the person authorized to make the inquiry considers appropriate for the conduct thereof but the hearing officer shall not exercise the power to punish any person unless, on application by the hearing officer, a judge of a superior or county court certifies that the power may be exercised in the matter disclosed in the application and the applicant has given to the person in respect of whom the applicant proposes to exercise the power 24 hours notice of the hearing of the application or such shorter notice as the judge considers reasonable.

(5) Any person who gives evidence in an inquiry authorized under subsection (1) is entitled to be represented by counsel and, on request made by the person to the Minister, to receive a transcript of the evidence given by the person.

(6) Any person whose affairs are investigated in the course of an inquiry authorized under subsection (1) is entitled to be present and to be represented by counsel throughout the inquiry unless the hearing officer appointed under subsection (2) in relation to the inquiry, on application by the Minister or a person giving evidence, orders otherwise in relation to the whole or any part of the inquiry on the ground that the presence of the person and the person's counsel, or either of them, would be prejudicial to the effective conduct of the inquiry.

Features and limitations of the *Income Tax Act* inquiry power are:

- the purpose of the inquiry must be for the administration or enforcement of the *Income Tax Act*;

- the Minister can authorize an inquiry officer to make any inquiry deemed necessary within the bounds of the prescribed purpose;

- that inquiry officer will then apply on behalf of the Minister to the Tax Court of Canada to appoint a hearing officer;

- the inquiry officer can then ask the hearing officer to issue subpoenas to relevant persons to give testimony and produce documents before the hearing officer;

- citations for contempt for failure to appear or answer questions are available, but only upon approval of a superior court judge;

- inquiry witnesses may be represented by counsel, and receive a transcript of their evidence upon request; and

- the target of an inquiry may be represented by counsel, and be present throughout proceedings, unless the hearing officer orders otherwise; excluding a target could later be held to be highly prejudicial to his rights.

In earlier days, investigators were responsible for setting up inquiries and questioning witnesses, but in today's increasingly legalistic world lawyers work with investigators to set things up, and it is the lawyers who ask the questions. Demystification of the law will assist investigators in navigating the inquiry process, but early investigator-prosecutor contact is vital to initiating a request to establish an inquiry.

3. The Legal Challenges of Inquiries

Witnesses and targets are increasingly contesting inquiry legitimacy on constitutional and procedural grounds. Collateral attacks on the inquiry process can delay the conclusion or even commencement of inquiries by many years and consume considerable resources, as happened to an extreme degree in one case I was involved with: *Del Zotto v. Canada*, (1994) 2 F.C. 640 (T.D.); [1995] 3 F.C. 507 (T.D.); [1997] 2 F.C. 428 (T.D.); [1997] 3 F.C. 40 (C.A.); [1999] 1 S.C.R. 3. The Supreme Court of Canada did in the end uphold the constitutional validity of regulatory inquiry procedures, adopting the reasons of the dissenting judge from the Federal Court of Appeal at paras. 65-66:

> What is striking about the offences described in paragraphs 239(1)(a) to (e) is that they all involve possible tax evasion through false returns, falsified documents, wilful evasion or conspiracy to commit any of the foregoing. This is not a typical criminal law but is a law designed to ensure compliance with the self-reporting requirements of the *Income Tax Act* and was characterized as part of what is really a regulatory scheme
>
> There cannot be the exaggerated claims to privacy connected with the administration of the *Income Tax Act* which the appellants assert. The Act requires all manner of disclosure.

The flexible *Charter* standards of the regulatory universe were again affirmed as a justifiable necessity for adequate compliance verification of Canada's myriad of regulatory laws. Inquiries remain a very useful tool where an inspection or search cannot be conducted because it is impossible to say where material relevant to verifying compliance would be found, and where demands for information are also not able to sufficiently advance an investigation.

The Cost and Use of Inquiries

Q&A

Q: While inquiries sound like a good tool to utilize, aren't they expensive to set up and run, and won't they just become bogged down in legal technicalities?

A: Inquiries are expensive since lawyers, a hearing officer, and staff must be retained, premises secured, and proceedings can drag on for a long time. They also suffer from legal challenges with respect to their initial establishment, and on the procedures they adopt in hearing evidence. But they can yield information that cannot be obtained in any other way. Their use should be restricted to very significant cases, and adequate resources need to be allocated to see an inquiry through to its conclusion.

ENSURING PROPER APPOINTMENT OF REGULATORY INVESTIGATORS

Although the requirement that an Act's regulatory compliance verification powers can only be utilized by an investigator properly appointed under the Act may seem like a minor formality, investigators and prosecutors face a serious problem if such an appointment never existed, expired or does not extend to the place, person or type of power involved in a case. For some Acts, simply being a peace officer will be sufficient to exercise its compliance verification powers. For other Acts, explicit appointment as a specific type of regulatory enforcement officer is necessary like appointment as a Fishery Officer to enforce the *Fisheries Act*:

> **5.** (1) The Minister may designate any persons or classes of persons as fishery officers or fishery guardians for the purposes of this Act and may limit in any manner the Minister considers appropriate the powers that a fishery officer or fishery guardian may exercise under this Act or any other Act of Parliament.
>
> (2) Each fishery officer and fishery guardian shall be provided with a certificate in a form the Minister considers appropriate certifying their designation as such and, where the powers of a fishery officer or fishery guardian are limited pursuant to subsection (1), specifying the powers that the officer or guardian may exercise under this Act or any other Act of Parliament.
>
> (3) On entering any place under this Act or any other Act of Parliament, a fishery officer or fishery guardian shall, on request, show the certificate of designation to the person in charge of the place.

If serious doubts are raised over an investigator's appointment, some kind of documentary evidence of that authority may need to be produced.

There is no limit to the number of cross-appointments that may be held. An RCMP officer could also be appointed a Fishery Officer, a provincial game warden, and a Canada Revenue Agency officer. Where multiple appointments do exist, knowing which "hat" is being worn during a particular investigation becomes all the more important since not all regulatory compliance verification powers are identical, and most of those powers have no equivalent when a *Criminal Code* investigation is being pursued.

Many regulatory investigators do *not* hold peace officer status permitting them to take advantage of enhanced peace officer powers under the *Criminal Code* like s. 495 *Code* arrest without warrant powers, s-s. 509(2) *Code* service of summons powers, and a variety of *Code* search and seizure powers available to investigate offences under any federal Act. If you will be routinely relying on powers only available to peace officers under the *Code*, formal appointment as a peace officer is likely required, but without such appointment you might in exceptional circumstances be able to rely on the *Code*'s powers and protections for peace officers to the extent you are acting in execution of your duties under the Act you are appointed to enforce, as noted in *R. v. Beaman,* [1963] S.C.R. 445 at 449:

> The situation appears to me to be that although the sphere of a game warden's authority is limited to the enforcement of a provin-

> cial statute, he is, nevertheless, for that purpose and by that statute, clothed with all the rights, powers and protections afforded to a peace officer by the *Criminal Code*. With all respect, this does not in my view mean that the province is giving to one of its law enforcement officers "the authority to act in criminal matters" and I cannot see that this legislation gives rise to any problem or conflict between the provincial and federal fields.

Any powers under the *Code* that you wish to rely upon will need to be interpreted in the context of the Act you are enforcing, which could place limits on those powers.

THE SPECIAL POSITION OF MILITARY INVESTIGATORS

Military investigators play an important role in regulatory compliance verification, as well as in criminal and regulatory law enforcement throughout Canada. Military investigators can definitely benefit from the demystification of the law and early investigator-prosecutor contact themes this book espouses. Non-military investigators will find a basic understanding of the unique position military investigations and prosecutions occupy in the Canadian legal system valuable because Canadian Forces personnel and property exist throughout Canada, and interact with non-military investigators when it comes to off-base and off-duty activities. It is most appropriate to deal with the situation of military investigators in this chapter because of the way they simultaneously wear the two hats of regulatory and criminal investigator, can utilize special forms of inspection, demand and inquiry powers in addition to traditional criminal investigation powers, and need to be equally adept at navigating the regulatory and criminal universes.

1. How the Special Structure of Military Investigations and Regulations Affects Powers

The federal government responded to the increasing pressures of the *Charter* and the difficulties identified in the report *Dishonoured Legacy: The Lessons Learned of the Somalia Affair* (Ottawa: Minister of Public Works and Government Services, 1997) by introducing many changes to the military justice system like the appointment of an independent Director of Defence Counsel Services to bring it more into line with the civilian system, but military law remains a distinct realm. While those who aren't part of the military might regard all those in the Canadian Forces tasked with regulatory compliance verification and offence investigation as "military police," in fact there are three classes of people who deal with such issues: the National Investigative Service who investigate serious or sensitive offences, the Military Police who investigate other offences, and individual operational units who investigate minor breaches of discipline. Military investigators perpetually wear two hats of regulatory compliance: verifier of the multitude of administrative regulations governing the daily lives of military personnel, and regulatory or criminal enforcer of the significant number of service offences inhabiting the regulatory and criminal universes. The split nature of their duties poses significant challenges to military investigators in interpreting predominant purpose and varying *Charter* standards when choosing from among the powers available to them.

Military investigators focus on the prohibitions of the *Code of Service Discipline*, being Part III of the *National Defence Act*, R.S.C. 1985, c. N-5, which tidily deals with everything from minor service disciplinary matters inhabiting the regulatory universe up to murder planted firmly in the criminal universe, and deems all offences under other federal Acts including the *Criminal Code* to be service offences. The *National Defence Act*, together with Volume II of the *Queen's Regulations and Orders*, is a complete code of procedure for military investigations and prosecutions. The justification for the unique position of wide-ranging military justice offences and expedient procedures rests, as described by *R. v. Stewart* (1993), 5 CMAR 205 at 212, in the unique purpose of the Canadian Forces:

> Military justice must not only promote good order but also high morale and discipline. In this way it has a more positive purpose than law in the purely civilian context. Discipline is defined as instant obedience to lawful orders, and the most essential form of discipline in the military environment is self-discipline — a person's willingness to carry out his or her assigned duties regardless of the danger, or lack of immediate supervision.

Do you hear echoes of the justification for flexible *Charter* standards and special rules applicable to anyone voluntarily choosing to be involved in a highly regulated industry?

2. The Person- and Territory-Specific Jurisdiction of Military Investigators

Questions of jurisdiction over offences, people and territory can arise at points of interaction between the military and civilian justice systems, requiring early investigator-prosecutor contact to answer. Sometimes military investigators will have authority that extends beyond military property or military personnel, but only where there is a close link to a military establishment and the authority is exercised within a reasonable time after an establishment offence occurred, as explained in *R. v. Nolan*, [1987] 1 S.C.R. 1212 at 1231-1232:

> Although the offence took place on a defence establishment, the actual detention of the accused occurred on a public highway after the military police had followed Mr. Nolan out of the gates of the base. The question arises whether the military police retained their status and authority as peace officers once they left C.F.B. Shearwater. On the particular facts of the instant case, I have no difficulty in concluding that they did. The accused was seen committing a traffic offence on the base. The officers only saw the accused as he was speeding out of the gates of the base and, in order to enforce the law, the military police officers had to follow Mr. Nolan off the base. There is absolutely no evidence that the accused attempted to evade the military police, so the circumstances do not really raise the issue of "hot pursuit". Given the instantaneous police warning to the accused to stop his vehicle and the detention immediately outside the gates of the base, there was such a clear nexus between the offence committed on the base and the detention off the base that I am convinced that the military police retained their status and authority as peace officers.

The limited person- and place-specific jurisdiction of military investigators is quite similar to the situation of regulatory investigators.

Because military policy seeks to adhere to the highest possible legal standards, even where the military justice system possesses jurisdiction over territory or an accused in some situations that jurisdiction will be deferred to the civilian justice system. For example, military investigators seeking search warrants in Canada will usually go to the civilian court system, even though the *Code of Service Discipline* provides they can be issued by a commanding officer. Likewise, certain offences like spousal assault and impaired driving will have charges laid and be prosecuted in civilian courts even when committed on military territory and by military personnel.

3. How the Predominant Purpose Test Affects Military Investigations

Three types of military administrative investigation exist: informal investigations, summary investigations, and boards of inquiry. While information compulsion powers might be employed to assist these administrative investigations, military law makes clear such investigations only have a fact find-ing rather than evidence gathering role, and goes so far as to specify that information collected during those investigations cannot be used in any sub-sequent prosecution. The Canadian Forces have even codified a version of the predominant purpose test in the *Inspection and Search Defence Regulations*, SOR/86-958, QR&O Vol IV, Appendix 3.3: inspections are to be conducted for purposes of maintaining military standards of health, hygiene, safety, security, efficiency, dress and kit, but cannot be conducted for the purpose of seeking incriminating evidence in a place where a privacy inter-est exists without a search warrant or other search authority being obtained. Military investigators are left with making similar choices as non-military investigators: conduct an exhaustive regulatory truth finding exercise by aggressively using all powers of information compulsion available in law and possibly forgo some prospects of a viable prosecution, or carefully scout out the state of regulatory compliance while being prepared to quick-ly switch to solely using powers of the criminal universe as soon as predom-inant purpose shifts to prosecution case building.

Civilian Versus Military Courts

Q & A

Q: I work as a police officer in a town adjacent to a large Canadian Forces base. If the military's *Code of Service Discipline* is so all encompassing in establishing offences, and providing for their investigation and prosecution by military tribunals, why do I occasionally see military personnel appear-ing in my local civilian provincial court charged with offences under the *Criminal Code*?

A: As a matter of policy, the Canadian Forces have chosen to let certain types of offences be tried in civilian courts for a variety of reasons. The fact such a policy choice has been made does not lessen the jurisdiction of the mili-tary to try those offences should military policy change. Those same offences if committed by Canadian Forces members overseas might be tried by a military tribunal.

WHEN IT MAKES SENSE TO EXERCISE RESTRAINT IN THE USE OF REGULATORY POWERS OF INTRUSION AND COMPULSION

Throughout this chapter I have urged investigators to embrace the use of regulatory intrusion and compulsion powers where available and appropriate to verify regulatory compliance. Such powers need not be methods of last resort, but investigators should realize there are advantages to avoiding their use where it's possible to secure compliance information of the same quality through abiding by the rules of the criminal universe. Playing by the criminal universe rules means any evidence you gather will be available for use in civil or criminal proceedings under any Act, and you avoid later arguments over your predominant purpose. However, limiting yourself to criminal universe powers might fail to advance more immediate compliance verification objectives. A balance must be struck between successful information gathering and successful subsequent legal proceedings.

In taking a middle course to obtaining regulatory information through means compatible with later court proceedings, a few guiding principles can be offered:

- where your predominant purpose clearly is regulatory compliance verification, and you do not contemplate any subsequent prosecution, you are free to embrace inspection and information demand powers where available;

- where your predominant purpose clearly is regulatory compliance verification, but a subsequent prosecution is a real possibility, be more cautious in using inspection and demand powers as you get close to the point of predominant purpose shift and RPG;

- once it appears predominant purpose has shifted, resort to search warrants and cautioned statements (for targets) instead of inspections and information demands;

- if you are concerned you are getting close to a predominant purpose shift, but have not reached that point, don't try to get a search warrant on existing sketchy information if you have regulatory inspection or demand powers available that might secure information of much higher quality that in turn can be used to support a much stronger warrant.

Sometimes you will have to make conscious choices between speedily and effectively pursuing regulatory compliance verification, or slowly advancing the laying of criminal or regulatory charges. Consider the public interest in making your choice.

Regarding the Boundaries of Regulatory Inspections, Information Demands and Inquiries

KEY POINTS

✓ Regulatory offences live in a different universe from criminal offences when it comes to *Charter* obligations, standards of proof, stigma associated with investigation, prosecution or conviction, and severity of punishment. It is often only through the use of inspection, information demand or inquiry powers that regulatory offences can be detected.

✓ Regulatory powers will only be available where explicitly authorized by legislation, an investigator is properly appointed under an Act to use them, and the predominant purpose of power use is regulatory compliance verification. The cut-off point for the use of regulatory compliance powers (with the exception of inquiry power) occurs where an investigator's predominant purpose shifts from verifying compliance to collecting evidence of an offence, which may be earlier or later than the point of reasonable and probable grounds.

✓ Investigators must be aware of the limits each Act authorizing an inspection power places on who and what can be inspected, plus where, when, why and how inspection may take place, including that inspection of a dwelling place will usually only be possible with consent or under an "inspection warrant." Investigators will often be able to make a statutory demand for information either orally or in writing, but may need to be flexible on the time allowed for and form of a response. The rarer inquiry power differs from an information demand in its formality, the "under oath" nature of its questioning, its ability to refer question refusals to a court for contempt sanctions, and its preparation of a report at the end of taking evidence.

✓ The *Charter* still applies to all activities of military investigators, but will be interpreted in a flexible manner depending on context. Military investigators have place-specific and people-specific jurisdiction that may coincide with the jurisdiction of non-military investigators, requiring agreement on who will investigate and prosecute particular matters.

✓ Sometimes it makes sense not to use powers of regulatory intrusion and compulsion even when they are available. Adhering to the information gathering restrictions of the most restrictive of the Acts that might have been infringed in a particular case permits later civil or criminal proceeding flexibility, but could be too limited for advancing more immediate compliance verification objectives.

FURTHER READING

Cases

British Columbia Securities Commission v. Branch, [1995] 2 S.C.R. 3. There is a reduced expectation of privacy in a regulatory inquiry.

Comité Paritaire v. Potash, [1994] 2 S.C.R. 406. Regulatory inspections may be conducted without prior judicial authorization.

Del Zotto v. Canada, [1999] 1 S.C.R. 3; affirming [1997] 3 F.C. 40. (C.A.). A subpoena issued as part of a regulatory inquiry is much less intrusive than a search, and the inquiry process is constitutionally valid.

R. v. Fitzpatrick, [1995] 4 S.C.R.154. The protection against self-incrimination should not be as rigidly applied in the regulatory compliance verification context as during criminal investigations.

R. v. Jarvis, [2002] 3 S.C.R. 757; *R. v. Ling*, [2002] 3 S.C.R. 814. The predominant purpose of regulatory inspections cannot be incrimination of the target.

R. v. White, [1999] 2 S.C.R. 417. Statements made under regulatory compulsion are inadmissible in collateral criminal proceedings.

R. v. Wilcox (2001), 192 N.S.R. (2d) 159; 2001 NSCA 45. Gives an overview of the challenges involved when executing search warrants based on information gathered through the exercise of inspection powers.

Books, Articles and Reports

T.L. Archibald, K.E. Jull & K.W. Roach, *Regulatory and Corporate Liability: From Due Diligence to Risk Management*, loose-leaf (Aurora, ON: Canada Law Book, 2005).

S. Berger, *The Prosecution and Defence of Environmental Offences*, loose-leaf (Aurora, ON: Canada Law Book, 1994).

I.S. Bloom et al., "Warrantless Techniques of Compelling Evidence: The Unique Rules of the Regulatory Universe" (2001) 13 N.J.C.L. 79.

I.S. Bloom, J. Vaissi Nagy & G.S. Campbell, "The Residual Protection Against Self-Incrimination in Canada: The Road Not Taken" (1995) 5 N.J.C.L. 363.

J.C. Clifford, *Administrative Policing: Some Unifying Ideas* (Ottawa: Law Reform Commission of Canada, 1990).

J.C. Clifford, *Inspection: A Case Study and Selected References* (Ottawa: Law Reform Commission of Canada, 1988).

Law Reform Commission of Canada, *Working Paper No. 44 — Crimes Against the Environment* (Ottawa: Law Reform Commission of Canada, 1985).

R. Libman, *Libman on Regulatory Offences in Canada*, loose-leaf (Saltspring Island, BC: Earlscourt, 2003).

W.J. Manuel & C. Donszelmann, *Law of Administrative Investigations and Prosecutions* (Aurora, ON: Canada Law Book, 1999).

R. Nadeau, *Compliance and Enforcement in Customs and Excise* (Ottawa: Law Reform Commission of Canada, 1982).

J. Swaigen, *Regulatory Offences in Canada: Liability and Defences* (Toronto: Carswell, 1992).

CHAPTER SIX

GENERAL PRINCIPLES FOR ENSURING SEARCH AND SEIZURE RESULTS ARE NOT LATER EXCLUDED AT TRIAL

The state's interest in detecting crime begins to prevail over the individual's interest in being left alone at the point where credibly-based probability replaces suspicion.

Hunter v. Southam, [1984] 2 S.C.R. 145 at 167.

In This Chapter

- The changed landscape of search and seizure
- Three questions to answer before searching or seizing
- Determining the purpose of the search
- Picking from the five authorities for search and seizure
- Steps to take before and during a search and seizure
- Steps to take after a seizure

THE CHANGED LANDSCAPE OF SEARCH AND SEIZURE

The *Canadian Charter of Rights and Freedoms* transformed search and seizure from the straightforward exercise of a set of powers rooted in statute and the common law into perhaps the most uncertain and complex part of criminal and regulatory investigation in Canada. Prior to the *Charter*, evidence collected by investigators when brought before the courts would almost never be excluded from evidence, even if it had been obtained in a questionable manner. The courts were quite resistant to the importation of concepts of remedial justice into the criminal trial process, as demonstrated in *R. v. Wray*, [1970] S.C.R. 272 at 293: "It is only the allowance of evidence gravely prejudicial to the accused, the admissibility of which is tenuous, and whose probative force in relation to the main issue before the court is trifling, which can be said to operate unfairly."

The position of the judiciary has since shifted so the courts have assumed a supervisory role over investigating and prosecuting authorities, as opposed to previously merely insuring a procedurally fair trial for the accused. Exclusion of evidence at trial has now become a routine event, and arguments of illegal investigative actions having been taken in good faith may carry little weight. The only way to ensure search and seizure results are not later excluded is to follow a few enduring search and seizure principles, and scrupulously comply with the most recent developments in the law.

Although the law of search and seizure continues to evolve concerning what practices are and are not permissible, demystification of that law is possible because search and seizure errors frequently violate legal developments of ten or twenty years ago. Even future developments in cutting edge legal areas like electronic surveillance can be somewhat predicted by paying attention to overall trends. If common mistakes are avoided, and attention is paid to trends, it should only be in exceptional circumstances that there will be any question as to whether seized evidence will be admitted at trial. Even exceptional circumstances can be dealt with through early investigator-prosecutor contact.

A common theme of protecting privacy values to the greatest degree possible runs through all search and seizure authorities in Canada. The greater the degree of privacy intrusion authorized, the more onerous the evidentiary and technical preconditions will be for such an authorization. This "burden proportional to intrusion" principle indicates that the least intrusive search and seizure authority should be chosen that satisfies your evidence collection needs in order to lesson the burden to be met to secure that authority.

THREE QUESTIONS TO ANSWER BEFORE SEARCHING OR SEIZING

Before conducting any type of search or seizure, all investigators must ask themselves three questions.

- What is the purpose of the search or seizure?

- What is my authority to conduct the search or seizure?

- What steps do I need to take before, during and after the search or seizure to ensure anything seized will not be excluded from evidence at trial?

Purpose leads to authority, which in turn leads to steps, so the order in which these questions are considered is important. Considering purpose will take the most time of all, so don't rush past it to impulsively grab an authority and proceed to look up its steps. There are for the most part only five authorities to choose from, while there are endless subtleties to what might be the purpose of a search or seizure. A detailed record of purpose, authority and steps is the key to successfully explaining at trial why a search or seizure action was properly authorized.

DETERMINING THE PURPOSE OF THE SEARCH

Authority completely flows from and follows purpose. If a search is being conducted for a purpose outside the recognized purposes of the authority being relied upon, then it will not be a lawful search. Plan out the search in your mind first, even if you only have a few moments to do so, and act only once you have settled on a purpose and thus understand the scope of your resulting authority. This point was driven home in *R. v. Caslake*, [1989] 1 S.C.R. 51 at para. 27:

> the police cannot rely on the fact that, objectively, a legitimate purpose for the search existed when that is not the purpose for which they searched. The *Charter* requires that agents of the state act in accordance with the rule of law. This means that they must not only objectively search within the permissible scope, but that they must turn their mind to this scope before searching.

Mismatched search purposes and authorities are common but avoidable problems. You cannot search a vehicle for contraband tobacco incidental to an impaired driving arrest because the purpose of the search is to look for tobacco, which cannot be matched with a search incident to arrest authority only extending to impaired driving and related offence evidence. Matching a tobacco purpose with a search warrant authority targeting tobacco could be acceptable, as could a consent search authority for tobacco.

Purpose of search governs not only which of the five search authorities are available, but also dictates within the warrant authority itself which type of warrant is required to provide the necessary authority to search. Tracking a person's movements is a different search purpose than searching that same person's residence; the first requires a s. 492.1 *Criminal Code* warrant, while a s. 487 *Code* warrant suffices for the second purpose. Purpose even dictates whether investigative actions constitute a search at all, rather than a regulatory inspection. The demystification of the law theme requires you not get too tied up by purpose worries, but some authorities are clearly more legally risky than others.

Unnecessary Warrants in Doubtful Cases Don't Imperil Prosecutions

Q & A

Q: What if I obtain a warrant when I don't really need one. Am I not putting the entire case at risk if the warrant is later found to be invalid?

A: As long as there is no bad faith or abuse of process involved in obtaining the warrant, its invalidity should be irrelevant to the outcome of a case if a trial court determines no warrant was needed to use a particular investigative technique. The work involved in preparing a warrant application should be more than compensated for by the assurance a valid warrant gives that any evidence obtained through it is unlikely to be later excluded as deriving from a privacy breach.

PICKING FROM THE FIVE AUTHORITIES FOR SEARCH AND SEIZURE

Of the five principal search and seizure authorities, four do not require prior court authorization, but three of those four fall into legally grey areas fraught with risks if a case goes to trial. We can count off those authorities in the order of how likely they are to hold up at trial.

1. Search by Search Warrant

Using a search warrant is the legally safest way to search for and seize anything because it is anchored in prior judicial authorization. Trial courts are much less likely to second guess a judge or justice's independent conclusion that there was a basis to issue a search warrant than they are to find fault with an investigator's unreviewed basis for a warrantless search. Even where a warrant is not absolutely necessary to conduct a search and seizure, obtaining one may be prudent to remove any doubt about authority. At a minimum, the warrant will articulate in an organized way all your grounds supporting a search and seizure, and show what a scrupulous investigator you are.

There will be times when a warrant is clearly neither necessary nor appropriate. Before you decide not to bother with a warrant, ask yourself whether it would be possible to get one to conduct your planned search and seizure. If the answer is no, then you had better be very sure into which of the statutory or common law exceptions to prior judicial authorization your actions fall. If the answer is yes, then you must figure out how, if challenged at trial, you are going to justify the fact you didn't get a warrant when one would have been available for the asking. Obtaining a warrant also protects an investigator from risks of civil liability arising out of illegal search and seizure. Warrants are a bit more work up front, but save a lot of work and greatly enhance case success in the long run.

Courts have frequently reaffirmed warrants as being useful tools that should be obtained wherever possible, as in *Hunter v. Southam*, [1984] 2 S.C.R. 145 at 160-61:

> A requirement of prior authorization, usually in the form of a valid warrant, has been a consistent prerequisite for a valid search and seizure both at common law and under most statutes. Such a requirement puts the onus on the state to demonstrate the superiority of its interest to that of the individual. As such it accords with the apparent intention of the *Charter* to prefer, where feasible, the right of the individual to be free from state interference to the interests of the state in advancing its purposes through such interference.
>
> I recognize that it may not be reasonable in every instance to insist on prior authorization in order to validate governmental intrusions upon individuals' expectations of privacy. Nevertheless, where it is feasible to obtain prior authorization, I would hold that such authorization is a precondition for a valid search and seizure.

"If in doubt, get a warrant" has always been the mantra I have urged on investigators.

2. Search Incidental to Arrest

Search incidental to arrest is the other legally solid search and seizure authority if it is connected to a preceding, legally valid arrest, but you need to be able to live within the narrow limitations of its authority instead of trying to extend its reach into territory needing a warrant. Search and seizure may, according to the common law, be conducted for three purposes incidental to arrest:

- to protect the safety of arresting investigators;

- to collect and preserve evidence of the offence being arrested for and of related offences;

- to prevent escape of the person under arrest.

The difficulty with searches incidental to arrest concerns how intrusive and broad they can be. Intrusiveness limits how far a search can go beyond a simple pat down escalating right up to a strip search or even a body cavity search. Breadth governs the geographic scope of the search extending to areas like the arrested person's clothing, a briefcase being carried, a vehicle or a room in which someone is arrested.

a. *Permissible Intrusiveness and Breadth of Search Linked to Purpose of Arrest*

There must be a reasonable basis to believe one of the three purposes of search incidental to arrest will be met by engaging in a more intrusive or broader search. Arresting someone in a vehicle on an outstanding warrant for failure to appear in court would necessarily include a power to search that person for weapons, which fulfills the purpose of investigator safety. It would not include a power to search the vehicle for drugs, which have nothing to do with the offence that is the basis of the arrest.

The courts have repeatedly cautioned about search incident to arrest powers exceeding their linkage to an arrest, as in *R. v. Caslake*, [1998] 1 S.C.R. 51 at para. 22:

> Requiring that the search be truly incidental to the arrest means
> that if the justification for the search is to find evidence, there must
> be some reasonable prospect of securing evidence *of the offence*

for which the accused is being arrested. For example, when the arrest is for traffic violations, once the police have ensured their own safety, there is nothing that could properly justify searching any further . . . .

Restraint on the part of investigators is the order of the day where search incidental to arrest is concerned.

Moderately intrusive, incidental-to-arrest personal searches of clothing and belongings being carried might be justified by the nature of the offence being investigated, but significantly intrusive strip and body cavity searches can only be conducted where there are compelling reasons to do so as noted in *R. v. Golden*, [2001] 3 S.C.R. 679 at para. 95: "a 'routine' strip search carried out in good faith and without violence will also violate s. 8 where there is no compelling reason for performing a strip search in the circumstances of the arrest." Extremely intrusive personal searches that interfere with bodily integrity, like the taking of blood samples, can never be conducted incidental to arrest and will always require a warrant or other explicit statutory authority because as found in *R. v. Stillman*, [1997] 1 S.C.R. 607 at para. 39, such searches "may constitute the ultimate affront to human dignity."

b. *Prefer a Warrant for an Intrusive or Broad Post-Arrest Search*

Why, you might ask, obtain a warrant where you don't absolutely need one? Because a trial court judge might later disagree with your interpretation of your own search incidental-to-arrest powers, because getting a warrant is not all that much work, and because your search might locate very important evidence you don't want excluded from admission at trial. If you've been working in law enforcement for any amount of time, you know lawyers and judges are always disagreeing among themselves about points of law, and can disagree with you. Certainly they have disagreed with me enough.

Broadening the area of a search incidental to arrest beyond the body and things carried by the person arrested to the area immediately surrounding the place a person is arrested can be done without a warrant, but it is best to obtain a warrant if a privacy interest could exist in the area to be searched. Different approaches might be called for to conduct a broad search of a public sidewalk (where there is no privacy interest), compared to a vehicle (where there can be a lessened privacy interest), or a residence (where there may be a very significant privacy interest) to minimize the risk a court will later find the breadth of the search to have exceeded the search incidental-to-arrest authority. The circumstances leading up to the arrest provide the grounds to get a warrant to search the location surrounding the arrest; if everyone in a target vehicle or residence has been detained or arrested, there will be time to obtain a warrant without risk of destruction of evidence.

c. *Examples of Valid and Invalid Searches Incident to Arrest*

A valid arrest remains the key precondition to reliance on the search incident-to-arrest authority. I can best illustrate this point through two contrasting cases I dealt with which both relied on search incident-to-arrest for discovery and seizure of drugs being carried by the accused. In the first case, the accused had fled a store after being observed shoplifting by a security guard. The police caught up with the accused, arrested him based on the first-hand account of the guard, and used the search incidental to arrest authority to look in a briefcase the accused was carrying at the time of arrest. The purpose of the search was to locate goods reported stolen by the guard. Instead of stolen goods, the police found heroin. The trial judge erroneously held the police needed a warrant to search the briefcase because the search extended beyond the accused's clothing, excluded the evidence, and acquitted the accused. I convinced an appeal court to overturn the acquittal because the police had both reasonable and probable grounds to arrest from the statement of the security guard, and reason to believe the stolen goods might be in the briefcase, which was not an overly broad place to search as an incident of arrest.

In the second case police stopped a person disembarking from a ferry and searched the bag he was carrying based on a vague informer tip of unknown reliability that the accused was transporting drugs. The police did find marijuana in the bag, but the search had been based only on a mere suspicion. The informer tip, while a good starting point for further investigation to develop grounds to arrest, did not by itself amount to reasonable and probable grounds of an offence. Although the search result proved the tip correct, the drugs could not add to arrest grounds after the fact. Sufficient grounds must exist before relying on the search incident-to-arrest authority. This time I stayed the charges because of the likelihood a court would find there to have been an illegal search and exclude all resulting evidence.

Scope of Search Incident to Arrest

Q & A

Q: Can I search a vehicle as a search incident to arrest when I arrest someone for impaired driving, or am I limited just to searching the clothing the person is wearing?

A: You must ask yourself what is the purpose of the search when searching incident to arrest. You are only authorized to look for items directly related to the offence you are arresting for or closely related offences, and items relevant to investigator safety or preventing flight of the arrested person. In an arrest for an impaired driving offence, you could search the vehicle for things like liquor, but you could not look for clothing connected to a sexual assault you suspect the driver was also involved in. For evidence of other offences, you will need a different search and seizure authority.

3. Seizure in Plain View

a. *Why Investigators Need to Have Authority to Be in Plain View Premises*

Plain view is really a common law power of *seizure*, not a power of search. No search is necessary, because the contraband item is in "plain view," but investigators must otherwise be lawfully in the premises where the plain view seizure takes place. Canadian courts have relied on the United States Supreme Court judgment of *Coolidge v. N.H.*, 403 U.S. 443 (1971) at 466, as accurately setting out the limitations on plain view seizure:

> the "plain view" doctrine may not be used to extend a general exploratory search from one object to another until something incriminating at last emerges. The plain view doctrine confers a seizure power not a search power. It does not permit an exploratory search to find other evidence.

According to *R. v. Buhay*, [2003] 1 S.C.R. 631 at para. 37: "the plain view doctrine requires, perhaps as a central feature, that the police officers have a prior justification for the intrusion into the place where plain view occurred." If there is no lawful authority to enter an area so a plain view seizure can be made, then a warrant must be obtained using as part of the grounds a description of the thing in plain view and the circumstances in which it was seen.

The two types of plain view are (1) from a public location, and (2) where an investigator is already lawfully in a private location. Public location plain view might occur where an inherently illegal item or an item that is evidence of an offence is viewed through a vehicle window during a routine traffic stop. Private location plain view could arise where investigators are already executing another search warrant or have been invited into private premises. While plain view may authorize you to reach into a vehicle to seize something because of the relatively minimal intrusion on privacy the reaching represents, it would likely not let you enter an apartment just because you saw something through an open street window. It appears to only allow seizure if you can reach out and touch the thing with the most minimal of privacy intrusions.

Ideally don't rely on plain view alone to seize unless you are in a public location. The best practice if you are in a private location, like a residence, without a warrant because of an invitation or emergency, and you see something in plain view you wish to seize is to secure the location and get a warrant. Without a warrant to back you up, it is too easy for the reasons you are in the private location to be later challenged in court, possibly leading to plain view evidence being excluded because of what the trial judge finds to have been an illegal search.

b. *Why the Illegality or Evidentiary Value of an Item Must Be Plain from a Mere View*

Illegality or evidentiary value must be "plain" from a mere "view" of an object, without further examination, analysis or opening of packaging, in order be seizeable under the plain view doctrine as explained in *R. v. Law*, [2002] 1 S.C.R. 227 at paras. 26-27:

> Corporal D. . . proceeded as though the safe had been abandoned by its owner and, for that reason, infringed the appellants' reasonable expectation of privacy.

> The respondent attempts to rely on the plain view doctrine, arguing that evidence that comes within the view of a "lawfully positioned" officer may be admissible if it is discovered inadvertently. . . . In this case, . . . the incriminating evidence was neither immediately obvious to Corporal D. . . nor discovered inadvertently. On the contrary, it came to light only after he examined, translated and photocopied several documents. Corporal D. . . admitted there was nothing facially wrong with the documents. He testified they contained a series of numbers and Chinese characters, and that he lacked both accounting expertise and proficiency in Chinese. Not having detected anything incriminating through the unaided use of his senses, Corporal D. . . cannot rely on the plain view doctrine either to establish reasonable and probable grounds to search, or to avoid the requirement of reasonable and probable grounds entirely . . . .

Since no illegality or evidentiary value was plain from documents written in Chinese that required financial analysis, even though they were ultimately connected to Goods and Services Tax offences, plain view could not be relied upon for their seizure. Remember to make sufficient notes of the exact state in which you found an object so you can convince a trial court that its illegality or evidentiary value was plain for all to see. The one-kilo block of cocaine sitting on the table just inside the open ground-floor apartment window that could be viewed by any passer-by taking a stroll on the sidewalk outside may in fact have been there, but a court will need some convincing that it was that plain.

c. *How Sometimes Plain View Really Is Obvious*

Don't take my cautionary words as discouraging you from ever using plain view. It is a solid common law seizure authority, you just need the right facts to make it work. For instance, in one of my cases a driver stopped for a traffic infraction produced his licence to police officers who noticed a lump of a black tar-like substance stuck to it. Upon closer examination, and a sniff or two, the officers formed the reasonable belief that it was a lump of hash, seized it, and charged the driver with possession of a controlled substance. At trial the driver argued that there had been an illegal search and he had been forced to incriminate himself by producing the licence, although he did admit he had received the hash at a party, and stuck it in his wallet for later use — sort of like sticking your chewing gum on the bedpost overnight. The court convicted him, finding the officers were hardly infringing his rights where he had been careless enough to produce a validly requested driver's licence with drugs stuck to it. When evidence literally drops into you lap, there is no rule of law to stop you from taking advantage of it.

Plain View is Only a Seizure Authority

Q&A

Q: If there is no such thing as a plain view search, and only a plain view seizure, then why do I hear the term "plain view search" all the time?

A: The misnomer "plain view search" leads to many misconceptions about the usefulness of this authority. Really plain view is only an ancillary seizure authority, but it will not always need to be attached to another valid search authority where investigators are in a public area or legitimately inside a private place as part of their duties and then come across an object in plain view that is clearly evidence of an offence.

4. *Search on Consent*

a. *The Risks Inherent in Consent Searches*

Although consent searches can still be validly performed in Canada, they are legally very risky because of being so dependent on the objective and subjective state of mind of the person giving consent, as affected by the exact words an investigator uses, any physical or psychological detention, and thus whether the decision to consent is informed and free from coercion. I believe consent to search should only be sought in rare circumstances due to the high standards to be met to obtain a free, fully informed, and unequivocal consent to waive the constitutional protection to be secure against unreasonable search and seizure. There are usually alternatives to a risky consent search.

If you already have reasonable and probable grounds to arrest a person, you could simply arrest and conduct a search incidental to the arrest so long as the search area and things to be searched for don't exceed the legal limits of a search incidental to arrest. If you already have reasonable and probable grounds to obtain a search warrant, the best thing to do is get the warrant. The doctrine of investigative detention discussed in Chapter 11 may allow you to detain a vehicle and its occupants pending the arrival of a warrant. Only if you have no grounds supporting a warrant or search incidental to arrest should you pursue a consent search, and even then you should think twice about the risk you are taking of later evidence exclusion.

Don't let yourself wind up in the situation of the investigators in *R. v. Calderon* (2004), 23 C.R. (6th) 1 (Ont. C.A.) at paras. 63 & 64:

> Within a few seconds of agreeing to a search of the car, Calderon withdrew his consent, as he was entitled to do. Although not then having the consent of either appellant, the officers nonetheless persisted in their search. They did not advise the appellants of their right to counsel. They did not consider obtaining a warrant. And they did not consider taking the appellants to the nearby police detachment.
>
> [The officers] found nothing in the interior of the car. However, after opening the trunk, they discovered marijuana in two sealed duffel bags. They then arrested the appellants, and advised them of their right to counsel.

There the appeal court found the seriousness of the *Charter* breach caused by the botched consent search required evidence exclusion, and acquitted the accused of all charges.

b. *The Conditions That Must Be Met for a Valid Consent Search*

A consent search will be found to be illegal if the person consenting was detained without rights to counsel being given at the time of the consent. Even without a detention, or after rights to counsel, according to *R. v. Wills* (1992), 52 O.A.C. 321 at para. 69, six primary conditions must be met in order for a waiver of constitutional rights to be free and voluntary:

> the application of the waiver doctrine to situations where it is said that a person has consented to what would otherwise be an unauthorized search or seizure requires that the Crown establish on the balance of probabilities that:
>
> (i) there was a consent, express or implied;
>
> (ii) the giver of the consent had the authority to give the consent in question;
>
> (iii) the consent was voluntary in the sense that that word is used in *Goldman*, supra, and was not the product of police oppression, coercion or other external conduct which negated the freedom to choose whether or not to allow the police to pursue the course of conduct requested;
>
> (iv) the giver of the consent was aware of the nature of the police conduct to which he or she was being asked to consent;
>
> (v) the giver of the consent was aware of his or her right to refuse to permit the police to engage in the conduct requested; and,
>
> (vi) the giver of the consent was aware of the potential consequences of giving the consent.

An investigator seeking consent to search a location over which a person has control and a privacy interest must explain the search purpose, potential consequences, and the right to refuse consent. No precise language need be used in asking for or giving consent, rather the informed nature of a consent is assessed based on all the circumstances.

What a consent to search comes down to for *Charter* purposes is the freedom to choose, as set out in *R. v. Borden*, [1994] 3 S.C.R. 145 at 162:

> In order for a waiver of the right to be secure against an unreasonable seizure to be effective, the person purporting to consent must be possessed of the requisite informational foundation for a true relinquishment of the right. A right to choose requires not only the

volition to prefer one option over another, but also sufficient available information to make the preference meaningful.

The only way of being virtually certain consent is fully informed is for the consent giver to obtain advice from a lawyer prior to giving consent.

Situations of voluntary consent after advice of counsel run a spectrum from the highly complex where a corporation being investigated for fraud voluntarily hands over its accounting records after consulting with its lawyers, to simpler cases where a vehicle driver calls a lawyer on a cell phone prior to letting the police look in the trunk. The fact legal advice was obtained tends to shut down trial arguments that consent was involuntary or misunderstood. Since obtaining legal advice takes time, it may be quicker for investigators to obtain a search warrant if grounds for one already exist rather than waiting for informed consent. Valid consent searches can take place in the absence of a lawyer's advice but are riskier. At a minimum, investigators need to take impeccable notes on the details of what was said when asking for the consent, and what the responses were of the person consenting — using portable video recording technology to record this exchange may greatly increase chances a court will find informed consent existed.

Are Consent Search Requirements Reasonable?

Q: Surely the law should permit any intelligent adult to consent to the search of his vehicle. The conditions that must be met for a valid consent search don't seem reasonable to me. Why are those requirements so complex?

A: The requirements of a valid consent search are rules of fairness that seek to level the playing field between state investigators and the persons asked to consent. Without those requirements, investigators could continually resort to consent searches by merely asking a question like "do you mind if I take a look in your trunk," instead of relying on the other search and seizure authorities available to them. The person being asked to consent would not know if there was any real choice *not* to consent.

5. Search in Exigent Circumstances

Reliance on exigent circumstances to justify search and seizure is legally riskiest of all because of uncertainty over what types of situations qualify. Exigent circumstances is not really an independent search authority by itself, but a largely statutory power contained in Acts stating something like "any power of search and seizure in this Act which may be authorized by warrant, may equally be exercised without a warrant by a person qualified to obtain such a warrant if the conditions for obtaining a warrant exist but by reason of exigent circumstances it would be impracticable to obtain a warrant." So reasonable and probable grounds of a thing in a place showing evidence of an offence are still needed for an exigent circumstances search, but it is left up to the searching investigators, instead of a judge or justice, to pass judgment on whether the requisite grounds exist.

A broad interpretation of exigent circumstances has been soundly rejected because of how this authority could justify almost any search and seizure. *R. v. Silveira*, [1995] 2 S.C.R. 297 at 369-70 & 374, found the existence of truly exigent circumstances will be rare:

> Yet, the question remains, how should the police act in a situation where they have a serious and valid concern pertaining to the preservation of evidence while awaiting a search warrant. As a result of this case, police officers will be aware that to enter a dwelling house without a warrant, even in exigent circumstances, constitutes a serious breach of *Charter* rights that will likely lead to a ruling that the evidence seized is inadmissible.
>
> . . .
>
> It will be rare that the existence of exigent circumstances alone will allow for the admission of evidence obtained in a clear violation of . . . s. 8 of the *Charter*.
>
> . . .
>
> The police must now know that exigent circumstance do not provide an excuse for failing to obtain a warrant.

The authority does, however, still have some life in it.

A burning building or sinking ship might be examples of true exigent circumstances sufficient to justify warrantless actions to preserve evidence inside the building or ship. Simple fear that the occupants of a residence have been tipped off and could destroy evidence before a warrant arrives does not appear to constitute exigent circumstances. Warrants are now available by telephone in most Canadian jurisdictions, so there need not be a lengthy delay between the time investigators form reasonable and probable grounds to search and the time a warrant is issued based on those grounds. Mere inconvenience or delay in getting a warrant will not justify an exigent circumstance search, but imminent risk of serious harm to human life or property could qualify.

Scope for an Exigent Circumstances Search

Q & A

Q: The *Criminal Code* and a lot of other Acts say that as a peace officer I can search and seize without a warrant in exigent circumstances. Why is the power there if you are telling me that there are very few times when I can use it?

A: The exigent circumstances authority has been around for a long time, and predates the *Charter*, which now circumscribes permissible investigative actions. The advent of telewarrants and investigative detention have reduced instances of true search urgency. Now only burning buildings full of evidence and other truly extreme situations are likely to qualify as exigent circumstances.

STEPS TO TAKE BEFORE AND DURING A SEARCH AND SEIZURE

The most important continuing series of steps that must be taken before, during and after any search or seizure is an assessment and reassessment of what will amount to relevant, reliable and necessary evidence worthy of your efforts. The law of evidence can be an extremely complicated and I like to think fascinating subject if you look at it up close, but take a step or two back and demystification of the law leaves you with a few fundamental principles you can work with in the field. Early investigator-prosecutor contact will cover off the more unusual situations where you need detailed advice on more nuanced questions of evidence law.

1. The Two Most Important Classes of Evidence to Search and Seizure

The two most important classes of evidence to search and seizure are known as "real evidence" and "documentary evidence," both of which loosely speaking could be termed physical evidence. Real evidence can be in any physical form like a gun or drug found in the possession of the accused, and is what most of us commonly think of when the word "evidence" is used. If a document is not being relied upon for the information it conveys, but rather for its physical existence, then it too could qualify as real evidence. In most cases, however, documents are governed by documentary evidence rules that can empower them to speak for themselves like witnesses, subject to issues of hearsay and solicitor-client privilege. Documentary evidence can extend beyond paper letters to include electronic files and recordings.

2. Focus on Relevance, Reliability and Necessity

Just because a search was legally conducted and evidence legally seized does not mean that evidence will necessarily be admissible at trial. While it may have potential for being admitted, translating that potential into actual admitted real or documentary evidence generally requires the prosecution to demonstrate:

- relevance;
- reliability; and
- necessity.

Relevance equals making a fact in dispute more or less likely, reliability demands a fairly low threshold of truthfulness, and necessity means the evidence doesn't exist in a better form readily available to the prosecution for production in court. The defence can also challenge evidence admissibly through reliance on common law and constitutional law principles of exclusion if it was obtained in an abusive way, its prejudicial effect outweighs its probative value, or it was obtained in contravention of *Charter* rights. I acknowledge I am generalizing from those detailed evidence law nuances you see up close, but a bit of generalization is necessary if demystification of the law is to be at all possible.

Seizing evidence that will never be admissible in court is largely pointless. Things irrelevant to any conceivable theory of a case, which are completely unreliable or have already been obtained in a better form, should not be seized. Seizing only the relevant, reliable and necessary stops accusations of abusive overseizure, lets searches proceed at an efficient pace, secures a manageable amount of material to analyze, and ensures investigators stay focused on the key elements of an investigation that will later have to be translated into admissible trial evidence if charges are laid.

a. *The Difference among Being Clearly Relevant, Possibly Relevant and Not Relevant*

The classic definition of relevance was repeated in *R. v. Seaboyer; R v. Gayme*, [1991] 2 S.C.R. 577 at 609:

> It is fundamental to our system of justice that the rules of evidence should permit the judge and jury to get at the truth and properly determine the issues. This goal is reflected in the basic tenet of relevance which underlies all our rules of evidence . . . . In general, nothing is to be received which is not logically probative of some matter requiring to be proved and everything which is probative should be received, unless its exclusion can be justified on some other ground.

It is the prosecution's job to convince a court of the relevance of evidence through submissions that link each piece of evidence to the prosecution's theory of the case. In the early stages of an investigation it might be impossible to distinguish the clearly relevant, from the possibly relevant and definitely irrelevant, but eventually investigators must face the reality that some material will turn out not to fit into any case theory.

Assessing relevancy is necessary to make informed charging decisions, prepare the prosecution brief and disclosure package, and develop a final theory of the case that can be presented in court. The real challenge in vetting material for relevance comes in deciding which items to toss into the possibly relevant category dependent on alternative theories of the case, including theories upon which the defence might rely. A case could self-destruct over disclosure deficiencies if investigators ignore possibly relevant material. Early investigator-prosecutor contact is highly advisable when making tough relevance choices, and will aid prosecutor understanding of how to present the big relevance picture at trial.

b. *The Onerous Burden of Establishing Reliability and Continuity*

Reliability is a much more onerous burden of evidence admissibility to satisfy than either relevance or necessity, but only "threshold reliability" need be initially established as noted in *R. v. Star*, [2000] 2 S.C.R. 144 at para. 215: "it is important when examining . . . reliability . . . to distinguish between threshold and ultimate reliability. Only the former is relevant to admissibility. . . . Threshold reliability . . . is concerned with whether or not the circumstances . . . provide circumstantial guarantees of trustworthiness." Ultimate reliability at the end of trial determines how much weight a court accords a piece of evidence when it is time to reconcile all evidence led by the prosecution and defence. Reliability is concerned with showing the thing you are seeking to be admitted into evidence is in fact what you say it is.

Physical evidence falls into four classes for the purposes of establishing reliability:

- unique items that speak for themselves;

- unique items that require test results;

- non-unique items that require a continuity chain; or

- unique and non-unique items that require the *viva voce* testimony of someone intimately familiar with the item in order to establish reliability.

A unique firearm with a serial number somewhat speaks for itself, although test results, continuity and *viva voce* testimony could further add to its reliability. By contrast, a non-unique block of a white powdery substance is a total unknown; its reliability as the cocaine the seizing investigator believed it to be is completely dependent on lab analysis, and precise continuity evidence that traces it from the time it was seized through to the time it was analyzed.

Continuity is an intangible factual spectre that haunts the legal halls of reliability. As its name implies, continuity is the qualification of continuous possession of an item from the time it was first seized until the time it passes into the hands of a court that marks it as an exhibit. Continuity is merely a factor affecting reliability, not a completely separate hurdle of admissibility. Any investigator upon first touching a seized item needs to be thinking about how he or she will later personally fit into the continuity chain. Figure 6-1, Maintaining an Evidence Continuity Chain, demonstrates what a proper chain looks like, with each time a piece of evidence is handled forming a link backwards and forwards in time. Continuity will only be maintained so long as those links remain unbroken.

The *Memorandum of Understanding Between the Royal Canadian Mounted Police and the Federal Prosecution Service Respecting the Conduct of Criminal Investigations and Prosecutions* (5 July 2001) at para. 3.1.9 explicitly acknowledges the importance of this continuity obligation and who bears the burden: "The obligation of the RCMP to preserve evidence and all relevant information that might assist defence continues during the prosecution stage. They maintain continuity and security of all physical evidence in their care." This is a burden that prosecutors cannot share for fear of becoming witnesses to continuity in the cases they prosecute.

Any seized item not sufficiently tied to the place and person from whom it was seized, and for which adequate continuity records are not kept to track its safe-keeping, can become an orphan devoid of any evidentiary value. Detailed investigator notes must describe:

Fig 6-1 | **MAINTAINING AN EVIDENCE CONTINUITY CHAIN**

START

Item located at search site by seizing officer.

Item seized and carried to another room by seizing officer. Seizing officer makes notes of item's description and location where item was found.

Item handed over to exhibits officer by seizing officer. Both exhibits and seizing officers make notes of handover. Exhibit officer places item in exhibit bag, seals bag, enters item in exhibit log, and writes pertinent seizure information on exhibit bag.

Item transported to investigator offices and placed in storage by exhibits officer. Sole key to secure storage given to lead investigator.

Item removed from storage and delivered to lab technician by lead investigator for purpose of forensic testing.

Item tested by lab technician and stored in secure area when not being tested.

Item picked up by lead investigator from lab technician after testing completed, and returned to secure storage under control of lead investigator.

New lead investigator takes over case; sole key to storage transferred from old lead investigator to new lead investigator.

Item removed from storage by lead investigator for meeting with prosecutor, and returned to secure storage by lead investigator after completion of meeting.

Item removed from storage and transported to courthouse by lead investigator. During trial, item kept in locked briefcase in lead investigator's possession until needed.

Prosecutor establishes continuity of item through evidence called at trial. Item marked as exhibit and court accepts custody.

END

Methods used to ensure continuity will vary according to the investigative agency and the item in question, but the continuity chain should remain unbroken in all cases.

- where each seized item was located;
- if the item was in anyone's possession;
- who seized it;
- what was the legal basis of the seizure;
- who ultimately took custody of it; and
- the complete continuity chain it passed along until the day it was tendered as evidence at trial.

You can shorten continuity chains through minimizing the number of people who handle seized material by designating a limited number of investigators who will actually seize evidence within a larger search team, and having one person take custody of all seized items after the search is concluded. This will in turn reduce the number of required trial witnesses, the number of trial adjournments due to absent witnesses, the number of witnesses exposed to potentially damaging cross-examination, and the overall time needed for trial.

There are three principles to keep in mind when retaining evidence over the long term while awaiting case developments or the start of trial:

- *Preservation*: keeping it in the same physical state it was first seized in, so it can be independently examined and tested;
- *Segregation*: keeping it separate from case materials or evidence from other cases, so its origins remain clear; and
- *Limitation*: keeping it in a location only a very limited number of people have access to, so continuity can be demonstrated at any trial.

Ideally, seized items will be secured in some kind of evidence locker for which only one person has a key. Investigative agencies need to devote resources to constructing or leasing evidence storage facilities instead of relying on *ad hoc* investigator solutions. Individual investigators cannot be expected to adequately preserve evidence without institutional resource support.

No matter how bad your in-office storage problems might be, don't do what an investigator in *R. v. Trang*, 2002 ABQB 744 at paras. 143-144, did by taking the evidence home:

> Crown counsel became aware of source and background materials used in drafting Affidavits 1631 and 1635 located in two boxes in

his home office, which staff Sgt. N. . . indicated was the only place available to him to store them.

From May 2001 until February 2002, he performed patrol duties as supervisor at the Downtown Division Operations Bureau where he was not assigned a storage facility. The sergeants' office was a large room with no dividers, just a series of 12 desks scattered around an office area with file cabinets and storage facility. He did not share his desk. He had access to one of two computers which were shared among all 12 sergeants and up to 100 other constables working in the same area. His duties often took him away from the office. He did not have a secure area within the office where he could store his two boxes. He had a portion of a file drawer that he could use for his own material, but that also included material he needed for the management of his squad. The nature of his duties as a patrol sergeant did not permit him to take time to review the Affidavits; he had to request time away from his duties in order to do that. He needed a secure place and ready access to the material in order to prepare, and therefore took the boxes to his house. He did not tell anyone about his lack of storage. He was not aware of any . . . management policy about taking work home and storing it at home. He did not consult with anyone before taking the boxes to his home office.

At home the preservation, segregation and limitation principles are all at risk. Serious disclosure problems arose in that case when material stored at home was omitted from the prosecution brief and disclosure package.

Reliability deficiencies must be dealt with through early investigator-prosecutor contact. Breaks in continuity or other reliability failings are usually not fatal to cases, but must be explained to a court in an open way. If these problems only come out in cross-examination, a court may be left with an impression of investigators being sloppy and secretive about all aspects of a case. A prosecutor who carefully presents reliability problems may be able to convince a court that any gaps are really minor imperfections in an otherwise impressive case. The courts do not demand perfection from investigators, but they do demand openness.

c. *Necessity Is Not Really Necessary*

To be necessary, evidence need only be the most readily available proof of a relevant fact. Technically speaking, proof of necessity is only required where hearsay evidence is being tendered, but hearsay necessity at times blends into the so-called "best evidence rule" (which isn't really a "rule" at all) applicable to other types of evidence. Demystification of the law dictates it is easiest to simply remember necessity is a factor.

Necessity is not an onerous factor to establish, as explained in *R. v. Smith* [1992] 2 S.C.R. 915 at 933-34:

> the criterion of necessity must be given a flexible definition, capable of encompassing diverse situations. . . . Wigmore, while not attempting an exhaustive enumeration, suggested . . .
>
>> The assertion may be such that we cannot expect, again or at this time, to get evidence of the same value from the same or other sources. . . The necessity is not so great; perhaps hardly a necessity, only an expediency or convenience, can be predicated.

If evidence is both relevant and reliable, it is rare for it to be excluded as unnecessary unless it is readily available in a more reliable form. Investigators still need to think about how each piece of evidence will be explained in court as being necessary in order to defend against criticism that better quality evidence was available for the taking but ignored by investigators.

Necessity establishes a pecking order of evidence, with oral first-hand testimony from a live witness usually being preferred first, followed by original physical evidence, and then overheard oral statements or copies of physical evidence. In this pecking order necessity requires not the best evidence, only the best readily available evidence. Where a witness is available to testify in court, but has previously made notes summarizing what the testimony will likely be, the notes are not necessary because a live witness is available to give the same evidence. Oral in-court evidence is usually treated as more reliable than written notes because it is under oath and its reliability can be tested through cross-examination. But if that same witness were to die before testifying, or give testimony different from the notes, then those notes might become necessary because they would be the only way to prove the facts recorded in them. Similarly, a photocopy of a document is not necessary if investigators have also seized the original document, but if the original is lost or cannot be obtained then the copy could be necessary. Sometimes necessity will be self-evident, while at other times a witness might need to explain why something is the best evidence that can be offered. Understanding the legal basis for admission of physical evidence in turn leads to an understanding of why precise procedures are required to perfect seizures for court presentation.

Dealing with Evidence Continuity Problems

Q & A

Q: The other day I seized a small packet of white powder. I kept it in my pocket while out on the road, but when I returned to the division I placed it on the top of my desk and forgot about it while I went to a brief meeting in another room. When I returned, the packet was still where I left it, and I processed it as an exhibit. Do I have a continuity problem with the packet?

A: You do have a weak point in continuity since others had access to a non-unique object while you were away from your desk. In theory, someone could have tampered with the evidence. But since you were in a supposedly secure building, the absence was not prolonged, and the packet appeared undisturbed when you returned, you do *not* seem to have a real problem. Ensure you make notes detailing the circumstances of your custody of the evidence which point to continued continuity.

STEPS TO TAKE AFTER A SEIZURE

The courts hold investigators to account for their seizures long before considering the admissibility of seized material at trial. If a search is conducted and nothing seized the law generally does not require investigators to take follow-up steps, but where things are seized with *or without* a warrant investigators must usually go before a court for a detention order. Follow the post-seizure procedural steps specified by the Act under which the seizure took place or under whose authority duties were being executed at the time of the seizure. The procedures enumerated in ss. 489.1 and 490 of the *Criminal Code* apply by default to any federal Act that does not contain its own post-seizure procedure. In most cases a formal application for detention of seized things must be brought, followed by application to extend that detention unless charges have been laid prior to the expiration of the initial detention.

1. File the Return to a Justice and Secure a Detention Order

Sections 489.1 and 490 of the *Criminal Code* give investigators two primary choices: keep the thing seized, or return it to the person from whom it was seized. Under s. 489.1 of the *Code*, if a seized thing is returned a receipt must be retained and a report filed with the court noting the seizure, the return and attaching a copy of the receipt. If the thing is detained then a report must likewise be filed with the court, but it will ultimately be up to the court to decide whether investigators can retain the thing over the long term. All of this must be done "as soon as is practicable:"

> **489.1.** (1) Subject to this or any other Act of Parliament, where a peace officer has seized anything under a warrant issued under this Act or under section 487.11 or 489 or otherwise in the execution of duties under this or any other Act of Parliament, the peace officer shall, as soon as is practicable,
>
> > (a) where the peace officer is satisfied,
> >
> > > (i) that there is no dispute as to who is lawfully entitled to possession of the thing seized, and
> > >
> > > (ii) that the continued detention of the thing seized is not required for the purposes of any investigation or a preliminary inquiry, trial or other proceeding,
> >
> > return the thing seized, on being issued a receipt therefor, to the person lawfully entitled to its possession and report to the justice who issued the warrant or some other justice for the same territorial division or, if no warrant was issued, a justice having jurisdiction in respect of the matter, that he has done so; or
> >
> > (b) where the peace officer is not satisfied as described in subparagraphs (a)(i) and (ii),
> >
> > > (i) bring the thing seized before the justice referred to in paragraph (a), or
> > >
> > > (ii) report to the justice that he has seized the thing and is detaining it or causing it to be detained
> >
> > to be dealt with by the justice in accordance with subsection 490(1).

Any investigator who is not a peace officer does not have the option of returning after seizure — instead according to s-s. 489.1(2) the options are only not to seize in the first place, or to file a detention report after seizure so that a justice can decide under s. 490 how the seized item should be dealt with. Because s. 489.1 is "subject to this or any other Act of Parliament," other Acts or provisions of the *Code* can contain their own detention procedures that should be followed in preference to ss. 489.1 and 490 for searches and seizures explicitly tied to those other Acts or provisions.

Section 489.1 imposes an obligation to make a return to a justice even for a search and seizure conducted incidental to arrest because of the purposes of s. 489.1 noted in *R. v. Backhouse* (2005), 195 O.A.C. 80 at paras. 107, 108, 110 & 112:

> It appears that one objective for the addition of s. 489.1 and some of the change in wording of s. 490 was to facilitate the return of items seized to their rightful owners. . . . The fact that the section covers a broad range of warrantless seizures indicates that it was not intended to be limited to seizures that arose out of some court process.
>
> The interpretation of s. 489.1 and related provisions that would best fulfill these objectives is to have the procedures apply to all seizures of property where police officers are in the execution of duties under the *Criminal Code* or other federal legislation.
>
> . . .
>
> Although s. 489.1 was an early enactment after proclamation of the *Charter* it reflects *Charter* values and principles. It favours judicial supervision. It is part of a scheme that includes s. 490 and that is designed to regulate state activity that interferes with privacy interests. As indicated, it also reflects an interest in protecting the rights of victims of crime.
>
> . . .
>
> Section 489.1 is part of a scheme to protect property and privacy interests that is more fully developed in s. 490. Section 490 provides that where things have been brought before a justice or a report made to a justice in respect of anything seized under s. 489.1, there is an obligation on the justice to supervise its detention. The section also sets out an elaborate scheme to facilitate the return of items seized to their lawful owners.

Failure to comply with s. 489.1 will not inevitably result in the exclusion of seized evidence, but could have adverse case consequences that investigators can easily avoid.

How soon is soon enough for filing a detention report with a justice depends on how many items were seized, and how long it reasonably takes to make an inventory of them. If only one or two items are seized, a report should likely be filed within a couple of days of the seizure. A delay of any longer than a week would require a good explanation. If thousands of items are seized a delay of a few weeks could be reasonable, but where proper inventories could take months investigators should file a general report grouping items by class, instead of making detailed lists of every item. It is uncommon for the preparation of a return to a justice to cause much difficulty, although it does require an adequate description of each of the items seized so a determination can be made of their relevance without having to examine the actual things seized.

2. Comply with the Burdens and Lengths of Detention

a. *Securing an Initial Detention Order*

In order to initially retain seized things investigators need to satisfy a court according to s-s. 490(1) of the *Criminal Code* "that the detention of the thing seized is required for the purposes of any investigation or a preliminary inquiry, trial or other proceeding." This is not a particularly high burden to meet, but nevertheless some evidence must be advanced that the thing is required, failing which the court will order return of the seized thing to the person lawfully entitled to its possession. If an item is ordered detained, s-s. 490(1)(b) of the *Code* requires "reasonable care to ensure that it is preserved until the conclusion of any investigation or until it is required to be produced for the purposes of a preliminary inquiry, trial or other proceeding." Negligence in safeguarding seized items could lead to a contempt of the court ordered detention made under s. 490 of the *Code*.

b. *Applying to Extend the Initial Detention Period*

The initial period of detention under s-s. 490(1) of the *Code* is only for three months. As the end of that period approaches, an investigator holding a seized thing has three options:

- lay charges that require continued detention of the thing;

- give the thing back; or

- make an application to a court (preferably with the help of a prosecutor) under s-s. 490(2) of the *Code* (or the appropriate section of the Act under which the initial detention was authorized) for a further detention order.

The burden of proof for the further detention order is on the investigator, just like it was at the initial detention stage. Unlike the initial 90-day detention where the thing only need be "required" for the case, after 90 days an investigator needs to show that the particular "nature of the investigation" requires further detention. This higher burden means an investigator must explain why the investigation is taking so long. Complexity of financial investigations, delays to protect ongoing viability of informers or other investigations, and waiting for third parties like banks or science labs to produce information could all contribute to the nature of the investigation requiring detention beyond the initial three-month period. All of this factual information will come before the court in the form of an affidavit sworn by a knowledgeable investigator and attached to the application for further detention.

After the further detention period grantable under s-s. 490(2) of the *Code*, which can range up to nine months, s-s. 490(3) of the *Code* requires an investigator to go to a superior court judge to demonstrate why the "complex nature of the investigation" requires yet more time before charges are laid. This even higher standard means you must be able to demonstrate significant case complexity through a particularly detailed affidavit. Simply explaining vague, unforeseen delays in a fraud investigation will not cut it. Much like drafting a warrant, while investigators can ask for and expect some prosecutor help in putting the first or subsequent applications for further detention together, the responsibility for factually justifying the detention ultimately rests with the investigators.

Because the burden is on the Crown to justify further detention of evidence, there will be times the Crown fails to discharge that burden as happened in *Bormley v. Canada*, 2002 BCSC 149 at paras. 22-23:

> There is a clear burden on the Crown, where things have been seized, to employ all reasonable resources that are required and to diligently press on with the investigation. I am satisfied that the investigation is time consuming, involving a multitude of transactions and individuals, with the added technical intricacies of deciphering whatever remains on the hard drive. Nevertheless, in the case before me there were avenues open to the Crown that may have ended the investigation within a one year time period. The Crown has failed to discharge the burden on it and the Crown's application to extend the time fails.

While the particular nature of the investigation in that case had convinced the court to extend the initial 90-day detention period up to the one year mark, the nature of the investigation was not by itself sufficient to discharge the greater s-s. 490(3) *Code* burden of showing a truly "complex" nature justifying detention without charge beyond one year. The court seemed to conclude that investigators had not been as diligent as they could have been in completing their inquiries, but still permitted investigators to make copies pursuant to s-s. 490(13) of the *Code* prior to returning the originals.

Investigators need a contingency plan if a further detention application fails, choosing among immediately laying whatever charges can be justified at that point, making certified copies under s-s. 490(13) of the *Code* of documents to be returned that according to s-s. 490(14) will have "the same probative force as the original document," or obtaining a new warrant to resieze all or some of the things after their return.

c. *How to Remedy a Failure to File a Detention Application*

You must move swiftly as soon as you realize there has been no detention application filed or a further detention application deadline has been missed in order to remedy the omission by bringing a court application including an explanation for the failure as provided for in s-s. 490(9.1) of the *Code*:

> **490.** (9.1) Notwithstanding subsection (9), a judge or justice referred to in paragraph (9)(a) or (b) may, if the periods of detention provided for or ordered under subsections (1) to (3) in respect of a thing seized have expired but proceedings have not been instituted in which the thing may be required, order that the thing continue to be detained for such period as the judge or justice considers necessary if the judge or justice is satisfied
>
> > (a) that the continued detention of the thing might reasonably be required for a purpose mentioned in subsection (1) or (4); and
> >
> > (b) that it is in the interests of justice to do so.

So long as the failure was not willful and the delay to file not excessive, in my experience a court will grant a late detention application. However, a total and unexplained failure to file a return to a justice could lead a court to order the return of the things seized or even grant *Charter* remedies as in *R. v. Martens*, 2004 BCSC 1450 at paras. 274-75:

> In this case, I am satisfied that the failure to file a return within seven days as required by 487.1(9) of the *Criminal Code* and the failure to at any time thereafter apply for an extension to allow the late filing of the return was a continuing breach of the telewarrant process. The failure to perfect the telewarrant process by filing a return left Ms. Martens' goods in the hands of the police while denying her the ability to apply for the return of any of the items seized by resort to the codified process by which she was entitled to make such an application. In my view, that continuing breach

was also a breach of Ms. Martens' s. 8 *Charter* rights to be free from unreasonable search and seizure because it was only by reason of that process that the police were entitled to obtain those good from Ms. Martens' residence.

3. Respond to Applications for Return of and Access to Seized Things

The lawful owner or possessor of a seized thing may apply under s-ss. 490(7) through 490(11) of the *Criminal Code* for its return. The onus is on the applicant to show that either the periods of detention have expired with no charges laid, or the seized thing is no longer required for the purposes of any investigation or legal proceeding. Prosecutors will require significant investigator input into defending a return application if it is to be argued the seized thing is still required for an ongoing investigation, notwithstanding charges have yet to be laid.

An application for access without return to seized things is possible under s-s. 490(15) of the *Code*. The person seeking access need not be the lawful owner or possessor, just "a person who has an interest in what is detained." Investigators can contribute to access applications by suggesting safeguards to ensure things accessed do not become altered, destroyed or go missing. It is all too easy during access to boxes containing hundreds of thousands of seized documents for a few documents to mysteriously go missing, or even more mysteriously to appear where they did not seem to be before. Investigators may need to personally supervise all access. A court order should specify access conditions that both protect the privacy of those accessing the documents, and the integrity of the documents being accessed. Any investigator who directly receives notice of an application for access or return must immediately contact a prosecutor.

4. Don't Assume a Power of Seizure Includes a Power of Destruction

Investigators do not possess inherent common law powers to destroy or otherwise dispose of items subject to search and seizure. Just because seized things like hydroponic grow equipment are difficult to store and apparently linked to criminal activity does not confer power on those who seized the equipment, as pointed out in *R. v. Waldron* (2003), 185 B.C.A.C. 310; 2003 BCCA 442 at paras. 17-18, quoting from the trial judgment:

because of lack of police storage space and since the equipment had already been examined and photographed, and in practice bulk equipment was not usually tendered as evidence in court, an internal administrative decision was made to destroy the seized marihuana cultivation equipment. He was under the mistaken legal impression that he was entitled to dispose of it. This was clearly contrary to s. 489.1 and s. 490 of the *Criminal Code,* and s. 15 of the *Controlled Drug and Substances Act,* which requires retention of the property seized until an order for disposal by the court.

. . .

the property manager's ignorance of the law respecting his duty to retain and preserve the seized equipment might be unacceptable negligence . . . .

Power to destroy or dispose will be found in legislation investigators administer, and generally can only be utilized upon a court or Ministerial order being granted.

a. *Discretionary Powers to Forfeit Perishable Things*

Occasionally an Act will grant investigators a discretionary power to dispose of perishable things provided the proceeds of disposition are paid over to the appropriate official pending final resolution of a case, like in s-s. 70(3) of the *Fisheries Act*:

> **70.** (3) A fishery officer or fishery guardian who has custody of any fish or other perishable thing seized under this Act may dispose of it in any manner the officer or guardian considers appropriate and any proceeds realized from its disposition shall be paid to the Receiver General.

It appears Parliament intended this provision to be restricted to items whose limits on continuing value could be measured in days or weeks, rather than months or years. Carefully read the language of any disposal or forfeiture provisions you think might be useful to your work, apply the statutory construction principles set out in Chapter 2 of this book, and resolve any doubts through speaking with a prosecutor.

If something is seized that does not fit squarely within a discretionary disposal provision, but whose value is declining rapidly and ongoing maintenance costs are very high, it might be possible to use a civil means of disposal depending on the facts of the case and what the thing is. For example, civil means were used to sell a seized boat implicated in an ongoing prosecution I was involved in called *R. v. Ulybel Enterprises Ltd.*, [2001] 2 S.C.R. 867. The court approved of the method of disposition because it followed proper admiralty law rules for seized vessels against which civil claims existed, even though disposal took place under the civil rules of the Federal Court, rather than as part of the prosecution process under the *Fisheries Act.*

b. *Disposing of Inherently Illegal Goods*

The *Controlled Drugs and Substances Act*, S.C. 1996, c. 19 (*CDSA*), contains provisions authorizing disposal of things whose possession is, in most cases, inherently illegal. Section 25 of the *CDSA* authorizes the Minister of Health to dispose of a seized controlled substance after waiting 60 days for a return application to be lodged by anyone claiming lawful possession. Section 26 of the *CDSA* authorizes a court to issue an immediate disposal order upon application by the Minister of Health where a potential security, public health or safety hazard is shown to exist. Section 29 of the *CDSA* additionally gives the Minister discretion to immediately destroy plants from which controlled substances can be extracted:

> **29.** The Minister may, on prior notification being given to the Attorney General, cause to be destroyed any plant from which a substance included in Schedule I, II, III or IV may be extracted that is being produced otherwise than under the authority of and in accordance with a licence issued under the regulations.

Thus no 60-day waiting period and no court order are necessary for bulky and possibly rapidly decomposing plant destruction, but s. 29 is of no help in destroying cocaine or heroin imported into Canada in refined form. The *CDSA* does not assist with pretrial destruction of marihuana grow-op equipment that is also bulky and difficult to store, but not inherently illegal — there one must look to the *Criminal Code* for help.

c. *Disposing of Goods No One Is Lawfully Entitled to Possess*

Sub-section 490(9) of the *Criminal Code* contains the basic disposal power applicable in all federal offence seizures not covered by disposal powers in other Acts. Only where no known person is entitled to possess a lawfully seized thing will court ordered forfeiture and disposal be possible under s-s. 490(9), like where everyone denies owning seized marihuana grow-op equipment. However, if someone steps forward and offers sufficient proof of lawful ownership, then the best the Crown can do is attempt to forfeit the equipment as offence-related property under ss. 16 or 17 of the *CDSA*.

Destruction or other disposal of seized items is no easy task. Parliament did not intend it to be easy, since an accused might be acquitted of an offence only to find that his seized legitimately owned property has already been destroyed. Investigators need not, however, be burdened with warehouses full of seized criminal junk that is not required as trial evidence if the courts agree disposal is appropriate.

To Ensure Search and Seizure Results Are Not Later Excluded at Trial

KEY POINTS

✓ Determine and record your authority, your purpose, and the steps you must follow before commencing any search or seizure. A warrant, incident to arrest, plain view, consent and exigent circumstances are the five principal search or seizure authorities, in increasing order of legal risk.

✓ All search and seizure authorities are limited in scope and breadth. Search pursuant to warrant is limited by the warrant power relied upon and the terms of the warrant issued. Search incident to arrest is limited to protecting the safety of those making the arrest, collecting and preserving evidence of the offences arrested for or related offences, and preventing escape of those being arrested. Plain view is only an authority for seizure, not an authority for search, and the evidentiary value of an item must be "plain." An investigator seeking a person's consent to search must explain the purpose, potential consequences, right to refuse or withdraw consent, and possibly provide rights and cautions. True exigent circumstances justifying a warrantless search will be rare, and likely limited to situations of imminent harm to a person or property.

✓ The most important continuing series of steps that must be taken before, during and after any search or seizure is an assessment and reassessment of what will amount to relevant, reliable and necessary evidence worthy of searching and seizing efforts. To be relevant, evidence must contribute in a positive or negative way to the proof of some fact in issue. To be reliable, evidence must have circumstantial guarantees of trustworthiness including a continuity chain to establish ultimate reliability for non-unique items. Necessity as a precondition to evidence admissibility requires not the best evidence, just the best readily available evidence.

✓ Within a reasonable time after a seizure investigators must usually file a report to a justice, and secure an initial detention court order that must be periodically renewed if charges requiring the seized things have not been laid by the time the order expires. Destruction or disposal of items discovered during a search can only take place with explicit statutory or court authority.

FURTHER READING

Cases

a. *The Standard to Meet to Conduct a Search*

Hunter v. Southam Inc., [1984] 2 S.C.R. 145. Search and seizure can be authorized by reasonable and probable grounds established on oath to believe an offence has been committed and there is evidence of that offence located at the place to be searched.

R. v. Debot , [1989] 2 S.C.R. 1140. Only reasonable probability or reasonable belief is required to form grounds to search, not proof beyond a reasonable doubt or a *prima facie* case.

R. v. Storrey, [1990] 1 S.C.R. 241. Reasonable and probable grounds has both a subjective and objective component: "a reasonable person placed in the position of the officer must be able to conclude that there were indeed reasonable and probable grounds."

The Queen v. Baron, [1993] 1 S.C.R. 416. "Reasonable grounds" and "reasonable and probable grounds" mean the same thing and require that the same standard be met.

b. *Searches without a Warrant*

R. v. Buhay, [2003] 1 S.C.R. 631. Pre-existing authority is needed for intrusion into any place where plain view seizure takes place.

R. v. Caslake, [1998] 1 S.C.R. 51. Search of an entire vehicle incident to arrest is permissible as long as the purpose of the search is consistent with the purpose of arrest.

R. v. Clement, [1996] 2 S.C.R. 289, affirming (1995), 83 O.A.C. 226. Confirms that a warrantless vehicle search can be based on informed voluntary consent.

R. v. Edwards, [1996] 1 S.C.R. 128. A person challenging a search must have a reasonable expectation of privacy in the place searched or an item seized; see also *R. v. Belnavis*, [1997] 3 S.C.R. 341.

R. v. Stillman, [1997] 1 S.C.R. 607. Bodily substances cannot be seized incident to a lawful arrest, and will always require judicial authorization for seizure.

R. v. Wills (1992), 52 O.A.C. 321. Sets out the test for free and informed consent to search.

Books and Reports

E. Ewaschuck, *Criminal Pleadings and Practice in Canada*, 2d ed., looseleaf (Aurora, ON: Canada Law Book, 1997). See particularly Chapter 3 (Search and Seizure) and Chapter 31 (Canadian Charter of Rights and Freedoms).

J. Fontana and D. Keeshan, *The Law of Search and Seizure in Canada*, 6th ed., (Toronto: LexisNexis Butterworths, 2005). Traces the law of search and seizure from its earliest origins and deals with the theory behind the law.

J. Fontana and D. Keeshan, *Police Guide to Search and Seizure* (Toronto: Butterworths, 2003). A scaled-down pocket-sized, but still detailed, version of the larger search and seizure book by the same authors.

C. Hill et al., *McWilliams' Canadian Criminal Evidence*, 4th ed., loose-leaf (Aurora, ON: Canada Law Book, 2003). A voluminous and comprehensive work on criminal evidence.

S.C. Hutchison, J.C. Morton & M.P. Bury, *Search and Seizure Law in Canada*, loose-leaf (Toronto: Carswell, 1993).

Law Reform Commission of Canada, *Report on Recodifying Criminal Law Procedure, Volume I — Police Powers: Title 1, Search and Related Matters* (Ottawa: Law Reform Commission of Canada, 1991).

Law Reform Commission of Canada, *Working Paper No. 30 — Police Powers: Search and Seizure in Criminal Law Enforcement* (Ottawa: Law Reform Commission of Canada, 1983).

J. Melnitzer & C. Bentley, *Disposition of Things Seized* (Ottawa: Law Reform Commission of Canada, 1982).

J. Sopinka, S. Lederman, & A. Bryant, *The Law of Evidence in Canada*, 2nd ed. (Toronto: Butterworths, 1999).

CHAPTER SEVEN

CHOOSING THE RIGHT WARRANT FOR YOUR CASE

At the investigative stage the authorities are charged with determining the following: What happened? Who did it? Is the conduct criminally culpable behaviour? Search warrants are a staple investigative tool for answering those questions, and the section authorizing their issuance must be interpreted in that light.

CanadianOxy Chemicals Ltd. v. Canada (Attorney General), [1999] 1 S.C.R. 743 at para. 21.

In This Chapter

- Starting with a warrant category

- Moving to a review of types of warrants

- Figuring out how a warrant authority operates

- The usefulness of telewarrants

- Proceeds of crime seizure, restraint and forfeiture

- Challenges of searching for and seizing electronic data

- Provincial and territorial powers of search and seizure

Investigators commonly hear the mantra from prosecutors of "get a warrant" and the unfortunate conclusion from judges of "should have gotten a warrant," but may be left searching for answers over what types of documents can be called warrants, what exactly can warrants authorize investigators to do, and how are warrants best defended when they later come under attack at trial. Being able to draw distinctions among the many types of warrants that for the most part don't involve electronic surveillance, and understanding the limitations of each type so you are capable of choosing the best warrant instrument for your investigative purpose, is what this chapter seeks to teach you. Once you have decided it is best not to rely on one of the common law search or seizure authorities, you need to think about both category and type of warrant, as well as whether special measures are needed to seize or forfeit proceeds of crime, or deal with electronic data.

STARTING WITH A WARRANT CATEGORY

Choosing the right warrant for your case usually begins with considering what kind of evidence you are looking for in what type of place in order to investigate what sort of offence, all of which will dictate the warrant category required. The three categories of warrants are:

1. those which provide for regular search and seizure of physical things in a normal place;

2. those which permit the gathering of an unusual type of evidence using a technique falling outside the normal sense of search or seizure of a thing in a place;

3. those limited to one offence or class of things.

The first category includes the traditional warrant authorizing actions like entry to a residence, searching it for evidence of drug trafficking, and seizing anything relevant to the drug investigation or related offences. The second category includes less conventional warrants authorizing less tangible actions like a demand to a bank to provide account records to support a fraud investigation where the records only exist electronically and are stored off-site in an unknown location. The third category includes very specific warrants like those only targeting obscene materials or proceeds of crime. Because the second and third category of warrants tend to be more difficult to draft and obtain, it is usually advisable to only move on to them if the first category does not meet your investigative needs.

MOVING TO A REVIEW OF TYPES OF WARRANTS

Having the required category in mind, an investigator can move on to a review of the types of appropriate warrants available within that category.

Since statutory interpretation principles say all legislative provisions were put there for a reason, it follows that investigators should first look to Act-specific warrant types when investigating offences under a particular Act. If Parliament had intended the *Criminal Code* to be the sole source of search or seizure warrant authorization for federal offences, warrant provisions could easily have been omitted from all other federal Acts — in fact warrant authorities are quite evident in other Acts.

For example, for drug offences look first to the warrant authority in s. 11 of the *Controlled Drugs and Substances Act*, S.C. 1996, c. 19 (*CDSA*), or for fishing offences check out s. 49.1 of the *Fisheries Act*, R.S.C. 1985, c. F-14. Only if those Act-specific authorities seem inadequate for your investigation should you fall back on the warrant authority of the *Criminal Code* available for all federal offences. Of course, if it is a *Criminal Code* offence being investigated, then the *Code* will be the first place to look for an appropriate type of warrant. Provincial and territorial warrant authorities may likewise rest in either specific or more general Acts. For some provincial or territorial offences no warrant authority may be available.

There are more types of warrants available under the *Code* than most people realize, with all three categories of warrants represented among the fifteen principal types of *Code* warrants:

- s. 164 *Criminal Code* — Obscene Material Warrant (seizure only);

- s. 199 *Criminal Code* — Gaming and Common Bawdy-House Warrant;

- s. 256 *Criminal Code* — Operation While Impaired Blood Sample Warrant;

- s. 320 *Criminal Code* — Hate Propaganda Warrant (seizure only);

- s. 395 *Criminal Code* — Valuable Mineral Warrant;

- s. 462.32 *Criminal Code* — Special Search Warrant for Proceeds of Crime;

- s. 487 *Criminal Code* — Basic Search and Seizure Warrant;

- s. 487.01 *Criminal Code* — General Warrant;

- s-s. 487.01(4) *Criminal Code* — Video Warrant;

- s. 487.012 *Criminal Code* — Production Order;

- s. 487.05 *Criminal Code* — DNA Warrant;

- s. 487.091 *Criminal Code* — Body Impression Warrant;

- s. 487.1 *Criminal Code* — Telewarrant for s. 256 or s. 487 Warrant;

- s. 492.1 *Criminal Code* — Tracking Warrant;

- s. 492.2 *Criminal Code* — Number Recorder Warrant.

In addition to choosing the right type of warrant, investigators also need to consider the utility of s. 487.3 *Code* sealing orders (applicable to all federal warrants), and s. 487.02 *Code* assistance orders (only applicable to *Criminal Code* warrants), both of which are explored in Chapter 8.

FIGURING OUT HOW A WARRANT AUTHORITY OPERATES

Once you have picked a category and reviewed the types of warrants that might suit your investigative needs, you still need to figure out how each of the possibly suitable search or seizure warrant authorities operates. Some work like s. 487 of the *Criminal Code* authorizing both search and seizure, while others like s. 49.1 of the *Fisheries Act* only authorize search with warrant and non-warrant seizure powers being contained elsewhere in the Act. The type of warrant you rely upon will dictate your pre-search, during search and post-search duties.

1. Warrants to Search for and Seize Physical Things in Normal Places

Warrants that fall into the most common category of searching for and seizing physical things in a normal place most often find their authority in s. 487 of the *Criminal Code*. All peace or public officers appointed to enforce any federal Act may seek a s. 487 *Code* warrant to investigate any federal offence. The demands of s. 487 are consistent with the three key elements that usually need to be satisfied to obtain any kind of warrant — a place, linked to offences, linked to things — and s. 487, like other warrant authorities, tells investigators the extent of its powers that do not go beyond conventional search and seizure:

> **487.** (1) A justice who is satisfied by information on oath in Form 1 that there are reasonable grounds to believe that there is in a building, receptacle or place

(a) anything on or in respect of which any offence against this Act or any other Act of Parliament has been or is suspected to have been committed,

(b) anything that there are reasonable grounds to believe will afford evidence with respect to the commission of an offence, or will reveal the whereabouts of a person who is believed to have committed an offence, against this Act or any other Act of Parliament,

(c) anything that there are reasonable grounds to believe is intended to be used for the purpose of committing any offence against the person for which a person may be arrested without warrant, or

(c.1) any offence-related property,

may at any time issue a warrant authorizing a peace officer or a public officer who has been appointed or designated to administer or enforce a federal or provincial law and whose duties include the enforcement of this Act or any other Act of Parliament and who is named in the warrant

(d) to search the building, receptacle or place for any such thing and to seize it, and

(e) subject to any other Act of Parliament, to, as soon as practicable, bring the thing seized before, or make a report in respect thereof to, the justice or some other justice for the same territorial division in accordance with section 489.1.

Investigators pursuing federal offences should be able to fit most of their search and seizure needs within the scope of a s. 487 *Code* warrant, but the warrant powers contained in other Acts could be an improvement on s. 487 powers.

Most other federal and provincial Acts that provide for warrants to search for or seize physical things in a normal place somewhat follow the structure of s. 487 of the *Code*, but there can be subtle differences in statutory wording that make a big difference to the drafting or execution of a warrant. The most commonly used warrant power found outside of the *Code* is probably s. 11 of the *CDSA*:

11. (1) A justice who, on *ex parte* application, is satisfied by information on oath that there are reasonable grounds to believe that

(a) a controlled substance or precursor in respect of which this Act has been contravened,

(b) any thing in which a controlled substance or precursor referred to in paragraph (a) is contained or concealed,

(c) offence-related property, or

(d) any thing that will afford evidence in respect of an offence under this Act

is in a place may, at any time, issue a warrant authorizing a peace officer, at any time, to search the place for any such controlled substance, precursor, property or thing and to seize it.

. . .

(5) Where a peace officer who executes a warrant issued under subsection (1) has reasonable grounds to believe that any person found in the place set out in the warrant has on their person any controlled substance, precursor, property or thing set out in the warrant, the peace officer may search the person for the controlled substance, precursor, property or thing and seize it.

Section 11 of the *CDSA* is narrower than s. 487 of the *Code* with respect to things that can be searched for and seized, but the powers that accompany the execution of a *CDSA* warrant go beyond those found in s. 487 to include execution at any time of the day or night (see *R. v. Saunders* (2003), 232 Nfld. & P.E.I.R. 22; 2003 NLCA 63; leave to appeal refused [2004] 3 S.C.R. 505), and ancillary powers to search people found at the location of a s. 11 *CDSA* warrant execution. Section 12 of the *CDSA* additionally provides that a peace officer executing a s. 11 warrant may "enlist such assistance as the officer deems necessary" (a s. 487 *Code* warrant needs to be accompanied by a separate s. 487.02 assistance order to have a similar power available) and "use as much force as is necessary in the circumstances" (a certain degree of force authorization is likely implicit in a s. 487 warrant, but s. 12 provides a broader force authority not requiring explicit reference in a warrant). As you can see, there is life beyond the s. 487 *Criminal Code* warrant.

2. Warrants to Gather Unusual Evidence in Unusual Places

a. *Section 487.01* Criminal Code *General Warrants*

The s. 487.01 *Criminal Code* "general warrant" authority is the most common way to obtain judicial authorization for gathering unusual evidence in unusual places by "authorizing a peace officer to . . . use any device or investigative technique or procedure or do any thing described in the warrant that would, if not authorized, constitute an unreasonable search or seizure in respect of a person or a person's property." Section 487.01 is the catch-all provision that can authorize devices, techniques and procedures not authorizeable elsewhere, best used when investigators aren't sure what form evidence may be in, or exactly where it is located. Because it is up to investigators to define in a s. 487.01 warrant application which type of investigative technique they want to use that would otherwise infringe privacy rights, Parliament has imposed a number of pre-conditions on the issuance of a s. 487.01 warrant that go beyond what is necessary for a s. 487 warrant:

- that the warrant be issued by a provincial or superior court judge, not by a justice of the peace;

- that issuing the warrant is in the best interests of the administration of justice;

- that the warrant authorizes investigative techniques not authorizeable elsewhere;

- that the warrant not interfere with the bodily integrity of any person;

- that the warrant stipulate terms and conditions to ensure the search and seizure is reasonable in the circumstances; and

- that notice of covert entry and search be given within three years of execution of the warrant.

Most notably, s. 487.01 can't be used as a way to get around the limitations of other search and seizure provisions. For example, a wiretap that can only be obtained for limited types of offences under s. 187 of the *Code* cannot alternately be obtained under the general warrant power of s. 487.01.

The seemingly endless potential but very restrictive reality of s. 487.01 general warrants has lead many investigators astray over the years, like in *R. v. Kuitenen* (2001), 45 C.R. (5th) 131; 2001 BCSC 677 at paras. 22-24, where investigators with the best of intentions misconstrued both the powers available and the standard of proof necessary for a s. 487.01 warrant:

The general warrant issued in this case is defective for a number of reasons. At the outset it should be noted that it is worded incorrectly. The form is wrong. There is no "General (Surreptitious Entry) Warrant". Furthermore, the wording of the warrant exceeds the scope of the section in that it authorizes a peace officer to search the property for evidence which 'may be obtained' as opposed to 'will be obtained'.

. . .

The fact remains, however, that on its face the warrant purports to give the police greater power than what is contemplated in the section.

The real problem with this warrant is that Constable C. . . did not have reasonable grounds to believe an offence had been committed. He admitted as much a number of times in his evidence. It is difficult to believe how he could have concluded that he lacked the reasonable grounds to obtain a warrant under s. 487 [of the *Criminal Code*] and under s. 11 [of the *Controlled Drugs and Substances Act*] and had reasonable grounds to obtain a warrant under the general warrant section. In order to obtain a warrant under the latter section greater safeguards are required in light of the highly intrusive nature of the authorization.

Don't jump to conclusions about warrant powers and standards of proof. Demystification of the law requires that you carefully read the statutory search and seizure provisions upon which you are relying. Early investigator-prosecutor contact should clarify any doubts about warrants to gather unusual evidence in unusual places.

b. *Section 487.012* Criminal Code *Production Orders*

Taking its cue from the information demand powers of regulatory compliance verification, s. 487.012 was recently added to the *Criminal Code* to provide for judicially authorizeable production orders "to produce documents, or copies of them certified by affidavit to be true copies, or to produce data; or . . . to prepare a document based on documents or data already in existence and produce it." Although powers similar in effect to the production order previously could be sought under a s. 487.01 general warrant, s. 487.012 production orders represent a simpler procedure with a lower threshold for authorization and a more explicit array of codified powers:

- any judge or justice can grant a production order;

- information cannot be demanded from a person under investigation for any federal offence — this is effectively only a third-party information demand power;

- only documents, certified document copies, data, or summaries of pre-existing documents or data can be demanded, not oral answers to questions or the creation of completely new documents;

- any time, place, and form for production of the documents can be specified, but a specific peace or public officer to whom they will be produced must be named;

- the application process is similar to the process for obtaining any kind of warrant, with a written affidavit submitted supporting issuance of an attached order;

- only a reasonable suspicion of an offence standard need be met, not a reasonable and probable grounds standard like for most other warrants — with the exception of tracking and number recorder warrants discussed in Chapter 10;

- the supporting affidavit must establish that the production order "will" afford evidence respecting the commission of an offence and the target of the order has possession or control of the documents or data sought — for tracking and number recorder warrants only a "could" afford evidence standard need be met;

- certified copies produced under a production order have the same probative value in court as original documents (thus avoiding reliance on *Canada Evidence Act* copy admissibility provisions).

Section 497.012 of the *Code* could be particularly useful in compelling a bank to produce a client's banking records, or an Internet service provider to produce data held in a customer's e-mail account. The reasonable suspicion standard for production orders is sure to attract *Charter* challenges, but those challenges could be defended on the basis that only third parties can be subject to a production order and only pre-existing documents or data can be sought.

3. Warrants Limited to One Type of Offence or One Class of Things

Hidden among substantive offences, far away from the *Criminal Code*'s Part XV "Special Procedures and Powers" where s. 487 warrants and their cousins live, are several little-known warrant provisions limited to investigating one type of offence or searching for and seizing one class of things. These diverse authorities were enacted by Parliament at different times in history to address varying social concerns of the day. Depending on the kinds of offences you investigate, you might find these specific provisions useful since they contain powers not found in s. 487 or s. 487.01 of the *Code*, especially in connection with forfeiture, but I urge you to seek out legal advice before relying on them. Because of the narrow application of warrants limited to one type of offence or class of things, a s. 487 or s. 487.01 warrant will usually be a better choice where a variety of offences or things to be searched for are involved.

a. *Betting Offence and Common Bawdy House Warrants*

Section 199 of the *Criminal Code* provides for betting offence and common bawdy house warrants that, upon reasonable grounds of such offences being shown, can authorize entry by day or night, search and seizure for evidence of those offences, and arrest of all persons found inside a target location. The automatic forfeiture provisions are the main attraction of s. 199, whose unusual features include:

- arrest powers applicable to all those found in the search site, and the requirement that all those arrested be brought before the judge or justice who issued the warrant;

- forfeiture powers running from 30 days after seizure if things seized are not required as evidence;

- the onus in a forfeiture application is on the person claiming return, not on the government seeking forfeiture;

- the Attorney General has full discretion over how something forfeited will be disposed of.

Those found committing offences in the course of a normal s. 487 *Code* search and seizure warrant execution could still be subject to arrest without warrant, those making such arrests would have greater discretion as to whether to release at the scene, and things seized under a normal warrant can also be subject to forfeiture, but the forfeiture test will be more onerous than that specified in s. 199.

A normal s. 487 search and seizure warrant could be enhanced by s-ss. 199(2) *Code* gaming device seizure, followed by s-s. 199(3) reverse onus forfeiture "if no person shows sufficient cause why it should not be forfeited," whether or not a conviction is obtained according to *R. v. Harb* (1994), 129 N.S.R. (2d) 123 (C.A.) at paras. 22-23:

> In my opinion the search and seizure made under *s. 487* of the *Code* in this case was a seizure within the meaning of *s. 199(2)* and therefore an order for forfeiture could have been made by the learned trial judge pursuant to *s. 199(3)*. . . . As a general rule gambling devices, being unlawful, should be forfeited unless the owner can show sufficient cause why they should not be.

Early investigator-prosecutor contact is advisable to weigh the pros and cons of proceeding under s. 199 of the *Code*.

b. *Hate Propaganda Warrants*

Section 320 of the *Criminal Code* provides for hate propaganda warrants if there are reasonable grounds to believe that copies of a publication kept for sale or distribution in premises within the jurisdiction of the court is hate propaganda. Unusual features of s. 320 warrants are:

- only a superior court judge can issue a hate propaganda warrant (except in Quebec), a restriction shared by intrusive wiretaps and general warrants;

- the warrant power only authorizes seizure, not search;

- the judge issuing the warrant must also issue a summons to the occupier of the seizure location requiring cause to be shown why anything seized should not be forfeited;

- the owner and author of the material alleged to be hate propaganda also has standing to appear to oppose forfeiture;

- the prior consent of the Attorney General of Canada or of a province is necessary to institute forfeiture proceedings.

Although it would seem reasonable to implicitly read a power of search into the measures a court can grant under s. 320, if a search power is not authorizeable then the intent of Parliament may have been to authorize seizures of publicly displayed materials like those in a retail store.

The practical use of a s. 320 *Code* warrant could be where investigators wish to destroy material they reasonably believe to be hate propaganda, but do not wish to institute a promotion of hatred prosecution that would require proof beyond a reasonable doubt. Section 320 firmly places the burden of proof on the occupier of the seizure location to show cause why the seized material should not be forfeited. However, the onerous requirement of consent of the Attorney General prior to bringing any s. 320 forfeiture application means other forfeiture provisions in the *Code* are easier to employ.

c. *Electronic Hate Propaganda Warrants*

Arguably much more practically useful than a s. 320 *Criminal Code* ordinary hate propaganda warrant is a s. 320.1 electronic hate propaganda warrant, which was added to the *Code* to address situations like that of Ernest Zundel who ran an extensive Internet site said to promote hatred. Section 320.1 of the *Code* is tailor-made for the control of hate Web sites upon showing reasonable grounds that hate propaganda is stored on and made available to the public through a computer system within the jurisdiction of the court. The vast advantages of a s. 320.1 warrant over a s. 320 warrant are:

- a provincial court judge can authorize a s. 320.1 warrant;

- seizure is accomplished through compulsory provision of a copy of the targeted material by its custodian, who will often be a legitimate Internet service provider;

- execution of a s. 320.1 warrant immediately terminates storage and public access to the target material;

- the provision of information necessary to identify and locate the person who posted the material can be compelled;

- a forfeiture hearing can proceed in the absence of the person who posted the material, so long as notice has been provided to that person or posted at the location where the material to be forfeited was stored;

- it is explicitly clarified that hate propaganda need only be proven on a balance of probabilities, not beyond a reasonable doubt;

- no consent of an Attorney General is necessary to institute forfeiture proceedings.

The utility of s. 320.1 is limited by the computer system needing to be "within the jurisdiction of the court," which will normally mean on Canadian territory although it is worth discussing with a prosecutor if some kind of novel jurisdictional argument could be made in any case you are wondering about. A s. 320.1 warrant would therefore still have trouble addressing the

Zundel situation where material was allegedly being posted on an Internet server in California by Mr. Zundel and his associates out of Toronto, but a s. 320.1 warrant could at least be used against Canadian computers used to prepare and transmit hate propaganda to a server beyond the jurisdiction of Canada's courts.

d. *Obscene Material Warrants*

Section 164 of the *Criminal Code* provides for obscene material, crime comic, child pornography and voyeuristic recording warrants that are similar to but easier to obtain than the warrants available for hate propaganda under s. 320 of the *Code*, provided there are reasonable grounds to believe that within the jurisdiction of the court (1) obscene material, a crime comic or voyeuristic recording is being kept for sale or distribution, or (2) that there is a representation, written material or recording that amounts to child pornography regardless of sale or distribution. Section 164 warrants have both similarities with and differences from s. 320 warrants:

- both require approval of a superior court judge (again except in Quebec);

- both only authorize seizure, not search;

- both require a summons to be issued to the occupier of the seizure location to show cause why seized material should not be forfeited;

- both permit the owner and maker to have standing to argue why the material should not be forfeited;

- unlike s. 320, prior consent of the Attorney General is *not* required to seek s. 164 forfeiture, but s-s. 164(7) of the *Code* does require consent to bring a prosecution based on any material seized under s. 164;

- also unlike s. 320, s. 164 clarifies that obscenity, a crime comic, child pornography or voyeuristic material only need be proved on a balance of probabilities.

Use of a s. 164 warrant leading to forfeiture seems to be more of an alternative to a s. 163 *Code* obscenity prosecution, rather than a prelude to prosecution in itself, because prior Attorney General consent is required to use s. 164 warrant evidence in a prosecution, but no such consent is required to launch a s. 163 obscenity prosecution.

All investigators should anticipate freedom of expression constitutional challenges when attempting to enforce obscenity laws. While the test of obscenity that had been rooted in community standards has now evolved to involve a harm-based analysis, the new test as described in *R. v. Labaye*, [2005] 3 S.C.R. 728 at para. 62, is perhaps not much easier to apply in practice than the old test:

> Indecent criminal conduct will be established where the Crown proves beyond a reasonable doubt the following two requirements:
>
> 1. That, by its *nature*, the conduct at issue causes harm or presents a significant risk of harm to individuals or society in a way that undermines or threatens to undermine a value reflected in and thus formally endorsed through the Constitution or similar fundamental laws by, for example:
>
>> (a) confronting members of the public with conduct that significantly interferes with their autonomy and liberty; or
>>
>> (b) predisposing others to anti-social behaviour; or
>>
>> (c) physically or psychologically harming persons involved in the conduct, and
>
> 2. That the harm or risk of harm is of a *degree* that is incompatible with the proper functioning of society.

The somewhat subjective nature of this test means it is difficult to predict the outcome of obscenity and indecency prosecutions.

e. *Electronic Child Pornography Warrants*

While s. 320.1 *Criminal Code* warrants electronically mirror s. 320 warrants in that both broadly target hate propaganda, s. 164 obscenity warrants have no broad electronic obscenity counterpart. Instead, s. 164.1 of the *Code* only targets electronic child pornography with warrants that are identical in all requirements to s. 320.1 electronic hate propaganda warrants. Notwithstanding the narrower scope, procedurally s. 164.1 warrants are simpler to employ than s. 164 warrants:

- approval by a provincial court judge is possible;

- seizure is authorized through compulsory provision of a copy of the objectionable material by the custodian;

- execution of the warrant immediately terminates storage of and public access to the target material;

- identification of the person who posted the material is compelled;

- a forfeiture hearing can proceed in the absence of the person who posted the material;

- child pornography need be proven only on a balance of probabilities.

The restriction of s. 164.1 warrants to child pornography seems to reflect a public policy decision not to target obscenity in its broadest sense unless it exists in a physical form "for sale or distribution" that will be covered by a s. 164 warrant. This policy choice may have been driven by the reality that there is greater agreement among Canadians and the international community over what constitutes child pornography and hate propaganda, than there is over what amounts to obscenity.

f. *Valuable Mineral Warrants*

Section 395 of the *Criminal Code* creates a rarely used warrant power to search for a "valuable mineral" provided there are reasonable grounds to believe that "contrary to this Act or any other Act of Parliament, any valuable mineral is deposited in a place or held by a person." The special features of a s. 395 warrant include:

- the thing searched for can only be a "valuable mineral";

- search of a person, as well as a place, can be authorized;

- the operation of ss. 489 and 490 of the *Code* are partly displaced by s. 395 having an internal detention and forfeiture code;

- restoration of the valuable mineral to the owner or forfeiture to the Crown if the owner cannot be located may occur even if charges are not laid.

Section 395 could certainly be quite useful in a mineral theft investigation at a mine, although I have never personally come across such a warrant being used.

Predicting Prospects of Warrant Trial Success

Q: How can I tell for sure in advance if a warrant I have obtained will later hold up at trial?

A: You can't. The best you can do to maximize your chances for trial success is give careful thought to preparation of all parts of the warrant and supporting information to obtain.

THE USEFULNESS OF TELEWARRANTS

Once category and type of warrant have been chosen, investigators still need to decide how they are going to seek out the proposed warrant. Some federal Acts now provide for certain types of warrants to be sought and issued by telephone or fax, following the basic form for telewarrants established in s. 487.1 of the *Criminal Code*:

> **487.1** (1) Where a peace officer believes that an indictable offence has been committed and that it would be impracticable to appear personally before a justice to make application for a warrant in accordance with section 256 or 487, the peace officer may submit an information on oath by telephone or other means of telecommunication to a justice designated for the purpose by the chief judge of the provincial court having jurisdiction in the matter.
>
> (2) An information submitted by telephone or other means of telecommunication, other than a means of telecommunication that produces a writing, shall be on oath and shall be recorded verbatim by the justice, who shall, as soon as practicable, cause to be filed, with the clerk of the court for the territorial division in which the warrant is intended for execution, the record or a transcription of it, certified by the justice as to time, date and contents.
>
> (2.1) The justice who receives an information submitted by a means of telecommunication that produces a writing shall, as soon as practicable, cause to be filed, with the clerk of the court for the territorial division in which the warrant is intended for execution, the information certified by the justice as to time and date of receipt.

Fax warrants are definitely permissible under s. 487.1, but e-mail warrants are not so clearly covered and are probably best avoided until the law is further clarified.

In addition to standard warrant conditions, telewarrants impose a few additional duties on investigators that ensure telewarrants do not simply become routine and insubstantial replacements for paper warrants:

- an explanation in the oral or fax information to obtain describing why it is impracticable to appear personally before a justice to secure the warrant;

- completion in duplicate of a copy of the warrant "noting on its face the name of the issuing justice and the time, date and place of issuance;"

- leaving a copy of the telewarrant at the place of execution as soon as is practicable; and

- filing a written report with the clerk of the court where the warrant was executed within at most seven days after execution stating the date and time of execution, the things seized and where they are being held.

The availability of telewarrants arguably has restricted what constitutes truly exigent circumstances justifying a warrantless search.

While s. 487.1 of the *Code* only explicitly applies to s. 487 and s. 256 *Code* warrants, other warrant provisions of the *Code* and other Acts identify whether they can also benefit from telewarrants like s-s. 11(2) of the *CDSA* which confirms: "an information may be submitted by telephone or other means of telecommunication in accordance with section 487.1 of the *Criminal Code*, with such modifications as the circumstances require." Investigators need to plan further in advance for any type of warrant lacking a telewarrant option, so that long delays are not incurred in drafting a paper warrant and physically locating a judge or justice to sign it.

Why Not Use Telewarrants All the Time

Q & A

Q: If telewarrants are so useful, why don't we use them all of the time and totally get rid of paper warrants?

A: There must be some urgency present in order to justify going the telewarrant route. Very complex facts supporting a warrant may be difficult to relay over the telephone, and when it comes time to later defend the warrant at trial a written information to obtain carefully prepared in advance of going to a justice might stand up better to vigorous attack. A warrant transmitted by fax does not share these weaknesses, but a fax machine may not be available in many urgent search situations. Moving to fully electronic warrants transmitted from an investigator's computer to a court computer would be a welcome future development in the law.

PROCEEDS OF CRIME SEIZURE, RESTRAINT AND FORFEITUE

Going after proceeds of crime involves a lot more than just choosing the right warrant to find and seize those proceeds, but some kind of warrant-like, judicially authorized, legal instrument will usually be required to achieve that aim. Proceeds may be of an intangible or immoveable nature not capable of conventional seizure, and be difficult to link to precise people or offences. The *Criminal Code* and the *CDSA* now contain special judicially-authorizeable powers to seize proceeds of crime not because they are evidence of an offence, but because there are reasonable grounds to believe they may be subject to forfeiture. Together those Acts provide for special search warrants, restraint orders and management orders to detain, control and perhaps eventually forfeit goods, real estate and bank balances. The rationale for the enactment of proceeds of crime legislation was succinctly put in *Quebec (Attorney General) v. Laroche*, [2002] 3 S.C.R. 708 at para. 25: "Parliament intended to neutralize criminal organizations by taking the proceeds of their illegal activities away from them. Part XII.2 intends to give effect to the old adage that crime does not pay. . . ."

1. Special Search Warrants and Restraint Orders

A "special search warrant" is available under s. 462.32 of the *Criminal Code* to search for and seize tangible and moveable proceeds of crime like vehicles or art subject to forfeiture, even where charges cannot be laid. Although the intangible nature of bank balances and immoveable nature of real estate mean they cannot be seized under a conventional warrant, notwithstanding they constitute a significant portion of proceeds of crime in Canada, s. 462.33 of the *Code* provides for "restraint orders" that ensure intangibles and immoveables don't disappear pending forfeiture applications before or after trial. What makes special search warrants and restraint orders so special is they:

- require a specific agent of the Attorney General to be the one who makes the application for a warrant or order;

- require the thing seized or restrained to be linked to designated offences;

- require reasonable and probable grounds that the thing seized or restrained may be subject to an order of forfeiture under either s-s. 462.37(1) or s-s. 462.38(2) of the *Code*;

- may require advance notice to any person having a valid interest in the target property if ordered by the issuing judge;

- involve a special duty to preserve seized property and require an undertaking by a senior prosecutor on behalf of the responsible Attorney General to pay damages or costs arising out of the making or execution of a special search warrant or restraint order;

- can only be issued by a superior court judge, except in Quebec where a provincial court judge can also issue them;

- additionally, a restraint order can be issued against property located outside Canada.

Parliament has clearly demonstrated it is concerned about limiting or compensating for any abusive use of these warrants or orders. Section 14 of the *CDSA* provides for restraint orders similar to s. 462.33 of the *Code*, but for drug offence related property.

The physical structure of the application for a special search warrant or restraint order is quite similar to a conventional warrant, naming:

- the designated offence under investigation;

- the building, place or receptacle where the thing to be searched for and seized is located, or the person believed to be in possession of the property if it is a restraint order being applied for, and the grounds for such belief;

- a description of the property;

- the grounds for the belief that an order of forfeiture may be made under s-ss. 462.37(1) or 462.38(2) of the *Code* against the property; and

- whether any previous applications for a special search warrant or restraint order against the target property have been made.

The focus on establishing grounds to believe a particular person is in possession of target property, rather than on grounds to believe the target property is located in a particular place, primarily distinguishes an affidavit supporting a restraint order from one supporting a special search warrant. The grounds supporting both restraint orders and special search warrants can be distinguished from those supporting conventional warrants in their focus on why the thing targeted may be subject to forfeiture, rather than why it will be evidence of an offence.

Demystification of the law has paid off with special search warrants and restraint orders, where as investigators have gained more experience with these legal instruments major high value property forfeiture successes have been achieved. Early investigator-prosecutor contact has been crucial for their drafting, bringing the applications and giving the undertakings on damages and costs. Because of that unique undertaking, prosecutors will be reticent to cooperate with investigators unless they have complete confidence that proper investigative procedures are scrupulously being followed.

Quebec (Attorney General) v. Laroche, [2002] 3 S.C.R. 708 at para. 55, found the execution of special search warrants on tangibles and restraint orders on intangibles constitute seizures that engage s. 8 *Charter* unreasonable search and seizure protections:

> the property is placed under the legal and actual control of the criminal justice system. Moreover, the objectives of this measure for exercising control are twofold. First, Parliament intended to facilitate criminal investigations, by enacting procedural provisions that make property, and information about it, more readily accessible to the police and the Crown. Second, the purpose of those procedures is to prevent the disappearance or wasting of the property. Doing this makes it possible to punish the crimes in question more effectively, and facilitates the enforcement of the orders of forfeiture that may be made in future. We can conclude from those characteristics, and the context and objectives, that a . . . order must be regarded as a seizure within the meaning of s. 8 of the *Charter*.

Deficient special search warrants and restraint orders will be challenged under the *Charter* just like deficient conventional warrants, so investigators need to ensure all technical requirements are covered, and that a sufficient factual basis is established through the supporting affidavit to justify their issuance.

2. Management Orders to Take Care of Tangible and Intangible Property

Investigators must remain concerned about what is happening to seized or restrained property pending any forfeiture application. Keeping a working farm operating so as to preserve both its ongoing income stream and market value while under restraint will require a highly skilled manager. A management order can be sought under s. 462.331 of the *Criminal Code* in respect of any property seized under a special search warrant or subject to a restraint order appointing "a person to take control of and to manage or otherwise deal with all or part of the property in accordance with the directions of the judge." Section 14.1 of the *CDSA* provides for similar management orders for drug offence related property. A management order application requires that a formal motion be brought before an appropriate court with an affidavit attesting to the grounds justifying the management order.

Section 463.331 of the *Code* gives a court a great deal of discretion over what kind of management to authorize, so investigators need to very explicitly stipulate in the management order application what they propose to do with the seized or restrained property, and what powers they need to accomplish that aim. Under s-s. 462.331(3)(a) sale is possible for perishable or rapidly depreciating seized property, and under s-s. 462.331(3)(b) destruction is possible for property of little or no value, but be prepared for opposing legal arguments that the property does not in fact qualify as perishable, rapidly depreciating, or fall into the realm of little or no value. Investigators need to be somewhat confident in the strength of their forfeiture arguments, and that they can preserve seized property at reasonable cost pending forfeiture, before taking action against proceeds of crime.

3. Forfeiture as the Consolation Prize to Conviction

Each federal, provincial or territorial Act under which a seizure is made or a charge laid must be individually examined in order to determine if, when and how forfeiture can take place. Forfeiture makes a lot of sense from a deterrence perspective, and enhances public confidence in the administration of justice when it can be shown that property has come into a person's hands through illegal means. Negotiated deals over forfeiture are often easier to conclude than negotiations with accused over lengthy terms of imprisonment that would result from guilty pleas to substantive charges. The prospects of conviction and the public interest ultimately guide any contemplated preference for forfeiture over prosecution.

a. *Forfeiture Independent of Charges under Any Act*

Forfeiture of seized items can be ordered under s-s. 490(9) of the *Criminal Code* where items are being detained pursuant to *Code* authority (usually because they have been seized under the authority of a federal Act), and no charges are being proceeded with in respect of that property. Sub-section 490(9) has become increasingly important to proceeds of crime investigations where other more technical forfeiture provisions are difficult to invoke. The preconditions to invoking s-s. 490(9) forfeiture proceedings in favour of the Crown are only:

- that there was a lawful seizure of a thing;

- that all periods of detention have now expired without charges being laid, or that the thing will not be required as evidence;

- that the thing was either seized from someone not in lawful possession of it or it was not in the possession of anyone; and

- that the lawful owner or possessor of the thing cannot be determined.

Investigators need to work closely with prosecutors in seeking s-s. 490(9) forfeiture by providing evidence that establishes reasonable efforts have been undertaken to locate the lawful owner or possessor of the things subject to forfeiture, and that any person from whom those things were seized does not have a lawful right to them. The greater the lengths investigators go to in attempting to locate a person lawfully entitled to possess the seized things, the more likely a court will be to find that forfeiture is justified.

b. *Forfeiture of Proceeds of Crime as Part of the Trial Process*

Where charges are proceeded with, it will be up to the trial judge to determine what will happen to seized property in accordance with the law. Sections 462.37 and 462.38 of the *Criminal Code* govern proceeds of crime forfeiture as part of a trial process for many federal indictable offences; ss. 16 and 17 of the *CDSA* similarly govern forfeiture of drug offence related property. Under these provisions where there is a conviction for a designated offence, the court hearing a forfeiture application need only be satisfied *on a balance of probabilities* that any property is proceeds of crime and that the designated offence conviction was committed in relation to that property, or for serious criminal organization or drugs offences that within the prior ten years the offender engaged in a pattern of criminal activity for material benefit or now has property whose value cannot be accounted for taking account of income not from designated offences, and the offender is unable to prove that property subject to forfeiture is *not* proceeds of crime. Where there is no conviction, an order of forfeiture is still possible but requires the court to be satisfied *beyond a reasonable doubt* that the property is proceeds of crime. Several innovative features have been incorporated into these provisions to ensure that forfeiture procedures are not frustrated by flight of the accused or proceeds from the court's jurisdiction, including the potential for an extraterritorial forfeiture order, or an order to substitute a fine equivalent to the value of the property subject to forfeiture where that property has been hidden, transferred, sent abroad, destroyed or commingled with other property.

The Complexity of Proceeds of Crime

Q&A

Q: The law on proceeds of crime seizure and forfeiture seems extremely complex. How can regular field investigators be expected to keep up with and enforce proceeds law?

A: The establishment of Integrated Proceeds of Crime units in the 1990s involving investigators, lawyers and accountants co-located in a single office recognized that successful proceeds of crime investigations are very much a joint effort. All investigators can, however, still benefit from a basic understanding of the proceeds tools available, since every case won't be handled by proceeds of crime specialists.

CHALLENGES OF SEARCHING FOR AND SEIZING ELECTRONIC DATA

Electronic data is already seized from sources as diverse as bookkeeping computers, navigation plotters and digital surveillance cameras, and could eventually become part of every search and seizure. Which powers are adequate to secure the data being sought, how to limit seizure scope, how to preserve continuity, and whether technical experts should accompany investigators during searches are all questions that need to be answered before commencing a search and seizure of electronic data.

1. Powers Aiding Electronic Data Seizure

Search and seizure warrants will be the primary means of getting at data stored in one fixed place, although common law powers and electronic surveillance authorizations could also be relevant. Common law search incident-to-arrest powers might be applicable when data is physically carried on someone's person, although if a notebook computer is like a room full of files search incident to arrest might not be a broad enough power to extend to every file a computer carries. Common law informed consent to search for data also might be useful, but needs to be treated with the same caution as any consent search. An electronic surveillance authorization could even be required to pluck out data travelling through the cyber ether if the data qualifies as a private communication under s. 183 of the *Criminal Code*.

a. Are Warrant Authorities Broad Enough to Include Data and Computer Operation?

The warrant provisions of many Acts are worded broadly enough to authorize the seizure of electronic data, however s. 487 of the *Criminal Code* comes with the added feature of amendments in s-ss. 487(2.1) and (2.2) which explicitly authorize the operation of computer equipment in the course of warrant execution:

> **487.** (2.1) A person authorized under this section to search a computer system in a building or place for data may
>
> > (a) use or cause to be used any computer system at the building or place to search any data contained in or available to the computer system;
> >
> > (b) reproduce or cause to be reproduced any data in the form of a print-out or other intelligible output;
> >
> > (c) seize the print-out or other output for examination or copying; and
> >
> > (d) use or cause to be used any copying equipment at the place to make copies of the data.
>
> (2.2) Every person who is in possession or control of any building or place in respect of which a search is carried out under this section shall, on presentation of the warrant, permit the person carrying out the search
>
> > (a) to use or cause to be used any computer system at the building or place in order to search any data contained in or available to the computer system for data that the person is authorized by this section to search for;
> >
> > (b) to obtain a hard copy of the data and to seize it; and
> >
> > (c) to use or cause to be used any copying equipment at the place to make copies of the data.

Just because another Act's search provisions do not have a computer operation section does *not* mean computer searches are somehow not permitted under that Act. No Act explicitly says investigators can open file cabinets in the course of their searching, but that is commonly done, so it follows computer operation is a necessary incident of exercising regular search and seizure powers in our modern world. However, seeking explicit authorization for computer operation in any warrant is always prudent, and ss. 487 (2.1) and (2.2) of the *Code* clarify any remaining computer operation doubts for s. 487 *Code* warrants.

b. *How Assistance Orders Can Aid Computer Searches*

An unusual computer configuration like a proprietary mainframe system, or data protected through passwords or encryption, could require a s. 487.02 *Criminal Code* assistance order to efficiently search for and seize electronic data:

> **487.02** Where an authorization is given under section 184.2, 184.3, 186 or 188, a warrant is issued under this Act or an order is made under subsection 492.2(2), the judge or justice who gives the authorization, issues the warrant or makes the order may order any person to provide assistance, where the person's assistance may reasonably be considered to be required to give effect to the authorization, warrant or order.

An assistance order could compel the disclosure of passwords or compel a business's information technology staff to assist investigators in operating computers for the purpose of finding information relevant to a *Criminal Code* authorized search. As regulatory Acts usually do not have assistance order provisions, a *Code* warrant may be the preferable route for computer searches predominantly connected to federal offences.

Assistance orders are not a cure all. People subject to such an order could frustrate its operation by claiming not to know passwords or computer procedures. Later contempt of court or obstruction of justice proceedings against the uncooperative will be of little assistance to investigators who need access to a computer system right now. Investigators still need their own experts to ensure those subject to assistance orders don't erase data or mislead investigators about computer contents, and experts will also be needed when attempting to gain direct access to targeted electronic data if no one is sufficiently cooperative or knowledgeable at a search site to respond to an assistance order.

c. Will Production Orders Revolutionize Electronic Data Search and Seizure?

The new s. 487.012 *Criminal Code* production order power will clearly be a great aid in the world of electronic data search and seizure, but will not completely replace s. 487 search warrants and s. 487.02 assistance orders for data searches because production orders cannot demand information from a person under investigation for any federal offence. Section 487 warrants will still be the instrument of choice to seek electronic data on the premises of investigative targets, as well as where investigators do not trust third parties to fully comply with a production order. But where their use is appropriate, production orders will be much less resource intensive to execute and will not require investigators to have advance knowledge of where data is located.

d. Are Computers a Means of Communication or a Repository of Documents?

Investigators who are only interested in computer data as a means of private communications between two or more parties need to consider whether a wiretap could be required to secure that data. Since communication files come to rest extremely quickly over the Internet, and semi-permanent records are usually created of Internet traffic, whether or how a wiretap application can be made to monitor the Internet may be purely an academic debate if most law enforcement agencies are better off just waiting for an Internet communication to stop travelling and then seize it from the destination computer, the computer of origin or any intermediary computer where a copy of the communication was retained. But where Internet chat or voice communication technologies facilitate communication without creating a permanent record that investigators can later seize, then a wiretap might be needed. By the time you read this, legislative amendments may have addressed some of the uncertainties concerning Internet information seizures, but new technology is sure to develop that will require further legal adaptation.

2. Competing Challenges of Limiting Electronic Data Seizure Scope and Preserving Continuity

Computer searches are particularly prone to over-seizures because of a computer's vast capacity to store unrelated data. Courts do not look favourably on smash and grab type searches, where all computer equipment at a target location is hauled away to be examined much later at investigator offices. Seizing all computer equipment is as objectionable as seizing an entire warehouse full of documents when only a few file boxes worth of material are sought under a warrant. The over-seizure problem is balanced by the need for continuity.

Simply copying a single file from a computer will not generate an electronic original because computer files are not saved in contiguous blocks, unlike individual paper files in a filing cabinet. Computer files are usually saved in scattered sectors across a disk, only being reassembled when a file is opened by an application capable of accessing it, so any copy other than a true "image copy" will scatter those sectors in different ways on different disks. It is like taking a document from a paper shredder, piecing it back together, and then tearing it up again.

Imaging an entire drive preserves all the bits in their original state at the time of seizure so that nothing is missed like the date a file was created or a deleted portion of a file. Image copies of entire drives will likely not be found to be over-seizures so long as they are made solely for continuity purposes, and not to impermissibly expand on the limited list of things to be searched for specified in a warrant. Occasionally seizures of entire original hard drives might be justified for similar reasons. Decisions on how to deal with seizure scope and continuity preservation will dictate the mode of computer search pursued.

3. The Four Modes of Computer Search

Investigators need to consider in advance of any search the type and extent of electronic data being sought, the power being relied upon to get at that data, and the goals of minimizing scope while maximizing continuity in order to determine the best mode of computer search and seizure to employ. Computer searches principally proceed by four modes:

- searching a computer storage drive and printing out copies of any relevant files;

- searching a storage drive and copying the relevant files to another disk;

- making an image copy of an entire drive, and later recreating the drive off-site; or

- seizing all hardware and software.

Section 8 of the *Charter* only offers protection against "unreasonable" search and seizure, so what amounts to a reasonable mode to accomplish electronic data seizure will depend on the circumstances of a particular case. Any application for a warrant to authorize a computer search should clearly explain in the "information to obtain" the justification for a particular mode of search, and include explicit authority in the warrant itself to pursue the proposed means of search and seizure.

The first two modes of printing or copying individual files have the value of limiting search scope where only a couple of documents are sought, but it may take an inordinate amount of time to locate or access those files and continuity problems could be created. The third mode of image-copying an entire drive pushes permissible search and seizure scope boundaries, but is efficient without likely being abusive. The fourth mode of seizing all hardware and software has a real potential for leading to claims of abuse and should be a last resort that is most appropriate where the hardware and software have evidentiary value themselves, or are necessary to access the data subject to seizure.

Seizing hardware and software could be justifiable if it was part of the means for committing offences, like creating and distributing child pornography, it was obtained through the commission of a crime, or it must be examined by an expert computer laboratory to recover difficult to locate or encrypted files. A warrant must explicitly list hardware and software as things to be seized, and the "information to obtain" must explain why such seizure is necessary. Sometimes providing replacement hardware will forestall claims that investigator actions have effectively put a legitimate organization out of business.

4. Personnel Necessary for Electronic Data Seizure

Technology experts may be required at the stages of drafting and executing a warrant seeking electronic evidence. Expert information describing the technology to be searched and the information to be obtained could justify the means of search and seizure. During execution experts can locate, gain access to and copy target data. Ideally, technology experts will also be peace officers or designated enforcement officers, but *R. v. Strachan*, [1988] 2 S.C.R. 980 at 997, established that undesignated assistants are permissible at a search and seizure site so long as they are there for a legitimate purpose connected to the warrant and directly under the control of the executing officers:

This requirement is met when the officer or officers named in the warrant execute it personally and are responsible for the control and conduct of the search. The use of unnamed assistants in the search does not violate the requirement of s. 10(2) so long as they are closely supervised by the named officer or officers. It is the named officers who must set out the general course of the search and direct the conduct of any assistants. If the named officers are truly in control, participate in the search, and are present throughout, then the use of assistants does not invalidate the search or the warrant.

Nevertheless, a best practice demonstrating the utmost good faith is to mention in the information to obtain the warrant that assistants who are not enforcement officers will be employed in the execution of the warrant, and explain why their presence is necessary.

Acceptable Scope for Computer Searches

Q & A

Q: What is the problem with seizing an entire computer during a search so long as it has one relevant file in it? Isn't this just the same as seizing an entire document where only one paragraph is relevant to the search?

A: No, it's not the same since a single personal computer can now store inordinate amounts of data, much more than any paper file folder or cabinet could ever hold. The law doesn't allow you to seize an entire roomful of documents when a warrant only authorizes search and seizure for one particular document. You must limit the scope of every search and seizure to what is truly necessary and within the scope of your powers to avoid accusations of abuse. Broader computer file seizure might, however, be permissible when technical requirements mean it could take several days or weeks to go through computer contents to locate the target document, or preserving continuity requires you seize more than just the document you are looking for.

PROVINCIAL AND TERRITORIAL POWERS OF SEARCH AND SEIZURE

Choosing the right warrant for your case could involve trolling through provincial or territorial Acts for a suitable search and seizure power instead of looking to federal legislation. Although the vast federal authorities covering search and seizure sometimes apply to the investigation of offences under any federal Act, they stop short of applying to provincial and territorial offences. Just as regulatory compliance verification powers of inspection, information demand or inquiry can be rooted in provincial or territorial legislation, and common law search or seizure powers can be invoked to aid provincial or territorial offence investigations, statutory search and seizure powers can also be found in provincial and territorial Acts. Some provincial or territorial search and seizure warrant powers may be found in general Acts like the Ontario *Provincial Offences Act*, R.S.O. 1990, c. P.33, or the Nova Scotia *Summary Proceedings Act*, R.S.N.S. 1989, c. 450, which contain procedural investigation and prosecution provisions similar to but more basic than those found in the *Criminal Code*. Just because a search and seizure power is supported by provincial or territorial legislation does not mean it is somehow less valid or useful than one that relies on federal legislation — it is usually the same justices and judges who issue both federal and provincial or territorial warrants. In joint-forces investigations, both federal and provincial warrants might even be sought at the same time for the same case.

There is no reason that one federal and one provincial warrant cannot be executed on the same premises, but consecutive execution avoids confusion over who is seizing what for which offences. If both provincial and federal investigators need the same piece of evidence, access by provincial authorities to federally held evidence can be obtained through a s-s. 490(15) *Criminal Code* application. The execution of warrants and inspections can even be mixed at the same location where different Acts or the same Act for different time periods are being enforced, with the best practice being to get the warrant executions out of the way first before moving on to the inspections. A larger site like a container terminal could be divided into quadrants with investigators utilizing different federal or provincial warrant or inspection powers simultaneously in different quadrants. Every investigator must, however, remain true to a permissible predominant purpose.

Investigators have lots of choices available when it comes to picking the right warrant or other power to use in a case. Your choices will be driven by the facts of your case, the predominant purpose of your inquiries, and the legislation under which you are operating. Creativity and broad mindedness are required to choose the best legal instrument to advance your case, rather than settling for the one everyone else seems to choose because that is the only one they know.

For Choosing the Right Warrant for Your Case

KEY POINTS

✓ Traditional warrants to search for and seize physical things located in a physical place usually represent the best balance between available search scope and preconditions for issuance. Other types of warrants like general warrants are available to gather unusual evidence in unusual places outside of the traditional sense of a thing in a place, but face additional preconditions for authorization. Offence and evidence-specific warrants tend to be narrow in scope, but may come with powers not provided for elsewhere. If available, consider getting a telewarrant in urgent search circumstances.

✓ A special search warrant is available to search for and seize tangible moveable property like art or vehicles for which there are reasonable and probable grounds to believe may be subject to forfeiture as proceeds of crime if they can be linked to a designated offence. A restraint order can be issued on a similar basis as a special search warrant, but can target both immoveable real estate and intangible property like bank balances, including property located outside of Canada. A management order can be issued in respect of any property seized under a special search warrant or subject to a restraint order.

✓ A court may authorize perishable or rapidly depreciating property to be sold, property of little value to be destroyed, and forfeiture of seized things if the lawful owner cannot be determined, if satisfied *on a balance of probabilities* the property is proceeds of crime connected to a proven designated offence, or without a conviction if satisfied *beyond a reasonable doubt* the property is proceeds of crime.

✓ Searching for and seizing electronic data poses unique challenges requiring advance planning, especially to avoid over-seizures and preserve continuity.

✓ Powers of search and seizure for provincial or territorial offences can either be found in the common law or in provincial and territorial legislation. Joint federal-provincial offence investigations should ideally decide in advance on consecutive or concurrent use of compliance verification or enforcement powers.

FURTHER READING

Cases

R. v. Brooks (2003), 15 C.R. (6th) 319 (Ont. C.A.). A s. 487.01 *Criminal Code* general warrant will be invalid if there was another federal search or seizure authority that would have provided for a warrant to authorize the action for which authorization was sought in the general warrant.

R. v. Erickson (2003), 192 B.C.A.C. 203; 2003 BCCA 693. While obtaining a s. 487.1 *Criminal Code* telewarrant requires that it is "impracticable" to appear personally before a justice to make a warrant application, no justice being available in the rural community where a police detachment is located may be sufficient to fulfill this requirement.

R. v. Multiform Manufacturing Co., [1990] 2 S.C.R. 624. Section 487 *Criminal Code* warrants can be used to investigate the breach of any federal Act, even an Act that contains its own search and seizure provisions.

Books, Articles and Reports

G.S. Campbell, "Emerging Issues of the Internet and Canadian Criminal Law" (1998) 3 Can. Crim. L. Rev. 101.

R.W. David and S.C. Hutchinson, *Computer Crime in Canada: An Introduction to Technological Crime and Related Issues* (Toronto: Carswell, 1997).

A.M. Gahtan, *Electronic Evidence* (Toronto: Carswell, 1999).

P.G. German, *Proceeds of Crime: The Criminal Law, Related Statutes, Regulations and Agreements*, loose-leaf (Toronto: Carswell, 1998).

R. Hubbard et al., *Money Laundering and Proceeds of Crime* (Toronto: Irwin Law, 2004).

S. Hutchinson, *Canadian Search Warrant Manual 2005* (Toronto: Thomson, 2004). Gives a concise summary of all the important aspects of search warrant drafting, focusing on warrants obtained under the *Criminal Code*.

W.T. Oppal, *Closing the Gap: Policing and the Community — The Recommendations* (Victoria, BC: Commission of Inquiry into Police in

British Columbia, 1992) [on-line: *www.pssg.gov.bc.ca/publications/oppal/ ClosingTheGap.pdf*].

Searching and Seizing Computers and Obtaining Electronic Evidence in Criminal Investigations (Computer Crime and Intellectual Property Section, United States Department of Justice, 2002) [on-line: *www. cybercrime.gov/s&smanual2002.htm*]. While some caution is required in relying on this publication because it is based on U.S. law, it contains a wealth of information on the procedures investigators need to consider for computer searches.

CHAPTER EIGHT

DRAFTING AND EXECUTING A BULLET-PROOF WARRANT

So long as the affidavit meets the requisite legal norm, there is no need for it to be as lengthy as *A la recherché du temps perdu*, as lively as the Kama Sutra, or as detailed as an automotive repair manual. All that it must do is set out the facts fully and frankly for the authorizing judge in order that he or she can make an assessment of whether these rise to the standard required in the legal test for the authorization. Ideally, an affidavit should be not only full and frank but also clear and concise. It need not include every minute detail of the police investigation over a number of months and even of years.

A corollary to the requirement of an affidavit being full and frank is that it should never attempt to trick its readers.

R. v. Araujo, [2000] 2 S.C.R. 992 at paras. 46-47.

In This Chapter

- The three duties of investigators seeking warrants
- What "reasonable and probable grounds" really means
- Nine fundamental principles for search warrant drafting
- How to avoid drafting confusion
- Techniques for spotting warrant errors
- Properly executing the warrant

In this chapter you will discover how to Kevlar-coat a warrant to please even the toughest critic. There is no quick dip method; the coating can only be achieved through painstaking preliminary research, collating and distilling all available facts, followed by careful wordsmithing so that you both say what you mean and mean what you say. What you might turn up when executing a warrant can never be fully predicted, but positive results when the legality of a warrant later gets challenged in court will in the vast majority of cases be a forgone conclusion if you have followed the bullet-proof principles.

THE THREE DUTIES OF INVESTIGATORS SEEKING WARRANTS

Because search or seizure warrants are authorized by courts, investigators owe those courts three principal duties occurring before the warrant is obtained, during its execution, and after anything has been seized:

- the pre-search duty of full and frank disclosure of relevant information to a judge or justice sufficient to support the application for a warrant;

- the during-search duty to execute the warrant in a respectful and non-abusive manner in accordance with its terms;

- the post-search duty to properly care for the seized goods, and to report back to the issuing court what was seized so that a determination can be made of whether the detention of each thing seized is justifiable.

Hunter v. Southam Inc., [1984] 2 S.C.R. 145 at 160, explained the importance of court supervision of search powers through prior judicial authorization:

> If the issue to be resolved in assessing the constitutionality of searches . . . were whether *in fact* the governmental interest in carrying out a given search outweighed that of the individual in resisting the governmental intrusion upon his privacy, then it would be appropriate to determine the balance of the competing interests *after* the search had been completed. Such a post facto analysis would, however, be seriously at odds with the purpose of s. 8. That purpose is, as I have said, to protect individuals from unjustified State intrusions upon their privacy. That purpose requires a means of *preventing* unjustified searches before they happen, not simply of determining, after the fact, whether they ought to have occurred

in the first place. This, in my view, can only be accomplished by a
system of *prior authorization*, not one of subsequent validation.

Breach of any of the pre-search, during-search, or post-search duties could
lead, before or after charges are laid, to evidence being ordered returned to
the owner or person from whom it was seized, or to that same evidence
being ruled inadmissible at trial.

Demystification of the law here tells you that warrants are not overly
complex creatures to be avoided if at all possible, but rather straightforward
tools to help investigators get the job done by extending their authority
beyond where the common law and legislators are comfortable providing
them full discretion. Early investigator-prosecutor contact for all but the
most routine warrant applications will ensure that the three duties of investigators seeking warrants are completely fulfilled.

WHAT "REASONABLE AND PROBABLE GROUNDS" REALLY MEANS

The key to obtaining a judicial authorization to search or seize generally lies in completing the connect the dots puzzle demonstrating reasonable
and probable belief linking (1) a thing to (2) a place to (3) an offence. The
Reasonable and Probable Grounds (RPG) Threshold Checklist, at the end of
this chapter, will help you in determining whether you do or do not have
RPG to conduct a search. Confusion over the point at which "credibly based
probability replaces suspicion" as described in *Hunter v. Southam,* [1984] 2
S.C.R. 145 at 167, is what causes much of the difficulty with warrants.

1. "Reasonable" and "Reasonable and Probable" Mean the Same Thing

Sometimes you will see the term "reasonable grounds" and at other
times "reasonable and probable grounds" used in legislation to tell you what
standard of proof you need to meet in order to conduct a search. Many
investigators quite reasonably assume provisions that add the words "and
probable" require a higher standard of proof to conduct a search. This is *not*
true. According to *R. v. Baron*, [1993] 1 S.C.R. 416 at 419: "'Reasonable' is
the same as 'reasonable and probable' and imports the same standard."
Forgetting to state that you either have reasonable grounds or reasonable
and probable grounds can be a serious problem in a warrant, where a court

might conclude that you only have a mere suspicion insufficient to obtain a warrant.

2. RPG Means Less Than Certainty and More Than Suspicion

The phrase "credibly based probability" implies the facts stated must have more than a 50-50 chance of being true in order to be probable, and must be convincing or worthy of belief. Certainty is not required, but more than a mere suspicion is necessary. RPG likely lies close to the midpoint between suspicion and certainty. Some of the facts recited in an information to obtain a warrant could be certain, while others might only amount to suspicions. It is the combination of all the facts, and the explanation of how solid the base is on which each of them rests, that leads to a totality of reasonable and probable grounds having been shown.

R. v. Saunders (2003), 232 Nfld. & P.E.I.R. 22; 2003 NLCA 63 at paras. 11 & 16, leave to appeal refused [2004] 3 S.C.R. 505, gives a good explanation of the correct test courts should apply in assessing the sufficiency of reasonable and probable warrant grounds:

> the trial judge engaged in a critique of the information to obtain . . . almost as if he were correcting a student's term paper . . . and not an assessment of the sufficiency of the information in the "totality of the circumstances". The approach taken by the trial judge was like that of a person who views a painting square centimetre by square centimetre to identify defects . . . which has its place . . . but then fails to step back and view the painting as a whole.
>
> . . .
>
> If one "deconstructs" each item of information from source "A" and then that from source "B" and then that from source "C" and applies the test as against each item individually, as did the Trial Judge, then the answer may well be "no", as the trial judge concluded. But, if one considers the "totality of the circumstances" one sees that the information from the three sources is corroborative *inter se;* because of this, the whole of their information becomes greater than the sum of its parts. To put it another way, the sequence of pictures drawn by the three sources tells a consistent story: Mr. Saunders sold hash oil, he kept it at his residence, he had hash oil at his residence on April 1, 2001. As such the whole could enable the justice of the peace to conclude that credibly-based probability had replaced suspicion.

So different parts of warrants can prop each other up. Each wall brace may, by itself, be insufficient to support the weight of the warrant wall, but working together all of the various braces can get the job done.

3. RPG Has a Subjective and an Objective Component

There are both subjective and objective components to the reasonable and probable grounds test. Subjectively, the person attesting to the belief really has to believe the facts and conclusions drawn from those facts being attested to are sufficient to support issuance of a warrant. Objectively, a hypothetical "reasonable person" must also find those facts and conclusions are sufficient grounds for the warrant to issue.

The subjective component means the person swearing to the affidavit in support of the warrant application can't simply sign it without truly knowing, understanding and believing what is in the document. Other investigators and lawyers can assist with its preparation, but the investigator swearing to the affidavit needs a considerable knowledge of its contents. To get that knowledge, an investigator has to be intimately involved in the warrant application's preparation, has to have carefully reviewed it to ensure it does not contain anything he or she would disagree with, and the application should use the style of language in which the investigator would normally write.

The investigator who swears the affidavit in support of the warrant application will later be the primary target of cross-examination in court about the factual basis supporting issuance of the warrant, and how that basis amounted to credibly based probability. Without having been closely involved in the affidavit's preparation, an investigator is easy prey during cross-examination through tripping up with contradictions, revealing a faulty memory of the warrant's contents, or simply coming across to the court as not credible. If during testimony the affiant fails to demonstrate subjective belief in the warrant's contents, it is unlikely the court will find the warrant to be objectively reliable.

Knowing When You Have Grounds for a Warrant

Q & A

Q: Isn't knowing whether or not you have reasonable and probable grounds for a warrant always a guessing game, where justices and judges are more than willing to second-guess investigators and each other over whether sufficient grounds really exist?

A: That is an unjustifiably pessimistic view of the warrant issuing and reviewing legal system. Usually after a quick read through I can tell in advance whether or not a warrant will stand up at trial. The burden resting on the defence to show a warrant should not have been issued will be very difficult to meet where investigators have established detailed and lucidly presented facts supporting the warrant.

NINE FUNDAMENTAL PRINCIPLES FOR SEARCH WARRANT DRAFTING

Assuming you already have enough evidence to satisfy the credibly based probability test, if you follow these nine principles of search warrant and information to obtain drafting you should not have a problem either getting a warrant issued, or in having its validity later upheld at trial.

1. *Draft Defensively for the Trial, Not Just for the Search*

Draft your search warrant and supporting information to obtain as if they will later be attacked with vigour, skill and cunning. You will find it is much more difficult to later defend a weak warrant at trial than it was to get a judge or justice to sign the warrant authorizing the search in the first place. Many warrants are sought on an urgent basis, possibly in the middle of the night. What looked good on a hot summer night in a justice's cramped office right before a major takedown may not look so good on a cold winter day the following year in an expansive courtroom with the public looking on. The details in your documents will get picked apart at trial since there will be months or even years available to the defence to go over the warrant in preparation for the cross-examination of the investigator who swore the information to obtain.

2. State the Basis for Your Belief by Setting Out Facts, Not Just Conclusions

The most important warrant drafting error to avoid, and the most common reason I have seen time and time again for warrants being struck down at trial, is a failure by the affiant to detail the basis for his or her belief in reasonable and probable grounds of a thing, in a place, giving evidence of or otherwise connected to an offence. Demonstrating the reliability of the information on which the belief is based — especially when information has been received from informers — is where drafters often run into trouble. Frequently problems arise not because drafters possess insufficient facts to show reliability, but because they do not include all of those facts when setting out in writing the basis for that reliability.

The law requires all relevant and credible information go into the information to obtain. Avoiding conclusory statements also means avoiding overly summarizing the facts. Lay those facts out in boring detail — within reason. Background facts can be summarized a bit, but it is far better to err on the side of too much detail rather than too little. Crucial information could be left out because of a rush in assembling the warrant, the inexperience of the drafting investigator, or the compartmentalized nature of the investigation where all collected information has not been pooled at the time a warrant is put together. It is very difficult to remedy these kinds of omissions at the trial stage of a case where a warrant is challenged as having been issued on insufficient grounds — the doctrine of amplification might allow some missed information to come before the trial court, but don't count on it.

In order to develop this detail, you will need to thoroughly go through the investigative file and take into account all investigator notes, common file notes, video and audio recordings, written statements, physical evidence, and anything else credible and relevant in the possession of your investigative agency, weaving it all into the information to obtain. This process of gathering and setting out the facts requires including information that both supports and does not support the warrant. Relevant and credible information that does not favour the issuance of a warrant can be explained and its negative impact thus minimized, but it cannot just be ignored.

There are many cases out there where courts found an information to obtain an already granted and executed warrant did not set out sufficient reasonable and probable grounds for the warrant to have been legally authorized, like in *R. v. Turcotte* (1987), 60 Sask. R. 289 (C.A.) at para. 10:

> The informant says that on or about the 17th day of November A.D. 1985 at Regina in the Province of Saskatchewan, a brown leather brief case containing Amway booklets, papers and contracts for First Choice Enterprises, pocket calculator and one hundred (100) business cheques for First Choice Enterprises, the property of Ed KURTZ, of a value not exceeding two (2) hundred dollars, was unlawfully stolen contrary to Section 294(b) of the Criminal Code, and that he has reasonable grounds for believing that the said things, or some part of them are in the dwelling-house, outbuildings and vehicles of 1728 St. John St. of Regina, in the said province. Lewis Leon TURCOTTE, a resident of 1728 St.

> John Street was arrested while attempting to negotiate a First Choice Enterprises cheque at the Toronto Dominion Bank, Victoria Square Mall, Regina, Saskatchewan.

Here the court found there was no evidence supporting the belief that the stolen goods would be found at the house to be searched, nor any evidence connecting the named target Turcotte to the alleged offence, and the information to obtain the warrant did not specify that the cheque the target attempted to negotiate was one of the stolen cheques. The dots of the offence, the place to be searched, and the things to be searched for were all set out in the affidavit, but the warrant failed because its drafters never explicitly connected those dots for the court by setting out sufficient factual detail.

3. Use as Many Words as Necessary to Include All Relevant Details

Some informations to obtain warrants are over 100 pages long, while others are only a few pages in length. How voluminous that document needs to be depends on the nature of the investigation and the amount of relevant information investigators have amassed. In order for the information to obtain to be compelling, detail is required that shows possession of a constellation of credible information leading to the conclusion that there is a particular thing in a particular place connected to a particular offence. All observations made, documents inspected, tips received and background information known is included if it is relevant to establishing the basis for issuance of the warrant.

If, after you are finished drafting, the information to obtain is extremely brief then you should be asking yourself whether you have forgotten to include anything. Describing the dots of offence, place and things to be searched for may be able to be done in a couple of pages, but sufficiently connecting them will almost always make your document much longer. Rarely have I seen a warrant that is too detailed and lengthy. I have seen a lot that are cursory and too short.

4. Establish the Basis for Reliability of All Informers

Information received from informers often makes up a significant part of the information to obtain a search warrant. I have seen many warrant and wiretap applications supported in part by very problematic informer-based grounds like: "Source A, Source B and Source C, all of whom are confidential reliable sources, informed me that drugs were being sold from 123 Maple St. within the last 48 hours." But why does the person swearing to this affidavit believe these sources are reliable? How do the sources know that information? How is a judge to know if Sources A, B and C are even different people?

When informers are used as any part of the basis for a warrant, the information to obtain affidavit should, in offering a detailed explanation of why the affiant believes each source to be reliable, answer the three questions posed in *R. v. Debot*, [1989] 2 S.C.R. 1140 at 1168:

> First was the information predicting the commission of a criminal offence compelling? Second, where that information was based on a "tip" originating from a source outside the police, was that source credible? Finally, was the information corroborated by police investigation prior to making the decision to conduct the search? I do not suggest that each of these factors forms a separate test. Rather, I concur with Martin J.A.'s view that the "totality of the circumstances" must meet the standard of reasonableness. Weaknesses in one area may, to some extent, be compensated by strengths in the other two.

Keep this 3-C triumvirate of compelling, credible, and corroborated in mind any time you are evaluating informer information.

Failing to be forthright in establishing the basis for informer reliability can especially imperil the validity of a warrant, as happened in *R. v. Philpott* (2002), 101 C.R.R. (2d) 87 (Ont. S.C.) at paras. 161, 179, 188, & 190:

> The law must vigorously maintain the distinction between acting on a tip from a reliable source and acting on a tip from an unproven source. Where there are scanty particulars provided by a tipster and his or her reliability is unknown, a relatively thorough investigation is essential so as to provide that critically important ingredient — corroboration.
>
> . . .
>
> Because the application for a search warrant is made in camera or ex parte, there is an obligation on the police to make full disclosure. This would include disclosure of everything said by the tipster and everything done by the police in the way of subsequent investigation (with exceptions for minute or unimportant steps).

. . .

> The most glaring and disturbing instance of non-disclosure of a
> material nature is that the "information to obtain" made no men-
> tion of the fact that the tipster was in custody at the time he spoke
> to the sergeant . . . .

. . .

> the justice of the peace was provided with a distorted picture and
> His Worship might well have assumed that the tipster was a con-
> cerned citizen with no ulterior motive. Lacking information
> whether a "deal" was offered to or expected by the tipster, it was
> impossible for the justice of the peace to determine whether there
> was a motivation to lie.

Material non-disclosure about the circumstances of the informer led the
reviewing judge to quash the warrant and exclude all evidence seized under
it.

The investigator drafting a warrant application must balance the compet-
ing interests of protecting the identity of the informer, with a full and frank
disclosure of the details of informer reliability. An unidentified informer with
no articulated basis for belief, no matter how much detail that informer provides, will never be a sufficient basis for obtaining a judicial authorization
for a warrant or wiretap without additional corroboration, usually obtained
through other investigative means or other informers.

Referring to the material you input in the Informer Checklist, reproduced
earlier in Chapter 4, should aid your assessment of an informer. Disclosure
of informer reliability details, where informer privilege will not be com-
prised, includes those factors discussed below.

- *The Informer's Means of Knowledge.* How does the informer
  know what she claims to know? Is she socially connected in specific criminal circles? Is she involved in the same criminal activity? Does
  she live in the same residence as investigative targets? Articulation of
  means of knowledge may need to stay vague to protect identity, but
  is a very powerful indicator of reliability that must be addressed.

- *The Informer's Motives and Current Relationship with
  Investigators.* Is the informer getting paid? If so, what are the
  details of payment? Is there a contract between the investigators and
  the informer? If so, what are the details of the contract? What other
  reasons does the informer have for cooperating with investigators?
  Setting out why the informer is doing what she is doing is very

important to an assessment of reliability. Just because the informer is only in it for the money does not make her unreliable, but the court must know this information so that it can look at all the factors in drawing reliability conclusions.

- ***The Informer's Criminal Record.*** In order to protect identity you don't have to provide precise details about the informer's criminal record like exact offences or dates, but the number and type of convictions should be specified in the information to obtain, particularly for convictions involving offences of dishonesty or offences against the administration of justice. For example: "the informer has three convictions for trafficking in narcotics, all from more than ten years ago, and one more recent conviction for dangerous driving." If an informer has no criminal record, this is an important factor to note as it enhances reliability. Only selectively disclosing informer convictions in an information to obtain by saying something like "the informer has no record for obstructing justice" is not helpful, since the informer could still have convictions for offences like fraud or breach of trust that would equally have an adverse affect on reliability.

- ***The Informer's History of Involvement Assisting Law Enforcement.*** Without compromising identity, give a detailed history of the informer's involvement with other investigations including involvement with yourself, other informer handlers in your organization, and with other law enforcement agencies if possible. Include numbers and types of investigations, length of involvement, circumstances of involvement such as payment or volunteered information, whether the informer was involved in the offences that information was being provided on, the significance the information provided played in the overall investigations, and the results like discovery of evidence or arrests made. The provision of past reliable information is probably the best way of establishing an informer is credible in a current case. Do you plan to use the informer in the future, and why or why not?

- ***The Accuracy of Past Information Provided by the Informer.*** Was the informer's past information detailed or vague? Was it possible to corroborate the information? Did the information prove correct all, most, or some of the time? When errors were made, what were the reasons for those errors like honest mistake or falsehood?

- *The Informer's Powers of Observation.* How careful an observer is the informer when it comes to details, numbers, distinguishing hearsay from first-hand knowledge, and following the directions of handlers?

- *Corroboration of Current Information Received from the Informer.* Do not force the judge or justice considering an application for a warrant to figure out whether informer information is corroborated elsewhere in the information to obtain. Explicitly set out all corroborating links between relevant information an informer has provided with other information known to investigators, be it from other informers or independent investigation.

The Required Level of Informer Reliability

Q & A

Q: How reliable does an informer have to be so that I can refer to him or her as a reliable confidential source in an affidavit in support of a search warrant or electronic surveillance application?

A: Instead of referring to the informer as simply being "reliable" in a general way, give very specific examples of reliability with the conclusion stated that from these examples you believe the informer to be reliable. The term "reliable confidential source" has to be the most overused term in the warrant world, and is devoid of meaning without supporting facts.

5. Make It Readable

Making a warrant and information to obtain readable means paying attention to the flow of the "story" and its organization. At worst, it should be possible to get through the story without being frustrated about the impossibly confusing plot, being unable to understand which characters engage in which actions, or failing to get the point of the story. Many drafts of an information to obtain a warrant may be necessary to have a well written story.

Follow these tips for warrant and information to obtain readability faithfully, and your prose will leap off the page with pizzazz:

- readability has nothing to do with legal skills, and everything to do with language skills;

- divide the overall warrant application into three sections:

     A — Description of People and Offences

     B — Description of Things to be Searched For and Place to be Searched

     C — Information Supporting the Basis for Belief;

- use introductory and concluding paragraphs to summarize the contents of the information to obtain;

- headings within the information to obtain are a great aid to readability that impose organization on your thoughts, make clear why information in a particular section is important, and permit the reader to recognize the interrelationships among sub-sections like:

     1. Background of Investigation
          a. *First Observations Conducted*
          b. *Initial Informer Tip Received*
          c. *Basis for Credibility of Informer*
     2. Current Status of Investigation;

- use short sentences;

- use short, consecutively numbered paragraphs throughout — restarting paragraph numbers with each new section leads to later confusion in court when the lawyers and judge are trying to navigate through the document by paragraph number;

- writing in the third-person is too confusing, instead always write in the first person as if you were testifying in court by saying "I met with the agent on . . ." instead of "the affiant/informant met with the agent on . . .";

- do not unduly repeat phrases, use overblown terms, or employ unnecessary words — always ask yourself, "is this word really necessary, and how does it advance what I am trying to say?";

- the most overused and unnecessary word is "said," like "the said informer" — while "said" used to have an honoured place in the legal vocabulary, what is known as the Plain Language legal movement now advocates a simpler and easier to understand style of legal writing;

- quote short statements verbatim, instead of paraphrasing them;

- using point form in some places makes sense, like when enumerating lists;

- define your terms;

- it is generally better to put in too much detail, rather than too little, but don't be repetitive and don't put in completely irrelevant details;

- synthesize the relevant information in your possession, don't just string together a series of notes;

- set out your information chronologically or thematically, but do *not* group it according to the source you received it from as that can lead to a jumbled picture where the reader has to fit the pieces of the puzzle together;

- the goal is to produce a warrant and information to obtain that can be understood after reading them once, in a fairly rapid manner.

6. Spelling and Grammar Count

Correct spelling and grammar throughout the warrant and information to obtain is fundamental to having credibility before any court. While this point may appear self-evident, there are countless examples of rushed warrant applications having atrocious spelling and grammar that both distract from the substance of the application, and leave one wondering if that substance can be trusted. If you are so careless that you don't bother correcting your spelling and grammar, a court will wonder what other details of the case you also may have been careless about.

There is one simple maxim that solves spelling problems: if in doubt, look it up. Electronic on-line dictionaries and thesauruses (a few of which are listed at the end of this chapter) greatly simplify spelling corrections and choosing the right word in the first place. Getting grammar just right is a little trickier, but carefully reading through each sentence to determine if it "sounds right" is a start; checking a reference work is better. Probably the best way to immeasurably improve your grammatical presentation in any document is to focus on punctuation.

Periods, commas, colons, semi-colons and dashes all need to be carefully placed. One comma can make the difference between: "the drugs were delivered, from Smith I got information" as compared to "the drugs were delivered from Smith, I got information." Leaving out apostrophes when you need them ("the informers vehicle"), or putting them in when you don't ("the vehicles belonging to the informer's") likewise conveys a message that you don't really care about what goes in your written material. If in doubt, shorten up your sentences with more periods, make your sentences flow more easily with fewer commas, avoid colons and especially semi-colons unless you know what you are doing, and employ the odd dash to improve meaning instead of going overboard with brackets or parentheses.

Do not rely solely on computer spelling or grammar checkers. Computer aids are a good start, but are not yet at a fully reliable level. They sometimes have problems distinguishing among British, Canadian and American spellings, occasionally miss misspelled words, will tell you some correct words are misspelled or ungrammatical, and are poor at picking up typing mistakes that are actually words like "bed revertible" instead of the "red convertible" you intended. The best advice I can offer on eliminating spelling and grammar errors is the same advice for eliminating any other kind of warrant error — carefully proofread every warrant and information to obtain that you draft, and ask at least one other person to look over the application as well for errors. You may still not wind up with a 100% error free application, but any errors should amount at worst to minor blemishes rather than dark stains.

7. Include and Abide by Other Details

a. *Time of Execution: Keep Your Eye on the Clock*

Specify the date and time during which the search warrant is to be executed. Usually a time of between 9 a.m. and 5 p.m. and one particular date will be used. A warrant can authorize a search at any time, even over a multi-day period, but the information to obtain the warrant must contain information justifying the necessity of a search outside of a normal timeframe. Section 488 of the *Criminal Code* imposes explicit time of day execution limitations on regular s. 487 search and seizure warrants and s. 487.1 telewarrants:

> **488.** A warrant issued under section 487 or 487.1 shall be executed by day, unless
>
> > (a) the justice is satisfied that there are reasonable grounds for it to be executed by night;
> >
> > (b) the reasonable grounds are included in the information; and
> >
> > (c) the warrant authorizes that it be executed by night.

Even though legislation authorizing other *Code* or non-*Code* warrants, and the case law interpreting that legislation, may not require explicit justification for searches outside normal daytime hours (see *R. v. Saunders* (2003), 232 Nfld. & P.E.I.R. 22; 2003 NLCA 63, leave to appeal refused [2004] 3 S.C.R. 505, for such an interpretation of s. 11 of the *Controlled Drugs and Substances Act* (*CDSA*)), it is still good practice to offer that justification since case law has not considered all types of warrants on this point. Nighttime warrant execution could be justified by informer information supporting that to be the only time stolen goods will be at a particular address, or an especially long duration warrant could be justified by explaining how tens of thousands of records must be examined during the search to locate the documents sought. A search must stop at the time a warrant expires, however an extension of that time could be sought from the issuing court.

b. *Place of Execution: Get the Description Right*

The place of execution for a search warrant must be precisely described, and all places to be searched covered by the scope of the warrant. In an urban area, this can be done through naming a street address in the warrant, and explaining in the information to obtain the factual basis for targeting that location. If a particular unit or apartment is to be searched at a larger address, a number or description of the unit must be given. The goal is always to keep the description of the search target location as narrow as possible, since a spatially limited search will later be easier to justify if challenged at trial than a much broader search that ranged across several units in one building, or several buildings on one property.

For rural areas provide a lot number and give a detailed physical description of the property in the warrant if street addresses are not in common use. Check the local registry of deeds and land surveys to avoid executing a warrant on a piece of property that is in fact adjacent to the property named in the warrant. The safest solution when the precise boundaries of a target property cannot be accurately determined without undertaking a formal survey is to seek a warrant with a broad area of search that encompasses all of the properties surrounding the target area, but which is limited to a search of the land and possibly outbuildings, and does not include dwelling places with their greater privacy interests. A subsequent warrant could always be sought to go after one dwelling place that becomes the focus of the investigation based on information gathered during execution of the broader warrant.

Clearly state in the information to obtain if the place to be searched is a dwelling house, or some kind of unconventional dwelling place like a boat or warehouse. Because of the greater privacy interest in all types of dwelling places, the legislation providing warrant powers may require announcement prior to entry by those executing such a warrant. Seek explicit authorization in the warrant for no prior announcement only if you can justify that omission.

Separate warrants are not needed for commonly owned and used buildings on a single piece of land targeted by a warrant (like a barn, garage or garden shed behind a house), but all buildings ideally should be described in the original warrant under places to be searched. General language like "and all structures located on the property" can be acceptable to avoid naming all of them, but the only way to completely prevent trial arguments over where the warrant did and did not apply is to list all of the places to be searched. The safest course of action to deal with previously unknown buildings that are discovered during the search of a property is to seek an additional warrant; there is an especially high risk of later evidence exclusion if an unknown building turns out to be a dwelling place whose search you have not justified in the original warrant.

Executing a warrant on the wrong address can be fatal to a search, as happened in *Sieger v. Avery* (1982), 34 B.C.L.R. 354 (S.C.) at paras. 5 & 7-8:

> Somewhere between 5:00 a.m. and 7:00 a.m. on 10th December 1981 four of the named . . . constables gained entrance through an unlocked front door of the premises at 523 Corbett Street. The house was in darkness. In a bedroom the officers "encountered" a male and a female in bed. The female was the petitioner, Colleen Avery. The male identified himself and informed the officers that Mr. Sieger lived next door!
>
> . . .
>
> The officers then withdrew and ascertained that the residence next door was 517 Corbett Street.
>
> Constable B. . . returned to his detachment office and telephoned the justice of the peace to advise that "the wrong number was on the warrant, and that I wished to have the warrant amended". The justice of the peace instructed him to come to her home. He then amended the warrant by striking out "523" and adding "517" and went to her residence. The justice of the peace confirms Constable B. . .'s evidence in this connection and initialled the change of address. She was not told that the warrant had already been executed. No oath was administered to Constable B. . . at that time.

The court held that at the very least the affiant on the warrant needed to swear a new oath as to the basis for his belief in the new address for the warrant, which he did not do, and so the warrant was quashed as not legally authorizing a search of the target location.

While in *Sieger* the court did not insist that a completely new warrant be obtained where an attempt to execute the old one had already been made, in *R. v. Silverstone* (1991), 2 B.C.A.C. 195 at para. 43, the executing officers realized their address mistake before entering a search site:

> I have concluded that in entering the duplex at 215 East 21st Avenue, knowing that he had a warrant for only 217 East 21st Avenue, Constable M. . . made a deliberate mistake which could, and should, have been avoided. Constable M. . . should have temporarily called off the search and applied for a second search warrant; subsequent events showed that this could have been accomplished easily and quickly.

Because they realized their mistake prior to execution, the court concluded a new warrant was needed — although all this would have required was changing the address in the warrant, adding a line to the information to obtain confirming that the address was now understood to be 215 East 21st Avenue because of the attendance there earlier in the day, reswearing the information to obtain affidavit, and asking a judge or justice to issue another warrant on that basis.

Unlike outbuildings that can all be included in a single warrant, vehicles come and go. Instead of trying to include all the vehicles found on a target property in a single search warrant, I urge you to seek separate warrants for each vehicle to be searched. The mere presence of third-party vehicles at a property search scene likely would not by itself justify their search. Failure to specify particular vehicles and justify their search during the search of a dwelling house, either as part of the dwelling house warrant or in separate warrants, can lead to exclusion of all evidence seized from such vehicles as in *R. v. Nguyen* (2004), 200 B.C.A.C. 59; 2004 BCCA 230 at paras. 20-22:

> On the face of the warrant I do not, with respect, see how it is possible to find that it authorized the search of a motor vehicle. The warrant recites that there are reasonable grounds to believe that evidence of an offence under the *Controlled Drugs and Substances Act* are "in a place, namely the dwelling house . . . ." The authority is "to enter the said place . . . ." The antecedent of place is clearly the dwelling house. That language cannot be stretched to include a vehicle.

Neither can it be said that the Information to Obtain provides a context for giving an expansive reading to the warrants such that it can include the Honda. There is reference in the Information to Obtain to the Pontiac but to no other vehicle.

Thus the search was not authorized by law: either by the warrant or by reason of exigent circumstances or a search incidental to an arrest. The appellant was not arrested at the time of the searches. It must follow in my judgment that the search of the vehicle violated s. 8.

Separate warrants permit specifically targeted vehicles to be stopped and searched wherever they are found if no longer located on the target property at the time of warrant execution.

What to Do with a Wrong Address in a Warrant

Q: What should I do if when I arrive at the target location to execute a warrant I realize the address appearing on the warrant is in fact for the house next door to the residence we want to search? Should I simply change the address by writing in the correct one, and proceed with the search?

A: Although any error in a warrant can jeopardize its validity, getting the address wrong is a particularly serious error. Your options are to seek out the issuing judge or justice and amend the defective warrant or get a new one. You can get a new warrant (which might be a telewarrant because of urgency) from a different judge or justice so long as you disclose the history of the first warrant. Where there is some delay in the arrival of a new or amended warrant, using powers of investigative detention or arrest might be justifiable to prevent destruction of evidence.

c. Name Persons Authorized under the Warrant

A specific person or persons who are to execute a warrant should usually be named in it. Those persons must meet the qualifications for the type of warrant, like being a peace officer or wildlife officer appointed to enforce an Act under which the warrant is sought in a particular province or territory. While some Acts may not explicitly require naming an executing investigator, courts might imply that requirement and there are enough wording variations in different Acts that naming is always a good idea.

The rationale for naming one of the investigators who will participate in the warrant's execution is so that someone is directly accountable to the authorizing court as noted in *R. v. Genest*, [1989] 1 S.C.R. 59 at 87:

> The naming requirement ensures that there is at least one officer who is responsible for the search, who must be personally present and must supervise the search. Because of the greater infringement of the individual's interests caused by the extensive power to search a dwelling-house, some officer must be accountable for the way the search is carried out.

But not all investigators who will execute the warrant need be named in the warrant, so long as at least one named person is clearly in charge according to *R. v. Fekete* (1985), 7 O.A.C. 152 at para. 12:

> it follows as a matter of common sense that if a power of search and seizure is conferred upon a named officer he is entitled to enlist aid in the execution of this power. That is not to say that he may assign or delegate this power, only that he may execute his power assisted by others. The fact of assistance does not change the essential fact that it remains the search and seizure of the named peace officer.

The best practice is to name a few investigators who may be involved in the warrant's execution, assisted by other unnamed peace officers, so that if one of the named investigators is unavailable at the time of warrant execution there can still be at least one named investigator present at the search site.

Since warrants do not give the state *carte blanche* to run amok in private premises, the people who are authorized to enter under a warrant are strictly limited. Television news crews cannot accompany police executing a search warrant at a residence, and the police agreeing to be so accompanied was found in *R. v. West* (1997), 100 B.C.A.C. 36 at paras. 19, 22 & 24-25, to be highly abusive:

> what happened here, therefore, was the state assisting the media to film the inside of a private residence where the media had no right to be . . . A search in these circumstances was unreasonable because it exceeded the authority of the warrant and it violated, for no investigatory or juridical purpose, the highest possible privacy interest of the accused in the security of his residence . . . it is unthinkable that officers of the state would undertake a search, even though they had a warrant, when they knew the inside of a private residence would be filmed and probably broadcast to the public. Even worse was the failure of the police to exclude the media and its cameras from filming and entering the accused's residence.

> . . .

> Our private residences are the places where we have the highest possible expectation of privacy against all intrusions except those authorized by law. The importance of all this is demonstrated when one thinks for a moment of the affront to democracy and decency if, as is sometimes the case, a search warrant is issued against an innocent person and a search of his or her residence is conducted with media coverage such as occurred in this case.

R. v. Strachan, [1988] 2 S.C.R. 980, mentioned in Chapter 7, did establish that investigators could take along technical support personnel to assist at a warrant execution, but only if the investigators named in the warrant are clearly in charge of the search.

d. *Detail is Needed in the List of Things to Be Searched For*

Although a detailed list of the things to be searched for must be included in the warrant, the list should *not* include things for which there is no reasonable belief that they either will be found in the premises to be searched or will afford evidence of an offence. You cannot simply reuse the same laundry list of things to be searched for in every search warrant application you produce. A brainstorming session among investigators to come up with all the things that need to be included in the things to be searched for list can be helpful. Remember that you have to say the things described "will afford evidence" of the listed offences, *not* "may" or "could" afford evidence.

The law requires detailed descriptions of the things to be searched for to prevent investigators from seizing everything found at a search site and later sifting through it all at a leisurely pace back in a secure facility in order to segregate the relevant from the irrelevant. Investigators executing a warrant must be able to quickly determine from checking the warrant's language whether something is or is not seizeable. It is the issuing court, and not the investigators, who has the discretion over what can and cannot be seized. Investigators must prepare a compelling information to obtain containing credible and sufficient facts to convince a court to authorize the search and seizure of all items contained in the list of things to be searched for.

The degree of specificity required in the list of things to be searched for depends on the breadth of the class of things described. For instance, saying "purchase invoices, sales invoices, cheques, bank statements, account books, inventory lists and all other documents related to the operation of ABC Realty Inc." will only be a sufficient description if the things to be searched for are (1) described in as much detail as the affiant's knowledge will permit, (2) identified by class, type or time frame, and (3) not left to the discretion of investigators at the time the warrant is executed. However, there is no need to name each individual document or item if a great deal of material is being searched for and it is really only possible to describe that material by class. Be as specific in the list as you reasonably can be.

Documents to be searched for and seized must be specified not only by their subject, but also by date range relevant for seizure. The narrower the time frame sought, the easier it will be to provide facts justifying it. The justification could be provided through the time period over which the alleged offences were committed, or through a technical explanation of an accountant as a sub-affiant that a longer time frame is needed to be able to fully appreciate the financial position and transaction history of a business.

e. *Properly Describe the Offences*

The offences detailed in a search warrant need not be the same as the offences eventually charged, but the offences referred to in the warrant should be drafted in the same way as would charges on an information laid against an accused. Name the Act and section contravened, the names of the accused (if known), and the place and date of the offences. All offences for which reasonable and probable grounds exist are normally listed in a warrant application, however there could be reasons not to list all of them so long as no attempt at deception is made. All persons who are believed on reasonable and probable grounds to have committed an offence need not be named at this point, but naming them is a good practice unless it would somehow compromise the investigation. Ideally at least one person should be named who can form a link to a place to be searched and things to be searched for, but the identity of potential accused can be uncertain at the search stage.

8. Use the Right Form and Statutory Provisions

Matters of both form and substance are important where search warrants are concerned. The *Criminal Code* and other Acts do not require much mandatory language in a warrant, but what is specified must be there. Some Acts specify a form to use for a warrant, while others only specify warrant requirements in the statutory provisions. Any form must be interpreted in light of an Act's provisions governing warrants, since all essential elements will be specified in the provisions but might not appear in a sample form that is only there to give the most general of guidance on drafting as confirmed in *R. v. Saunders* (2003), 232 Nfld. & P.E.I.R. 22; 2003 NLCA 63 at paras. 25-26, leave to appeal refused [2004] 3 S.C.R. 505:

> Where, however, Parliament otherwise authorizes the issuing of a search warrant, as it has by section 11 of the *CDSA* and by other provisions of the *Criminal Code*, the requirements for its issue must be determined by reference to the specific statutory provisions relied upon as authority for issuing the warrant being sought.
>
> Section 11 of the *CDSA* contains comprehensive provisions respecting the issuing and execution of search warrants. Unlike section 487 of the *Criminal Code*, it does not specify a form which may be used or varied to suit the circumstance.

Investigators confusing s. 487 *Code* and s. 11 *CDSA* warrants is a common problem, resulting in situations like the one in *R. v. Schedel* (2003), 184 B.C.A.C. 166; 2003 BCCA 364 at para. 18:

> As the trial judge remarked in his reasons, some of the officers involved in the search were surprisingly vague about the distinction between the search warrant provisions of the *Code* and the *Drug Act*. In relation to that, it is of some interest that four of the officers engaged in this raid were aware that the warrant was issued under the *Code*, while the other four thought they were acting under the *Drug Act*.

You need to remain aware of the differences among warrant powers present in different Acts in order to accomplish valid searches and seizures.

9. Consider Sealing and Assistance Orders

a. *The Impermanency of Sealing Orders*

A sealing order can be sought under s. 487.3 of the *Criminal Code* for a warrant issued under *any* federal Act, with the order application either rolled up as part of the application for the warrant, or made separately at a later time. If the warrant and sealing are pursued as a package, then the information to obtain the warrant will have to specify the grounds justifying the sealing, and the warrant itself will contain the order for sealing. If a separate sealing application is brought, an affidavit in support of that application, a notice of application and a separate order seeking the sealing must also be filed.

In justifying sealing, s-s. 487.3(2) of the *Code* requires the supporting affidavit to establish that the ends of justice would be subverted by the disclosure of the warrant and information to obtain because it would:

- compromise the identity of a confidential informer;

- compromise the nature and extent of an ongoing investigation;

- endanger a person engaged in particular intelligence gathering techniques, thereby prejudicing future investigations in which similar techniques would be used;

- prejudice the interests of an innocent person;

- be used for an improper purpose; or

- any other sufficient reasons.

In addition, the enumerated interests justifying sealing must outweigh other interests in access to the information. The affidavit supporting the application for the sealing order needs to lay out one or more of the six interests listed, point to specific facts or past experience supporting belief in those interests, and then explain why the interests are of great importance.

Toronto Star Newspapers v. Ontario (2003), 178 O.A.C. 60 at paras. 18-19, stressed the reasons to apply a strict test when seeking and maintaining a sealing order:

> Once a search warrant is executed and something has been seized pursuant to that search warrant, the warrant and the information to obtain the warrant are available to the public unless a party seeking a sealing order can demonstrate that public access would subvert the ends of justice . . . .The narrow grounds upon which a sealing order may be obtained and the requirement that the sealing order be carefully tailored so as to minimize restriction on public access are demonstrated in s. 487.3 of the *Criminal Code* . . . .
>
> The importance of freedom of expression, including freedom of the press, is obvious. The significant intrusion on that freedom effected by sealing orders such as the order in issue here cannot be minimized. It is the importance of the freedom infringed by this sealing order and the significance of the contemplated infringement that combine to require that any request seeking an order sealing court documents must be subject to close scrutiny and meet rigorous standards.

It is very difficult to maintain sealing beyond the point at which charges are laid because disclosure obligations kick in. Sometimes it is possible to do court supervised editing of the unsealed material prior to disclosure, but interests in full and frank disclosure could outweigh sealing interests at this point.

Sealing cannot be relied upon as a perfect tool to indefinitely protect the identity of a confidential informer. Instead, don't include informer identifying material in the information to obtain a warrant in the first place. A compromise has to be struck between including detail sufficient to establish a informer's reliability, and not including so much detail as to reveal informer identity. Sealing a warrant is most useful when investigators do not wish investigative targets to know the full extent of an on-going investigation, and so need temporary protection for undercover investigators, informers or investigation plans.

b. *The Propriety of Assistance Orders*

Assistance orders most commonly compel third parties who are not targets of an investigation to produce certain items sought under a s. 487.01 *Criminal Code* general warrant whose location is not known to investigators although s. 487.02 *Code* assistance orders can compel assistance with *any* type of *Code* warrant or wiretap:

> **487.02.** Where an authorization is given under section 184.2, 184.3, 186 or 188, a warrant is issued under this Act or an order is made under subsection 492.2(2), the judge or justice who gives the authorization, issues the warrant or makes the order may order any person to provide assistance, where the person's assistance may reasonably be considered to be required to give effect to the authorization, warrant or order.

Without a s. 487.02 assistance order, a warrant or authorization might have no life as explained in *Canada Post Corp. v. Canada (Attorney General)* (1995), 95 C.C.C. (3d) 568 (Ont. C.J.(Gen. Div)) at para 19:

> In my view, the order of assistance attached to the warrant does not exceed the bounds of s. 487.02 of the *Criminal Code*. It is within the letter and spirit of the section; it allows the police to utilize an investigative technique to obtain information which, if not authorized, might constitute unreasonable search of a person's property. In my view, without the assistance order, the warrant would be reduced to words on paper; it would be devoid of any ability to accomplish its purpose. It would be useless as a device or investigative technique. The order for assistance breathes life and muscle into the frame of the Second Warrant.

The assistance order is not, however, a stand-alone compulsion power similar to those available to pursue compliance verification of regulatory matters. It only helps with implementation of a judicially authorized search, like through compelling a person to assist with the installation of a wiretap.

HOW TO AVOID DRAFTING CONFUSION

With all the talk in the *Criminal Code* and other Acts of reasonable suspicion, reasonable belief, reasonable grounds, reasonable and probable grounds, proof on a balance of probabilities, and proof beyond a reasonable doubt, it is easy to become confused about what standard of proof is applicable to the authorization of a desired investigative technique. It is likewise easy even for experienced investigators to become confused by the multiple forms, wording variations and approval standards applicable to different types of judicial authorizations. Well intentioned investigators may still wind up relying on defective past precedents, demonstrating it is best to build each warrant application from the ground up avoiding dreaded "boilerplate" language. Embracing the demystification of the law and early investigator-prosecutor contact themes is the only way to be relatively certain that a warrant will stand up to challenge at trial.

Following the Search Warrant and Information to Obtain Checklist, at the end of this chapter, should prevent major errors in the form or content of a warrant or information to obtain. Demystification of the law teaches that the legal standard for an investigative technique will always be clearly stated in the section of the Act authorizing that technique and that if a particular form is required it too will be specified. Early investigator-prosecutor contact should resolve cases of doubtful drafting, and serve as a final check for a warrant that investigators are confident has been drafted correctly.

Drafting confusion over even one word can invalidate an entire warrant. In *R. v. Guilbride* (2003), 10 C.R. (6th) 243; 2003 BCPC 177 at para. 14, investigators became confused about the legal test to be applied to link the belief in offences to the belief that evidence would be found in the target search location:

> AND UPON BEING SATISFIED that there are *reasonable grounds to believe* offences contrary to the *Controlled Drugs and Substances Act* and the *Criminal Code of Canada* have been or will be committed and that *information that is relevant to the commission of these offences could be obtained* through the covert entry and search of the residence and the business known as Black Nugget Museum located at 12 Gatacre Street in the City of Ladysmith, Province of British Columbia.

The court found the use of the word "could" concerning whether relevant evidence would be found at the proposed search site, rather than using the word "will," meant the investigator swearing the information to obtain the warrant and the justice issuing it may have proceeded on a reasonable suspicion instead of reasonable and probable grounds standard, and therefore the warrant was invalid. Confusion could have been avoided through the demystification of the law technique of closely reading the applicable legislation in s. 487.01 of the *Code* that specifies the words "will be" as the required standard, and directly copying those words from the legislation into the warrant application.

Who Should be Drafting Warrant Documents

Q & A

Q: It seems to me that lawyers know more than investigators about the legal requirements for a valid warrant. Wouldn't it be a lot quicker if a lawyer simply wrote up the warrant and information to obtain, and then I swore to it when the lawyer was finished?

A: You may need the assistance of a lawyer on some of the technical points, but the warrant and information to obtain documents you prepare contain your own story, and must be in your own words if you are going to survive extensive trial cross-examination over their contents. The vast majority of an information to obtain is factual, not legal, and you already know the facts of your investigation better than any lawyer will.

TECHNIQUES FOR SPOTTING WARRANT ERRORS

In order to test yourself on your understanding of the points outlined in this chapter, here is a hypothetical sample search warrant and information to obtain combining several deficiencies. Assume you have been asked by a colleague to review the warrant shortly before it is taken to a court for authorization. The language is closely modeled on warrants I have come across that not only were issued and executed, but made it right to the point of trial before running into serious difficulties. See how many problems you can spot, and how you would suggest fixing those problems. You may wish to try the Search Warrant and Information to obtain Checklist with this sample warrant. The material with an "XXX" through it is information your colleague believes would reveal source identity, and thus, although to be included in the application to the court, is proposed to be deleted prior to disclosure and trial.

FORM 5 — WARRANT TO SEARCH
(Section 487)

Canada,

Province of Prince Edward Island

To the peace officers of Prince Edward Island:

Whereas it appears on the oath of Constable Guy Smith of Pleasantville, Prince Edward Island, that there are reasonable grounds for believing that controlled drugs and related paraphernalia are in the premises and vehicle of Shamus Jones, hereinafter called the premises;

This is therefore, to authorize and require you to enter into the said premises between 9 o'clock and 4 o'clock and search for the said things and to bring them before me or some other justice.

Date this 26th day of April, 2006, at Pleasantville, Prince Edward Island.

_____

A Justice of the Peace in and for Prince Edward Island.

APPENDIX "A"

Constable Guy Smith, hereinafter referred to as the informant, is a member of the Queen's County Regional Police stationed in Pleasantville, Prince Edward Island. As such I have personal knowledge of all information relating to this investigation and where information is received from a confidential source I verily believe the information to be true.

Cst. Smith has been stationed in Pleasantville for app. 2 1/2 years and has received information during the past year from sources that Shamus Jones is dealing drugs in the Pleasantville area. He sells drugs from his residence in Pleasantville. On 2004-09-04 Shamus Jones was charged with possession of a controlled substance sec 4(1) CDSA and a stay of proceedings was entered in relation to the charge on 05-05-05.

On September 23, 2005, Cst. B. Rowe of the Queen's County Regional Police received information from a confidential human source, hereinafter referred to as Source A. Source advised that Shamus Jones supplies several persons with drugs and they in turn sell the drugs to area residents as well as one high school.

On October 25th, 2005, Cst. Smith of the Queen's County Regional Police received information from a confidential human source hereinafter referred to as Source B. Source advised that Shamus Jones is selling drugs from his apartment in Pleasantville.

On April 24th, 2006, Cst. G. Smith of the Queen's County Regional Police received information from a confidential human source, hereinafter referred to as Source C. Source advised that Shamus Jones is growing marijuana plants in his upstairs apartment. XXXXXXXXXXXXXXXXXXXXXXXXXXXXXXXXXXXXXXXXXXXXXXX XXXXXXXXXXXXXXXXXXXXXXXXXXXXXXXXXXXXX.

Source C also advised that the windows are covered with garbage bags and that they were cracked open XXXXXXXXXXXXXXXXXX XXXXXXXXXXXXXXXXXXXXXXXXXXXXXXXXXXXXXXXXXXXXXXX XXXXXXXXXXXXXXXXXXXXXXXXXXXXXXXXXXXXXXXXXXXXXXX XXXXXXXXXXXXXXXXXXXXX.

On April 15, 2006, Cst. Smith and Cpl. White made a patrol by the apartment building and noted the windows covered and several slightly open as described by Source C.

Selected Errors in the Warrant to Search

- Although reference is made to "s. 487" and "Form 5," the warrant should explicitly refer to the Act and section it is being sought under, preferably being s. 11 of the *CDSA* since it is predominantly targeting evidence of drug offences.

- The warrant does not name an offence for which there are reasonable grounds to believe has been committed.

- The things to be searched for are far too vague.

- The place to be searched is also far too vague, with no address or other means of limiting where the search will take place, plus the vehicle needs to be much more precisely identified and should likely be the subject of a separate warrant.

- The times for execution are stated in a confusing way that require clarification, and the warrant should also preferably set out specific dates for its validity.

- The warrant ideally should have at least one named officer responsible for its execution, in addition to other peace officers of Prince Edward Island.

Selected Errors in the Information to Obtain

- Where is the sworn information to obtain? This is only an Appendix, which is not even mentioned in the warrant.

- There is no reference justifying an address or description of the search location.

- Reference to the prior charge leading to a stay is irrelevant.

- Mixing of the 1st person and 3rd person writing perspective in the same document is confusing — only the easier to understand 1st person should be used.

- The affiant seems to be claiming personal knowledge of everything — more particulars are necessary in specifying the sources of information.

- It is not made clear whether the three sources are three different people.

- No basis for source reliability is articulated — the basis for each source's information needs to be shown to be beyond mere gossip and rumour.

- There were no attempts by investigators to corroborate the source information, other than one drive by of the target's residence.

- The information to obtain should have been drafted in a way that no information needs to be blacked-out for disclosure and trial. Here, deletions from what is already a very skimpy document jeopardize upholding the warrant at trial.

- Much of the information given is out of date.

- Overall, this is a very vague information to obtain a warrant.

Using Precedents to Draft Warrants

Q&A

Q: There are a couple of search warrant precedents in the office that we have been using for years. Recently a judge struck down a warrant based on these precedents, but we are still using them since we don't know what else to do. Do you think we could lose another warrant this way, or was this some kind of fluke where the judge was having an off day?

A: Stop using the precedents right now. They may never have been any good in the first place. I have even seen defective warrant precedents included in training materials. You need to start from scratch in putting together new precedent documents. The time you spend doing so will pay off hundreds of times over in the future. List out the warrant preconditions in the governing Act, ask other detachments of investigators or your headquarters for precedents they recommend, see if a prosecutor can help you revise your materials, and work up a new precedent based on the principles articulated in this book.

PROPERLY EXECUTING THE WARRANT

Properly executing a search or seizure warrant means complying with the legal requirements of the *Charter*, the common law, the Act under which the warrant was issued, and the warrant itself. A search warrant must be in the possession of the investigator executing it, unless it is a telewarrant. For dwelling houses, a demand for entry must be made prior to execution (at least in the case of *Criminal Code* warrants), unless the warrant explicitly waives this obligation. The executing investigator must produce the warrant to the person occupying the location being searched, and permit that person to examine the warrant. The terms of the warrant specifying where investigatiors may search for evidence, what kinds of evidence may be seized, and to what offences that evidence may relate all must be respected. Only reasonable force can be used in the execution of a warrant. Any evidence seized during the execution of an otherwise valid warrant may wind up being excluded at trial if the court finds the warrant to have been executed contrary to the law.

For instance, failure to make prior announcement was found to be a serious breach of *Charter* rights justifying exclusion of evidence in *R. v. Schedel*, 12 C.R. (6th) 207, 2003 BCCA 364 at para. 45, which quoted with approval from W.T. Oppal, *Closing the Gap: Policing and the Community — The Recommendations* (Victoria, BC: Commission of Inquiry into Police in British Columbia, 1992):

> Most people are aware of the instruments of force available to police, and the need to avoid even presenting the appearance of danger to entering officers. The knock-notice rule permits the householder, such as the young man shot in the 1992 drug raid, to prepare to be safely detained or arrested and to put down toy guns, channel changers, or other objects that have the potential to mistakenly signal life-threatening danger to the entering police officers.

> In general, the safety of the police is also enhanced by compliance with the knock-notice rule. People are much less likely to act violently toward police when, before entering, they announce their presence, authority and purpose. This tells the householder not only that the police, as statutory peacekeepers, are present, but also that this specific police attendance has been explicitly authorized by a judicial official.

Exceeding what amounts to reasonable force while executing a warrant can also amount to an abuse, as *R. v. Genest*, [1989] 1 S.C.R. 59 at 89, confirmed:

> whether the circumstances of the case show a real threat of violent behaviour, whether directed at the police or third parties. Obviously, the police will use a different approach when the suspect is known to be armed and dangerous than they will in arresting someone for outstanding traffic tickets. The consideration of the possibility of violence must, however, be carefully limited. It should not amount to a

carte blanche for the police to ignore completely all restrictions on police behaviour. The greater the departure from the standards of behaviour required by the common law and the Charter, the heavier the onus on the police to show why they thought it necessary to use force in the process of an arrest or a search. The evidence to justify such behaviour must be apparent in the record, and must have been available to the police at the time they chose their course of conduct. The Crown cannot rely on ex post facto justifications.

Over-seizure is another form of potential abuse where irrelevant classes of material need to be avoided, and accidental seizure of the irrelevant must be remedied by returning the material as soon as reasonably possible unless there is other applicable authority like common law plain view or s. 489 *Criminal Code* authority to seize things believed on reasonable grounds to be evidence of any federal offence. Drafting and executing a bullet-proof warrant is even more of a challenge where the "special places" discussed in the next chapter are the targets of search and seizure.

For Drafting and Executing a Bullet-Proof Warrant

KEY POINTS

✓ The three duties of investigators seeking warrants are full and frank disclosure before the warrant is issued, respectful and non-abusive execution of the warrant, and post-seizure care, reporting and application for detention of anything seized.

✓ Reasonable and probable grounds for a warrant require subjective and objective credibly based probability that is more than mere suspicion but less than certainty that evidence or something relevant to an offence is in a particular place.

✓ The fundamental principles of warrant drafting include draft defensively, state the basis for your belief, use as many words as are necessary, establish the basis for reliability of all informers, make it readable, spelling and grammar count, include and abide by other details, use the right form and statutory provisions, and consider sealing and assistance orders. Specific details to address on the face of the warrant and support in the information to obtain include the time of execution, the place of execution, naming persons authorized to execute the warrant, the list of things to be searched for, and a proper description of the offences.

✓ The reviewing trial judge is much more likely to find fault with a warrant than is the issuing judge or justice, so carefully check a warrant and supporting information to obtain for errors before seeking to have it issued.

KEY POINTS

✓ Properly executing a warrant generally requires that it be in possession of the investigator executing it, a demand for entry be made prior to execution at a dwelling house, the warrant be produced to the occupant of the target premises and that person be permitted to inspect the warrant, and that the terms of the warrant limiting what can be searched for, where it can be searched for, and what offences it relates to are respected.

REASONABLE AND PROBABLE GROUNDS (RPG) THRESHOLD CHECKLIST

A   RPG TEST TO APPLY

❏ Reasonable grounds = reasonable and probable grounds = credibly-based probability

❏ Subjective component = do I personally believe RPG exists?

❏ Objective component = would others believe RPG exists?

B   FACTS THAT SUPPORT RPG

❏ I have received information from _____ that leads to RPG

   ❏ This information is credible because _____

   ❏ This information is corroborated by _____

❏ I have observed events of _____ that lead to RPG

   ❏ These observations are credible because _____

   ❏ These observations are corroborated by _____

❏ I have located items in/on _____ that lead to RPG

   ❏ These items are credible because _____

   ❏ These items are corroborated by _____

C   CONCLUSIONS ON RPG

❏ I have more than a mere suspicion

❏ The commission of an offence is probable, not just possible

❏ I can seek a warrant because RPG links:

   ❏ particular evidence to ❏ a particular offence at ❏ a particular place

❏ I can lay a charge because RPG links:

   ❏ a particular person with ❏ a particular offence ❏ at a specific time and to ❏ a particular place

❏ RPG exists against _____ for offences of _____

   _____   _____

   _____   _____

   _____   _____

   _____   _____

   _____   _____

❏ RPG does not exist for any other targets

A CONTENT OF WARRANT AND INFORMATION TO OBTAIN

❏ No conclusory statements

　❏ Stated all supporting facts

　❏ Stated relevant unsupporting facts, and then dealt with those facts

❏ Basis for reliability of all informers established

　❏ Informers' motives and current relationships with investigators specified

　❏ Informers' criminal records specified

　❏ Informers' history of involvement assisting law enforcement specified

　❏ Accuracy of past information provided by informers specified

　❏ Informers' powers of observation specified

　❏ Corroboration of current information received from informers specified

❏ No unsourced statements

　❏ Stated sources of all information, whether known from direct experience or learned from a person or piece of evidence

❏ Details of all relevant facts included: names, times, dates, addresses, descriptions and activities

❏ History and background to investigation included to give context

❏ Suspected offences specified including names of accused, offence names and legislative sections, place and dates of commission of offences

❏ Targets of warrant named

❏ Things to be searched for specified in detail:
　　　　　❏ electronic records
　　　　　❏ document date ranges
　　　　　❏ classes of things not overly broad

❏ Place to be searched specified in detail:
　　　　　❏ municipal address
　　　　　❏ physical description of place
　　　　　❏ verified place named in warrant matched location searched

❏ Time of warrant execution specified and justified if necessary

❏ Persons linked to offences linked to things to be searched for linked to place to be searched

❏ Persons named who are authorized to execute warrant

❏ Identity of informers protected

❏ Past unsuccessful attempts to obtain a warrant disclosed

❏ Clearly articulated reasonable and probable grounds supporting issuance of warrant

❏ No irrelevant information included

B | **FORM AND READABILITY OF WARRANT AND INFORMATION TO OBTAIN**

❏ Correct form used according to Act warrant sought under

❏ Told a reasonable "story" with: ❏ an introduction

❏ a body

❏ a conclusion

❏ Topic headings inserted throughout text

❏ Short sentences and paragraphs used

❏ Paragraphs and pages consecutively numbered throughout

❏ Short statements quoted verbatim, not paraphrased

❏ Point form used when enumerating lists

❏ All terms defined

❏ Information synthesized, not just strung together

❏ Information arranged chronologically or thematically, not by source
   from which information was received

❏ Double-spaced with adequate margins

❏ Spelling, grammar and readability checked not only by computer, but also
   through careful re-reading by drafter

❏ Spelling, grammar and readability checked by someone other than drafter

❏ Easy-to-read computer font used

❏ Text left-aligned, not justified

C | **NECESSITY OF ANCILLARY ORDERS**

❏ Considered whether sealing order really necessary

❏ Sealing order required: ❏ until execution of warrant

❏ until charges laid

❏ until a certain date

❏ until investigation complete

❏ Sealing not being relied upon solely to protect informer identity

❏ Detailed justification for sealing order given

❏ Considered necessity of other ancillary orders like writ of assistance

FURTHER READING

Cases

R. v. Garofoli, [1990] 2 S.C.R. 1421. A judge reviewing the validly of a warrant cannot simply substitute his or her own view for that of the issuing judge or justice. The review test is not whether the reviewing judge "would" have issued the warrant, but rather whether the issuing judge or justice "could" have issued it taking into account any evidence of fraud, non-disclosure, misleading evidence and new evidence.

R. v. Greffe, [1990] 1 S.C.R. 755. Confidential information provided by a reliable informer can provide reasonable and probable grounds to support a warrant, but in order for a warrant to validly issue the information to obtain the warrant must go far beyond including a mere conclusory state that information was provided and the affiant believes that information.

R. v. Shiers (2003), 219 N.S.R. (2d) 196; 2003 NSCA 138. A case that is instructive on the limits to which a reviewing judge can find fault with the way a warrant is drafted, where the Court of Appeal at para. 23 disagreed with the trial judge that the warrant was deficient: "The issuing judge, by drawing reasonable inferences from the quantity of drugs said to be in Shiers possession at the time of the transaction and the way in which they were packaged, the evidence that Shiers was known to be involved in the drug trade, the fact that the transaction took place on the street in front of his residence and other facts and opinions disclosed in the Information to Obtain, could conclude that there were reasonable grounds to believe that the items targeted by the search were in his residence."

Books and Articles

C. Hill, S. Hutchinson, & L. Pringle, "Search Warrant: Protection or Illusion?" (2000) 28 C.R. (4th) 89. Reports on the results of a study conducted by the authors where 100 randomly selected search warrants and informations to obtain on file at the provincial courthouse in downtown Toronto were examined. While warrants had been refused in only 7% of cases, the authors concluded that 61% of examined warrants would not have survived s. 8 *Charter* challenges should their cases have made it to trial because of substantive defects and a generally evident lack of understanding of warrant drafting principles.

S. Hutchinson, *Canadian Search Warrant Manual 2005* (Toronto: Thomson, 2004). Gives a concise summary of all the important aspects of search warrant drafting, focusing on warrants obtained under the *Criminal Code.*

J. Fontana and D. Keeshan, *The Law of Search and Seizure in Canada,* 6th ed., (Toronto: LexisNexis Butterworths, 2005). Traces the law of search and seizure from its earliest origins and deals with the theory behind the law.

L. Truss, *Eats, Shoots and Leaves — The Zero Tolerance Approach to Punctuation* (New York: Gotham Books, 2003). There are lots of grammar books out there that I could recommend, but in this chapter I will suggest to you only this one charming work that may actually make you like the finer points of punctuation.

On-line Resources

There are now many useful free on-line spelling and grammar reference works available to assist you with your writing that are quicker to use than any work available in print; here I list only a sampling of what is available.

www.andromeda.rutgers.edu/~jlynch/Writing — home of university English professor Jack Lynch's *Guide to Grammar and Style.*

www.cctc.comment.edu/grammar — home of the *Community Capital College Foundation Guide to Grammar and Writing* that includes an easy to navigate grammar guide.

www.dictionary.cambridge.org — home of the *Cambridge Advanced Learner's Dictionary.*

www.englishplus.com/grammar — home of the *Grammar Slammar* help file.

www.askoxford.com — home of the 145,000 word *Compact Oxford English Dictionary.*

www.m-w.com — home of the *Marriam-Webster Online Dictionary and Thesaurus.*

CHAPTER NINE

CORRECTLY APPROACHING SPECIAL PLACES FOR SEARCH AND SEIZURE

[T]here are places for which authorization to search should generally be granted only with reticence and, where necessary, with more conditions attached than for other places. One does not enter a church in the same way as a lion's den, or a warehouse in the same way as a lawyer's office. One does not search the premises of a third party who is not alleged to have participated in the commission of a crime in the same way as those of someone who is the subject of such an allegation.

Descôteaux v. Mierzwinski, [1982] 1 S.C.R. 860 at 889.

In This Chapter

- The special place of the human body
- The special place of the bank
- The special place of the law office
- The special place of the international border and airport
- Other special places

"A man's home is his castle" has never been an entirely accurate statement of the law (gender issues aside), although residences are accorded a few more protections from inspection and search than other locations. The real castles of today are places whose protected uses play fundamental roles in the functioning of our society: the human body, banks, law offices, other professional offices — particularly media offices — and government offices. International borders and airports render Canada a kind of castle itself, but unlike the other special places discussed in this chapter they are accompanied by a far lesser expectation of privacy. It is what amounts to a reasonable expectation of privacy, together with the operation of statutory and common law privileges, that create "special places" for search and seizure purposes. While search and seizure is still possible in special places, investigators need to take extraordinary care in approaching them because special rules must be complied with, warrants will almost always be necessary, and courts may hold the value of protecting the privacy of people connected to those places outweighs investigative interests of searching and seizing inside them.

THE SPECIAL PLACE OF THE HUMAN BODY

The seizure of any bodily substance is considered by the courts to be highly intrusive. While some cases have found a warrant was not needed where the accused had "abandoned" a bodily substance, true abandonment is rare. In *R. v. Stillman*, [1997] 1 S.C.R. 607 at paras. 51 & 91, a majority of the court believed it was a breach of a suspect's rights to seize hair samples, dental impressions and even a used tissue abandoned in a police station without the suspect's informed consent or a warrant:

> It was the ultimate invasion of the appellant's privacy. . . . In the case at bar to proceed in the face of a specific refusal to compel the accused to submit to the lengthy and intrusive dental process, to force the accused to provide the pubic hairs and to forcibly take the scalp hairs and buccal swabs was, to say the least, unacceptable behaviour that contravened both s. 7 and s. 8 of the *Charter*. It was a significant invasion of bodily integrity. . . . If there is not respect for the dignity of the individual and the integrity of the body then it is but a very short step to justifying the exercise of any physical force by police if it is undertaken with the aim of solving crimes.

The high value placed by the courts on bodily integrity means a warrant will almost always be required for any search seeking to seize a bodily substance unless there is truly informed consent or the seizure is of breath or blood samples for an impaired driving investigation.

1. Consent to Seizure of Bodily Substances

It is possible to obtain bodily substances through consent, but the same problems about whether the consent was really informed arise here as they do in other types of consent searches. If the target of the search and seizure has discussed the consequences of a proposed consent search with a lawyer, then a court will likely conclude any consent to search subsequently given was informed. Without the target receiving a lawyer's advice, proceeding to search and seize bodily substances solely with a consent authority is legally risky. With the exception of drug or alcohol impairment cases where there is some urgency, DNA or other bodily substances will not disappear in the time it takes a target to seek legal advice or investigators to obtain a warrant.

Generally, it is only the person from whom substances were removed for testing purposes who can give investigators consent to seize those substances. Where there is no informed consent, investigators will need a warrant even to get hospital blood test results that have already been created for medical treatment purposes. *R. v. Dersch*, [1993] 3 S.C.R. 768 at 779 was highly critical of a physician voluntarily releasing a patient's blood samples to the police:

> The net result of the *Charter* violation by police in the particular circumstances of this case, was to take advantage of the improper conduct by his doctors in taking the blood sample contrary to the specific instructions of the patient. When this factor is taken together with the seriousness of the *Charter* violation by police and the importance of guarding against a free exchange of information between health care professionals and police, in my view the impugned evidence should be excluded by application of s. 24(2) of the *Charter*.

While consent can be a viable authority for bodily substance search and seizure, alternative authorities should be pursued where possible.

2. Warrant Requirements for Bodily Impressions and DNA

a. *Bodily Print or Impression Warrants*

Any type of print or impression of a body is available under a s. 487.092 *Criminal Code* warrant to investigate any federal offence, be it criminal or regulatory, with the preconditions being not much more onerous than for a normal search and seizure warrant:

487.092. (1) A justice may issue a warrant in writing authorizing a peace officer to do any thing, or cause any thing to be done under the direction of the peace officer, described in the warrant in order to obtain any handprint, fingerprint, footprint, foot impression, teeth impression or other print or impression of the body or any part of the body in respect of a person if the justice is satisfied

(a) by information on oath in writing that there are reasonable grounds to believe that an offence against this or any other Act of Parliament has been committed and that information concerning the offence will be obtained by the print or impression; and

(b) that it is in the best interests of the administration of justice to issue the warrant.

(2) A warrant issued under subsection (1) shall contain such terms and conditions as the justice considers advisable to ensure that any search or seizure authorized by the warrant is reasonable in the circumstances.

Investigators must explain in the information to obtain how "information concerning the offence will be obtained by the print or impression," like by setting out how a footprint was found at the scene of the crime, the warrant target was observed near the crime scene close to the time of the offence, and taking a foot impression of the target would provide information concerning the offence. Some kind of justification that an impression warrant is in the best interests of the administration of justice must also be offered, which could amount to explaining how the proposed technique will be effective at confirming or eliminating the target as a suspect. Because the warrant must also contain conditions making the search "reasonable in the circumstances," it is helpful to include limiting terms like stipulating that an expert trained in the taking of foot impressions will be employed. The taking of dental impressions would especially require technical expertise, and is the most invasive procedure that can be authorized by this type of warrant.

b. *DNA Warrants*

In contrast to bodily impression warrants, the DNA warrants provided for under s. 487.05 of the *Criminal Code* are limited to a select list of designated offences and subject to a host of procedural hoops that investigators must jump through before and after execution of the warrant. Although more intrusive than bodily impression warrants, DNA warrants have been found to be constitutional because of the factors described in *R. v. B. (S.A.)*, [2003] 2 S.C.R. 678 at para. 61:

> In light of the high probative value of forensic DNA analysis, the interests of the state override those of the individual. Forensic DNA analysis is capable of both identifying and eliminating suspects, a feature that seriously reduces the risk of wrongful convictions. The DNA provisions contain procedural safeguards that protect adequately the multiple interests of the suspected offender.

Like wiretap authorizations, DNA warrants are limited to designated offences, although the list of offences eligible for DNA warrants as set out in s-s. 487.04 of the *Code* are aimed at a broad array of violent and sexual offences quite different from the primarily economic and occasionally violent offences permissible for wiretaps.

Section 487.04 of the *Code* sets up lists of "Primary Designated Offences" and "Secondary Designated Offences" that both qualify for DNA warrants, but differ in the applicability of s. 487.051 DNA databank provisions. Primary designated offences require mandatory sampling from an offender unless the offender shows a grossly disproportionate impact on his privacy and security as compared to the protection of society and proper administration of justice. Secondary designated offences leave sampling to the discretion of the court according to what is in the best interests of the administration of justice.

The s. 487.05 *Code* authority for a DNA warrant varies a bit in its preconditions for authorization from the "thing in a place connected to an offence" formula because of the very precise purpose of DNA samples, requiring instead a bodily substance already found in a place, object or person connected to a designated offence, and that DNA analysis of a bodily substance from a person believed to be a party to the offence will reveal whether that person's DNA matches the DNA already linked to the offence. Additional preconditions include:

- only a provincial or superior court judge can issue a DNA warrant;
- the warrant must be in "the best interests of the administration of justice";
- the issuing judge must consider the nature of the offence, circumstances of its commission and whether a qualified person is available to take the samples;
- hair, saliva and blood are the only types of DNA samples that can be obtained;

- the issuing judge may impose any terms and conditions so that the taking of samples is "reasonable in the circumstances."

Even though informed consent is not a factor, investigators also have a considerable duty under s. 487.07 of the *Code* when executing a DNA warrant to inform the target of:

(a) the contents of the warrant, order or authorization;

(b) the nature of the investigative procedures by means of which the samples are to be taken;

(c) the purpose of taking the samples;

(d) the authority of the peace officer and any other person under the direction of the peace officer to use as much force as is necessary for the purpose of taking the samples; and

(e) in the case of samples of bodily substances taken in execution of a warrant,

(i) the possibility that the results of forensic DNA analysis may be used in evidence, and

(ii) if the sample is taken from a young person, the rights of the young person under subsection (4).

Under s-ss. 487.07(2) & (3) an investigator may detain and transport a person for the purpose of taking a sample, but "must ensure that the person's privacy is respected in a manner that is reasonable in the circumstances."

To further drive home the extent Parliament went to in protecting DNA privacy, s. 487.09 of the *Code* requires the results of DNA warrants to be destroyed:

- where the sample does not match the DNA obtained from the scene of the crime;

- where the target of the warrant is finally acquitted of the designated offence or a related offence; or

- where one year has passed since discharge at preliminary inquiry, dismissal, withdrawal or stay of the information charging the offence, and no new information has been laid or direct indictment preferred.

Destruction can only be prevented by judicial order finding that the DNA results "might reasonably be required in an investigation or prosecution of the person for another designated offence or of another person for the designated offence or any other offence in respect of the same transaction."

The Sanctity of the Human Body

Q & A

Q: Why is the integrity of the human body regarded as so sacrosanct that it is so difficult to search and seize there? People abuse their bodies every day for no good reason other than to have fun, whereas with legitimate search and seizure of the body the interests of all Canadians are served.

A: We all can make the free choice to abuse our bodies, but others cannot choose that for us. If privacy interests range up an increasing scale from public places, to businesses, vehicles and residences, then the human body is the ultimate temple of privacy — some might even say the last refuge.

3. The Impairment Exception to Warrant Requirements for Breath and Blood Samples

Breath and blood samples are the one exception to the "get a warrant or get informed consent" rule for bodily substances, but only where the statutory requirements of s. 254 of the *Criminal Code* can be met. Sub-section 254(2) of the *Code* requires an investigator to have reasonable suspicion of alcohol in the body before a warrantless demand for a screening device breath sample can be made. Reasonable suspicion is a lower standard than the reasonable and probable grounds needed for most warrants, but still requires some evidence to raise the level of belief of alcohol in the body above a mere possibility. Impaired driving defences often focus on the officer making the demand for a sample not having had sufficient grounds to do so, thus investigators must carefully make detailed notes of their basis for the breath sample demand so that basis can later be testified to at trial. The courts will not, however, impose standards of belief on investigators that are impossible to meet as confirmed in *R. v. Lindsay* (1999), 40 M.V.R. (3d) 225 (Ont. C.A.) at para. 2:

> The trial judge accepted the officer's evidence that she smelled alcohol on the respondent's breath. This observation led her to suspect that the respondent had alcohol in his body and she made the ALERT demand accordingly. An officer may make an ALERT demand where she reasonably suspects that a person who is operating a motor vehicle has alcohol in his or her body (s. 254(2) of the *Criminal Code*). There need only be a reasonable suspicion

and that reasonable suspicion need only relate to the existence of alcohol in the body. The officer does not have to believe that the accused has committed any crime. We see no need to put a gloss on the words of s. 254(2). The fact that there may be an explanation for the smell of alcohol does not take away from the fact that there exists a reasonable suspicion within the meaning of the section.

Before a demand for a full breath or blood sample can be made to definitively test for the presence of alcohol in the body, s-s. 254(3) of the *Code* requires an investigator to meet the higher standard of having reasonable and probable grounds to believe the offence of operating a vehicle while impaired has been committed within the last three hours as a result of the consumption of alcohol, but a major component of this RPG will often be a screening device result. Taking blood samples under s-s. 254(3) requires a qualified medical practitioner, whereas the taking of a DNA blood sample does not — presumably because the usual method of DNA collection by pricking the skin is less invasive, and because prior-judicial authorization of DNA sampling means a court can impose whatever conditions it thinks appropriate in the circumstances including a medical practitioner requirement. Breath samples under s-s. 254(3) require a "qualified technician." If it were not for the time-sensitive nature of blood-alcohol readings, it is likely Parliament would have imposed a warrant requirement on at least the blood samples, if not the breath samples.

4. Impaired Driving Blood Sample Warrants

Warrants to obtain blood samples are available under s. 256 of the *Criminal Code* for investigating operation of a motor vehicle while impaired offences under s. 253 of the *Code*, but only need be resorted to when a warrantless alternative is not available. The three fairly onerous preconditions to obtaining a s. 256 warrant are:

- a s. 253 offence must have taken place at most four hours prior to the application for the warrant;

- the target of the seizure must have been involved in an incident causing death or bodily harm;

- a qualified medical practitioner must be of the opinion that the target is unable to consent to the taking of samples of his or her own blood due to incapacitation from the incident (like a vehicle collision) or drug or alcohol consumption, and that the taking of samples would not endanger the person's health.

The prevalence of s. 253 offences makes this an invaluable class of offence and thing-specific warrants that will no doubt be relied on much more frequently than other offence or purpose-specific warrant types described in Chapter 8.

Justifying Impaired Driving Exceptions

Q & A

Q: Why all this talk about the sanctity of the body, and then ignore it when it is expedient for the purposes of impaired driving investigations? Isn't this hypocritical?

A: *Charter* rights are not absolute, with s. 7 guaranteeing life, liberty and security of the person and the right not to be deprived thereof *except in accordance with the principles of fundamental justice*, s. 8 guaranteeing protection against *unreasonable* search and seizure, and s. 1 making all *Charter* rights subject to such reasonable limits prescribed by law as can be demonstrably justified in a free and democratic society. The narrow exceptions to warrant requirements created for impaired driving investigations have been found to be justified because of the minimally intrusive nature of breath samples, and the high public importance of reducing the numbers of impaired drivers on the roads.

THE SPECIAL PLACE OF THE BANK

Sub-section 29(7) of the *Canada Evidence Act*, R.S.C. 1985, c. C-5 (*CEA*), grants any bank or other financial institution that accepts deposits of money in Canada substantial immunity from seizure of its original books and records, subject to the exception that seizure of originals can be authorized if a warrant explicitly states it is not limited by s-s. 29(7). Only copies of originals are obtainable, but s-ss. 29(1) and (2) of the *CEA* gives them the same effect as originals so long as they are properly authenticated through an affidavit or trial witness. Investigators must ensure a bank employee, manager or accountant is lined up before a preliminary inquiry or trial to provide such authenticating evidence. Investigators need to be prepared for considerable delays in obtaining a response to a s. 487.012 *Criminal Code* production order or s. 487.01 general warrant compelling a bank to produce its records, and should track reasons for any delays if further detention applications may be required while awaiting bank documents.

Courts have for some time been willing to give a broad interpretation to what will amount to a bank record copy admissible under s. 29 of the *CEA*, as in *R. v. Bell* (1982), 35 O.R. (2d) 164 (C.A.) at paras. 7-10:

> Because of the rapidly changing nature of the technology, it would be impossible to lay down general rules to govern every case. It is always a question of fact whether any recorded information (in whatever form) is a "record kept in any financial institution", but I think the following general propositions have so far emerged:
>
> 1. A record may be in any, even an illegible, form.
>
> 2. The form in which information is recorded may change from time to time, and the new form is equally a "record" of that kind of information.
>
> 3. A record may be a compilation or collation of other records.
>
> 4. It must have been produced for the bank's purposes as a reference source, or as part of its internal audit system and, at the relevant time must be kept for that purpose.

So electronic, microfilm or paper records could equally qualify under s. 29, and could take any form of compilation so long as they were produced by the bank for bank purposes, rather than simply being third-party records stored at a bank like contracts kept in a bank safety deposit box. Seizure of original bank documents might be necessary in the unlikely case where the bank itself or its employees are suspected of involvement in criminal activity or some kind of forensic testing of documents is contemplated.

THE SPECIAL PLACE OF THE LAW OFFICE

Cases ranging from money laundering, to immigration fraud, to murder sometimes either implicate lawyers directly in offence commission, or lead investigators to believe a lawyer possesses evidence of an offence. The key role in business transactions played by many of the over 85,000 lawyers in Canada means that inevitably some of them will become involved, at least unwittingly, in illegal activity. The elevated position of solicitor-client privilege is what makes the seizure of any information connected to a lawyer fraught with complexity.

The rationale for that privilege was explained in *Smith v. Jones*, [1999] 1 S.C.R.455 at para. 46:

> Clients seeking advice must be able to speak freely to their lawyers secure in the knowledge that what they say will not be divulged without their consent. It cannot be forgotten that the privilege is that of the client, not the lawyer. The privilege is essential if sound legal advice is to be given in every field. It has a deep significance in almost every situation where legal advice is sought whether it be with regard to corporate and commercial transactions, to family relationships, to civil litigation or to criminal charges. Family secrets, company secrets, personal foibles and indiscretions all must on occasion be revealed to the lawyer by the client. Without this privilege clients could never be candid and furnish all the relevant information that must be provided to lawyers if they are to properly advise their clients. It is an element that is both integral and extremely important to the functioning of the legal system. It is because of the fundamental importance of the privilege that the onus properly rests upon those seeking to set aside the privilege to justify taking such a significant step.

The privilege is a practical one that keeps the legal system working and free from every defence lawyer becoming a potential witness for the prosecution, and likewise protects every prosecutor from becoming a witness for the defence. If lawyers and their files were always fair game for the uncovering of evidence relevant to any court case, clients — be they organized criminals seeking out defence counsel advice, or police seeking out advice from prosecutors — could no longer freely discuss their legal problems. The law generally recognizes that the more Canadians are able to find out about it, the better and more just a place Canada will be to live.

1. Where Does Solicitor-Client Privilege Originate?

Just because you are a lawyer doesn't confer any special immunity to search and seizure. It is the work-product of a lawyer, or the material that the lawyer receives to produce that product, that can acquire special status if it is created for the purpose of giving or seeking legal advice, or for purposes connected to litigation. That special status is usually called "solicitor-client privilege," although you may also hear the terms "litigation privilege" or "communication privilege" used occasionally to distinguish between two sub-classes of solicitor-client privilege. While other types of privilege exist under Canadian law, it is rare for them to inhibit the operation of judicially authorized search and seizure through a warrant.

Lavallée, Rackel & Heintz v. Canada (Attorney General); White, Ottenheimer & Baker v. Canada (Attorney General); R. v. Fink, [2002] 3 S.C.R. 209 at para. 24 described the effect of the privilege:

> all information protected by the solicitor-client privilege is out of reach for the state. It cannot be forcibly discovered or disclosed and it is inadmissible in court. It is the privilege of the client and the lawyer acts as a gatekeeper, ethically bound to protect the privileged information that belongs to his or her client. Therefore, any privileged information acquired by the state without the consent of the privilege holder is information that the state is not entitled to as a rule of fundamental justice.

Questions of relevance, reliability and necessity become moot if what could otherwise qualify as evidence is protected by solicitor-client privilege, and thus inadmissible at any trial.

2. How to Know If a Record Is Protected by Solicitor-Client Privilege

Not everything found in a law office is privileged, and privileged documents may be found outside of a law office. Just because someone has written "SOLICITOR-CLIENT PRIVILEGE" in bold type across the top of a document does not mean it is privileged, and just because a document contains no reference to that term does not mean it isn't privileged. Solicitor-client privilege can apply to documents in the possession of the solicitor, the possession of those assisting the solicitor, or the possession of the client in any location, be it a home, a warehouse, or an automobile. Lawyers often disagree among themselves over what is and is not privileged, so as an investigator you won't be able to say at the time of a search that any privilege claim you face is or is not reasonable.

Although fundamentally important to Canadian society, three significant exceptions to solicitor-client privilege exist:

- when disclosure of privileged material is necessary because the innocence of the accused is at stake and the privileged material would assist the accused in making a defence;

- when the solicitor-client communications are themselves criminal, like when both the lawyer and client are part of a conspiracy, or the client seeks to obtain legal advice to assist with the commission of a crime;

- when a compelling public safety or other public interest outweighs the fundamentally important protection of solicitor-client privilege.

Any of these exceptions may be relevant to the preparation of a search warrant against a law office. Early investigator-prosecutor contact is imperative to clarify how this sensitive area of the law applies to the facts of your case.

3. The Procedure to Follow When a Solicitor-Client Privilege Claim Is Made

Section 488.1 of the *Criminal Code* used to specify a procedure to follow when privilege claims were raised during a law office search, but *Lavallée, Rackel & Heintz v. Canada (Attorney General); White, Ottenheimer & Baker v. Canada (Attorney General); R. v. Fink*, [2002] 3 S.C.R. 209, struck down that procedure as unconstitutional. Until Parliament enacts new legislation to resolve solicitor-client privilege claims, everyone must for the moment rely on the common law privilege principles summarized in that case at para. 49:

1. No search warrant can be used with regard to documents that are known to be protected by solicitor-client privilege.

2. Before searching a law office, the investigative authorities must satisfy the issuing justice that there exists no other reasonable alternative to the search.

3. When allowing a law office to be searched, the issuing justice must be rigorously demanding so to afford maximum protection of solicitor-client confidentiality.

4. Except when the warrant specifically authorizes the immediate examination, copying and seizure of an identified document, all documents in possession of a lawyer must be sealed before being examined or removed from the lawyer's possession.

5. Every effort must be made to contact the lawyer and the client at the time of the execution of the search warrant. Where the lawyer or the client cannot be contacted, a representative of the Bar should be allowed to oversee the sealing and seizure of documents.

6. The investigative officer executing the warrant should report to the justice of the peace the efforts made to contact all potential

privilege holders, who should then be given a reasonable opportunity to assert a claim of privilege and, if that claim is contested, to have the issue judicially decided.

7. If notification of potential privilege holders is not possible, the lawyer who had custody of the documents seized, or another lawyer appointed by either the Law Society or by the court, should examine the documents to determine whether a claim of privilege should be asserted, and should be given a reasonable opportunity to do so.

8. The Attorney General may make submissions on the issue of privilege, but should not be permitted to inspect the documents beforehand. The prosecuting authority can only inspect the documents if and when it is determined by a judge that the documents are not privileged.

9. Where sealed documents are found not to be privileged, they may be used in the normal course of the investigation.

10. Where documents are found to be privileged, they are to be returned immediately to the holder of the privilege, or to a person designated by the court.

These principles are implemented by the way investigators draft and execute warrants, and the way prosecutors resolve privilege claims.

When drafting an information to obtain a search warrant to seize documents in a law office or in the possession of a lawyer you must include information that demonstrates that it is at least arguable the material sought is not privileged, and there is no other reasonable way to obtain the same information — like by searching a corporation's offices instead of its lawyer's offices — and the warrant's terms must maximize the protection of solicitor-client privilege. The "no other reasonable source" and "maximum protection of privilege" conditions were called in *Maranda v. Richer*, [2003] 3 S.C.R. 193 at para. 17 a "duty to minimize":

> The existence of the principle of minimization must be reflected in the way that the application for authorization is worded, and in particular in the wording of the affidavits presented in support. The affidavit must contain allegations that are sufficiently precise and complete that the authorizing judge is able to exercise his or her jurisdiction with full knowledge of the facts. . . . It is then up to the judge to exercise his or her jurisdiction carefully, to ensure that the application for authorization properly establishes that there are no reasonable alternatives, and to define a procedure to be followed

in executing the search that will preserve solicitor-client privilege to the greatest possible extent. This is not a matter of fulfilling formalities or laying out boilerplate allegations. Where privilege could be breached, it must be shown to the judge's satisfaction that the duty to minimize can be met in carrying out the proposed procedure.

The obligation to define a procedure that will preserve solicitor-client privilege to the greatest degree possible appears to be more important than the obligation to exhaustively look for other sources — especially if one interprets these obligations in light of the wealth of case law that has built up in the wiretap field.

If you are determined to get a warrant to search a lawyer's office, make sure you only target a very narrow class of information and don't wind up hauling away file cabinets of material as was disapproved of in *Maranda*. It can be very helpful to have a prosecutor available by telephone during a law office search to provide on-going advice as the search progresses. Seal any potentially privileged documents upon seizure, immediately contact the lawyer and client connected to those documents, allow a reasonable opportunity for privilege to be asserted, and return all clearly privileged documents without delay. Section 487.012 *Criminal Code* production orders might eventually become a common substitute for search and seizure warrants targeting law offices, but will still have to deal with issues of solicitor-client privilege.

4. The Risky and Frustrating Road of Privilege Claim Negotiations

Do not attempt to negotiate a solicitor-client privilege claim yourself as an investigator — you will get burned. I cannot stress enough the importance of contacting a prosecutor or other legal advisor as soon as any privilege claim is made. Do insist the person first asserting the privilege claim explain its basis to you in at least basic terms, and record that explanation as it will be important to the court process that will attempt to resolve the claim of privilege. It is the prosecutor's duty to seek to have unworthy privilege claims dismissed by a court, but if it initially appears that there could be some legitimacy to a claim then it is prudent for investigators to consider alternate ways to advance their inquiries in case they never get to examine the disputed documents. In one of my cases the privilege claim resolution process dragged on in court for almost three years over two boxes of documents that hadn't been seized from a law firm, but were located in an accounting firm that occasionally assisted lawyers.

THE SPECIAL PLACE OF THE INTERNATIONAL BORDER AND AIRPORT

Unlike the other special places discussed in this chapter that are subject to more restricted search and seizure than normal, *Charter* standards governing search, seizure and detention are much more flexible at international entry points to Canada than elsewhere in Canada. These entry points deserve mention in this chapter because their distinct *Charter* position is capable of creating confusion if you don't understand why different standards apply there. The *Customs Act*, R.S. 1985, c. 1 (2nd Supp.), contains unique powers that fall outside of what would normally be described as either a search or a regulatory inspection. These powers were justified in *R. v. Simmons*, [1988] 2 S.C.R. 495 at 528: "the degree of personal privacy reasonably expected at customs is lower than in most other situations. People do not expect to be able to cross international borders free from scrutiny." Defences to smuggling offences usually focus on the accused's knowledge of the contraband goods, be they hidden in a car door, welded into the bottom of a metal pot, or taped to the accused's body, rather than on privacy violations.

According to s. 2 of the *Customs Act* those qualifying for powers include anyone "employed in the administration or enforcement of this Act, the *Customs Tariff* or the *Special Import Measures Act* and includes any member of the Royal Canadian Mounted Police." Sections 98 and 99.2 of the *Customs Act* authorize a search of any person recently arrived in or about to leave Canada, or leaving a customs controlled area, if a customs officer

> suspects on reasonable grounds that the person has secreted on or about his person anything in respect of which this Act might be or has been contravened, anything that would afford evidence with respect to a contravention of this Act or any goods the importation or exportation or which is prohibited, controlled or regulated under this or any other Act of Parliament.

The ss. 98 and 99.2 statutory search without warrant authorities *do* require reasonable and probable grounds of an offence because of the possibly intimate nature of a personal search, but do not depend on arrest, consent, exigent circumstances or prior judicial authorization.

Section 99 of the *Customs Act* authorizes examination, opening and sampling of any goods, packages or mail in the process of being imported, *without* the need for reasonable grounds of *any* offence — the authority is not applicable to people, although its use could give rise to grounds for a s. 98 or 99.2 search. Section 99 also authorizes examination and opening of any goods, packages or mail in the process of being exported, as well as the stopping and examination of any conveyance, but only if a customs officer "suspects on reasonable grounds" that federal Acts or regulations "have been or might be contravened in respect of" the goods or conveyance. This "might be" standard appears to be similar to the reasonable suspicion standard of investigative detentions. Mail that weighs 30 grams or less may not, however, be opened under the *Customs Act* without the consent of either the sender or recipient.

Section 99.1 of the *Customs Act* covers those who may have recently made it past a border or international airport checkpoint into Canada without reporting:

> **99.1.** (1) If an officer has reasonable grounds to suspect that a person has entered Canada without presenting himself or herself in accordance with subsection 11(1), the officer may stop that person within a reasonable time after the person has entered Canada.
>
> (2) An officer who stops a person referred to in subsection (1) may
>
> (a) question the person; and
>
> (b) in respect of goods imported by that person, examine them, cause to be opened any package or container of the imported goods and take samples of them in reasonable amounts.

Again, examination of goods is authorized without reasonable grounds of imported goods being involved in an offence, but this power cannot be abused to justify warrantless searches long after people have entered Canada — reasonable grounds are needed that the target did not report when entering Canada, and a stop may only occur within a "reasonable time" after entry. Once items or people are well beyond the border, the special inspection and search powers of ss. 98, 99 and 99.2 of the *Customs Act* no longer apply and search warrants for inside Canada or international assistance for outside Canada may be required. *Customs Act* inspection and search authorities provide good illustrations for demystification of the law purposes of just how flexible *Charter* standards can be.

> **Q & A**
>
> ## Compelling Reasons for Search Discretion at Borders
>
> **Q:** If international airport or border inspection and search powers are so effective at locating things like heroin that are extremely harmful to all Canadians, then why can't at least some of those powers whose exercise is left to the discretion of customs officers also be extended to police officers operating inside Canada?
>
> **A:** The way s. 8 *Charter* protection against unreasonable search and seizure is applied depends on what expectation of privacy is reasonable at a particular place. Canadians have a very low expectation of privacy at a border, and there is a compelling public interest to protect those in Canada from the myriad of things that might illegally cross Canada's frontiers — not just drugs, but also things like disease bearing plants and goods on which no duty has been paid. Inside Canada, Canadians have a much higher expectation of privacy, and there is a less compelling public interest in conducting warrantless searches.

OTHER SPECIAL PLACES

The human body, banks, law offices and entry points to Canada are for the most part the only commonly searched places consistently given special status in the law. The offices of other professionals, particularly medical professionals and journalists, sometimes attract special status because the maintenance of confidential relationships is instrumental to conducting their important duties, but those offices do not attract the same privilege protection as law offices. While not commonly searched for, investigators need to be aware that material located in government offices may be inadmissible in court proceedings because of public interest privilege. The future could see more classes of information endowed with some sort of privilege. Demystification of the law is there to alert you to privilege issues, but early investigator-prosecutor contact is required to resolve them.

1. Searching Other Professional Offices

Most professionals owe duties of confidentiality to their clients. This confidentially is necessary to permit the free exchange of information and opinions inherent in a healthy professional-client relationship, be the relationship with a medical professional, accountant, architect or engineer. *R. v.*

Gurenke, [1991] 3 S.C.R. 263 at 284, approved of four preconditions to the formation of any kind of privilege:

(1) The communications must originate in a *confidence* that they will not be disclosed.

(2) This element of *confidentiality must be essential* to the full and satisfactory maintenance of the relation between the parties.

(3) The *relation* must be one which in the opinion of the community ought to be sedulously *fostered.*

(4) The *injury* that would inure to the relation by the disclosure of the communications must be *greater than the benefit* thereby gained for the correct disposal of litigation.

Satisfying all those conditions will not necessarily make material privileged under Canadian law, but it sets up a potential finding of privilege that could lead a court to decide certain material deserves protection in the specific circumstances of a case.

Material seized from any professional office also runs a risk of being covered by solicitor-client privilege because of the frequency by which professionals either are the clients of lawyers, or are employed by lawyers to give professional advice relevant to ongoing litigation. Don't jump to hasty conclusions about the validity of privilege claims over material not in the possession of a lawyer. In one case I argued the report of a private vehicle accident expert employed by an insurance company could not be privileged from examination by federal investigators just because it had been prepared to assist with possible civil litigation between private parties, but the court found that because it had been prepared in contemplation of litigation at the request of a lawyer solicitor-client privilege should apply. Investigators at least can insist that anyone making a privilege claim articulate its basis so it is clear from the start whether solicitor-client privilege is being dealt with, or some other kind of less recognized professional privilege, and that privileged material be segregated from non-privileged material as the courts have disapproved of blanket privilege claims.

2. Searching Media Offices

Investigators must especially watch out for media privilege claims that have become increasingly common as advancing technology and the skill of investigative journalists lets the media record more and more information of potential interest to regulatory or criminal investigators. While the law does not yet recognize a freestanding "media privilege" category, the media may owe a duty of confidentiality to its sources and executing warrants on media offices to search for and seize items like raw video footage of a riot or the research files of an investigative journalist tends to provoke indignation and legal challenges. The courts will sometimes side with the media in protecting its sources if the public interest in access to the material does not outweigh the interests in keeping it confidential.

Canadian Broadcasting Corp. v. New Brunswick (Attorney General), [1991] 3 S.C.R. 459 at 475, recognized the special societal role that the media play:

> The media have a vitally important role to play in a democratic society. It is the media that, by gathering and disseminating news, enable members of our society to make an informed assessment of the issues which may significantly affect their lives and well-being. . . . The importance of that role, and the manner in which it must be fulfilled, gives rise to special concerns when a warrant is sought to search media premises.

Investigators need to consider if searching a media office is an absolute necessity, whether there is an alternate source of similar information available, and whether they even have solid grounds to get a media warrant in the first place.

In the course of my work consulting with investigators contemplating media warrants targeting places like television stations, I discovered it was often difficult to say there were reasonable and probable grounds to believe information of an offence *would* be found in a media office. Saying only that evidence *might* be found there is not sufficient since search warrants cannot authorize fishing expeditions. Just because a videographer is present at the scene of a riot or an investigative journalist writes a story involving interviews with organized crime figures does not necessarily mean either is in possession of evidence of an offence.

To establish grounds for a warrant targeting the office or residence of a journalist, it might take a reliable informer detailing exactly what evidence is in the journalist's hands. Information possessed by journalists is often independently available, sometimes directly from a journalist's source. Going after journalist information is a shortcut to that information, but one fraught with legal peril.

Courts are particularly strict in scrutinizing applications for warrants against media offices, and will apply the principles set out in *Canadian Broadcasting Corp. v. New Brunswick (Attorney General)*, [1991] 3 S.C.R. 459 at 476:

> Whether the search of a media office can be considered reasonable will depend on a number of factors including the nature of the objects to be seized, the manner in which the search is to be conducted and the degree of urgency of the search. It is of particular importance that the justice of the peace consider the effects of the search and seizure on the ability of the particular media organization in question to fulfil its function as a news gatherer and news disseminator. If a search will impede the media from fulfilling these functions and the impediments cannot reasonably be controlled through the imposition of conditions on the execution of the search warrant, then a warrant should only be issued where a compelling state interest is demonstrated.

Investigators must adopt warrant conditions for media offices that minimize interference in the business of the media as news gatherers and disseminators, or else demonstrate "a compelling state interest," which can be a very difficult burden to meet. There are obvious parallels to the law office search duty to minimize. Section 487.012 *Criminal Code* production orders might become a substitute for some search and seizure warrants targeting media offices, but will run into the same claims of confidentiality and privilege.

3. Searching Government Offices

The mere fact that an office is controlled by a government does not make it a special place for search and seizure purposes, but the government information contained within that office may attract a public interest privilege rendering it inadmissible in court due to the operation of ss. 37, 38 or 39 of the *CEA*. Section 37 of the *CEA* is the general section used to claim public interest privilege:

> **37.** (1) Subject to sections 38 to 38.16, a Minister of the Crown in right of Canada or other official may object to the disclosure of information before a court, person or body with jurisdiction to compel the production of information by certifying orally or in writing to the court, person or body that the information should not be disclosed on the grounds of a specified public interest.

Although s. 37 does not limit the types of "public interest" that may be asserted, s. 38 of the *CEA* provides for a particular kind of public interest privilege concerning "sensitive information," which is defined as:

> information relating to international relations or national defence or national security that is in the possession of the Government of Canada, whether originating from inside or outside Canada, and is

of a type that the Government of Canada is taking measures to safeguard.

The s. 38 sensitive information public interest privilege rules are more complex and difficult to overcome than the s. 37 rules governing other types of public interest, but most notable is s. 39 of the *CEA*, which confers absolute public interest protection on Privy Council confidences:

> **39.** (1) Where a minister of the Crown or the Clerk of the Privy Council objects to the disclosure of information before a court, person or body with jurisdiction to compel the production of information by certifying in writing that the information constitutes a confidence of the Queen's Privy Council for Canada, disclosure of the information shall be refused without examination or hearing of the information by the court, person or body.

These confidences include memorandums and discussion papers to cabinet and draft legislation. Public interest privilege can be waived, or evidence of similar value might be obtained through another source, but where ss. 37, 38 or 39 of the *CEA* apply, not all relevant, reliable and necessary material seized from a government office will be admissible in court.

Scope and Purpose of Privilege

Q&A

Q: I understand the concept of solicitor-client privilege, but why do lawyers get special status over other professionals? Why isn't a similar type of privilege extended to doctors, accountants, or the clergy? Is it simply because lawyers write the laws in their own best interests?

A: The justice system would collapse without lawyers being able to communicate in true confidence with their clients. Although the relationships other professionals have with their clients are also highly confidential, it cannot be said that the justice system would collapse without those professionals having similar privilege protection. There are already several exceptions to solicitor-client privilege that ensure lawyers are not immune from investigation. Judges will carefully scrutinize the grounds supporting warrants where any professional offices are involved.

For Correctly Approaching Special Places for Search and Seizure

KEY POINTS

✓ Seizures of bodily substances are usually not permissible without a warrant, except for breath and blood samples in impaired driving investigations or where truly informed consent has been obtained. The *Criminal Code* provides for bodily impression or print warrants under s. 487.092, DNA warrants under s. 487.05, and impaired driving blood sample warrants under s. 256.

✓ Banks have qualified immunity from seizure of original documents under s. 29 of the *Canada Evidence Act*, however a warrant can explicitly authorize the seizure of original records and properly authenticated copies of bank documents will have the same probative value as original documents.

✓ The work product a lawyer produces, or material the lawyer receives to produce that product, can acquire solicitor-client privilege status if it is created for the purpose of giving or seeking legal advice, or for purposes connected to litigation. Searches of law offices must therefore minimize and justify the intrusion to the greatest degree possible, but exceptions exist to solicitor-client privilege where the innocence of the accused is at stake, where communications are made for a criminal purpose, or where a compelling public interest takes precedence.

✓ All privilege claims made during a search and seizure must be taken seriously and referred to a court for determination, regardless of where the search is being conducted. Ascertain what type of privilege is being asserted, seal any material over which privilege is claimed, allow a reasonable opportunity for a privilege claim to be advanced in court, and return all material found to be privileged without delay.

✓ *Charter* standards governing search, seizure and detention are treated in a much more flexible manner at international entry points to Canada than elsewhere in Canada. The *Customs Act* contains unique place-specific powers that fall outside of what normally would be described as either a search or a regulatory inspection.

✓ Searching non-lawyer professional offices still comes with the risk of privilege being asserted, although it is less likely that a court would uphold such a claim. No free-standing media privilege has been recognized in Canada, but courts are keen to protect the continued operation of the media as part of a free and democratic society so any warrant needs to minimize interference with media operations, and may need to demonstrate a compelling state interest. Searches of government offices may trigger claims of public interest privilege over information pertaining to confidential investigative techniques, international relations, national defence, national security, memorandums to cabinet and draft legislation.

FURTHER READING

Cases

Desôcteaux v. Mierzwinski, [1982] 1 S.C.R. 860. Solicitor-client privilege is a substantive right going beyond merely rendering privileged documents inadmissible at trial, and in some cases extends to preventing state authorities from even examining privileged material.

R. v. Gruenke, [1991] 3 S.C.R. 263. There is no broad class of common law religious communication privilege, although some jurisdictions have established statutory privileges and the existence of a religious communication privilege may be assessed on a case-by-case basis.

R. v. Meuckon (1990), 78 C.R. (3d) 196 (B.C.C.A.). The exact interest must be specified when objecting to disclosure of information under the s. 37 *Canada Evidence Act* public interest privilege. The privilege will be upheld if the trial judge considers that information would not alter the outcome of the trial. The prosecution will be stayed where the trial judge determines that upholding the privilege will prevent the accused from making full answer and defence to the charges.

Books and Articles

G.M. Chayko & E.D. Guilliver, eds., *Forensic Evidence in Canada*, 2nd ed. (Aurora, ON: Canada Law Book, 1999).

M.S. Gorbert, "The Accidental Consistency: Extracting a Coherent Principle from the Jurisprudence Surrounding Solicitor-Client Privilege between the Police and the Crown" (2004) 41 Alta. L. Rev. 825.

C.M. Hageman, D. Prevett & W. Murray, *DNA Handbook* (Toronto: Butterworths, 2002).

R.D. Manes & M.P. Silver, *Solicitor-Client Privilege in Canadian Law* (Markham, ON: Butterworths, 1993).

R. Pomerance, "Compelling the Message from the Medium: Media Search Warrants, Subpoenas and Production Orders" (1997) 2 Can. Crim. L. Rev. 5.

D. Rose & L. Goos, *DNA: A Practical Guide*, loose-leaf (Toronto: Carswell, 2004).

CHAPTER TEN

DEFINING PRIVACY INTERESTS AND JUSTIFYING INTRUSIVE ELECTRONIC SURVEILLANCE

A society which exposed us, at the whim of the state, to the risk of having a permanent electronic recording made of our words every time we opened our mouths might be superbly equipped to fight crime, but would be one in which privacy no longer had any meaning.

R. v. Duarte, [1990] 1 S.C.R. 30 at 44.

In This Chapter

- Making an informed decision to pursue electronic surveillance
- Is prior judicial authorization needed?
- Do the facts and procedures meet the threshold for a wiretap?
- The very limited exigent circumstances wiretap
- Less intrusive forms of electronic surveillance

The term "wiretap" has taken on a mystical air unlike any other investigative technique, perhaps because of the James-Bond-planting-a-listening-device-in-a-martini-olive spy allure with which wiretaps are associated. That air may also have come about because of the exclusive club wiretaps inhabit, requiring special agents to apply for them, particular judges to consider them, and precise rules limiting when they can be authorized. However, placed in their proper context wiretaps are simply another investigative tool available in the *Criminal Code* tool box. Wiretaps don't sit on the top tray when you first open that box, but might be able to be lifted out of the box after you have rummaged around a bit to make sure there aren't more appropriate tools in there. Demystification of the law can lay bare the underpinnings of electronic surveillance authorizations, but early investigator-prosecutor contact is necessary because of the intrusive and evolving nature of this area of law.

MAKING AN INFORMED DECISION TO PURSUE ELECTRONIC SURVEILLANCE

The broad term "electronic surveillance" now includes more than just wiretap communications intercepts, also encompassing less intrusive forms of surveillance like tracking devices and number recorders, as well as almost equally intrusive video monitoring. Before making a decision to proceed with any form of electronic surveillance ask yourself: is non-electronic surveillance just as effective and much less hassle? The factual complexity that can tie up several investigators for weeks at a time, the cost of recording and translating thousands of conversations, and the effort of supporting a complex prosecution mean, especially prior to seeking a true wiretap authorization, you have to consider what you realistically can expect to accomplish. My personal experience in dealing with wiretap cases at the prosecution end has been that months worth of wiretaps will sometimes secure information of little evidentiary value to a court proceeding. The recorded conversations of targets may be just too cryptic, or targets may avoid making important communications by telephone. If you do decide to go the electronic route, has the right form of electronic surveillance been chosen? Will the judicial authorization and its supporting affidavit hold up at trial?

IS PRIOR JUDICIAL AUTHORIZATION NEEDED?

Prior judicial authorization for electronic surveillance is needed when artificial enhancement of human powers of perception exceeds *reasonable* expectations of privacy. Although the *Charter* protects the privacy interests of people and not places, it is generally the place electronic surveillance will be conducted at and the technology deployed to pursue that surveillance that governs the need for prior authorization. This is because the reasonableness of any expectation of privacy is contextual, so that two people conferring at a mall food court table could have a reasonable expectation that their conversations will not be overheard by electronic means, but not that they will be immune from video surveillance in such a public place (especially if video warning signs are posted) or from being observed by an investigator sitting at a neighbouring table who only uses his natural senses of sight, smell and hearing.

Section 184 and s-s. 487.01(4) of the *Criminal Code* codify the main restrictions on audio and video monitoring. Section 184 implies that any electronic or mechanical hearing enhancement requires prior authorization to intrude on a "private" conversation: "Every one who, by means of any electro-magnetic, acoustic, mechanical or other device, willfully intercepts a private communication is guilty of an indictable offence and liable to a term of imprisonment for a term not exceeding five years." Sub-section 487.01(4) requires a video warrant for any observation "by means of a television camera or other similar electronic device" of a person "engaged in activity in circumstances in which the person has a reasonable expectation of privacy." Thus only electronic devices are regulated for visual imaging, not mechanical ones like binoculars.

It is impossible for the courts to exhaustively determine in advance whether a privacy interest exists in every unique human life situation, but they have issued many rulings that allow prosecutors to draw general conclusions about where the line lies for prior judicial authorization. For example, the context of a hotel room was determined in *R. v. Wong*, [1990] 3 S.C.R. 36 at 47, to be sufficiently private that a reasonable expectation to be free from video surveillance could arise:

> George Orwell in his classic dystopian novel 1984 paints a grim picture of a society whose citizens had every reason to expect that their every movement was subject to electronic video surveillance. The contrast with the expectations of privacy in a free society such as our own could not be more striking. The notion that the agencies of the state should be at liberty to train hidden cameras on members of society wherever and whenever they wish is fundamentally irreconcilable with what we perceive to be acceptable behaviour on the part of government.

Early investigator-prosecutor contact should be able to guide you on what private situations require prior authorization for electronic surveillance, and which public situations do not.

Although the mantra "if in doubt, seek a warrant" applies just as strongly to electronic surveillance as to more conventional forms of search and seizure, not every act of electronic surveillance will run roughshod over privacy. For example, the minimally intrusive electronic FLIR (forward looking infra-red device) has, after some legal shifting to and fro, been found not to require prior judicial authorization when used to gather heat signature information about the interior of buildings, even when those buildings are dwelling places. FLIR devices were initially believed not to engage privacy rights, but briefly fell afoul of an apparent presumption that electronic enhancement equaled privacy breach in *R. v. Tessling* (2003), 168 O.A.C. 124 (C.A.) at para. 79: "the nature of the intrusiveness is subtle but almost Orwellian in its theoretical capacity." Thus a different court using the same Orwell literary reference as in *Wong* came to a similar finding that warrantless conduct of investigators breached the *Charter* — obviously a book that has become a cultural privacy protection icon.

The following year the warrantless use of current FLIR technology was rehabilitated as not so Orwellian after all in *R. v. Tessling*, [2004] 3 S.C.R. 432 at paras. 30 & 63:

> the reasonableness line has to be determined by looking at the information generated by *existing* FLIR technology, and then evaluating its impact on a reasonable privacy interest. If, as expected, the capability of FLIR and other technologies will improve and the nature and quality of the information hereafter changes, it will be a different case, and the courts will have to deal with its privacy implications at that time in light of the facts as they then exist.
>
> . . .
>
> External patterns of heat distribution on the external surfaces of a house is not information in which the respondent had a reasonable expectation of privacy. The heat distribution, as stated, offers no insight into his private life, and reveals nothing of his "biographical core of personal information". Its disclosure scarcely affects the "dignity, integrity and autonomy" of the person whose house is subject of the FLIR image.

It is tough to know which other devices that enhance the senses like night-vision scopes or aerial gyroscopically stabilized telescopes will presumptively be found to intrude on privacy rights until each piece of new technology is vetted by the courts. The best that can be said in pursuit of demystification of the law is that the more intrusive the technology, the greater likelihood its use will require prior judicial authorization.

Precision of the "Reasonable Expectation of Privacy" Standard

Q & A

Q: Why couldn't Parliament just set out in the *Charter* or the *Criminal Code* the places or situations where a person does and does not have privacy rights? This concept of "reasonable expectation of privacy" seems awfully imprecise for investigators to be able to figure out when court authorized warrants and wiretaps are and aren't needed.

A: An enumerated privacy list admittedly would be a far more elegant solution, but no matter how long the list was it too would be subject to constant interpretation as to whether a factual situation fell inside or outside its boundaries. An easier approach is for investigators to remember broad categories encompassing the relative order of places and aspects of the person where there is a good chance a privacy interest exists.

DO THE FACTS AND PROCEDURES MEET THE THRESHOLD FOR A WIRETAP?

When drafting a true wiretap application to intercept private communications and its supporting affidavit under the Part VI "Invasion of Privacy" provisions of the *Criminal Code*, there are many additional hoops you have to jump through to secure a valid wiretap compared to a normal search warrant. Sub-section 186(4) of the *Code* spells out what the authorization must deal with:

184. (4) An authorization shall

(a) state the offence in respect of which private communications may be intercepted;

(b) state the type of private communication that may be intercepted;

(c) state the identity of the persons, if known, whose private communications are to be intercepted, generally describe the place at which private communications may be intercepted, if a general description of that place can be given, and generally describe the manner of interception that may be used;

(d) contain such terms and conditions as the judge considers advisable in the public interest; and

(e) be valid for the period, not exceeding sixty days, set out therein.

Sub-sections 185 (c) – (h) of the *Code* set out the affidavit requirements to support an authorization:

185. . . . .shall be accompanied by an affidavit, which may be sworn on the information and belief of a peace officer or public officer deposing to the following matters:

(c) the facts relied on to justify the belief that an authorization should be given together with particulars of the offence,

(d) the type of private communication proposed to be intercepted,

(e) the names, addresses and occupations, if known, of all persons, the interception of whose private communications there are reasonable grounds to believe may assist the investigation of the offence, a general description of the nature and location of the place, if known, at which private communications are proposed to be intercepted and a general description of the manner of interception proposed to be used,

(f) the number of instances, if any, on which an application has been made under this section in relation to the offence and a person named in the affidavit pursuant to paragraph (e) and on which the application was withdrawn or no authorization was given, the date on which each application was made and the name of the judge to whom each application was made,

(g) the period for which the authorization is requested, and

(h) whether other investigative procedures have been tried and have failed or why it appears they are unlikely to succeed or that the urgency of the matter is such that it would be impractical to carry out the investigation of the offence using only other investigative procedures.

Both the authorization and the supporting affidavit need to cover most of the same details, but the authorization states the legal limits to the wiretap, while the affidavit states the factual basis supporting those limits. The two details the affidavit especially needs to cover that aren't replicated in the authorization are previous related wiretap authorization applications, and the existence of investigative necessity. Those wiretap statutory requirements lead to nine key questions you must ask yourself during the drafting stage.

1. Does the Offence Being Investigated Qualify?

The special nature of wiretaps derives not from what they can do, but from what they cannot do. Section 183 of the *Criminal Code* strictly limits the types of offences for which true wiretaps and video warrants are available:

> **183.** In this part . . . "offence" means an offence contrary to, any conspiracy or attempt to commit or being an accessory after the fact in relation to an offence contrary to, or any counselling in relation to an offence contrary to (a) any of the following provisions . . .and includes any other offence that there are reasonable grounds to believe is a criminal organization offence or any other offence that there are reasonable grounds to believe is an offence described in paragraph (b) or (c) of the definition "terrorism offence" in section 2.

Very few regulatory offences qualify, even though regulatory offences are prone to conspiracies, and can merit terms of imprisonment of many years. Make sure you check an up-to-date version of the *Code* for new offences that are occasionally added to the s. 183 list that includes:

- almost 100 of the more serious offences involving violence, fraud, property, and public morals under the *Criminal Code*;

- one offence under the *Bankruptcy and Insolvency Act*, R.S.C. 1985, c. B-3;

- most *Controlled Drugs and Substances Act* offences;

- one offence under the *Corruption of Foreign Public Officials Act*, S.C. 1998, c. 34,

- any offence under the *Crimes Against Humanity and War Crimes Act*, S.C. 2000, c. 24,

- a few offences under the *Competition Act*, R.S.C. 1985, c. C-34;

- two offences under the *Customs Act*, R.S.C. 1985, c. 1 (2nd Supp.);

- a few offences under the *Excise Act 2001*, S.C. 2002, c. 22;

- a few offences under the *Export and Import Permits Act*, R.S.C. 1985, c. E-19;

- a few offences under the *Immigration and Refugee Protection Act*, S.C. 2001, c. 27;

- any offence under the *Security of Information Act*, R.S.C. 1985, c. O-5;

- any "criminal organization" or "terrorism" offence.

Wiretap Applications for Non-Designated Offences

Q&A

Q: I'm a Canada Revenue Agency investigator looking into serious allegations of tax evasion that also involve investor fraud. I'm afraid that the only way I can further advance my case is through wiretaps. Can I bring an application for a wiretap authorization if I link in fraud charges in addition to tax evasion offences?

A: No. You could turn the criminal fraud component of the case over to the appropriate police service who independently might pursue a wiretap authorization for a fraud investigation, but for an investigation whose predominant purpose is the gathering of tax evasion evidence, you cannot use a wiretap even if other charges are involved.

2. Does Investigative Necessity Exist?

While wiretaps are not truly a method of last resort, there must be a certain degree of investigative necessity because of the degree to which they intrude on privacy. According to s-s. 185(1)(h) of the *Criminal Code* the affidavit filed in support of the wiretap application must state either:

- whether other investigative procedures have been tried and have failed; or

- why it appears other procedures are unlikely to succeed; or

- that the urgency of the matter is such that it would be impractical to carry out the investigation of the offence using only other investigative procedures.

Investigative necessity has not been interpreted as requiring absolute necessity, just that there is a good reason for going the wiretap route rather than choosing a more conventional investigative technique as confirmed in *R. v. Araujo*, [2000] 2 S.C.R. 992 at para. 33:

> Recent jurisprudence has confirmed that such language is to be interpreted in a practical commonsense fashion, so that courts may issue wiretap orders even when the government has not pursued all other investigative techniques. Courts have found a variety of grounds for allowing that normal investigative techniques are unlikely to succeed. These include: a showing by the government that those techniques would not reveal key information . . . ; when it can be shown that those techniques are ineffective against a large-scale crime organization . . . ; . . . a close-knit family . . . or a drug conspiracy; or when counter-surveillance methods employed by the defendants made such methods unlikely to succeed . . . .

An overly involved explanation is not usually required to satisfy investigative necessity, but something must be said since investigative necessity cannot simply be assumed to exist. This is one of the most common places for a defence attack on the validity of an authorization, so you can't claim necessity without explaining "why" through explicit reference to the factual situation of your own unique investigation. Do not just repeat some *pro forma* clause here that you found in another wiretap affidavit of times gone by.

Parliament decided in s-s. 186(1.1) of the *Code* that the mere investigation of two particular classes of offences is itself sufficient to show investigative necessity without any further rationale:

- those involving criminal organizations;

- those involving terrorism offences.

Sub-section 467.1(1) of the *Code* defines a criminal organization as:

> a group, however organized, that

> > (a) is composed of three or more persons in or outside Canada; and

> > (b) has as one of its main purposes or main activities the facilitation or commission of one or more serious offences that, if committed, would likely result in the direct or indirect receipt of a material benefit, including a financial benefit, by the group or by any of the persons who constitute the group.

> It does not include a group of persons that forms randomly for the immediate commission of a single offence.

> "serious offence" means an indictable offence under this or any other Act of Parliament for which the maximum punishment is

imprisonment for five years or more, or another offence that is pre-scribed by regulation.

"Terrorism offences" are set out in ss. 83.02-83.04 & 83.18-83.23 of the *Code*, which include any federal indictable offence committed for the benefit of, at the direction of or in association with a terrorist group. Check a recent version of s. 83.01 of the *Code* for the latest definition of what amounts to a terrorist group, as it is a complicated formulation that is evolving over time.

3. Is There a Designated Wiretap Agent Available to Make the Application?

Not just any peace officer can bring an application for a wiretap. Sub-section 185(1) of the *Criminal Code* requires a specially appointed agent of the Attorney General or Solicitor General of Canada to bring the application:

> **185.** (1) An application for an authorization to be given under sec-tion 186 shall be made *ex parte* and in writing to a judge of a supe-rior court of criminal jurisdiction or a judge as defined in section 552 and shall be signed by the Attorney General of the province in which the application is made or the Solicitor General of Canada or an agent specially designated in writing for the purposes of this section by
>
> > (a) the Solicitor General of Canada personally or the Deputy Solicitor General of Canada personally, if the offence under investigation is one in respect of which proceedings, if any, may be instituted at the instance of the Government of Canada and conducted by or on behalf of the Attorney General of Canada, or
> >
> > (b) the Attorney General of a province personally or the Deputy Attorney General of a province personally, in any other case . . . .

Usually these agents are a small number of prosecutors scattered through-out the country. Non-agents, including investigators and other lawyers, can still work on preparing a wiretap application and any investigator with the required knowledge can swear the affidavit filed in support of the applica-tion, the wiretap agent is only required to bring the application itself before the appropriate court.

4. Is the Application Being Brought before the Appropriate Court?

Another rare requirement of s-s. 185(1) of the *Code* is that only a superior court judge can grant a wiretap application — not a provincial court judge, and especially not a justice of the peace. Only the most serious of offences must be tried by a superior court judge and only the most significant of court applications need the approval of such a judge. The special status of both the person who may apply and the person who may grant the authorization underlines the highly intrusive nature of wiretaps, and the serious scrutiny that every wiretap application receives.

5. Have the Persons Whose Communications Are to Be Intercepted Been Particularized?

The place to be searched in a regular search warrant is not left to the discretion of investigators after the warrant has been issued. So too with the choice of persons whose communications are to be intercepted under a wiretap authorization. Sub-section 185(1)(e) of the *Code* requires every wiretap application to include: "the names, addresses and occupations, if known, of all persons, the interception of whose private communications there are reasonable grounds to believe may assist the investigation of the offence."

a. *How to Construct a Basket Clause for Unknown Persons Subject to Interception*

Any persons who are targets of the wiretap, and known persons who might also be incidentally intercepted like spouses or friends of the targets, should be named in the application and supporting affidavit. Other unknown persons who could be intercepted are specified in a "basket clause" that sets a limit on that class of persons, like all persons speaking to a particular target at a certain place. The key is to be as specific as possible in describing the persons whose communications you intend to intercept.

What must be avoided is a basket clause containing no real limits as described in *R. v. Grabowski*, [1985] 2 S.C.R. 434 at 445-46:

> paragraph 3(b), read with paragraph 4(b), means that this authorization allowed the conversations of anyone to be intercepted anywhere.

The persons whose communications can be intercepted are William Murphy and certain other persons whose identity is unknown at present, provided the latter are in collusion with Murphy or in collusion with someone at one of the places mentioned in paragraph 4. According to paragraph 4(b), this includes anywhere that a person mentioned in paragraph 3 may be found, thus including persons whose identity is unknown.

In my opinion, the authorization consequently contains no limitation as to persons or place.

Basket clauses are not a substitute for a careful review of all names known to investigators. A good example of those who could legitimately fall into a basket clause are people not previously known to investigators who telephone a target's cell phone number to order drugs.

b. *The Benefits and Goals of Specificity in Naming Targets*

It is an irony of wiretap authorization drafting that the best wiretaps from a legal perspective are the ones most restricted as to from who or where they can collect information. Investigators must ask themselves: just how many calls can we reasonably sort through anyway, especially if interpreters will be needed to translate some of those calls? I personally think of wiretaps as hand held dip nets that carefully pick among all species of fish and that can only be used to fish at a very small number of locations. Wiretaps are not ocean-going factory freezer trawlers that sweep telephone networks clean of all their communications so that the state can keep the few interesting conversations, and throw back the rest.

Lack of specificity in naming targets can invalidate an authorization, as in *R. v. Paterson* (1985), 7 O.A.C. 105 at paras. 22 & 24, affd. [1987] 2 S.C.R. 291, where the authorization read in part:

3) (b) Authorization is also hereby given to intercept the private communications of persons whose identities are presently unknown, in accordance with the terms of this Authorization, provided that there are reasonable and probable grounds to believe that the interception of such private communications may assist the investigation of any of the offences stated in paragraph I above, whether or not any such person described in paragraph 3(a) above is party to such private communications.

4) That, in relation to the places at or from which the private communications of the above described known and unknown persons

may be intercepted and in respect of which a general description of the places of interception may be given, the places of interception are as follows:

. . .

(e) All other places either stationary, portable or mobile, that may become apparent to the police as a result of their investigation to which they believe that the persons mentioned in paragraph 3 are resorting or attending at.

The court concluded:

In my view the "basket clause" is invalid. It vests in the police the discretion to intercept the private communications of any or all persons if there are reasonable and probable grounds to believe that the interception of such private conversations may assist in the investigation of any of the offences specified in the authorization. That constitutes a delegation of the judge's function to the police.

To use yet another analogy, there is a difference between a basket capable of containing a few additional bad apples, and a horn of plenty capable of containing the entire population of a province.

c. *Focusing the Wiretap on People*

The focus of the wiretap is on people, unlike the search warrant which is focused on a place. A solid wiretap goes to great lengths to get the description right of the people whose communications are to be intercepted, and links their communications to particular offences for which wiretaps are available. By contrast, the search warrant must correctly describe the place to be searched, and link its contents to specific offences for which the type of warrant sought is available. Wiretaps still need to be connected to a place, and search warrants are ultimately looking for evidence of offences committed by real people, but I believe it helps to start off thinking about wiretaps by thinking about the people they will legitimately intercept, instead of all the ripe locations at which listening devices can be installed.

d. *Naming and Factually Justifying the Inclusion of Everyone in the Supporting Affidavit*

The affidavit supporting the authorization must provide facts sufficient to support reasonable belief that communications of the people to be intercepted will provide evidence of a designated offence. Name everyone in the affidavit for whom there are reasonable grounds to believe that their private communications may assist the investigation of the offence in question. Some of those named may be people innocent of any wrongdoing. Even if the exact name of a person whose communications are to be intercepted is unknown, a description of that person's appearance can be used in the affidavit. The affidavit's facts also must support the boundaries of any basket clause, by explaining how the named class of people would be communicating in a way that will provide evidence of the offences under investigation.

6. Have the Places Where Interceptions Can Occur Been Particularized?

Sub-section 185(1)(e) of the *Code* requires: "a general description of the nature and location of the place, if known, at which private communications are proposed to be intercepted," so that a court can decide on its appropriateness, instead of location choice being left to the later discretion of investigators. Ideally, a specific property address will be given if it is tied to a land-based telephone line associated with those persons targeted by the wiretap. In less than ideal situations locations unknown at the time a wiretap is initially applied for can still be targeted, but broadly naming any place where a named target can be found is not sufficient. A proper "resort to clause" could read something like "any place within the province of British Columbia which is believed, on reasonable grounds during the currency of this authorization, to be a place resorted to by Johan Smith." Using a resort to clause for places is the equivalent of using a basket clause for people — they are both good ways to deal with unknowns, but neither can be open-ended.

R. v. Thompson, [1990] 2 S.C.R. 1111 at 1141, gave examples of what would and would not amount to reasonable grounds that justified a "resort to" clause:

> The case at bar provides examples of situations in which the police obviously proceeded with sufficient evidence of "resorting to" and a situation equally obviously without sufficient evidence. There is evidence that the targets made use of public telephones and employed a code to inform one another of where they could be reached. In several cases the police placed taps on telephones because the numbers of the telephones were referred to in other calls. In my view this is sufficient evidence to act upon, and

amounts to reasonable and probable grounds that the target will resort to that place. This is subject to its being established that the private communication relied on is itself the product of a lawful interception. In another situation, however, the police placed taps on four public telephones because of their proximity to where one of the targets was staying. In my view, this is insufficient evidence to act upon, and amounts to little more than indiscriminate monitoring based on a hunch.

Restrictions on people to be intercepted will inevitably restrict places of interception, and restrictions on places of interception will likewise restrict people to be intercepted. A lack of practical restrictions in the authorization on places of interception is a strong signal that any basket clause present covering unknown people may also be deficient.

a. *Disclosure of Places That Become Known*

Where a place resorted to does subsequently become known, it must be explicitly named in any wiretap renewal or new related wiretap authorization as noted in *R. v. Moore*, (1993), 27 B.C.A.C. 253 at paras. 30-31, affd. [1995] 1 S.C.R. 756:

> The evidence is clear that from May 26, 1989 onward Surrey Stereo was a location to which the appellant and other targets had resorted — to such an extent that a manually controlled intercepting device had been installed on the telephone at that location.

> While giving evidence on the voir dire, Constable K. . . asserted that having initially utilized the "resort to" clause as authority to install the intercepting device, the police could rely on that same clause in the second authorization. I do not agree. At the time the second authorization was applied for, Constable K. . . and others directly involved knew, or must be presumed to have known, that private communications would continue to be intercepted at the Surrey Stereo location on and after June 22, 1989 when the second authorization would be in effect. Under the circumstances, that location and the specific telephone number could have been disclosed to the authorizing judge. That disclosure would have permitted him to address his mind to the imposition of whatever conditions he thought appropriate to minimize indiscriminate interceptions at Surrey Stereo.

The *Criminal Code* gives investigators lots of flexibility to intercept communications of unknown persons falling within a basket clause, and at unknown locations coming within a "resort to" clause, but demands in return that when investigators learn the identity of anyone or the location of any place being so intercepted, they name the person or place in all renewal or new authorizations so a court has the opportunity to rule on their appropriateness. The courts control the scope of the wiretap process, investigators only control wiretap implementation.

b. *Mobile Communications and Places of Interception*

As many specifics as possible regarding wiretap target locations need to be given, like listing all home or business addresses commonly frequented by a target, but the advent of mobile communications technology increasingly requires a bit of flexibility on how intercept locations are specified. Generally, the place of interception for a cell phone will be the phone itself and the switching station that the call is routed through, but even the switching station can become an uncertainty with multiple cell phone companies using differing cell networks. *R. v. Willock* (1998), 64 Alta. L.R. (3d) 354 (C.A.), confirmed that a cellular telephone registered in the name of and used by a particular person would qualify as a place to name as a wiretap target location, and it did not matter where the telephone was located at the time of the intercept. But place continues to create confusion as in *R. v. Nguyen* (2001), 294 A.R. 201 (Prov. Ct.) at para. 29, which seemed to contradict the higher court in *Willock*:

> "place" means the locations of the two telephones at opposite ends of the conversations. If it is a land line, the "place" is the address where the land line is installed. If it is a cellular phone, the "place" description may be more general, i.e., "This call was serviced by cell towers 'A' and 'B' located at X (address) and Y (address) respectively, in the city of Calgary, Alberta."

Notwithstanding the conflicting law, naming the phone and switching station seems sufficient.

For Internet-based communications, the location of a wiretap might be the address of the Internet service provider, the address of the computer that could change each time a user logs in, or the address of a wireless hub from which that computer accesses the Internet. Satellite phones pose yet another set of problems over location, particularly because both the service provider and the satellite relay may be located outside of Canadian territory. Uncertainties over evolving law governing emerging communications technologies requires early investigator-prosecutor contact to resolve.

c. *Affidavit Support for Places of Interceptions*

The affidavit supporting the wiretap authorization must provide factually solid grounds for the choice of places for interception, setting out the facts investigators possess to reasonably believe that particular targets make calls from certain telephone numbers. Relevant facts could include that target telephone numbers are registered in the names of the people being targeted, or that those numbers are assigned to places where the targets are known to reside from visual observations conducted by investigators or tips received from informers. Where a "resort to" clause is used, the affidavit should set out detailed facts supporting the belief that certain locations may be resorted to for the purposes of communication by the targets. Don't just state conclusions, state the underlying facts supporting those conclusions, the sources of those facts, and why those sources are worthy of belief.

7. Has the Time Period During which the Authorization Is Valid Been Specified?

Wiretap authorizations are governed by statutory time limits at the end of which they must be renewed or will expire. Specifying on the face of an authorization the dates between, or for how many days, it is valid enables anyone later dealing with it to determine when it was legally in effect, and is consistent with the requirement in s-s.185(1)(g) of the *Code* to name: "the period for which the authorization is requested." Investigators need to quickly get legal advice if unsure about whether an important communication was legally intercepted around the time of an authorization's expiry. Generally speaking, s-s. 186(4)(e) of the *Code* limits a single authorization's validity to 60 days, subject to renewal for additional 60-day periods. In the case of criminal organization or terrorism offences, s. 186.1 of the *Code* permits an authorization or its renewals to have a maximum validity of one year. Given that the planning of complex conspiracies can stretch over much more than 60 days, the one-year period for validity is a great aid to investigative efforts where previously a lot of time was spent seeking wiretap renewals to continue monitoring developing criminal plans. If you are not certain the offences or targets you are investigating fit into the criminal organization or terrorism exceptions to the 60-day limit, you should limit your authorization to 60 days to avoid later trial challenges to the authorization's validity.

8. Have the Types of Communications, Manner of Interception and Ways Privacy Intrusions Will Be Minimized Been Specified?

The last of the wiretap technical details to be addressed are covered in s-ss. 185(1)(d) & (e) of the *Code*: "the type of private communication proposed to be intercepted . . . [and] a general description of the manner of interception proposed to be used" must be particularized, at least in a general sense. In naming the type of communication, the current practice is simply to name all types of communication falling within the definition of "private communication" in s. 183 of the *Criminal Code*: oral communications and telecommunications, including radio-based (cell) phone communications. In addition, briefly describe the technical means proposed for interception. Internet communications may not currently be covered by the language of the *Code*, but legislative amendments could address this problem. Section 487.01 *Code* general warrants might already cover the Internet to some degree, particularly if you view the Internet as predominantly containing data and documents, rather than communications covered by s. 183 *Code* wiretaps.

Investigators must also set out conditions in the authorization to ensure people who aren't legitimate targets of investigation will not be subject to privacy intrusions. Failure to minimize intrusions has been severely criticized, as in *R. v. Thompson*, [1990] 2 S.C.R. 1111 at 1145-46, where a wiretap authorization permitted the recording of all telephone calls made from a number of public pay telephones regardless of who was making a call:

> On these facts, given the breadth of the authorizations, hundreds of private conversations may have been intercepted when not one target was involved . . . At minimum, I would think that such an authorization would provide that conversations at a public telephone not be intercepted unless there were reasonable and probable grounds for believing that a target was using the telephone at the time that the listening device was activated. The police cannot simply install a listening device and leave it running indiscriminately in the hope that a target may come along.
>
> . . .
>
> Interceptions which were made pursuant to these authorizations, which were simply fishing expeditions and not based on reasonable and probable grounds for believing the target would be utilizing the pay telephones at the time, were, in my opinion, unreasonable. In most instances, it would be preferable to have actual phys-

ical surveillance of the public telephone to ensure that it is being used by the target.

The minimization obligation goes beyond merely specifying appropriate persons and locations as targets, or drafting limited "basket" and "resort to" clauses. Minimization extends to working out technical ways to limit intrusions, be they physical surveillance of public telephones, live monitoring of private telephones used by many people who aren't targets, checks that targets' privileged conversations with their lawyers aren't recorded, or new and novel means of ensuring the state is only using a hand dip net and not a factory trawler to gather private information.

The accompanying affidavit should offer factual support for why there is reasonable belief the targets use particular types of communications at certain telephone numbers. The affidavit should also describe the basic physical workings of wiretap technology to satisfy the court of the means of interception and the steps investigators will follow to minimize intrusion into non-target communications. In addressing the means of interception and minimization, a balance must be struck between revealing enough detail to fulfill the requirements of the *Criminal Code*, and not revealing so many details that investigators later feel it necessary to edit the affidavit to protect confidential investigative techniques prior to its disclosure.

9. Has the Affidavit Been Drafted in a Way That Sufficiently Supports the Authorization?

The general principles of search warrant information to obtain drafting detailed in Chapter 8 are equally applicable to wiretap affidavit drafting, so long as the wiretap's additional preconditions are addressed. Because wiretap affidavits are generally far lengthier than warrant informations to obtain, drafters of wiretaps run a greater risk of coming up with a confusing affidavit that is factually insufficient to support an authorization. Worst of all, wiretap drafters often wind up resorting to stultifying boilerplate language that does nothing to advance their cases.

a. *Avoiding Over Mixing of Your Affidavit*

I have seen both wiretap and search warrant affidavits that were like stews, with lots of carefully chopped ingredients all blended together and left to simmer for a bit, with the occasional new ingredient being added during the cooking process. After they come off the stovetop those affidavits initially seem like a pleasant enough hearty meal because of their extensive content. Dipping into them results in a pleasing first taste, but after a couple of more mouthfuls it quickly becomes apparent that the individual ingredients cannot be distinguished from one another. The cook cannot even recite the recipe since ingredients were just randomly thrown in as they became available, and a few extra spices used to cover over any inadequacies. This mixing of flavours might sometimes work in cooking, but it definitely does not make for a good affidavit supporting a wiretap or search warrant application, no matter how big a pot of stew is the end result.

Each factual ingredient going into the wiretap affidavit needs to be carefully matched up with each separate offence, person and location so the authorizing judge can be certain all required grounds are present. Additionally, time and means of execution and investigative necessity need to be addressed as discrete factual topics, and not be buried under the weight of offence-person-location facts. It is not sufficient that all of those ingredients do in fact exist and might after days of careful study be found to be quietly lurking somewhere within the affidavit's text; they must be clearly and separately listed off in the affidavit if investigators want to be sure that they count towards issuance of the authorization.

b. *Ensuring the Affidavit is Factually Complete*

It will be a lot easier to figure out whether you have included all of the required facts if you avoid the over mixed affidavit. As with regular search warrants, it is vital to set out *all* underlying facts relevant to supporting the request for a wiretap authorization, and not just state conclusions. There is really no way around supporting affidavit factual complexity, particularly when incorporating relevant information gathered during previous authorizations; it comes with the territory of getting involved in wiretaps, but complexity need not sacrifice readability.

Affidavit readability must not, however, be confused with oversimplification. Investigators cannot simply say "trust me" when setting out the intricacies of case facts in the affidavit. Parliament set up the *Criminal Code*'s wiretap provisions to provide a completely independent review of the facts said to support issuance of a wiretap, and it tasked superior court judges with conducting the review, so investigators have no choice but to give those judges *all* of the relevant facts. It is always that one important detail left out of the supporting affidavit that defence counsel can later turn into a key non-disclosed fact which it is argued invalidates the entire wiretap. While the most relevant facts of other authorizations should still be included in the body of a new affidavit, attaching related prior authorizations as appendices to a new affidavit permits some summarization of the old affidavits' facts to improve readability of the new affidavit.

c. *Avoiding the Dreaded Boilerplate*

While there clearly are a lot of set requirements for a wiretap affidavit, resist being tempted by dangerous blind reliance on "boilerplate" that can wind up being inapplicable, out of date, or improperly drafted in the first place. There is a great difference between relying on sound precedent to guide your hand at drafting a fresh and thoughtful affidavit where each included phrase is carefully considered and fully understood, as compared to dropping vast tracts of boilerplate of unknown origin into an affidavit whose only originality comes from the names of the people and places being targeted. Precedent turns into boilerplate when human beings do not assess and adapt past precedent to current facts, and instead pump a new affidavit full of catch phrases like "reliable confidential informer," even though that person may not be reliable, his identity may not be confidential, and he may not even really be an informer.

R. v. Araujo, [2000] 2 S.C.R. 992 at paras. 46-47, succinctly and somewhat poetically summed up the correct approach to drafting an affidavit that supports an application for a wiretap:

> Looking at matters practically in order to learn from this case for the future, what kind of affidavit should the police submit in order to seek permission to use wiretapping? The legal obligation on anyone seeking an *ex parte* authorization is *full and frank* disclosure of *material facts* . . . .
>
> At best, the use of boiler-plate language adds extra verbiage and seldom anything of meaning; at worst, it has the potential to trick the reader into thinking that the affidavit means something that it does not. Although the use of boiler-plate language will not automatically prevent a judge from issuing an authorization (there is, after all, no formal legal requirement to avoid it), I cannot stress enough that judges should deplore it. There is nothing wrong—and much right—with an affidavit that sets out the facts truthfully, fully, and *plainly*. Counsel and police officers submitting materials to obtain wiretapping authorizations should not allow themselves to be led into the temptation of misleading the authorizing judge, either by the language used or strategic omissions.

I intentionally do not include a sample wiretap authorization and supporting affidavit in this book so it cannot be turned into boilerplate. Drafting any type of wiretap or warrant is much more an exercise in substance rather than form. Early investigator-prosecutor contact can set you on the right path with regard to form, but it will be up to you as the investigator who best understands your own investigation to create the substance that can then be checked over by a prosecutor once it is in decent shape from following the principles set out in this book.

The Length and Complexity of Wiretap Supporting Affidavits

Q & A

Q: It seems to a lot of us that no matter how much material we include in an affidavit supporting a wiretap, it is never enough. These affidavits now run to hundreds of pages and still courts find fault with their completeness. What do they want, 100,000 page affidavits?

A: The sufficiency of wiretap supporting affidavits is, like many things in life, more a question of the quality of the facts, rather than their quantity. Advance planning before the actual writing starts, concerning how the facts will be laid out toward the goal of securing a court authorization, will pay off.

THE VERY LIMITED EXIGENT CIRCUMSTANCES WIRETAP

Section 184.4 of the *Criminal Code* provides an exigent circumstances exception to the highly intrusive tool of the wiretap, but only makes that tool available in a very constrained way — sort of a wiretap-light version:

> **184.4.** A peace officer may intercept, by means of any electromagnetic, acoustic, mechanical or other device, a private communication where
>
> (a) the peace officer believes on reasonable grounds that the urgency of the situation is such that an authorization could not, with reasonable diligence, be obtained under any other provision of this Part;
>
> (b) the peace officer believes on reasonable grounds that such an interception is immediately necessary to prevent an unlawful act that would cause serious harm to any person or to property; and

> (c) either the originator of the private communication or the person intended by the originator to receive it is the person who would perform the act that is likely to cause the harm or is the victim, or intended victim, of the harm.

Because s. 184.4's requirements are cumulative, wiretaps without prior judicial authorization are restricted to truly exceptional, emergency situations, and are limited to the communications of the victim or perpetrator of the harm, *not* of third parties who for example could have knowledge of the location of a kidnap victim. Investigators will bear a heavy burden when tendering evidence collected under s. 184.4 at a trial.

LESS INTRUSIVE FORMS OF ELECTRONIC SURVEILLANCE

In the ever-expanding world of electronic surveillance, communications intercepts remain the ultimate crime fighting weapon in the investigator tool box. That every other electronic tool is considered to be less intrusive on privacy interests is demonstrated by the progressively lower requirements that must be met for prior judicial authorization to use those tools. Consent intercepts, tracking devices, number recorders and the infinite variety of techniques available under the general warrant, including video surveillance, are all there in the tool box just waiting to be picked out when right for the job, but you must understand each of their respective legal requirements in order to make effective use of them during your investigations. The Electronic Surveillance Checklist, at the end of this chapter, should help ensure you have considered all the major wiretap and non-wiretap electronic surveillance options, and that a sufficient legal and factual basis exists to support a chosen option.

1. Why Consent Intercepts Are Different

I don't know if it is art imitating life, or life imitating art, but it seems at times in television, movies and real life everyone is recording everyone else — be it the disgruntled employee, the jealous spouse, or the professional hit man wannabe. It is not a crime in Canada for one party to a conversation to secretly record a conversation with someone else, but state investigators cannot use or encourage others to use such techniques without prior judicial authorization. *R. v. Duarte*, [1990] 1 S.C.R. 30 at 48, found there was a difference between an investigator repeating in court what she had heard someone else say, and the same investigator playing a voice recording of the other person for the court:

> I am unable to see any similarity between the risk that someone will listen to one's words with the intention of repeating them and the risk involved when someone listens to them while simultaneously making a permanent electronic record of them. These risks are of a different order of magnitude. The one risk may, in the context of law enforcement, be viewed as a reasonable invasion of privacy, the other unreasonable. They involve different risks to the individual and the body politic. In other words, the law recognizes that we inherently have to bear the risk of the "tattletale" but draws the line at concluding that we must also bear, as the price of choosing to speak to another human being, the risk of having a permanent electronic recording made of our words.

An investigator making notes of a conversation overheard at a restaurant without electronic enhancement requires no prior judicial authorization, while that same investigator covertly making an electronic recording of the conversation for the purpose of later using it as evidence in court does require authorization, even if the investigator is a party to the conversation.

Section 184.2 of the *Criminal Code* now provides for a simplified process to obtain judicial authorization for a "consent intercept" to secretly record the conversation of another person where one party knows the recording is being made:

> **184.2.** (1) A person may intercept, by means of any electro-magnetic, acoustic, mechanical or other device, a private communication where either the originator of the private communication or the person intended by the originator to receive it has consented to the interception and an authorization has been obtained pursuant to subsection (3).
>
> . . .
>
> (3) An authorization may be given under this section if the judge to whom the application is made is satisfied that
>
> (a) there are reasonable grounds to believe that an offence against this or any other Act of Parliament has been or will be committed;
>
> (b) either the originator of the private communication or the person intended by the originator to receive it has consented to the interception; and

> (c) there are reasonable grounds to believe that information concerning the offence referred to in paragraph (a) will be obtained through the interception sought.

These are consent intercepts because at least one party to the conversation has consented to its interception. As a result of the lesser privacy intrusion, the burden for judicial authorization is lower than where wiretaps are involved. There is *no limitation on the types of offences* for which a consent intercept may be sought, so long as it pertains to the investigation of an offence under *any* federal Act, and there is *no requirement for investigative necessity* to be shown. It is more like an application for a regular search warrant than for a wiretap because any peace officer may apply, a provincial court judge (although not a justice of the peace) may authorize the intercept, and a telewarrant-like procedure is available under s. 184.3 of the *Code*.

a. *Using Consent Intercepts as Officer Protection Kits*

Section 184.1 of the *Criminal Code* permits the use of officer protection kits to listen in on an undercover investigator's conversations with targets *without judicial authorization* so long as three conditions are met:

> **184.1.** (1) An agent of the state may intercept, by means of any electro-magnetic, acoustic, mechanical or other device, a private communication if
>
> > (a) either the originator of the private communication or the person intended by the originator to receive it has consented to the interception;
> >
> > (b) the agent of the state believes on reasonable grounds that there is a risk of bodily harm to the person who consented to the interception; and
> >
> > (c) the purpose of the interception is to prevent the bodily harm.

The trade-off for no prior authorization is that any evidence obtained through the officer protection kit interception is inadmissible in court except for charges relating to actual, attempted or threatened bodily harm, and any recordings made pursuant to s. 184.1 must be destroyed as soon as is practical in the circumstances of a case. Section 184.1 is only useful when using some kind of evidence gathering powers found elsewhere.

b. *Use of Consent Intercepts by Private Parties*

Since it is only people working for or at the direction of the state who must obtain judicial authorization for consent intercepts, recordings of conversations made by private parties where the recording party was also a party to the conversation can be completely admissible as evidence in court without any prior judicial authorization so long as they were not made under the direction of any state agent. What are in effect consent intercepts created by private parties could contain valuable evidence of serious offences, like attempts to extort money or threats of violence, made long before any crime is reported to investigators and thus long before investigators can seek some kind of judicial authorization to investigate such a crime. In order to authenticate it, investigators should take a detailed statement from anyone who makes such a private recording, check into the circumstances of its recording, verify what happened to the recording from the time it was made to the time it was given to the investigators, and confirm the identity of the other voices on it. Any state involvement in the making of unauthorized private party intercepts could taint their admissibility, and would illegally circumvent the restrictions on what investigators can directly do themselves.

In *R. v. Coburn* (2003), 108 C.R.R. (2d) 173; 2003 BCSC 243 at paras. 26-27, a consent intercept lacking prior authorization was admitted into evidence because it had been recorded by a private party without the involvement of state authorities:

> There was no dispute that although Mr. Hewitt intercepted two of his private communications with Mr. Coburn with the intent of providing them to the police, the police did not know of Mr. Hewitt's existence or of these interceptions until after the event. As was set out in *R. v. Broyles* [1991] 3 S.C.R. 595 (S.C.C.), at 608, "A relationship between the informer and the authorities which develops after the statement is made . . . will not make the informer a state agent for the purposes of the exchange in question." In other words, at the very least a person is not considered to be acting as an agent of the state until a peace officer has formed a relationship with them.

> As the relationship between the police and Mr. Hewitt developed after the interceptions had occurred, I conclude that Mr. Hewitt was not an agent of the state at the time of those interceptions. As Mr. Hewitt was acting as a private citizen, the *Charter* has no application.

If Hewitt had gone to the police first, and the police had asked Hewitt to make the recordings of his conversations with Coburn, then prior judicial authorization under s. 184.2 of the *Code* would have been required. Completely covert freelance wiretaps set up by a private party to secretly monitor the conversations of others, none of whom know they are being monitored, are an entirely different matter that could constitute a serious criminal offence under s. 184(1) of the *Code* — although they might survive *Charter* scrutiny.

The Usefulness of Recordings Made by Private Parties

Q: An anonymous source recently e-mailed me a digital audio recording of what sounds like the voice of a target I am currently investigating for some minor offences and an unknown voice discussing the planning of a murder. If this recording was made without a wiretap authorization, could it still be admissible in court?

A: So long as you can show it was not made at the direction of the state, a court might find it to be admissible, but if you don't know how or in what context the recording was made its lack of authentication will greatly limit its value as evidence.

---

c. *Proof of Voluntariness in Consent Intercepts*

Where it is an investigator who is the consenting party, proof of valid consent will usually be as simple as calling that investigator to the stand to testify at trial. Where it is an informer-agent or other private party who is offering consent, proof of consent requires a bit more caution since the consent needs to be informed consent. The standards applicable to wiretap consent aren't necessarily the same as for consent to give a voluntary statement or waive *Charter* rights, although it is s. 8 *Charter* rights to be secure against unreasonable search and seizure that are being waived, so following principles similar to those used for consent searches might be appropriate. There is always the possibility that a person consenting to an intercept could later become a co-accused, thus raising self-incrimination problems if the consent was not of the most informed and proper nature.

2. Why Tracking Devices Are Minimally Intrusive

Probably a lot more use by both regulatory and criminal investigators could be made of the factually revealing and fairly easy to obtain tracking device warrant than currently takes place. I have heard of tracking devices being planted in vehicles suspected of driving to criminal conspiracy meeting points, on clothing belonging to a person believed to be travelling to a location where evidence of a crime was disposed of, or even on animals subject to poaching. Whether there is a reasonable expectation of privacy in the place or thing that the tracking device is planted in or on will largely determine whether or not prior judicial authorization is necessary.

Tracking devices are defined under s-s. 492.1(4) of the *Criminal Code* as "any device that, when installed in or on any thing, may be used to help ascertain, by electronic or other means, the location of any thing or person." Sub-section 492.1(1) of the *Code* sets out the parameters of tracking device authorization:

> **492.1.** (1) A justice who is satisfied by information on oath in writing that there are reasonable grounds to suspect that an offence under this or any other Act of Parliament has been or will be committed and that information that is relevant to the commission of the offence, including the whereabouts of any person, can be obtained through the use of a tracking device, may at any time issue a warrant authorizing a peace officer or a public officer who has been appointed or designated to administer or enforce a federal or provincial law and whose duties include the enforcement of this Act or any other Act of Parliament and who is named in the warrant
>
> > (a) to install, maintain and remove a tracking device in or on any thing, including a thing carried, used or worn by any person; and
> >
> > (b) to monitor, or to have monitored, a tracking device installed in or on any thing.

Investigators will need to make an additional application under s-s. 491.1(5) to covertly remove any device that is still installed at the time its authorization expires.

R. v. Wise, [1992] 1 S.C.R. 527 at 535, 538 & 542, confirmed the minimal infringement on privacy that vehicle tracking devices represent:

> It has been seen that there is a reduced expectation of privacy by those using a motor vehicle. In addition, the intrusion on any remaining expectation of privacy as a result of the device used in this case is minimal. This particular beeper was a very rudimentary extension of physical surveillance. It must be remembered as well that the device was attached to the appellant's vehicle, not to the appellant. How very different a device such as this is, in its

> operation and in its effect on the individual, from a hidden video camera or an electronic monitor that surreptitiously intercepts private communications.
>
> . . .
>
> In this case, it has been fairly conceded that the installation of the beeper in the interior of the motor vehicle constituted a search which breached the provisions of s. 8 of the *Charter*. Since the beeper monitoring of the appellant's vehicle invaded a reasonable expectation of privacy, this police activity also constituted a search. Absent prior authorization, such a search will be prima facie unreasonable and therefore in violation of s. 8. As there was no prior authorization for the installation and use of the beeper device, the monitoring violated the appellant's s. 8 right to be free from unreasonable search. At the same time, however, the lessened privacy interest combined with the use of an unsophisticated device establish that the search was only minimally intrusive.
>
> . . .
>
> It has been conceded that visual surveillance of motor vehicles by the police is permissible. Further, there is agreement that visual surveillance may properly be augmented by the use of binoculars. The use of this particular beeper, similarly, simply augments visual surveillance. The installation and use of the beeper did not affect in any way the movement of the car. It simply enhanced the ability of the police to observe its movements.

The privacy intrusion is so minor that there are no limitations on the types of federal offence investigations for which tracking warrants can be issued, and even a standard lower than reasonable belief is used as the factual threshold for the warrant.

a. *The Reasonable Suspicion Standard for Tracking Devices*

Only *reasonable suspicion* is necessary to secure a tracking warrant, as explained in *R. v. Briggs* (2001), 149 O.A.C. 244 at para. 32:

> the reasonableness standard under s. 8 of the *Charter* fluctuates with the context. The specific wording of a section is informed by its history, purpose, structure and function. Section 8 of the *Charter* does not require that each and every search and seizure be done only on the basis of the existence of reasonable grounds. See . . . ss. 492.1 and 492.2 of the *Criminal Code*. Thus, the reasonableness

> of a search and the surrounding standards of belief must be assessed in the context of each case.

If reasonable belief is more than suspicion and less than certainty, then reasonable suspicion is more than a mere hunch, but less than reasonable belief. The "reasonable" suspicion must still be based on objectively discernable facts explained in an affidavit that support that suspicion, like an informer tip whose detail and basis for reliability do not rise to the level of reasonable belief but is still worthy of at least some credibility.

Especially pay attention to explaining how a tracking warrant will help advance your particular investigation into a federal offence. For example, that you have reason to suspect a certain warehouse is being used to disassemble stolen vehicles, the target of the tracking warrant application is suspected of being involved in a conspiracy to steal those vehicles, and a tracking device planted in the target's vehicle will obtain information regarding involvement of the target in the conspiracy by showing whether or not he stops to visit the warehouse when driving about town.

b. *How to Particularize Necessary Tracking Warrant Powers*

As with any warrant, investigators need to particularize the powers of the tracking warrant from those available in s. 492.1 of the *Code*:

* install a tracking device;

* maintain a tracking device;

* monitor a tracking device;

* remove a tracking device.

Set out facts in the information to obtain that justify those powers, without going into so much detail as to reveal public interest privileged material.

Not explaining at least the general procedures investigators will follow in executing a tracking warrant can lead to warrant invalidity, as happened in *R. v. Gerrard*, 2003 CarswellOnt 421 (S.C.) at para. 47, where investigators had neither sought authority to remove the target vehicle from its location for device installation, nor authority to actually monitor the device:

> a major flaw in my view in this case is that the warrant on its face does not grant any authorization to surreptitiously remove the vehicle. Furthermore, Section 492.2(1)(a) gives the authority to install the tracking device. However, Section 492.1(1)(b) authorizes monitoring of the device. The warrant on its face in this case refers solely to the installation of the device and does not make

> any reference to monitoring. Furthermore, the only reference to the moving of the vehicle is in the affidavit where D/C B. . . states that, "It is proposed to remove the vehicle. . ." Any warrant should state on its face the enabling power and authorization in sufficient terms to reasonably inform the subject of the nature and object of the search. There is nothing on the face of the warrant as issued to authorize moving or monitoring.

Don't take any power for granted — ask for whatever powers you need so long as they are within the bounds of the applicable Act and not already implicitly part of warrant execution.

3. Why Number Recorders Are Minimally Intrusive

Like tracking warrants, number recorder warrants are also *available for all federal offences* even though they involve electronic surveillance, and *only require reasonable suspicion* because of their minimal intrusion on privacy. They are capable of establishing links among people in conspiracy cases where a wiretap cannot be obtained either because wiretaps are not available for the type of offence being investigated, or because the evidence collected to date does not meet wiretap thresholds. Courts have rejected arguments that the lower reasonable suspicion standard of number recorder warrants is unconstitutional, such as in *R. v. Cody*, 2005 CarswellQue 182 (C.S.) at para. 21:

> D.N.R. records show phone calls made to a residential or business phone (or to a cell phone). They also show the phone calls which are made from that residence, business or cell phone. Should the police be authorized to obtain such D.N.R. records upon a reasonable ground to suspect a crime or reasonable grounds to believe a crime? In other words, does the nature of this information and the methods used to retrieve it require a standard higher than the standard set out in section 492.2, namely the standard of reasonable grounds to believe that a crime has been committed, rather than reasonable grounds to suspect? . . . I think the answer must be no.

Nonetheless, a warrant is still required to electronically record or obtain records of numbers called because of a reasonable (albeit fairly low) expectation of privacy in what numbers a person telephones.

Statutory authority for number recorder warrants is found in s-s. 492.2(1) of the *Criminal Code*:

> **492.2.** (1) A justice who is satisfied by information on oath in writing that there are reasonable grounds to suspect that an offence

under this or any other Act of Parliament has been or will be committed and that information that would assist in the investigation of the offence could be obtained through the use of a number recorder, may at any time issue a warrant authorizing a peace officer or a public officer who has been appointed or designated to administer or enforce a federal or provincial law and whose duties include the enforcement of this Act or any other Act of Parliament and who is named in the warrant

> (a) to install, maintain and remove a number recorder in relation to any telephone or telephone line; and

> (b) to monitor, or to have monitored, the number recorder.

The actual content of a call cannot be monitored with a number recorder warrant. Like tracking devices, number recorder warrants are only valid for a maximum of 60 days, but additional number recorder warrants can be applied for to extend their time of operation. In many cases, only recording numbers called instead of actually hearing what is said during the calls will be of little assistance to an investigation, so as with tracking warrant applications investigators need to carefully explain how a number recorder warrant will assist the investigation by obtaining relevant information.

In addition to the s-s. 492.2(1) *Code* power to record numbers as calls are placed, s-s. 492.2(2) empowers a judge to authorize telephone record compulsion:

> **492.2.** (2) When the circumstances referred to in subsection (1) exist, a justice may order that any person or body that lawfully possesses records of telephone calls originated from, or received or intended to be received at, any telephone give the records, or a copy of the records, to a person named in the order.

A s. 487.01 *Criminal Code* general warrant would not be available to get the same records because of the existence of the s. 492.2 power, and would have to meet more onerous preconditions, but a s. 487.012 *Code* production order might also be useful here.

4. How General Search Warrants Also Facilitate Electronic Surveillance

Already discussed in Chapter 7 in the context of warrants to search for and seize tangible or intangible goods, s. 487.01 *Criminal Code* general search warrants can also authorize types of electronic surveillance not provided for elsewhere in the *Code*. With s. 487.01 general warrants we are back to a reasonable belief standard, but they enable investigators to use a great deal of creativity in developing new investigative techniques that would breach s. 8 of the *Charter* without prior judicial authorization. Demystification of the law here teaches that the law does not exist to stifle investigator creativity, all the law asks is that *Charter* interests be addressed and statutory limits be respected.

5. Why Video Warrants Are Subject to Many of the Same Standards as Wiretaps

Although video warrants fall within the s. 487.01 *Criminal Code* general warrant provisions, s-ss. 487.01(4) and 487.01(5) of the *Code* require video warrants to meet standards that are almost as high as wiretaps because of the potentially Orwellian intrusiveness that video and audio surveillance is considered to represent:

> **487.01.** (4) A warrant issued under subsection (1) that authorizes a peace officer to observe, by means of a television camera or other similar electronic device, any person who is engaged in activity in circumstances in which the person has a reasonable expectation of privacy shall contain such terms and conditions as the judge considers advisable to ensure that the privacy of the person or of any other person is respected as much as possible.

> (5) The definition "offence" in section 183 and sections 183.1, 184.2, 184.3 and 185 to 188.2, subsection 189(5), and sections 190, 193 and 194 to 196 apply, with such modifications as the circumstances require, to a warrant referred to in subsection (4) as though references in those provisions to interceptions of private communications were read as references to observations by peace officers by means of television cameras or similar electronic devices of activities in circumstances in which persons had reasonable expectations of privacy.

Whether images are recorded or not is irrelevant — it is investigators conducting observations using any kind of electronic device similar to a television camera, coupled with a reasonable expectation of privacy, that triggers the warrant requirement. Also like wiretaps, the discretion given to the judge to protect the privacy of the target and third parties "as much as possible" means investigators must consider including video warrant conditions that amount to a minimization clause in wiretap terms.

a. *The Less Onerous Conditions for Video Surveillance*

Representing a bit less of a privacy intrusion than wiretaps, video warrants do not require investigative necessity or a specially designated official to bring the application, and can be issued by either a provincial court or superior court judge (but not by a justice of the peace). More importantly, many video surveillance situations do not require a warrant where no reasonable expectation of privacy is engaged, and thus unlike wiretaps warrantless video surveillance is available to a broad spectrum of regulatory and criminal investigators. Video surveillance is already employed without a warrant in many public places like parking lots and shopping malls, whereas no electronic surveillance by investigators of audio communications could take place in those locations without prior judicial authorization (except for officer protection kits). So fishery officers could install a video camera in a government controlled lighthouse to remotely view and record open fishing wharf activity given the extremely low expectation of privacy in such a place, but they could not install tiny microphones around the wharf to listen to wharf-side conversations as this would require a wiretap that is unavailable for fishing offences.

b. *The Importance of Not Confusing the Purpose of Different Court Authorizations*

Don't confuse video warrants with regular s. 487 *Code* warrants, as happened in the warrant cited in *R. v. Mero* (2003), 109 C.R.R. (2d) 34; 2003 BCSC 964 at para. 19:

> IT is hereby ordered that Constable C. . . of the . . . General Investigation Section and any other Peace Officers, acting in good faith, in aid thereof, are hereby authorized to surreptitiously enter and search the property and outbuildings, excluding any residences, permanent or temporary of . . . situated on . . . near Quesnel, British Columbia (hereinafter referred to as "the premises") for the purpose of video-taping and/or photographing any structures, vehicles and equipment used on the said property, without entering any such structures, vehicles and equipment used if they exist on the said premises, to gather evidence relating to the

criminal offenses pursuant to the provisions of Section 487.01 of the Criminal Code of Canada. No notice to any person is required prior to, during, or subsequent to any such entry.

Was the purpose of the warrant to conduct video surveillance, or to gather physical evidence? Why did the warrant refer to the term "surreptitious entry" since that term isn't used in s. 487.01, although covert entry is mentioned in s-s. 487.01(5.1)? Why did it seek to authorize no notice of entry ever being given, in express contradiction to the requirements of s-ss. 481.01(5.1) and (5.2) of the *Code*? Was the reference to officers "acting in good faith" an attempt to predetermine for a future reviewing court whether the executing officers were indeed acting in good faith? The understandably confused reviewing court found the warrant to be invalid, and excluded its evidence. Here a routine s. 487 *Criminal Code* warrant could likely have accomplished investigator objectives, which appear merely to have been a perimeter search including incidental photography.

Video Surveillance of Public Places

Q&A

Q: The drug squad that I'm a member of has mounted surveillance cameras in a variety of locations around a shopping mall, aimed at recording illicit drug trafficking activity. Some cameras are in the parking lot, some in stairwells, and some in the public washrooms of the food court. Because we have the permission of the mall owner, are we correct in assuming we don't need video warrants?

A: There likely is no reasonable expectation of privacy in the parking lot or stairwells, and so no warrant requirement, but it is preferable if signs are posted telling mall patrons that by choosing to be in these areas they may be subject to video surveillance. However, according to the case law even "public" washrooms and particularly washroom stalls do come with a reasonable expectation of privacy. A camera covering the sink area might be permissible with a warning posted, but stall surveillance would almost certainly violate s. 8 of the *Charter* and even a video warrant would be very difficult to obtain for such a location.

For Defining Privacy Interest and Justifying Intrusive Electronic Surveillance

KEY POINTS

✓ Before employing any form of electronic surveillance, ask yourself whether more legally certain conventional investigation techniques or a lesser form of electronic surveillance having fewer preconditions could accomplish your goals.

✓ Whether prior judicial authorization is required for audio, video or other forms of electronic surveillance depends on whether the targets of the surveillance have a reasonable expectation of privacy to be free from such surveillance. Authorization for the electronic interception, viewing, and recording of any form of communication or image is limited to explicitly enumerated serious federal offences and non-enumerated serious offences connected to organized crime and terrorism.

✓ A true wiretap requires investigative necessity, a designated wiretap agent to make the application, and a superior court judge to grant it. The wiretap authorization must place reasonable limits on the who and where of communications intercepts as well as specify the time period of validity, the types of communications to be intercepted, the ways they will be intercepted, and the ways privacy intrusions will be minimized. The supporting affidavit must demonstrate reasonable belief in an enumerated offence, that the communication intercepts will lead to evidence of that offence, and include all relevant underlying case facts.

✓ Other electronic surveillance techniques generally have lower standards for approval than wiretaps. A s. 184.2 *Code* consent intercept still requires prior authorization unless it is being used as an officer protection kit under s. 184.1 or solely at the instigation of a private party, but that authorization is available for any federal offence without proof of investigative necessity. Section 492.1 *Code* tracking device and s. 492.2 number recorder warrants only require reasonable suspicion that use of the technique can lead to evidence of any federal offence. A s. 487.01 *Code* general warrant can authorize a grab-bag of creative electronic surveillance techniques not provided for elsewhere, including video warrants under s-s. 487.01(4), which have preconditions lower than wiretaps but higher than other techniques.

A — INITIAL ASSESSMENT OF ELECTRONIC SURVEILLANCE

❏ Judicial prior-authorization is required to employ this electronic surveillance technique

    ❏ Principle of electronic enhancement triggers prior-authorization requirement

    ❏ Reasonable expectation of privacy triggers prior-authorization requirement

❏ Statutory authority exists for this type of electronic surveillance:

_____

❏ Facts of this case meet statutory preconditions for this type of electronic surveillance:

_____

B — WIRETAP ASSESSMENT

❏ Offence being investigated qualifies: _____

❏ Reasonable and probable grounds of designated offence exist

❏ Investigative necessity exists: _____

❏ Designated wiretap agent available to make application: _____

❏ Application brought before appropriate court: _____

❏ Persons whose communications are to be intercepted particularized:

_____

❏ Places where interceptions can occur particularized:

_____

❏ Period during which authorization is valid particularized: _____

❏ Types of communications specified: _____

❏ Ways in which intercepts will be conducted specified: _____

❏ Ways privacy intrusions will be minimized specified: _____

❏ Supporting affidavit addresses all required issues

C — CONSENT INTERCEPT ASSESSMENT

❏ Reasonable and probable grounds of federal offence exist

❏ Originator or recipient of communication has consented to interception

❏ Information concerning offence will be obtained through consent intercept

❏ Application brought before appropriate court:_____

❏ No prior judicial authorization required because consent intercept only used as officer protection kit

❏ Supporting affidavit addresses all required issues

D | TRACKING DEVICE ASSESSMENT

❏ Tracking warrant necessary because of privacy interest in target location

❏ Reasonable suspicion standard met for tracking warrant

   ❏ Explained how information from tracking device would assist investigation of federal offence

❏ Installation power requested and justified

❏ Maintenance power requested and justified

❏ Monitoring power requested and justified

❏ Removal power requested and justified

❏ Supporting affidavit addresses all required issues

E | NUMBER RECORDER ASSESSMENT

❏ Reasonable suspicion standard met for number recorder warrant

   ❏ Explained how information from number recorder would assist investigation of federal offence

❏ Installation power requested and justified

❏ Maintenance power requested and justified

❏ Removal power requested and justified

❏ Order to compel production of telephone records requested and justified

❏ Supporting affidavit addresses all required issues

F | GENERAL SEARCH WARRANT ASSESSMENT

❏ Desire to use electronic surveillance technique requiring prior judicial authorization and not provided for elsewhere in federal legislation

❏ Application brought before appropriate court

❏ Reasonable and probable grounds of federal offence exist

❏ Electronic surveillance technique will be useful in collecting information concerning that offence

❏ Granting warrant to use electronic surveillance technique in the best interests of the administration of justice

❏ Supporting affidavit addresses all required issues

G | VIDEO WARRANT ASSESSMENT

❏ Offence being investigated qualifies: _____

❏ Reasonable and probable grounds of designated offence exist

❏ Video surveillance will be useful in collecting evidence concerning that offence

❏ Application brought before appropriate court: _____

❏ Way in which video surveillance will be conducted specified

❏ Ways privacy intrusions will be minimized specified

❏ Supporting affidavit addresses all required issues

FURTHER READING

Cases

R. v. Araujo, [2000] 2 S.C.R. 992. A wiretap authorization may be granted if other investigative techniques were tried and failed, other techniques are unlikely to succeed, or urgency means it is impractical to carry out other techniques.

R. v. Duarte, [1990] 1. S.C.R. 30. A consent intercept requires judicial authorization, other than in exceptional circumstances covered by statute.

R. v. Garofoli, [1990] 2 S.C.R. 1421. Assessing reliability of informer tips used in support of an electronic surveillance authorization is to be based on degree of detail, informer's source of knowledge, past reliability, and corroboration from other investigative sources.

R. v. Grabowski, [1985] 2 S.C.R. 434. A wiretap authorization must contain limits on persons, places and methods of interception.

R. v. Thompson, [1990] 2 S.C.R. 1111. A wiretap authorization could be constitutionally invalid if not supported by sufficient grounds or if it authorizes unreasonable surveillance techniques; the authorization must name the offences, persons and places for which the authorization is sought.

R. v. Wong, [1990] 3 S.C.R. 36. Video surveillance requires a warrant where a reasonable expectation of privacy exists.

Books and Articles

G.S. Campbell, "Emerging Issues of the Internet and Canadian Criminal Law" (1998) 3 Can. Crim. L. Rev. 101.

E. Ewaschuk, *Criminal Pleadings and Practice in Canada*, 2nd ed., loose-leaf (Aurora, ON: Canada Law Book, 1997). See particularly Chapter 4 ("Protection of Privacy").

R. Hubbard, P. Brauti, & S. Fenton, *Wiretapping and Other Electronic Surveillance: Law and Procedure*, loose-leaf (Aurora, ON: Canada Law Book, 2000). Includes comprehensive coverage of both the theory and practice of drafting electronic surveillance applications and later defending them in court.

R.W. Hubbard, S. Magotiaux & M. Sullivan, "The State Use of Closed Circuit TV: Is There a Reasonable Expectation of Privacy in Public?" (2004) 49 Crim. L.Q. 222.

R.W. Hubbard, P. DeFreitas & S. Magotiaux, "The Internet: Expectations of Privacy in a New Context" (2000) 45 Crim. L.Q. 170.

Y. Rahamin, "Wiretapping and Electronic Surveillance in Canada: the Present State of the Law and Challenges to the Employment of Sophisticated and Intrusive Technology in Law Enforcement" (2004) 58 Windsor Rev. Legal & Social Issues 87.

CHAPTER ELEVEN

MAKING SOUND DECISIONS ABOUT DETENTION, ARREST AND RELEASE

Police officers, when acting or purporting to act in their official capacity as agents of the State, only act lawfully if they act in the exercise of authority which is either conferred by statute or derived as a matter of common law from their duties. The reason for this is the authoritative and coercive character of police action. An individual knows that he or she may ignore with impunity the signal to stop of another private individual. That is not true of a direction or demand by a police officer.

R. v. Dedman, [1985] 2 S.C.R. 2 at 28.

In This Chapter

- The challenge of defining detention and arrest
- Navigating the uncertainty of investigative detention
- How to exercise powers of arrest
- Use of force in making an arrest
- Avoiding abusive detention or arrest
- Adapting detention or arrest procedure to place
- Release burdens, reasons and conditions

It's as if state investigators have magnetic powers emanating from their bodies, powers that may start exerting themselves to draw in and root others to the spot, resulting in a detention. Sometimes even before the magnetic powers have had a chance to take effect, investigators will physically take control of someone that at a minimum will amount to a detention and usually results in an arrest. With those powers typically comes responsibility — the admissibility of evidence discovered as a result of search incident to arrest, consent search, plain view seizure as well as the admissibility of statements made by an accused can all be affected by the legality of a preceding detention or arrest. Demystification of the law here comes down to understanding your grounds to detain or arrest before acting, recording them so they can later be recalled in court, and scrupulously complying with all your legal obligations while a person is in your custody, if you hope to be successful with charges and avoid civil or criminal liability. Detention and arrest have immediate serious consequences for both the detainee who loses freedom of action, and for investigators who must, as described in Chapter 12, caution a detained or arrested person before questions are posed or statements otherwise elicited — subject to a few contextually specific exceptions like impaired driving checks.

THE CHALLENGE OF DEFINING DETENTION AND ARREST

Determining whether or not a detention or arrest has occurred is no easy task. Getting a handle on definitions is your best protection against winding up with detentions and arrests you never intended.

1. The Broad Definition of Detention

The legal definition of detention is extremely broad, with both psychological as well as physical detention being possible. For instance, if a pedestrian subjectively believes she cannot leave the presence of a peace officer who has approached her on the street, and objectively it appears a reasonable pedestrian would likewise feel compelled to stay put, then a detention is underway, as was explained in *R. v. Therens*, [1985] 1 S.C.R. 613 at 642 & 644:

> In addition to the case of deprivation of liberty by physical constraint, there is in my opinion a detention within s. 10 of the *Charter* when a police officer or other agent of the state assumes

control over the movement of a person by a demand or direction which may have significant legal consequence and which prevents or impedes access to counsel.

. . .

The issue, as I see it, is whether that compulsion need be of a physical character, or whether it may also be a compulsion of a psychological or mental nature which inhibits the will as effectively as the application, or threat of application, of physical force. The issue is whether a person who is the subject of a demand or direction by a police officer or other agent of the state may reasonably regard himself or herself as free to refuse to comply.

. . .

The element of psychological compulsion, in the form of a reasonable perception of suspension of freedom of choice, is enough to make the restraint of liberty involuntary. Detention may be effected without the application or threat of application of physical restraint if the person concerned submits or acquiesces in the deprivation of liberty and reasonably believes that the choice to do otherwise does not exist.

It is those magnetic attraction powers at work.

Clearly not every contact between state investigators and private citizens amounts to a detention. *R. v. Moran* (1987), 21 O.A.C. 257 at para. 82, set out factors to take into account in assessing the existence of detention for a person who later becomes an accused, including:

- the precise language used by investigators;

- the location of the contact between investigators and the accused;

- whether investigators escorted the accused to the point of contact or did the accused come in response to an investigator request;

- whether the accused left at the end of the contact or was arrested;

- was the stage of investigation at the point where investigators were only conducting general inquiries, or had they already decided a crime was committed so that questioning sought out incriminating statements;

- whether reasonable and probable grounds (RPG) of an offence existed against the accused at the time of the contact;

- were the questions general in nature, or was the accused being confronted with evidence of guilt;

- personal circumstances of the accused affecting subjective belief in a detention.

Using non-coercive language, making contact where a person feels comfortable, inviting a person for contact, not arresting at the end of contact, only being at the general inquiry stage of a case, not having RPG of an offence against the person being dealt with, and only asking general questions all favour a conclusion that a detention did not take place.

R. v. Nicholas (2004), 184 O.A.C. 139, is a good example of investigators doing everything they could to minimize prospects for detention in the course of contacting over 100 persons against whom they had no evidence to link break and enter, assault and sexual assault charges they were investigating, but who had become of interest mainly through informer tips. Investigators attended at the home of one of those people in the evening, were invited inside by another resident, spoke with the person who was eventually to become the accused, told him he was a person of interest in the offences being investigated, and asked if he would speak with them. The accused replied "sure, no problem." They eventually sat down together in the basement of the house where the following exchange took place, recounted at paras. 12-15 of the judgment:

> D/Cst. Dyck again explained to Mr. Nicholas that they were investigating a series of sexual assaults and that he was a person of interest they wanted to speak to. D/Cst. Dyck read the consent form to him and Mr. Nicholas agreed to provide a buccal swab. D/Cst. Dyck then turned the audiotape on, read the consent form again, and asked Mr. Nicholas if he understood it. Mr. Nicholas answered "yes".

> The key portion of the audiotape transcript reads as follows:

> Dyck: I'm just gonna read something to you here. It's a consent form, and-ah I'm just gonna read this. Toronto Police Service is investigating a series of break and enters which have occurred between the twenty-third of June and twenty-first of August Nineteen-ninety-nine, inclusive. During the course of these break and enters female persons have been subjected to either physical or sexual assault. We are seeking permission from you to obtain bodily samples including blood or saliva for scientific testing, including DNA analysis. The samples obtained from you will be scientifically tested and analysed and compared with evidence obtained from the other crime scenes. The purpose of this analy-

sis and comparison is to enable investigators to attempt to positively identify the person responsible for the break and enters, sexual assaults and to also enable the investigators to eliminate the persons as possible suspects. You understand that so far Sir?

. . .

Nicholas: Yes

Dyck: You are not required to give us these samples. You may refuse to provide these samples. If you agree to provide samples for analysis, the results of the analysis may be used against you in criminal proceedings. You may wish to discuss this request with anybody including a lawyer and you are free to do so now. Do you understand what I've just read to you sir?

Nicholas: Yes Sir.

Dyck: Do you have any questions?

Nicholas: No.

Mr. Nicholas's mother, who had come into the kitchen at some point during the interview, then asked the police "[S]houldn't he have a lawyer?" The officers replied that it was "up to him" and told her that Mr. Nicholas had stated that he understood his opportunity to speak "to a lawyer or anyone else for that matter".

Mr. Nicholas then signed the form, swabbed the inside of his mouth, and handed the swabs to the officers. The officers left his house at approximately 10:32 p.m.

The court concluded there was no psychological compulsion, no detention, and the accused had provided a voluntary and informed consent to the DNA sample. The consent was audio recorded as well as obtained in writing, the consent's purpose was made clear, it was requested in circumstances not giving rise to the appearance of a detention, investigators ensured the accused understood what was being requested including consequences and lack of obligation, and gave an opportunity to speak with a lawyer.

When about to approach and question anyone, ask yourself — would I feel compelled due to my words or actions if I was this person? Your best bet if you fear factors are present that could later lead to a detention finding at trial is to attempt to break the detention. Tell the person you have stopped that she doesn't have to answer any of your questions, and that she is free to leave. Don't physically impede her leaving your presence in any way. And only then ask her if she doesn't mind voluntarily answering a couple of questions.

2. The Equally Broad Definition of Arrest

What amounts to an arrest was concisely summed up in *R. v. Asante-Mensah*, [2003] 2 S.C.R. 3 at para. 43, quoting from a Privy Council judgment:

> An arrest occurs when a police officer states in terms that he is arresting or when he uses force to restrain the individual concerned. It occurs also when by words or conduct he makes it clear that he will, if necessary, use force to prevent the individual from going where he may want to go.

Physical control need not have been firmly established for a lawful arrest to have been made. Grabbing a driver's arm and telling him he is under arrest as he pulls out of a parking space can be an arrest, even if the driver breaks the peace officer's hold by speeding away.

An implied *de facto* arrest is possible, as happened in *R. v. Latimer*, [1997] 2 S.C.R. 217 at para. 25:

> On the facts of this case, a *de facto* arrest occurred through the use of words that conveyed clearly that Latimer was under arrest, the conduct of the officers, and Mr. Latimer's submission to the authority of officers C. . . and L. . . . Mr. Latimer was told that he was being detained, and that he would be taken back to North Battleford to be interviewed. The police officers informed him of his right to silence and his right to counsel. They accompanied him back into his house while he changed his clothes, telling him that they were doing so because he was now in their custody. Finally, at no point did Mr. Latimer protest or resist the police—he submitted to the authority of the arresting officers.

If as an investigator you are acting like an arrest has been made, a court may later find that you did indeed make an arrest even if you never intended to do so. The longer the detention, and the more directed movement involved, the more likely an arrest will be found to have occurred.

Implicit Detentions and Arrests

Q: I don't understand why, if I don't have any intention of detaining or arresting someone, a court could still find that I did conduct a detention or arrest. Why do the courts keep inventing these legal fictions to make my job more difficult?

A: Your powers of detention or arrest are purely a creation of the law, so it is up to the courts as interpreters of the law to determine when those powers exist, and when they don't. Factually, you could go ahead and attempt to restrain anyone you choose to, but you would not have any legal authority to do so unless you are acting in a manner consistent with the law governing detention and arrest. As an investigator, you are stuck with the detention and arrest rules as you find them, but you can influence the way the courts apply those rules to your facts by carefully recording and later articulating your grounds for detaining or arresting.

NAVIGATING THE UNCERTAINTY OF INVESTIGATIVE DETENTION

Most arrest powers grounded in the common law are now statutorily codified, but the law of detention (more properly called "investigative detention") in Canada remains an uncodified evolving common law concept defined by the courts and possibly authorizing brief restraints on a person's liberty for purposes of questioning, preventing potential offences or flight from future arrest. While there is now no doubt investigative detention is available to Canadian investigators, the case law remains unsettled on precisely when the tool can be used where RPG does not yet exist to make an arrest.

1. The Articulable Cause or Reasonable Suspicion Standard

R. v. Simpson (1993), 12 O.R. (3d) 182 (C.A.) at 200, looked to United States law in finding the threshold for investigative detention to be "articulable cause," said to "require a constellation of objectively discernible facts which give the detaining officer reasonable cause to suspect that the detainee is criminally implicated in the activity under investigation." *R. v.*

Mann, [2004] 3 S.C.R. 59 at paras. 34 & 45, somewhat clarified the unsettled law 11 years later by focusing on "reasonable suspicion":

> The detention must be viewed as reasonably necessary on an objective view of the totality of the circumstances, informing the officer's suspicion that there is a clear nexus between the individual to be detained and a recent or on-going criminal offence. Reasonable grounds figures at the front-end of such an assessment, underlying the officer's reasonable suspicion that the particular individual is implicated in the criminal activity under investigation. The overall reasonableness of the decision to detain, however, must further be assessed against all of the circumstances, most notably the extent to which the interference with individual liberty is necessary to perform the officer's duty, the liberty interfered with, and the nature and extent of that interference. . . .
>
> . . .
>
> Police officers may detain an individual for investigative purposes if there are reasonable grounds to suspect in all the circumstances that the individual is connected to a particular crime and that such a detention is necessary.

A valid investigative detention generally requires:

- a recent or ongoing criminal offence;
- reasonable suspicion the individual to be detained is implicated in the offence;
- necessity of the detention to the investigator's duties;
- that the detention be brief in duration; and
- justification for the nature and extent of the liberty interference.

As noted in *R. v. Calderon* (2004), 23 C.R. (6th) 1 (Ont. C.A.) at para. 69: "An officer cannot exercise the power to detain on a hunch, even a hunch born of intuition gained by experience."

2. Investigative Detention Is Not a Search or Questioning Authority

What investigative detention does *not* do is provide general authority to search or question a person being detained, a point made clear in *R. v. Mann*, [2004] 3 S.C.R. 59 at paras. 40 & 45:

The general duty of officers to protect life may, in some circumstances, give rise to the power to conduct a pat-down search incident to an investigative detention. Such a search power does not exist as a matter of course; the officer must believe on reasonable grounds that his or her own safety, or the safety of others, is at risk. I disagree with the suggestion that the power to detain for investigative searches endorses an incidental search in all circumstances. . . . The officer's decision to search must also be reasonably necessary in light of the totality of the circumstances. It cannot be justified on the basis of a vague or non-existent concern for safety, nor can the search be premised upon hunches or mere intuition.

. . .

Both the detention and the pat-down search must be conducted in a reasonable manner. In this connection, I note that the investigative detention should be brief in duration and does not impose an obligation on the detained individual to answer questions posed by the police. The investigative detention and protective search power are to be distinguished from an arrest and the incidental power to search on arrest . . . .

Investigative detention allows temporary control to be exerted over a person, during which time questions can be asked without any power to compel answers, facts checked from other sources, or inspection and search powers utilized that are independent of the investigative detention.

Problems with the Promise of Investigative Detention

Q&A

Q: Investigative detention sounds really useful, almost too good to be true. Is there a downside to making regular use of it?

A: I fear the whole concept of investigative detention may one day disappear through courts ruling against it, and even now it is questionable just how useful it is. You still need sufficient grounds to be able to use it, in most cases you still need to fully caution a detained person if you are going to ask detailed questions, and no one knows how long an investigative detention can continue before it is abusive. The preventive arrest powers found in the *Criminal Code* may be more useful and are definitely more certain. Legislative amendments in Canada could codify investigative detention to make it a more certain power, as has been done elsewhere.

HOW TO EXERCISE POWERS OF ARREST

Powers of arrest have existed for centuries, but have now mostly been incorporated into federal, provincial and territorial legislation, with the *Criminal Code* containing the most important arrest authorities. Regardless of whether an arrest is made with or without a warrant, the standard upon which an arrest can be made requires both subjective and objective belief that an offence has been committed, as explained in *R. v. Storrey*, [1990] 1 S.C.R. 241 at 250-51:

> In summary, then, the *Criminal Code* requires that an arresting officer must subjectively have reasonable and probable grounds on which to base the arrest. Those grounds must, in addition, be justifiable from an objective point of view. That is to say, a reasonable person placed in the position of the officer must be able to conclude that there were indeed reasonable and probable grounds for the arrest. On the other hand, the police need not demonstrate anything more than reasonable and probable grounds. Specifically, they are not required to establish a prima facie case for conviction before making the arrest.

> In the case at bar, the trial judge specifically stated that "Sergeant Larkin had reasonable and probable grounds" to make the arrest. In my view there was ample evidence on which the trial judge could very properly make that finding. The reasonable grounds could be based subjectively on the testimony of Larkin and objectively upon the cumulative effect of the following items: (a) the possession and ownership by Storrey of a 1973 blue Thunderbird, which was a relatively unusual and uncommon car and was the type of car used in the infraction; (b) the fact that he had been stopped by the police on several occasions driving that car; (c) his past record of violence; (d) the fact that two of the victims picked out a picture of Cameron as someone who looked like their assailant; and (e) the remarkable resemblance of Storrey to Cameron. These factors taken together clearly were sufficient in their cumulative effect to constitute reasonable and probable grounds for Sergeant Larkin to arrest the appellant.

Whereas the courts encourage search warrants to be sought out in all appropriate situations, the use of arrest warrants is discouraged where there is a reasonable alternative authority available to assume control over a person and compel his appearance in court.

1. Justifying Arrest without a Warrant

Most arrest without warrant powers in Canada flow from s. 494 (exercisable by anyone) and s. 495 (exercisable only by peace officers) of the *Criminal Code*. Although s. 494 is often referred to as the "citizen's arrest" power, it is also extremely useful to peace officers and regulatory investigators who do not hold peace officer status. A peace officer's s. 495 powers are an expansion of s. 494 powers, rather than s. 494 somehow being a narrowing of s. 495, as noted in *R. v. Asante-Mensah*, [2003] 2 S.C.R. 3 at paras. 39-40:

> Powers of arrest have been conferred on ordinary citizens by statute from early times, for example, to arrest for the misdemeanours of "night walking" and "riding armed". . . . The citizen's power of arrest survives under s. 494 of the *Criminal Code* (*Cr. C.*). As will be seen, many federal and provincial statutes authorize a citizen's arrest but few give any explicit guidance about its procedures and consequences. The explanation is that legislators presuppose that the term has a well-known legal significance (i.e., is a term of art) derived from the common law.
>
> The development of modern police forces brought about a transfer of law enforcement activities from private citizens to peace officers. But it is the peace officer's powers which are in a sense derivative from that of the citizen, not the other way around.

Therefore investigators should always look to s. 494 powers to see if those meet their needs.

a. *Reasons Justifying Arrest without a Warrant by Anyone*

There are only three types of situation where s. 494 of the *Code* may be used to arrest without a warrant:

- where the arrestor makes the arrest while the arrestee is committing an indictable offence;

- where the arrestor believes on reasonable grounds that the arrestee has committed *any* criminal offence and "is escaping from and freshly pursued by persons who have lawful authority to arrest"; or

- where the arrestor who owns, is in possession or has authorization in respect of a property, finds the arrestee committing any criminal offence on or against that property.

Sub-section 494(3) requires as a duty following arrest that "Anyone other than a peace officer who arrests a person without warrant shall forthwith deliver the person to a peace officer." Remember all hybrid indictable-summary offences are included within the bounds of the first situation of "found committing an indictable offence," so the third property offence situation need only be relied upon for uniquely summary offences.

b.   *Reasons Justifying Arrest without a Warrant by a Peace Officer*

Section 495 of the *Code* authorizes a peace officer to make the same kinds of arrests as are available under s. 494, but additionally authorizes arrest in four other situations:

- a person believed on reasonable grounds to have committed a still outstanding indictable offence in the past;

- a person believed on reasonable grounds to be about to commit an indictable offence;

- a person found committing any criminal offence, regardless of the location of the offence; or

- a person believed on reasonable grounds to be subject to an outstanding arrest or committal warrant valid in the jurisdiction in which the person is found.

This expansion to past and future indictable offences, current summary offences, and warrants gives peace officers a lot more flexibility in going after offences they don't actually witness or offences of a minor nature, however s. 495 does not confer a power of arrest without warrant for past or anticipated summary-only offences. There are a few other arrest without warrant powers scattered throughout the *Code* exercisable by peace officers, but only if ss. 494 or 495 appear insufficient or you are a regulatory investigator not holding peace officer status do you really need to concern yourself with them.

c.   *Why s. 494 Arrest Powers Can Be Better Than s. 495 Arrest Powers*

The greatest difficulty with s. 495 powers is that they can only be exercised in the normal execution of arresting officer duties, whereas s. 494 doesn't suffer from that limitation. Fishery Officers who witness an assault in a restaurant during their lunch break would, for example, have difficulty relying on s. 495 to arrest because the investigation of *Criminal Code* offences is not part of their duties if not tied to fishing offences. Those same officers would definitely qualify for s. 494 arrest powers, available to anyone who witnesses an assault because assault is a hybrid offence under s. 266 of the *Code*.

2. Justifying Arrest with a Warrant

There is a presumption in the *Criminal Code* in favour of a promise to appear or summons as the preferred ways to compel attendance of an accused at court, thus investigators need to demonstrate very good reasons for issuance of an arrest warrant. Form 7 found in s. 894 of the *Code* contains not only the template for a "Warrant for Arrest," but also a very useful summary of the nine leading reasons and related *Code* section authorities under which an arrest warrant can issue:

(a) there are reasonable grounds to believe that it is necessary in the public interest to issue this warrant for the arrest of the accused [507(4), 512(1)];

(b) the accused failed to attend court in accordance with the summons served on him [512(2)];

(c) (an appearance notice or a promise to appear or a recognizance entered into before an officer in charge) was confirmed and the accused failed to attend court in accordance therewith [512(2)];

(d) it appears that a summons cannot be served because the accused is evading service [512(2)];

(e) the accused was ordered to be present at the hearing of an application for a review of an order made by a justice and did not attend the hearing [520(5), 521(5)];

(f) there are reasonable grounds to believe that the accused has contravened or is about to contravene the (promise to appear or undertaking or recognizance) on which he was released [524(1), 525(5), 679(6)];

(g) there are reasonable grounds to believe that the accused has since his release from custody on (a promise to appear or an undertaking or a recognizance) committed an indictable offence [524(1), 525(5), 679(6)];

(h) the accused was required by (an appearance notice or a promise to appear or a recognizance entered into before an officer in charge or a summons) to attend at a time and place stated therein for the purposes of the Identification of Criminals Act and did not appear at that time and place [502, 510];

(i) an indictment has been found against the accused and the accused has not appeared or remained in attendance before the court for his trial [597];

These arrest warrant authorities can be broken down into two classes: (1) those that initiate the court process leading to the court acquiring jurisdiction over the accused, and (2) those that further the court process after an accused has initially appeared. A warrant can be "endorsed" in advance under s-s. 506(6) of the *Code* to authorize the accused's release by the officer in charge pending the next court appearance, or under s-s. 511(3) issued with discretion "to allow the accused to appear voluntarily before a judge or justice having jurisdiction in the territorial division in which the warrant was issued" prior to a certain date.

Investigators need to place a sufficient evidentiary basis for an arrest warrant in front of a judge or justice to prevent the warrant from later being successfully challenged in court, as happened in *R. v. Henry*, 1997 CarswellBC 1085 (S.C.) at paras. 5-8 & 11-12:

An Information was laid and a summons was issued charging that offence returnable September 17, 1993. The respondent's address was Nanaimo and a Constable G . . . attempted to serve the summons. She made three attempts in all, the first on August 19, 1993 and two on August 25, 1993. Personal service was not accomplished and she never saw the respondent on any of the attempts.

Constable G. . . apparently made no phone calls and there is no record of any attempt by her to gather information about the respondent, and after the attempts described she set out that information in affidavit form which would appear to be a form of affidavit used when an application for substituted service is contemplated although no such application was pursued here.

On September 23, 1993 a Justice of the Peace in Vancouver issued a warrant to arrest the respondent. . . .

> The accused was arrested on October 26, 1993 in Vancouver on the basis of that arrest warrant. The accused was searched and . . . incidental to the arrest the knife and handgun were found on the person of the respondent.
>
> . . .
>
> The trial judge concluded . . . that on the evidence that was available to her she could not have had reasonable and probable grounds to believe that it was necessary that a warrant to arrest be issued in the public interest.
>
> He found the warrant of arrest to be unlawful and that the foundation for the arrest and the search of the respondent had ceased to exist. He conceded that the police were acting in good faith, which they clearly were, but found that they had not had any legal authority to arrest or to search the accused. He found the search to have been unreasonable and that it had been a breach of the accused's Section 8 *Charter* rights.

Both the trial judge and judge hearing the appeal appear to have believed additional efforts should have been made to serve the summons, such as through substitutional service, before an arrest warrant was issued for an offence so minor as a traffic offence that turned out in the end not even to have been committed by the accused.

3. Justifying Arrest in Regulatory Investigations

A summons or appearance notice will be the usual means used to compel appearance in court to answer for regulatory offences, but powers to arrest are embedded in some regulatory Acts, in the *Criminal Code* for federal regulatory offences, and sometimes in provincial or territorial procedural legislation. For example, the *Highway Traffic Act*, R.S.O. 1990, c. H.8, has a narrow arrest power at s-s. 217(7) for making a false application statement, defacing a number plate, failing to identify self when unable to produce licence, and driving while suspended:

> **217.** (7) Any police officer who, on reasonable and probable grounds, believes that a contravention of any of the provisions of subsection 9 (1), subsection 12 (1), subsection 13 (1), subsection 33 (3), subsection 47 (5), (6), (7) or (8), section 51, 53, 130, 172 or 184, subsection 185 (3), clause 200 (1) (a) or subsection 216 (1) has been committed, may arrest, without warrant, the person he or she believes committed the contravention.

Section 24 of the *Provincial Offences Act*, R.S.O. 1990, c. P.33, more generally provides for an arrest warrant to compel court attendance to answer a charge to be issued by a justice "where the arrest is authorized by statute and where the allegations of the informant or the evidence satisfy the justice on reasonable and probable grounds that it is necessary in the public interest to do so. . . ."

4. The Contents of an Arrest Warrant

An arrest warrant is quite a simple document to create, that explicitly and accurately states five things:

- who is authorized by the warrant to make an arrest;
- the territorial application of the warrant;
- the name and address of the person to be arrested;
- the offences connected to the warrant; and
- the reason the warrant was issued.

Although Form 7 of the *Code* should generally be followed in drafting an arrest warrant, s. 849 of the *Code* offers form flexibility: "The forms set out in this Part, varied to suit the case, or forms to the like effect are deemed to be good, valid and sufficient in the circumstances for which they are provided."

Investigators dealing with an already issued arrest warrant should pay particular attention to its provisions specifying who can execute it, its territorial jurisdiction and its return radius (which might not be specified on its face). While a Canada-wide arrest warrant may issue for serious federal offences, most warrants are directed to peace officers in a single territorial jurisdiction and confusingly may have a narrower return radius. For example, a police service obtaining a warrant directed to all peace officers in Alberta may only wish it be given effect within an 80 km return radius of Edmonton because of a lack of resources to pick-up prisoners. It is pointless to execute an arrest warrant for a person who will not be returned to the location issuing the warrant.

Detentions or Arrests and Regulatory Compliance Verification

Q & A

Q: As a regulatory investigator, I often serve information demands on people who voluntarily work in the industry governed by the Act I monitor. I also require the assistance of these same people during inspections which I conduct. If these people are compelled to immediately comply with an information demand or inspection, isn't there an element of detention or arrest present?

A: So long as the predominant purpose of your information gathering is compliance verification, not collecting evidence for a prosecution, no impermissible detention or arrest should arise solely because the assistance of managers or employees of a business is statutorily compelled. Cautioning a person to whom an information demand is directed would defeat the purpose of the demand, however regulatory information gathering powers will not usually authorize restrictions on movement or directions to attend an investigator's office for questioning.

USE OF FORCE IN MAKING AN ARREST

While each investigative agency will have its own use of force policy, ss. 25 and 27 of the *Criminal Code* contain basic statutory protections for all investigators. Sub-section 25(1) arguably covers off every aspect of use of force in an investigator's duties, but use of force during specific duties is also mentioned later in s. 25 and in s. 27:

25. (1) Every one who is required or authorized by law to do anything in the administration or enforcement of the law

(a) as a private person,

(b) as a peace officer or public officer,

(c) in aid of a peace officer or public officer, or

(d) by virtue of his office,

is, if he acts on reasonable grounds, justified in doing what he is required or authorized to do and in using as much force as is necessary for that purpose.

(2) Where a person is required or authorized by law to execute a process or to carry out a sentence, that person or any person who assists him is, if that person acts in good faith, justified in executing the process or in carrying out the sentence notwithstanding that the process or sentence is defective or that it was issued or imposed without jurisdiction or in excess of jurisdiction.

(3) Subject to subsections (4) and (5), a person is not justified for the purposes of subsection (1) in using force that is intended or is likely to cause death or grievous bodily harm unless the person believes on reasonable grounds that it is necessary for the self-preservation of the person or the preservation of any one under that person's protection from death or grievous bodily harm.

(4) A peace officer, and every person lawfully assisting the peace officer, is justified in using force that is intended or is likely to cause death or grievous bodily harm to a person to be arrested, if

(a) the peace officer is proceeding lawfully to arrest, with or without warrant, the person to be arrested;

(b) the offence for which the person is to be arrested is one for which that person may be arrested without warrant;

(c) the person to be arrested takes flight to avoid arrest;

(d) the peace officer or other person using the force believes on reasonable grounds that the force is necessary for the purpose of protecting the peace officer, the person lawfully assisting the peace officer or any other person from imminent or future death or grievous bodily harm; and

(e) the flight cannot be prevented by reasonable means in a less violent manner.

(5) A peace officer is justified in using force that is intended or is likely to cause death or grievous bodily harm against an inmate who is escaping from a penitentiary within the meaning of subsection 2(1) of the *Corrections and Conditional Release Act*, if

(a) the peace officer believes on reasonable grounds that any of the inmates of the penitentiary pose a threat of death or grievous bodily harm to the peace officer or any other person; and

(b) the escape cannot be prevented by reasonable means in a less violent manner.

The general preconditions s. 25 of the *Code* imposes for the valid use of force are:

- legal authorization to pursue action furthering administration or enforcement of the law;

- action is based on reasonable grounds;

- only as much force is used as is necessary for the purpose pursued;

- investigators are acting in good faith should the action later turn out to be part of an erroneous judicial process or criminal sentence; and

- reasonable belief on the part of investigators that use of force is necessary for preservation of self, or another under protection, if the force used is intended or likely to cause death or grievous bodily harm.

Section 27 of the *Code* deals with using force to prevent the commission of an offence:

27. Every one is justified in using as much force as is reasonably necessary

(a) to prevent the commission of an offence

(i) for which, if it were committed, the person who committed it might be arrested without warrant, and

(ii) that would be likely to cause immediate and serious injury to the person or property of anyone; or

(b) to prevent anything being done that, on reasonable grounds, he believes would, if it were done, be an offence mentioned in paragraph (*a*).

According to s-s. 25(1), use of force would still have to be otherwise authorized by law. Because ss. 25 and 27 stress use of force proportionate to the situation, making notes about the factual basis surrounding your decision to use force is very important.

Section 26 of the *Code* makes it perfectly clear that while ss. 25 and 27 give investigators a lot of discretion when it comes to using force, they will be held accountable for any error in judging how much force is appropriate in a given situation:

> **26.** Every one who is authorized by law to use force is criminally responsible for any excess thereof according to the nature and quality of the act that constitutes the excess.

Sections 25 and 27 of the *Code* will also not provide absolute protection from civil liability, as explained by *Green v. Lawrence*, (1998) 129 Man. R. (2d) 291 (C.A.) at paras. 46-47:

> The provision was intended to provide an exclusion from liability where the police officer uses force to effect an arrest, but where no more force than necessary is employed. Where more force than necessary is used, as in the present case, the trespass to the person is actionable.
>
> In the present case, there was an intentional application of force, rather than an unintended or accidental occurrence. Negligence, therefore, does not arise. But if this case could be seen as one sounding in negligence, s. 25 would afford the police officer no relief from liability.

You must have been acting reasonably in the lawful execution of your duties to benefit from ss. 25 and 27 *Code* protection. It is prudent for investigators to obtain early legal advice about their liability exposure, although it will be lawyers other than prosecutors who can provide such advice.

AVOIDING ABUSIVE DETENTION OR ARREST

Conduct that would shock the conscience of the community at large can render an otherwise valid detention or arrest illegal. In determining what is shocking, courts will look to the way the detention or arrest was conducted and to its underlying purpose. Most objectionable is an improper purpose for initiating a detention or arrest. The inquiry into what can constitute an abuse is thus much broader than merely looking at whether excessive force was used; excessive force alone may render the investigator who used it civilly or criminally liable, but will not always undermine the legal validity of a detention or arrest.

A number of recent findings of abusive detention and arrest deriving from an improper purpose involve racial profiling, whose origins and consequences were explained in *R. v. Campbell*, 2005 CarswellQue 243 (C.Q.) at paras. 26, 101 & 115:

> Racial profiling was adopted originally in the United States as an investigatory technique in drug trafficking cases. The practice was subsequently adopted by certain Canadian forces . . . . Factors such

as age, gender, race, location, dress, perceived life style and socio-economic status are among the indicators used to target suspects. Other indicators are associated with specific activities such as driving. Case law reveals that young black men driving expensive cars is one profile of drug dealer suspects; at the other end of the spectrum, young black males who are poor are also profiled as drug dealers.

. . .

Proof of racial profiling is proof of improper purpose and vitiates the lawfulness of the detention.

. . .

While the racial profiling may have been practiced unconsciously, the good faith of the officers does not restore the right of all citizens to non discriminatory treatment.

R. v. Khan (2004), 24 C.R. (6th) 48 (Ont. S.C.) at paras 68-69, examined the *Charter* consequences of abusive detention or arrest, again in the context of racial profiling:

> Mr. Khan has proven to be a reliable and credible witness. I accept his evidence that he did nothing to cause the officers to stop him. In any event, even if there had been some minor thing about his driving, I do not believe that was the real reason he was stopped. The police stopped him for an improper purpose. Mr. Khan was targeted for this stop because of racial profiling; because he was a black man with an expensive car.
>
> Mr. Khan's rights under both s. 8 and 9 of the *Charter* were violated. The Crown fairly conceded that if there was a finding of racial profiling, it would not be appropriate to admit the evidence of the cocaine under s. 24(2) of the *Charter*. I agree entirely. Conduct of this kind by the police is reprehensible. It cannot be condoned or excused. It is a most serious breach of Mr. Khan's human rights, as well as his rights under ss. 8 and 9 of the *Charter*. The evidence of the cocaine is excluded. In the absence of the drugs, the Crown has no case. The charge against Mr. Khan is dismissed.

Because of close ties between a valid detention or arrest, and a valid search, once the vehicle stop in *Khan* was found to be illegal, the search also became illegal.

R. v. Brown (2003), 170 O.A.C. 131 at paras. 4, 10, & 44-46, examined the means of proving abusive detention or arrest, yet again in the context of racial profiling:

> The attitude underlying racial profiling is one that may be consciously or unconsciously held. That is, the police officer need not be an overt racist. His or her conduct may be based on subconscious racial stereotyping.
>
> . . .
>
> If a police officer stops a person based on his or her colour (or on any other discriminatory ground) the purpose is improper (*Brown v. Durham Regional Police Force* (1998), 131 C.C.C. (3d) 1 (Ont. C.A.), at 17) and clearly would not be an articulable cause.
>
> . . .
>
> A racial profiling claim could rarely be proven by direct evidence. This would involve an admission by a police officer that he or she was influenced by racial stereotypes in the exercise of his or her discretion to stop a motorist. Accordingly, if racial profiling is to be proven it must be done by inference drawn from circumstantial evidence.
>
> The respondent submits that where the evidence shows that the circumstances relating to a detention correspond to the phenomenon of racial profiling and provide a basis for the court to infer that the police officer is lying about why he or she singled out the accused person for attention, the record is then capable of supporting a finding that the stop was based on racial profiling. I accept that this is a way in which racial profiling could be proven. I do not think that it sets the hurdle either too low (which could be unfair to honest police officers performing their duties in a professional and unbiased manner) or too high (which would make it virtually impossible for victims of racial profiling to receive the protection of their rights under section 9 of the *Charter*).
>
> In the present case, in addition to submitting that the facts (a young black person wearing a baseball hat and jogging clothes driving an expensive new car) fit the phenomenon of racial profiling, the respondent refers to several features of the evidence which support the argument that the officer was not being truthful about the real reasons for the stop. . . Briefly, the record includes: the respondent's evidence that the officer looked into his car before

> following and stopping him; evidence of the second set of notes
> prepared by the officer to firm up his reasons justifying the stop
> after he became aware the person under arrest was a well-known
> sports figure likely to undertake a defence of the charge against
> him; a licence check that the officer made before he stopped the
> respondent; and discrepancies between the times recorded in his
> notebook and those which he gave to the breathalyzer technician.

Before conducting any detention or arrest, every investigator needs to think twice about the reasons. Is there any chance that you are, either consciously or unconsciously, about to detain or arrest for an improper purpose? Thinking twice does not mean constantly second guessing all your decisions so you become paralyzed from taking any action. If you do decide to proceed with a proper detention or arrest, make sure you write down as soon as possible the reasons on which you relied.

ADAPTING DETENTION OR ARREST PROCEDURE TO PLACE

While the basic principles applicable to detention and arrest are consistent regardless of where an individual is approached by investigators, the practical application of those principles varies according to the reasonable expectation of privacy inherent in the place of contact. Public areas, motor vehicles, business premises, and dwelling places all give rise to different detention and arrest considerations.

1. The Easiest Procedure of Detention or Arrest in Public Places

Approaching a pedestrian walking in a public area like a sidewalk and asking a few simple questions is less likely to involve a detention than situations where investigators physically stop a person or enter a location where someone is located prior to questions being asked. *R. v. H. (C.R.)*, 2003 MBCA 38 at paras. 31-32, 49-51, & 57, confirmed that merely approaching a pedestrian to ask basic questions will not constitute a detention, and whether a detention existed must be assessed by looking at all the circumstances:

> there can be no question that there was no detention in the first
> half of the encounter, before the police asked for identification.
> Other than the fact that the questioning took place in the early
> hours of the morning, there is nothing else that would lead one to

conclude a demand was being made. The police did not block their path with their car or even get out of the car. They did not impede the youths' progress at all. The location of the questioning was not, aside from the time of night, oppressive. It did not take place in a back alley, back of a police car or a police station. According to the evidence, the language and tone of questioning were casual. They asked for no incriminating information (e.g., do you have any outstanding criminal charges, do you have any drugs on you?) and the youths voluntarily came over to the police car. Up until then, it is clear there is no detention.

At that point, the police officer asked them for identification and proceeded to check that information in the police computer. It is not clear from the evidence whether they supplied their names and addresses because they had no identification or whether that is what they were asked for. The police officer indicated that it was a request, not a demand, that they would have let the accused move on had he refused and that the "casual chat" continued through this process.

. . .

in this case, there was no crime committed and no investigation taking place. In such a situation, a pedestrian has the expectation of complete freedom of movement. To be stopped randomly in those circumstances without explanation by a figure of authority is contrary to one's expectations and an inference of compulsion may be easier to establish than in other situations. As well, evidence of improper motive might reinforce an atmosphere of harassment or oppression and lead to a conclusion that the accused reasonably believed he had no other choice but to comply. While the police serve the community and perform vital law enforcement and peacekeeping functions, these objectives can be open to abuse in the form of racial profiling, harassment or other improper motives.

. . .

However, in this case, there is no evidence for such an inference.

. . .

the duration of the interaction prior to the arrest was brief and the degree of intrusiveness minimal. Even while the identifying information was run through the computer, the evidence was that the accused was not asked to wait, but rather that one of the police officers engaged the youths in "casual chat."

. . .

> In speaking to an individual on the sidewalk, a police officer does
> not obviously assume control over the movements of an individual
> in the same way as stopping the driver of a motor vehicle. More
> importantly, on the sidewalk, unless there is evidence to the con-
> trary . . . there is no compulsion to speak and one can walk away.

In order to avoid an unintentional pedestrian detention, investigators
should:

- go over to the pedestrian, rather than calling the pedestrian over to
  them;

- not block the path of the pedestrian;

- not use a threatening or commanding tone of voice; and

- make clear the pedestrian need not answer any questions and is free
  to go at any time.

The legal thresholds for investigative detention (reasonable suspicion) or
arrest (reasonable and probable grounds) are, however, no different for
pedestrians than for those located in other more private locations.

The Threshold for Detention

Q & A

Q: Are you saying that my merely approaching and speaking with someone
on a public street could later be found by a court to have been a detention?

A: Probably not, unless there are other factors present that would lead a reasonable person to believe she was not free to leave.

2. The Relatively Easy Procedure of Detention and Arrest in a Business

As with pedestrians, all those approached and questioned by investigators in a business will not necessarily be detained. Certainly those questioned under the compliance verification authority of a regulatory Act are
not detained in the sense of triggering the full panoply of *Charter* protections. During the execution of most types of search or seizure warrants at a
business there is no accompanying authority to detain or arrest those found
in the business unless they are required pursuant to the terms of the warrant to assist investigators, are observed committing offences, or RPG to
arrest them is formed as a result of the search.

Standard warrantless and warranted arrest authorities are likely exercisable in the public areas of a business without any further authority. Arguably even for areas of a business where a reasonable expectation of privacy exists, one could infer a lawful power to arrest includes a power to enter solely for the purpose of making an arrest because of the lessened expectation of privacy inherent in a business. The *Criminal Code* only provides for special entry warrants to make an arrest inside a residence. However, entering a private area of a business to execute an arrest warrant is likely more defensible than exercising powers of arrest without a warrant. A s. 529 *Code* dwelling place arrest warrant would be the prudent route to follow for a mixed-use residence/business.

3. The Challenging Procedure of Detention or Arrest in a Moving Vehicle

The detention and arrest legality battle is hardest fought where motor vehicles are involved. Investigators can legally speak to vehicle occupants and look at contents in plain view if a vehicle is already stopped, they stop a vehicle based on reasonable suspicion to detain, or there is RPG to arrest an occupant. It is when there is no reasonable suspicion or RPG to stop, or where investigators stop a vehicle for one purpose but that purpose shifts during the stop, that problems arise.

Unlike pedestrian approaches, most vehicle stops will initially amount to a detention with inherent limitations on voluntariness of answers to questions including consent to search. Some arbitrary vehicle detentions like random stops and roadblocks can be justified under the *Charter* if for a compelling purpose like an impaired driving check, but investigators walk a legal tightrope of not using that purpose as a pretext to conduct a wider investigation. Investigators must have a legitimate purpose to stop a vehicle in their minds before taking action, and make notes of that purpose.

a. *Compelling Justification Needed for Random Vehicle Stops*

Completely random vehicle stops for either regulatory or criminal investigative purposes will violate s. 9 of the *Charter* as an arbitrary detention, but the lessened expectation of privacy in vehicles combined with compelling public safety purposes might justify the *Charter* breach as explained in *R. v. Hufsky*, [1988] 1 S.C.R. 621 at 636-37:

> In view of the importance of highway safety and the role to be
> played in relation to it by a random stop authority for the purpose
> of increasing both the detection and the perceived risk of detec-
> tion of motor vehicle offences, many of which cannot be detected
> by mere observation of driving, I am of the opinion that the limit
> imposed by s. 189(1) of the *Highway Traffic Act* on the right not
> to be arbitrarily detained guaranteed by s. 9 of the *Charter* is a rea-
> sonable one that is demonstrably justified in a free and democrat-
> ic society. The nature and degree of the intrusion of a random stop
> for the purposes of the spot check procedure in the present case,
> remembering that the driving of a motor vehicle is a licensed activ-
> ity subject to regulation and control in the interests of safety, is pro-
> portionate to the purpose to be served.

Permissible random stops are clearly limited in their purpose according to
R. v. Mellenthin, [1992] 3 S.C.R. 615 at 624:

> Check stop programs result in the arbitrary detention of motorists.
> The programs are justified as a means aimed at reducing the terri-
> ble toll of death and injury so often occasioned by impaired driv-
> ers or by dangerous vehicles. The primary aim of the program is
> thus to check for sobriety, licences, ownership, insurance and the
> mechanical fitness of cars.

Neither powers of questioning nor powers of searching extend beyond the
justifiable highway traffic safety (or other) purposes of random stops.

On questioning limits *R. v. Ladouceur*, [1990] 2 S.C.R. 1257 at 1287 said:
"Once stopped the only questions that may justifiably be asked are those
related to driving offences. Any further, more intrusive procedures could
only be undertaken based upon reasonable and probable grounds." As for
searching *R. v. Mellenthin*, [1992] 3 S.C.R. 615 at 629, found:

> A check stop does not and cannot constitute a general search war-
> rant for searching every vehicle, driver and passenger that is pulled
> over. Unless there are reasonable and probable grounds for con-
> ducting the search, or drugs, alcohol or weapons are in plain view
> in the interior of the vehicle, the evidence flowing from such a
> search should not be admitted.

Highway traffic purposes especially cannot be used as a pretext to stop for
what is really an investigation into a criminal offence like drug trafficking,
or even to check for regulatory offences like payment of park admission
fees. *R. v. Schaeffer* (2005), 257 Sask. R. 219; 2005 SKCA 33 at para. 48,
found police stopping every vehicle still at-large in a provincial park after
10 p.m. "as part of a general effort to discourage crime, to maintain quiet

and to confirm that Park users had passes" was not a justifiable infringement on *Charter* rights because the purpose was far too nebulous.

To avoid allegations of an improper stop you may not need very substantial grounds to establish reasonable suspicion, but you will need something more than a mere hunch. In *R. v. Wilson*, [1990] 1 S.C.R. 1291 at 1297, sufficient grounds were found to be contextual:

> in this case the stopping of the appellant was not random, but was based on the fact that the appellant was driving away from a hotel shortly after the closing time for the bar and that the vehicle and its occupants were unknown to the police officer. While these facts might not form grounds for stopping a vehicle in downtown Edmonton or Toronto, they merit consideration in the setting of a rural community.

Thus rural investigators may be capable of establishing reasonable suspicion more readily than urban investigators.

b. *Roadblocks as Difficult to Justify Random Stops*

A roadblock is an extreme version of the random stop. Just because everyone is being stopped doesn't render the stop any less random — there is no reasonable suspicion to conduct *any* of the stops. There may be occasional special circumstances that will justify roadblocks, but these will be rarer than circumstances justifying selective random stops, including "that a serious crime has been committed and a roadblock may apprehend the perpetrator" as explained in *R. v. Clayton*, (2005) 196 O.A.C. 16 at para. 53:

> Where the police do not have grounds to suspect any specific person or persons, the use of a roadblock stop cannot be justified in furtherance of the police duty to investigate and prevent crime unless the police have reasonable grounds to believe both that a serious crime has been committed and that the roadblock stop may apprehend the perpetrator. The significant interference with liberties of an indeterminate number of people occasioned by the roadblock stop, combined with the fact that the individuals stopped are targets of a police investigation and may face criminal jeopardy as a result of the police action, demands a strong state interest to justify police interference with individual liberties. The state interest in the investigation of crime and the apprehension of criminals is sufficiently strong to justify the kind of interference necessitated by a roadblock stop only where the police have reasonable grounds to believe that a serious crime has been committed and reasonable

grounds to believe that the roadblock stop will be effective in that it will apprehend the perpetrator.

There the *Charter* rights of the two accused who were stopped at a roadblock set up in response to a 911 call to look for weapons among those exiting a bar were found to have been violated, firearms in their possession were excluded from evidence, and they were acquitted of all charges because the court was not satisfied with justification for the stop.

Examples of situations where roadblocks have been successfully justified include:

- where there is solid information from a reliable source like another police service that a bank has been robbed, and suspects are heading down a particular road in the direction of the roadblock;

- where a roadblock's primary aim is protecting life and safety, instead of simply pursuing the investigation of crime;

- to elicit information from the public about a crime, rather than targeting vehicles as containing suspects in a crime.

But even a justifiable roadblock must be limited both in duration and intrusiveness.

A general search of vehicles or occupants stopped at a roadblock is *not* permitted. What is permissible is:

- questioning the occupants about matters connected to the reason for the stop;

- conducting a visual examination of the interior of the vehicle without entering it; and

- removing the occupants from the vehicle to facilitate interior visual examination.

Those actions could lead to RPG to arrest, in which case a search incident to arrest might be conducted or a search warrant obtained, but could likewise come up with nothing — even if the stopped vehicle had ten kilos of heroin and a dead body securely hidden away in its trunk. With roadblocks, just like with other investigative actions, it is not sufficient to argue the end justifies the means. Investigators who have reasonable suspicion to stop a vehicle are legally better served by setting up roadside observations to wait for the vehicle to appear, rather than stopping every vehicle in the hope that one will fit the description of the target vehicle.

c. *Examples of How to and How Not to Conduct Vehicle Stops and Searches*

The two contrasting cases of *R. v. France*, 2002 NWTSC 32, and *R. v. Whitford*, 2004 NWTSC 38, illustrate how to and how *not* to establish grounds to detain and search a moving vehicle. Both cases come from the Northwest Territories. Both involved vehicle stops leading to the discovery of drugs. But in one, all seized evidence was excluded at trial and the accused acquitted, whereas in the other the evidence was admitted and convictions secured. The difference between the cases lies in the strength of the grounds to stop, and what means were employed to detect and secure evidence.

In *R. v. France*, 2002 NWTSC 32, police believed drugs were being moved from Alberta to the NWT by a female in a red Jeep Cherokee. The police stopped a vehicle that was neither red, nor a Jeep Cherokee, and not containing any females, ultimately discovering 84 pounds of marihuana and over $10,000 in cash. The police relied on what they argued was their reasonable suspicion to stop the vehicle because:

- an unknown rental vehicle with British Columbia plates was observed in the Northwest Territories at a gas stop where the driver did not exit the vehicle, paid for gas in cash, and there appeared to be luggage in the vehicle;

- the rear windows of the vehicle were open even though it was a cold day; and

- when stopped earlier in the day for a highway traffic check the driver had been nervous and overly friendly, stated that he and his passenger were driving straight through from British Columbia to the Northwest Territories, and asked the officer who stopped them about the conditions on an ice road.

The court concluded at para. 51:

> what Constable L. . . had was nothing more than a hunch, . . . and much less than reasonable cause for suspicion. What have been described in this case as indicators seem to me to amount to nothing more than hunches based on intuition perhaps gained by experience. Obviously, Constable L. . .'s hunch turned out to be correct, but that does not alter the fact that it was a hunch, not articulable cause.

This lack of grounds to stop amounted to a s. 9 *Charter* breach, compounded by a s. 8 *Charter* breach because of a defective consent search request that was not sufficiently documented or informed as described in paras. 61-68:

> At most, Mr. France acquiesced; he did not consent or waive his s. 8 right. In my view, Mr. France's s. 8 right was breached unless it can be said that he authorized Winter to waive his right. There is no evidence of that.
>
> I also find that the evidence is less than clear as to what exactly Mr. Winter said in giving his consent to Constable L. . . . The problem is that he made no notes at the time of exactly what Mr. Winter said.
>
> Constable L. . .'s evidence is that he told Winter he could withdraw his consent or stop the search at any time without penalty or without legal consequences . . . that is not the same as telling a person they do not have to consent to the search at all.
>
> . . .
>
> Constable L. . . had standard . . . consent forms in his police vehicle which he did not use, because, he said, he felt he did not have to use them where the search was offered to him. It seems to me, however, that a police officer would want to obtain a written consent as the best evidence that a consent was in fact given and an acknowledgement that the individual understood the terms of the consent. . . .
>
> . . .
>
> In my view, the . . . policy recognizes what the law says: that the information to be given includes two components: the right to refuse to consent and the right, if consent is given, to withdraw consent. Constable L. . . told Mr. Winter of only one of those components. For that reason alone, the consent given was not fully informed.

The serious nature of the *Charter* breaches led to the exclusion of all evidence at trial.

In *R. v. Whitford*, 2004 NWTSC 38, the police again believed drugs were being moved in a vehicle from Alberta into the Northwest Territories. Again, police stopped a vehicle in which drugs were ultimately found (this time 48 grams of crack cocaine and $3,000 in cash). But there the similarities in the cases end. The reasonable suspicion to stop in *Whitford* was composed of:

- several sources who had provided information over the course of one year that the accused was bringing crack from Alberta into the Northwest Territories for purposes of sale;

- one of those sources, who provided details that the accused carried the crack in a fanny pack and sold from a particular address, had information from personal knowledge, and had previously provided reliable information leading to the prosecution and conviction of others;

- on the day of the stop a source indicated he personally saw the accused as a passenger in a black vehicle travelling south into Alberta, and that the driver of the vehicle who the source identified by name took possession of a package at a gas stop before driving back north; and

- that a records check revealed the driver on whom the source had provided information in fact owned a black Chrysler.

Thus the court held there to be ample reason to stop.

Instead of attempting a consent search, in *Whitford* the lead investigator sought a search warrant for the vehicle. There were some drafting problems with the warrant identified at para. 19 of the judgment: "Cst. I. . . himself acknowledged that he made a mistake by relying on 'boilerplate' wording instead of modifying it to the circumstances." But the court ultimately supported the warrant at para. 26:

> In the case before me, Cst. I. . . was not careful in his drafting of the Information. He failed to specify that there were three sources, not one, and he failed to specifically associate the reasons he gave for their reliability to each of the three sources. So there was the potential to mislead the Justice of the Peace. However, I am satisfied that these errors were inadvertent, as opposed to a deliberate attempt to mislead, and that Cst. I. . .acted in good faith throughout. But this case should serve as a warning about over-reliance on "boilerplate" wording. Nevertheless I am satisfied that, even with these errors, there was reliable evidence that might reasonably be believed so as to justify issuance of the warrant. The evidence provided by amplification, going as it does to the totality of the circumstances, reinforces this conclusion.

Solid grounds to stop, followed by a warrant, although not perfect, supported the valid seizure of evidence, and led the court to overlook warrant imperfections because investigators demonstrated the utmost of good faith throughout the stop and search.

d. *Avoiding Mixed Purposes in Vehicle Stops*

Mixed highway traffic and criminal investigation purposes cause just as many legal difficulties at roadblocks as they do in single random stops. In *R. v. Ladouceur* (2001), 223 Sask. R. 161; 2001 SKCA 73, the court gained direct insight into the original investigative purpose from the "Regional Highway Patrol Traffic Plan — April 1999 — Operation Recovery" attached as Appendix A to the judgment:

> Numerous offences under the Highway Traffic Act are detected daily by law enforcement agencies within Saskatchewan, Canada and North America. In an attempt to combat these problems, and to insure the safe use of our Highways, it is our intention to check all traffic using #1 Highway near . . . Saskatchewan. It has also been noted that illegal contraband is being transported via passenger vehicles, power units, recreation vehicles and uhaul rental vehicles, across the province of Saskatchewan along Highway #1. Contraband has consisted of illegal drugs, tobacco, alcohol, wildlife, firearms, etc. . . .
>
> . . .
>
> By holding a ROADBLOCK for a 10 hour period, we will attempt to combat and detect vehicle infractions, driver infractions and the transportation of illegal contraband. By applying our investigative skills and observation, we will attempt to locate traveling criminals and locate illegal contraband being transported on our highways.
>
> . . .
>
> Priorities will consist of enforcement and prosecution of offences detected during this period. Checks will be conducted for the following: PROHIBITED/IMPAIRED DRIVERS, CVSA INSPECTIONS, DRUGS, TOBACCO, FIREARMS, ALCOHOL and any other infractions under Provincial Legislation and Criminal Code.
>
> . . .
>
> There have been numerous stolen vehicles, drugs, cigarettes and cash seizures on this busy route and we will work together to produce a thorough Check Stop. All sections of the Criminal Code and Highway Traffic Acts will be available to use.

Notwithstanding that 4.55 kilos of marihuana had been located in the accused's vehicle in a check during this roadblock, the court held at paras. 53-54 & 65:

> The police wrongly forced Mr. Ladouceur to participate in the discovery of evidence by: (i) requiring him to stop at a program designed in part for the search for illicit drugs; (ii) subjecting him to questioning by Sgt. U. . . at the initial stop, which questioning pursued a purpose beyond road safety concerns; (iii) compelling him to bring his vehicle to the "safety zone" where a more extensive search of his vehicle was conducted; (iv) questioning him further at the safety zone; and (v) requiring him to exit his vehicle. . . .Thus, the trial judge's conclusion that admitting this evidence would render the trial unfair is not unreasonable.

> When I pass to the issue of whether the seriousness of the breach commands the attention of this Court, I agree with the trial judge's reaction that the operation was fatally flawed from the outset. The police believed themselves capable of conducting an intensive operation which resembles that of a border search. They set out to find reasonable and probable grounds and viewed their operation as steps in an investigative process, and . . . planned to charge Mr. Ladouceur with obstruction if he did not cooperate.

> . . .

> Our society is not the kind where in the interests of reducing criminal activity generally or a particular genus of criminal activity, we authorize our police to detain citizens arbitrarily or indiscriminately on the highway or the street or wherever with a view to identifying former or potential criminals in the hope of detecting some criminal activity on their part should it happen to be then taking place. While it is true that the members of our society desire security they also desire freedom.

The court concluded at para. 66: "it is important not to encourage the establishment of check-stops where a nominally lawful aim is but a plausible façade for an unlawful aim."

If drug investigation is your purpose, observing a vehicle and running its details through your records will not violate the rights of any occupant, may ultimately prove sufficient to develop reasonable suspicion to stop, and can be followed by conversations with vehicle occupants and plain view into the vehicle interior that might lead to RPG to conduct a search or seizure (preferably with a warrant). For example, in one case with which I was involved three off-duty police officers with previous drug investigation experience were driving together on a highway in a personal vehicle when they observed another vehicle travelling in the adjacent lane with what appeared to be a large baggie of marihuana on the dashboard. The passenger of the other vehicle was for some inexplicable reason video recording the baggie and its rapid progress down Canada's highways and byways. The officers made a cell phone call to a local police detachment that dispatched a marked cruiser to stop the target vehicle, subsequently leading to a seizure, arrest and charges. No purpose problem arose in that stop because either reasonable suspicion or reasonable and probable grounds had been developed solely from the observations the officers had made.

Executing programs of illegal goods interdiction on Canada's roads and in Canada's domestic airports, bus and train stations is legally challenging because investigators do not possess the same lawful authority to comprehensively check vehicles and people as exists upon entering or exiting from Canada at border points. If you stick with the two themes of this book, first examining the demystified basic principles of detention, arrest, search and seizure law, and second contacting a prosecutor or other legal advisor prior to executing any major operation that pushes legal boundaries, you will maximize prospects for case success.

Sticking to Legitimate Vehicle Stop Purposes

Q: How can I best ensure the legitimate highway traffic stops I make, which sometimes lead to discovering evidence of unrelated offences, aren't later found to be illegal pretext stops not conducted for highway traffic purposes?

A: Think through your predominant purpose before making a vehicle stop, then stick to and make notes of that purpose. Be prepared to respond to cross-examination questions in court challenging your actual purpose.

4. The Most Difficult Procedure of Detention and Arrest in a Dwelling Place

a. Reasons for Investigators to Be Inside a Dwelling Place When Making an Arrest

Because a residence has the greatest expectation of privacy of any place other than the human body, detention or arrest may only occur when investigators have legal authority to be there beyond the mere grounds to make a detention or arrest. Section 2 of the *Code* gives a broad definition to a "dwelling house:"

> "dwelling-house" means the whole or any part of a building or structure that is kept or occupied as a permanent or temporary residence, and includes
>
> (a) a building within the curtilage of a dwelling-house that is connected to it by a doorway or by a covered and enclosed passageway, and
>
> (b) a unit that is designed to be mobile and to be used as a permanent or temporary residence and that is being used as such a residence;

I sometimes use the terms dwelling house, dwelling place and residence interchangeably, but you should use whatever language is specified in any legislation under which you are seeking judicial authorization.

There can be several lawful reasons for investigators to be inside a residence at the time they decide to make an arrest:

- they are already on the premises because of an invitation to enter;
- grounds supporting a detention or arrest are observed during execution of a search warrant;
- they are in the residence because of a threat to public health or safety that required urgent entry, like in response to a 911 call;
- they are engaged in hot pursuit of a fleeing suspect;
- they have obtained a s. 529 or s. 529.1 *Code* dwelling house entry warrant.

Suspicion alone was never a sufficient basis upon which to enter and search a residence for evidence of an offence, and it is also an insufficient basis upon which to enter and search for a suspected offender.

Relying on s. 529 of the *Code* only adds a residence entry authority at the time another type of federal arrest warrant is issued:

> **529.** (1) A warrant to arrest or apprehend a person issued by a judge or justice under this or any other Act of Parliament may authorize a peace officer, subject to subsection (2), to enter a dwelling-house described in the warrant for the purpose of arresting or apprehending the person if the judge or justice is satisfied by information on oath in writing that there are reasonable grounds to believe that the person is or will be present in the dwelling-house.

(2) An authorization to enter a dwelling-house granted under subsection (1) is subject to the condition that the peace officer may not enter the dwelling-house unless the peace officer has, immediately before entering the dwelling-house, reasonable grounds to believe that the person to be arrested or apprehended is present in the dwelling-house.

By contrast, a s. 529.1 *Code* warrant is an independent instrument that supplements another arrest warrant already in force or enhances arrest without warrant powers:

529.1. A judge or justice may issue a warrant in Form 7.1 authorizing a peace officer to enter a dwelling-house described in the warrant for the purpose of arresting or apprehending a person identified or identifiable by the warrant if the judge or justice is satisfied by information on oath that there are reasonable grounds to believe that the person is or will be present in the dwelling-house and that

(a) a warrant referred to in this or any other Act of Parliament to arrest or apprehend the person is in force anywhere in Canada;

(b) grounds exist to arrest the person without warrant under paragraph 495(1)(a) or (b) or section 672.91; or

(c) grounds exist to arrest or apprehend without warrant the person under an Act of Parliament, other than this Act.

The mandatory conditions to obtaining and executing either a s. 529 or 529.1 warrant are:

- reasonable belief that the person sought is or will be present in a named dwelling house; and

- prior announcement of investigator intention to enter (s. 529.4), unless explicitly waived by the court because of risk of bodily harm or destruction of evidence.

The information to obtain s. 529 or s. 529.1 *Code* powers can be simpler than the average warrant to search since only one thing is being sought (the target of the arrest), the thing is in a clearly defined location (a particular dwelling house), the offence has been determined (because charges will usually have been laid prior to the arrest), and supporting grounds will often derive from direct investigator or informer observations of the target recently entering the residence named in the warrant.

b. *Exceptions to the Dwelling Place Warrant Requirement*

Hot pursuit and imminent harm are two long-standing exigent circumstances common law exceptions to dwelling place arrest warrants. Investigators who witness the commission of an arrestable offence, or arrive shortly after its commission, witness the offender fleeing, and then conduct a fresh and continuous pursuit have been entitled to enter a residence without a warrant to make an arrest under the hot pursuit doctrine, as explained in *R. v. Macooh*, [1993] 2 S.C.R. 802 at 815-16:

> The offender is then not being bothered by the police unexpectedly while in domestic tranquility. He has gone to his home while fleeing solely to escape arrest. In such circumstances, the police could not be obliged to end the pursuit on the offender's doorstep . . . . The flight of the offender, an act contrary to public order, also should not be thus rewarded.

> From a more practical standpoint, it is not desirable for offenders to be encouraged to seek refuge in their homes or those of third parties. Significant danger may be associated with such flight and the pursuit that may result. Thus, in the present case the appellant by his flight unnecessarily threatened the safety of those who might have been in his way.

> . . .

> In short, the basis for this exception is common sense, which is opposed to the offender being able to escape arrest by fleeing into his home or that of a third party. This is why if an arrest without a warrant is permissible at the outset, the offender's flight into a dwelling-house cannot make it unlawful. The entry of the police in hot pursuit is then perfectly justified.

This exception cannot be stretched to include situations where a pursuit earlier in the day was broken off.

The doctrine of imminent harm likewise authorizes investigators to enter a residence without a warrant for the purpose of preventing death or serious bodily harm, whereby investigators might incidentally make an arrest of the person who poses the threat of harm, as explained in *R. v. Godoy*, [1999] 1 S.C.R. 311 at para. 22:

> the importance of the police duty to protect life warrants and justifies a forced entry into a dwelling in order to ascertain the health and safety of a 911 caller. The public interest in maintaining an effective emergency response system is obvious and significant

enough to merit some intrusion on a resident's privacy interest. However, I emphasize that the intrusion must be limited to the protection of life and safety. The police have authority to investigate the 911 call and, in particular, to locate the caller and determine his or her reasons for making the call and provide such assistance as may be required. The police authority for being on private property in response to a 911 call ends there. They do not have further permission to search premises or otherwise intrude on a resident's privacy or property.

Imagined risks not having a solid basis in reality don't justify imminent harm entry.

Section 529.3 of the *Code* has now somewhat codified dwelling house exigent circumstances arrest warrant exceptions, explicitly mentioning imminent harm or evidence loss, but not hot pursuit, which arguably is implicitly included:

> **529.3.** (1) Without limiting or restricting any power a peace officer may have to enter a dwelling-house under this or any other Act or law, the peace officer may enter the dwelling-house for the purpose of arresting or apprehending a person, without a warrant referred to in section 529 or 529.1 authorizing the entry, if the peace officer has reasonable grounds to believe that the person is present in the dwelling-house, and the conditions for obtaining a warrant under section 529.1 exist but by reason of exigent circumstances it would be impracticable to obtain a warrant.
>
> (2) For the purposes of subsection (1), exigent circumstances include circumstances in which the peace officer
>
> (a) has reasonable grounds to suspect that entry into the dwelling-house is necessary to prevent imminent bodily harm or death to any person; or
>
> (b) has reasonable grounds to believe that evidence relating to the commission of an indictable offence is present in the dwelling-house and that entry into the dwelling-house is necessary to prevent the imminent loss or imminent destruction of the evidence.

Just because the exceptions have been codified does not mean investigators have *carte blanche* in relying on them to avoid obtaining s. 529 or s. 529.1 warrants.

Even investigators knowing the location of a murder suspect does not inexorably lead to exigent circumstances, as noted in *R. v. Feeney*, [1997] 2 S.C.R. 13 at para.168:

> The circumstances surrounding the police entry into the trailer were similar to those following any serious crime: a dangerous person is on the loose and there is a risk that he or she will attempt to destroy evidence linking him or her to the crime. To define these as exigent circumstances is to invite such a characterization of every period after a serious crime. In my view, exigent circumstances did not exist when the police entered the trailer. Consequently, even if there is an exception to the warrant requirement in exigent circumstances generally, rather than only in hot pursuit, which I refrain from deciding in the present case, the forcible entry in this case required a warrant.

Exigent circumstances really have to be exceptional circumstances. Reliance on them should be avoided if there is any other alternative like setting up residence observations while securing a warrant. Section 529.5 of the *Code* provides for telewarrants to enter residences to make arrests, thus speeding the judicial prior authorization process.

RELEASE BURDENS, REASONS AND CONDITIONS

As important as the decision to detain or arrest is, the decision on whether to release after arrest and on what terms may be more important. Because s-s.11(e) of the *Charter* guarantees the right "not to be denied reasonable bail without just cause," as noted in *R. v. Morales*, [1992] 3 S.C.R. 711 at 737, detention cannot be a routine event:

> Bail is not denied for all individuals who pose a risk of committing an offence or interfering with the administration of justice while on bail. Bail is denied only for those who pose a "substantial risk" of committing an offence or interfering with the administration of justice, and only where this "substantial likelihood" endangers "the protection or safety of the public". Moreover, detention is justified only when it is "necessary" for public safety. It is not justified where detention would merely be convenient or advantageous.

R. v. Hall, [2002] 3 S.C.R. 309, further explained:

> The right conferred "is a basic entitlement to be granted reasonable bail unless there is just cause to do otherwise" . . . . This entitlement rests on the presumption that an accused person is innocent until found guilty at trial. However, s. 11(e) also recognizes that, notwithstanding the presumption of innocence, "just cause" may exist for denying liberty to an accused person pending trial.

Before you make an arrest, you should ideally consider what form of release and conditions, if any, would be appropriate.

1. The Ladder System of Release

The *Criminal Code* sets out a ladder system of incremental release steps, where release must be made on the lowest appropriate ladder rung:

- at the ladder base where no arrest took place is s. 496 authorizing an appearance notice issued at the scene to compel appearance in court to answer a charge;

- on the first ladder rung where an arrest did occur is s. 497 that again authorizes an appearance notice issued at the scene or alternatively release with no notice because appearance will later be compelled by summons, which maintains flexibility over the court date;

- the second rung up the ladder is release at the detachment by the investigator in charge pursuant to s. 498 with a promise to appear or a recognizance not to exceed $500, pursuant to s. 499 if arrest was made with an endorsed warrant in which case release conditions can be imposed, or under s-s. 503(2.1), which authorizes release on an undertaking with conditions;

- the third rung on the ladder is bringing the accused before a judicial official under s. 515 for a bail hearing, where a prosecutor can take the position that the accused should be detained in custody or released on conditions.

Detention above the lowest appropriate rung by lodging someone in cells overnight to await a bail hearing where there is no reason to do so may constitute a breach of s. 9 of the *Charter*, and lead to the exclusion of all evidence connected to the offence arrested for as happened in *R. v. Kime*, (1985) 41 Sask. R. 35 (Prov. Ct.) at paras. 3 & 9:

> The accused had been apprehended on a shoplifting charge and when searched certain drugs were found in her possession. She was arrested by peace officers and was taken to the . . . City Police offices around 6:00 p.m. on October 27, 1984. After being questioned by drug section officers in respect to the drug matter, she testified that she felt that she would be released soon. She had been encouraged in this belief by some of the officers with whom she dealt. She made several telephone calls and arranged for a friend to attend at the police station for the purpose of establish-

ing her identity and to give her a ride to her residence from the police station. Notwithstanding that all police investigation in respect to the shoplifting and the drug charge appear to have been complete well before midnight on that date, the accused was not released on any process to compel her appearance in court at a later date. She was released the following day on an undertaking without special conditions given before a Justice of the Peace. Neither on examination or cross-examination were the accused or the investigating officers able to supply any reason why the accused's continued custody was necessary past the evening of October 27th.

. . .

The accused ought to have been released before an officer in charge pursuant to s. [498] or in the unlikely event that there was no officer in charge at the . . . Police office, the arresting police officer should have released her pursuant to s. [497].

Release must follow an arrest unless investigators can satisfy one or more of the *Code*'s specified reasons for moving up the rungs of the release ladder.

Sub-section 498(1.1) of the *Code* enumerates some of the public interest reasons that could justify moving up the ladder to:

- establish identity of the person arrested;

- secure or preserve evidence related to the offence;

- prevent continuation of the offence or commission of new offences;

- ensure security of victims or witnesses;

- ensure the person arrested will attend court.

If none of these reasons apply in your case, you usually should be releasing anyone in your custody post-haste unless a serious indictable offence is involved or there are other legal reasons not to release. Figure 11-1, Compelling Appearance, Arrest and Release Decision-Making Matrix, will assist you in deciphering the best method to compel appearance and determining how the chosen method will dictate your release options. For example, if you compel appearance by way of summons, then conditions on release will not be possible. Sometimes it is best to first figure out what form of release would be appropriate, and then work back to choose a means to compel appearance.

Fig 11-1	COMPELLING APPEARANCE, ARREST AND RELEASE DECISION-MAKING MATRIX				
Type of power	Summons without arrest	Appearance notice	Arrest without warrant - Anyone power	Arrest without warrant - peace officer power	Arrest with warrant
Section of *Code*	ss. 507 & 509	s. 496	s. 494	s. 495	s. 519
Limits on use	Charge laid, not in custody, not otherwise bound to appear	Found committing criminal offence, has or will commit indictable offence, or outstanding warrant	Found committing indictable offence, escaping criminal offence, or property owner	Found committing criminal offence, has or will commit indictable offence, or outstanding warrant	Valid warrant in jurisdiction or freshly pursued from that jurisdiction
Forms of release and conditions that may be imposed	None	None	Deliver person arrested forthwith to peace officer	Unconditional release s-s.503(1)	Unconditional release s-s.503(1)
				No conditions	No conditions
				Promise to appear by OIC s-s.498(1)(b)	Promise to appear by OIC if warrant endorsed s-s.499(1)(a)
				No other conditions	Limited conditions s-s. 499(2)
				Release own recognizance up to $500 by OIC s-ss.498 (1)(c)&(d)	Release own recognizance up to $500 by OIC if endorsed warrant s.499
				No other conditions	Limited conditions s-s. 499(2)
				Release by justice on undertaking without conditions s-s.515(1)	
				No conditions	
				Release by justice on undertaking with conditions s-s. 515(2)	
				Sureties and all reasonable conditions may be imposed	
				Release by justice on recognizance with conditions s-s.515(2)	
				Sureties and all reasonable conditions may be imposed	
Detention and review process				Detention in custody by justice s-s.515(10)	
				Bail review in Superior Court ss.520 & 521	
				Appeal of bail review to Court of Appeal	

2. Who Bears the Burden for Post-Arrest Release or Detention in Custody?

The prosecution bears the burden of justifying detention under s. 515 of the *Code*, except s-s. 515(6) of the *Code* places a reverse onus on the accused to justify release when:

- charged with committing an indictable offence while already on release for another indictable offence;

- charged with a criminal organization or terrorism offence;

- the accused is not ordinarily resident in Canada;

- charged with breaching a condition of a prior release or failing to appear;

- charged with a serious drug offence.

Notwithstanding having appeared as a prosecutor at hundreds of bail hearings, I have never been sure whether placing the onus for detention on the Crown or accused makes a great difference. There ultimately needs to be a compelling reason to detain anyone.

3. The Three Main Reasons for Post-Arrest Detention

There are three questions known as the primary, secondary and tertiary grounds of detention set out in s-s. 515(10) of the *Code* determining whether an accused will be released at a bail hearing.

1. Is the accused likely not to attend court appearances?

2. Is the accused likely to commit additional offences if released?

3. Is detention necessary to maintain public confidence in the administration of justice?

The tertiary ground can be useful in cases like *R. v. Hall*, [2002] 3 S.C.R. 309, where the accused had ample community and family ties, proposed significant security for his release, and there was no fear that he would commit offences while on bail, but the vicious nature of the first degree murder charge, the strong evidence linking him to the offence, and the post-murder fear prevalent in the community led the court to detain him solely on the tertiary ground.

Reasons To Seek Post-Arrest Detention

Q&A

Q: Especially in reverse-onus situations, why wouldn't a prosecutor seek to detain all accused in custody pending their trial? Isn't pretrial detention an effective tool to force accused to plead guilty?

A: Both investigators and prosecutors act in the public interest. Investigators and prosecutors should seek an accused's detention where it is in the public interest or there is another legal reason to do so. Where detention that could possibly last for months or years pending trial is not absolutely required, it may be better to make a deal for strong release conditions rather than have an accused let out on basic conditions after the court rejects demands for detention. It is true that those detained prior to trial have a significant incentive to plead guilty, but the extraction of a plea is not a legitimate reason to seek detention.

4. Crafting Appropriate Bail Conditions

Investigators are in the ideal position in the judicial system to know which bail conditions might be most effective to ensure court attendance and prevent new offences. In a bail order issued by a justice or judge under s. 515 of the *Code* and in an undertaking imposed by a peace officer pursuant to s-s. 503(2.1) conditions can include:

- remain in a particular territorial jurisdiction;

- notify the authorities of any change of address;

- abstain from communicating with certain persons, or from attending specified places;

- deposit passport;

- surrender firearms and related permits;

- report to a specified person at specified times;

- abstain from consuming alcohol or drugs;

- comply with "any other condition specified in the undertaking that the peace officer or officer in charge [or justice] considers necessary to ensure the safety and security of any victim of or witness to the offence."

A justice or judge can additionally order an undertaking to include cash deposit or sureties, depending on the circumstances, and impose "such other reasonable conditions specified in the order as the justice considers desirable," instead of just conditions to ensure the safety and security of victims or witnesses.

Bail conditions can be stacked one upon the other until reaching dizzy heights, but I have always advised investigators not to make bail orders so mind-numbingly complex as to be essentially inviting a breach by an accused. Strictness is still possible without complexity by picking a few carefully crafted provisions like:

- do not at any time enter the area of Toronto bounded by Bloor St. to the North, the Don River to the east, Runnymede St. to the West, and Lake Ontario to the south;

- report in person to the reporting centre located at 123 Ash St., Centreville, Quebec, every day between the hours of 10 a.m. and 4 p.m.; or

- remain in his residence 24 hours a day, seven days a week, except for four hours between noon and 4 p.m. every Wednesday for the purpose of shopping and attending to other personal matters.

5. The Short and Sweet Bail Brief

Investigators who wish an accused detained or subject to strict release conditions must provide the prosecution and court with lots of supporting factual information about the current offence and accused's background, which is best presented in a bail brief including:

- a summary of the offence facts;

- a list of prior, still outstanding charges the accused faces and the bail conditions on those charges (including their occurrence reports if they are serious and especially if the new bail brief relates to a domestic assault where there are prior assault charges);

- the complete criminal (and sometimes relevant regulatory) record of the accused;

- background information on the accused;

- any justification for detention; and

- recommendations for conditions of release in case the prosecution or court decides release is appropriate.

Using inflammatory language in the bail brief will not help secure the accused's detention because the prosecutor will not be able to use that language in court, and may come to the conclusion that you have tunnel vision incapable of assessing whether detention really is justifiable. Asking for every accused that you bring before a justice to be detained, rather than asking for at least some of them to have strong conditions of release imposed upon them, is another way to guarantee a prosecutor will not take your recommendations seriously. Attending the bail hearing in person, thereby being available to answer last minute prosecutor questions and possibly give testimony, will greatly enhance your chances of securing detention or strict conditions of release.

If you are still working on ascertaining facts relevant to whether an accused should be detained at the time an accused is first brought before a justice, s-s. 515(1) of the *Code* gives the prosecution the ability to request a delay in holding a bail hearing for up to three days. Not being certain about the accused's identity, criminal record, or other charges for which the accused may already be out on bail are all good reasons to seek a bail hearing delay.

For Making Sound Decisions about Detention, Arrest and Release

KEY POINTS

✓ Detention can occur during physical constraint, following a demand or direction with the risk of significant legal consequences accompanied by impeded access to counsel, and in the course of psychological detention. An arrest occurs when an investigator takes control of a person in a way where it is explicitly or implicitly made clear an arrest is intended and force will be used to prevent that person from leaving. Rights to counsel and cautions must generally be provided upon detention or arrest, although the exact point by which they absolutely must be delivered will vary according to the context.

✓ Investigative detention may be available where there is a recent or ongoing criminal offence, reasonable suspicion that a person is implicated in the offence, necessity for the detention to the investigator's duties, the detention will be brief in duration, and justification for the nature and extent of the liberty interference. Investigative detention is not an authority to search or compel answers.

✓ An arrest without a warrant can be made under s. 494 of the *Criminal Code* by anyone witnessing the commission of an indictable offence, who has reasonable grounds to believe the person arrested is escaping from and freshly pursued by those who have authority to arrest, or who arrests in respect of an offence being committed on or against that person's property. An arrest without a warrant can be made by a peace officer under s. 495

KEY POINTS

of the *Code* of a person believed to have previously committed or who is about to commit an indictable offence, a person found committing any criminal offence, or a person subject to an arrest or committal warrant. Before executing an arrest warrant issued under any Act, check its territorial validity, who can execute it, and the prisoner return radius.

✓ Only reasonable and legally authorized force is permissible in the execution of an investigator's duties. Sections 25, 26 and 27 of the *Code* cover the protections and liabilities arising from investigator use of force. Abusive detention or arrest that amounts to an improper purpose like racial profiling may undermine the validity of a detention or arrest.

✓ Avoid unintentional detention of pedestrians by approaching them rather than calling them over to you, not blocking their path, not using a threatening or commanding tone of voice with them, making clear that they do not have to answer any questions, and are free to go at any time. Powers of detention and arrest in a business depend on the circumstances of investigator interaction with those present in the business, and the degree of privacy in the area of the business. A random vehicle stop violates the constitutional rights of those stopped absent a truly compelling justification for the stop. Arrest in a dwelling place requires a special s. 529 or s. 529.1 *Criminal Code* warrant, unless there is hot pursuit, public safety is at risk, or other exigent circumstances exist.

✓ The *Criminal Code* sets out a ladder of incremental post-arrest release steps dependent on the likelihood of the accused attending court appearances or committing additional offences if released, and whether detention is necessary to maintain public confidence in the administration of justice. Without compelling reasons to seek detention, you are better off trying to secure strong conditions for bail. A bail brief can provide detailed justification and evidence for detention or conditions of release.

FURTHER READING

Cases

R. v. Asante-Mensah, [2003] 2 S.C.R. 3. Arrest when made by a citizen with statutory authority to conduct the arrest is "a continuing status initiated by words accompanied by physical touching or submission and ending with delivery to the police, maintained as necessary with a force that is no more than reasonable in all the circumstances" (at para. 80).

R. v. Dedman, [1985] 2 S.C.R. 2. A peace officer must have lawful authority in order for an arrest to be valid.

R. v. Feeney, [1997] 2 S.C.R. 13. An arrest warrant is generally required to make an arrest in a dwelling place due to the privacy interest present in such a place, but hot pursuit is an exception to this principle.

R. v. Mann, [2004] 3 S.C.R. 59. Investigative detention may take place where "reasonable grounds" exist.

R. v. Moran (1987), 21 O.A.C. 257. Sets out the factors to consider in assessing whether a detention exists.

Books, Articles and Reports

G. Arcaro, *Basic Police Powers*, 3rd ed. (Toronto: Nelson, 2003).

N. Bala, *Youth Criminal Justice Law* (Toronto: Irwin Law, 2003). Provides a detailed explanation of the different rules that apply when detaining and arresting young persons.

P. Ceyssens, *Legal Aspects of Policing*, loose-leaf (Saltspring Island, BC: Earlscourt Legal Press, 1994). Comprehensive coverage of the civil and administrative law of policing, including the potential civil liability and disciplinary consequences of exceeding criminal and regulatory powers as an investigator.

E.G. Ewaschuk, *Criminal Pleadings and Practice in Canada*, 2nd ed., loose-leaf (Aurora, ON: Canada Law Book, 1997). See particularly Chapter 5 ("Arrest") and Chapter 6 ("Release from Custody").

Law Reform Commission of Canada, *Working Paper No. 41 — Arrest* (Ottawa: Law Reform Commission of Canada, 1985).

Law Reform Commission of Canada, *Working Paper No. 55 — Compelling Appearance, Interim Release and Pre-Trial Detention* (Ottawa: Law Reform Commission of Canada, 1988).

R. Salhany, *The Police Manual of Arrest, Seizure and Interrogation,* 8th ed (Toronto: Carswell, 2002).

J. Stribopoulos, "Unchecked Power: The Constitutional Regulation of Arrest Reconsidered" (2003) 48 McGill L.J. 225.

G. Trotter, *The Law of Bail in Canada,* 2nd ed. (Toronto: Carswell, 1999). A comprehensive work on release from custody.

CHAPTER TWELVE

TAKING AND USING GREAT STATEMENTS

It has long been established as a positive rule of English criminal law that no statement by an accused is admissible in evidence against him unless it is shewn by the prosecution to have been a voluntary statement, in the sense that it has not been obtained from him either by fear of prejudice or hope of advantage exercised or held out by a person in authority.

Ibrahim v. The King, [1914] A.C. 599 at 609.

In This Chapter

- Meeting the criteria for statement voluntariness
- Content and timing of rights and cautions
- Duties accompanying rights and cautions
- Why make a record of all statements
- The use in court that can be made of a statement
- The enduring value of creativity in questioning

Despite extensive research, we are still unable to discover another human being's inner-most thoughts without that person choosing to reveal them to us. Some might argue it is this one area of ultimate sanctity from state intrusion that protects us from a society of Thought Police. Investigators are entitled to persuade people to reveal thoughts relevant to an investigation, but there are strict rules to protect a statement's voluntariness and a person's guarantee of rights on what is and is not acceptable persuasion. The law seeks to obtain the truth from people's thoughts, rather than what the state wants to hear.

The genuineness of physical evidence can often be determined through scientific means — not so with inner thoughts. A lie frequently sounds just like the truth when it is spoken. It is only by examining the circumstances surrounding the saying of a thought that we can hope to determine its truthfulness. What was known as the hearsay rule had previously tried to control the floodgates that kept most out of court statements from being entered as trial evidence for the truth of their contents because of fundamental reliability fears. Whatever might be left of that rule has been transformed by a "principled approach" generally requiring a statement to be relevant, reliable and necessary in order to be admissible, subject to certain other limitations of fundamental fairness.

The Detention, Arrest and Statement Rights to Counsel and Caution Checklist, at the end of this chapter, together with accurate and preferably electronic recording, will assist you with taking admissible statements of the highest possible value. Notwithstanding the rules investigators must follow to ensure statement admissibility, there remains a great deal of room for creativity in questioning.

MEETING THE CRITERIA FOR STATEMENT VOLUNTARINESS

According to the common law, the prosecution always bears the burden of proving voluntariness beyond a reasonable doubt when tendering a statement made by an accused to a person in authority. *R. v. Oickle*, [2000] 2 S.C.R. 3 at para. 48, advocated that courts conduct a wide-ranging review of factors relevant to voluntariness to take account of the diverse factual situations surrounding the making of statements:

> The common law confessions rule is well-suited to protect against false confessions. While its overriding concern is with voluntariness, this concept overlaps with reliability. A confession that is not voluntary will often (though not always) be unreliable. The application of the rule will by necessity be contextual. Hard and fast rules simply cannot account for the variety of circumstances that vitiate the voluntariness of a confession, and would inevitably result in a rule that would be both over-and under-inclusive. A trial judge should therefore consider all the relevant factors when reviewing a confession.

Ah, another helpful test you say, telling me that there are no hard and fast rules. Investigators can at least focus on a few factors courts have found to be especially relevant to circumstantial voluntariness, and generally consider what would be the fair and humane course of questioning. While these voluntariness factors are focussed on accused who make confessions, I suggest you give them some consideration in all instances of interviewing witnesses since it is impossible to be sure a mere witness will not later turn into an accused. An incriminating statement can be very powerful evidence at trial.

1. Avoiding Threats, Promises, Bad Treatment, or Intimidation

Proof of statement voluntariness is usually adduced in court by asking a series of questions of all investigators who had significant contact with the person who made the statement, covering the time from first contact up to and including the time of the statement. From these questions a prosecutor seeks to show whether investigators made any threats or promises in exchange for a statement, whether any weapons were drawn or worn by investigators, how investigators treated the person making the statement, and whether any investigator actions might constitute intimidation or inducement sufficient to render the statement involuntary.

R. v. Oickle, [2000] 2 S.C.R. 3 at paras. 49 & 57, explained the reason threats or promises are a problem:

> Intuitively implausible as it may seem, both judicial precedent and academic authority confirm that the pressure of intense and prolonged questioning may convince a suspect that no one will believe his or her protestations of innocence, and that a conviction is inevitable. In these circumstances, holding out the possibility of a reduced charge or sentence in exchange for a confession would raise a reasonable doubt as to the voluntariness of any ensuing confession. An explicit offer by the police to procure lenient treatment in return for a confession is clearly a very strong inducement, and will warrant exclusion in all but exceptional circumstances.
>
> . . .
>
> The most important consideration in all cases is to look for a *quid pro quo* offer by interrogators, regardless of whether it comes in the form of a threat or a promise.

Vague assurances that investigators will look at any statement after it has been given, or after court testimony has been provided, to see if it is appropriate to offer some kind of consideration for it will usually not create problems for voluntariness, because there is no direct link between the statement and a positive or negative outcome for the person making the statement. Moral encouragement that telling the truth might clear an accused's conscience has been found to be permissible because no tangible benefit is being offered. Investigators must proceed with extreme caution where consideration is offered in a more explicit way, like through an assistance or immunity agreement. The best question to ask yourself is: "just how much of an incentive to lie are we giving this person?" If the answer you come up with is "possibly quite a bit" then you have reason to worry, and should consider whether there are any alternative ways to secure a statement.

Common Courtesies as Inducements

Q & A

Q: If anything I say or do could later be found by a court to be an inducement that renders a statement involuntary, does this mean I can't even offer an accused a cup of coffee during an interview?

A: Common courtesies like coffee won't usually be found to be inducements, but what amounts to an inducement really depends on the context. If an accused asks for a coffee, and you tell him you will get it for him, but only after he confesses, then that coffee could be an inducement. The key is to be scrupulous about not making any offers of courtesies contingent upon the giving of a statement.

2. Ensuring the Mental and Physical Fitness of the Person Giving the Statement

An investigator must be confident a person being interviewed is both mentally and physically able to give a voluntary statement, which involves having an operating mind capable of choosing whether or not to give a statement, as explained in *R. v. Whittle*, [1994] 2 S.C.R. 914 at 941:

> The operating mind test, which is an aspect of the confessions rule, includes a limited mental component which requires that the accused have sufficient cognitive capacity to understand what he or she is saying and what is said. This includes the ability to understand a caution that the evidence can be used against the accused.

> The same standard applies with respect to the right to silence in
> determining whether the accused has the mental capacity to make
> an active choice.

A very high degree of intoxication from drugs or alcohol, or a very poor
physical state, could render a statement inadmissible because it was not
taken from a truly operating mind.

Medical attention must be sought for any reasonable signs of mental or
physical unwellness. If there is any doubt about mental or physical fitness
to give a statement, questions need to be asked about how the person is
mentally or physically feeling. Doubts about impairment from alcohol or
drugs should be followed up with questions about whether the person has
recently taken alcohol or drugs — so long as such questions do not give
rise to self-incrimination difficulties. If there are still doubts about fitness, a
medical practitioner can be brought in to do an examination, or a breathalyzer might be administered by a qualified investigator. The purpose of mental and physical examination is *not* to gather evidence against a suspect, but
rather to ensure any statement is the voluntary product of a properly functioning mind.

A voluntary statement could still be taken from someone with minor
alcohol or drug impairment. A voluntary statement could likewise be taken
from a person who has physical injuries, so long as adequate medical treatment has been provided for those injuries. The key to all aspects of voluntariness is the ability to choose. Your notes should ideally reflect your
assessment of the mental and physical state of the person giving the statement so a court can later be confident the person's mind was sufficiently
operating to make a choice about whether to say anything, and to understand what was being said.

3. Avoiding an Atmosphere of Oppression

A person giving a statement must be made as comfortable as is possible
in the circumstances. Undue discomfort could lead to an atmosphere of
oppression, which a court might find compelled an involuntary statement.
R. v. Oickle, [2000] 2 S.C.R. 3 at para. 58, explained the problem an atmosphere of oppression creates for voluntariness:

> If the police create conditions distasteful enough, it should be no
> surprise that the suspect would make a stress-compliant confession
> to escape those conditions. Alternately, oppressive circumstances
> could overbear the suspect's will to the point that he or she comes

to doubt his or her own memory, believes the relentless accusations made by the police, and gives an induced confession.

The four basic things all statement makers might require to avoid an atmosphere of oppression are clothing, food, water and shelter. Providing clothing to wear is necessary if original clothing was seized as evidence, destroyed in a fight, or never present in the first place. Providing food and water is necessary if the detention lasts for more than a short period of time. Being seated in an interview room should qualify as adequate shelter; being questioned outside in the cold rain could be interpreted as oppressive duress.

4. Avoiding Conduct That Shocks the Community

Even though all the foregoing conditions for a voluntary statement may exist, *R. v. Oickle*, [2000] 2 S.C.R. 3 at para. 67 concluded: "There may be situations in which police trickery, though neither violating the right to silence nor undermining voluntariness *per se*, is so appalling as to shock the community." Conduct that shocks the community will render a statement inadmissible because of the way it undermines the integrity of the criminal justice system. Examples the court cited in *Oickle* were an investigator posing as a lawyer or priest in order to gain the trust needed to secure a confession, or injecting truth serum into a diabetic telling him it was insulin. In certain respects, the "shock the community" test can be understood as another admonishment to investigators to avoid oppression when seeking a confession.

The courts have emphasized that use of tricks and deceit are only acceptable where they neither render a statement involuntary nor shock the community. Saying some tricks are fine, and others are not, makes the jobs of investigators very difficult in figuring out where it is acceptable to push for a confession, and where investigators must sit back to hope a confession spontaneously emerges from a suspect. Among acceptable tricks likely not to undermine voluntariness or shock the community is the practice of investigators posing as criminal figures to gain the trust of a suspect and thereby extract a confession, so long as those criminal figures do not unreasonably induce commission of an offence or giving a statement. Another acceptable trick that requires considerable caution is the practice of investigators lying about known facts in a case or about what other witnesses said in order to get a reaction from someone they wish to give a statement.

5. Complying with the Four Special Requirements for Statements from Young Persons

A young person is potentially more vulnerable and susceptible to suggestion than the average adult, so different language or people may have to be employed to ensure voluntariness than when taking a statement from an adult. In addition to giving a normal caution, investigators have four duties under s. 25 of the *Youth Criminal Justice Act*, S.C. 2002, c. 1:

- to determine if someone is a young person through questioning or other means;

- to notify a parent, an adult relative or another appropriate adult if a young person is under arrest or detained;

- to inform the young person of the right to consult a parent or other appropriate adult, and to have counsel, the parent or other adult present during questioning; and

- to ensure any waiver of the right to counsel by a young person is video or audio recorded or in writing.

Although compliance may delay questioning somewhat, failure to follow these requirements could render a statement from a young person inadmissible in court.

CONTENT AND TIMING OF RIGHTS AND CAUTIONS

1. The Role of the *Charter* in Statement Admissibility

The *Charter* has added a constitutional component to common law statement voluntariness requirements. This constitutional component is made up of a set of rights to detention information and counsel, as well as two cautions (all of which are often referred to collectively as either "rights to counsel" or "the caution"), to be delivered in most situations of detention or arrest. The rights to detention information and counsel derive from s. 10 of the *Charter*.

10. Everyone has the right on arrest or detention

(a) to be informed promptly of the reasons therefore;

(b) to retain and instruct counsel without delay and to be informed of that right . . . .

The cautions are predominantly connected to s. 7 of the *Charter.*

> **7.** Everyone has the right to life, liberty and security of the person, and the right not to be deprived thereof except in accordance with the principles of fundamental justice.

Because the burden of proving a *Charter* breach rests on the accused, if there is no arrest or detention, or the accused does not raise a *Charter* argument challenging statement admissibility, then only common law statement voluntariness will be an issue at trial.

Is the *Charter* the Most Onerous Requirement of Statement Taking?

Q & A

Q: It seems to be that the *Charter* has made the jobs of investigators overly complicated when it comes to taking statements. Is the Canadian public really any better off after the introduction of all of these artificial rules on rights and cautioning?

A: Complying with the long-standing common law requirement of voluntariness is a much more onerous obligation than delivering *Charter* rights. It is avoiding inducements and oppression, and verifying mental and physical fitness of the subject that are the real challenges in obtaining an admissible statement.

2. The Content of the Rights and Cautions

There is no magic formula for perfect delivery of rights and cautions. They must cover all elements the law requires and appropriate language be used so a suspect *understands* what is being said. While adequate delivery of rights and cautions can take different forms, a consistent version should be used by all members of an investigative agency. All questions from a suspect about rights, cautions and the statement process must be answered until investigators are satisfied that person understands the rights available. The basic investigator duties in delivering information on s. 10 *Charter* rights are that the suspect must be informed of the nature of investigation or charge, of the right to immediately consult a lawyer of choice or legal aid duty counsel using the toll-free direct line available 24 hours per day, 7 days a week (or whatever the hours of local availability are), and the availability of legal aid representation if qualifying factors are met. Particularly pay attention to conveying the concept that the right to counsel can be exercised "now," not later in the day, or on Monday morning.

The "primary caution" following on s. 10 rights delivery requires investigators to inform the person being cautioned that there is no obligation to say anything, and that anything said may later be used in evidence. The "secondary caution" must be provided each time a separate statement is taken from someone in order to guard against previous voluntariness difficulties affecting all future statements made by the same person. It can take a form similar to: "You must understand that anything said to you previously should not influence you or make you feel compelled to say anything at this time. If you felt influenced or compelled to say anything earlier, you are not now obliged to repeat it, nor are you obliged to say anything further, but whatever you say now can be used in evidence."

Many investigator field notebooks now incorporate the required warnings right on the inside front cover or first couple of pages. Some investigative agencies print the warnings on laminated cards that investigators can carry with them. It is best to read to suspects straight from these notebooks or cards in all cases, rather than summarizing, paraphrasing or trying to deliver their contents from memory so that you can testify you always read from the card, and because you made an indication like "11:39 p.m. RTC given" in your notebook you have complete confidence about exactly what you said.

Watch out for changes in the standard rights and cautions required by developments in the case law — changes should at most only happen once every few years. Failure to adopt them could render detentions, arrests or statements inadmissible. For example, *R. v. Bartle*, [1994] 3 S.C.R. 173 at 203, held the local toll free 1-800 number for legal aid must be read as part of the warning: "in today's highly technological and computerized world, 1-800 numbers are simple and effective means of conveying the sense of immediacy and universal availability of legal assistance which . . . must be conveyed as part of the standard s. 10(b) warning in jurisdictions where such a service exists." All standard warning cards had to be changed after the ruling, and investigative agencies scrambled to make sure every one of their members knew about the change.

To ensure the person being told of these rights and cautions understands them, it's good practice to pose direct follow-up questions.

- Do you understand?

- Do you want to call a lawyer right now?

Providing rights and cautions is more of a dialogue than a speech. You will not get very far by simply reading them off a card without looking at their recipient, listening to anything said in response, and recording that person's understanding. If you can show you did pay attention to this dialogue, courts will usually back you in the face of claims by the accused that he wasn't informed of his rights, didn't understand them, or wasn't given an opportunity to exercise them.

3. Knowing When to Provide Rights and Cautions

Generally speaking, without a detention or arrest fairly extensive questions can be asked without delivering rights and cautions, but with a detention only the briefest questions can be delivered prior to cautioning. A spontaneous utterance by a suspect upon first seeing investigators is admissible without rights and cautions because the statement was not given in response to any question posed by a person in authority. A statement of someone who at the time was not the target of an investigation, against whom no reasonable and probable grounds (RPG) of an offence existed, and who was not being detained can also be admissible without rights and cautions even if the statement was made in response to direct questioning by investigators. There is no need for investigators to overcaution everyone they speak with, but there is also no legal harm in erring on the side of cautioning when in doubt.

Rights and cautions may need to be given to a person (or given again if they have already been provided) at the point where the nature of an investigation changes, that person advised of the possibly greater criminal jeopardy now being faced from RPG of new offences having arisen, and an opportunity to stop speaking with investigators provided. While a person may voluntarily choose to speak with investigators for one purpose, when the purpose of investigators changes that person must be given the freedom to choose whether to continue providing information. Freedom of choice to voluntarily give a statement requires a general idea about the state of an investigation, and thus the risks being taken in talking to persons in authority.

Is There Such a Thing as Overcautioning?

Q & A

Q: Wouldn't it be safer for me just to assume that everyone I talk to while I am in uniform is detained, and that they should always be given their rights and cautions before I ask any questions?

A: While erring on the side of giving too many cautions rather than too few is a good policy, cautioning everyone may unnecessarily impede your gathering of information. If you are verifying regulatory compliance, cautioning without a detention could directly undermine your information demand powers. Carefully exercising discretion when cautioning is necessary.

DUTIES ACCOMPANYING RIGHTS AND CAUTIONS

Although the informational component of what needs to be said when providing rights and cautions is well settled, there is ongoing legal debate concerning the obligations investigators must fulfill to give effect to those rights and cautions.

1. The Duty to Cease Questioning

After rights and cautions have been provided, investigators can proceed with questioning unless the person detained or arrested expresses a desire to exercise those rights. A suspect saying something like: "Prove it. I ain't saying anything until I see my lawyer. I want to see my lawyer" amounts to expressing a desire to call a lawyer. At that point investigators need to provide access to a telephone and telephone directory, privacy to call a lawyer, and cease questioning until a reasonable opportunity has been given to contact a desired lawyer.

It is not acceptable to continue questioning after rights have been invoked, as happened during interrogation in *R. v. Manninen*, [1987] 1 S.C.R. 1233 at 1238:

> Q. What is your full name?
>
> A. Ronald Charles Manninen.
>
> Q. Where is your address?
>
> A. Ain't got one.
>
> Q. Where is the knife that you had along with this [showing the respondent the CO2 gun found in the car] when you ripped off the Mac's Milk on Wilson Avenue?
>
> A. He's lying. When I was in the store I only had the gun. The knife was in the tool box in the car.

There the court found at 1242-44 that a *Charter* breach had occurred:

> The respondent clearly asserted his right to remain silent and his desire to consult his lawyer. There was a telephone immediately at hand in the office, which the officers used for their own purposes. It was not necessary for the respondent to make an express request to use the telephone. The duty to facilitate contact with counsel

included the duty to offer the respondent the use of the telephone. Of course, there may be circumstances in which it is particularly urgent that the police continue with an investigation before it is possible to facilitate a detainee's communication with counsel. There was no urgency in the circumstances surrounding the offences in this case.

Further, s. 10(b) imposes on the police the duty to cease questioning or otherwise attempting to elicit evidence from the detainee until he has had a reasonable opportunity to retain and instruct counsel. The purpose of the right to counsel is to allow the detainee not only to be informed of his rights and obligations under the law but, equally if not more important, to obtain advice as to how to exercise those rights. In this case, the police officers correctly informed the respondent of his right to remain silent and the main function of counsel would be to confirm the existence of that right and then to advise him as to how to exercise it. For the right to counsel to be effective, the detainee must have access to this advice before he is questioned or otherwise required to provide evidence.

. . .

It seems that he did not intend to waive his right, as he clearly asserted it at the beginning and at the end of the questioning. Rather, the form of the questioning was such as to elicit involuntary answers. The police officer asked two innocuous questions followed by a baiting question which led the respondent to incriminate himself. In addition, where a detainee has positively asserted his desire to exercise his right to counsel and the police have ignored his request and have proceeded to question him, he is likely to feel that his right has no effect and that he must answer. Finally, the respondent had the right not to be asked questions, and he must not be held to have implicitly waived that right simply because he answered the questions. Otherwise, the right not to be asked questions would exist only where the detainee refused to answer and thus where there is no need for any remedy or exclusionary rule.

The court found that all evidence of the statement should have been excluded at trial.

The courts have taken a moderate position in recognizing it is not reasonable to expect investigators to remain mute after rights to counsel are provided, or the right to silence is invoked. Questioning can continue until rights are invoked and engaging a suspect in general conversation is permissible even after invocation of the right to silence. Courts seem willing to assume a suspect knows what he or she is doing when choosing to voluntarily speak with investigators. The voluntariness criteria ensure speaking is a free choice, and *Charter* requirements ensure it is an informed choice. Where investigators expect to take an important formal statement, ensuring a suspect has exercised the right to speak with counsel will best guarantee a trial court finds any decision to waive the right to silence to be a fully informed choice.

2. The Duty to Facilitate Communication with Counsel of Choice

The right to counsel includes the right to speak with counsel of choice. A reasonable opportunity must be given to contact counsel of choice and the technical means to accomplish that contact must be provided. What will amount to reasonable opportunity and means depend on the circumstances of each case.

If an arrest is made at night, where there is no urgency in taking a statement, then waiting until regular office hours in the morning to proceed with questioning so that the accused has an opportunity to contact counsel of choice is the reasonable course of action. This did not happen in *R. v. Leclair*, [1989] 1 S.C.R. 3, where the accused were afforded their opportunity to contact counsel at 2 a.m. and not surprisingly received no answer from their counsel of choice. Instead of waiting until morning to proceed with further investigation, police asked the accused to participate in a line-up at 3 a.m. which they did without advice of counsel; the court concluded at 11-12:

> Reasonable diligence in the exercise of the right to choose one's counsel depends upon the context facing the accused or detained person. On being arrested, for example, the detained person is faced with an immediate need for legal advice and must exercise reasonable diligence accordingly. By contrast, when seeking the best lawyer to conduct a trial, the accused person faces no such immediacy. Nevertheless, accused or detained persons have a right to choose their counsel and it is only if the lawyer chosen cannot be available within a reasonable time that the detainee or the accused should be expected to exercise the right to counsel by calling another lawyer.
>
> . . .
>
> Having seen that the appellants got no answer to their telephone calls, the police officers placed them in police cells, and a few min-

utes later the appellants were told to participate in a line-up, which they did.

> The police were mistaken to follow such a procedure. As this court held in *Manninen*, supra, the police have at least a duty to cease questioning or otherwise attempting to elicit evidence from the detainee until he has had a reasonable opportunity to retain and instruct counsel. In my view, the right to counsel also means that, once an accused or detained person has asserted that right, the police cannot in any way compel the detainee or accused person to make a decision or participate in a process which could ultimately have an adverse effect in the conduct of an eventual trial until that person has had a reasonable opportunity to exercise that right. In the case at bar, it cannot be said that the appellants had a real opportunity to retain and instruct counsel before the line-up was held. Nor can it be said that there was any urgency or other compelling reason which justified proceeding with the line-up so precipitously.

Where, however, there is urgency to secure evidence like in the impaired driving context a reasonable opportunity to contact counsel of choice will not mean waiting until the morning. An accused must also be reasonably diligent in tracking down counsel of choice.

With respect to the means for consulting counsel, investigators should do whatever they can to provide access to a telephone at the earliest reasonable opportunity. This could be a telephone at a search location in which the accused is found, a cell phone carried by an investigator, or a phone back at a detachment with holding facilities — it all depends on the facts of the case as to how soon access must be provided. The advance of mobile communications technology, which has led to reliable telephone connections becoming available in more remote areas, may lead the courts to increasingly find access to a telephone should be provided sooner rather than later. An exception to the "now" element of exercising rights to counsel has been created for administering approved screening device tests and other roadside investigative measures such as physical sobriety tests, but not for the breath samples taken at the detachment according to *R. v. Thomson*, [1988] 1 S.C.R. 640 at 655:

> The important role played by roadside breath testing is not only to increase the detection of impaired driving, but to increase the perceived risk of its detection, which is essential to its effective deterrence. In my opinion the importance of this role makes the necessary limitation on the right to retain and instruct counsel at the roadside testing stage a reasonable one that is demonstrably justified in a free and democratic society, having regard to the fact that

the right to counsel will be available, if necessary, at the more serious breathalyzer stage.

Where a telephone is provided, but it cannot make long distance telephone calls — even at the detainee's own expense on his calling card — then a violation of the right to counsel of choice may have occurred as in *R. v. Hansen*, 2005 ABPC 111 at para. 53:

> While the accused was able to consult with two other lawyers before he provided the breath samples, he remained unable to consult with his first lawyer of choice. He was forced to choose from local legal resources in whom he obviously did not find initial trust, since he decided to get a second opinion. It is up to the Crown to establish that the accused would not have acted differently if his access to counsel of his choice had been properly facilitated. That onus has not been met. While the accused consulted with two other lawyers and ultimately provided samples of his breath for analysis, it would be speculation to find he would not have acted differently had he spoken to counsel of his choice. I find the admission of the Certificate of Analysis, in these circumstances, would adversely affect the fairness of the trial.

Since particularly in motor vehicle cases a suspect may be outside the local calling area of his lawyer of choice, the police must provide access to a telephone with long distance capability, and assist the person with making the call. It is debatable whether investigators need to provide free access to a long distance line, although I would suggest that with plummeting long distance rates the courts might hold there to be such a duty.

Although demystification of the law can generally explain how to give rights and cautions, and how to ensure statements are voluntary, early investigator-prosecutor contact is necessary for advice on precisely when, where and how you do this depending on what duties you are undertaking. Regulatory investigators might rarely need to provide rights and cautions, patrol officers engaged in impaired driver screening will have a delayed obligation, and prudent homicide squad investigators could wind up providing rights and cautions to everyone they interrogate believed to be a suspect.

3. Giving Cautions and Taking Statements in an Understood Language

Without a common language, statements and the cautions that render them admissible lose all value. Rights and cautions that have not been understood due to language difficulties have not been delivered. Likewise, a waiver of rights cannot be valid if the person doing the waiving does not understand and cannot convey what is being waived. Section 10 *Charter* obligations have been found to have a language component, as in *R. v. Vanstaceghem* (1987), 21 O.A.C. 210 (Ont. C.A.) at para. 20, quoting with approval from *R. v. Michaud* (1986), 45 M.V.R. 243 (Ont. Dist. Ct.) at 248-49:

> The police may not be required to go to extreme means in order to respect an accused's rights under s. 10 of the Charter. It is necessary, however, in order to comply with the section that an accused be meaningfully informed of the rights. The accused must understand what is being said to him or her and understand what the options are in order that he or she may make a choice in the exercise of the rights guaranteed by the Charter.
>
> It is not sufficient for a police officer upon the arrest or detention of a person to merely recite the rights guaranteed by s. 10 of the Charter. As s. 10(*b*) stipulates, the accused or detainee must be informed. This means that the accused or detainee must understand what is being said to him or her by the police officer. Otherwise, he or she is not able to make an informed choice with respect to the exercise or waiver of the guaranteed rights.
>
> If the rights are read in English only, and the accused's or detainee's knowledge of the English language does not allow sufficient comprehension of the matter, those are "special circumstances" which alert the officer and oblige him to act reasonably in the circumstances.

An accused who seems to understand what is said may later be found by a court to not really have understood, so investigators must address even a hint of language or comprehension problems.

a. *Situations Giving Rise to Language Problems*

R. v. Oliynyk, 2003 CarswellOnt 6335 (C.J.) at paras. 29-30, enumerated examples of language difficulties encountered in the course of giving rights and cautions sufficient to require action on the part of investigators:

> Marin J. provided a helpful summary of some of the instances in which "special circumstances" have been found to exist in *R. v. Shmoel*, [1998] O.J. NO. 2233 (Ont. Prov. Div.);
>
> • where it is clear to the officer that an accused person's first language is not English and there is difficulty comprehending the demand for samples of breath: see *Vanstaceghem, supra;*

- the accused's failure to respond to questions dealing with the right to counsel coupled with statements to the effect that "I don't speak the best English": see *R. v. Lukavecki,* [1992] O.J. No. 2123 (Ont. Gen. Div.);

- the necessity of speaking slowly to an accused who speaks English "a little bit": *R. v. Ly,* [1993] O.J. No. 268 (Ont. Prov. Div.);

- the accused's negative response when asked if the right to counsel is understood and thereafter, the failure to provide verbal or written instruction about that right in the first language of the accused: *R. v. Lim,* (unreported judgment of His Honour Justice Bigelow, October 14, 1993 [1993 CarswellOnt 714 (Ont. Prov. Div.)]);

- the failure to honour the accused's request for an interpreter or an officer or a lawyer who speaks his or her first language: *R. v. Ferreira,* (unreported judgment of His Honour Justice Wren, December 6, 1993 [(Ont. Gen. Div.)]).

In *Shmoel,* Justice Marin found that the accused had a "day to day" comprehension of the English language but she was not satisfied that his comprehension of English extended to legal technicalities. Although he eventually understood that he could speak to a lawyer, he did so in English and was confused about whether he had spoken to a lawyer. The court found that there were "special circumstances", and that the police had not taken the necessary steps so that he understood his right to counsel.

There are a great variety of factual scenarios involving language where investigators might need to take action to verify a suspect's understanding or else find an interpreter.

b. *Dealing with People Who Hide Behind a Language Barrier*

I have heard investigators complain with some justification of accused who seem to perfectly understand English or French at the time of an arrest, but develop a feeble grasp of the language by the time the trial rolls around. While this might appear to be a credibility issue for the trial court to sort out, judges have generally not been willing to second guess just how much an accused understood at the time of her initial encounter with investigators. Courts for the most part will give an accused the benefit of the doubt if she is able to demonstrate at trial that her first language was not the language spoken to her by investigators, that her first language skills are far superior to the language she attempted to communicate in at the time rights and cautions were delivered, and she credibly claims she did not understand the rights and cautions given. Take the example *R. v. Oliynyk*, 2003 CarswellOnt 6335 (C.J.) at paras. 35-36:

> After reviewing all the evidence in this case, I think it is fair to say that Mr. Oliynyk hid behind the language barrier from time to time during the course of his trial. I did not find him to be a credible witness. I am aware that to some extent, he may have also hidden behind the language barrier on the night of his arrest. However, having considered the evidence of the civilian witnesses, the police officers and having watched the video myself, I find that I do not share Cst. D. . .'s confidence that Mr. Oliynyk's language barrier was a sham. To the contrary, I find there was a real and legitimate concern about his ability to comprehend what was going on. At the very least, I find that it was incumbent upon the police to make further inquiries about the accused's ability to understand the demand and his rights to counsel.
>
> Mr. Rother has satisfied me on the balance of probabilities that Mr. Oliynyk's right to counsel was violated in this case.

So even an accused who may have hidden behind his language barrier can be found to have had his *Charter* rights violated if the trial court is not confident he understood what was going on, because investigators made insufficient inquiries to ascertain whether in fact he understood and did not provide an interpreter.

c. *Providing Quality Interpretation*

While the interpretation provided at the detention, arrest and statement taking stages of a case might be a little more basic than that offered in a trial, minimum standards must still be met. *R. v. Tran*, [1994] 2 S.C.R. 951 at 998, addressed quality of interpretation in the context of the s. 14 *Charter* right to an interpreter at trial:

> The scope of the right to interpreter assistance guaranteed by s. 14 of the *Charter* may be stated in the following broad terms. The constitutionally guaranteed standard of interpretation is not one of perfection; however, it is one of continuity, precision, impartiality, competency and contemporaneousness. An accused who does not understand and/or speak the language of the proceedings, be it English or French, has the right at every point in the proceedings

in which the case is being advanced to receive interpretation which meets this basic standard. To establish a violation of s. 14, the claimant of the right must prove on a balance of probabilities not only that he or she was in need of assistance, but also that the interpretation received fell below the basic, guaranteed standard and did so in the course of the case being advanced.

Sections 7, 10, and 11 of the *Charter* implicitly impose competent interpretation obligations during investigations by requiring that people be informed of their rights in a language they understand, be it Spanish, Punjabi or American Sign Language.

Sometimes an investigator who is a speaker of another language might fulfill the interpreter role, sometimes it will be a fluent speaking civilian who is not a professional interpreter, and at other times only a professional interpreter will do. Both interviewer and accused need to be relatively fluent in the language used for rights, cautions, questions and answers, or be assisted by an interpreter with that fluency. I am not suggesting you need native-like fluency to give a caution, but I have seen many misunderstandings arise from language difficulties, like a Portuguese speaking officer being the sole means of communication with a Spanish speaking accused, which are sufficient to later put statement voluntariness and *Charter* requirements in doubt at trial.

d. *Overcoming Statement Language Difficulties in Ways That Make for Good Evidence*

Delay all statement taking until an appropriately qualified interpreter is available. Even with an interpreter, record the statement in the original language in which it is given. For example, don't have a witness give a statement in French, which an interpreter simultaneously translates into English, and which the interviewer then records only in English, since the words written down in English will be the words of the interpreter, not the words of the witness.

There are primarily three ways to create an adequate record of an interpreted interview:

- audio or video record the whole oral interview in both languages;

- have the witness write out and sign a statement in the original language;

- have the interpreter write out the statement in the original language, which is then read back to and signed by the witness who agrees it is accurate.

These techniques permit a more precise translation of the statement to be prepared later for use at trial, and guard against disputes over translation nuances. The interpreter can still provide a rough translation to investigators at the time the statement is made, which facilitates asking follow-up questions. It will ultimately be up to the trial court to determine with the aid of prosecution or defence translators what the original statement meant.

Language Challenges in Taking Statements

Q & A

Q: We don't have some kind of universal computer translator like they did in Star Trek. How can investigators be expected on short notice to find someone to speak the language of a suspect or witness before reading a caution or taking a statement?

A: If you believe a person does not have sufficient facility in English or French to understand a caution and follow questions you might ask, you are going to need a translator. Go ahead and give the caution in English, or French, or whatever language you can manage that the person might best understand, but hold off on your questioning until you have secured some translation help, and offer the caution again at that point. Competent interpretation can be done over the telephone.

WHY MAKE A RECORD OF ALL STATEMENTS

It is very important that all questions and answers be completely recorded by written, audio or video means, even if a formal signed written statement is not provided. Recording statements is arguably the most important aspect of note-taking, and in my experience the area where investigators encounter some of the greatest difficulties. These difficulties derive from failure to realize a short remark might later be important, failure to realize the caution, response to the caution, questions asked as well as answers given are all important, and failure to realize each and every word uttered by an accused in a longer statement can be equally important.

1. Electronic Solutions to the Challenge of Accurately Recording a Statement

Fully recording questions and answers can be a very difficult process when speaking and writing are simultaneously required by one investigator. Missing out a word or two asked or answered in your notes will not necessarily invalidate a statement, but in order to later tender that statement as trial evidence for the truth of its contents you must be able to demonstrate to a court that what you wrote down accurately reflects what was said. There is a big difference between the muffled and sobbing voice of a suspect mumbling into his hands "I killed her" and "I didn't kill her." Your uncorroborated recollection of what was said, without some form of recording to back you up, may be insufficient to prove a statement in court.

Video recording flash freezes a statement in a better state of freshness than any other preservation technique currently available. Audio recording freezes a bit less of the statement, and note-taking freezes even less than audio recording. With any form of statement recording, the aim is to be able to repeatedly thaw out the statement at later times as if the statement was being freshly made all over again. The staler the statement appears to be when thawed out, the less likely the judge or jury will believe it was voluntarily made, or that it reflects what really was said.

Miniature audio or video recording equipment is a good technological solution to the problem of recording accurate statements in the field. Recording basic statement details in your notebook, like the time a statement commenced, the time it stopped and how it was recorded is still good practice so that the electronic record can later be verified as accurate. To avoid common video statement problems:

- check the audio and video recording quality of all devices;

- check the video view to ensure it has an unobstructed view of the witness' face;

- keep the recording going, even if you or the witness need a short break, to forestall later questions about what happened during a pause in recording; and

- don't edit recordings — aim for a recording that creates the experience of being present in the interview room with the witness, complete with interruptions.

I once watched a murder confession stretching over several hours that had been recorded by a camera mounted on the ceiling of a small brightly lit interrogation room where the only microphone was attached to the camera. The suspect sat slumped over on a chair with his head in his hands for most of the statement, so all that could be viewed of his features was the top of his head, and all that could be heard from him a lot of the time were snatches of words and broken phrases. A check of the equipment during the recording would have revealed investigators either needed to convince the suspect to look up and speak more clearly, get better equipment, or start taking comprehensive notes.

2. The Burden on Investigators to Explain Why a Statement Was Not Recorded

We have not yet reached the point in Canada where courts demand all statements taken from accused be audio or video recorded as there will always be situations of casual remarks or malfunctioning equipment that do not lend themselves to recording, but courts have started to express significant reluctance over admitting statements where it was possible to electronically record a statement and investigators chose not to do so. In *R. v. Moore-McFarlane* (2001), 152 O.A.C. 120, the court found at para. 65 amid allegations of physical abuse and oppression to obtain a statement:

> where the suspect is in custody, recording facilities are readily available, and the police deliberately set out to interrogate the suspect without giving any thought to the making of a reliable record, the context inevitably makes the resulting non-recorded interrogation *suspect*. In such cases, it will be a matter for the trial judge on the *voir dire* to determine whether or not a sufficient substitute for an audio or video tape record has been provided to satisfy the heavy onus on the Crown to prove voluntariness beyond a reasonable doubt.

Other courts have made similar findings like *R. v. Lafrance*, 2004 ONCJ 302 at para. 87:

> In this case, there was no reason advanced to explain the decision not to record by way of electronic means save a question of personal preference, there was no urgency demonstrated much less suggested, and the Court was left with a highly contentious factual debate about what occurred initially surrounding the provision of rights to counsel, leaving aside what was said after the advice in this respect. In the result, I cannot determine which version is accurate and, more to the point, I cannot conclude that the state of the record permits me to find that the prosecution has shown beyond a reasonable doubt that the statement is voluntary in the sense of being free of inducements, and the product of a freely arrived at choice (and a fully informed one) to waive the right to silence.

The report on the *Inquiry Regarding Thomas Sophonow* (Winnipeg: Manitoba Justice, 2001) in its summary of recommendations on police interviews went even further:

I would recommend that videotaping of interviews with suspects be made a rule and an adequate explanation given before the audio taping of an interview is accepted as admissible. This is to say, all interviews must be videotaped or, at the very least, audio taped.

Further, interviews that are not taped should, as a general rule, be inadmissible. There is too great a danger in admitting oral statements. They are not verbatim and are subject to misinterpretation and errors, particularly of omission. Their dangers are too many and too serious to permit admission. Tape recorders are sufficiently inexpensive and accessible that they can be provided to all investigating officers and used to record the statements of any suspect.

Even where the accused insists he will only speak to investigators if the statement is not audio or video recorded, at the very least investigators need to get that refusal on an audio or video recording (preferably together with delivery of rights and cautions), or else the refusal might not be believed by the trial court.

THE USE IN COURT THAT CAN BE MADE OF A STATEMENT

Just because someone tells you something does not necessarily mean you can then give testimony in court about what you were told — it may be completely irrelevant to a case before the court, completely unreliable, its prejudicial effect may outweigh its probative value, it may simply not be necessary to repeat it, or there could be some other reason like immunity for a statement to be inadmissible. There is nothing stopping investigators from collecting all information by way of statements they think might be helpful to an investigation, but statement triage is necessary to sort through the useful and not so useful with an eye on admissibility.

1. The Limits Imposed by the Hearsay Rule

Hearsay is literally what it sounds like: hearing something from a source, and then saying what you heard to another source, without having firsthand knowledge of the thing said — like hearing from Bill that he saw Bob rob the local convenience store last Tuesday, and then repeating to the court what you heard from Bill. Documentary, audio and video hearsay are also possible. The hearsay rule used to exclude all sorts of out of court statements from being admitted into evidence primarily because of reliability concerns over statements not under oath, lacking contemporaneous cross-examination, and where a judge or jury is not able to observe the statement maker's demeanour. Like a lot of "rules" in law, the hearsay rule was subject to a myriad of exceptions like "admission against interest," which admitted confessions. *R. v. Star*, [2000] 2 S.C.R. 144, adopted a "principled approach" to hearsay that requires (1) relevance, (2) reliability, and (3) necessity for an out of court statement to be admissible at trial, instead of fitting a hearsay statement into a pigeon hole exception.

The relevance factor for hearsay admissibility requires some probative value so a statement makes a disputed fact in a case either more or less likely to be proven. Necessity can be established where evidence of the same value cannot otherwise be offered, like where a witness is unavailable or recants, or a document summarizes complex calculations that cannot be recalled from memory. The real challenge with hearsay admissibility is assuring a court of reliability.

Without an oath, contemporaneous cross-examination, or demeanour observation, the principled approach to the hearsay rule relies on other circumstantial indicators of reliability. You should ask yourself when taking a statement or examining a document: "why do I believe this person, and how can I later explain in court why the statement should be believed?" The old exceptions to the hearsay rule like admission against interest and dying declaration offered circumstantial reliability through a person's motives for giving a statement, but the most solid way to now establish reliability is by preserving the oath and demeanour factors through video recording the statement.

2. The Admissibility of Video Recorded Hearsay for the Truth of Its Contents

A driving force behind changes to the hearsay rule was the spread of video recording technology that enables courts to independently assess out of court statement credibility. You may have heard talk about "K.G.B. statements" that have nothing to do with a former communist intelligence service; the term originated in the case of *R. v. B.(K.G.)*, [1993] 1 S.C.R. 740, which established a prior inconsistent out of court statement could, under certain circumstances, be admitted into evidence for the truth of its contents. Cases since *K.B.G.* have broadened the trial use and admissibility of prior video recorded statements, but *K.G.B.* remains the authority on how to take such a statement. The terms "KGB statement" and "video recorded statement" are now often used interchangeably, even though technically *K.G.B.* statements only include prior inconsistent statements made by third parties.

Figure 12-1, Video Statement-Taking Room Set-Up, suggests one way to arrange a room used to video record a statement that maximizes the fairness to and visibility of all participants in the statement, and thus also maximizes the likelihood the statement can later be tendered into evidence at trial for the truth of its contents. The ideal two camera with videographer statement taking set-up of Figure 12-1 was explicitly approved of in *R. v. B.(K.G.)*, [1993] 1 S.C.R. 740 at 792-93. The set-up provides for an overall view of the room to verify the conditions under which the statement is being made, a zoomed-in view of the facial expressions and other body language of the giver of the statement, and a separate camera operator who can best ensure both the audio and video are clearly recorded throughout the statement. I concede that most day-to-day operations will likely only have one camera and no operator, which is still quite acceptable and vastly superior to a solely audio-recorded or handwritten statement, but will require a compromise somewhere in the middle of a zoomed-in and zoomed-out view that guarantees there is an unobstructed view of the statement giver's face.

The Video Statement Checklist (also applicable to audio statements), located at the end of this chapter, gives you the basic procedure and script to use, including how to administer an oath and warnings over the serious consequences flowing from failing to tell the truth. Whether an oath and warnings are actually administered will, however, depend on the context of a statement. They would be very appropriate for an accused or witness who has a motive to lie, whereas for a crime victim or vulnerable witness they might not be given — although you should at least consider administering an oath.

Video statements generally do not address the lack of contemporaneous cross-examination inherent in out of court statements. While not advisable in most cases, cross-examination during a video statement could further bolster reliability in rare cases where it is virtually guaranteed the video testimony will be the only testimony possible from that witness at trial — like where the witness is suffering from a terminal illness. Video statement cross-examination can be achieved if investigators, working through prosecutors, invite counsel representing a suspect or accused to attend a witness interview (with the permission of the witness) to ask cross-examination type questions on video after investigators have finished their questioning of the witness.

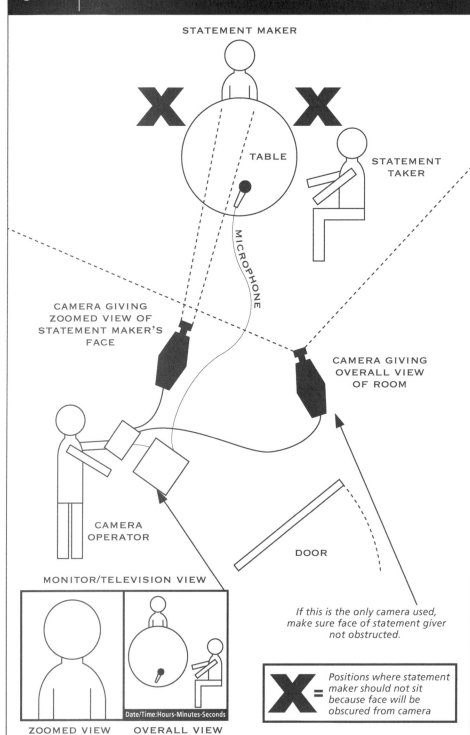

Fig 12-1 | VIDEO STATEMENT-TAKING ROOM SET-UP

STATEMENT MAKER

TABLE

STATEMENT TAKER

MICROPHONE

CAMERA GIVING ZOOMED VIEW OF STATEMENT MAKER'S FACE

CAMERA GIVING OVERALL VIEW OF ROOM

CAMERA OPERATOR

DOOR

MONITOR/TELEVISION VIEW

Date/Time:Hours-Minutes-Seconds

ZOOMED VIEW   OVERALL VIEW

If this is the only camera used, make sure face of statement giver not obstructed.

X = *Positions where statement maker should not sit because face will be obscured from camera*

3. The Limits Imposed by Statement Immunity

The use of some statements in court may be limited by constitutional, statutory or negotiated immunity. Part of the reason constitutional and statutory testimonial immunities exist in Canada is because of the general rule that a witness *can* be forced to incriminate herself in court if not a defendant in the case where testimony is compelled. Sub-section 5(1) of the *Canada Evidence Act*, R.S.C. 1985, c. C-13, states the general statutory immunity rule for witnesses:

> No witness shall be excused from answering any question on the ground that the answer to the question may tend to criminate him, or may tend to establish his liability to a civil proceeding at the instance of the Crown or of any person.

Sections 7, 10(c) and 13 of the *Charter* additionally provide constitutional self-incrimination protections for both accused and witnesses. Making early choices about whether a person is to be treated only as a witness, or as a potential prosecution target, greatly aids negotiated immunity decisions as discussed in Chapter 4 when combined with early investigator-prosecutor contact.

Working with Immunity

Q&A

Q: Where I have a witness who will be testifying under a grant of immunity, are there any special measures I have to take to make sure we live up to our side of the bargain, and the witness lives up to her side?

A: Carefully tracking the witness' testimony against prior statements she made will assist the prosecutor in knowing whether the witness is fulfilling the typical duty of testifying truthfully and consistently with prior statements. Any inconsistencies can then be sorted out right on the stand. Fulfilling your side of transactional immunity is as easy as not laying charges for the identified transactions. Living up to use immunity is still fairly simple — just don't directly use anything said in earlier statements directly against that person. Fulfilling derivative-use immunity obligations is more difficult unless all investigations into past possible illegal conduct of the witness have already been concluded, since there is always a chance some immunized evidence will influence the discovery of future evidence.

4. The Inadmissibility of Lie Detector Test Results

There is nothing illegal about administering a lie detector test as part of the statement taking process to someone who has voluntarily agreed to take a test, but don't expect test results to be admissible in court. Lie detector results are inadmissible *not* because they fail to meet the reliability requirement for the admission of any evidence (although their reliability is a source of active debate), but because as the court said in *R. v. Beland*, [1987] 2 S.C.R. 398 at 417-18, they usurp the truth-finding function of the trier of fact:

> however scientific it may be, its use in court depends on the human intervention of the operator. Whatever results are recorded by the polygraph instrument, their nature and significance reach the trier of fact through the mouth of the operator. Human fallibility is therefore present as before, but now it may be said to be fortified with the mystique of science. Then, it may be asked, what does it do? It provides evidence on the issue of the credibility of a witness. This has always been a collateral issue and one to be decided by the trier of fact. Is the trier of fact assisted by hearing, firstly from witness "A" that he was not present at the scene of the crime, and then from witness "B", a polygraph operator, that "A" was probably truthful? What would the result be, one may ask, if the polygraph operator concluded from his test that witness "A" was lying? Would such evidence be admissible, could it be excluded by witness "A", could it be introduced by the Crown? These are serious questions and they lead to others. Would it be open to the opponent of the person relying upon the polygraph to have a second polygraph examination taken for *his* purposes? If the results differed, which would prevail, and what right would there be for compelling the production of polygraph evidence in the possession of a reluctant party? It is this fear of turmoil in the courts which leads me to reject the polygraph. ... I would not wish to see a return to the method of pre-Norman trials where parties relied heavily upon oath-helpers who swore to their veracity. ... I would seek to preserve the principle that in the resolution of disputes in litigation, issues of credibility will be decided by human triers of fact, using their experience of human affairs and basing judgment upon their assessment of the witness and on consideration of how an individual's evidence fits into the general picture revealed on a consideration of the whole of the case.

If you do decide to resort to a lie detector test in the course of an investigation, you must be especially careful not to mention it in your testimony. Courts have even held that where investigators overstate lie detector results to a suspect and present that, as a complete certainty, investigators know the suspect is lying, an atmosphere of oppression can be created, which undermines the voluntariness of a confession.

5. The Difficulty with Line-Up Evidence

Still a staple of crime movies, the classic line-up of similar looking suspects filing one at a time into a one-way glass theatre with black on white height markings behind them has now been superceded by the photo line-up because of advances in technology as well as logistical and self-incrimination problems concerning informed consent with the traditional line-up. These photo line-ups still play a crucial role in proving identity that is an essential element any offence. A line-up must be conducted prior to the commencement of court proceedings (even if you do the line-up months after the offence was committed); in-court identification often carries very little weight by itself.

Arranging for a witness to view any sort of line-up is a very directed form of statement taking prone to investigators being told what they want to hear. Identification witness contamination through external information or unfair presentation of choices has long been recognized by the courts to be a major problem, as noted in *R. v. Mezzo*, [1986] 1 S.C.R. 802 at para. 40, citing *R. v. Smierciak* (1946), 87 C.C.C. 175 (Ont. C.A.) at 177:

> of the utmost importance, is the method used to recall or refresh the recollections of a witness who is to be relied upon to identify a person suspected of wrongdoing or who is under arrest. If a witness has no previous knowledge of the accused person so as to make him familiar with that person's appearance, the greatest care ought to be used to ensure the absolute independence and freedom of judgment of the witness. His recognition ought to proceed without suggestion, assistance or bias created directly or indirectly. Conversely, if the means employed to obtain evidence of identification involve any acts which might reasonably prejudice the accused, *the value of the evidence may be partially or wholly destroyed.* Anything which tends to convey to a witness that a person is suspected by the authorities, or is charged with an offence, is obviously prejudicial and wrongful. Submitting a prisoner alone for scrutiny after arrest is unfair and unjust.

Courts continue to struggle with the weight to accord line-up evidence because of factors that can influence a witness to pick out one person over all the others, or inflate the certainty of identification, including the following: too limited a group of people to choose from; one person not looking like any of the others; words or actions that give a witness a hint of which person to choose; a desire by the witness to pick someone; picking one person being interpreted as a certainty rather than just a possibility; or investigators reinforcing a witness' choice after the choice has been made.

The Inquiry Regarding Thomas Sophonow (Winnipeg: Manitoba Justice, 2001), under "Eyewitness Identification" made recommendations to address problematic line-up practices which could result in false identifications:

Live line-up

- The third officer who is present with the prospective eyewitness should have no knowledge of the case or whether the suspect is contained in the line-up.

- The officer in the room should advise the witness that he does not know if the suspect is in the line-up or, if he is, who he is. The officer should emphasize to the witness that the suspect may not be in the line-up.

- All proceedings in the witness room while the line-up is being watched should be recorded, preferably by videotape but, if not, by audiotape.

- All statements of the witness on reviewing the line-up must be both noted and recorded verbatim and signed by the witness.

- When the line-up is completed, the witness should be escorted from the police premises. This will eliminate any possibility of contamination of that witness by other officers, particularly those involved in the investigation of the crime itself.

- The fillers in the line-up should match as closely as possible the descriptions given by the eyewitnesses at the time of the event. It is only if that is impossible, that the fillers should resemble the suspect as closely as possible.

- At the conclusion of the line-up, if there has been any identification, there should be a question posed to the witness as to the degree of certainty of identification. The question and answer must be both noted and recorded verbatim and signed by the witness. It is important to have this report on record before there is any possibility of contamination or reinforcement of the witness.

- The line-up should contain a minimum of 10 persons. The greater the number of persons in the line-up, the less likelihood there is of a wrong identification.

Photo pack line-up

- The photo pack should contain at least 10 subjects.

- The photos should resemble as closely as possible the eyewitnesses' description. If that is not possible, the photos should be as close as possible to the suspect.

- Everything should be recorded on video or audiotape from the time that the officer meets the witness, before the photographs are shown through until the completion of the interview. Once again, it is essential that an officer who does not know who the suspect is and who is not involved in the investigation conducts the photo pack line-up.

- Before the showing of the photo pack, the officer conducting the line-up should confirm that he does not know who the suspect is or whether his photo is contained in the line-up. In addition, before showing the photo pack to a witness, the officer should advise the witness that it is just as important to clear the innocent as it is to identify the suspect. The photo pack should be presented by the officer to each witness separately.

- The photo pack must be presented sequentially and not as a package.

- In addition to the videotape, if possible, or, as a minimum alternative, the audiotape, there should be a form provided for setting out in writing and for signature the comments of both the officer conducting the line-up and the witness. All comments of each witness must be noted and recorded verbatim and signed by the witness.

- Police officers should not speak to eyewitnesses after the line-ups regarding their identification or their inability to identify anyone. This can only cast suspicion on any identification made and raise concerns that it was reinforced.

- It was suggested that, because of the importance of eyewitness evidence and the high risk of contaminating it, a police force other than the one conducting the investigation of the crime should conduct the interviews and the line-ups with the eye-witnesses. Ideal as that procedure might be, I think that it would unduly complicate the investigation, add to its cost and increase the time required. At some point, there must be a reasonable degree of trust placed in the police. The interviews of eyewitnesses and the line-up may be conducted by the same force as that investigating the crime, provided that the officers dealing with the eyewitnesses are not involved in the investigation of the crime and do not know the suspect or whether his photo forms part of the line-up. If this were done and the other recommendations complied with, that would provide adequate protection of the process.

Key features in these recommendations are fairness in presenting the choices, lack of pressure to make any choice, preventing contamination of the witness by post-event information influencing a particular choice, and recording line-up presentation.

THE ENDURING VALUE OF CREATIVITY IN QUESTIONING

Like a lot of other rules mentioned in this book, the rules surrounding questioning of accused and witnesses are rules of fairness that enhance the value of evidence. The rules do not ruin the basic questioning process that has remained unchanged for thousands of years: ask a question, receive an answer, evaluate that answer, then ask another question taking into account the answers already received. The Canadian legal system promotes fairness in questioning by providing an incentive to follow the rules — evidence admissibility — and a disincentive not to follow them — evidence exclusion.

Creativity is still very much a part of investigative questioning. Investigators can come up with creative ways to pose single questions, invent creative paths of questioning that will best draw out information from a witness or suspect, try multiple questioning paths to approach the same set of desired answers, or keep going down the same path over and over again to see if answers change as time drags on. Investigators can even be misleading in their questioning — to a point. But the confessions rule insists a statement must be voluntary, so threats, bad treatment, intimidation, an atmosphere of oppression, conduct that shocks the community or inducements cannot be used, and sufficient mental and physical fitness is also required. Additional requirements must be met for young persons. Plus rights and cautions obligations must have been fulfilled. Finally, each statement must be recorded in a way a court will accept as accurate.

Will all of these preconditions to a valid statement result in some statements not taking place? Sure they will. That's the whole point. Think of the preconditions like a screen, through which only the best of statements can pass. A majority of statements should still get through the screen if investigators are scrupulous in their statement taking practices. Among the justifications for those preconditions is that reliable investigations should *not* be based solely on statements — there needs to be other independent and objective evidence going beyond the frailties of the human mind. Nonetheless, where a statement does pass the admissibility test, it can be some of the most powerful evidence available to prove an offence.

For Taking and Using Great Statements

KEY POINTS

✓ Voluntariness of a statement taken from an accused sufficient for court admissibility is achieved through a lack of inducements, mental and physical fitness to give a statement, lack of an atmosphere of oppression, lack of conduct that shocks the community, and a few additional statutory requirements if the statement is taken from a young person. The exact point in a detention at which rights and cautions must be given will depend on the context, but rights and cautions must be understood by the person giving the statement. If those rights are invoked, questioning must cease and communication with counsel of choice facilitated.

✓ An accurate, permanent and preferably electronic record should be made of every statement. A video recorded statement taken under oath with the necessary rights and cautions best maximizes prospects of later admission into evidence for the truth of its contents regardless of whether the statement maker remains only a witness or becomes an accused.

✓ Constitutional, statutory or negotiated immunity may limit the use of some statements.

✓ Lie detector test results are not admissible in Canadian courts because they usurp the truth finding function of the trier of fact. Properly conducted photo line-ups with enough similar subjects where investigators do not influence a witness' choice are far superior to live line-ups in avoiding self-incrimination problems and controlling conditions of presentation. Use of an unreliable single person line-up may taint all future identification by a witness.

✓ Notwithstanding all the rules governing taking admissible statements, creativity is still very much a necessary part of successful investigative questioning.

A — REASON FOR RIGHTS AND CAUTIONS

❑ Suspect under investigation — predominant purpose of questioning is gathering evidence of offences, and RPG possibly exists

❑ Suspect under investigative detention — reasonable suspicion of offence exists

❑ Suspect under arrest — reasonable and probable grounds of offence exist

> ❑ Arrested by citizen and placed in peace officer custody
>
> ❑ Arrested by peace officer without warrant
>
> ❑ Arrested by peace officer with warrant

B — CONTENTS OF RIGHTS AND CAUTIONS

RIGHTS

❑ Informed of reason for detention or arrest, including any charge that will be laid

❑ Informed of the right to retain and instruct counsel without delay

❑ Informed that legal aid duty counsel is available, and provided with 1-800 number to contact duty counsel immediately

❑ Asked suspect: "Do you now wish to call a lawyer?"

> ❑ Ceased questioning until reasonable opportunity given to contact desired lawyer
> ❑ Asked: "Do you now wish to call a lawyer?"
> ❑ Provided telephone, privacy and other assistance to facilitate access to lawyer of choice

PRIMARY CAUTION

❑ Advised there is no obligation to say anything to investigators, and that anything said may later be used in evidence

SECONDARY CAUTION

❑ Advised that if a police officer or other person in authority has previously been spoken with in connection to the case, then nothing said previously should influence making a statement now

C — LANGUAGE

❑ Confirmed suspect understands language spoken by interviewer

> ❑ Used interpreter to interpret from _____ language
>
> ❑ Suspect cautioned in understood language
>
> ❑ Statement recorded in original language

D   PROTECTING VOLUNTARINESS

❏ Confirmed understanding of rights and cautions

❏ Avoided threats, promises, bad treatment or intimidation

❏ Ensured mental and physical fitness of statement giver

   ❏ Medical attention offered for any ailment requiring immediate attention

❏ Confident suspect not intoxicated or impaired by drugs

   ❏ Suspect asked whether drugs or alcohol recently taken
(if no self-incrimination problem)

   ❏ Breathalyser administered to suspect

   ❏ Suspect examined by medical practitioner

❏ Avoided an atmosphere of oppression

❏ Suspect made comfortable, and depending on circumstances provided:

   ❏ Food and water

   ❏ Clothing to wea r

   ❏ Shelter

❏ Avoided conduct that shocks the community

E   ADDITIONAL OBLIGATIONS TO YOUNG PERSONS

❏ Confirmed if suspect is a young person

   ❏ Informed young person of right to consult parent or other appropriate adult person, and to have counsel, parent or other appropriate person present during questioning

   ❏ Waiver of right to counsel by young person either video recorded or in writing

F   RECORD OF RIGHTS, CAUTIONS AND STATEMENTS

❏ Rights and cautions used and responses showing understanding written down or audio/video recorded

❏ All questions posed and answers given during taking of statement written down or audio/video recorded

A TECHNICAL SET-UP AND IDENTIFICATION

❏ One camera set-up

❏ Two camera set-up

❏ Camera operation confirmed

❏ Recording device operation confirmed

❏ Clear field of view to witness' face

❏ Clear field of view of both witness and statement taker together

❏ Good audio quality confirmed

    ❏ Microphones clipped to clothing of witness and statement taker

    ❏ Microphones placed in front of witness and statement taker

❏ Camera operator available for all of statement taking

❏ Investigator on video states date, time, location and purpose of meeting

❏ Each person in room (other than camera operator) identifies self on video

B VIDEO STATEMENT CAUTION

❏ Witness warned that statement to be taken under oath and video recorded:

- "You must understand that this statement will be taken under oath, solemn affirmation or solemn declaration and will be video recorded."

- "Do you have any questions about the taking under oath, solemn affirmation, or solemn declaration of this statement, or the fact that it will be video recorded? "

      ❏ No questions, or questions asked and answered to satisfaction of witness

- "Do you understand that this statement will be taken under oath, solemn affirmation or solemn declaration, and will be video recorded?"

      ❏ Positive response given

❏ Witness warned of severe criminal penalties for not telling the truth:

- "You must understand that giving a false statement during this interview may constitute the criminal offence of obstructing justice under section 139 of the *Criminal Code*. You must further understand that you may be a witness at a subsequent proceeding concerning the events you describe in this statement and if at that time you recant your statement or claim it to be false, it can and will be used at that trial and you may be liable to prosecution under section 137 of the *Criminal Code* for fabricating evidence. You must additionally understand that giving a false statement to a peace officer may constitute the criminal offence of mischief under section 140 of the *Criminal Code*."

- "Do you have any questions about the criminal consequences of making a false statement?"
    - ❏ No questions, or questions asked and answered to satisfaction of witness
- "Do you understand the severe criminal consequences of making a false statement? "
    - ❏ Positive response given

❏ Witness warned that no obligation to give statement:

- "You must understand that you are not obliged to give this statement and if any person has by words or acts attempted to persuade you to provide it, you are to disregard those words or acts and only give this statement if you freely choose to do so."

- "Do you have any questions about your freedom of choice to give this statement?
    - ❏ No questions, or questions asked and answered to satisfaction of witness

- "Do you choose then to voluntarily give a statement?
    - ❏ Positive response given

| C | CONDUCT OF VIDEO STATEMENT |

❏ Witness makes oath, solemn affirmation or solemn declaration with appropriate official to tell the truth:

"Do you solemnly swear/affirm/declare that in the statement you are giving today you will tell the truth, the whole truth, and nothing but the truth (so help you God)?"

❏ Non-leading questions asked of witness

❏ Witness allowed to complete all answers, and to clarify any questions that are not understood

❏ Documents shown to witness also shown to camera and if possible copies made to keep with recording

❏ Continuous video recording throughout statement-taking session, even if brief break taken

❏ At conclusion of video statement, investigator states date, time and that statement now concluded

FURTHER READING

Cases

R. v. B. (K.B.), [1993] 1 S.C.R. 740. Video recording an out of court statement, preferably under oath, will later permit a trial court to readily assess the reliability of the statement for the purpose of its admission into evidence.

R. v. Bartle, [1994] 3 S.C.R. 173. Any waiver of rights to counsel must be fully informed and unequivocal.

R. v. Brydges, [1990] 1 S.C.R. 190. Advising of rights to counsel includes informing a suspect of the existence of legal aid and how to contact legal aid.

R. v. Hodgson, [1998] 2 S.C.R. 449. A confession to a person in authority must be proven beyond a reasonable doubt to have been given voluntarily.

R. v. Oickle, [2000] 2 S.C.R. 3. Contains a good discussion of the principles of voluntariness necessary to render confessions admissible.

R. v. Prosper, [1994] 3 S.C.R. 236. Advising a suspect of rights to counsel includes facilitating access and giving the opportunity to contact counsel.

R. v. Starr, [2000] S.C.R. 144. The principled approach to the hearsay rule requires that in order to be admissible at trial, any out of court statement must have circumstantial guarantees of reliability and be necessary, in addition to being relevant.

R. v. Therens, [1985] 1 S.C.R. 613. A detention that requires the giving of rights to counsel can be psychological, not just physical.

Books, Articles and Reports

G. Arcaro, *Criminal Investigations — Forming Reasonable and Probable Grounds*, 4th ed. (Toronto: Nelson, 2004).

N. Bala, *Youth Criminal Justice Law* (Toronto: Irwin Law, 2003). Provides a detailed explanation of the different rules that apply when taking statements from young persons.

I.S. Bloom, J. Vaissi Nagy & G.S. Campbell, "The Residual Protection Against Self-Incrimination in Canada: The Road Not Taken" (1995) 5 N.J.C.L. 363.

P. Calarco, "What Happens When Evidence has not Been Recorded?: Staying Charges to Ensure a Fair Trial" (2001) 44 Crim. L.Q. 514.

J. Euale & J. Turtle, *Interviewing and Investigation* (Toronto: Edmond Montgomery, 1998).

A. Grant, *The Audio-Video Taping of Police Interviews with Suspects and Accused Persons by Halton Regional Police Force, Ontario Canada* (Ottawa: Law Reform Commission of Canada, 1987).

R. Marin, *Admissibility of Statements*, 9th ed., loose-leaf (Aurora, ON: Canada Law Book, 2003). An extensive survey of the principles and case law of admitting statements into evidence at trial.

I.D. Scott, "Taking Statements from Police Officers Suspected of Criminal Misconduct: A Proposed Protocol" (2004) 49 Crim. L.Q. 166.

R.S. Woods, *Police Interrogation* (Toronto: Carswell, 1990).

CHAPTER THIRTEEN

ADVANCING INTERNATIONAL INVESTIGATIONS

The investigation, prosecution and suppression of crime for the protection of the citizen and the maintenance of peace and public order is an important goal of all organized societies. The pursuit of that goal cannot realistically be confined within national boundaries.

United States v. Cotroni, [1989]
1 S.C.R. 1469 at 1485.

In This Chapter

- Deemed extraterritorial application of Canadian laws
- Options for conducting investigations outside of Canada
- Foreign investigations inside Canada
- Options for return of accused located outside of Canada
- Options for returning foreign fugitives found in Canada

Banking records held in a small island state that are required for a tax evasion investigation, a drug importing conspiracy stretching between two continents, or an accused in a sexual assault case fleeing prosecution in Canada are all examples of how the increasing movement of information, goods and people across borders has led to transnational issues arising more frequently in investigations of criminal and regulatory offences. Every investigator now needs to know at least the basics of what can be done to gather evidence from other states, lay charges for offences committed abroad, arrest accused outside Canada's borders, and understand the limits on foreign investigative actions within Canada. Canada's international law enforcement obligations are of a reciprocal nature, where just as Canadian investigators are restricted by foreign law in what they can accomplish abroad, Canadian law places similar restrictions on foreign investigators operating inside Canada.

International legal proceedings frequently involve untested points of law, implications for diplomatic relations, and unpredictable outcomes. Over the last few years Canada has experienced many high profile legal battles arising from international investigations like the case of the *Maersk Dubai* where Romania sought to extradite from Canada six detained Taiwanese ship's officers accused of murdering two Romanian stowaways by casting them adrift on a flimsy raft on the high seas. After protracted legal proceedings the extradition judge found in *Romania v. Cheng* (1997), 158 N.S.R. (2d) 13 (S.C.); affd. (1997), 162 N.S.R. (2d) 395 (C.A.), that he did not have any jurisdiction to commit the fugitives for extradition because the extradition treaty Canada had concluded with Romania back in 1893 only covered crimes committed within the actual territory of each state:

> **Art. 1.** The High Contracting Parties engage to deliver up to each other those persons who, being accused or convicted of a crime or offence committed in the territory of the one Party, shall be found within the territory of the other Party, under the circumstances and conditions stated in the present Treaty.

Investigations with an international element require the earliest investigator-prosecutor contact of all, but demystification of the law affirms that investigators should not be deterred from exploring all angles of how a successful investigation and prosecution can be conducted, even if a suspected offence, its evidence or the accused is located outside of Canada's territory. See Figure 13-1, Ways to Advance International Investigations, for a summary of the main methods.

DEEMED EXTRATERRITORIAL APPLICATION OF CANADIAN LAWS

The *Criminal Code* effectively gives Canadian courts extraterritorial jurisdiction over offences and offenders through deeming certain acts to have been committed within Canada even when they occurred on the high seas, in the air or in another country. These *Code* provisions do not actually extend Canada's laws abroad, but do empower Canadian courts to assume jurisdiction over certain offences and accused. Section 7 of the *Code* creates

Fig 13-1 | WAYS TO ADVANCE INTERNATIONAL INVESTIGATIONS

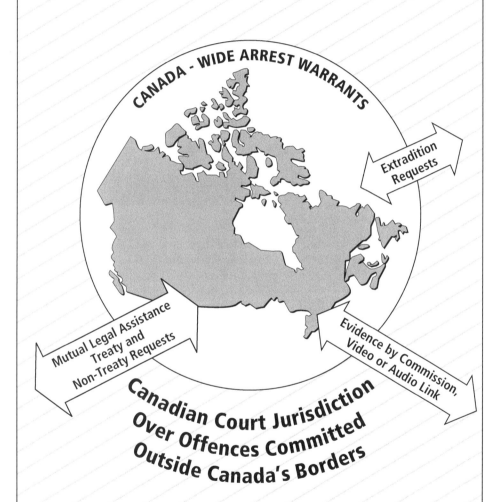

act-specific and person-specific deemings for terrorist offences, sexual offences against children, offences against internationally protected persons, hostage taking, offences against nuclear material, air or sea piracy, and bombing offences. All of these offences are deemed to have been committed within Canada if committed by or against Canadian citizens, or against a Canadian government, subject to other technical criteria being met. Section 7 also creates place-specific deemings for Canadian aircraft while in flight, for any in-flight aircraft whose flight terminates in Canada, for offshore fixed platforms anchored to Canada's continental shelf, and for Canadian ships, all of which are deemed to be within Canadian court jurisdiction regardless of who the offence is committed by or against. Section 477.1 of the *Code* likewise deems offences committed on board a ship to come within Canadian jurisdiction if the ship is registered in Canada, or where there is hot pursuit of the ship from Canadian waters.

To give an example of just how complex extraterritorial deeming language can get, and how it must be continually amended to keep up with changes in technology, take a look at the space station deeming language in s-ss. 7(2.3)-(2.34) of the *Code*:

> **7.** (2.3) Despite anything in this Act or any other Act, a Canadian crew member who, during a space flight, commits an act or omission outside Canada that if committed in Canada would constitute an indictable offence is deemed to have committed that act or omission in Canada, if that act or omission is committed
>
> (a) on, or in relation to, a flight element of the Space Station; or
>
> (b) on any means of transportation to or from the Space Station.
>
> (2.31) Despite anything in this Act or any other Act, a crew member of a Partner State who commits an act or omission outside Canada during a space flight on, or in relation to, a flight element of the Space Station or on any means of transportation to and from the Space Station that if committed in Canada would constitute an indictable offence is deemed to have committed that act or omission in Canada, if that act or omission
>
> (a) threatens the life or security of a Canadian crew member; or
>
> (b) is committed on or in relation to, or damages, a flight element provided by Canada.

. . .

(2.34) The definitions in this subsection apply in this subsection and in subsections (2.3) and (2.31).

. . .

"Space Station" means the civil international Space Station that is a multi-use facility in low-earth orbit, with flight elements and dedicated ground elements provided by, or on behalf of, the Partner States.

Extraterritorial jurisdiction in most cases will only apply if the facts of an offence have some kind of tie to Canada.

The act-specific, person-specific and place-specific deemings found in the *Code* are consistent with international conventions Canada is a party to and with principles of customary international law. *Libman v. R.*, [1985] 2 S.C.R. 178 at paras. 74 & 76-77, explained the justness of Canadian laws having *de facto* extraterritorial application:

> all that is necessary to make an offence subject to the jurisdiction of our courts is that a significant portion of the activities constituting that offence took place in Canada. As it is put by modern academics, it is sufficient that there be a "real and substantial link" between an offence and this country, a test well-known in public and private international law.
>
> . . .
>
> Just what may constitute a real and substantial link in a particular case, I need not explore. There were ample links here. The outer limits of the test may, however, well be coterminous with the requirements of international comity.
>
> . . .
>
> the common interests of states have grown proportionately. Under these circumstances, the notion of comity, which means no more nor less than "kindly and considerate behaviour towards others," has also evolved. How considerate is it of the interests of the United States in this case to permit criminals based in this country to prey on its citizens? How does it conform to its interests or to ours for us to permit such activities when law enforcement agencies in both countries have developed cooperative schemes to prevent and prosecute those engaged in such activities? To ask these questions is to answer them. . . . we should not be indifferent to

the protection of the public in other countries. In a shrinking world, we are all our brother's keepers. In the criminal arena this is underlined by the international cooperative schemes that have been developed among national law enforcement bodies.

It seems Canada is willing to authorize its courts to become seized with jurisdiction over a considerable number of offences committed throughout the world, so long as doing so does not antagonize other states and so breach international comity.

OPTIONS FOR CONDUCTING INVESTIGATIONS OUTSIDE OF CANADA

1. Getting the Most Out of Mutual Legal Assistance Treaty (MLAT) Requests

Powers held by Canadian investigators do not extend beyond Canada's borders. Investigators must rely on what is known as "mutual legal assistance" to conduct a lawful investigation outside of Canada. The *Mutual Legal Assistance in Criminal Matters Act*, R.S.C. 1985, c. 30 (4th Supp.), was primarily enacted to implement numerous bi-lateral mutual legal assistance treaties, and a smaller number of multi-lateral conventions to which Canada is a party. The term "MLAT request" is a bit of a misnomer because a formal treaty is not required for a mutual legal assistance request to be made, but any request is more likely to succeed if made under the authority of a treaty that delineates the rights and duties of the parties.

The *Mutual Legal Assistance in Criminal Matters Act* also enables evidence gathered abroad to be admitted in Canadian court proceedings if it would have been admissible under the laws of the state in which it originated. The Act authorizes judges to take a flexible approach to evaluating the probative value of foreign evidence:

> **36.** (2) For the purpose of determining the probative value of a record or a copy of a record admitted in evidence under this Act, the trier of fact may examine the record or copy, receive evidence orally or by affidavit, or by a certificate or other statement pertaining to the record in which a person attests that the certificate or statement is made in conformity with the laws that apply to a state or entity, whether or not the certificate or statement is in the form of an affidavit attested to before an official of the state or entity, including evidence as to the circumstances in which the information contained in the record or copy was written, stored or repro-

duced, and draw any reasonable inference from the form or content of the record or copy.

Canadian rules of evidence may, however, get in the way of admission of foreign evidence if it is not relevant, reliable or necessary.

Foreign evidence gathering can face interminable but somewhat understandable delays while formal requests make their way up the approval process to the Canadian Minister of Justice, are transmitted to a foreign justice minister, and then make their way down to the local foreign investigators and prosecutors who will carry them out. Once the evidence has been gathered the process must be reversed. For most cases it will be far too late to initiate a foreign evidence gathering request after charges have been laid in Canada. Sometimes informal requests for information are more expedient than using the treaty process, but some states prefer to use a formal process for all requests.

While mutual legal assistance requests are limited by Canada's reciprocal treaty obligations and the requirements of Canadian legislation, the *Charter* does not apply to the procedures used by foreign states in gathering evidence on behalf of Canada according to *R. v. Terry*, [1996] 2 S.C.R. 207 at paras. 18-20:

> The practice of cooperation between police of different countries does not make the law of one country applicable in the other country. Bilateral Mutual Legal Assistance Treaties negotiated under the authority of the *Mutual Legal Assistance in Criminal Matters Act*, R.S.C., 1985, c. 30 (4th Supp.), stipulate that the actions requested of the assisting state shall be undertaken in accordance with its own laws, not those of the requesting state . . . . Thus, if the Santa Rosa police in this case had been responding to a treaty request, they would not have been governed by the *Charter*.

> Still less can the *Charter* govern the conduct of foreign police cooperating with Canadian police on an informal basis. The personal decision of a foreign officer or agency to assist the Canadian police cannot dilute the exclusivity of the foreign state's sovereignty within its territory, where its law alone governs the process of enforcement. The gathering of evidence by these foreign officers or agency is subject to the rules of that country and none other. Consequently, any cooperative investigation involving law enforcement agencies of Canada and the United States will be governed by the laws of the jurisdiction in which the activity is undertaken . . . .

> It follows that the *Charter* did not apply to the California police when they detained the appellant. They were subject only to

American law. Their conduct cannot amount to a breach of the *Charter.*

The *Charter* will, however, apply to Canadian investigators working directly with local investigators in a foreign state who undertake actions like interviewing a Canadian detained there as occurred in *R. v. Cook*, [1998] 2 S.C.R. 597 at para. 25: "the *Charter* applies to the actions of the Vancouver detectives in interviewing the appellant in New Orleans."

There is nothing the Minister of Justice or a Canadian court can do to force a foreign state to comply with a request for legal assistance, other than invoke treaty obligations or other principles of international law. A subpoena issued by a Canadian court has no power to compel a reluctant witness to attend and give evidence unless that witness can be served with the subpoena inside Canada, or a foreign court somehow gives effect to the subpoena. Even a witness served with a subpoena inside Canada who does not show up for trial will be unaffected by a material witness warrant issued by a Canadian court if the witness has left Canada. Fortunately, options are available to compel and facilitate witness testimony abroad.

The Limits of Subpoenas

Q: Why are subpoenas issued in Canada not effective elsewhere?

A: Sovereign state immunity and limits on the jurisdiction of Canadian judges mean that a subpoena cannot have extraterritorial effect, unless a foreign court gives it effect.

2. How to Take Testimony Abroad through Commission Evidence

Investigators need not be deterred from vigorously pursuing an investigation just because key witnesses refuse to come to Canada for trial. Sections 709, 712, 713 and 713.1 of the *Criminal Code* provide for "commission evidence" to be taken where a witness is located outside of Canada, with s. 713.1 clarifying the admissibility rules to be used:

> **713.1.** Evidence taken by a commissioner appointed under section 712 shall not be excluded by reason only that it would have been taken differently in Canada, provided that the process used to take the evidence is consistent with the law of the country where it was

taken and that the process used to take the evidence was not contrary to the principles of fundamental justice.

The procedure for taking commission evidence involves a judge, prosecutor and defence counsel along with necessary assistants travelling to the jurisdiction where the witness is located and receiving evidence as if the witness had testified in Canada. A mutual legal assistance request can lead to a foreign court granting an order to compel the attendance and testimony of the witness, but any examination must be conducted according to the terms of the order.

The enormous costs of a court party travelling anywhere outside of Canada can't be ignored when deciding whether to undertake commission evidence. Costs will quickly climb proportionate to the complexity of the evidence and thus length of time required for the commissioner to take that evidence. But where there is a compelling public interest to pursue an investigation and prosecution, the commission evidence procedure can ensure a trial court has all the necessary facts before it to come to a fully informed decision about the guilt or innocence of an accused.

Investigators seeking to take commission evidence need to work out a host of details so that both the rights of a Canadian investigative target and the requirements of a foreign legal system are respected. Considerable negotiations may be necessary between Canadian and foreign authorities before the taking of commission evidence commences, as happened in *R. v. Baker*, 2001 CarswellOnt 4480 (S.C.) at paras. 11, 15 & 24, where the state in which the commission evidence was to be taken initially placed severe restrictions on what questions could be asked and who could ask them:

> With respect to the Bahamas, the respondent points to a number of concerns about significant restrictions that may be placed on the procedure for the taking of commission evidence. These restrictions are set out in a letter from Sheena A. Wilson, Chief Counsel of the Office of the Attorney General of the Bahamas, dated September 12, 2001. For example, she suggests that a list of questions must be filed with the court in advance and those questions made available to the witnesses in any court order compelling attendance of such witnesses. The role of the Canadian commissioner, court reporter and Canadian counsel would be limited to observer status. The proceedings would be presided over by a Bahamian judicial officer and recorded by a Bahamian court reporter. Only attorneys called to the Bahamian bar would be allowed to put questions. Bahamian defence counsel, *with the permission of the examiner*, would be able to put additional questions arising out of the examination of the witness. While a request for

> videotaping may be made, there is no guarantee that it will be granted.
>
> . . .
>
> It seems to me that . . . the ultimate issue is whether the process proposed for the taking of commission evidence is consistent with the principles of fundamental justice for purposes of a Canadian trial and whether it will cause unfair prejudice to the accused.
>
> . . .
>
> The appropriate way to proceed is by way of a letter of request from this Court to the Bahamian Court, setting out the procedure contemplated by Canadian law for the taking of commission evidence in a criminal trial. This will allow the Bahamian Court to respond formally to the request and may initiate, if necessary, a dialogue between the two court systems.

State-to-state dialogue is the key to successful commission evidence collection. The hurdles involved in securing the required approvals and working out logistical details for a Canadian court to take evidence on foreign soil means investigators should first examine other possible legal avenues to secure evidence of the same value before pursuing the commission evidence route.

3. The Advantages of Evidence by Video or Audio Link

Use of the revolutionary provisions found in ss. 714.2 and 714.4 of the *Criminal Code*, which authorize the taking of evidence from witnesses outside of Canada by way of electronic link, can cut through the huge logistical problems faced by commission evidence. The use of these provisions is not yet common, but they could be of immeasurable value in cases like one I prosecuted where I contemplated using s. 714.2 to take the evidence of Russian sailors who were fishing off the coast of Africa at the time of a trial I was conducting in Newfoundland. True, there were still the logistical hurdles of contacting the sailors and arranging for them to be in a port with video conference facilities at the time of the trial, but doing so would have been potentially easier and less costly than having an entire court party show up to take their evidence in Africa.

The s. 714.2 *Code* video link provision is the easier one to invoke; a Canadian court *must* receive s. 714.2 evidence taken at a distance unless one of the parties demonstrates that receiving the evidence would violate the principles of fundamental justice:

> **714.2.** A court shall receive evidence given by a witness outside Canada by means of technology that permits the witness to testify in the virtual presence of the parties and the court unless one of the parties satisfies the court that the reception of such testimony would be contrary to the principles of fundamental justice.

By contrast, the s. 714.4 *Code* audio link provision can only be used at the discretion of the court involved:

> **714.4.** The court may receive evidence given by a witness outside Canada by means of technology that permits the parties and the court in Canada to hear and examine the witness, if the court is of the opinion that it would be appropriate, considering all the circumstances including
>
> (a) the nature of the witness' anticipated evidence; and
>
> (b) any potential prejudice to either of the parties caused by the fact that the witness would not be seen by them.

The mandatory versus discretionary distinction between s. 714.2 and s. 714.4 reflects the fact that admission of out of court sworn video testimony is now well established in Canada, while out of court audio testimony has not been found to be as reliable because of the difficulty in judging credibility from a voice alone without the assistance of body language. The obvious upside to s. 714.4 is that even the most remote corners of the earth now have some kind of telephone service, whereas video conferencing facilities are still not widespread and entirely reliable even in Canada.

Canadian courts have generally been supportive of the use of technology in enhancing the ability of both the prosecution and defence to present evidence at trial, so long as that technology has explicit legislative authorization. The mere fact that a witness is testifying in another country by video link will not be contrary to the principles of fundamental justice as confirmed in *R. v. Turner*, 2002 BCSC 1135 at paras. 11-13 & 16:

> While it cannot be said that the virtual presence of a witness in the courtroom is equivalent to the actual presence, that, with respect, does not appear to me to be the only question. As I suggested to counsel during submissions, Parliament must have intended that the court receive such evidence except where it is demonstrably contrary to the principles of fundamental justice. In enacting the section, Parliament must have considered the impact of technolo-

gy generally on the ability to conduct cross-examination and the ability of the court to assess credibility.

As to the assessment of credibility, sometimes members of the public, lawyers, and perhaps even judges make the mistake of concluding that the assessment of credibility depends on observations of physical demeanour during the course of the witness testifying. In my experience, those observations are rarely determinative of credibility, as a judge who relies solely on physical observations of demeanour is likely to err.

Having said that, the possibility of interruptions in the operation of the technology could lead to the judge and counsel missing key parts of an answer. There are undoubtedly other examples of how the technology might fail to operate in a given case in such a way as to impact on the fairness of the trial. In my respectful view, most of those risks can be minimized by ensuring that counsel make appropriate arrangements for the operation of the technology subject to the directions of the trial judge.

. . .

In all the circumstances, I am not persuaded that it would be contrary to the principles of fundamental justice, as I conclude that the trial judge will be in a position to make such directions as are necessary to ensure that the concerns raised by defence counsel are met.

One can even see outright enthusiasm expressed over the use of video technology to take testimony in *R. v. Heynen*, 2000 YTTC 502 at para 315:

I was most impressed by the use of video testimony and believe it will soon become essential to the conduct of court business. I found no significant difficulty in evaluating testimony, but rather noted several advantages. Camera angles and close-up views, in many respects, enhance the ability to evaluate demeanour. Although not required in this case, the opportunity for a video replay affords many advantages over audio replays.

These affirmations of the constitutional protections and enhancements to evaluating credibility that video testimony offers are further proof to investigators that all statements should be video recorded, regardless of whether those statements are taken downtown or on the other side of the world.

FOREIGN INVESTIGATIONS INSIDE CANADA

A common misconception among investigators is that any response to an inquiry from a foreign investigative agency, no matter how innocuous, about a person's activities in Canada somehow requires the approval of the Minister of Justice or a Canadian court. In fact, only foreign inquiries that intrude on the privacy interests of a target require Ministerial and court approval, as described below. So a request for some basic surveillance of a target in a public place, or commonly known information about the target like a home address or publicly listed telephone number, does not amount to an international mutual legal assistance request. When privacy rights are not implicated, information sharing with foreign agencies will only be subject to Canadian investigative agency internal policies.

In the case of true international mutual legal assistance requests made to the Minister of Justice, *Re Pokidyshev* (1999), 124 O.A.C. 24 at paras. 18-19, explained the distinct roles of the Minister who will always be required to make a decision on whether to support the foreign request for investigative assistance within Canada and the Canadian courts who will sometimes be involved in approving implementation of a supported request:

> Under the [Mutual Legal Assistance] *Act*, the Minister of Justice serves as the guardian of Canadian sovereignty interests. She effectively controls both ends of the process. No request goes forward without her approval and no sending order is implemented without her approval. The central role of the Minister of Justice in the process reflects the essentially political nature of decisions involving international relations. These decisions properly rest with the executive arm of the federal government which is responsible for the conduct of Canada's foreign relations . . . .

> The judiciary also plays a role under Part I of the *Act*. . . .These compulsory measures can be invoked only where a judge of the Superior Court of the province so orders . . . . In making the order, the judge must be satisfied that the statutory conditions precedent to the order have been met. Any information obtained under these orders can be sent to the foreign jurisdiction only if the court so orders . . . . In exercising its jurisdiction to order information sent to the foreign jurisdiction, the court may place terms and conditions on the sending order . . . . In deciding what terms, if any, to impose, the court must consider both the interests of parties affected by the order and the need to give effect to the request made by the foreign state.

Like the extradition process, foreign investigations proposed to be conducted inside Canada are subject to far more political considerations than are domestic investigations where political interference would usually be considered improper. This political approval process is considered fundamental to safeguarding Canada's sovereignty, but the courts are required to sanction the two principal means of search warrants and evidence gathering orders by which those foreign investigations can be pursued in Canada.

1. Assisting with the Execution of International Search Warrants

Sections 10 through 16 of the *Mutual Legal Assistance in Criminal Matters Act* contain unique search warrant provisions usable by foreign states with prior approval of the Canadian Minister of Justice and a Canadian superior court to obtain the types of warrants that appear in the *Criminal Code* and other Canadian legislation. The Minister acts under s-s. 11(1) of the *Act* as a conduit for the foreign investigation request:

> **11.** (1) When the Minister approves a request of a state or entity to have a search or a seizure, or the use of any device or investigative technique or other procedure or the doing of any other thing to be described in a warrant, carried out regarding an offence, the Minister shall provide a competent authority with any documents or information necessary to apply for a search warrant or other warrant.

The competent authority is any federal or provincial prosecution service in Canada, who will apply to a superior court judge on behalf of and under the name of the requesting state for a warrant. Local Canadian investigators will then be required to execute any warrant that is issued. The court issuing the warrant must hold a hearing after its execution to consider whether anything seized should be sent abroad, and can impose conditions to ensure the preservation and eventual return of those things to Canada. An important limitation on these foreign investigation warrants is that the granting judge must first be satisfied an evidence gathering order is not appropriate in the circumstances, presumably because evidence gathering orders are less intrusive than search warrants.

2. Facilitating International Evidence Gathering Orders

If it is the testimony of witnesses rather than physical evidence that is sought by a foreign state, the desired physical evidence is in an unknown location so that a search warrant cannot be executed, or it is a mere examination rather than a search and seizure that is desired, then ss. 17 through 23.1 of the *Mutual Legal Assistance in Criminal Matters Act* can be employed to obtain an evidence gathering order. Again, the Minister of Justice must first approve the request, and will then refer the matter to appropriate prosecutors who will apply to a local superior court judge for an order that can include wide-ranging powers as specified under s-s. 18(2) of the Act. The scope of an evidence gathering order is similar to a domestic subpoena *duces tecum* for a Canadian trial or preliminary inquiry, and is also similar to a regulatory inquiry power, but is in some respects broader than either of those powers because of its available features:

- it must be directed at a named person;

- the named person may be ordered to attend a specified place for examination and remain until excused;

- examination may or may not be under oath;

- it can be accompanied by an order to make a copy of a document or electronic data;

- the named person can be ordered to bring to an examination any copy or original of a thing in possession and produce it to the person conducting the examination;

- the named person can be ordered to provide information for an affidavit or certificate that has been requested to accompany a copy, record or thing sought;

- the named person can be compelled to answer the questions of the designated person conducting the examination;

- the questions answered and things produced can be required to take a form complying with the laws of evidence of the foreign state which made the request.

On the one occasion when I acted as the designated person under s-s. 18(2)(c) of the *Mutual Legal Assistance in Criminal Matters Act* in a request to gather evidence on Canadian soil, investigators played an important role in finding the witness, serving the evidence gathering order on him, arranging for a local court reporter to take down a transcript of the evidence, ensuring a commissioner of oaths was present to swear the witness, and providing a location to conduct the interview, but didn't need to be involved in the actual questioning because I was not going to be serving in a prosecutorial role for this foreign case and so it was acceptable to run the risk of becoming a witness. A Canadian judge will be the first to determine whether any refusals to answer questions were well-founded in law, and will ultimately decide if evidence gathered under an order should be sent abroad.

a. Order to Give Evidence by Video or Audio Link

A variation on the evidence gathering order is an order under s. 22.1 of the *Mutual Legal Assistance in Criminal Matters Act* to give foreign evidence from within Canada via video or audio link, again with prior approval of the Minister of Justice and authorization of a superior court judge:

> **22.1** (1) If the Minister approves a request of a state or entity to compel a person to provide evidence or a statement regarding an offence by means of technology that permits the virtual presence of the person in the territory over which the state or entity has jurisdiction, or that permits the parties and the court to hear and examine the witness, the Minister shall provide a competent authority with any documents or information necessary to apply for the order.

Section 22.1 is the foreign proceedings counterpart to ss. 714.2. and 714.4 of the *Criminal Code* that enable evidence from abroad to be taken for Canadian proceedings. A witness giving evidence under s. 22.1 lives in a strange dual world, being subject to the laws of evidence and procedure of the foreign state's court hearing the evidence, but subject to Canadian laws of privilege and contempt of court.

A basic s-s. 18(2) order seems sufficient to video record the evidence being gathered, although it is preferable if the evidence gathering order stipulates that evidence is to be taken by means of video recording. A s. 22.1 order is only required for taking live testimony in Canada for use in another jurisdiction by some technological means of video conferencing or teleconferencing. Section 22.1 is intentionally vague on the type of technology that can be used because of the ever evolving nature of establishing a virtual presence in another place.

b. Arrest Warrant for Failure to Attend Evidence Gathering

Investigators may occasionally have to execute a s. 23 *Mutual Legal Assistance in Criminal Matters Act* arrest warrant for a person who failed to attend an evidence gathering session. There are a number of technical preconditions for such a warrant that go beyond those of a normal arrest warrant:

- the order to attend was personally served on the witness;

- the witness likely has material evidence to give; and

- the witness did not attend or remain in attendance pursuant to the order.

The high standards required for evidence gathering arrest warrants are consistent with foreign evidence gathering being an extraordinary procedure, unlike the routine nature of investigations and prosecutions taking place within Canada.

c. *Orders for Lending of Exhibits*

Orders for the foreign lending of exhibits already in the custody of a Canadian court are available under s. 30 of the *Mutual Legal Assistance in Criminal Matters Act.* An exhibit loan order proceeds through the Minister of Justice who must first approve the request and transmit it to a local prosecutor who will apply to the court that has possession of the exhibit for an order that must specify:

- a description of the exhibit;

- the person to whom it will be given;

- any tests that can be performed on the exhibit, and where they will be conducted;

- the place where the exhibit will be taken; and

- the length of time the exhibit may be held.

Investigators need not be too concerned about continuity problems arising for exhibits lent to other states because of a very helpful deeming provision in s. 34 of the *Act*:

> **34.** The burden of proving that an exhibit lent to a state or entity pursuant to a loan order made under subsection 31(1) and returned to Canada is not in the same condition as it was when the loan order was made or that it was tampered with after the loan order was made is on the party who makes that allegation and, in the absence of that proof, the exhibit is deemed to have been continuously in the possession of the court that made the loan order.

Without s. 34, dozens of witnesses might have to be brought to Canada in order to prove continuity any time the exhibit was later needed at new Canadian court proceedings.

Foreign Law Enforcement Within Canada

Q: Are foreign law enforcement officials allowed to operate within Canada?

A: The *Mutual Legal Assistance in Criminal Matters Act* provides a mechanism whereby foreign officials can be provided assistance by Canadian law enforcement authorities in conducting investigations within Canada. The foreign officials do not have investigative powers inside Canada, but could be present to render technical support while an investigation is conducted on their behalf. Like extradition, sometimes mutual legal assistance will be governed by a particular treaty with a foreign state, and at other times it will be done on a case-by-case basis.

OPTIONS FOR RETURN OF ACCUSED LOCATED OUTSIDE OF CANADA

1. Inexpensive and Uncomplicated Voluntary Return with Canada-Wide Arrest Warrant

Charges may have been laid, and sometimes an entire trial already concluded, only to find the accused now beyond Canada's borders. The easiest, though perhaps least effective, way to bring an internationally-at-large accused to justice in Canada is to wait for the accused's return to trigger a previously issued Canada-wide arrest warrant. A Canada-wide arrest warrant will remain in force indefinitely until either executed or withdrawn, and can be obtained under s. 507 of the *Criminal Code* if investigators demonstrate why it is in the public interest to issue a warrant instead of a summons:

> **507.** (4) Where a justice considers that a case is made out for compelling an accused to attend before him to answer to a charge of an offence, he shall issue a summons to the accused unless the allegations of the informant or the evidence of any witness or witnesses taken in accordance with subsection (3) discloses reasonable grounds to believe that it is necessary in the public interest to issue a warrant for the arrest of the accused.

That the accused is beyond Canada's borders and it would be impossible to serve a summons should be a more than sufficient reason for a Canada-wide arrest warrant.

It could, however, be a very long wait for an accused to return to Canada. In the small number of cases where I have been consulted on this procedure and the accused had no ties to Canada, I never heard back from investigators that the accused had been arrested so a prosecution could proceed. But for some individuals with extensive ties to Canada, eventual voluntary return to face Canadian justice is inevitable. A Canada-wide warrant can be an effective low-cost procedure that avoids the legal and political complexities of initiating a formal extradition request, and does not require that investigators even know the foreign whereabouts of a fugitive.

2. Playing the Extradition Waiting Game

Extradition is a much more proactive, effective and complex option for securing an accused's return to answer charges in Canada. Since the extradition process is generally a two way street, a lot of the law relevant to extradition to Canada is also relevant to extradition from Canada. Section 78 of the *Extradition Act*, S.C. 1999, c. 18, contains the basic authority for the Minister to initiate action to return a fugitive to Canada:

> **78.** (1) The Minister, at the request of a competent authority, may make a request to a State or entity for the extradition of a person for the purpose of prosecuting the person for—or imposing or enforcing a sentence, or making or enforcing a disposition . . ., in respect of—an offence over which Canada has jurisdiction.

No court authorization is required for the Minister to initiate an extradition request from another state, but that state must qualify as an "extradition partner," which s. 2 of the *Extradition Act* defines as: "a State or entity with which Canada is party to an extradition agreement, with which Canada has entered into a specific agreement or whose name appears in the schedule." Canada has many important non-treaty extradition partners listed in the "Schedule" found at the end of the *Extradition Act*, including the United Kingdom.

Usually it will be the Attorney General of a province or the Attorney General of Canada who is the competent authority to start the extradition request, which will be forwarded to the foreign state through the International Assistance Group of Justice Canada in Ottawa after the Minister of Justice has concurred in the request. Canadian investigators work with local prosecutors to pass an extradition request through the appropriate Attorney General, and then wait — and sometimes wait and wait and wait. There is really no way to get around the waiting. The complexities of international law and the desire of states, including Canada, to ensure their nationals are not forced to face baseless charges in hostile foreign lands means that internal legal procedures in the state where a fugitive has taken refuge require time to work themselves out.

There are frequent lengthy legal battles fought over extradition, but at least in Canada there are really very few points of law that can be argued in those disputes. *United States of America v. McAmmond* (2005), 193 O.A.C. 129 at para. 8, explained how extradition is more a political than a legal decision:

> At its core, extradition is a political process in which primary responsibility rests with the executive branch of government. It is a means by which nations honour their international obligations and the principles of comity through a framework of treaties and domestic legislation. In Canada, the process is two-staged. The first stage involves judicial input in the form of a screening mechanism whereby a judge decides whether the requesting state has put forth sufficient evidence to warrant a committal for surrender. If that is so, the Minister determines in the second stage whether the individual whose extradition is sought should be surrendered for that purpose.

Whether or not extradition is possible in a particular case depends on the type of offence charged, the severity of the potential punishment, and the country from whom extradition is sought.

a. *Double Criminality and Minimum Available Punishment Requirements*

Many states have laws similar to Canada's s-s. 3(1) of the *Extradition Act* that requires that the type of offence charged in Canada be able to be equated to an offence under the laws of the state from whom extradition is sought (known as double criminality), and be punishable by two or more years imprisonment in the requesting state (unless otherwise specified by treaty — in the case of Canada's most important extradition partner, the threshold has been lowered by treaty with the United States of America to one year), in order for Canada to contemplate extradition. While Canada's early extradition treaties specified particular offences for which each state party would grant extradition, more modern treaties now use double criminality and minimum punishment standards to avoid constant amendment as new offences are created.

Extradition from a non-treaty state is much more difficult to secure, depending on the political will of that state, and the type of offence for which Canada is seeking extradition. Sub-section 10(1) of the *Extradition Act* authorizes the consideration on a case-by-case basis of extradition to non-treaty states under what is known as a "specific agreement." The challenges of non-treaty extradition requests are compounded by the s-s. 3(1)(b)(i) *Extradition Act* requirement that specific agreement requests be connected to offences punishable by at least five years imprisonment, instead of the usual two years imprisonment required for treaty requests.

b. *The Requirement of Prosecution Only for the Offence Returned For*

The *Extradition Act* also imposes significant limitations on what can be done with a fugitive after that person's return to Canada. The goal is to allow the extraditing state some control over what happens to those being shipped abroad who are often its own citizens. According to s. 80 of the *Act*, a returned fugitive can usually only be prosecuted for the offences he was explicitly returned for, and cannot in turn be extradited to a third country.

Lack of control over trial fairness and conditions of punishment prevents many civil law based European states from extraditing any of their nationals to Canada or anywhere else. If a Canadian fugitive is a resident national in one of these states, the only alternatives are to either wait for the fugitive to travel to a state with which Canada does have an extradition relationship, or discuss with the non-extradition state whether the Canadian crimes alleged are of such a serious nature that a prosecution could be brought within its own court system under its laws for offences which transpired in Canada.

If extradition is granted by a foreign state, the usual practice is for Canadian investigators to travel to the surrendering state to take custody of the fugitive. Section 81 of the *Extradition Act* does, however, permit the Minister to authorize foreign investigators to bring a fugitive into Canada for a handover on Canadian soil. Such a procedure could make sense if foreign investigators are already travelling to Canada on other business, and avoids the sometimes considerable cost of Canadian investigators travelling abroad. Some states might prefer to personally deliver a fugitive, rather than have Canadian investigators intrude onto foreign soil. The *Extradition Act* even gives foreign investigators the power to arrest in Canada when in fresh pursuit of a fugitive who escapes prior to a handover to Canadian authorities.

OPTIONS FOR RETURNING FOREIGN FUGITIVES FOUND IN CANADA

Prosecutors bear the heavier burden when extraditing *from* Canada because of the extensive legal proceedings they have to deal with on behalf of the requesting state. Investigators bear the greater burden in extraditing *to* Canada because of the documentary record of evidence that must be put together for the foreign state holding the fugitive. Investigators do need to understand at least the basics of extraditing a fugitive from Canada, as in the course of your routine duties you may run across an international fugitive driving down a quiet suburban Canadian street, or you may be asked to coordinate the take down of one of America's most wanted.

Investigators also need to be prepared for considerable media attention when dealing with cases of extradition from Canada, especially since a number of those cases arise due to television shows like *America's Most Wanted* or *Unsolved Mysteries.* In one case I dealt with, a fugitive from the United States wanted for serious sexual offences against children had lived undetected in Canada for several years, but one wintry Prince Edward Island night his luck ran out when fellow island residents learned of his background from a rerun of an American television show and immediately telephoned the F.B.I. That call triggered a series of events starting with American authorities forwarding sufficient material upon which we could seek a provisional warrant for the fugitive's arrest pending a formal extradition request, and ending with American law enforcement officials travelling to Canada to take custody of this reluctant television star.

1. The First Step of Obtaining a Provisional Arrest Warrant

Since an international fugitive may have gone to some effort to flee from foreign law enforcement authorities, it is naïve to expect the fugitive to stay put while a polite diplomatic exchange drags on over whether Canada should return that person to face foreign justice. The provisional arrest warrant can bring the fugitive under Canadian control, even before a formal extradition request has been received. All that is required from foreign authorities is enough information to enable the swearing of an affidavit supporting a provisional warrant as provided for under ss. 12-13 of the *Extradition Act*:

> **12.** The Minister may, after receiving a request by an extradition partner for the provisional arrest of a person, authorize the Attorney General to apply for a provisional arrest warrant, if the Minister is satisfied that
>
> > (a) the offence in respect of which the provisional arrest is requested is punishable in accordance with paragraph 3(1)(a); and

(b) the extradition partner will make a request for the extradition of the person.

13. (1) A judge may, on ex parte application of the Attorney General, issue a warrant for the provisional arrest of a person, if satisfied that there are reasonable grounds to believe that

(a) it is necessary in the public interest to arrest the person, including to prevent the person from escaping or committing an offence;

(b) the person is ordinarily resident in Canada, is in Canada or is on the way to Canada; and

(c) a warrant for the person's arrest or an order of a similar nature has been issued or the person has been convicted.

In addition to the diplomatic process at work in convincing the Minister to authorize the seeking of the warrant, Canadian investigators can play an important role in the provisional arrest warrant's preparation as well as in its execution. They can make use of their informal contacts with foreign law enforcement authorities to aid the inter-agency and international dialogue involved in scraping together enough information on short notice to satisfy the public interest test required by s. 13 of the *Extradition Act.*

The fact that Canadian courts will sometimes release an arrested international fugitive on bail conditions while the extradition process plays out may seem counterintuitive, but prospects for release depend on a variety of circumstances like whether the person is ordinarily resident in Canada, poses a real flight risk, or is a danger to the Canadian public. Investigator involvement is important at the extradition bail hearing in order to present both the history of the fugitive's conduct in Canada, and the alleged or proven conduct in the foreign jurisdiction requesting extradition. Considerable quick and challenging investigation may be required to gather a fugitive's background history if he has been living in Canada under several different names. Investigators can also contribute to suggestions for what will usually be quite strict conditions placed on release should bail be granted. I have found that a fugitive's keenness for release is often proportionate to ties to the local community in which the arrest is made, and that some fugitives with minimal community ties will consent to their detention.

One example of just how complex and contentious even provisional arrest and extradition bail can get involved three Russian sailors from the tanker ship *Virgo* who were accused by American authorities of murder in the course of allegedly running down an American fishing boat off the

United States coast. The sailors were arrested under provisional arrest warrants in St. John's, Newfoundland and Labrador, when their ship docked there, and the court saw fit to release them on a bail with severe movement restrictions keeping them far from their families pending resolution of lengthy legal proceedings to extradite them to the United States.

The most unusual twist in the case came when the extradition judge eventually agreed the sailors could return to Russia while on bail to await the outcome of the extradition process, a finding upheld on appeal in *United States of America v. Ivanov* (2003), 223 Nfld. & P.E.I.R. 44; 2003 NLCA 11 at paras. 12 & 13:

> a combination of factors including the best efforts of the Russian government combined with the influence of the respondents' employer and, indeed, the integrity of the respondents themselves led [the extradition judge] to believe that they would not fail to return when required.

> At first blush, it seems counterintuitive to permit persons subject to proceedings under the *Extradition Act* to leave the Country, at least when they are not citizens of Canada. After all the whole purpose of such proceedings is to require, in proper cases, that individuals face prosecution in a place to which they do not wish to go and when these individuals return to Russia there is no way of compelling their return. However, I have not been shown any authority, either statutory or judicial which says that permitting someone who is on judicial interim release to leave the Country is contrary to law.

After lengthy diplomatic negotiations among Russia, Canada and the United States, the extradition request for the sailors was eventually withdrawn, showing how closely law and politics may interact in international investigations and extradition matters.

The Legality of Bounty Hunting

Q & A

Q: What does Canadian law say about private bounty hunters from foreign states coming here to capture and return fugitives wanted outside of Canada?

A: Canada has recognized a legal process under the *Extradition Act* through which foreign states can secure the return of fugitives, either under a treaty or on a case-by-case basis. So-called bounty hunters could have statutory authority for their actions inside their home jurisdictions, but that authority does not extend into Canada where similar actions can constitute serious offences under the *Criminal Code*.

2. Respecting Time Limitations and Evidentiary Burdens for Extradition

What can be termed the 60-30 Extradition Rule plays an important role in ensuring a fugitive is not left locked up in Canada for unreasonable lengths of time while complex case materials are assembled, assessed, translated and transmitted from the requesting state to Canada. The state requesting extradition has 60 days from the time of execution of the provisional arrest warrant to supply to Canada all certified material required by the *Extradition Act* to initiate a formal extradition request. Investigators or prosecutors may need to informally check in with their foreign counterparts to make sure the 60-day limitation period isn't missed. Canada's Minister of Justice then has 30 days to decide on whether to proceed with an extradition hearing. Investigators should also track this 30-day limitation period, and check with prosecutors close to the time of its expiry on the status of the decision-making process. An extradition court hearing in Canada will usually be held soon after an Authority to Proceed is issued by the Minister.

At the extradition hearing, counsel for the Attorney General of Canada represents the state requesting extradition and presents the materials supporting extradition, leading to case names like *United States of America v. Sheppard.* The fugitive has an opportunity to present evidence and legal argument at the hearing, but the jurisdiction of the extradition judge is limited. Nothing close to a trial on the merits of the offences for which extradition is sought takes place. The process is predominantly about whether the formal requirements of the *Extradition Act* have been complied with.

If the extradition judge finds the submitted material complies with the *Extradition Act*, and the foreign state has made out a *prima facie* case of an offence committed by the fugitive that qualifies as an extraditable offence, then the judge can issue an order for committal that is forwarded to the Minister of Justice. The fugitive then has 30 days in which to make final submissions directly to the Minister on whether surrender should take place and if any conditions should be imposed on the surrender — like a no death penalty guarantee. This 30-day waiting period further emphasizes the predominantly political character of the process, where the court does not have the final say.

Investigators and prosecutors must work in complete harmony to advance international investigations; neither group has the power to pluck evidence or fugitives from abroad, and all are at the mercy of diplomatic processes. Investigators and prosecutors are also implementers of Canadian sovereignty when foreign states use diplomatic channels to secure permission for the gathering of evidence or fugitives from Canada. Although political and judicial decision making can consume a lot of time in international investigations, investigators and prosecutors must be ready to act extremely quickly once decisions to proceed are taken so people and evidence don't slip away into yet another foreign jurisdiction.

KEY POINTS

On Advancing International Investigations

✓ Canadian law does not have general extraterritorial effect, but depending on the offence, who it was committed by or against, and where it took place, certain offences and offenders located abroad can nonetheless be subject to Canadian court jurisdiction.

✓ Mutual legal assistance requests facilitate Canadian investigations in foreign states and foreign investigations inside Canada. The *Charter* does not apply to the procedures used by foreign states in gathering evidence on behalf of Canada, but does apply to Canadian investigators operating directly in a foreign state in conjunction with local investigators. The *Criminal Code* provides authority for court testimony and related evidence to be taken outside of Canada by commission, by video link or by audio link. International search warrants and evidence gathering orders are available to foreign states under the *Mutual Legal Assistance in Criminal Matters Act* upon the approval of the Minister of Justice and a local superior court who will determine if any seized or gathered evidence should be sent abroad, and what conditions should be imposed on the eventual return of the evidence to Canada.

✓ A Canada-wide arrest warrant is a simple way to bring a foreign fugitive to justice if it is likely that person will eventually voluntarily return to Canada. Extradition both to or from Canada can take place either under a treaty Canada has concluded with a foreign state or on a case-by-case basis under a specific agreement where there is no treaty. Requirements of minimum punishment levels and double criminality limit the types of offences for which extradition can be sought or granted. Where an extradition request is forthcoming, a provisional arrest warrant can be issued in Canada for a fugitive in or on the way to Canada if such a warrant is found to be in the public interest and a warrant or conviction exists elsewhere against that person.

✓ Mutual legal assistance and extradition are predominantly political processes where in Canada the Minister of Justice plays the key decision-making role, and the courts ensure procedural standards are met.

FURTHER READING

Cases

R. v. Cook, [1998] 2 S.C.R. 597. The *Charter* applies to Canadian investigators directly conducting investigative duties outside of Canada, but not to foreign investigators working outside of Canada as agents of Canadian investigators.

R. v. Terry, [1996] 2 S.C.R. 207. Bilateral mutual legal assistance is undertaken in accordance with the laws of the assisting state, not the requesting state, so the *Charter* does not apply to evidence gathering by a foreign state at the request of Canada.

Schrieber v. Canada (Attorney General), [1998] 1 S.C.R. 841. No judicial authorization is required for a Canadian request to gather foreign evidence.

United States v. Burns, [2001] 1 S.C.R. 283. Assurances from the requesting state that the death penalty will not be sought are required in all cases of extradition from Canada where a fugitive is charged with a capital crime, other than in exceptional circumstances.

United States of America v. Lépine, [1994] 1 S.C.R. 286. A fugitive's conduct must have a real and substantial link to the country requesting extradition in order for extradition to proceed.

Books, Articles and Reports

G. Botting, *Canadian Extradition Law Practice* (Markham, ON: LexisNexis Butterworths, 2005).

R.J. Currie, "*Charter* Without Borders?: The Supreme Court of Canada, Transnational Crime, and Constitutional Rights and Freedoms" (2004) 27 Dalhousie L.J. 235.

R.J. Currie, "Search Warrants Under the *Mutual Legal Assistance in Criminal Matters Act*" (2003) 12 C.R. (6th) 275.

E.G. Ewaschuk, *Criminal Pleadings and Practice in Canada*, 2nd ed., loose-leaf (Aurora, ON: Canada Law Book, 1997). See particularly Chapter 32 ("Extradition and Fugitive Offenders").

R. Goldstein and N. Dennison, "Mutual Legal Assistance in Canadian Criminal Courts" (2001) 45 Crim. L.Q. 126.

E.F. Krivel, T. Beveridge and J.W. Hayward, *A Practical Guide to Canadian Extradition* (Toronto: Carswell, 2002).

Law Reform Commission of Canada, *Working Paper No. 37 — Extraterritorial Jurisdiction* (Ottawa: Law Reform Commission of Canada, 1984).

P. Morris, *Territoriality and Extraterritoriality: Some Comments on the Ambit of the Criminal Law of Canada* (Ottawa: Law Reform Commission of Canada, 1981).

CHAPTER FOURTEEN

DECIDING TO CHARGE, DRAFTING CHARGES, AND SPEAKING TO THE MEDIA

> It is undeniable that the theory of our criminal law is that all persons should be prosecuted in the name of the Sovereign who is "the proper person to prosecute for all public offences and breaches of the peace, being a person injured in the eyes of the law."
>
> *R. v. Deveraux* (1966), 49 C.R. 194 (Ont. C.A.) at 196.

In This Chapter

- How to make the decision to charge
- How to draft the charge
- The twelve fundamental principles of charge drafting
- Deciding on and drafting conspiracy charges
- Compelling court attendance
- The notice of intent to seek greater punishment
- Speaking to the media

Did you know that theft of cattle is a straight indictable offence under s-s. 388(2) of the *Criminal Code*, punishable by ten years imprisonment? How about that according to s. 2 of the *Code* a goat qualifies as cattle, so even goat theft is an indictable offence? By comparison, the more general offence of theft under s. 322 of the *Code* is only a hybrid offence and attracts a lesser punishment depending on the value of the theft. Why should I care, you ask? Because being familiar with all charges that can be based on a given set of facts, the procedures surrounding the laying of those charges, and the maximum punishments available after conviction is crucial to the process of deciding if charges should be laid in the first place, and how they should be drafted.

When you lay charges, you lay them on behalf of the state as represented by the sovereign as head of state. Whether or not to lay charges, and what form a charge will take, are *the* most crucial decisions that will be made in the course of any investigation. The fruits of all investigative labours are funneled into the charging decision and shape whether a charge is supported by evidence. After the charge is laid, the prosecution has to proceed according to that charge, not according to the charge that should have been laid.

From the thousands of offences available to be charged, and the millions of possible variations in the wording of a charge that may be employed, drafting a charge can seem a daunting task. It need not be so. The checklists and principles of good practice included in this chapter will help you determine whether it is appropriate to lay charges, and ensure that you cover all the key elements when drafting charges you have decided to lay.

HOW TO MAKE THE DECISION TO CHARGE

1. Deciding If Charges Should Be Laid

In Canada there is a marked separation between charging decisions, and prosecution decisions. The minimum standard required to lay a charge is reasonable and probable grounds (RPG) an offence has been committed by an identified person within the territorial jurisdiction of the court where the charge will be laid, but significantly greater certainty of an offence than that bare RPG threshold is needed to sustain a charge as highlighted in *R. v. Kearley*, 2004 CanLII 20256 (N.L.P.C.): "The evidence in this case clearly met the threshold necessary for the laying of the charges. However, the test for conviction is much higher . . .The Accused may well have been responsible, but that has not been proven beyond a reasonable doubt." Because of the high threshold for conviction, investigators must think beyond the RPG threshold.

Although the job of an investigator is quite distinct from that of a prosecutor, when laying charges investigators need to think somewhat like prosecutors. Prosecutors primarily look at two factors when assessing whether a charge should proceed in court.

- Is there a reasonable prospect of conviction?
- Is the prosecution in the public interest?

The wording of the first factor can vary a bit depending on which prosecution service is involved, with a "reasonable likelihood of conviction" standard sometimes being used, which seems to mean probable but not necessarily highly probable, instead of "reasonable prospect," meaning more than just possible but not necessarily probable. In this chapter I use the more commonly relied on "reasonable prospect." Investigators are well advised to occasionally consult the publicly available policy manuals produced by most prosecution services that guide prosecutors in exercising their wide discretion to proceed with or decline charges.

Krieger v. Law Society (Alberta), [2002] 3 S.C.R. 372 at paras. 43-46, confirmed the core aspects of prosecutorial discretion:

> "Prosecutorial discretion" is a term of art. It does not simply refer to any discretionary decision made by a Crown prosecutor. Prosecutorial discretion refers to the use of those powers that constitute the core of the Attorney General's office and which are protected from the influence of improper political and other vitiating factors by the principle of independence.
>
> . . .
>
> As discussed above, these powers emanate from the office-holder's role as legal advisor of, and officer to, the Crown. In our theory of government, it is the sovereign who holds the power to prosecute his or her subjects. A decision of the Attorney General, or of his or her agents, within the authority delegated to him or her by the sovereign is not subject to interference by other arms of government. An exercise of prosecutorial discretion will, therefore, be treated with deference by the courts and by other members of the executive, as well as statutory bodies like provincial law societies.
>
> Without being exhaustive, we believe the core elements of prosecutorial discretion encompass the following: (a) the discretion whether to bring the prosecution of a charge laid by police; (b) the discretion to enter a stay of proceedings in either a private or public prosecution, as codified in the *Criminal Code*, R.S.C. 1985, c. C-46, ss. 579 and 579.1; (c) the discretion to accept a guilty plea to a lesser charge; (d) the discretion to withdraw from criminal proceedings altogether . . . and (e) the discretion to take control of a

private prosecution. . . . While there are other discretionary decisions, these are the core of the delegated sovereign authority pecu-
liar to the office of the Attorney General.

All of the identified core elements relate to controlling the gates of the justice process.

a. *The Two Charge Approval Factors*

There are two possible questions to ask yourself in looking at the first
factor of reasonable prospect of conviction.

- Will the evidence I collected be admissible in court?

- Were any investigative actions taken which might compromise the
  prosecution because of abuse of process or breach of *Charter* rights?

The second factor of public interest involves more diverse and concrete
considerations like:

- the seriousness of the offence and likely sentence;

- the mental or physical health, personal circumstances and coopera-
  tiveness of the accused;

- the availability and appropriateness of alternatives to prosecution;

- the attitude of the victim to the prosecution;

- the expense of the prosecution;

- the likely effect of the prosecution on public confidence in the
  administration of justice.

I urge you to consult a prosecutor before laying a charge to better understand what these factors mean in your jurisdiction. Consulting a prosecutor
will be compulsory in provinces where mandatory charge screening exists,
which is currently limited to British Columbia, Quebec and New Brunswick.

The primary goal of prosecutors is not to stop too many charges from
proceeding to trial. In fact, prosecutors might at times wish investigators had
laid additional charges if the evidence additionally or alternately appears
better to support them. Following the theme of early investigator-prosecutor contact will ensure you have canvassed all possible charges in advance
of making a charging decision. Following the theme of demystification of
the law guarantees your charges will be well drafted.

Using Figure 14-1, Charge Decision-Making Matrix, will help you decide among charging options. You should believe that both the reasonable prospect of conviction and public interest factors can be satisfied before going to the trouble of preparing a complete prosecution brief. Charge analysis need not be overly complicated or time consuming, however in cases of urgency a charge could be laid or recommended solely based on RPG so that the judicial interim release process can commence.

b. *Reasons to Argue with the Prosecutor's Decision Not to Proceed*

There are many technical legal issues at play working for and against charge viability. Where you disagree with a prosecutor's decision not to proceed with charges, you will be on firmer ground arguing over the public interest factor than on whether there is a reasonable prospect of conviction. Certainly prosecutors should hear you out, but one argument not compelling to them is: "let the court decide about whether a conviction is appropriate." Prosecutors and investigators are duty bound not to let charges proceed that do not meet the required legal standards. If the prosecutor does not believe charge standards have been met, and investigators cannot change her mind, it would not be ethical to simply leave it to the court to decide whether to throw out the charges. Leaving it to the court clogs already overburdened court dockets with unnecessary trials, and puts accused and sometimes fragile witnesses through needless proceedings.

The Exercise of Prosecutorial Discretion

Q & A

Q: I have compelling evidence of three different offences committed by four people, but the prosecutor says I should only lay one charge against two of the four people. I don't agree with his advice, and want to go ahead to charge all of them with all possible offences. What should I do?

A: A prosecutor who articulates well-founded reasons for believing there is no reasonable prospect of conviction or that it is not in the public interest to proceed with particular charges will almost certainly withdraw or stay those charges, even if an investigator is working in a jurisdiction where it is in his discretion to lay them. Reasoned dialogue, rather than confrontation, is the preferred route to resolving charging disagreements.

Fig 14-1 | # CHARGE DECISION-MAKING MATRIX

Potential Accused:_____

Evidence Gathered	Links	Potential Charges	RPG of Offence	Charge Weaknesses	Reasonable Prospect of Conviction	Charge in Public Interest
1. _____ •	•	1. _____	❑	_____	❑	❑
_____		_____		_____		
2. _____ •	•	2. _____	❑	_____	❑	❑
				_____		
3. _____ •	•	3. _____	❑	_____	❑	❑
_____		_____		_____		
4. _____ •	•	4. _____	❑	_____	❑	❑
_____		_____		_____		
5. _____ •	•	5. _____	❑	_____	❑	❑
_____		_____		_____		
6. _____ •	•	6. _____	❑	_____	❑	❑
_____		_____		_____		
7. _____ •	•	7. _____	❑	_____	❑	❑
_____		_____		_____		
8. _____ •	•	8. _____	❑	_____	❑	❑
_____		_____		_____		
9. _____ •	•	9. _____	❑	_____	❑	❑
_____		_____		_____		
10. _____ •	•	10. _____	❑	_____	❑	❑
_____		_____		_____		

Draw a linking line between each piece of evidence and every potential charge to which it can be connected. The number and type of links show the strength of charges, and whether additional charges might arise from evidence not linked to current charges.

2. Deciding When Charges Should Be Laid

Deciding *when* to charge is almost as important as deciding *if* to charge. The crucial rule applicable to charging timelines is that *all charges must be laid prior to the expiration of their respective time limitation periods*. There is no such thing as a general "Statute of Limitations" for prosecutions in Canada; limitation periods are separately specified for different types of offence.

For indictable offences there is *no* limitation period. For most summary offences found in the *Criminal Code* and certain other federal, provincial or territorial Acts, the limitation period is a mere six months from the time the offence was committed. Sub-section 786(2) of the *Code* contains the general rule: "No proceedings shall be instituted more than six months after the time when the subject-matter of the proceedings arose, unless the prosecutor and the defendant so agree." Some provincial or municipal summary offences have limitation periods as short as 90 days, but other federal summary regulatory offences have two year or longer charging limitations reflecting the extended times they require to be discovered and investigated. For hybrid offences where the prosecution can choose to proceed either by way of summary conviction or on indictment, a charge can be laid after the summary offence limitation period has expired, but the prosecution will have to proceed by indictment with its attendant greater time and expense requirements.

3. Avoiding Limitation Periods Contingent on Minister's Awareness of Offence

The most complicated charge limitation periods are the ones measured from the time the offence came to the attention of the responsible Minister, like s. 275 of the *Canadian Environmental Protection Act*, 1999, S.C. 1999, c. 33:

> **275.** (1) Proceedings by way of summary conviction in respect of an offence under this Act may be instituted at any time within, but not later than, two years after the time when the Minister became aware of the subject-matter of the proceedings.

> (2) A document purporting to have been issued by the Minister, certifying the day on which the Minister became aware of the subject-matter of any proceedings, shall be received in evidence and, in the absence of any evidence to the contrary, the doc-

> ument shall be considered as proof of that fact without proof of the
> signature or of the official character of the person appearing to
> have signed the document and without further proof.

The original intent of provisions like this one seems to have been to give the government a reasonable period of time to investigate and decide on charging after learning about a difficult to detect offence, but the practical operation of these moving target limitations has been to fuel courtroom arguments over whether charges are out of time.

Great controversy can surround when exactly an offence came to light, and who in the government first learned about it. Prosecutors who work with these kinds of cases tend to advise investigators to lay charges within two years (or whatever period the Act stipulates) of the commission of the actual offence if possible, rather than relying on arguable Ministerial certificates attesting to when the Minister learned of the offence. Knowledge by any part of the government could be argued to be equivalent to the Minister's knowledge. Sub-section 244(4) of the *Income Tax Act*, R.S.C. 1985, c. 1 (5th Supp.), has considerably extended its summary offence limitation period to "8 years after the day on which the matter of the information or complaint arose" to avoid arguments over Ministerial certificates. I anticipate other regulatory Acts could move to longer fixed summary limitation periods in the future, so check a recent copy of the legislation you are dealing with before making any charge limitation assumptions.

4. The Clock Starts Running Once Charges Are Laid

The clock on getting to trial within a reasonable time starts ticking the moment a charge is laid, but an accused is generally only prejudiced by post-charge delay as noted in *R. v. Finta*, [1994] 1 S.C.R. 701 at 875: "In the present case, I am unable to see any merit in the respondent's arguments that he suffered prejudice as a result of the pre-charge delay. Indeed, it is far more likely that the delay was more prejudicial to the Crown's case than it was that of the defence." Unless a limitation period or making an arrest forces you into laying charges before you are completely ready to proceed, try to avoid charging until you can answer "yes" to three questions.

- Is the investigation complete?

- Can disclosure be provided soon after charges are laid?

- Can a trial be proceeded to without delay?

In marked contrast to pre-charge delay, post-charge delay is one of the four horsemen of the case destroying apocalypse, the other three horsemen being disclosure problems (often the cause of delay in the first place), search problems, and statement problems. Yes, cases can disintegrate for many other reasons beyond investigator control, but these four horsemen are firmly within your control and can be prevented from doing damage if you embrace demystification of the law and early investigator-prosecutor contact.

The infamous case of *R. v. Askov*, [1990] 2 S.C.R. 1199, led the Attorney General of Ontario to stay or withdraw over 47,000 charges as being beyond what the Supreme Court of Canada said was the maximum acceptable eight month gap between the laying of charges and the start of a trial. The Supreme Court has since backed off on specifying firm maximum post-charge delay periods, moving to a more flexible approach in *R. v. Morin*, [1992] 1 S.C.R. 771 at 787:

> While the Court has at times indicated otherwise, it is now accept-ed that the factors to be considered in analyzing how long is too long may be listed as follows:
>
> 1. the length of the delay;
>
> 2. waiver of time periods;
>
> 3. the reasons for the delay, including
>
>> (a) inherent time requirements of the case,
>>
>> (b) actions of the accused,
>>
>> (c) actions of the Crown,
>>
>> (d) limits on institutional resources, and
>>
>> (e) other reasons for delay; and
>
> 4. prejudice to the accused.

The key factor in this list is prejudice to the accused, but all these factors play an important role in the assessment of how long is too long to wait for a trial to start. Lower courts continue to dismiss charges in significant num-bers because they cannot be brought to trial within a "reasonable time" as is required by s-s. 11(d) of the *Charter*.

Systemic trial delays, because of court scheduling problems, do in theory count against the prosecution, but I have found that "normal" delays tend to establish the benchmark of reasonableness in a local jurisdiction. My experience practicing in a number of different provinces, in both urban and rural areas, is that what courts will tolerate as reasonable trial delay is directly proportional to the case burden of the court involved. Quieter, more rural courts may be able to set a trial date within a few months of the first appearance and so believe a trial starting much beyond that point through no fault of the accused is unreasonable; busier more urban courts may be setting trial dates over a year in the future and so think that isn't unreasonable delay. The circuit courts that cover the most geographically remote areas of Canada may have quite long trial delays if circuits are infrequent or delayed because of bad weather, and thus trial delay arguments may only become a problem where the prosecution has asked for multiple adjournments because of missing evidence or witnesses. Where a case proceeds by indictment and a preliminary inquiry is held, the acceptable period of delay until the start of trial will be significantly longer than without a preliminary inquiry. It is sometimes impossible to say with certainty how much delay will be too much because of the role prejudice to the specific accused plays in delay assessment, but investigators can be confident that if a case is almost ready to go to trial at the time charges are laid, it is much less likely any subsequent delay arguments will be successful.

Dealing with Charge Delay

Q & A

Q: How am I supposed to know how much charge delay is too much delay?

A: The sooner a case can go to trial the better — ideally a case will proceed on the first available court date. A best investigative practice would be to electronically track the delay all your outstanding cases have incurred to date, with warnings popping up with increasing urgency as a case surpasses particular delay thresholds at which point investigators could check on the cause of delay and see if anything can be done about it.

HOW TO DRAFT THE CHARGE

The investigator who makes the initial decision to charge, is also the one who should draft the charge. Having a prosecutor do all the drafting could be perceived as an impermissible infringement on the legal distinction between the roles of investigators and prosecutors. This is not a prosecutor's plea to worm out of legitimate work — you can of course still get help from prosecutors in drafting charges — but I have found if prosecutors control the charge drafting process, investigators can get sidelined from their legitimate role of initially deciding which charges get laid.

Relying on precedents for drafting charges can be helpful, but as is the case with warrants and wiretaps all too often the precedents are unreliable or out of date. Investigators are usually better off just drafting charges from scratch, while being guided by a basic template like the one presented in this chapter. Charge precedents can still be an aid, just don't slavishly follow them without giving thought to whether they make sense. The Charge Drafting Checklist, at the end of this chapter, will help ensure you cover all the key elements when drafting charges from scratch, or reviewing the accuracy of precedents.

It is always a good idea to run the wording of a charge by a prosecutor before you swear out the charge, particularly when you are charging an offence you haven't dealt with before. It is all too easy to make a serious charge drafting mistake. Fortunately the law grants judges considerable discretion to amend defective charges, but getting the charge right the first time is far preferable to pleading with a court to amend in the face of vigorous defence opposition. When I have run across serious wording problems in already laid charges, I have usually advised investigators to relay the information if the limitation period hasn't run out rather than risk a court denying a motion to amend.

Subject to slight regional variations in what a charging information looks like, the same basic elements must always be present when setting out each offence. There is theoretically no limit to the types of offences or number of accused appearing on one information so long as there is a factual nexus among the accused and offences charged. If there is insufficient space in the standard charging form your local courts use to list a multitude of accused or charges, just type "See Appendix A" where you would normally list charges in the form. The attached Appendix A could then run to as many pages as needed.

The flexibility available to charge drafters was explained in *R. v. Sault Ste. Marie*, [1978] 2 S.C.R. 1299 at 1307:

> To resolve the matter one must recall, I think, the policy basis of the rule against multiplicity and duplicity. The rule developed during a period of extreme formality and technicality in the preferring of indictments and laying of informations. It grew from the humane desire of judges to alleviate the severity of the law in an age when many crimes were still classified as felonies, for which the punishment was death by the gallows. The slightest defect made an indictment a nullity. That age passed. Parliament has made it abun-

dantly clear in those sections of the *Criminal Code* having to do with the form of indictments and informations that the punctilio of an earlier age is no longer to bind us. We must look for substance and not petty formalities.

Willful ignorance of formalities will, however, only lead to endless legal arguments over charge validity. Both form and substance remain important to any valid charge.

THE TWELVE FUNDAMENTAL PRINCIPLES OF CHARGE DRAFTING

While very few things in life may be perfect, in charge drafting perfection is possible. You don't want to simply bulletproof the charges, you want them to be of a model nature. Perfection is achieved through a golden rule and several principles flowing from that rule. Although search warrant drafting may be more art than science, by contrast charge drafting is a straightforward, scientific process if you adhere to the twelve principles discussed in the sections below. You may have survived for years as an investigator laying charges that don't precisely follow these principles because those charges have not been repeatedly challenged in court; that doesn't mean you won't have trouble in the future.

1. Charge Drafting Principle #1: Follow the Golden Rule of Charge Drafting

The Golden Rule of charge drafting is "the simpler, the better, but include the who, where, when and what." All other rules flow from, or build on, this rule. The rule ensures all accused receive fair notice of the charges being faced. To give this notice, establish the court's jurisdiction over the alleged offence and offender, and set up the essential elements of the offence to be proved, the charge must answer the questions: *who* is the accused, *where* did the offence occur, *when* did it happen, and *what* is the nature of the offence. *How* exactly the offence transpired should *not* be included, unless required by the nature of the charge.

2. Charge Drafting Principle #2: Include the Who

Set out the accused's full legal name in the charge. If there is uncertainty over two or more names, include them all with the term "also known as" written between each name. A separate charge is not placed on an information for each accused alleged to have committed an identical offence; rather, a series of names can appear at the start of a single charge, with the next different charge listed in the information having a different set of names preceding it. Where a group of people are all charged with identical offences, then the names can simply be set out at the top of the information in one block, and the charges enumerated underneath. It is possible to mix and match this technique with say five names followed by two charges they all face, then two names followed by four charges those accused face, finally followed by a single name with a unique charge only faced by that person. This way all the charges in a case can fit on one information so long as there is a factual nexus among the offences and offenders for a single trial.

3. Charge Drafting Principle #3: Include the Where

Be as general about the place as is necessary to ensure all possible places of commission of the offence are covered, providing the territorial jurisdiction where the charge is to be laid is included. For example, in an immigration conspiracy case you could stipulate "did at the City of Vancouver, and elsewhere is British Columbia, and elsewhere in Canada and elsewhere in the world commit the offence of . . . ." Some offence locations like those committed on the water can pose special drafting challenges. Check the Act you are charging under for unique territorial terms that you may wish to refer to, like "within Canadian Fisheries Waters" or "within Canada's territorial sea" in conjunction with "adjacent to the province of (insert name of province)." As discussed in Chapter 13, even offence locations completely outside of Canada can amount to a sufficient place to anchor a charge if there is a statutory deeming provision giving a Canadian court jurisdiction over the facts of your case.

4. Charge Drafting Principle #4: Include the When

Use a wide date range if there is any doubt about the start or stop date of an offence, like "between 1 January 2005 and 31 December 2005." Courts tend not to be critical of wide date ranges so long as the accused receives fair notice of the offence charged. If you are certain about the precise date, then say something like "on the 2nd of July 2005." If citing an ongoing offence as having taken place between two or more exact dates, always use the term "(inclusive)" after the dates, otherwise the charge will not include the first and last dates you name.

5. Charge Drafting Principle #5: Include the What

a. *Getting the Citation Right*

Use the correct name and citation applicable to the Act or Regulation charged. Look near section one or two of an Act or Regulation for the short form way to cite it. Referring to the *Criminal Code of Canada* is a common mistake; s. 1 of that Act tells you its legal name is the *Criminal Code* and the preamble tells you its citation is "R.S.C. 1985, c. C-46." The name of an Act or Regulation is always rendered in italics, but the rest of the citation appears in plain text. In this age of computers underlining is no longer an acceptable substitute for italics, which were not available on most typewriters.

Use the proper citation *every time* an Act or Regulation is mentioned in the charge. I know I haven't done that in this book, but this is a less formal and much longer work than a charging information. The citation is necessary to distinguish among federal and provincial Acts or Regulations having similar names, and between older and newer versions of enactments.

For Acts, cite to the last Revised Statutes and include the specific chapter number. There is no need to list amendments or even to say "as amended"; incorporated amendments are considered to be implicit in the citation. For any federal Act in existence as of 1985 the citation will be "Revised Statutes of Canada 1985, chapter [*x*] ," which is abbreviated to "R.S.C. 1985, c. [*x*]." For federal Acts passed after 1985, cite to the sessional statutes where the Act first appears like "Statutes of Canada 1990, chapter [*x*]," which again is abbreviated to "S.C. 1990, c. [*x*]." Of course there is the odd exception to this rule, with a couple of frequently amended federal Acts being cited as a supplement to the 1985 Revised Statutes like the *Income Tax Act*, R.S.C. 1985, c. 1 (5th Supp.). Most provincial and territorial statutes follow similar forms of citation as federal statutes.

For federal Regulations, the form of citation is "Standing Orders and Regulations/[*x*]," abbreviated to "SOR/[*x*]." Note there are no periods between the letters SOR, in contrast to R.S.C., and a "/" instead of a space appears between the SOR and the number of the Regulation. You might occasionally see other ways of citing Acts and Regulations, but the one I'm showing you here is currently the most widely accepted Canadian standard. Forms of citation may evolve as we move to completely electronic statutes.

b. *Getting the Wording of the Charge Right*

Use as close as possible to the exact wording appearing in the Act or Regulation being charged. Make changes only for grammatical reasons like converting the present to past tense. If you essentially copy a charge right from the legislation, you will usually only have to insert names of accused, dates of commission, places of commission, and possibly a mode of commission. Charge drafting is not a place to get creative with your job — save that creativity for searching out evidence or questioning suspects.

The appropriate sections or sub-sections of an Act or Regulation need to be named so an accused knows precisely what she is accused of, and what punishment is faced. Each charge must refer to the prohibition contravened and the provision creating an offence for that contravention. Sometimes the prohibition and offence are contained within the same section or sub-section of an Act, like for forcible confinement under s-s. 279(2) of the *Criminal Code*:

> **279.** (2) Every one who, without lawful authority, confines, imprisons or forcibly seizes another person is guilty of
>
>> (a) an indictable offence and liable to imprisonment for a term not exceeding ten years; or
>>
>> (b) an offence punishable on summary conviction and liable to imprisonment for a term not exceeding eighteen months.

Here the charge would only need to refer to s-s. 279(2), and not further specify s-s. 279(2)(a) or s-s. 279(2)(b) because the discretion to make an election over whether to proceed by indictment or summary conviction lies with prosecutors.

At other times the prohibition and offence are separated by several sections of an Act, like for theft where s-s. 322(1) of the *Code* contains the basic prohibition:

> **322.** (1) Every one commits theft who fraudulently and without colour of right takes, or fraudulently and without colour of right converts to his use or to the use of another person, anything, whether animate or inanimate, with intent

(a) to deprive, temporarily or absolutely, the owner of it, or a person who has a special property or interest in it, of the thing or of his property or interest in it;

(b) to pledge it or deposit it as security;

(c) to part with it under a condition with respect to its return that the person who parts with it may be unable to perform; or

(d) to deal with it in such a manner that it cannot be restored in the condition in which it was at the time it was taken or converted.

Several sections later the offence of theft is created in s. 334:

334. Except where otherwise provided by law, every one who commits theft

(a) is guilty of an indictable offence and liable to imprisonment for a term not exceeding ten years, where the property stolen is a testamentary instrument or the value of what is stolen exceeds five thousand dollars; or

(b) is guilty

(i) of an indictable offence and is liable to imprisonment for a term not exceeding two years, or

(ii) of an offence punishable on summary conviction,

where the value of what is stolen does not exceed five thousand dollars.

Intervening between s. 322 and s. 334 of the *Code* are several sections that establish different kinds of specific theft prohibitions that legislators were presumably concerned might not be covered by the general s. 322, as well as some operational provisions setting out under what kinds of conditions theft may occur.

Both ss. 322 and 334 of the *Code* need to be referenced in a charge for theft. Section 322 without s. 334 only tells you a theft may have occurred, but not that an indictable or summary charge can be laid as a result. Section 334 without s. 322 tells you punishments are available for theft, but does not describe what one must have done to merit those punishments. Investigators can elect to lay the s-s. 334(a) charge of theft over $5000 if the facts support it, which will by default make it a straight indictable offence, but a s-s. 333(b) charge should not be further particularized to s-ss. 333(b)(i) or 334(b)(ii).

If you have doubts over which sub-section is applicable to a charge, cite to the appropriate section and not the sub-section. It is better to be a bit too general, rather than charging the wrong offence or only naming the punishment sub-section instead of the substantive offence. To use a s. 322 *Code* theft example again, there is no need to specify a s-s. 322(1)(c) prohibition in order to have a valid charge. Citing s-s. 322(1) should be sufficient, although you could particularize s-s. 322(1)(c) if you are absolutely certain it is the only mode of commission of theft that may have transpired in your case. Some statutory provisions are relevant to whether an offence took place by serving as interpretive aids or deeming devices, but should not be cited as part of a charging document — for example s. 323 of the *Code* aids the prosecution of oyster theft by clarifying property and jurisdictional issues.

Contravention of a Regulation must be tied back to an offence creating section in an Act. For example, s. 43 of the *Maritime Provinces Fishery Regulations*, SOR/93-55 says:

> **43.** (1) Subject to subsection (2), no person shall fish for gaspereau in the inland waters of Nova Scotia by any means other than angling during the period beginning at sunset and ending at sunrise.
>
> (2) Subsection (1) does not apply in the inland waters of Halifax and Yarmouth Counties to a person who holds a licence to fish for gaspereau with a dip net at a dip stand.

You won't find any offence-creating language in the Regulations; you have to look to s. 78 of the *Fisheries Act*, R.S.C. 1985, c. F-14, for that: "Except as otherwise provided in this Act, every person who contravenes this Act or the regulations is guilty of . . . ."

6. Charge Drafting Principle #6: Usually Do Not Include the How

Do not specify the exact mode of commission or factual details of an offence in the charging information unless required by the type of charge. The offence details will be included as part of disclosure. Significant factual detail placed inside the language of a charge could lead to an acquittal if the evidence at trial supports contradictory details. For example, for a charge involving theft of an automobile do not specify the VIN or plate number in the charge — these are factual details useful to prove the offence in court, but not essential elements of the offence. Likewise, specifying how a robbery was committed or how a drug was trafficked just isn't necessary in a charge, but don't confuse an unnecessary *how* with a necessary *what*, like what type of drug was trafficked. The *what* can affect which charge may be laid and the penalties flowing from it, whereas the *how* will usually only be part of the trial evidence.

7. Charge Drafting Principle # 7: Globalize Charges

Global charges are those involving a date range, like "did commit fraud between date x and date y." Where multiple occurrences of the same offence are alleged to have been committed by the same individual(s) over a period of time, consider globalizing all the charges into one charge with a broader date range. Globalizing charges greatly simplifies prosecutions, maximizes prospects of conviction, and does not undermine the sentencing tariff.

When globally charging, there is nothing wrong with charging as many *different types* of offences as possible. What global charging does not do is charge the *same offence* over and over again distinguished only on the basis of date (or occasionally on the basis of some other repetitive factor like identical item stolen). The two factors governing when a globalized charge will be appropriate are penalty sufficiency and charge complexity.

Globalize where the maximum available penalty for one count is considerably above the total penalty sought for all combined counts, so long as the charge does not become too complicated to understand because of the number of modes or places of commission and accused. As a prosecutor I liked to recommend globalization where the aggregate penalty available for all charges exceeded the penalty sought by at least 100%. For example, where an individual is likely to receive a fine in the $50,000 range for a set of offences, and the maximum penalty available is $100,000 per count, laying 20 identical charges covering different dates with a combined maximum possible penalty of $2 million is overkill. One count with a request for a fine at 50% of the maximum level is sufficient. But if you decided $100,000 was the appropriate and likely fine to be imposed, you should not globalize down to one charge as it is highly unlikely a fine at 100% of the maximum will be imposed since it is reserved for the worst offence committed by the worst offender. Instead, you might distill those 20 charges to two or three charges putting you back at the 50% fine level.

The "not putting all your eggs in one basket" principle could, however, favour laying more than one or two counts. A compromise between pure global charging and maximizing charge numbers is to group date ranges. If illegal transactions occurred throughout the course of a year, five transactions could be listed as one charge from 1 January to 30 April, four included in a second charge from 1 May to 31 August, and two included in a 1 September to 31 December charge.

Not globalizing charges is only acceptable if the number of counts remains reasonable. I once was faced with an information containing 865 counts of alleged breaches of the *Copyright Act*, which was definitely not manageable. One charge had been laid for each pirated music CD copy seized. The charging information was spiral-bound and the arraignment would have taken a good part of the morning if it hadn't been waived. Instead of laying one count for every illegal copy, investigators could have just grouped the charges as one count for each different CD recording seized leading to about 12 charges with a very adequate maximum total available fine of $12 million, rather than $865 million.

8. Charge Drafting Principle #8: Charge Jointly

Always jointly charge multiple accused and multiple offences on one information, so long as there is a factual nexus among the accused and the offences charged. For example, acts of civil disobedience committed by five protesters who each individually caused damage to five different vehicles during the same march on the same street within a 20-minute period should be jointly charged. But all accused on the same information need *not* be charged with the same offences.

In theory an unlimited number of accused and charges can be listed on a single information, but practically speaking I like to keep the number to about 20 accused and 100 charges because beyond that point a case tends to collapse under its own weight of courtrooms full of defence lawyers, a proliferation of motions, and practical evidence presentation difficulties. Numbers lower than the 20-100 guide are preferable. Keeping charge and accused numbers down can be done through global charging and by dividing large numbers of accused into smaller groupings on separate informations according to some common element like date, place or type of offence.

Don't initially put accused on separate informations solely for the purpose of being able to call one accused as a witness against other accused at their separate trials, unless you have already secured a compelling statement from one of them that is crucial to proof of the case against the others. More often, separate charging is a futile attempt to salvage a marginal case by hoping one accused will incriminate the others, even though no solid incriminating statement has been taken. If the prosecution does later decide to call one accused against the others, charges can be severed or a completely new information laid if limitation periods have not run out.

Charging each accused on a separate information can cause a series of related prosecutions to self-destruct due to delay. I became involved in one set of regulatory offence cases where approximately 50 separate trials needed to take place because investigators had laid 50 separate informations. Around eight months after the offences were committed, only three trials had started (and none had finished) in a rural area where only one provincial court judge regularly sat. All the cases, other than those whose trials had already commenced, wound up being stayed by the court for unreasonable delay contrary to the *Charter*. Since the cases involved connected offences allegedly committed as a protest against government regulation, investigators could have laid two or three informations grouping accused by geographical location of protest and greatly shortened the trial time required.

Calculating Charge Numbers

Q&A

Q: For statistical purposes we keep track of how many charges each of us lay in my office. My supervisor is reluctant to embrace the suggestion of global charges on joint informations for multiple accused. In many of our cases, following that practice would lead to only one or two charges being laid, even when there are twenty accused. Is there any way to increase the charge numbers?

A: Global and joint charging are more issues of form rather than substance. If twenty accused appear on one information charged with the same offence, then in substance there are at least twenty charges there but only one charge will be listed as a matter of form. For statistical purposes it is fair to count a joint or global charge as a separate count against each accused who faces that charge.

9. Charge Drafting Principle #9: Consider Multiple Offence Charging

As an investigator, your charging discretion may let you lay many different charges against the same individual arising out of the same incident.

Multiple offence charging, where possible and appropriate, maximizes prospects for conviction on at least some counts. I am by no means advocating overcharging, since doing so leads to the two or three strongest charges being lost among and undermined by the dozen weak charges. Laying multiple charges relating to the same act committed in a single time frame may not significantly improve sentence prospects because concurrent sentences could be given for a single set of facts. Demystification of the law enables you to be aware of the variety of offences that might be charged, while early investigator-prosecutor contact will ensure you have help in picking the best offences to charge.

Laying Multiple Charges in One Information

Q&A

Q: I want to charge five accused all on one information, but the local justice of the peace has refused to swear the information, claiming at most two people can be charged in one information because that is all there is space for in the standard information form used in our jurisdiction. To avoid trouble, should I just do as she says and hope the informations can be joined together later?

A: The justice of the peace has a misconception about the law. Charging multiple accused on one information only requires a sufficient factual nexus among the accused and their offences. If, after discussing the situation with the JP, she is still not willing to swear the single information, you could go and locate another JP to swear it out. This second JP should be informed of what transpired with the first JP. A prosecutor could also be contacted to make legal representations to the JP on why a joint information is a proper procedure in your case.

10. Charge Drafting Principle #10: Exercise Charging Discretion over Who to Charge

While the justice system would break down if everyone was charged in every case with every possible offence, no one need be automatically eliminated from charging consideration just because of falling into a particular category like "corporation," or "passenger" or "young person." Those directly participating in an offence, aiding or abetting an offence, or conspiring to commit an offence may be candidates for charging. Because s. 21 of the *Criminal Code* deems those aiding or abetting to be principals to an offence, no one is ever charged as aiding or abetting. Unlike aiding and abetting, conspiracy to commit any offence under a federal Act is a separate charge under s. 465 of the *Code*, but investigators need to decide where to draw the line in naming co-conspirators, and whether it is worth laying conspiracy charges if it is easier to prove the substantive offence. When an organization like a corporation is to be charged, consider if it is appropriate to also jointly charge at least one natural person like the president or a manager closely involved with the offence to avoid the organization being dissolved to escape punishment. The strength of the case and the public interest govern who should be charged.

11. Charge Drafting Principle #11: Use the Simplest Language Possible

Track the language the legislation uses to create the prohibition and offence whenever you draft a charge, making sure all essential elements are included. Adding extraneous wording is dangerous. At best a court may become confused by the extra words, and at worst will interpret them as essential elements the prosecution must prove. You can state alternative modes of commission for an offence within the same charge, or break the alternative modes up into separate charges if that is easier to understand — a prosecutor will usually only seek conviction on one of the alternatives as supported by the evidence, but the trial could proceed on all alternate charges.

12. Charge Drafting Principle #12: Put It All Together

The Charge Drafting Checklist, at the end of this chapter, includes all the principles mentioned above. The general formula to use for putting a charge together is: "That [name of accused], at or near [place of offence], on or about [date of offence], did [describe offence], contrary to s. [specify section and name of Act, Regulation or other provision contravened], thereby committing on offence under s. [list offence creating section and name of Act]." There is no need to refer in the charge to the sections of an Act that promulgate Regulations, to variation orders that modify a particular Regulation, to amendments that have changed the wording of an Act, to schedules or appendices to an Act, or to any other additions to an Act. Simply state the offence in its current form.

Amending Charges

Q & A

Q: I was reaching the end of the six month limitation period to lay a summary charge of forgery, so I quickly drafted an information and had it sworn. I've now discovered that not only did I misspell the accused's name, I also cited the section of the *Criminal Code* for high treason, not forgery. I did use the word "forgery" when drafting the charge. It is now past the six month limitation. Should I tell the prosecutor to forget about the case because of the defective information?

A: The powers of a court to amend an information are very broad. Only informations that constitute absolute nullities can't be amended. In this case, so long as the accused received fair notice of the charge, amendment should be possible.

DECIDING ON AND DRAFTING CONSPIRACY CHARGES

During the early stages of an investigation it will sometimes not matter whether you are investigating a true conspiracy in the legal sense, or just a group of people cooperating in some way to commit an illegal act, but a decision on whether conspiracy charges are legally supportable needs to be made at the charging stage. *R. v. Carter*, [1982] 1 S.C.R. 938 at para. 86, set out the definition of conspiracy:

> A conspiracy consists not merely in the intention of two or more, but in the agreement of two or more to do an unlawful act, or to do a lawful act by unlawful means. So long as such a design rests in intention only, it is not indictable. When two agree to carry it into effect, the very plot is an act in itself, and the act of each of the parties . . . punishable for a criminal object.

Members of a conspiracy need not know about each other's existence and a conspiracy's membership can change over time while still constituting the same conspiracy. Multiple interlinked conspiracies might be charged on a single information, although conspirator triage is advisable so only the most important conspirators are charged with the most provable offences.

The "Carter Test" requires three questions be positively answered to establish membership of an accused in a conspiracy.

1. On all of the evidence, is it proved beyond a reasonable doubt that the conspiracy as charged existed?

2. Based on the evidence independently admissible against each accused, was the accused on a balance of probabilities a member of the conspiracy?

3. Based on the acts and declarations of all the conspirators in further-ance of the conspiracy, is membership of the individual in the con-spiracy proven beyond a reasonable doubt?

The test means you cannot use the statements of one member of the con-spiracy as the sole proof of membership of another member of the conspir-acy — the other members must do or say something that shows them at least on a balance of probabilities to also be members.

It may not be worth charging anyone with conspiracy if there are other easier to prove substantive charges that can be laid. Although the s. 465 *Criminal Code* conspiracy offence can be charged for conspiring to violate any federal Act, the punishment under s. 465 is no greater than the punish-ment available for the substantive offence being conspired about:

> **465.** (1). . . (c) every one who conspires with any one to commit an indictable offence not provided for in paragraph (a) [murder] or (b) [false prosecution] is guilty of an indictable offence and liable to the same punishment as that to which an accused who is guilty of that offence would, on conviction, be liable; and

> (d) every one who conspires with any one to commit an offence punishable on summary conviction is guilty of an offence punishable on summary conviction.

Conspiracy charges are most useful for a "dry conspiracy" like importing drugs where the drugs never actually arrive in Canada and where not all individuals involved in the conspiracy directly committed the substantive offence — but consider whether they alternately can be linked-in as aiders or abettors. When conspiracy charges are chosen and substantive charges also laid, at least you can fall back on the substantive charges if proof of conspiracy fails.

The place of offence and location of accused capable of supporting con-spiracy charges is very broad, with s. 465 of the *Code* making it an offence to conspire:

- within Canada to commit any indictable or summary offence, even an offence planned to take place outside Canada, so long as the planned act is an offence under the law of the intended place of commission and the conspirator is located in Canada;

- to commit any indictable or summary offence, even if the conspirator is located outside Canada, so long as the planned act is to take place inside Canada.

Where there is an alleged conspiracy to commit an act outside of Canada, or by a conspirator located outside Canada, charges for that conspiracy can be laid anywhere in Canada. The location of a transnational conspiracy need not always be precisely defined, so long as investigators can establish a substantial link with Canada.

COMPELLING COURT ATTENDANCE

Some legal process is required to compel an accused to attend a court appearance after a charge is laid. Without that process, there is no recourse if the accused doesn't show up to answer the charge. As described in Chapter 11, the options available are the promise to appear, the appearance notice, the recognizance, the summons and the arrest warrant. Section 507 of the *Criminal Code* gives the option to either seek a summons or warrant to arrest from the judicial official before whom you are swearing out a charging information, but unless you can offer compelling evidence of why "it is in the public interest to issue a warrant for the arrest of the accused" you will only get a summons, whose precise content and means of service are specified in s. 509 of the *Code*.

A summons is the principal means of compelling a corporation or other organization to attend court to answer a charge since an organization is not capable of being arrested. Sections 621, 623 and 800 of the *Code* go so far as to authorize the *ex parte* trial of an organization that does not show in response to a properly served summons. Section 703.2 of the *Code* specifies the people on whom service of a summons (or other legal document connected to a prosecution) will constitute personal service on an organization:

> **703.2** Where any summons, notice or other process is required to be or may be served on an organization, and no other method of service is provided, service may be effected by delivery
>
> > (a) in the case of a municipality, to the mayor, warden, reeve or other chief officer of the municipality, or to the secretary, treasurer or clerk of the municipality; and
> >
> > (b) in the case of any other organization, to the manager, secretary or other senior officer of the organization or one of its branches.

Before attending at the offices of an organization, investigators should figure out through a corporate or Internet search exactly who are the appropriate senior officers. The summons will not be validly served if it is only left with a receptionist.

THE NOTICE OF INTENT TO SEEK GREATER PUNISHMENT

The notice of intent to seek greater punishment by reason of prior conviction required by s-s. 727(1) of the *Criminal Code* opens a new world of sentencing options for certain offences:

> **727.** (1) . . . where an offender is convicted of an offence for which a greater punishment may be imposed by reason of previous convictions, no greater punishment shall be imposed on the offender by reason thereof unless the prosecutor satisfies the court that the offender, before making a plea, was notified that a greater punishment would be sought be reason thereof.

While Chapter 17 deals with the five other most common pretrial notices investigators may be required to prepare or serve, the notice of intent to seek greater punishment is a pre-plea notice required so long before trial that it really must be dealt with at the charging stage of a case. Giving this notice for a second offence could, for example, mean mandatory imprisonment for at least fourteen days in the case of the s-s. 255(1)(a)(ii) *Criminal Code* offence of driving while impaired, as compared to only a mandatory fine on a first offence. Even greater disparities can exist between sentences available for first and subsequent regulatory offences, like two years imprisonment becoming available under s. 78 of the *Fisheries Act* for a second offence, as opposed to no imprisonment for a first offence.

There is no specified form for the notice to seek greater punishment, but you must be able to later prove it was given to an accused. If you discover from checking an accused's prior record that a notice to seek greater punishment is required, the four options open on or before the first court date (when a plea might be entered) are:

- provide a written notice directly to the accused;

- provide the prosecutor with a written notice to give to the defence;

- indicate to the prosecutor as part of the prosecution brief that a notice to seek greater punishment must be given to the accused; or

- tell the prosecutor about the need to inform the accused verbally on the record in open court about the intention to seek greater punishment.

Each of these options has advantages and limitations, depending on if and how investigators interact with prosecutors before or at first court appearances. Ideally, the notice requires prosecutor input, must be consistently given in a timely way for appropriate cases, not lead to the prosecutor becoming a potential witness to the notice, and not unduly add to investigator workloads. Definitely do not assume just because you include the criminal record of the accused at page 47 of the 68-page prosecution brief that a prosecutor will have time or even think to check the brief to see if a notice to seek greater punishment should be given prior to plea.

SPEAKING TO THE MEDIA

The investigation and laying of serious charges, or any charges involving prominent individuals or organizations, can trigger media demands for information. Part of the process of putting a more human face on government, including the justice system, has been to provide the public with information about government's internal workings. A very fine line needs to be walked in any media communications concerning active cases between providing enough information so the media can accurately inform the public, and not providing so much information or information with a "spin" on it that the accused's fair trial rights or anyone's privacy rights are prejudiced.

1. The Rise of Media-Friendly Communications Policies

The many prosecution services and investigative agencies operating in Canada have differing media relations policies, but it seems moving towards more open media relations is a general trend as expressed in the *Federal Prosecution Service Deskbook*, loose-leaf (Ottawa: Supply and Services Canada, 2000) at chapter 10:

> The obligation of the justice system to inform the public is an essential ingredient of a fair and equitable justice system. In February 1998, the Minister of Justice affirmed this principle by publicly stating that it is a priority for the Department of Justice to restore the public's confidence in the system of criminal justice.

Public confidence in the administration of justice depends on access to full and accurate information on court proceedings. A misinformed media can convey misleading messages, thereby undermining public confidence.

By providing appropriate information, Crown counsel can help ensure that citizens have a fair opportunity to determine whether the justice system is functioning effectively.

In the past, communications with the media have largely been handled by official spokespersons. Crown counsel, who are often the most knowledgeable persons about the information requested, should be able to respond directly, to ensure that accurate information is presented to the public.

Subject to the overriding duty to the administration of justice to ensure that trials are fair, Crown counsel are encouraged to provide the media with timely, complete and accurate information on matters relating to the administration of criminal justice in which the Attorney General of Canada is involved.

The goal of the policy is to enhance public understanding of, and confidence in, the administration of justice by providing available information. Crown counsel should respond to all reasonable requests for such information.

The only way to ensure balanced media coverage of a case is for investigators or prosecutors to respond in a meaningful but measured way to media inquiries. Such responses could range from providing basic facts already in the public domain, to briefly setting out the legal issues at play, to explaining the procedural chronology of a case.

2. The Inherent Dangers in Media Communications about an Ongoing Case

There are two overriding dangers in any media communication connected to a case:

- expressing an opinion about the guilt of the accused;

- revealing facts only available through disclosure not in the public domain.

Investigators or prosecutors who offer an opinion about the guilt of the accused signal they may have been biased in conducting their investigation or prosecution since ultimate guilt or innocence is something only a court can determine. Revealing facts investigators have learned in the course of their investigation may breach the accused's or a third party's privacy, breach a privilege, contaminate the minds of potential witnesses and jurors, runs the risk of getting the facts wrong, and could even amount to libel or slander.

Holding a news conference or sending out a press release at the time seizures or arrests occur, or charges are laid, can be very flashy from a publicity perspective, but very damaging to prospects of conviction. It is not in the public interest to avoid these dangers by always remaining mute in the face of media inquiries, but an appropriate middle ground to take in media friendly communications is sticking to reactive communications that only respond to media inquiries prior to the trial court rendering final judgment. Save proactive communications until after conviction or acquittal, when they can be a great aid to sentencing objectives like general deterrence.

In *Uni-Jet Industrial Pipe Ltd. v. Canada (Attorney General)* (2001), 156 Man. R. (2d) 14; 2001 MBCA 40 at paras. 2-6, $65,000 in damages (including punitive damages) were awarded when a senior investigator tipped off journalists that search warrants were being executed at particular businesses, thus generating considerable adverse publicity for the business owners even though charges were never laid:

> The defendant Staff Sgt. J. . . . was a designated media relations officer . . ., and it is his conduct with which we are concerned. . . .

> On May 23, 1997, R. . . was an investigator in the Commercial Crimes Section . . . . He obtained warrants for a search of the premises of the plaintiffs (Baziuk and Uni-Jet) and two other companies engaged in the sewer contracting business. The warrants were in furtherance of an investigation into allegations of fraud respecting sewer construction jobs in several urban and rural municipalities in Manitoba.

> On the morning of May 26, 1997, based on information received from R. . ., J. . ., unsolicited and on his own initiative, volunteered to three of his media contacts that the search warrants were about to be or were in the course of being executed. There was no denial by J. . . that, as was suggested to him in cross-examination, his objective was to curry favour and enhance his own relationship with the working press.

> The alerted journalists and photographers attended upon the plaintiffs' premises that same morning. Subsequently thereto there was extensive reporting of the event including newspaper stories, pho-

tographs and television coverage describing police officers carrying boxes out of the premises. . . .

> It was not until mid-February 1998 that the plaintiffs or the public were advised that no charges would be laid against Baziuk personally or his corporation. The plaintiffs believe that they have been aggrieved by J. . .'s conduct and have claimed general, punitive, exemplary and special damages, since it is not contested that people in the construction industry, customers and friends of the plaintiffs were aware of what was happening as a result of the media coverage.

The plaintiff relied upon the Operational Manual of the police service involved for the quite reasonable general principles: "Do not reveal the names of suspects until charges have been laid" and "Ensure the information released to the media does not . . . result in injury, injustice or embarrassment to the innocent or accused."

Improper disclosures in proactive pretrial media communications can play a role in trial court assessment of whether investigators were acting in good faith throughout an investigation, like in *R. v. Wise*, [1992] 1 S.C.R. 527 at 571:

> It might be noted that the search in this case appears to have been part of a larger pattern of disregard for the appellant's rights. The police actually held a press conference where they all but identified the appellant as a suspect (the press identified him the next day) even though they admitted that they did not have enough evidence at that time to arrest him. The appellant was, not surprisingly, "hounded" by the media from that point forward.

A pretrial press conference can also trigger a trial being moved to another venue at great expense, as occurred in *R. v. Feeney*, 1998 CarswellBC 347 (S.C.) at paras. 1-3:

> We all know, of course, and it is very basic, that persons ought to be tried in the community in which the crime was alleged to have occurred. It is, until recently at least, a rare thing for that not to occur. We go to a great deal of trouble to ensure that the justice system applies on a universal basis and that the rules are the same whether it be in Fort St. John or in Cranbrook.

> There are situations, of course, where it is not possible to try persons in the community in which the alleged crime occurred because of circumstances. In recent times, for example, the . . . Police have, in various communities and probably for various reasons have held, what I refer to, as a press conference sometime

during the investigatory stage of a crime, and generally speaking, that press conference is publicized throughout the province by television. I personally have been involved in three or four applications, perhaps more, where defence counsel apply for a change of venue when that occurs, and on each occasion the defence have been successful in persuading me that the trial ought not to take place in the area where that press conference was held which is in the area where the alleged crime occurred. I do not know why it is necessary for there to be press conferences either by the police or counsel or anybody else in cases of this nature.

I have made my objections known, they are on the record, and the police, for whatever reason, persist in this sort of activity. As recently as this morning, I made an order moving a trial again from Williams Lake to Vancouver for precisely that reason. It is a very, very important case. . . for the community. It is again a murder case. There was a great deal of animosity expressed by members of the community, but I am convinced from the material that was filed in that case, a lot of the animosity was due to the sort of activities that the police engaged in during the investigatory stage.

The best way to ensure smooth media relations in the course of investigations and prosecutions is through development of a joint investigator-prosecutor media strategy.

3. Developing a Joint Investigator-Prosecutor Media Strategy

The need for an advance media strategy, combined with restraint, was recognized in the *Memorandum of Understanding Between the Royal Canadian Mounted Police and the Federal Prosecution Service Respecting the Conduct of Criminal Investigations and Prosecutions* (5 July 2001):

8.1 The parties recognize the need for a comprehensive and cooperative media strategy.

8.2 Absent compelling circumstances, the parties do not comment publicly on ongoing investigations.

A media strategy can set out in advance the boundaries of what may be said to the media about investigations or prosecutions, and who will say it. While not commenting on ongoing investigations is usually an easy enough principle to agree to, a number of other media situations also need advance agreement.

- Can overall strategies taken to combat particular forms of crime be discussed?

- Can anything be said when charges are laid?

- How can the risk of prejudice to ongoing investigations be minimized when speaking about related charges?

- What can be said about the court process a case is following?

- Can anything be said about broader policy issues in a case?

- Should it be investigators or prosecutors who comment on particular aspects of a case?

- At which point will the risk of prejudice to a case from media communications have passed?

For routine cases a generic strategy can be applied, but for high-profile cases investigators and prosecutors should discuss developing a case-specific media strategy.

When a decision is made to communicate with the media, all information must be delivered in a timely manner or it will lose its value once a story deadline is missed. No "off the record" comments should be offered, since it is easy to question the motives of an official who is willing to share information but not his name, and it is also easy for misunderstandings to develop so what was thought off the record is really on the record and makes the front page of the next day's newspaper. "No comment" is never an appropriate answer, since it appears the person giving such an answer is trying to hide something — instead, a comment explaining why a question cannot be answered at this time is more appropriate. Be particularly diligent in determining whether a total or partial court imposed publication ban or statutory information disclosure affects the proceedings before saying anything.

Restricting What Is Said to the Media

Q & A

Q: Doesn't the public have a right to know about offences committed in the community, who committed them, and what the authorities are doing to deal with those offences?

A: Most certainly the public interest does favour disclosure to the public of case facts, but until those facts are proven in court they are only allegations. Sometimes evidence at trial comes out quite differently than anyone anticipated. Both investigators and prosecutors need to be very careful about what they say to the media so as not to prejudice an accused's or anyone else's rights. Cases need to be tried in courts of law, not in courts of public opinion.

For Deciding to Charge, Charge Drafting, and Speaking to the Media

KEY POINTS

✓ Before laying a charge ask yourself whether there is a reasonable prospect of conviction and will a prosecution be in the public interest.

✓ The timing of when charges should be laid must balance being within the limitation period, and not proceeding until the investigation, prosecution brief and disclosure package are as complete as possible in the circumstances. There is no limitation period for indictable offences, but for summary offences the limitation period could be under six months. Avoid limitation periods contingent on Ministerial knowledge of an offence. Pre-charge delay is generally irrelevant, whereas post-charge delay is very relevant.

✓ Use you own skills and judgment to draft charges in as simple a manner as possible — include the who, where, when and what, but usually not the how. Consider globalizing date ranges of identical offences into one charge, charging multiple accused jointly on one information possibly with multiple different offences, charging a natural person where an organization is to be charged, charging those aiding or abetting an offence as principals, and whether conspiracy charges are appropriate.

✓ Pick the most appropriate means to compel an accused's attendance in court from among the promise to appear, appearance notice, recognizance, summons or arrest warrant.

✓ Speaking to the media about ongoing investigations or prosecutions must be approached with extreme caution. The rise of media friendly communication policies dictate that the media be provided with relevant case information when possible, but any information provided prior to conviction runs the risks of prejudicing the accused's trial and breaching the privacy of both accused and third parties. Expressing an opinion about the guilt of the accused or revealing information not in the public domain can be particularly damaging. Engaging only in reactive rather than proactive media communications will greatly lessen the risks, as will developing a joint investigator-prosecutor media strategy.

CHARGE DRAFTING CHECKLIST

A — GOLDEN RULE

- ❏ Charge drafted as simply as possible with no unnecessary details included
    - ❏ "Who" specified
        - ❏ Accused's full legal name indicated
        - ❏ Also-known-as used if uncertainty over name
    - ❏ "Where" specified (location or jurisdiction)
    - ❏ "When" specified (date(s) of offence)
        - ❏ Term "inclusive" used when citing between exact dates
    - ❏ "What" specified
        - ❏ Exact wording of charge taken from Act or Regulations, with changes made only for grammatical reasons
        - ❏ Correct citation used for Act or Regulation (e.g. R.S.C. 1985, c.____ or SOR/____)
    - ❏ "How" only specified if required by nature of offence

B — STANDARD FORMAT

- ❏ Standard format of charge drafting followed:

    "That (name of accused) on or between (date(s) of offence) at or near (place of offence) did (describe offence) contrary to (section, subsection, name and citation of Act or Regulation contravened), thereby committing an offence under (section, subsection, name and citation of Act that actually creates offence for provision contravened)."

C — OTHER NECESSARY CONSIDERATIONS

- ❏ Considered charge globalization using broad date range
- ❏ All accused engaged in common action jointly charged on one information
    - ❏ Very large numbers of accused broken up into separate charging groups on separate informations according to common elements
- ❏ Considered multiple offence charging
- ❏ Those aiding or abetting charged as principals to offence
- ❏ Considered also charging natural person where corporation or other organization to be charged
- ❏ Where conspiracy charges to be laid, substantive offence charges considered as an addition or alternative
- ❏ Whether proceeding by indictment or summarily not specified in charges
- ❏ Limitation periods checked

FURTHER READING

Cases

R. v. Carter, [1982] 1 S.C.R. 938. Conviction on a conspiracy charge requires three stages of proof: proof of the existence of a conspiracy, proof of probable membership of the accused in the conspiracy based solely on that accused's acts and declarations, and then proof of the accused's membership in that same conspiracy beyond a reasonable doubt based on the acts and declarations of all conspirators.

R. v. Moore, [1988] 1 S.C.R. 1097; *R. v. Webster*, [1993] 1 S.C.R. 3. A technically defective information can be cured by amendment, unless it fails to give the accused fair notice of the offence and thus amendment would work an injustice.

Books, Articles and Reports

T. Brucker, *The Practical Guide to the Controlled Drugs and Substances Act*, 3rd ed. (Carswell, 2002). Outlines all the fundamentals of drug charges.

E.G. Ewaschuk, *Criminal Pleadings and Practice in Canada*, 2nd ed., loose-leaf (Aurora, ON: Canada Law Book, 1997). See particularly Chapter 9 ("Form and Content"), Chapter 10 ("The Information") and Chapter 11 ("Preferring Indictments").

B.A. Grosman, *Discretion in the Initiation of Criminal Proceedings* (Ottawa: Law Reform Commission of Canada, 1974).

P. Harris, *Weapons Offences Manual*, loose-leaf (Aurora, ON: Canada Law Book, 1990). Covers the elements of all weapons charges.

W. Holland, *The Law of Theft and Related Offences* (Toronto: Carswell, 1998). Explains the different modes of commission and legal requirements for proof of theft charges.

Law Reform Commission of Canada, *Working Paper No. 55 — The Charge Document in Criminal Cases* (Ottawa: Law Reform Commission of Canada, 1987). Recommends simplification of the current distinctions between informations and indictments to establish a common "charge document."

Law Reform Commission of Canada, *Working Paper No. 52 — Private Prosecutions* (Law Reform Commission of Canada, 1986). Advocates expanding the rights of private prosecutors.

D. Layton, "The Prosecutorial Charging Decision" (2002) 46 Crim. L.Q. 447.

R. Libman, *Libman on Regulatory Offences*, loose-leaf (Saltspring Island, BC: Earlscourt, 2003). Provides a detailed discussion of regulatory charge elements.

B. MacFarlane, R. Frater and C. Proulx, *Drug Offences in Canada*, 3rd ed., loose-leaf (Aurora, ON: Canada Law Book, 1996). Long the standard work on drug charges in Canada.

McGill Law Journal, *Canadian Guide to Uniform Legal Citation*, 6th ed. (Toronto: Carswell, 2006). Forms of citation for Acts and Regulations.

B. Nightingale, *The Law of Fraud and Related Offences*, loose-leaf (Toronto: Carswell, 2000). Focuses on the elements required to prove fraud charges.

J. Swaigen, *Regulatory Offences in Canada: Liability and Defences* (Carswell, 1992). Discusses the elements of regulatory charges.

CHAPTER FIFTEEN

PREPARING A COMPLETE PROSECUTION BRIEF THAT STILL MAKES SENSE

The RCMP provide prosecutors with appropriate briefs in a timely way. The obligation to provide all relevant reports and briefs continues throughout the judicial phase.

> *Memorandum of Understanding Between the Royal Canadian Mounted Police and the Federal Prosecution Service Respecting the Conduct of Criminal Investigations and Prosecutions* (5 July 2001) at 3.1.14.

In This Chapter

- Minimum prosecution brief contents
- Exceptions to inclusions in the prosecution brief
- What the brief should look like
- Being more efficient through rolling briefs and protocols

The prosecution brief is the culmination and distillation of hours, weeks or sometimes years of hard investigative work. The importance of the brief cannot be stressed enough. It doesn't matter how good the evidence is if it is not accurately and clearly presented in the brief. A prosecutor might have to make a quick decision on the merits of proceeding with a case; all that prosecutor will usually have on which to base the decision to proceed is the brief you provided. The realities of prosecutors carrying heavy case-loads, and sometimes not being assigned to a case until the night before trial, means there may be little or no other investigator-prosecutor contact prior to trial than through the written prosecution brief.

The prosecution brief will also later be the basis for the disclosure package provided to the defence. Incomplete prosecution briefs lead to incomplete disclosure. Incomplete disclosure can in turn result in a judicial stay of proceedings for breach of the accused's right to make full answer and defence under the *Charter*. It is not sufficient to provide a skimpy prosecution brief in the hope the accused will plead guilty, with the intention of eventually getting around to putting together a more complete disclosure package. All a skimpy brief will guarantee is that prosecutors won't have a clue what your case is about, won't understand the importance of the charges, and if prosecutors don't drop your insubstantial looking case, they still won't have any foundation on which to base solid sentencing submissions should a guilty plea take place.

The exact categories of information included in a prosecution brief vary depending on the offence charged and law enforcement agency preparing the brief, but there are good practices common to the preparation of all briefs. Every brief has a similar aim: to quickly and comprehensively inform a prosecutor who has never seen the case before what it is all about, and how proof of the offences charged can best be offered in court. This chapter does *not* describe a wish list for a prosecution brief, but rather the bare minimum brief contents necessary for prosecutors to be able to take a case to trial.

Over the years of working as a prosecutor I slowly learned about the various practical and systemic difficulties that can make brief and disclosure production an extremely difficult task from the investigator perspective. I learned that there was nothing to gain from developing an adversarial relationship with investigators over briefs and disclosure — my adversarial relationships with defence counsel and occasionally with the courts were enough to contend with. But prosecution brief and disclosure completeness remain a great source of frustration for investigators and prosecutors alike, so be prepared for tension to arise, and think about how you might defuse that tension. Investigators and prosecutors have the right to demand respect from each other in the course of requests for additional brief or disclosure information, or explanations of why that material cannot be provided. I found in-person meetings or teleconferences to resolve disagreements much more fruitful than simply trading increasingly curt letters or e-mails.

The Prosecution Brief and Disclosure Package Checklist, at the end of this chapter, will help you check off initial prosecution brief requirements and eventual disclosure delivery needs in one complete form. Show the checklist to the prosecutors you work with to determine if there are things not listed there that they require, or things listed that they don't require. Better yet, jointly develop a negotiated prosecution brief and disclosure checklist with those prosecutors.

Prosecution Briefs and Guilty Pleas

Q&A

Q: If I know the accused if going to plead guilty, why do I have to prepare a prosecution brief at all? Even if I need a brief, why do I need to include all the detail you are suggesting here?

A: A prosecutor will not be able to give you an informed opinion about whether your case meets the threshold required to take it to court without having *all* the facts. Even if you can convince a prosecutor to look at a case without having a full brief, it is much more likely the prosecutor will find the case does not meet the required tests for prosecution if pieces of evidence are missing. The lack of a complete brief could mean a case does not even get to a first appearance where an accused could plead guilty. In addition, prudent defence counsel will not suggest a guilty plea to a client until the disclosure package has been reviewed. Where an accused does plead guilty, an incomplete brief can lead to a low sentence being imposed due to inability of the prosecutor to provide evidence of prior offences or properly articulate the facts supporting the seriousness of the offence. Most importantly, you can never be sure an accused will plead guilty.

MINIMUM PROSECUTION BRIEF CONTENTS

1. Include a Summary of Facts

A full and accurate factual synopsis is the single most important item in any prosecution brief. Regrettably, factual synopses are often cursory, omit vital details, or entirely absent from briefs. I usually found it impossible to piece together the theory of the case solely from investigator notes, which were not created to tell a lucid story. The synopsis tells a story in as plain and uncomplicated language as possible. Sometimes this means it will read like a simple Doctor Seuss children's book, and at other times like a complex Russian novel, depending on the length and scope of the investigation.

The factual synopsis included in the prosecution brief might differ from the violation report prepared immediately after the offence was discovered. Some violation reports are rushed so charges can be laid or bail hearings held; the synopsis in the brief can be more thought out. There is no need to make the synopsis sound legalistic, just use your own writing style and be complete.

The goal of the synopsis is to integrate all the relevant facts of the case into a detailed, chronological, and cohesive whole. Sequentially stringing together all investigator notes is not a synopsis, and is not helpful. Doing so is like writing a script for a movie where none of the characters ever meet and are restricted to talking to themselves in separate locked rooms. The first five minutes of the movie would have a monologue by one character, followed by another five minutes from a second character, and then a third character might appear for two or three minutes. In the course of preparing the prosecution brief, you must sift through and distill all investigator notes, physical evidence, and statements taken in order to extract and weave together the relevant information. A good synopsis gives anyone reading it a full understanding of who did what, when, and where, and offers compelling proof of those facts.

2. Include a Witness List Specifying Roles Played

Like a program handed out at the start of a play that lists all the actors and their respective roles, a good prosecution brief offers a list of all the players in a case, even those playing very minor parts. A prosecutor requires that list to be able to indicate to a court how many and which witnesses will be required for a preliminary inquiry or trial, and to be able to quickly appreciate respective witness roles when calling evidence in court. The roles must be both detailed and accurate; listing three investigators as "Exhibits Officer" is not giving a helpful level of detail if there is no indication of what items they each took into custody. Saying "Exhibits — cocaine," "Exhibits — pager and cellphone" and "Exhibits — money" is more helpful. Accuracy means two investigators cannot be listed as "Arresting Officer" for the same accused; only one of them can have formally made the arrest, and who it was will be especially important if a *Charter* challenge to arrest validity arises. Entire squads of investigators can become tied up in court from a lack of proper investigator role enumeration, or exposed to needless cross-examination if a prosecutor puts incorrect witnesses on the stand.

3. Include a List of All Exhibits

A separate list of all exhibits is a crucial part of the prosecution brief. Itemize and break down the list into every separate item seized, the location it was seized from, and the investigator who seized it. Like archaeological treasures, the value of evidence is context-dependent on the location in which it was found. Orphaned evidence devoid of place, lacking continuity and that cannot be linked back to the accused will have little value in court. The prosecutor also needs to know whose testimony will be required to get an exhibit admitted into evidence. Without comprehensive exhibit lists, prosecutors may wind up sending investigators on last minute hunts for key missing evidence, or ask for voluminous amounts of superfluous evidence to be lugged into court.

4. Include Copies of All Investigator Notes

Field notes help case assessment, disclosure and trial preparation by providing a great degree of factual detail recorded directly by each investigator close to the time of original events. Missing investigator notes are the most common problem I have observed with prosecution briefs. I acknowledge there can be reasons why investigator notes go missing that have nothing to do with the diligence of the lead investigator: some investigators may be slow to submit notes, some notes may get lost, and some investigators may not tell the lead investigator that they made any notes. If you are having problems pulling together investigator notes when preparing a prosecution brief, just say so in the brief. Identifying missing material and when or if you might be able to obtain it will greatly enhance your relationships with prosecutors, all of whom like to avoid surprises at trial.

Only "relevant" notes need be included in a prosecution brief and disclosure, not every single jotting on paper or in a computer file that has some vague connection to a case. One helpful way to determine how far relevance extends into the internal workings of an investigation is to consider what amounts to the "fruits of the investigation" as discussed in *R. v. Chan*, (2002) 6 Alta. L.R. (4th) 364; 2002 ABQB 588 at para. 41:

> fruits of the investigation are disclosable. The fruits consist of facts, information, and material emanating from the investigation which may be of some use to the defence. If the fruits are contained within a document, the document itself is disclosable as context, in my view, has been and always will be of potential relevance. Mr. Justice Binder in *Trang* recognized that form may be of importance. I would go further in stating that an accused is entitled to the fruits of the investigation in all forms.

It doesn't matter whether the fruit is oranges, apples, or durian — it needs to find its way into the prosecution brief. Generally speaking, if it doesn't amount to fruit you don't have to include it. Although demystification of the law suggests erring on the side of prosecution brief and disclosure inclusion if there is any doubt about relevance, this is tempered by the early investigator-prosecutor contact theme that says serious doubts are best dealt with by a call to the local prosecutor's office to resolve questions concerning this still developing area of the law.

The Status of E-Mails

Q&A

Q: What about my e-mails? They often contain information that seems relevant to an investigation. Should they be part of the prosecution brief and eventually included in disclosure?

A: Not necessarily, but the answer depends on their relevance. E-mails falling into the category of "internal investigator memoranda" may not be relevant for disclosure if they only deal with administrative issues, but e-mails making a record of telephone calls or face-to-face conversations with witnesses that previously would have been recorded in a field notebook could be relevant "fruit" of the investigation. It will definitely be necessary to disclose e-mails if they contain relevant information not repeated elsewhere in a more complete form. This is a rapidly evolving area of the law where you should seek current legal advice.

5. Include Copies of Rough Notes of Investigators If Available

Include rough notes in the prosecution brief if they still exist at the time the brief is prepared. Final notes may be more complete and eloquent, but as discussed in Chapter 3 the court, defence or prosecution may have concerns over whether missing rough notes differed from final notes. These concerns can be completely eliminated if the rough notes are preserved. *R. v. La*, [1997] 2 S.C.R. 680 at para. 22, established a general obligation on investigators to preserve all relevant evidence:

> serious departures from the Crown's duty to preserve material that is subject to production may also amount to an abuse of process notwithstanding that a deliberate destruction for the purpose of evading disclosure is not established. In some cases an unacceptable degree of negligent conduct may suffice.

It is best not to run the risk of a court finding that the destruction of rough notes denied the accused the ability to make full answer and defence.

6. Include "Can-Say" or "Will-Say" Statements for All Witnesses

Even though photocopies of notes are being provided, "can-say" or "will-say" statements as described in Chapter 3 should also be supplied in the prosecution brief except in very simple cases where a list of investigator roles may suffice. Think of can-says or will-says as being a bit like hockey or baseball cards. They provide the name, team, position played and basic statistics for each player. They can be easily arranged and rearranged in any order or laid out next to each other so the whole team can be seen at one time. The witnesses are players, whose order may need to be shuffled and roles quickly assessed without delving into dense field notes or detailed statements. Chances for prosecution success are greatly enhanced by can-say or will-say creation.

7. Include Copies of All Expert Reports

An expert report can be *the* key document in a prosecution because it brings objectivity to a case by someone who has no first-hand experience with the facts but who is uniquely qualified to give an opinion about portions of those facts. Experts can enhance physical evidence, provide testimony about patterns of criminal activity, interpret criminal jargon, or give a technical analysis of how death or serious injury occurred. On one occasion, I even had to locate a meat identification expert for a moose poaching case where there wasn't a whole lot of evidence left to determine what sort of animal had been hunted and killed.

An expert is needed when a fact must be proved by way of opinion evidence beyond what an ordinary investigator can offer, provided certain admissibility criteria are satisfied as explained in *R. v. D.D.*, [2000] 2 S.C.R. 275 at paras. 11 & 21:

> Four criteria must be met by a party which seeks to introduce expert evidence: relevance, necessity, the lack of any other exclusionary rule, and a properly qualified expert. Even where these requirements are met, the evidence may be rejected if its prejudicial effect on the conduct of the trial outweighs its probative value.
>
> . . .
>
> When it comes to necessity, the question is whether the expert will provide information which is likely to be outside the ordinary experience and knowledge of the trier of fact.

The law restricts the topics on which an expert can be called to testify, and governs the qualifications a person must have to be declared an expert in a particular field. Consult with a prosecutor when assessing what kind of experts and qualifications are most suitable for a case, and carefully check out the background of different experts — don't be caught at the last minute as I was with an expert being called for his honesty who turns out to have a criminal record for fraud.

Starting the search for an expert cannot wait until after charges are laid. The entire viability of an investigation and prosecution can hinge on the contents of an expert report. In relatively routine cases involving an offence like drug possession a prosecutor may be able to work on some assumptions pending receipt of the report, but in not so routine cases like a murder or workplace fatality a prosecutor may be unwilling to make a decision to proceed until an expert report is received.

The expert report included in the prosecution brief need not always be lengthy, but will be definitive, written in the expert's own words, and bear the expert's signature. The report will set out the still unproven facts of the case presented to the expert, the expert's method for analyzing the facts, any assumptions the expert has made, and the conclusions arrived at from the analysis. The professional qualifications of the expert, usually in the form of a *curriculum vitae*, should be attached to the report. Sub-section 657.3(3) of the *Criminal Code*, discussed in more detail in Chapter 17, has now imposed an advance trial notice requirement for experts and their reports that makes the early retention of an expert all the more important. You might be surprised by just how many trials you have previously testified at which would have been enhanced by an expert if the investigators and prosecutors involved had turned their minds to how an expert could help.

Finding Experts

Q&A

Q: How am I supposed to know where to find an expert and what am I supposed to do if the prosecutor doesn't like the expert I find?

A: Finding an appropriate expert should not be done on a case-by-case basis. Any investigative agency engaged in the types of investigations that require experts needs to develop pre-approved lists of experts who are willing to independently review evidence and give testimony in court within their respective fields. Investigators will then only have to refer to a list to pick an expert. Some experts will be university academics, others private consultants, and a few might work in-house for an investigative agency — a lot of flexibility is available on who can qualify as an expert so long as you don't try to overly stretch a person's field of expertise. There will still be cases where going beyond the list will be necessary, but those cases should be the exception rather than the rule.

8. Include Copies of All Statements Taken from Accused or Civilian Witnesses

The simplest of statements are often contained within an investigator's notebook, while the most complex are video recorded under oath, but all statements from accused and witnesses can have great significance to the outcome of a trial. No matter how inconsequential a statement may seem to be, a copy of it should be provided in the prosecution brief if it has the least bit of relevance to a case. If the statement was originally video or audio recorded, a copy of the recording together with a full written transcription is required. A prosecutor who only has a non-transcribed recording could find parts of it inaudible, or of such a lengthy and meandering nature that it is extremely difficult to spot the one vital admission made in the statement. If the statement was originally taken in a language other the common language in use in the jurisdiction of the prosecution (English or French), a full translation must be provided. Include a list in the prosecution brief of who gave statements, who they were taken by, and where they are located in the brief; a statement lurking in the photocopied pages of an investigator's notebook might be missed by a prosecutor unless there is a note somewhere else in the brief directing the prosecutor to look in that notebook.

9. Include Copies of All Warrants and Other Judicial Investigative Authorizations

The second most common problem I have observed with prosecution briefs is missing warrants and the informations to obtain that support their issuance. Sometimes the warrant is included, but the information to obtain is missing. At other times, any reference to the fact a warrant was even executed is absent. The misconceptions leading to these omissions, shared by lawyers and investigators alike, rest on two false assumptions about the private or public nature of warrants.

- *False Assumption #1: Based on Warrants Fundamentally being Private Documents.* Any information to obtain a warrant containing confidential informer information can be indefinitely protected from disclosure, and so is not relevant to either the prosecution brief or subsequent disclosure.

- *False Assumption #2: Based on Warrants Fundamentally being Public Documents.* Because a warrant and information to obtain are already publicly on file at a courthouse, and are only tools used to collect evidence of an offence rather than constituting evidence themselves, they again are not relevant for inclusion in the prosecution brief or disclosure package.

Without the warrant and supporting documents, prosecutors cannot assess whether they will run into *Charter* difficulties with seized evidence because of deficiencies in the judicial authorization for search and seizure. Likewise, the defence will not be able to assess the validity of evidence collection methods used by investigators. The law requires that the defence have the opportunity to challenge investigative methods that are contrary to the law, and the prosecution needs to prepare for such challenges. Because warrants and the informations to obtain them will almost always be relevant to an investigation, neither investigators nor prosecutors have any discretion to completely omit them from the disclosure package.

For complex cases, include an index in the prosecution brief of all warrants or other judicial investigative authorizations executed, the date, time and place of execution, and names of the affiant(s) and granting judicial officer(s). Clearly indicate if the information to obtain a warrant is still under court seal at the time the brief is submitted, on what date the sealing order expires, and that a copy of the information to obtain will be provided after it is no longer under seal. An unsealing application will be necessary if a warrant is under indefinite seal. If a warrant contains information whose disclosure would breach informer privilege, a court supervised process is available to edit that information prior to disclosure; ideally warrants will be drafted in a way that requires no editing, striking a balance between providing enough detail about the basis of the informer's reliability to support the warrant and not so much as to identify the informer. Discuss any concerns over the disclosure of confidential or privileged warrant information with a prosecutor prior to finalizing the prosecution brief.

10. Include Copies of All Key Evidence

There is no substitute for being able to experience evidence first hand. A prosecutor can read the best investigator-prepared case summary of the facts in the world, and still not have a good sense of how the case will actually play out in court. Experiencing the evidence means looking at signatures on documents, examining details in photographs, listening to the tone of voice and studying the facial expressions of an accused during a video statement. I have found that only with such direct evidentiary experience of those sorts of details made possible by receiving copies of all key evidence in the prosecution brief could I conduct a proper assessment of the relative merits of cases assigned to me, and thereby determine whether there was a reasonable prospect of conviction.

In a simple case involving minimal evidence, all evidence eventually to be provided in disclosure will also initially be included in the prosecution brief. In a complex case involving thousands of documents where copying those documents will be very resource intensive, the prosecution brief could initially contain something less than all documents so long as at least the key evidence is included, but since every last piece of relevant evidence will usually have to be provided in the disclosure package it may be easiest to get all the copying out of the way at the prosecution brief preparation phase. Disputes over what went into or was omitted from the prosecution brief can sour productive investigator-prosecutor relationships more quickly than just about any other dispute because of frustrations that build up on both sides. Early investigator-prosecutor contact before you prepare a large brief will allow you to reach agreement with the prosecutor in advance on what amounts to the key evidence.

11. Include Records of Past Offences and Other Sentencing Range Information

Past offences aren't usually relevant to assessing whether there is a reasonable prospect of conviction the next time round, but they can be extremely relevant to assessing whether it is in the public interest to pursue a new prosecution. They can also be significant aggravating sentencing factors on new charges, as found in *R. v. Taylor* (2004), 189 O.A.C. 388 at para. 39:

> it is a misconception to say — as the respondent submits — that a criminal record may not be an aggravating factor in sentencing. Certainly, it would be wrong to punish a person for his or her past crimes by using a criminal history in effect to impose a "double punishment" on that person, i.e., to impose a sentence for the offence in question and then to add something more for the criminal record . . . .Thus, it is not proper to treat the record of the accused as an aggravating factor in the sense that the trial judge is entitled to raise the sentence beyond what would otherwise be a fit sentence . . . . However, a criminal record, depending on its nature, may be an "aggravating" factor in the sentencing context in the sense that it renders a stiffer sentence "fit" in the circumstances because it rebuts good character and because of what it tells the trial judge and society about the need for specific deterrence, the chances of successful rehabilitation, and the likelihood of recidivism.

Past convictions can thus motivate new prosecutions leading to higher sentences that might prevent the commission of even more offences.

The prosecution brief requires up-to-date copies of the criminal or regulatory offence records of all accused. Canadian Police Information Centre (CPIC) database printouts are a good place to start in gathering past offence information, but may not include all prior convictions — particularly convictions for regulatory offences. For significant criminal cases and for all regulatory cases investigators are best served by getting the case disposition reports located at the agency that laid the earlier charges. Not only will those reports reveal convictions not recorded elsewhere, they will also provide background information capable of establishing similar facts and patterns of conduct.

For more unusual offences, or more significant cases, including an entire sentencing section in the prosecution brief is a good idea. This sentencing sub-brief can concisely set out all the aggravating and mitigating factors involved in a case, cite examples of recent sentences handed out by courts in the same jurisdiction for similar offences, and specify the sentencing range recommended by the lead investigator. One sentence range could be for an early guilty plea, and a different range for a sentence imposed after a trial. So long as those recommendations are reasonable, prosecutors will take them into account in formulating their own submissions to the court. One way for investigators to ensure their recommendations get ignored by prosecutors is to always request a sentence at the high-end of the statutory range.

Dealing with Prosecutors

Q&A

Q: Regardless of what information I and the other investigators I work with provide in a prosecution brief, it seems prosecutors always want more information and have personal preferences for the best way to organize a brief. Isn't my trying to be obsessively complete in a brief simply a waste of time?

A: If a reasonable prosecutor is confident the brief is complete, there won't be anything else to ask for. At most, the prosecutor will ask you to explain some of the included materials. A complete brief prevents prosecutor requests constantly interrupting new investigative tasks. I concede there could be unreasonable prosecutors out there, but negotiating a prosecution brief and disclosure preparation protocol between your investigative agency and the prosecution services it deals with will prevent prosecutor personal preferences getting in the way of your brief preparation.

EXCEPTIONS TO INCLUSIONS IN THE PROSECUTION BRIEF

Although I am clearly advocating a "more is more" approach to prosecution brief preparation, there are a few notable exceptions. Some material will be privileged, while other material will not be relevant. You don't have to open up your entire investigative file, shovel its contents into a dump truck, and drive it over to the prosecutor's office. For example, an investigator's personnel form claiming pay for overtime worked in relation to a case would not be provided because it is not on its face relevant to the prosecution or defence of the case — unless the defence later makes out a case for relevance. Investigators do, however, need to be very cautious about not jumping to conclusions over what can be excluded. I am tempted to tell you "if in doubt, include it," but issues of privilege and the risk of burying the prosecution under an irrelevant mountain of material lead me instead to tell you "if in doubt, ask a prosecutor."

Aside from confidential case instructions directed to the prosecutor, you generally should not be providing prosecutors with anything you would have a problem with being passed on to defence counsel. Privilege may in theory prevent the disclosure of sensitive material past the point of the prosecutor, but exceptions exist to those privileges and prosecutors are not always in a position to vet all material provided by investigators before it is disclosed to the defence. Everything included in a prosecution brief may wind up going out the door as a disclosure package if local practice involves administrative staff making complete copies of briefs to provide to the defence. Having effective gate keeping systems in place may be the most important aspect of an effective prosecution brief and disclosure package preparation process: systems that make sure what needs to get to the prosecution or defence does get there, and what shouldn't go to one or both of them stays behind. Information left in a single page of disclosed investigator field notes that tends to identify a confidential informer could put that informer's life at risk.

1. The Privileged Material Exception

Confidential instructions for the prosecution are best contained in a separate sealed package marked "CONFIDENTIAL INSTRUCTIONS FOR THE CROWN" accompanying the prosecution brief. These instructions might discuss issues like proposed charges, proposed sentences, potential defences, or legal problems with the case. They can usually remain confidential instead of being disclosed because of their solicitor-client privileged nature, and also because they are not relevant to disclosure.

Chapter 9 already discussed the concept of solicitor-client privilege for materials seized from a private sector lawyer or client. That privilege applies equally to advice given to government bodies like police services by publicly employed lawyers, as confirmed in *R. v. Campbell*, [1999] 1 S.C.R. 565 at para. 49 :

> The solicitor-client privilege is based on the functional needs of the administration of justice. The legal system, complicated as it is, calls for professional expertise. Access to justice is compromised where legal advice is unavailable. It is of great importance, therefore, that the RCMP be able to obtain professional legal advice in connection with criminal investigations without the chilling effect of potential disclosure of their confidences in subsequent proceedings.
>
> . . .
>
> Cpl. R. . . consultation with Mr. L. . . of the Department of Justice falls squarely within this functional definition, and the fact that Mr. L. . . works for an "in-house" government legal service does not affect the creation or character of the privilege.

But just because you have placed troubling facts about a case in the confidential Crown instructions will not protect those facts from disclosure, as *R. v. Campbell* found at para. 50: "Whether or not solicitor-client privilege attaches in any of these situations depends on the nature of the relationship, the subject matter of the advice and the circumstances in which it is sought and rendered." The confidential instructions only exist for a free exchange of *opinions*; all *facts* relevant to a case usually have to be disclosed unless covered by some other type of privilege.

Notes of meetings or correspondence with prosecutors will likewise usually be exempt from disclosure so long as they were not created in the course of evidence gathering as explained in *R. v. Dempsey*, 2000 BCSC 1677 at para. 7:

> Notes made by Crown counsel while undertaking fact finding must be disclosed as a matter of routine. Notes made by Crown counsel for purposes of trial preparation need not be disclosed. However, if a witness changes his or her evidence from what has already been disclosed to the defence during an interview with Crown counsel preparing for trial, Crown counsel must disclose that change in the form of a "will say" statement. If there is an issue about the "will say" statement, "the Court will peruse the Crown notes and compare it . . . to the 'will say' statement".

Black out portions of notes or other documents protected by privilege before they find their way into the brief. As a prosecutor I didn't want to know the particulars of information covered by a privilege if I could avoid it, since yet another person knowing only increased the risk of inadvertent or court ordered disclosure, but I did need to know about its existence so I could take steps to protect it consistent with the rights of the accused.

2. The Internal Memoranda Exception

Investigative internal planning documents will not usually be included in the prosecution brief or disclosure package because most are not relevant, and those having tangential relevance might be reproduced elsewhere in a more complete form or covered by a public interest privilege as found in *R. v. Trang* (2002), 1 Alta. L.R. (4th) 247; 2002 ABQB 19 at paras. 48 & 55:

> The Crown has asserted privilege status for investigative techniques, ongoing investigations, police intelligence, police internal communications, and information potentially affecting the safety of individuals. Defence counsel submits that in order for public interest privilege to justify non-disclosure this Court must find that the information, if disclosed, would cause damage to either national security or international relations. I cannot accept this position, since investigative techniques, ongoing investigations and safety of individuals have been accorded common law privilege status in the jurisprudence, as well as statutory privilege status in relation to editing of wire-tap applications before being disclosed to the accused.
>
> . . .
>
> In accordance with the jurisprudence, these privileges are subject to review and balancing by the Court of the public interest served by the privilege against the importance of the information to the right of an accused to make full answer and defence.

Courts have been reticent to order disclosure of internal investigative records that don't amount to "fruits of the investigation" unless the defence can demonstrate relevance. Internal memoranda are best managed by creating two files at the start of any large investigation: one for factual material relevant to the case, and another for administrative documents not to be forwarded to the prosecution or defence.

WHAT THE BRIEF SHOULD LOOK LIKE

Even if a prosecution brief is complete, providing a jumble of disorganized papers is a good way to ensure an acquittal. There is no one right way to organize a brief unless you are bound by a prosecution brief preparation protocol, but the brief must be laid out in a logical fashion that makes sense to you and others. An organized brief has a table of contents, consecutive page numbers, and tabs separating the major sections. Using brightly coloured paper on the cover will help it stand out from the pestilence of other paper that plagues all offices. Moving from the general to the specific, in a chronological fashion, will allow the brief to flow from overview facts, to early stages of case development, to specific material seized during searches conducted later in the investigation. Highlighting key passages in the brief like incriminating statements in field notes is extremely helpful.

Prosecution briefs suffer such abuse at the hands of harried prosecutors and investigators that they must be secured together in a durable fashion. Some briefs I have dealt with in high-volume court houses looked like they had been run over, laundered, and then employed as a microwave dinner tray. A brad for shorter packages or cerlox binding for more voluminous materials are preferred methods of binding. Relying only on a staple invites the end pages to drift away, never to be seen again, without anyone noticing until the middle of trial. While three-ring binders are also acceptable, their alterable nature makes them more prone to pages getting out of order, going astray, or exploding across the courtroom. Imagine, if you will, a heavy evidence binder sailing out of my hands in the middle of a trial, hitting a table, the rings crisply popping open, and its 500 pages simultaneously performing aerial acrobatics to celebrate their new found freedom. Although perhaps it was no worse than my knocking over the large water glass I had just refilled onto original affidavits about to be handed up to the court. I now avoid water in court, and likewise avoid easy-open binders.

If you provide a totally or partially electronic prosecution brief, it must be in a format accessible and useable by prosecutors. Prosecutors may need software to access the information, hardware capable of running that software, and training to use the software efficiently. Technology costs triggered by electronic brief and disclosure preparation can lead to disputes between investigators and prosecutors (not to mention defence counsel) over who will pay. A compromise I have seen work is for investigators to loan prosecutors the required document management software, and for prosecutors to bear their own hardware costs.

BEING MORE EFFICIENT THROUGH ROLLING BRIEFS AND PROTOCOLS

To avoid brief preparation becoming an insuperable task at the end of an exhausting investigation, some law enforcement agencies internally achieve efficiency through brief preparation as an ongoing part of the investigation, usually with the aid of some type of computer database that electronically categorizes, indexes, summarizes and perhaps stores copies of all evidence as it is collected. A rolling brief can even be prepared without the aid of case management software by placing copies of case material into a tabbed and indexed binder as it comes into the office. A bit of later reorganizing to ensure all pieces of the investigative puzzle fit together, and some tweaking for relevance and privilege, may be required but the time spent will be a fraction of what it would take to put in order piles of jumbled together material.

Concluding a prosecution brief and disclosure preparation protocol between investigators and prosecutors will eliminate protracted case-by-case negotiations over inclusions and costs. The start of this chapter set out the basic principles of a protocol between the RCMP and FPS who agreed on "appropriate briefs" in a "timely way" throughout the "judicial phase" of a case. Because it is a national protocol it sticks to fairly general principles covering a host of investigator-prosecutor relationship issues; at a local level much more detailed protocols are possible. A protocol could be based on a checklist like the one at the end of this chapter. Protocols are efficient instruments to ensure the relevant is included, the superfluous excluded, and that briefs serve the needs of both investigators and prosecutors.

For Preparing a Complete Prosecution Brief that Still Makes Sense

KEY POINTS

✓ Every prosecution brief requires a summary of the facts, a witness list specifying roles, an exhibits list, investigator notes including rough notes if available, can-says or will-says, expert reports, all statements, all warrants or other judicial authorizations including the affidavits supporting them, all key evidence, records of past offences, and sentencing information. Among exceptions to what would be routinely included in the prosecution brief are privileged material and internal investigative memoranda that are either privileged or not relevant.

✓ An organized prosecution brief will have a table of contents, consecutive page numbers, tabs separating the major sections, and be held together in a durable fashion. A totally or partially electronic prosecution brief must be

KEY POINTS

provided in a readily accessible format that prosecutors can use. There is no one right way to structure a prosecution brief, so long as it is complete and laid out logically.

✓ Compile a rolling prosecution brief as the investigation progresses to cut down on brief preparation work at the point charges are to be laid.

✓ Concluding a prosecution brief and disclosure preparation protocol between your investigative agency and the prosecution services it frequently deals with will avoid future protracted negotiations and disagreements over what should go into a brief.

✔ Keep one copy on investigation file and include one copy with prosecution brief.
✔ All applicable sections must be completed. Indicate N/A if not applicable.

Accused:_____

_____

_____

Defence counsel: _____

Address, Tel & Fax:_____

_____

Date(s) of offence(s):_____

Charge(s):_____

_____

_____

_____

Lead investigator:_____

Detachment:_____

Tel: _____ Fax: _____

Cell:_____ E-mail: _____

Prosecutor (if assigned):_____

A   **FACTS, WITNESSES AND NOTES**

❏ Summary of facts (include all relevant facts in detailed chronological order)

❏ Witness list including investigator roles (e.g. P/C Smith — seized cocaine; P/C Boudreau — arrested buyer)

❏ Exhibit list (include what was seized, who seized, where seized from, and who ultimately took custody)

❏ Copies of all investigator notes; ❏ privileged information in notes blacked out

B   **STATEMENTS**

❏ Summary "will-say/can-say" statements for all witnesses prepared by investigator-in-charge

❏ Copies of all formal or informal statements taken from accused/civilian witnesses, including video/audio recordings with transcripts:

____ statement(s) from _____
❏ in investigator notes ❏ audio recorded ❏ video recorded ❏ translator ❏ under oath

____ statement(s) from _____
❏ in investigator notes ❏ audio recorded ❏ video recorded ❏ translator ❏ under oath

____ statement(s) from _____
❏ in investigator notes ❏ audio recorded ❏ video recorded ❏ translator ❏ under oath

___ statement(s) from_____

❏ in investigator notes ❏ audio recorded ❏ video recorded ❏ translator ❏ under oath

Total video recordings **x**___ ❏ with transcript(s)_____

Total audio recordings **x**___ ❏ with transcript(s)_____

Translator(s) involved:_____

Investigator notes containing statement(s):_____

C   WARRANTS AND AUTHORIZATIONS

❏ Copies of all executed warrants   ❏ with informations to obtain as sworn

❏ s. 487 *Criminal Code* search warrants **x**___

❏ s. 487.01 *Criminal Code* general warrants **x**___

❏ Electronic intercept authorizations **x** ___

❏ Other judicial authorizations **x** ___ (e.g. Tracking Warrants, Production Orders)

❏ List of all executed warrants and authorizations, including date, place, affiant and granting judicial officer

D   REAL, DOCUMENTARY AND EXPERT EVIDENCE

❏ Indexed copies of all evidence:

❏ ___ seized documents **x** ___ pages in total:_____

❏ Photos **x** ___ ❏ Edited videos **x**___

❏ Unedited videos **x** ___ with time index of relevant material (not including statements)

❏ Expert reports **x** ___ prepared by_____

❏ Copies of licences **x**___ ; ❏ Corporate/business registration(s) **x** ___ with ❏ *Canada Evidence Act* affidavits as required

❏ Descriptions and values of non-documentary seized evidence (e.g. vehicles, drugs with weights, merchandise, cash, firearms)

❏ Other:_____

E   CHARGES, DEFENCES AND SENTENCING

❏ Draft/Actual charging Information (include full wording of charges/persons to be charged)

❏ Young Person(s): _____

❏ Potential mental disorder issue   ❏ Potential constitutional defence

❏ Any confidential instructions for prosecutor, clearly marked in sealed envelope

❏ Copies of criminal records for _____

❏ Copies of past regulatory violation reports for _____

❏ Suggested sentence on early plea and after trial indicated for all accused

  ❏ Rationale given for proposed sentence(s)

  ❏ Sentencing evidence included:

      ❏ Expert Report(s) **x** ____   written by_____

      ❏ Victim advised of opportunity to provide victim impact statement
        by_____on _____

      ❏ Victim/Community Impact Statement(s) **x** _____
        made by_____

      ❏ Other_____

F | **PROSECUTION REFERRAL**

❏ Appearance notice given ❏ Summons served on_____
  for first appearance date of_____ at_____

❏ Notice to seek greater punishment by reason of prior conviction provided to

  ❏ _____ by _____ on _____

❏ Referral of prosecution brief on _____ to _____
  delivered by_____

❏ Prosecutor response on_____ by _____ stating:

      ❏ no prosecution because: _____

      ❏ more information needed: _____

        ❏ information provided on: _____

      ❏ prosecution to proceed

G | **DISCLOSURE**

❏ Complete disclosure package provided to:

  ❏ _____ by _____ on _____

  ❏ _____ by _____ on _____

  ❏ _____ by _____ on _____

  ❏ _____ by _____ on _____

  ❏ Statutory notices to produce evidence at trial included in disclosure package:
  _____

  ❏ Items missing from disclosure package:

  _____
  because _____
  to be available by_____

  ❏ Copy of disclosure package is retained in secure custody by_____
Other Comments _____

FURTHER READING

I cannot recommend much in the way of further reading specifically dedicated to prosecution brief preparation, although a number of readings on disclosure discussed in the next chapter might be helpful. The most important works to read are those devoted to how to write well because the more organized your thoughts and evidence, the more effective your brief will be in getting the prosecutor to understand the case. Looking at works on expert witnesses will also assist you in choosing an adequate expert and connecting the expert's report to the rest of the brief.

Books

G. Araco, *Principles of Law Enforcement Report Writing*, 2nd ed. (Toronto: Thomson, 2004).

R.L. Bintliff, *How to Write Effective Law Enforcement Reports* (Englewood Cliffs, NJ: Prentice Hall, 1991).

D. Hacker, *A Canadian Writer's Reference* (Toronto: Nelson, 1996).

K. Jakob, *A Guide to Police Writing*, 3rd ed. (Toronto: Carswell, 2002).

K.M. Matthews ed., *The Expert — A Practitioner's Guide*, loose-leaf (Toronto: Carswell, 1995).

K. Rogers-Rupp, *Police Writing: A Guide to the Essentials* (Upper Saddle Rive, NJ: Pearson/Prentice Hall, 2005).

L. Truss, *Eats, Shoots and Leaves — The Zero Tolerance Approach to Punctuation* (New York: Gotham Books, 2003).

J. Venoilia, *Write Right: A Desktop Digest of Punctuation, Grammar and Style*, 4th ed. (Ten Speed Press, 2001).

R.B. White, *The Art of Using Expert Evidence* (Aurora, ON: Canada Law Book, 1997).

CHAPTER SIXTEEN

INCLUDING EVERYTHING IN THE DISCLOSURE PACKAGE EXCEPT THE IRRELEVANT AND THE PRIVILEGED

The way in which disclosure of evidence was viewed in the past — as an act of goodwill and cooperation on the part of the Crown — played a significant role in catastrophic judicial errors.

. . .

Little information will be exempt from the duty that is imposed on the prosecution to disclose evidence.

> *R. v. Taillefer, R. v. Duguay,* [2003] 3 S.C.R. 307 at paras. 1 & 60.

In This Chapter

- How this book can help you
- Allocating sufficient resources to disclosure preparation
- Similar prosecution briefs and disclosure packages
- Organized disclosure benefits everyone
- Making sure disclosure is complete
- Making sure disclosure is timely
- Taking care of ongoing disclosure obligations

- Technical issues of disclosure to consider
- Dealing with pretrial notices as accompanying disclosure
- The consequences of non-disclosure or late disclosure

"Disclosure." Does the mere mention of the word send shivers down your spine? It has certainly been the source of considerable grief for investigators and prosecutors alike in the cases in which I have been involved — all from one short word; not even a mysterious or difficult to define word. Investigators and prosecutors have for a long time made some kind of disclosure of their cases to the defence prior to trial — it clarified issues in dispute, encouraged guilty pleas, and forestalled defence adjournment requests to study the prosecution's evidence, but prior to the *Charter* the defence did not have strong remedies available if displeased over receiving arguably inadequate case details. Post-*Charter*, the defence acquired considerable leverage to compel disclosure sufficient for an accused to make full answer and defence to charges.

You might be wondering why disclosure problems continue to occasionally spiral out of control when the *Charter* has been in existence since 1982, and *R. v. Stinchcombe*, [1991] 3 S.C.R. 326 at 336, confirmed the constitutional obligation to provide comprehensive disclosure back in 1991:

> This review of the pros and cons with respect to disclosure by the Crown shows that there is no valid practical reason to support the position of the opponents of a broad duty of disclosure. Apart from the practical advantages to which I have referred, there is the overriding concern that failure to disclose impedes the ability of the accused to make full answer and defence. . . . The right to make full answer and defence is one of the pillars of criminal justice on which we heavily depend to ensure that the innocent are not convicted.

Ongoing disclosure failures appear to have two primary causes: a lack of understanding of the law as it now stands, and a Canada-wide trend towards conducting more complex forms of criminal and regulatory investigations involving unprecedented numbers of co-accused and volumes of evidence. The first cause can be addressed by embracing demystification of the law, the second by implementing very disciplined case management and material tracking procedures. Developing adequate disclosure systems, allocating sufficient time and resources to those systems, and custom designing disclosure strategies for complex cases will best forestall *Charter* claims.

THE ONE SIMPLE RULE OF DISCLOSURE

In a world full of complexity, there is one surprisingly simple rule for disclosure as confirmed in *R. v. Taillefer, R. v. Duguay*, [2003] 3 S.C.R. 307: subject to issues of privilege, everything relevant to a case in the possession of the Crown must be included in the disclosure package and provided to the defence. Relevant material is everything tending to prove or disprove the case against an accused, or material having a reasonable possibility of being useful to an accused in making full answer and defence. Today it is clear that only the privileged and the *clearly* irrelevant should not be disclosed.

Ultimately it is up to the prosecutor to decide on relevance, subject to review by the courts. As a prosecutor I constantly found this rule of relevance to be endlessly appealing in theory, and infinitely frustrating in its practical application. How is a prosecutor in the best position to judge relevance? Investigators are in the best position to know about the existence of material that could be relevant. Defence counsel are in the best position to know what is relevant to defence arguments. I found myself left in the middle, knowing neither what evidence had been collected by investigators nor what arguments would be used by the defence to rebut that evidence. This state of prosecutor ignorance is why disclosure is everyone's responsibility. The price to pay for an error in judging disclosure relevance can be ignominious case implosion.

The prosecutor will never have as intimate a knowledge of the contents of the case file as do the investigators. A close disclosure relationship between investigators and prosecutors is necessary to make the relevance rule work, leading to a few prosecutors now being co-located in investigator offices to provide disclosure advice on a full-time basis. The *Memorandum of Understanding Between the Royal Canadian Mounted Police and the Federal Prosecution Service Respecting the Conduct of Criminal Investigations and Prosecutions* (5 July 2001) at section 4.1 provides an excellent example of an investigative agency and prosecution service coming to terms with their joint disclosure obligations: "The parties share the Crown's constitutional responsibility and ongoing obligation to disclose to the accused all material and information in their possession or control which is not privileged or clearly irrelevant, irrespective of whether the prosecutor intends to introduce it into evidence." Fulfilling this responsibility requires investigators carefully track everything created or collected that could be relevant to a case. Very small undisclosed items tend to have a habit of being turned into key pieces of missing evidence by defence counsel at trial.

ALLOCATING SUFFICIENT RESOURCES TO DISCLOSURE PREPARATION

Courts have recognized that preparing disclosure represents an additional investigator workload beyond preparing the prosecution brief, as mentioned in *R. v. Chenier*, 2002 CarswellOnt 5010 (S.C.) at para. 5:

> Accuracy, editing, and the need for completeness of the materials, particularly in light of the high level for concern for witness security, led to Sgt. S. . . taking personal responsibility for detailed scrutiny and review of materials being prepared for disclosure. It must also be recognized that in addition to organizing materials in some coherent fashion, Sgt. S. . . was at the same time preparing and organizing the prosecution brief for the Crown Attorney. While the two tasks were inevitably on similar tracks, they were by no means co-incidental or duplicative, the one of the other.

While the disclosure package will not take as much time to prepare as did the prosecution brief if that brief was well prepared, you still need to anticipate disclosure preparation consuming considerable investigative resources.

Resource challenges specific to disclosure include ensuring materials are precisely duplicated in a useable form, delivering those materials to the accused, and quickly responding to the demands of further disclosure. Practice varies as to who physically produces and pays for copies of the disclosure package given to all accused, but preparation of the initial package by necessity is the responsibility of the investigating agency. The investigators are the ones who are in possession of the original evidence to be disclosed, best understand that evidence, and will have to testify in court if relevant material fails to make it into the disclosure. Allocating adequate resources to disclosure pays off in how quickly charges can be proceeded with to trial, and overall trial success. Provided you keep an eye on any charging limitation period, there is little point in quickly laying a routine charge only to have it stall in a series of set-date court appearances because the disclosure package cannot be completed until months later.

SIMILAR PROSECUTION BRIEFS AND DISCLOSURE PACKAGES

Think of the prosecution brief and disclosure package as fraternal twins. Not quite identical, but sharing many traits. The disclosure package may be a little lighter without confidential instructions to the Crown, or it may be a little heavier in complex fraud or conspiracy cases where not every piece of evidence could be reproduced for the prosecution brief. Keeping the prosecution brief and disclosure package as similar as possible will ensure both complete and timely disclosure is made.

Because the prosecution brief contained the following items enumerated in detail in Chapter 15, so will the disclosure package:

- a summary of the facts;
- a list of the roles of all witnesses;
- a list of all exhibits;
- copies of all investigator notes;
- copies of rough notes of investigators if available;
- can-say or will-say statements for all witnesses;
- copies of all expert reports;
- copies of all statements taken from accused or civilian witnesses;
- copies of all warrants or other judicial investigative authorizations;
- copies of all other evidence — not just key evidence, since this is disclosure; and
- records of past offences committed by the accused.

Only a small amount of material relevant to a case will be left out of disclosure because it is privileged.

The Difference between Disclosure and the Prosecution Brief

Q: How is the disclosure package any different from the prosecution brief?

A: Usually there will be no difference, other than for any confidential instructions to the prosecutor included in the prosecution brief but not in disclosure, material included in the prosecution brief that the prosecutor tells you to delete from disclosure (because of relevance or privilege), or material missing from the prosecution brief that the prosecutor asks you to add to disclosure.

ORGANIZED DISCLOSURE BENEFITS EVERYONE

Organized disclosure helps investigators respond to additional disclosure requests or accusations that certain items were not provided in disclosure. Organized disclosure helps prosecutors present the case to the court.

Organized disclosure helps the defence make full answer and defence to the charges. In short, organized disclosure ensures that justice is done.

To be organized, disclosure needs to meet physical as well as conceptual requirements. Physically, the disclosure package will be very similar to the prosecution brief with a table of contents, page numbers, and tabs all held together with some kind of binding. Conceptually, the simpler the disclosure package is to read for both the defence and prosecution, the more likely the case will be resolved through a guilty plea or at least won't result in a multi-month trial. A confusing package composed of a morass of material that is not self-explanatory only serves to delay a case from proceeding to trial, and prolongs or possibly derails proceedings once the trial has started. Courts have found extremely disorganized disclosure can amount to no disclosure at all, like in *R. v. Rajalingam* (2004), 190 O.A.C. 270 at paras. 1-3:

> The trial judge stayed the criminal charges against the respondent on the basis that they would constitute an abuse of process and on the basis that the disclosure failings by the Crown breached s. 7.
> . . .
>
> The trial judge's finding that the prosecution approach to disclosure in this case was "disorganized", "haphazard" and "indifferent" was fully supported by the evidence.
>
> While some judges might have held that the prosecution conduct in this case, while worthy of condemnation, did not warrant a stay of proceedings, we cannot say that the trial judge's decision to order a stay was "clearly wrong", thereby warranting our intervention.

Evidence is best collected by investigators who are thinking about their eventual disclosure obligations. The *Memorandum of Understanding Between the Royal Canadian Mounted Police and the Federal Prosecution Service Respecting the Conduct of Criminal Investigations and Prosecutions* (5 July 2001) agrees at section 3.1.2: "The RCMP preserve and organize information and evidence collected in the course of their investigation, in contemplation of the Crown's obligation to disclose and in recognition of the benefits of early disclosure." It is far easier to set up a file at the start of a case in a way that serves the interests of both investigators and prosecutors, than it is to later completely restructure a voluminous investigation file so it can be used to support a prosecution.

To measure whether your disclosure package is sufficiently organized before you finalize it, try giving it to one of your colleagues not involved in the case and ask her to find a particular item, like the notes of a named investigator. Time how long it takes. Assuming this is a standard one binder case, over a minute is way too long. Ten seconds is great. Allow extra time for each additional binder of disclosure. The longer it takes, the more additional work you need to do on your master index, tabs or overall organization.

MAKING SURE DISCLOSURE IS COMPLETE

Despite your best efforts as an investigator, the evidence may just not pan out. This can happen long before any charges are laid, or right in the middle of a trial when a witness recants. Evidentiary case failures are sometimes unavoidable. Investigators cannot discover evidence that doesn't exist. But where the evidence in a case is sound, I have found *among the most common difficulties imperiling case success has been incomplete disclosure.* The mere omission of one page of investigator notes, forgetting to list one witness, or misplacing one seized document can compromise a case. The Prosecution Brief and Disclosure Package Checklist in Chapter 15 will help you ensure the disclosure package is complete.

Some sort of system is required to manage and collate in one case file all the information collected during an investigation. In contentious disclosure disputes, an investigator must be able to say under oath in court something like: "I know everything relevant in this case has been disclosed to these parties on *x* date." To ensure all relevant material not only makes it into the master disclosure package, but also into each copy of the package provided to the accused, the master copy will ideally be duplicated by a reliable technician who is later available to testify about the accuracy of the duplication technique, be it with a photocopier, computer or other device. The copies could be compared to the originals before being disclosed to confirm pages did not stick together, double-sided pages were not copied only on one side, and any one of dozens of other possible copying errors did not happen. In very voluminous cases it is not necessary to compare every copy with every original, but at least sample spot checks should be made. The spread of electronic disclosure should cut down on copy problems in the future.

Completeness also requires preserving the master disclosure package in an unaltered and secure state. Except during duplication, that package is locked in a limited access location so it can later be used to prove what in fact was disclosed. In increasingly complex cases, accused or defence counsel commonly cannot find material in the disclosure package. Sometimes their frustration will result in a motion to compel disclosure or stay proceedings, even though the material has already been provided. Good organization of the disclosure package will forestall most claims of missing disclosure.

Disclosure of Checklists
Q: Just how far can the relevance rule be taken? For instance, are the checklists in this book, once completed, subject to disclosure?
A: It depends on the information they contain. Usually they will qualify as internal investigative planning documents with no relevance to the prosecution or defence of the case. The relevant information they contain will already be stated elsewhere in the disclosure materials, like in the notes of the investigators. If prepared as confidential instructions solely for the use of the prosecutor, some of the checklists could qualify as being subject to solicitor-client privilege. Discuss all doubtful disclosure issues with a prosecutor. Ask yourself: "why shouldn't I disclose this item?" rather than "why should I disclose it?"

MAKING SURE DISCLOSURE IS TIMELY

If not provided in a timely manner, the most complete disclosure package in the world is worthless. A date usually cannot be set for a preliminary hearing or trial, and a pretrial conference among the prosecution, defence and a judge to clarify the issues cannot take place, unless the disclosure package has been finalized. Once charges have been laid, providing disclosure should be the number one case priority of the lead investigator. Because investigators understandably have many ongoing investigative duties having nothing to do with disclosure, appointing a disclosure coordinator in each investigative unit makes sense to handle prosecution requests for updates on the status of initial or subsequent disclosure, and to enforce internal deadlines governing the delivery of disclosure.

How late is too late for disclosure is a matter of much debate, and depends on the circumstances of each case. Investigators need to be able to justify anything more than a short delay after charging because of the complexity of the case, volume of disclosure, or difficulty in duplication. Warning a prosecutor in advance about disclosure delays helps forestall a court taking drastic remedies born of intense frustration and lack of knowledge. Insist prosecutors take your calls or meet you to resolve disclosure issues.

TAKING CARE OF ONGOING DISCLOSURE OBLIGATIONS

Disclosure does not end with dropping off the finished disclosure package. Any relevant information subsequently received by investigators, be it in addition or contrary to previous disclosure, must be sent out as a further disclosure package. The more disclosure packages created, the more difficult it becomes to later prove who received what and when. My rule of thumb has been to try to limit a case to two disclosure packages per accused. The first package would be provided shortly after it seems all relevant information is available. The second package is provided at least one month prior to trial and includes things missed or unavailable when the first package was prepared.

The two packages principle is at least good theory. In practice I have had cases suffer through a dozen disclosure packages per accused, which quickly became a logistical nightmare to track. Many extra deliveries can be avoided by delaying the second package until there is some confidence in it containing almost all missing material. That delay is balanced by the obligation to disclose new material in a timely manner.

A failure to meet ongoing disclosure obligations can have equally serious consequences as an omission made during the initial stages of disclosure, as confirmed in *R. v. Chaplin*, [1995] 1 S.C.R. 727 at para 21: "Failure to comply with this initial and continuing obligation to disclose relevant and non-privileged evidence may result in a stay of proceedings or other redress against the Crown, and may constitute a serious breach of ethical standards." Keeping a running computerized index of what was disclosed on what date, and what still needs to be disclosed, assists in meeting these ongoing obligations.

Dealing Directly with the Defence

Q & A

Q: Defence counsel has written to me, and requested I disclose not only the name of the informer in one of my cases (which I will likely have to do since he participated as an agent and has agreed to waive informer privilege), but also the contents of the case files for all prior occasions that informer had contact with me or my investigative agency. What should I do? Isn't responding to disclosure requests the job of the prosecutor?

A: Yes, the prosecution is responsible for the legal aspects of disclosure, including negotiating defence requests for that disclosure. Immediate contact with the prosecution service responsible for a case is imperative when a disclosure request is directly made to investigators. To be disclosable, prior files would have to be relevant to the present case.

TECHNICAL ISSUES OF DISCLOSURE TO CONSIDER

The amount disclosure costs to produce flows from the format in which information is disclosed, which in turn gives rise to technical questions of how copies will be produced, who will produce them, who will pay for them, who will deliver them, and ultimately what forms of disclosure are acceptable to trial courts. Must copies of everything relevant to a prosecution be made? What should be done with material that is incapable of being copied? Although disclosure uncertainties are often approached on a case-by-case basis, it is far better to conduct disclosure pursuant to a protocol jointly developed by investigative agencies and the prosecution services with whom they work.

1. Providing Disclosure in an Accessible Form

A failure to disclose material in a readily accessible form will breach disclosure obligations just as surely as a failure to disclose any material, like in *R. v. Cheung* (2002), 272 A.R. 332; 2000 ABPC 86 at paras. 93-97 & 105:

> It is urged that there is nothing in law requiring that disclosure be under any particular form. That may be so. But if the information and material are disclosed in a form which an accused is unable to access, then it has not been disclosed. It is not meaningful.
>
> As has been noted, disclosure is disclosure to the accused, not to counsel.
>
> The Crown is not being asked to do anything unusual in terms of the form of disclosure. Disclosure is usually made in the form of hard copy.
>
> Nothing is being requested by the applicants in terms of creating new material. That would be the case if the accused could not understand one of Canada's two official languages, and were requesting a translation of all proposed Crown disclosure into a third language. That is not what is being applied for here. All that is requested here is the exact reproduction of already existing material.
>
> The only extraordinary factor which has resulted in the Crown disclosure to this date in electronic or soft copy, is the extraordinarily large volume of the data, and the resulting extraordinarily high cost of reproducing the data in the usual way.

. . .

> The several extraordinary factors about this case are such that the
> Crown must accept that there are going to be extraordinary costs
> associated with every aspect of its prosecution.

There is no set rule for disclosure to be in a particular format, only that it
be sufficiently accessible depending on the circumstances of the case to
enable the accused to make full answer and defence. If an accused is in custody with limited access to computers as in *Cheung*, then non-electronic
copies of disclosure might be required.

2. Managing Disclosure Costs

Who bears the cost of disclosure is a crucial question in increasingly
complex cases with ever-increasing costs running into the hundreds of thousands of dollars. In voluminous cases, copies of items of only tangential relevance need not necessarily be provided in disclosure so long as access is
offered, but copies of all fundamentally relevant evidence must be included
as confirmed in *R. v. Blencowe* (1997), 118 C.C.C. (3d) 529 (Ont. Ct. (Gen.
Div.)) at 543:

> The disclosure which is sought lies at the core of the prosecutor's
> case. It is what the prosecutor alleges is child pornography or
> obscene. It is the prosecutor's obligation to provide such funda-
> mental or basic disclosure. It is the prosecutor's further obligation,
> in my respectful view, to pay for it.
>
> To impose upon the prosecutor the obligation to pay the costs of
> disclosure of copy tapes, in the circumstances of this particular
> case, coincides with general principle. Disclosure is a constitution-
> al right of every person accused of crime. There is a correlative
> obligation upon the state to respect that right, as fully as it is given.
> The state's duty involves providing a benefit to the accused, not
> merely refraining from interference with the right. The obligation
> is unconditional. It does *not* come with a price tag, at all events,
> for disclosure of what is *fundamental* to the prosecutor's case. This
> is *not* an exceptional case where disclosure may be accomplished
> by providing an adequate opportunity to view the relevant record-
> ings.

Assume that disclosure time and financial expenditures will increase directly in proportion to the amount of resources expended on the investigation.
Investigator disclosure practices need to be able to adapt not only to

changes in the law of disclosure, but also to changes in the type of investigation being conducted.

3. Formulating a Disclosure Strategy

Formulate a disclosure strategy as early on in an investigation as possible, considering the questions of how, who and how much. Modify that strategy as the case progresses and different types of evidence are collected. Always remember that material organized to work for the investigation may need to be reorganized to work for the prosecution. Ideally, index all investigative material in a way that works for both investigators and prosecutors, holds evidence in a form that is readily disclosable, and that will not destroy annual budgets or attract court condemnation. The strategy needs to extend to how the disclosure will be served as well as structured.

In *R. v. Trang* (2002), 329 A.R. 241; 2002 ABQB 990 at paras. 9 & 10, there was a disclosure system in place that impressed the court:

> Sgt. B. . ., a member of the . . . Police . . . was in charge of disclosure and service of the Notices, Transcripts, Statements and updated or corrected versions of these (collectively the "Material") on each accused.
>
> Sgt. B. . . testified regarding the system he developed to ensure that the Material was served. He described: the process of selection of Calls, the request to the Crown for the appropriate Notice, the designation of groups of Calls into rounds ("Rounds") as they became available, the system for maintaining continuity, the verification process used to ensure that correct copies of the Material were served, the organization of the Rounds, the system established for delivery of the Material to each accused, his counsel or designate by members of the . . .Police Service . . ., the maintenance of a control copy of the Material in a secure area, the system of note-taking used by the officers serving the Material, the instructions given to those officers, and the system of reporting back so that Sgt. B. . . and Cst. L. . ., a member of the . . . who assisted him in these tasks, could be satisfied that service was effected as they had instructed.

Because a system had been put in place, the court was convinced disputed material actually had been disclosed to the defence. *Trang* still ran into serious disclosure difficulties because of the complex and voluminous nature of the case; compliance with the system needed improvement and more careful tracking of material was required at an earlier stage of the case, but the system was still worthwhile.

Even when you have a system, your disclosure strategy must be prepared to react to serious failures like the debacle that unfolded at an earlier hearing of *R. v. Trang*, 2001 ABQB 1091 at paras. 1 & 24:

> On October 1, 2001, the Court . . . learn[ed] that 25 boxes of additional disclosure had come to the attention of the Crown. The Court was informed on October 9, 2001 that the number of boxes had grown to 36.
>
> . . .
>
> As we have seen, late disclosure is likely to occur in a prosecution such as this, which is unprecedented in this Province having regard to the number of police officers (the estimate ranges from 300 to 600) having taken part in the investigation and over 281,000 calls intercepted, many of which required translation. In short, the fruits of the investigation turned out to be enormous and overwhelming.

Thirty-six missing boxes is an awful lot of disclosure gone astray, even in a highly complex prosecution. The remedy granted for late or absent disclosure will ultimately depend on how it affects an accused's right to make full answer and defence, but the better the disclosure procedures in place, the less likely large disclosure gaps will develop, and the less likely significant remedies will be granted against the Crown. Documents, electronic recordings and physical non-documentary evidence are the three main classes of information that require specific procedures to facilitate complete, timely and understandable disclosure.

The Necessity of a Disclosure Strategy

Q&A

Q: Why should I bother with a disclosure strategy? I can understand the need for an investigation strategy, and even a prosecution strategy, but a disclosure strategy? Disclosure seems like an awfully small part of the greater investigation and prosecution to merit going to a lot of trouble to plan out a strategy.

A: Disclosure has become such a problematic aspect of investigations and prosecutions — it may currently be *the* number one curable problem leading to case failure — that it is imperative to make some kind of plan for how it will happen in a way that is satisfactory to all the players in a case. In minor cases with small amounts of disclosure you will not need any kind of elaborate disclosure strategy, whereas for mega cases it may take weeks just to design the disclosure system that will be used.

4. How to Disclose Documents

Documents are the heart and soul of every investigation, ranging from original evidence like letters seized from co-conspirators to field notes intended only to refresh investigator memories. Even audio and video recordings add to the document pile when transcripts are prepared. There are primarily three options for document disclosure:

- provide photocopies;

- provide them in an electronic form; or

- only provide access, not copies.

Making photocopies of every relevant document is currently the most accepted method of disclosure preparation, and also the most costly. Where a case only involves a few hundred documents, and only a few accused, providing photocopies will usually be the preferred option until electronic disclosure standards become universal.

Disclosure in electronic form is a better option where thousands of documents and many accused are involved, avoiding the massive copying costs and difficult to manage reams of paper produced in mega-cases. Electronic disclosure involves scanning into a database all relevant documents as image copies, as well as full-text searchable copies using optical character recognition (OCR) technology. Greater or lesser amounts of human intervention are then required to organize and index the scanned copies, depending on the software used, level of document organization and searchability investigators intend to achieve. Disclosure can then be made by CD-ROM, other emerging mass storage technology, or e-mail.

Defence counsel object to electronic document disclosure for various reasons. They say they or their clients lack computer literacy, or lack hardware or software capable of reading the material. These technology-based objections can usually be addressed through providing the necessary training and technology to the defence, which is still often cheaper than providing traditional paper disclosure. More troubling are the "paper is superior to deal with" objections that electronic documents are difficult to locate, read or verify their completeness in their electronic-only form. These difficulties can become acute if the electronic documents were organized solely to serve the needs of the investigation, and not with an eye to the later prosecution.

Only providing access to documents was a method of disclosure sometimes employed before a broad disclosure obligation under the *Charter* was recognized. Today, providing actual copies in either paper or electronic form is widely accepted as being necessary. Only offering access could, however, be reasonable where documents are apparently not relevant, but might arguably have some tangential connection to a case.

Only providing access where documents are admitted by the prosecution to be relevant has been disapproved of, as in *R. v. Hallstone Products Ltd.* (1999), 46 O.R. (3d) 382 (S.C) at para. 39, where the prosecution had provided 4,900 pages of documents in hard copy, and offered access to the complete 853,000 pages secured in government facilities:

> in this case I find that the right of inspection is of little help to the defendants. Although I understand fully the concerns with the safety of the documents as expressed by Revenue Canada, there can be no question that if it is necessary to access hard copies and discuss them freely, doing so in a facility with the restrictions and limitations as exist here is very difficult. I accept the reasonableness of the contention that documents and discussion surrounding them will need to occur with frequency and continuously as this matter proceeds through the criminal justice system. There is also the added difficulty that some of the materials are secured in Scarborough while others are secured in Vancouver. As well some of the defendants are located in Toronto while others are in Vancouver and one is a resident in the United States. Clearly the right of inspection under these conditions and in these circumstances, again while of assistance, is not an adequate substitute for possessing hard copies.

All documents had been scanned onto CD-ROMs to be offered as disclosure, but the court found at paras. 28 and 38 there were problems with the software used to access those documents:

> On the issue of disclosure through the CD-ROMs, it became clear from the evidence . . . that, while helpful and useful, it is a less than perfect system. I do not believe that any of the parties would take issue with my findings on this point. In any event, my findings in respect of the CD-ROMs and the computer program are: (i) not all of documents contained in the program could be readily found, and some not at all; (ii) not all of the seized documents have been scanned into the computer program; (iii) efficiency and accessibility of documents is directly related to the level of skill and expertise of the operator; and (iv) information retrieved will only be as good as the commands or instructions used to retrieve it.

> . . .

> I wish to be clear that I am not suggesting that disclosure by way of a computer program such as that presented in this case would

not, in other circumstances, be totally appropriate and reliable. On the contrary, I find it to be impressive in its potential and use in cases where there are large numbers of documents. However, as I have found herein, I also believe that its potential in this specific case can only be that of an aid to disclosure and not a substitute for hard copies.

The form disclosure takes must be fair and reasonable in the circumstances of the case.

Where specialized software was used by investigators to search for electronic documents, providing exact copies of the source material searched through, and access to the software used to conduct the search, is likely sufficient disclosure according to *R. v. Cassidy* (2004), 180 O.A.C. 355 at paras. 11-14:

> We agree that in this case the proper disclosure order is that the Crown provide copies of the hard drives to the respondent and access on the basis proposed to the two software programs used to retrieve the material which is the subject of these charges.
>
> This will allow the defence to replicate in privacy the process used by the police to obtain the material underpinning the charges and to explore other matters that might reasonably be relevant to making full answer and defence, such as the context in which the material was found, or the dates on which it was saved to the hard drives.
>
> It is unnecessary for the Crown to go beyond that to purchase copies of the programs for the respondent or to pay for training the respondent's expert in their use. The evidence does not suggest that either step would permit the accused to do anything with the hard drives relevant to the defence that could not be done with the disclosure proposal now being made by the Crown.
>
> We suspect that an order similar to the one we would propose will be sufficient to ensure that the Crown meets its disclosure obligation in most cases involving electronic information. However, if there are cases in which the Crown's disclosure obligation can be met only by providing the accused with copies of software and the training to use it, that will be for the trial judge to consider when those cases arise.

In that case the software didn't need to be provided because the court found it was only a document search tool, not a document access tool. Where the mere accessing of electronic documents subject to disclosure requires specialized software, then an actual copy of the software will likely need to be provided. Investigator-prosecutor contact needs to take place at an early stage in large document-based investigations to determine the full extent of evolving disclosure obligations.

5. How to Disclose Video or Audio Recordings

The copying of video or audio recordings can be a particularly costly proposition where many recordings and multiple accused are involved. Recordings primarily fall into one of two categories:

- records of statements made by accused or third parties to investigators; and

- records of surveillance of accused or third parties covertly conducted by investigators.

Unedited copies of all recordings of statements connected to a case must be provided to the defence as statements are always important and usually not too numerous, but some discretion exists over the copying of covert surveillance recordings of questionable relevance where only access could be offered. Any recording transcripts, as well as edited copies of recordings the prosecution intends to use, should also be disclosed.

Fears surrounding the improper use of disclosure materials by accused, such as by distributing them to the public in order to embarrass a victim, are particularly serious where audio or video recordings are involved. Very difficult victim statements recounting traumatic events like sexual assaults may be part of disclosure. Courts have upheld limitations being placed on the way an accused can access disclosure materials where there is a risk disclosure will be improperly used, as in *R. v. Papageorgiou* (2003), 172 O.A.C. 50 at para. 14:

> The risk of harm from the improper use of disclosure materials is particularly pronounced, in our view, in cases involving sexual abuse. The *Report* of the Advisory Committee, in the context of such cases, reflects the important public policy concern that sensitive materials, including statements by complainants, not be exposed to misuse by unrepresented litigants during or after pending criminal proceedings. For that reason, the Committee endorsed the provision by the Crown to an unrepresented accused of private access to disclosure materials, including videotaped witness statements, under controlled circumstances.

Where accused are represented by counsel, the Crown might demand disclosure safeguarding undertakings from them in order to provide copies instead of just access to sensitive disclosure. But the courts have disapproved of the prosecution demanding blanket trust obligations for all disclosure where there is no sensitive information involved, as in *R. v. Little* (2001), 304 A.R. 15; 2001 ABPC 13 at paras. 54-56:

> I have taken into consideration the particulars of this case and find that these are straight forward drinking and driving and manner of driving offences under the *Criminal Code* and that there is no evidence to support concerns with regards to public safety, the security or privacy of witnesses or victims, or the need to protect the integrity of the administration of justice, in the circumstances of this particular case.
>
> I also considered the nature, extent, and effect of the trust conditions and find that these particular trust conditions are unnecessary because the obligations that the Crown seeks to impose are already provided for in the existing duties or obligations owed by defence counsel as officers of the court with regards to the use, delivery and dissemination of disclosure materials.
>
> Lastly, I have considered the balancing of the rights and interests of the accused and those that the Crown seeks to protect and find that there are no significant rights or interests that the Crown needs to protect in the circumstances of this particular case. Since there are no such interests to protect, there is no justification for restrictions or trust conditions being placed on disclosure in this case. The circumstances of this case do not disclose any realistic risk of misuse of the disclosure materials thereby making restrictions on the use of disclosure materials unnecessary.

Investigators need to flag for prosecutors where there are disclosure sensitivities that might require access or use restrictions, instead of leaving it to prosecutors to take a one-size-fits-all approach to disclosure restrictions. Other alternatives to only providing access are to provide a written transcript of a sensitive recording, together with access to the recording, or to include a privacy statement in the cover letter to the disclosure package indicating all disclosure remains the property of the Crown, is provided solely for the purposes of preparing a legal defence, and it is an offence to disseminate it to others.

Possession of Disclosure as an Offence

Q&A

Q: I sometimes investigate cases involving obscene or hateful material. How can disclosure be made, if possession of the disclosure itself is an offence?

A: Allegedly obscene or hateful material is different for disclosure purposes than inherently illegal substances like heroin. Receiving samples of what is thought to be seized heroin does not assist with preparation of a defence, other than for testing by an independent lab where results will be largely conclusive. Because there are no lab tests for whether materials are obscene or hateful at law, the defence will require extensive access to the materials. A prosecutor could ask a court for directions in these types of cases, including what limitations on the use of disclosure would be appropriate if copies are provided.

6. How to Disclose Physical Non-Documentary Evidence

Physical non-documentary evidence disclosure should aim to provide sufficient information for the defence to ascertain whether the evidence is indeed what it purports to be, like the murder weapon used to kill the deceased or drugs found on the accused. For the proverbial smoking gun, photographs, measurements, descriptions, forensic testing reports and carefully controlled access are the closest to copies of the item that can be provided. Even access is largely pointless for non-unique physical evidence like narcotics, unless the evidence is to be released under court order for independent lab testing.

An investigator forgetting to mention a seizure somewhere in the myriad of disclosable investigation reports is the greatest risk involved in the seizure of physical non-documentary evidence where no copy will be provided to the defence. Without a disclosed record of seizure, neither the defence nor prosecution may learn about a piece of evidence until halfway through the cross-examination of the seizing investigator at trial. Such a "pop-up seizure" problem is not a happy moment in court for anyone. The best way to address this risk is to openly disclose all exhibit logs specifying what evidence was seized, where it was seized from, who seized it, and who retained custody of it.

7. How to Deliver Disclosure

There is no requirement for formal "service" of disclosure, making disclosure unlike a summons or notice of appeal which have service requirements stipulated by the *Criminal Code*. It's possible disclosure obligations may in the future be formally codified by Parliament, but at the moment all you have to guide you is case law, local practice and rules of court, and any disclosure protocol concluded between your investigative agency and local prosecution service. Disclosure can be properly delivered by a variety of methods:

- by delivery to an accused at his residence or defence counsel at her office;

- by making it available for pick up from the prosecutor's office;

- by handing it over in court; or

- by delivering it through the mail or by courier.

Because it is the accused who has the right to pretrial disclosure, not the accused's lawyer, the prosecution must be satisfied a lawyer is formally retained to represent the accused and will accept disclosure on the accused's behalf before disclosure is provided by any method to counsel. The key to an acceptable method of delivery is the ability to later prove the accused actually received the disclosure, usually accomplished through notes made by investigators or disclosure clerks, court transcripts or signed delivery receipts. Receipt of disclosure does not have to be proved at every trial, but I have observed an increasing number of challenges to the means of disclosure delivery.

The prosecution can set some reasonable rules on how disclosure must be applied for and how it will be delivered, but insisting on unreasonable preconditions to delivery can amount to an impairment of an accused's right to make full answer and defence, as was the case in *R. v. Guiducci,* 2005 CarswellOnt 5 (S.C.) at paras. 7 & 10:

> In the present case, I have found on the stay application that the policy and practice of the Crown's Office . . . in refusing to deliver to an accused the Crown's disclosure materials in a situation where there was no private or sensitive information was without rational justification and constituted a breach of the accused's rights under s.7 of the *Charter* to make full answer and defence to the charges. In essence, the Crown's declining to deliver to these applicants the disclosure package respecting charges of impaired driving and related offences upon confirmation that the applicants had retained counsel on those charges effectively delayed the applicants in their decision as to how to plead to the offences charged and determine the appropriate response to those charges.
>
> . . .

The correspondence between counsel for the accused and the Crown Attorney's Office appearing in the materials filed for the substantive application establishes that it was the policy of the . . . Crown's Office not to deliver disclosure packages to an accused person or persons where the Crown's Office had knowledge or notice that the accused was represented by counsel. In this situation, the refusal to deliver a disclosure package for an offence for which there was no sensitive or private information concerns to an accused whom the Crown knew to be represented by counsel, inadvertent or careless on the part of the Crown's Office must be considered as 'well beyond inadvertent or careless failure to discharge a duty'. In sum, the act or failure to act was advertent.

The Crown's office subsequently changed its disclosure policy in response to the court's ruling, and the accused was awarded costs. The one simple rule of disclosure cannot be frustrated by unreasonable delivery requirements.

What If an Accused Refuses Disclosure?

Q&A

Q: What should I do with the disclosure if I arrive at a self-represented accused's residence with a box of disclosure, and the accused says he doesn't want it, and absolutely refuses to take it?

A: Make notes about your attempt to provide disclosure, what you told the accused about the disclosure, and what the accused said in response. If you can convince the accused to let you leave the disclosure on his front porch, or in his garage, then that would be the best course of action since he might later change his mind about wanting disclosure, or his lawyer might ask him for it. Otherwise, take the disclosure back to your office and file it away — you did your best to comply with a constitutional obligation that benefits the accused. It is important to let the prosecutor know about this refusal so he is able to respond to any later trial disclosure complaints.

DEALING WITH PRETRIAL NOTICES AS ACCOMPANYING DISCLOSURE

Statutory pretrial notice requirements are often most efficiently delivered together with the disclosure package as they can then be directly tied to related evidence, thus avoiding overly complicated notices that attempt to describe extremely lengthy numbers of documents or recordings by name. Proof of notice provision is facilitated, accused or counsel do not have to be tracked down more than once to be provided with disclosure and notice, and notices will not be forgotten if checked off as part of a larger disclosure "to do" list. As discussed in Chapter 17, the *Canada Evidence Act* notice of intention to produce documents at trial, the *Criminal Code* notice of intention to call an expert witness, notice of analyst on impaired driving, notice of weapons analyst and notice to introduce intercepts, as well as the *Controlled Drugs and Substances Act* analyst notice could all appropriately be part of disclosure so long as they are prominently identified. However, disclosure should not be unduly delayed solely to accommodate a pretrial notice if the notice will take some time to finalize — it can always be provided separately at a later time before the statutory notice deadline.

THE CONSEQUENCES OF NON-DISCLOSURE OR LATE DISCLOSURE

The consequences of non-disclosure or late disclosure run the full gamut of remedies from brief adjournment up to stay of proceedings. Because there are few hard and fast rules about disclosure other than the one simple rule, it is sometimes difficult to say what amounts to non-disclosure or late disclosure other than situations where there has been a failure to provide clearly relevant and not privileged material within a reasonable time prior to trial. The burden is on the defence to demonstrate the accused's right to make full answer and defence to a charge has been hampered due to a disclosure lapse amounting to a *Charter* breach, and it is the defence who must also demonstrate why a particular remedy is justified.

Once a breach concerning disclosure has been established, the full panoply of remedies contained in s. 24 of the *Charter* can be invoked. *R. v. O'Connor*, [1995] 4 S.C.R. 411 at para. 77, covered the principal disclosure remedies:

> Thus, where the adverse impact upon the accused's ability to make full answer and defence is curable by a disclosure order, then such a remedy, combined with an adjournment where necessary to enable defence counsel to review the disclosed information, will generally be appropriate.

> There may, however, be exceptional situations where, given the advanced state of the proceedings, it is simply not possible to remedy through reasonable means the prejudice to the accused's right to make full answer and defence. In such cases, the drastic remedy of a stay of proceedings may be necessary.

Section 24 *Charter* remedies are only limited by the creativity of counsel and the court.

Other possible remedies include the right to recall witnesses, exclusion of non-disclosed evidence and even costs against the Crown, a rare event in criminal matters which happened in *R. v. Peekeekoot* (2002), 311 A.R. 95; 2002 ABPC 23 at para. 71-73:

> In my view, the non-disclosure in this case is flagrant and unjustified. Requests for disclosure of information available by a few key strokes (the criminal records of Crown witnesses only produced some 5 months after being requested, statements from the accused on one occasion lost and on another occasion after an aborted trial date were still not produced for another month and some days, photographs taken on the date of the alleged offences were only produced on the morning of trial) all qualify as flagrant and unjustified. Due to this non-disclosure, a trial date was lost and Peekeekoot remained in custody awaiting trial for another 5 and 1/2 months.
>
> In my opinion, a cost award is appropriate in addition to an accelerated trial date. But for the fact that Defence Counsel made no applications to deal with disclosure before the aborted November 29, 2001 trial date, the award of costs would be substantially higher.
>
> However, taking all the circumstances into account, I assess costs against the Crown in the sum of $2,500.00 payable forthwith. This award is reflective of the non-disclosure particulars set forth above.

Disclosure failures are entirely preventable if the material is in your possession.

Discovery of a disclosure omission prior to trial, no bad faith in withholding the information, missing disclosure being provided with dispatch, and no substantial prejudice suffered by the accused will usually lead to an adjournment and at most to a costs award. Discovery during or after trial, and willful or negligent withholding or destruction of relevant evidence could lead to a more severe remedy including the stay of proceedings as described in *R. v. O'Connor,* [1995] 4 S.C.R. 411 at para. 82, as being "appropriate 'in the clearest of cases', where the prejudice to the accused's right to make full answer and defence cannot be remedied or where irreparable prejudice would be caused to the integrity of the judicial system if the prosecution were continued."

The boundaries of disclosure are now well defined, subject to relevance and privilege. The negotiation of disclosure protocols and implementation of reliable disclosure systems are capable of reducing disclosure failures to minor annoyances from the blight they sometimes currently represent. If standard categories of relevant evidence were to be identified for all types of cases, then that evidence could be automatically collated and reproduced after being vetted for privilege. A copy of the charge, its particulars, witness statements, criminal records, expert witness reports, a copy of the physical evidence, search warrants and wiretaps plus their informations to obtain are all usually required for basic disclosure. Only once the job of producing disclosure is substantially complete can investigators and prosecutors turn their attention to the pressing task of preparing for the actual conduct of the trial.

For Including Everything in the Disclosure Package Except the Irrelevant and the Privileged

KEY POINTS

✓ All material relevant to a prosecution must be disclosed to the defence, subject to issues of privilege. Disclosure must be organized, complete and timely. While disclosure is an ongoing obligation, try to limit the number of separate disclosure packages you need to track. The circumstances of a case will dictate what amounts to an accessible form of disclosure. Disclosure costs must be budgeted into every major investigation financial plan, and an agreement reached with prosecution authorities as to who will bear those costs.

✓ A disclosure strategy will ensure the disclosure demands of many minor cases or a couple of major cases do not overwhelm the ability of investigators to collect, organize, review, copy and deliver the reams of relevant disclosure the law now requires be provided to the defence.

✓ Photocopies, electronic copies or only providing access are the primary options available for the disclosure of documents. Copies of audio or video recordings should be disclosed in an unedited form, where all recorded statements connected to a case will be relevant for disclosure, but access only might be offered to certain arguably irrelevant surveillance recordings. The best disclosure that can usually be offered of physical non-documentary evidence is photographs, descriptions, measurements, test reports and controlled access.

✓ Deliver disclosure by a means through which you can later prove the accused received it. Providing pretrial notices at the same time as disclosure ensures timeliness and allows them to be tied into the physical documents of which they give notice.

✓ The consequences of non-disclosure or late disclosure can run a full gamut of remedies right up to a stay of proceedings, depending on how the accused's ability to make full answer and defence to charges is affected.

FURTHER READING

Cases

R. v. Carosella, [1997] 1 S.C.R. 80. Non-disclosure may lead to the remedy of a stay of proceedings where the ability to make full answer and defence is impaired.

R. v. O'Connor, [1995] 4 S.C.R. 411. Private records in possession of a third party must be established to be "likely relevant and necessary" to make full answer and defence in order for disclosure to be required.

R. v. Stinchcombe, [1991] 3 S.C.R. 326. This is the case that started it all, at times interpreted more broadly than its actual pronouncements justify. It generally holds that material relevant to a prosecution, and not privileged, must be disclosed to the defence.

R. v. Taillefer; R. v. Duguay, [2003] 3 S.C.R. 307. There only need be a reasonable possibility of information being useful to the accused in making full answer and defence in order for disclosure to be required, regardless of whether the prosecution intends to introduce the information as evidence at trial.

Books, Articles and Reports

Attorney General of Ontario's Advisory Committee, *Report of the Attorney General's Advisory Committee on Charge Screening, Disclosure and Resolution Discussions* (Toronto: Queen's Printer, 1993).

I. Carter, "Chipping Away at Stinchcombe: The Expanding Privilege Exception to Disclosure" (2002) 50 C.R. (5th) 332.

Department of Justice Canada, *Disclosure Reform Consultation Paper* (November 2004), on-line: *www.canada.justice.gc.ca/en/cons/disc-ref/*. Floats some interesting ideas on how to fix many of the long-standing procedural problems that lead to protracted litigation.

Law Reform Commission of Canada, *Discovery in Criminal Cases* (Ottawa: Law Reform Commission of Canada, 1974). An interesting older look at extending civil litigation discovery processes into criminal procedure.

P. Rosenthal, "Disclosure to the Defence After September 11: Sections 37 and 38 of the *Canada Evidence Act*" (2003) 48 Crim. L.Q. 186.

M.D. Segal, *Disclosure and Production in Criminal Cases*, loose-leaf (Toronto: Carswell, 2000). A one-volume supplemented book that references the major cases.

C. Sherrin and P. Downes, *The Criminal Lawyer's Guide to Disclosure and Production* (Aurora, ON: Canada Law Book, 2000). This short volume offers a good overview.

CHAPTER SEVENTEEN

WORKING WITH THE PROSECUTOR TO PREPARE FOR TRIAL: YOU ARE ALL ON THE SAME TEAM

This process of developing logical, consistent positions on disputed facts is what counsel call developing a theory of the case.

> T.A. Mauet, D.G. Casswell & G.P. Macdonald, *Fundamentals of Trial Techniques — Canadian Edition* (Boston: Little Brown, 1984) at 8.

In This Chapter

- The necessity of distinct investigator and prosecutor roles
- The necessity of an early meeting with the prosecutor
- A unified theory of the case: keep it simple and sensible
- The necessity of doing pretrial witness interviews
- The necessity of doing follow-up investigation
- The necessity of serving subpoenas and pretrial notices
- Respective roles in discontinuing proceedings

The historic separation between investigators and prosecutors can foster harmful isolationism if each group thinks of itself as an independent, competitive camp. Each camp then can blame the other camp for its problems and failures, and feels no need to take responsibility for what happens to a case before it enters or after it leaves its own camp. The camp mentality leads to two solitudes that are not at all conducive to maximizing prospects for investigation and prosecution case success.

A team mentality is necessary to maximize case success. To use a sports analogy, think of investigators and prosecutors as part of a football team. At the initial stages the only players on the field are investigators. The quarterback is also an investigator. But the players may find prosecutor coaching advice helpful in advancing their game. The ball is the evidence. As the evidence gets moved toward the mid-field, the prosecutor-coaches may become more and more useful in advancing the game. After the ball passes the mid-field point a prosecutor takes over as quarterback, calling all the plays now that charges have been laid. The same investigators are still playing on the field, but the game becomes more controlled as the ball gets closer to the end zone. Only a few yards might be gained on every play. The prosecutor-quarterback might decide to give the ball to a running back, or throw a long pass to a wide receiver. The team might fumble the ball. Only a concerted team effort will lead to success. Just because the quarterbacks switch mid-way should not undermine the unity of the team.

Preparing the prosecutor for trial involves more than just submitting the prosecution brief and sending out the disclosure package. The evidence must be reviewed with the prosecutor, a theory of the case developed, evidence confirmation and witness rapport interviews conducted with civilians, follow-up investigation conducted, subpoenas served, and pretrial notices provided. Each of the many pretrial tasks may by themselves seem insignificant, but taking care of them collectively makes the difference between a mishap-filled case that could bring discredit and doom to investigators and prosecutors alike, and a case that moves like a star running back, relentlessly driving towards the end zone.

THE NECESSITY OF DISTINCT INVESTIGATOR AND PROSECUTOR ROLES

Having to go to all this effort to brief someone else on the facts of a case that you already know inside-out leads to the question of why investigators don't prosecute their own cases. There are two fundamental difficulties with combining the investigative and prosecutorial functions: (1) the *Canadian*

Charter of Rights and Freedoms in 1982 resulted in the technicalization of the criminal law so that it is now very difficult even for specialist criminal lawyers to keep up with new legal developments, and (2) our common law system is based upon independent prosecution review and conduct of all charges by the responsible Attorney General, as represented by the Attorney General's prosecutors. Independent review does *not* establish that prosecutors know better than investigators whether charges should proceed. Rather, the system is built so that there are two checks on whether charges *must* proceed: one at the charge laying stage where the investigator has full discretion (other than in British Columbia, Quebec and New Brunswick) over whether to lay the charge, and another at the prosecution stage where the discretion belongs to the prosecutor. This double veto makes sense for a system that wishes to avoid being overwhelmed by even greater numbers of charges than it already faces, charges that might be proceeding on weak evidence or could even lead to wrongful convictions, and shields charging and prosecution decisions from political pressure.

The marked separation between investigators and prosecutors was justified in *R. v. Regan*, [2002] 1 S.C.R. 297 at para. 66, quoting from the report of the Royal Commission on Donald Marshall Jr.:

> We recognize that cooperative and effective consultation between the police and the Crown is also essential to the proper administration of justice. But under our system, the policing function—that of investigation and law enforcement—is distinct from the prosecuting function. We believe the maintenance of a distinct line between these two functions is essential to the proper administration of justice.

The distinct line is tempered by the need for cooperation — investigators and prosecutors are in a co-dependent relationship. Just because there is a legal line separating them does not mean they cannot practically function as a team. *R. v. Regan*, [2002] 1 S.C.R. 297 at para. 64, found flexibility is built into the separation of roles: "while the police tasks of investigation and charge-laying must remain distinct and independent from the Crown role of prosecution, I do not think it is the role of this Court to make a pronouncement on the details of the practice of *how* that separation must be maintained." So investigators and prosecutors can work out their own cooperative working arrangements.

There has been a trend over the last few decades towards Canadian prosecutors becoming more involved at the early stages of investigations as newer investigative techniques like wiretaps and newer offences like proceeds of crime prove to be legally very complex. Likewise, the increasing factual complexity of trials has required investigators to remain more actively involved in cases after referrals to prosecutors have taken place. The Integrated Proceeds of Crime (IPOC) units established in the early 1990s involving co-located RCMP commercial crime investigators and Federal Prosecution Service prosecutors, and the more recent advent of Integrated Market Enforcement Teams (IMET) to deal with criminal capital markets fraud are examples of the blurring line between investigation and prosecution, but even there police-prosecution separation is maintained by co-located lawyers only playing an advisory role that generally does not extend to prosecuting the cases on which they advise.

THE NECESSITY OF AN EARLY MEETING WITH THE PROSECUTOR

After charges have been laid, the prosecution brief submitted, disclosure made, and it is clear the case will proceed to preliminary inquiry or trial, investigators should take the initiative and offer to meet the prosecutor before the trial date, or at least have contact by telephone. Investigators can find out which parts of their evidence to focus on as being most important to the legal issues in dispute, which parts of the case are weak so that additional investigation can be conducted, and assist the prosecutor in reviewing the evidence. The bigger the case, the earlier a meeting needs to take place.

Investigators will have completed their comprehensive review of evidence sufficiency at the time they lay charges, whereas prosecutors may only be able to turn their minds to how to present the evidence close to the time of trial. Without investigator involvement, a prosecutor might only amount to a bundle of legal principles lacking the fundamental factual understanding of a case that makes the difference between evidence admission and exclusion. In major cases, an initial joint review of the evidence needs to be conducted before disclosure (and possibly before charging) to determine what material is relevant or whether disclosure exceptions are required for privileged material. The pretrial preparation phase of a case builds on the team concept whereby prosecutors help investigators understand the law during their investigations, and investigators help prosecutors understand the facts during their prosecutions. Lead investigators should follow the Trial Preparation Checklist at the end of this chapter.

The *Memorandum of Understanding Between the Royal Canadian Mounted Police and the Federal Prosecution Service Respecting the Conduct of Criminal Investigations and Prosecutions* (5 July 2001) includes formal agreement on pretrial meetings at 3.1.11: "Lead RCMP investigators, to the extent reasonably possible, make themselves available to review with prosecutors the facts of the case and disclosure issues prior to preliminary hearing or trial." My prosecutions with the best outcomes have always been the ones where I met with investigators prior to trial. Investigator-prosecutor rapport was established. Surprises and stress at trial were reduced for both prosecutors and investigators. Working relationships were enhanced.

When the Prosecutor is Too Busy To Meet

Q&A

Q: I used to work in a rural detachment where the local prosecutor was always more than happy to meet with me before trial, and all the investigators and prosecutors knew each other by their first names. Now I work in a highly urbanized detachment where very few of the investigators and prosecutors know each other, and prosecutors tell me they are too busy doing court appearances to meet with me before the trial date. How can I follow your advice of setting up an early meeting with the prosecutor if the prosecutor won't agree to attend such a meeting?

A: Prosecutors in high case volume urbanized offices may have set up a division of labour where some prosecutors spend more time in court, and others devote more of their time to vetting files or specializing in certain types of cases like sexual assault or proceeds of crime. Investigators should be able to meet with these vetting or specialist prosecutors to discuss case problems considerably before trial, even if different prosecutors will be appearing in court on the day of trial.

A UNIFIED THEORY OF THE CASE: KEEP IT SIMPLE AND SENSIBLE

The single most important task faced by both investigators and prosecutors preparing for any criminal or regulatory trial is the development of a rational and cohesive theory of the case. This theory at the prosecution stage may or may not be the same as the theory investigators held during the investigation. Investigators could base their theory on all information discovered during the investigation, whereas prosecutors must base their theory solely on admissible trial evidence. Excluding inadmissible informer information, inadmissible statements, and inadmissible seized evidence could require the case theory to be reinvented to meet the requirements of the court process.

Developing a theory of the case is necessary for the prosecution to possess internal consistency, and for the defence to know exactly what case it has to answer as noted in *R. v. Rose*, [1998] 3 S.C.R. 262 at para. 61:

> The right to prior knowledge of what is contained in the Crown's evidence and theory of the case is fundamental because it is the Crown's burden to present evidence sufficient to show guilt beyond a reasonable doubt. Without knowing the Crown's basic case, the defence would have to put forward its case in a vacuum, and could not even begin to answer it.

Depending on how the evidence comes out, there might be some theory refinements or changes in direction during the course of a trial, but a radical mid-trial theory shift indicates an inadequate theory in the beginning.

Investigators who work with prosecutors in the initial development of the prosecution theory of the case will prevent fundamental factual flaws appearing in the theory as the evidence unfolds at trial. The theory should be simple, so the judge or jury can keep it in mind throughout the calling of evidence. The theory should also make sense, so the judge or jury are not asked to overly stretch their powers of belief. All too often case theories violate these rules.

Defence theories based on reasoning like "(1) he wasn't in the country at the time of the murder, but if he was (2) he had never met the deceased, but if he did (3) it was only a casual acquaintance, but if it was more than that (4) they were sexually intimate on only a few occasions and he would never do anything to harm her, and if he did harm her (5) it was self-defence!" are particularly prone to violating the keep it simple and sensible rules. Prosecutor theories can fall into similar traps. Particularly in conspiracy cases, it will sometimes be necessary to get rid of peripheral charges or accused from the bulk of a case in order to present a unified theory supported by evidence of all required elements of each offence, and tie those elements to each accused by explaining their actions and interactions in a way that makes sense. The theory is a brief summary of the story the prosecution will tell; ideally it will be an interesting and perhaps even fascinating story. It is the true life stories that are, after all, often the most interesting.

The Value of a Theory of the Case

Q & A

Q: Why do we need a theory of the case if we already have a mountain of evidence that will prove the case?

A: The more evidence you have, the more you need a theory of the case. Not understanding the case because of the evidence is like not seeing the forest because of the trees. The theory of the case clarifies and focuses the evidence, demonstrating why the prosecution has proven beyond a reasonable doubt that the accused committed the offences as charged.

THE NECESSITY OF DOING PRETRIAL WITNESS INTERVIEWS

1. Investigator-Led, Civilian-Witness Evidence-Confirmation Interviews

Conducting civilian-witness interviews close to the time of trial to confirm witnesses still hold to statements they made months or years before, and possibly to pin down details that remain vague in previous statements or that have only recently become relevant due to developments in the theory of the case, is vital to avoid surprises when those witnesses take the stand at trial. The prosecutor can not attend such interviews because of the risk of becoming a witness to the statements. Any new relevant information that comes to light in evidence confirmation interviews must of course be disclosed to the defence along with older relevant statements.

All is not lost if a witness claims to have no memory or a different memory of important facts given in an earlier statement, but prosecutors need to be informed about the problem so they can make additional disclosure and consider tendering the earlier recorded statement directly into evidence as a past recollection recorded, supplemented by whatever live testimony can be offered of facts the witness still remembers. People's recollections legitimately change over time, with details tending to fade but sometimes important pieces of information being newly remembered. Securing video recorded statements from key witnesses as discussed in Chapter 12 is especially helpful in guarding against witnesses becoming unavailable, forgetful or recanting at trial.

2. Prosecutor-Led, Witness-Rapport Interviews

Ideally all witnesses will also be met by the prosecutor prior to the trial date to go over each witness' testimony, explain court procedures, and establish a rapport that can be further built on at trial. These prosecutor-led, witness-rapport interviews could be conducted immediately following investigator-led, evidence-confirmation interviews. Investigators are sometimes surprised to learn they must be present at all meetings between civilian witnesses and prosecutors to prevent the prosecutor becoming a witness in the proceedings and being forced to withdraw from the case if a civilian reveals relevant new case information at a meeting and later tells a contradictory story on the witness stand. The presence of investigators is also valuable because they are the ones who will already have some kind of rapport with the civilians, and can assist in making them feel at ease in answering the prosecutor's questions about possibly quite traumatic events. The *Memorandum of Understanding Between the Royal Canadian Mounted Police and the Federal Prosecution Service Respecting the Conduct of Criminal Investigations and Prosecutions* (5 July 2001) recognizes the requirement for investigator involvement in prosecutor interviews with civilian witness at 3.1.10: "As requested and where reasonably possible, the RCMP attend and participate in post-charge interviews of prospective witnesses by prosecutors and maintain notes of such interviews for disclosure purposes."

Some prosecutor-civilian witness meetings may even happen as early as the pre-charge stage so that the prosecutor can assess the strength of the case. In *R. v. Regan*, [2002] 1 S.C.R. 297 at para. 64, the propriety of pre-charge prosecutor-civilian witness meetings was put in question:

> The question before this Court is whether the Crown's objectivity is necessarily compromised if Crown counsel conduct pre-charge interviews of witnesses without the single, express intention of screening out charges before they are laid. In essence, this Court has been asked to consider whether, at law, Crown prosecutors must be prevented from engaging in wide-ranging pre-charge interviews in order to maintain their essential function as "Ministers of Justice".

Ultimately the court upheld the practice, but stressed prosecutors cannot play an investigative role by gathering new evidence in those meetings. Any investigator acting as a witness to prosecutor meetings with civilians should take careful notes of what is said by the witnesses in order to be in the best position if necessary to offer disclosure and testify at trial about the meeting. It is not that prosecutors have something to hide in this pretrial preparation, but the administration of justice would grind to a halt if prosecutors continually became witnesses in their own cases purely due to the case preparation in which they must engage.

Prosecutor Hand Holding

Q&A

Q: Why do I need to waste my time holding the prosecutor's hand while she meets with witnesses?

A: Civilian witnesses change their stories. If a civilian witness gives a new version of events to a prosecutor during a pretrial meeting without an investigator present, it would fall to the prosecutor to record the changed statement, disclose it and possibly become a witness if the civilian later denies the new story told to the prosecutor.

THE NECESSITY OF DOING FOLLOW-UP INVESTIGATION

Through no fault of investigators, there may be evidentiary holes in a case that need to be plugged immediately before or even during the trial, requiring a committal of significant investigative resources. These demands could be caused by missing prosecution evidence, a recanting or unavailable witness, a court's refusal to admit evidence necessary to prove an essential element of the charge, or unanticipated defence evidence and theories requiring rebuttal evidence. It will usually be the prosecutor who suggests last minute follow-up investigation.

Sometimes investigative resources are in short supply, but the reasons for the request for additional investigation need to be fully explored with prosecutors before a decision is made *not* to investigate. Investigators also need to consider the consequences to the prosecution arising from a decision not to investigate further. The preferable approach to dealing with follow-up investigation requirements is through a comprehensive investigator-prosecutor memorandum of understanding on principles to guide the deployment of resources, rather than approaching each case in an *ad hoc* and possibly inconsistent manner. For example, the *Memorandum of Understanding Between the Royal Canadian Mounted Police and the Federal Prosecution Service Respecting the Conduct of Criminal Investigators and Prosecutions* (5 July 2001) states at 3.1.8 "The RCMP carry out additional investigative steps that are reasonably required by prosecutors to ensure they can effectively present their case and carry out their duties."

Overcoming Mutual Lack of Understanding

Q&A

Q: While I realize my role as an investigator isn't over until a court gives final judgment in a case, it seems some prosecutors want me to be at their beck and call, doing trivial tasks like hunting down and disclosing one additional page of not very relevant notes. Don't they realize I'm also working on other cases, and have a limited role after charges are laid?

A: A lack of mutual understanding between prosecutors and investigators can doom cases. In a perfect world, prosecutors and investigators would perhaps be required to exchange jobs for a couple of years, or even for a couple of days, in order to better understand why requests that seem simple to the requester are not in fact as simple for the doer. It is only through improved communication that the situation can change. Prosecutors need to clearly explain case requirements, and investigators need to just as clearly articulate available resources.

THE NECESSITY OF SERVING SUBPOENAS AND PRETRIAL NOTICES

Investigators will also sometimes be required to prepare and provide subpoenas and pretrial notices as part of their trial preparation duties. In larger urban areas investigative agencies may have staff devoted to such duties, but in smaller agencies or areas with lower charge volume these duties may fall to the lead case investigator. If you don't ask prosecutors about pretrial subpoena and notice obligations, you might wind up assuming prosecutors are preparing them, and they might assume you are doing so, with the result that no one learns until the day of trial that no subpoenas or notices were prepared.

With any subpoena or notice, investigators need to be concerned with three factors:

- the document is drafted in a way that accords with statutory requirements;

- the document names the correct person, offences, place and date for appearance in court (if applicable); and

- all reasonable efforts are made to serve or provide the document in a way that is acceptable under the relevant Act for that type of document.

Demystification of the law says getting these three factors right only requires finding the language of the applicable Act, reading through it, and checking off that its requirements have been met. Early investigator-prosecutor contact will clarify pretrial subpoena or notice requirements not specified in detail by an Act, like what "reasonable" means where an Act only stipulates "reasonable notice" must be provided.

1. The Subpoena

Sub-section 698 of the *Criminal Code* provides an uncomplicated subpoena power for any federal offence prosecution:

> **698.** (1) Where a person is likely to give material evidence in a proceeding to which this Act applies, a subpoena may be issued in accordance with this Part requiring that person to attend to give evidence.

Subpoenas can also be sought under provincial or territorial legislation. Subpoenas should be sought from the court before which you intend to bring a witness.

Section 700 of the *Code* specifies the scope of subpoena power:

> **700.** (1) A subpoena shall require the person to whom it is directed to attend, at a time and place to be stated in the subpoena, to give evidence and, if required, to bring with him anything that he has in his possession or under his control relating to the subject-matter of the proceedings.
>
> (2) A person who is served with a subpoena issued under this Part shall attend and shall remain in attendance throughout the proceedings unless he is excused by the presiding judge, justice or provincial court judge.

The main distinction to watch for in the world of subpoenas is between a normal subpoena only requiring a witness to attend court and testify on the date specified, and a subpoena *duces tecum* additionally requiring the witness to bring documents or other things relevant to a case, including anything explicitly named in the subpoena. Usually there will be a box to check off on the subpoena form if it is a subpoena *duces tecum*. Subpoenas can only be served by a peace officer or other person qualified to serve civil process, so regulatory investigators may need to engage the services of a local police detachment or find some other means of service if none of them are designated as peace officers or process servers.

2. The *Canada Evidence Act* Notice

The *Canada Evidence Act*, R.S.C. 1985, c. C-5 (*CEA*), contains a grab-bag of evidentiary provisions that assist in the admission of evidence of judicial proceedings, official government or corporate documents, public documents, and business records at trials of federal offences, but also impose obligations on those seeking such admission. Although the common law now affords more scope for admission of documentary evidence than when the *CEA* was first passed, prosecutors continue to rely on the *CEA* as an alternate means of admitting evidence in document intensive cases. Sections 28 and 30 of the *CEA* require the prosecution to provide advance notice of any documents it intends to introduce pursuant to a variety of provisions in the Act:

> **28.** (1) No copy of any book or other document shall be admitted in evidence, under the authority of section 23, 24, 25, 26 or 27, on

any trial, unless the party intending to produce the copy has before the trial given to the party against whom it is intended to be produced reasonable notice of that intention.

(2) The reasonableness of the notice referred to in subsection (1) shall be determined by the court, judge or other person presiding, but the notice shall not in any case be less than seven days.

. . .

30. (7) Unless the court orders otherwise, no record or affidavit shall be admitted in evidence under this section unless the party producing the record or affidavit has, at least seven days before its production, given notice of his intention to produce it to each other party to the legal proceeding and has, within five days after receiving any notice in that behalf given by any such party, produced it for inspection by that party.

It is good practice to give a *CEA* notice for all disclosed documents not already having some other clear means of admissibility, since it is tough to know in advance of trial when reliance on the Act might become necessary.

By far the easiest way to deal with drafting and providing the *CEA* document notice is to include it as part of the disclosure package. Title any *CEA* document notice "Notice of Intention to Produce Documents at Trial Pursuant to the *Canada Evidence Act*" without specifying the *CEA* sections being relied upon, as there are often alternative *CEA* sections available for admission of the same document, and no requirement to name the precise section in the notice. If you have a short number of documents, they could all be listed in the notice or copies of those documents simply attached to it. You may have to accurately describe numerous documents by group unless you provide the notice at the same time as disclosure, where you could reference the number of binders or boxes the notice applies to and perhaps attach their respective tables of contents to the notice. According to s-s. 30(7) of the *CEA*, the notice of intention to produce documents must be given at least seven days prior to production of the documents at trial — meaning notice could be given after the trial starts, so long as no documents are introduced until seven days after notice.

3. The Expert Notices

The most common way to tender expert evidence in court is to call a live witness. To forestall some experts having to give evidence thousands of times per year, certain Acts let them attest to certificates containing the basic opinions they would give on narrow subjects were they called as witnesses. Where either a live expert will be called to the stand, or a certificate of an expert will be relied upon to prove a fact in issue, the prosecution is usually required to provide the defence with advance notice together with a copy of the certificate of analyst or summary of the proposed expert testimony so that the defence has an adequate opportunity to assess the evidence and prepare a response.

a. *Notice of Intention to Call an Expert Witness*

A pretrial notice of intention to call an expert witness notice is required under s-s. 657.3(3) of the *Criminal Code*:

> **657.3.** (3) For the purpose of promoting the fair, orderly and efficient presentation of the testimony of witnesses,
>
>> (a) a party who intends to call a person as an expert witness shall, at least thirty days before the commencement of the trial or within any other period fixed by the justice or judge, give notice to the other party or parties of his or her intention to do so, accompanied by
>>
>>> (i) the name of the proposed witness,
>>>
>>> (ii) a description of the area of expertise of the proposed witness that is sufficient to permit the other parties to inform themselves about that area of expertise, and
>>>
>>> (iii) a statement of the qualifications of the proposed witness as an expert;
>>
>> (b) in addition to complying with paragraph (a), a prosecutor who intends to call a person as an expert witness shall, within a reasonable period before trial, provide to the other party or parties
>>
>>> (i) a copy of the report, if any, prepared by the proposed witness for the case, and
>>>
>>> (ii) if no report is prepared, a summary of the opinion anticipated to be given by the proposed witness and the grounds on which it is based;

These requirements can be challenging to meet because of the lengthy 30-day pretrial notice period, the particular person named as the proposed expert could wind up being unavailable by the time the trial rolls around, defining the area of expertise might be difficult where the prosecution has not yet fully developed its theory of the case, and providing a qualifications summary could require obtaining a *curriculum vitae* from the expert. However, the expert report or opinion summary only need be provided to other parties a "reasonable" time before trial, which could be later than 30 days in advance.

Early investigator-prosecutor contact is needed to ascertain if a formal expert will be required for a case. Advances in science make expert opinions increasingly relevant in proving essential elements of a wide array of offences. It is usually the lead investigator who will locate the expert, commission any report, and prepare or at least contribute to the preparation of the expert witness notice. No s-s. 657.3(3) *Code* expert notice will be required where another statutory provision authorizes an expert's certificate to be filed as evidence, although such certificates usually require their own notices as seen below.

b. *Notice of CDSA Analyst*

Section 51 of the *Controlled Drugs and Substances Act* (*CDSA*) creates a statutory deeming rule for admission of evidence of a drug analyst, but only after "reasonable notice" prior to tendering a certificate or report of an analyst:

> **51.** (1) Subject to this section, a certificate or report prepared by an analyst under subsection 45(2) is admissible in evidence in any prosecution for an offence under this Act or the regulations or any other Act of Parliament and, in the absence of evidence to the contrary, is proof of the statements set out in the certificate or report, without proof of the signature or official character of the person appearing to have signed it.
>
> (2) The party against whom a certificate or report of an analyst is produced under subsection (1) may, with leave of the court, require the attendance of the analyst for the purpose of cross-examination.
>
> (3) Unless the court otherwise orders, no certificate or report shall be received in evidence under subsection (1) unless the party intending to produce it has, before its production at trial, given to

the party against whom it is intended to be produced reasonable notice of that intention, together with a copy of the certificate or report.

52. (1) For the purposes of this Act and the regulations, the giving of any notice, whether orally or in writing, or the service of any document may be proved by the oral evidence of, or by the affidavit or solemn declaration of, the person claiming to have given that notice or served that document.

(2) Notwithstanding subsection (1), the court may require the affiant or declarant to appear before it for examination or cross-examination in respect of the giving of notice or proof of service.

Here notice can be provided after the start of trial, although it must still be a "reasonable" time prior to producing the certificate. In the hundreds of drug prosecutions I conducted, I rarely encountered notice and service problems with drug analysis certificates but the lack of problems was hardly good luck, rather it was the result of good systems put in place by investigators.

c. *Notice of Blood-Alcohol Analyst*

There are several provisions for admission of evidence of analyst by certificate contained within s-s. 258(1) of the *Criminal Code* pertaining to impaired driving offences, all of which ultimately tie into proving blood-alcohol quantum:

258. (1)(e) a certificate of an analyst stating that the analyst has made an analysis of a sample of the blood, urine, breath or other bodily substance of the accused and stating the result of that analysis is evidence of the facts alleged in the certificate without proof of the signature or the official character of the person appearing to have signed the certificate;

(f) a certificate of an analyst stating that the analyst has made an analysis of a sample of an alcohol standard that is identified in the certificate and intended for use with an approved instrument and that the sample of the standard analyzed by the analyst was found to be suitable for use with an approved instrument, is evidence that the alcohol standard so identified is suitable for use with an approved instrument without proof of the signature or the official character of the person appearing to have signed the certificate;

(g) where samples of the breath of the accused have been taken pursuant to a demand made under subsection 254(3), a certificate of a qualified technician stating

(i) that the analysis of each of the samples has been made by means of an approved instrument operated by the technician and ascertained by the technician to be in proper working order by means of an alcohol standard, identified in the certificate, that is suitable for use with an approved instrument,

(ii) the results of the analyses so made, and

(iii) if the samples were taken by the technician,

. . .

(B) the time when and place where each sample and any specimen described in clause (A) was taken, and

(C) that each sample was received from the accused directly into an approved container or into an approved instrument operated by the technician,

is evidence of the facts alleged in the certificate without proof of the signature or the official character of the person appearing to have signed the certificate;

(h) where a sample of the blood of the accused has been taken pursuant to a demand made under subsection 254(3) or otherwise with the consent of the accused or pursuant to a warrant issued under section 256,

(i) a certificate of a qualified medical practitioner stating that

(A) the medical practitioner took the sample and that before the sample was taken he was of the opinion that the taking of blood samples from the accused would not endanger the life or health of the accused and, in the case of a demand made pursuant to a warrant issued pursuant to section 256, that by reason of any physical or mental condition of the accused that resulted from the consumption of alcohol, the accident or any other occurrence related to or resulting from the accident, the accused was unable to consent to the taking of his blood,

(B) at the time the sample was taken, an additional sample of the blood of the accused was taken to permit analysis of one of the samples to be made by or on behalf of the accused,

(C) the time when and place where both samples referred to in clause (B) were taken, and

(D) both samples referred to in clause (B) were received from the accused directly into, or placed directly into, approved containers that were subsequently sealed and that are identified in the certificate,

(ii) a certificate of a qualified medical practitioner stating that the medical practitioner caused the sample to be taken by a qualified technician under his direction and that before the sample was taken the qualified medical practitioner was of the opinion referred to in clause (i)(A), or

(iii) a certificate of a qualified technician stating that the technician took the sample and the facts referred to in clauses (i)(B) to (D) is evidence of the facts alleged in the certificate without proof of the signature or official character of the person appearing to have signed the certificate; and

(i) a certificate of an analyst stating that the analyst has made an analysis of a sample of the blood of the accused that was contained in a sealed approved container identified in the certificate, the date on which and place where the sample was analyzed and the result of that analysis is evidence of the facts alleged in the certificate without proof of the signature or official character of the person appearing to have signed it.

. . .

(7) No certificate shall be received in evidence pursuant to paragraph (1)(e), (f), (g), (h) or (i) unless the party intending to produce it has, before the trial, given to the other party reasonable notice of his intention and a copy of the certificate.

Here "reasonable" notice must be provided prior to trial, not just prior to producing the certificate.

d. *Notice of Weapons Analyst*

Working similarly to the other notice of analyst provisions, s. 117.13 of the *Criminal Code* authorizes the introduction into evidence of a certificate of an analyst concerning weapons and related devices:

> **117.13** (1) A certificate purporting to be signed by an analyst stating that the analyst has analyzed any weapon, prohibited device, ammunition, prohibited ammunition or explosive substance, or any part or component of such a thing, and stating the results of the analysis is evidence in any proceedings in relation to any of those things under this Act or under section 19 of the *Export and Import Permits Act* in relation to subsection 15(2) of that Act without proof of the signature or official character of the person appearing to have signed the certificate.
>
> (2) The party against whom a certificate of an analyst is produced may, with leave of the court, require the attendance of the analyst for the purposes of cross-examination.
>
> (3) No certificate of an analyst may be admitted in evidence unless the party intending to produce it has, before the trial, given to the party against whom it is intended to be produced reasonable notice of that intention together with a copy of the certificate.
>
> (4) For the purposes of this Act, service of a certificate of an analyst may be proved by oral evidence given under oath by, or by the affidavit or solemn declaration of, the person claiming to have served it.
>
> (5) Notwithstanding subsection (4), the court may require the person who appears to have signed an affidavit or solemn declaration referred to in that subsection to appear before it for examination or cross-examination in respect of the issue of proof of service.

Again, notice need only be provided a "reasonable" time before trial.

4. The Wiretap Notice

Section 189 of the *Criminal Code* not only requires "reasonable notice" of intent to introduce wiretap evidence be given prior to it being tendered in court, but that a transcript of the recording or "full particulars" be provided, including the time, place, date and parties of the intercept:

189. (5) The contents of a private communication that is obtained from an interception of the private communication pursuant to any provision of, or pursuant to an authorization given under, this Part shall not be received in evidence unless the party intending to adduce it has given to the accused reasonable notice of the intention together with

> (a) a transcript of the private communication, where it will be adduced in the form of a recording, or a statement setting out full particulars of the private communication, where evidence of the private communication will be given viva voce; and

> (b) a statement respecting the time, place and date of the private communication and the parties thereto, if known.

Because of the complexity and long terms of imprisonment often at stake in wiretap cases, whether the s. 189 notice requirements have been complied with is frequently the source of lengthy disputes at trial. How s. 189 modifies disclosure requirements of other wiretap conversations the prosecution does *not* intend to introduce at trial also needs to be considered. Early investigator-prosecutor contact is necessary to guarantee a proper understanding on the current law governing s. 189 and ensure its requirements are met.

Whose Job Is It to Look After the Pretrial Notices?

Q&A

Q: Why is it my job as an investigator to provide pretrial notices? This seems like a very "legal" aspect of a prosecution where the duty to prepare and provide the notices falls squarely on the shoulders of the prosecutors.

A: I am not suggesting the duty to prepare and provide pretrial notices is solely an investigator task; it needs to be a shared duty. These notices can become legally quite technical, so prosecutors will almost always have to be involved in their preparation. But prosecutors also have to be able to prove in court that notice was provided to the defence, so investigators will become required witnesses to the notices. Because of the tie many of these notices have to particular items provided as part of disclosure, where possible it makes sense to package the notices and disclosure together.

RESPECTIVE ROLES IN DISCONTINUING PROCEEDINGS

An assessment or reassessment by prosecutors of whether a case meets the legal tests to proceed to trial is part of the trial preparation process. It may have made perfect sense at one point in time to lay a charge that appeared to be well supported by the evidence, but later factual and legal developments might dictate that charge not proceed to trial. Ideally investigators and prosecutors will work together at both the investigation and prosecution stages of a case to ensure charge judgment calls are fully informed by the facts and the law.

I have come to understand the high level of frustration investigators feel when prosecutors precipitously terminate cases that represent months of investigative work. No reasonable prosecutor will be offended by an investigator closely questioning reasons for discontinuing proceedings, but a prosecutor will usually not offer a detailed explanation for legal decisions unless asked to do so, just like investigators do not usually explain the underlying reasons for their investigative actions. One of the goals of this book is to arm investigators with legal tools to enhance their participation in and analysis of the outcome of case assessment decision making.

Sometimes as an investigator you will be so dissatisfied with the prosecutor's decision to discontinue proceedings that you will want to challenge it. Going directly to the prosecutor's supervisor to complain about the decision is not warranted without first speaking with the prosecutor. If you are still not satisfied after discussing the case, you must consider what you hope to accomplish by lodging a complaint after the fact over the discontinuance of proceedings. A better approach is to make contact with the prosecutor at an early stage of the case before a final decision on proceeding has been taken, and set out in writing the compelling evidentiary and public interest reasons for proceeding. This justification will ideally be included in the original prosecution brief. A written justification like that is difficult to ignore, and you will be more likely to be consulted before any decision not to proceed is taken.

Some Crown Counsel policy manuals make clear that prosecutors have a duty to consult in advance with investigators, where possible, about decisions on whether to proceed with a case. *The Federal Prosecution Service Deskbook*, loose-leaf (Ottawa: Justice Canada, 2000) states at 11.5:

> After consultation, investigators and Crown counsel will usually agree on the charging decision. If they disagree, the issue should be resolved through discussion at successively more senior levels on both sides.
>
> Normally, assessments respecting whether a case should commence or continue should be made at the regional level. Access to witnesses, investigators and physical evidence make this a practical reality. Disagreements that are not resolved should be referred to the Prosecution Group Head and then, if necessary, to the Regional Director or the Senior Regional Director. Where the unre-

solved disagreement is between a Crown agent and the police, the matter should be referred to the Agent Supervisor in the Regional Office. If the matter cannot be resolved at this level, it should be referred to the Group Head.

In rare circumstances, senior managers at Headquarters may need to review a case in which there is a disagreement. First, the appropriate Senior General Counsel in the Criminal Law Branch should assess the case. Then, if necessary, the Assistant Deputy Attorney General (Criminal Law) and, finally, the Deputy Attorney General may need to provide advice.

Advance consultation on discontinuing proceedings makes sense since investigators may be able to provide additional information that can change opinions about case viability. But just because investigators refuse to agree to the discontinuance of a prosecution does not mean prosecutors are paralyzed from acting.

Maintaining the distinct legal roles of laying charges and taking those charges to trial should not be permitted to ruin a mutually beneficial spirit of cooperation between investigators and prosecutors. Each group must realize that in working towards the common goal of seeing that justice is done, investigators may at times insist certain charges be laid or not be laid, and prosecutors may insist particular charges proceed or not proceed to trial. Each group is only doing the job the law has assigned it, and only if those jobs are done diligently while maintaining a cooperative spirit will justice be done.

For Working with the Prosecutor to Prepare for Trial

KEY POINTS

✓ Investigators and prosecutors are ultimately in a co-dependent relationship. The active involvement of the lead investigator in the pretrial case preparation of the prosecution is vital to the success of any trial. That involvement includes an early investigator-prosecutor meeting to develop a unified theory of the case that ties evidence of all required elements of each offence to each accused by explaining their actions and interactions in a way that is simple, makes sense, and can be readily presented in court.

✓ Investigators need to conduct pretrial interviews to confirm that each civilian witness' evidence hasn't changed between the time of an original interview and the months or years later that a trial finally commences. Ideally, all witnesses will also be met by the prosecutor to explain court procedures, clarify unclear evidence, and establish a rapport, but investigators need to be present for these prosecutor-led interviews to ensure the prosecutor does not become a witness in the case.

KEY POINTS

✓ Investigators must plan for the contingency of significant investigative resources being required immediately prior to or even during the trial to pursue follow-up investigation that becomes necessary because of unanticipated trial developments like a court finding crucial evidence to be inadmissible or the accused raising an unanticipated defence. Investigators preparing for a trial should also discuss with prosecutors whether any subpoenas or pretrial notices are required and who is expected to draft and provide or serve them.

✓ Part of the pretrial preparation of prosecutors will involve an assessment or reassessment of whether a case meets the legal tests to be able to proceed to trial. Investigators should have input into a prosecutor's decision to continue or discontinue proceedings, but lack of investigator agreement will not stop a prosecutor from terminating a case, so investigators must put forward a compelling case to proceed right in the prosecution brief.

Accused: _____

Charges: _____

Date(s) of offence(s): _____

Lead investigator: _____

Prosecutor: _____ Defence counsel: _____

Court: _____ Judge (if assigned): _____

A   DOCUMENT PREPARATION

❏ Prosecution brief complete

❏ Warrants/wiretaps unsealed or prosecutor informed of need to edit

❏ Updated criminal record checks done on all accused and civilian witnesses

❏ Disclosure complete

    ❏ Items of disclosure still to be provided:
    ❏ _____
    ❏ _____
    ❏ _____
    ❏ _____

    ❏ Accused still to be provided with disclosure:
    ❏ _____
    ❏ _____
    ❏ _____
    ❏ _____

❏ All witnesses subpoenaed

    ❏ Witnesses still to be subpoenaed: ❏ _____
    ❏ _____
    ❏ _____
    ❏ _____

❏   All affidavits required for trial requested

❏   All affidavits required for trial received and provided to prosecutor

    ❏ Outstanding affidavits: ❏ _____
    ❏ _____
    ❏ _____
    ❏ _____

❏ All notices required for trial prepared and provided to accused

   ❏ Outstanding notices: ❏ _____

                                 ❏ _____

                                 ❏ _____

                                 ❏ _____

B   CASE STRATEGY, WITNESS AND EVIDENCE PREPARATION

❏ Trial preparation meeting held with prosecutor

❏ Unified theory of the case developed

❏ Evidence reviewed with prosecutor

   ❏ Evidence still to be reviewed
      with prosecutor: ❏ _____

                                 ❏ _____

                                 ❏ _____

                                 ❏ _____

❏ Investigator-prosecutor pretrial meetings with all witnesses conducted or attempted

	Evidence Confirmation	Witness Rapport
❏ Witnesses to meet with:		
_____	❏	❏
_____	❏	❏
_____	❏	❏
_____	❏	❏

❏ Follow-up investigation necessary _____

_____

❏ Investigators to testify have reviewed their notes and are available on trial dates

❏ Sentencing evidence and range discussed with prosecutor

FURTHER READING

Cases

R. v. Campbell, [1999] 1 S.C.R. 565. A Government lawyer's legal advice to investigators might not be privileged where an investigator relies on that advice in court in arguing that illegal investigative actions were taken in good faith, or where disclosure of that advice is required for an accused to make full answer and defence.

R. v. Regan, [2002] 1 S.C.R.297. The interviewing of witnesses by the prosecutor in the presence of investigators is permissible to assess credibility, but the prosecutor should not assume the function of investigators by gathering new evidence.

Books and Articles

J.D. Brooks, "The Ethical Obligations of the Crown Attorney — Some Guiding Principles and Thoughts" (2001) 50 U.N.B. L.J. 229.

D.G. Burrow, *A Practical Guide to Criminal Prosecutions* (Toronto: Carswell, 1992).

Federal Prosecution Service Deskbook, loose-leaf (Ottawa: Justice Canada, 2000) [on-line: *www.canada.justice.gc.ca/en/dept/pub/fps/fpd*].

R.J. Frater, "The Seven Deadly Prosecutorial Sins" (2002) 7 Can. Crim. L. Rev. 209.

B.A. MacFarlane, "Sunlight and Disinfectants: Prosecutorial Accountability and Independence Through Public Transparency" (2001) 45 Crim. L.Q. 272.

CHAPTER EIGHTEEN

TESTIFYING AT TRIAL: BEING AND SOUNDING TRUTHFUL AND PRECISE

After all, a witness will be believed and remembered because of the manner and content of his testimony, not because the questions asked were so brilliant. Witness credibility is determined by who the witness is (background), what he says (content) and how he says it (demeanour).

> T. A. Mauet, D.G. Casswell & G.P. Macdonald,
> *Fundamentals of Trial Techniques — Canadian Edition*
> (Boston: Little Brown, 1984) at 61-62.

In This Chapter

- There is no shame in preparation
- The two fundamental principles of being a good witness
- Do not use your notes as a crutch
- How to deal with defence cross-examination tactics
- Do not assume knowledge
- Do not speculate
- Do not start an answer with a "yes" or "no"

- Stick to your answer
- Concede when you are mistaken
- Do not offer hearsay unless it is explicitly asked for
- Do not give privileged testimony
- Do not get too hung up on titles
- The prosecutor is not your lawyer
- Have fun and be yourself when testifying

While acting in a theatre is make believe, and testifying in court is very real, there are some useful parallels that can be drawn between the two. You must be very well prepared for both, knowing not only exactly what you are going to say, but also how you are going to say it. For both, you must be able to step into another role or improvise if someone becomes ill, a prop disappears, or something else does not go as expected. For both, the performance is live, so you have only one chance to get it right.

THERE IS NO SHAME IN PREPARATION

As an investigator, preparing your testimony means reading and rereading your notes, checking with other investigators to confirm details that are missing or no longer make sense, and meeting with the prosecutor to learn what sorts of questions you will be asked and explore potential weaknesses in your testimony. Preparing your testimony means more than just developing a mastery of the facts, it also involves developing the ability to deliver those facts, so rehearsing how you will speak about the facts is important. Ideally your preparation will be done with the prosecutor, but it can also be done with fellow investigators, or even in front of a mirror.

1. Preparation Is Not the Same as Witness Coaching or Collusion

There is nothing improper about extensive preparation of testimony. If asked by defence counsel or the judge if you prepared, you should freely admit if you did. But no one should have told you what to say. What is forbidden is witness coaching or collusion among witnesses in giving testimony, like that found to have taken place in *R. v. Singh*, 2000 ABPC 149 at paras. 12-13:

> Particularly, with respect to many of his answers, the accused's friend parroted, almost word for word the evidence of the accused. In my experience, the accused's friend's demeanour and responses held the clear aspect of assisted coaching and rehearsed answers. When the question was a familiar one, his response was immediate. On questions he had not been coached on, the responses were tentative and inconsistent with the accused's responses. The friend would often look to the accused, as if the accused might help him with the correct response. One example of his response was when he was asked whether or not he and the accused had talked about the event since the night it occurred. His response to this unrehearsed question was totally different from that of the accused, yet both of them used the exact times of 10:05 p.m. to 10:10 p.m. as the time they stopped drinking. The accused's friend gave this precise and consistent time, notwithstanding he testified he was not paying any attention to the time. Consistently, he looked to the accused, as if to confirm he was doing a good job and giving the correct answers.
>
> Between the two of them, the accused and his friend gave the definite impression they had colluded and connived their evidence to coincide with the version that would most assist the accused. I found neither of them credible or believable.

Your testimony needs to be based on your independent recollection of events as you experienced them. In putting together your notes you may quite properly have received details, sorted out event sequences or resolved points of confusion with other investigators like a central note-taker that will *not* constitute collusion to give identical answers. But copying whole passages from the notes of another investigator where you have utterly no independent recollection of the events, perhaps because you forgot to make any notes at the time, or changing a note of a fact you still believe to be correct — like a key time — purely so it agrees with other investigator notes would be improper collusion.

Talking to a prosecutor about what testimony you will give, and receiving helpful hints on how to deliver that testimony, likewise does not amount to witness coaching. Improper coaching would occur if a prosecutor told you what to say, rather than how to say it. The only thing a prosecutor should ever tell you to say is the truth. If the prosecutor does tell you that, you will then have a good response to a line of defence questioning, such as outlined here.

Q: Did you meet with the prosecutor on this case prior to coming to testify today?

A: Yes.

Q: Did you discuss the testimony you would give?

A: Yes.

Q: Did the prosecutor tell you what to say?

A: Yes.

Q: And what did the prosecutor tell you to say?

A: Only to tell the truth.

The final answer in this not uncommon exchange halts further questioning along this line, and may even fluster the defence sufficiently to cause some flailing around for where to go next.

2. Be Flexible in Your Preparation

Preparation also extends to flexibility in your mastery of the case facts, and your ability to deliver those facts regardless of how questions are phrased, in which order they are delivered, or on what areas of the case those questions focus. If another investigator is unable to attend court, but an adjournment of a case is not possible, you ideally must be prepared to testify in another role. While you cannot use another investigator's notes, your own role will often overlap other investigator roles. For example, you may have heard a statement made by the accused, even though you were not the investigator taking the statement, possibly permitting you to fill in for that other statement-taking role. Being able to recite a good overview of the entire case will make you a very useful witness, and also give you a better perspective on where your own testimony fits into the rest of the case evidence.

Being prepared for the unexpected means not simply memorizing a script by rote. Rote learning will only lead to disaster if new developments in a case supercede what you have memorized. Rote learning will also not stand up to close cross-examination. The improvisational theatre element to delivering your testimony requires both mastery of the original facts, and also the ability to reason beyond those facts. You must be able to figure out on the stand when you should concede, or hold firm, on a particular point. Always try to look ahead to where a particular line of questioning is leading you and the court.

3. Practice May Not Make Perfect, but It Makes Testimony a Whole Lot Better

Being good at giving testimony takes practice. Investigators who work as police patrol officers might give testimony many times per year, but those who work as regulatory investigators, or who only work on major cases, may rarely testify. If you don't have much courtroom experience, setting up some mock testimony with the prosecutor, your office colleagues, or in front of a mirror can be very helpful practice. Have others ask you difficult questions, or write some down yourself on separate cards, shuffle the cards and then randomly turn them face up one at a time on a table. These can be questions specific to a particular case in which you are involved, or generic questions of a tricky nature like how you handled evidence, took a statement, or what your grounds were for arresting someone.

Instead of making your testimony sound scripted, advance practice will make your courtroom testimony come across as more natural. Practice teaches you not only how to answer questions, but how you are going to look and sound to others. You may not think you are talking in a whisper, or in a roar, and you may not think you present an aggressive posture, or a meek one, but practice will tell you this.

Video recording your practice sessions is the best way to review how you look and sound to others. You may be shocked at what you see — certainly I used to be disconcerted by the sound of my recorded voice and physical gestures, none of which were like I imagined them to be. You do get used to seeing recordings of yourself after a while. Those recordings make it possible to identify weaknesses in the way you present yourself, and then review different styles of speaking or gestures that could compensate for those weaknesses. You may think there is a big difference between your old whisper voice, and your new assertive voice, but a recording may reveal the difference is all in your head and you need to work harder at improvement. Or you may think one style of presenting yourself is unprofessional, but it might turn out to look great on a recording.

Convincing friends or colleagues to be brutally honest about your performance is helpful in getting a broader perspective on how others see you and to identify specific voice or gesture problems you haven't noticed on your recordings — like tapping a pencil or foot throughout your testimony. Getting professional public speaking help is best of all. I have taken media training sessions I found to be invaluable in teaching me how to answer media questions and speak on camera. An investigative agency could bring in a professional trainer or use in-house expertise to deliver a one- or two-day "how to testify" course, including examination and cross-examination exercises in a mock courtroom for a variety of types of cases.

Unscripted Testimony

Q: I have always believed all I needed to do at trial was show up, and tell the truth. The preparation you seem to be suggesting makes giving testimony sound like a very scripted process.

A: The unpredictable elements of cross-examination mean you can never have a script for your testimony, but practice is required on how you will deliver your message and react to surprises. Without that practice, you could be completely truthful, but not be believed by the court.

THE TWO FUNDAMENTAL PRINCIPLES OF BEING A GOOD WITNESS

There are two fundamental principles of being a good witness when giving testimony. Both these principles have the aim of being and sounding truthful and precise when on the witness stand. The two principles are easy to remember:

1. always listen to the question; and

2. don't be helpful.

The principles mean you answer only what is asked — nothing more, nothing less. They require you to pause briefly after a question is finished being asked in order to consider your answer. This pause will additionally give the prosecutor the opportunity to object to the question if necessary. There is no rush. Take your time. The transcript records every word you say, but not your pauses. No one will later know how long you took to answer. An answer that takes a while to start shows you have put great thought into it, and comes across to the court as more credible than one you rush into.

These two principles of giving testimony apply equally to testifying in-chief and being cross-examined. If only the exact question asked is answered, and nothing more volunteered, guessed at or readily agreed to, you will stay out of trouble. Listening to the question lets you avoid traps set by others. Not being helpful means you will not run afoul of traps you set for yourself. The first principle ensures you tell the whole and complete truth, but that your words aren't twisted by the way the question was asked. The second principle guards against you straying down irrelevant paths that will confuse the judge and jury, blunt the force of the relevant part of your answer, or open new fields for cross-examination. If a simple question is asked, calling for an answer of a few words, that is what you should give. But do not simply be agreeable with counsel, whether counsel is working for the prosecution or defence, by telling her what she wants to hear.

DO NOT USE YOUR NOTES AS A CRUTCH

Ask the court's permission if you wish to consult your notes or examine exhibits in order to help you answer a question. Also ask permission if you wish to refer to an item that has not already been made an exhibit. Permission will likely be granted. You don't need to do everything from memory, but don't be so dependent on your notes that your entire testimony consists of word-for-word reading of what you previously wrote down. Extensive reading may lead a court to conclude you really don't have an independent memory of the events in question, and will reduce the credibility of your testimony.

A favourite and at times effective defence counsel technique is to ask to look at the notes you are holding when on the witness stand, and then walk away with those notes while asking you detailed questions. If you ask for the notes back before answering, you appear to need them as a crutch. If you answer while defence counsel is holding onto them, you could get the answer wrong. The balance to strike is to have memorized the general and most important facts of the case, while relying on your notes for the precise details.

Do not bring anything to court with you that you have not already disclosed or could not publicly disclose, unless you first speak to the prosecutor about it. I once had a witness pull out reams of undisclosed, privileged and irrelevant papers from a briefcase in the middle of a cross-examination, and start flipping through them to help him with an answer. I was apoplectic with shock, while a smile spread across the face of opposing counsel. The papers wound up locked in a safe while we spent months arguing over their relevance and privileged status. Any disclosure problems need to be dealt with long before you get on the witness stand.

HOW TO DEAL WITH DEFENCE CROSS-EXAMINATION TACTICS

Defence counsel can ask you leading questions in cross-examination, where the question suggests the answer to you. The prosecution generally cannot do so, unless it is the defence that has called you as a witness. While a hectoring, sarcastic and confrontational cross-examination style is the style most likely to make you angry, the pleasant, complimentary and sly cross-examination style is more dangerous. With either style, you might say things you didn't mean to say, say them in a way you didn't intend, forget to mention details you know, or agree with suggestions you would not agree with if given more time to consider the implications of your answers. There may be more to admire in the devious cross-examiner than in the bully, but you must be prepared for either.

Courts will give a lot of leeway to the prosecution and particularly to the defence in the way they conduct their cross-examinations, as affirmed in *R. v. Fanjoy*, [1985] 2 S.C.R. 233 at 238:

> There is, of course, no doubt that in cross-examination in criminal cases, particularly where questions of credibility of witnesses are in issue, a wide latitude is accorded to counsel and too fine a line should not be drawn to confine or limit a detailed and searching inquiry into the matters raised by the evidence given by the accused and other witnesses.

Aggressive cross-examination is permissible, even encouraged if it helps get at the truth, but abusive cross-examination, like repeatedly asking a witness why another witness would lie about a particular fact now being contradicted by the current witness, is not acceptable. Every judge does have the discretion to limit cross-examination, but it is usually only when the fair trial rights of the accused are being imperiled that a judge will exercise that discretion. A judge intervening to protect professional investigator witnesses from defence cross-examination runs the risk of a successful appeal from an accused who later claims he was improperly restricted in his right to make full answer and defence to the charges.

Most good cross-examiners have been practicing the required skills for a long time, and have learned through trial and error what works and what doesn't. As a prosecutor I did not get much practice at cross-examination because in the types of cases I tried the accused tended not to testify, but I did encounter some very skilled defence bar cross-examiners who had spent decades honing their skills cross-examining investigators. The very good cross-examiners rarely ask exactly the same questions in two trials, and instead are able to constantly adapt to probe the weaknesses of any testimony.

Regardless of a lawyer's skill at asking questions, I have noticed that using the "let them talk" tactic of cross-examination is highly effective. This technique simply asks open-ended questions and doesn't use a new question for a long time. This tends to encourage a witness to fill periods of silence with more testimony. Witnesses wind up volunteering pieces of information that were never requested, but which are very helpful to the cross-examiner's case. Various other cross-examination techniques that might be employed against you include:

- inviting you to argue with defence counsel — you will not win such an argument, so avoid being drawn into one;

- asking hypothetical questions, often starting with "is it possible that . . . ?" — never speculate, stick to certainties;

- asking if you have discussed the case with particular persons — do not deny discussing the case with anyone you in fact discussed it with, the purpose of the question is to make you feel it was somehow wrong to discuss the case, even though it wasn't;

- alleging contradictions by other witnesses — if you are told other witnesses disagree with your testimony, do not speculate why those witnesses might disagree since if you did not actually hear their testimony, you do not even know for sure they did disagree;

- long periods of silence inviting you to fill the gaps — resist — if you have finished your answer, stay silent until the next question, however long it takes to come;

- distracting the witness — stay focused;

- flattery — don't drop your guard;

- threats — preparation blunts fear;

- rapid fire questioning — do not allow yourself to be cut off, and if the defence does manage to cut you off before you have finished answering, ask the court to be permitted to answer;

- standing close to you or behind you with the intent to intimidate you — making strong eye contact with defence counsel can prompt a retreat.

There are a number of basic principles for giving testimony discussed below that will keep you out of trouble regardless of whether you are facing examination-in-chief by the prosecution or cross-examination by the defence.

Dealing with Unfair Questions

Q: Sometimes questions put to me by the defence seem unfair or even downright nasty. Isn't it the prosecutor's job to protect me from those kinds of questions by objecting to them?

A: The prosecutor has the right to object to illegal questions, but not all difficult questions are illegal. Even for the illegal questions, a prosecutor must not waste opportunities to object. There are no theoretical limits to the number of objections that can be raised in a trial, but too many will only antagonize the court, and gives the impression you are too fragile to protect yourself. The prosecutor can throw you a life ring from time to time, but cannot teach you how to swim while you are on the stand — those lessons need to come before the trial.

DO NOT ASSUME KNOWLEDGE

Don't assume the judge, or anyone else, knows anything about the facts of the case, or even about the kind of offence about which you are testifying. It is easy to become so immersed in one investigation that lasts several years, or several short similar investigations, that you assume the others in the courtroom must know at least a little bit about the subject matter of the case. Perhaps you assume that from working in the justice industry, reading, watching television or just general chit chat in the community, everyone present must have picked up some background details about the subject of your testimony, be it drug use, money laundering, domestic violence or fishing methods. It is very dangerous to presume knowledge. Yes, you should assume basic intelligence on the part of others, and the willingness to learn, but not knowledge.

Some witnesses also err by assuming lack of interest. They assume that those in the courtroom must have heard similar case details so many times that repeating background details that are similar to other cases the court routinely hears will put everyone to sleep, and so they gloss over relevant details leading up to the key events in issue. These witnesses forget it is the job of most of those present in court to listen to the details, and that providing details can best set the stage for how an arrest or seizure came about. Some in court, including the judge, may never have heard any of those kinds of details before and in fact find them quite fascinating. For example, to a judge who rotates from a court that does not hear drug cases, or who has never heard an occupational health and safety case before, all background details in drug or safety cases will be new and exciting.

Since your starting point for giving evidence will be assuming complete ignorance and enthralled interest on the part of your audience, be as detailed as necessary in explaining the facts of the case. Start by providing an overview of the investigation and type of offence being investigated, so long as you have personal knowledge of all the facts you are giving, and don't stray into giving opinion evidence unless you have first been qualified as an expert. If you are asked open-ended questions, like what happened during a particular day, feel free to go into great detail. While "let them talk" may also be a cross-examination technique, I have found using it during examination-in-chief often brings out the most comprehensible version of the story the court needs to hear. The lawyer asking the questions will stop you if you are giving too much detail, or if you need to clarify a particular point.

DO NOT SPECULATE

Only give answers of which you are certain. Do not speculate or speak in possibilities. Either you know, or you don't know. If you know, say so. But one of the best answers you can possibly give is "I don't know." There are very few follow-up questions that can be asked from an "I don't know" answer. Following with a question like "why don't you know?" does not really make sense, and should be met with another polite but firm "I have already told you, I don't know."

If you *do* know, be firm in your knowledge. If asked a question like "isn't it possible that you are wrong?" do not answer with a response like "anything is possible." Instead, simply say "no." Once you start to concede anything is possible, you will soon be conceding the possibility that pink elephants were roaming the local highways on the day of the offence.

If asked to speculate, or comment on a hypothetical question, refuse unless you have been qualified as an expert witness in the field. Simply say you can only stick to the facts and certainties. Only offer opinions if they are about everyday activities and observations like visibility, distances, weather conditions or other matters within "common knowledge." Your estimation of the time a person died would, by contrast, require you to be a qualified expert.

DO NOT START AN ANSWER WITH A "YES" OR "NO"

By commencing an answer with the word "yes" or "no," you run the risk of getting cut off by counsel who assumes or demands that your answer is satisfactory without further elaboration on your part. This can happen to you even if it is the prosecution asking the questions. This one-word answer trap often follows a common form.

Q: Were you armed that night?

A: Yes, but . . .

Q: Thank you, that's I all need to know.

A better way to answer if you want to qualify your "yes" by noting no one could have observed your weapon is:

A: My service pistol was concealed in a shoulder holster under my jacket.

If defence counsel demands a "yes" or a "no" in response to any question put to you, and you feel such a simple answer is not sufficient, you are fully within your rights to politely refuse to fall into the one-word answer trap. Here is how to deal with defence frustration.

Q: I asked you a yes or no question! I just want you to answer yes, or no in your answer.

A: I am unable to answer the question with a yes, or a no. It is simply not possible to do so.

Q: Look, I am not telling you what to answer. You have a choice. Is it yes, or is it no?

A: And I am telling you, it is neither yes nor no. The only way to answer your question is with a more complete answer than simply yes or no.

Q: I don't care about complete. Just give me a yes, or no.

A: I am happy to answer your question. I'm not trying to be difficult here. Just let me answer with my own words, and I will fully respond to your question.

Throughout this kind of exchange with defence counsel, focus on successfully conveying to the court the best answer you have formulated in your head. Stay calm. Be polite, even if counsel is not — it will only make you look good, and your cross-examiner look bad. If defence counsel does not eventually back down from insisting on a yes or no answer, it is likely either the prosecutor will eventually intervene to ask the judge to let you answer the question, or the judge will intervene of her own accord to order defence counsel to let you answer.

STICK TO YOUR ANSWER

If a question is asked again in precisely the same way, give precisely the same answer. If the next question put to you is slightly different than the one before it, you must determine if a slightly different answer is called for. Stick to your position once you have stated it, unless you are absolutely certain you made an error earlier. Do not allow yourself to be brow beaten into submission. Review this example and be prepared.

Q: Exactly what time was it when you arrested my client?

A: It was 10:00 p.m.

Q: Are you sure it was 10:00 p.m.?

A: Yes, I am sure.

Q: Exactly 10:00 p.m.?

A: It was exactly 10:00 p.m.

Q: How did you know it was 10:00 p.m.?

A: I looked at my watch.

Q: How do you remember looking at your watch eight months after the arrest?

A: I wrote the time of arrest down in my field notebook, which you have a copy of, and it is my usual practice to look at my watch when I conduct an arrest to verify the time. I am still wearing that watch today, and I have always found it to be accurate.

Q: But on the night in question, isn't it possible that your watch wasn't working properly? Isn't it possible it could have been off by five or ten minutes?

A: No, it's not possible.

Q: But you aren't some kind of watch expert, are you? You didn't set your watch against one of the atomic clocks in Greenwich, England, did you?

Q: I don't need to be a watch expert to know that whenever I have compared my watch to the National Research Council time signal on CBC Radio, it has always been accurate.

Q: But isn't it possible your watch was a bit off on that one day.

A: No.

Here defence counsel attempted to shake belief not just in this one answer concerning the time of arrest, but for all answers this witness had and would give. The witness stuck by the answer and successfully defended his overall credibility.

The goal of sticking to your answer is consistency, not unrelenting precision. In the example given, if the witness knew his watch was prone to running five minutes fast or slow, but never more inaccurate than five minutes, then an acceptable first answer would have been:

A: It was between 9:55 p.m. and 10:05 p.m.

Defence cross-examination would likely have then focused on the general unreliability of the watch, and made suggestions to the witness that couldn't it have possibly been at 9:30 p.m. or 10:30 p.m. that the arrest took place? So long as you are certain of your answer before your give it, there is no need to agree to possibilities posed by defence counsel — just stick to the first answer, be it 10:00 p.m. (if you know your watch to be completely accurate) or 9:55 p.m. to 10:05 p.m. (if you know your watch to have a five minute margin of error).

CONCEDE WHEN YOU ARE MISTAKEN

Quickly conceding when you have been mistaken, either in a prior answer, in making notes, or in other aspects of your duties, is an important companion principle to sticking to your answer. You cannot let prosecution or defence counsel tell you when you have been mistaken, you have to decide that for yourself. Only when you are certain you have made a mistake should you offer a correction. But once you have come to that point of mistaken certainty, quickly make the concession and move on.

If you realize of your own accord that you were mistaken in earlier testimony, like while reading over your notes during a break, you can correct a past answer.

A: Before I answer that question, I would like to correct an answer I gave earlier this morning. When I said that I observed the accused enter the passenger side of a red car at 3:30 p.m. on August 30th, 2004, I should have said that I observed the accused enter the passenger side of a green car at that date and time. I had made the entry of a green car in my notebook, and now have an independent recollection of the car being green, but when giving my testimony I was not referring to my notes and had confused the colour of car noted on August 30th with the colour of the car the accused entered on August 29th which was red.

Here the witness picked an appropriate time to offer the correction, gave enough detail so those present could know exactly what answer was being corrected, and provided a reasonable explanation about why the error in testimony had been made. Certainly the defence might then launch into a series of questions around whether there are any other answers the witness would like to correct, and how can the court be sure the witness is correct about any testimony if a mistaken car colour was given, but if you follow the "stick to your answer" principle for all other answers that you are sure of, you and your credibility will survive.

It is by sticking with an incorrect answer, or by refusing to admit you made an error in your notes, that you will erode the credibility of the rest of your testimony. Even where it is defence counsel who first points out an error in your earlier testimony, you can still maintain your credibility by agreeing an error was made if that was indeed the case. In the following example a witness takes defence counsel's observation of an error in stride, corrects the earlier answer, offers an explanation for the error, and moves on.

Q: Even though you earlier testified that the amount of income unreported by my client in the 2003 taxation year was $79,359, I am now showing you printouts of computer entries from your office that say otherwise. They say that for the 2003 year, the amount of unreported income was $53, 819. How do you explain the discrepancy between these computer records and your testimony? Weren't you the one who made the computer entries?

A: (after taking a suitable pause or even asking for a break to consider the figures) The correct figure for unreported income for the 2003 taxation year was $53, 819 as indicated in the computer entries. I was mistaken in my earlier answer because I was looking at a figure on my spread sheet for gross income, not net taxable income after deductions. You already have a copy of that spreadsheet, which I think has been marked as exhibit 3. You will see there are two columns for each taxation year in question — gross income and net taxable income.

If the witness had been headstrong and initially insisted the original answer was correct when in fact it wasn't, a much deeper credibility hole would have been dug that would only have been climbed out of with much greater effort. Asking for a break to consider your answer is completely reasonable if an apparent error in your testimony is pointed out to you, and demonstrates you are a witness who takes answering each question seriously. Try to offer an explanation for why an error was made, but don't make excuses. Just take responsibility for the error and move on — it will likely not be your first or last error in giving testimony.

The longer you refuse to admit an error in the face of incontrovertible proof to the contrary, the more damage your credibility will suffer. An error can be corrected at any time. Even after you have finished testifying, you can tell the prosecutor about what you believe to be any error in your earlier testimony. The prosecutor can then decide how to best approach the court and defence so the error can be corrected.

Reconciling Sticking to an Answer and Conceding Mistakes

Q & A

Q: You say that I should stick to my answer, and then you tell me to concede when I am mistaken. What if I am not sure whether I am mistaken or not? Should I then insist I am right, or concede I harbour doubts about whether I am right?

A: Never offer doubtful answers in the first place. Doubtful answers pave the road to wrongful convictions. Either you are sure about an answer, or you should not be giving that answer. Resolve any doubts before testifying by reviewing your notes, and discussing the case with your fellow investigators. If you are asked an unexpected question when testifying whose answer you are not sure about, it is far better to say you don't know the answer than to offer a speculative answer.

DO NOT OFFER HEARSAY UNLESS IT IS EXPLICITLY ASKED FOR

Demystification of the law says investigators need not worry too much about the technical ambit of the hearsay rule that was discussed in greater detail in Chapter 12, just don't repeat on the witness stand what other people have told you unless specifically asked in a question to repeat what was said. You can, however, freely refer to the fact that others said things to you, and what you did in response.

Q: And why did you go to the garage that morning?

A: It was because I was told to by my supervisor, who had received a tip from an informer.

Do not then go on to relate in detail what your supervisor told you, or what the supervisor told you that the informer told her. Your supervisor is in the best position to testify to what she said or what information she received.

If the prosecutor asking you the questions believes a hearsay answer would be admissible, a follow-up question will be asked.

Q: And can you please tell the court, exactly what did your supervisor say to you?

Defence counsel might raise an objection at this point, so you might need to wait a few minutes to give the answer if the lawyers and court need to sort out the answer's admissibility. But subject to being stopped by the lawyers or the court, go ahead and provide the hearsay if it is explicitly asked for — you may be giving it for a non-hearsay purpose, or it may not actually amount to hearsay if it satisfies the principled approach to the hearsay rule.

DO NOT GIVE PRIVILEGED TESTIMONY

Do not testify about the contents of your conversations with the prosecutor or other government-retained lawyers you have dealt with in the course of the investigation and trial preparation. As already discussed in Chapter 9 in the context of private lawyers and their clients, communications between lawyers and investigators, for the purpose of giving or seeking legal advice, are usually protected by solicitor-client privilege rooted in strong reasons of public policy, but as affirmed in *R. v. McClure*, [2001] 1 S.C.R. 445 at para. 37: "only communications made for the legitimate purpose of obtaining lawful professional advice or assistance are privileged."

There is no need to deny having spoken with lawyers about the investigation or prosecution, just don't reveal the contents of those conversations. Once you have blurted out in court a privileged conversation, it is too late to take it back and it may be implied that you have waived privilege. In *R. v. Shirose*, [1999] 1 S.C.R. 565 at paras. 47 & 48, an investigator relying on a conservation with a prosecutor to justify police action was found to have waived the privilege, and forced revelation of the advice:

> We have no reason to think the [police service] ignored the advice it was given, but as the [police service] did make an issue of the legal advice it received in response to the stay applications, the appellants were entitled to have the bottom line of that advice corroborated.

It appears, therefore, that the only satisfactory way to resolve the issue of good faith is to order disclosure of the content of the relevant advice. This should be done (for the reasons to be discussed) on the basis of waiver by the [police service] of the solicitor-client privilege.

That privilege breach could have been avoided by investigators freely admitting advice had been sought, but refusing to make any reference in their testimony to the content of that advice, and not seeking to rely upon it for justification of their actions.

Since lawyers themselves spend years arguing in court over what may or may not be privileged — at least I certainly did — when facing the stress of giving live testimony it is best if you don't try to figure out the niceties of solicitor-client privilege exceptions by yourself. Assume the contents, but not the existence, of all conversations with lawyers are privileged. The court or prosecutor will tell you if you should give details in your testimony about a particular conversation you had with a lawyer.

DO NOT GET TOO HUNG UP ON TITLES

What to call the variety of judicial officials you will run into over the course of your investigative career can be perplexing at the best of times. The tried and true terms "Your Lordship" and "Your Ladyship" (which confusingly you sometimes have to substitute with "My Lord" and "My Lady" depending on the way you are using the terms) are falling into disuse with superior courts. Today many courts simply use the term "Your Honour" for all judges, be they sitting in provincial, superior, or appeal courts. But some courts persist with more traditional forms of address, so ask the lawyers what terms you should use.

You will earn great goodwill by calling the judge or justice by his or her proper title. If you forget to check on what term should be used, there are worse words to use than "Sir" and "Madam." Justices of the Peace, who you will encounter in some jurisdictions in bail court or during trials of provincial offences, are usually addressed as "Your Worship." Switching courts requires concentration to keep the different forms of address straight. It's best to get titles straight in your head before you walk through the courtroom doors, but if you get them wrong it won't be the end of your case. While we are on matters of showing respect to the court, I should mention that it is also good practice to bow slightly towards the judge when entering or leaving the courtroom.

THE PROSECUTOR IS NOT YOUR LAWYER

Once you are under oath, you cannot speak to the prosecutor about the case until after all of your testimony is finished. This includes during court breaks, and continues for as long as you are on the stand, which could extend over a long time-period. If you don't know how to answer a question because of some legal difficulty like informer privilege, ask for the assistance of the court, not the assistance of the prosecutor. The court may give you leave to speak privately with the prosecutor to inform yourself on a legal topic, and the extent of your obligation to answer.

You must realize the prosecutor is not your lawyer. The prosecutor represents the Attorney General and the public interest, not your interests or the interests of other investigators. If you still believe you have a legal difficulty that is unresolved by asking for the assistance of the court and speaking with the prosecutor, ask the court for permission to seek independent legal advice through lawyers employed by your investigative agency, or through a private lawyer. A public interest privilege claim opposing disclosure of an investigative technique is an example of an area where investigator-prosecutor disagreement could arise, necessitating investigators to retain outside counsel to independently argue for maintaining the privilege without prosecutor support.

Why the Prosecutor Isn't Your Lawyer

Q: You talk a lot about investigators and prosecutors being part of the same team, and the need for them to work together, so how can you then say that the prosecutor is not my lawyer?

A: Just because you are on the same team doesn't mean the prosecutor works for you, or you work for the prosecutor. You are working cooperatively in the public interest, but you each have separate reporting relationships. By contrast, your own lawyer will follow your instructions within the boundaries of professional ethics, and vigorously represent your own interests, or the interests of your investigative agency. So long as investigators and prosecutors are both pursuing the same aim of successfully concluding a prosecution that is in the public interest, then those investigators can rely on legal advice received from prosecutors with whom they will have a solicitor-client relationship. But when investigator and prosecutor interests diverge, investigators may need to retain their own lawyers.

Q & A

HAVE FUN AND BE YOURSELF WHEN TESTIFYING

As strange as it might sound, try to have fun and be yourself while testifying. If you try to feel nothing at all, most likely you will feel nervous, which will cause you to rush answers and forget important details. Having fun means enjoying being the centre of attention, enjoying the importance of your role (much more important than the lawyers who can only bring out and not give evidence), and enjoying that your case has made it this far in the justice process.

Defence counsel may try to make you mad, or afraid, or feel one of many other emotions. Remaining calm, and remembering that you can take all the time you want to compose yourself and your answers, will be of great assistance to you. When you are on the stand, you are calling the shots. Just focus on your role as star witness, and don't drift into the role of defence counsel, prosecutor or judge.

Speak clearly and slowly. Speak in the general direction of the microphone if there is one. Look at the judge (and jury if there is one) at least occasionally. If you are sitting, put your hands in your lap and keep them there unless you are examining notes or exhibits. If you are standing, hold onto the witness box with your hands. Hand gestures are prone to conveying nervousness or annoying others. Your testimony need not be devoid of emotion, but your body language should remain as neutral as possible.

KEY POINTS

For Testifying at Trial

✓ Advance preparation with a lawyer does not amount to witness coaching. Be flexible in your preparation so that ideally you can testify in a variety of roles.

✓ Always listen carefully to the question, but don't be helpful in giving your answers, just answer the questions that are asked. Do not continually read from your notes when giving testimony, they are only there to refresh your memory.

✓ Effective cross-examination can make you say things you did not mean to say, say them in a way you did not intend, forget to mention details you know, or agree with suggestions that you would not have agreed with if you had more time to consider the implications of your answers.

✓ Do not assume knowledge on the part of the judge or anyone else. Do not speculate. Do not start an answer with a "yes" or a "no," if you intend to use more than one word in giving your answer, to avoid the risk of being cut off by counsel who assumes or demands your answer is satisfactory without further elaboration.

KEY POINTS

✓ Stick to your answer. Do not allow yourself to be brow beaten into conceding that you might be mistaken when you know you are correct. But when you are absolutely convinced you made a mistake, quickly concede the mistake, offer an explanation and correction, and move on. Sticking with an answer after it becomes clear a mistake was made will undermine the credibility of all your other answers.

✓ Do not offer hearsay unless it is explicitly asked for. Do not give privileged testimony unless ordered to do so by the court. Try to sort out in your mind the appropriate judicial titles to use.

✓ There may be times when investigator and prosecutor interests sufficiently diverge in court that investigators will need to retain their own counsel.

✓ Try to have fun and be yourself when testifying.

FURTHER READING

Giving testimony is more art than science. While the admission of testimony into evidence is governed by a myriad of legal rules, it is important that any witness not become bogged down in those rules or else the witness may wind up never uttering a word for fear of saying something inadmissible. I therefore won't refer you to any particular cases to read on this topic, just a small selection of useful books.

Books

D. Bellemare, *How to Testify in Court: The Police Officer's Testimony* (Cowansville, Que.: Yvon Blais, 1985).

B. Finlay & T.A. Cromwell, *Witness Preparation Manual*, 2nd ed. (Aurora, ON: Canada Law Book, 1999). Written for lawyers who are tasked with preparing witnesses for trial. This is also a useful short work to read as a prospective witness.

E. Levy, *Examination of Witnesses in Criminal Cases*, 4th ed. (Toronto: Carswell, 1999). A book that gives lots of examples, especially surrounding how to cross-examine, that can show investigators how lawyers think when they formulate questions.

T.A. Mauet, D.G. Casswell & G.P. Macdonald, *Fundamentals of Trial Techniques — Canadian Edition*, 2nd ed. (New York: Aspen, 1995). A thorough discussion of the process of witness examination and cross-examination, entering exhibits, raising objections and lawyer openings and closings.

CHAPTER NINETEEN

WORKING WITH THE PROSECUTOR AT TRIAL: YOU ARE STILL ALL ON THE SAME TEAM

It cannot be over-emphasized that the purpose of a criminal prosecution is not to obtain a conviction; it is to lay before a jury what the Crown considers to be credible evidence relevant to what is alleged to be a crime.

Boucher v. The Queen, [1955] S.C.R. 16 at 23.

In This Chapter

- Staying happy assisting with an appeal-proof trial
- Assisting with the preliminary inquiry
- Assisting with the pretrial motions
- Assisting with jury selection
- Marshalling the witnesses and evidence while communicating with the prosecutor
- Avoiding exclusion of assisting investigators
- Assisting with sentencing submissions after a conviction

The success of any trial is the result of a lengthy team effort. Prosecutors are not lone wild-west gunslingers; hopefully you will not run into any who have delusions about such a role. The prosecutor's role at trial is to make certain key decisions concerning how to present the case in court, in consultation with the investigators, and to proceed with the trial in the fairest but also most effective manner possible.

The prosecutor is the manager of the law at the trial. The legal calls the prosecutor makes dictate how the facts are presented, but the prosecutor does not control those facts. The lead investigator is the marshal of the facts before and during the trial, corralling all required facts into one suitable place, answering prosecutor questions about them and making sure they stay put until no longer needed. As those facts will determine the outcome of the preliminary inquiry, pretrial motions, jury selection, trial itself, and any sentencing process, it is incumbent on investigators to marshal the facts in a way that facilitates them being presented to their full effect.

The Importance of the Lead Investigator at Trial

Q & A

Q: The prosecutor doesn't come along with me on surveillance operations, and isn't directly involved in most other aspects of the investigation phase of a case. Why should I be required to be in court helping the prosecutor for the duration of the prosecution phase of a major case just because I'm the lead investigator?

A: The case is still as much your case now that it is in a trial court as it was at the earliest of investigative stages. Cases cannot be completely handed off by an investigator to a prosecutor for trial. The lead investigator provides the continuity of history a case needs to successfully make the transition from investigation to prosecution.

STAYING HAPPY ASSISTING WITH AN APPEAL-PROOF TRIAL

A goal in any trial is to maximize the potential for a conviction of the accused being upheld throughout the appeal process. A goal is not to shovel in as much damning evidence as possible, regardless of its prejudicial nature, or to make highly inflammatory statements to a jury that are likely to goad its members into convicting. To be happy being involved in criminal or regulatory trial work as either a prosecutor or investigator, you have to accept that the overall goal of a trial is not to secure a conviction at any cost, but rather to see that justice is done which is the true measure of case success.

It also helps to like surprises. Not just happy surprises, but any surprises. The unpredictability of trial work means you never know what the next day or minute is going to bring. Some people naturally like predictability, to have a day fully planned out, and take great satisfaction from the day unfolding as planned, but things just don't work like that at trials full of misplaced evidence, recanting witnesses, novel legal defences, mercurial personalities, and even the occasional bomb threat. You need to roll with the surprises, quickly figure out solutions, and incorporate them into your original trial plan. Surprises can be so devastating to trial work that if you don't keep a sense of humour and embrace the challenge of seeing that justice is done, the work will quickly become very depressing. The road to justice is an unpredictable one.

ASSISTING WITH THE PRELIMINARY INQUIRY

Although you may have heard talk about the imminent death of the preliminary inquiry, I can assure you that it is still alive and well. Applicable only in indictable offence cases proceeding to a superior court trial, the preliminary inquiry ensures an accused is not subject to a full trial for an alleged crime the prosecution cannot even make out a *prima facie* case against, and provides limited discovery of the prosecution case by testing some of its witnesses and evidence. The threshold for demonstrating a *prima facie* case was defined in *United States of America v. Sheppard*, [1977] 2 S.C.R. 1067 at 1080:

> this is to be determined according to whether or not there is any evidence upon which a reasonable jury properly instructed could return a verdict of guilty. The "justice", in accordance with this principle, is, in my opinion, required to commit an accused person for trial in any case in which there is admissible evidence which could, if it were believed, result in a conviction.

Early investigator-prosecutor contact allows determination of exactly which witnesses and evidence will be required for the preliminary inquiry — usually considerably fewer witnesses and less evidence than for the trial — depending on the type of charges and respective roles witnesses played during the investigation.

Preparation is definitely required for a preliminary inquiry. It's a great embarrassment to both investigators and prosecutors when a case fails even to make it past the preliminary inquiry threshold. While neither the weight of evidence — including continuity — nor the *Charter* are in issue at a preliminary inquiry, showing "some" evidence on all essential elements of each charge can still pose a challenge. To take a drug possession charge as an example, there must be some evidence that:

- the substance seized was a controlled substance included under the schedules to the *Controlled Drugs and Substances Act*;

- the accused had control over the substance; and

- the accused had knowledge of the substance.

Most preliminary inquiries last less than a day, but some can continue for several months, so investigators need to be prepared for a courtroom effort that could approach that of the trial itself. Investigator assistance at preliminary inquiries is invaluable to overall case success.

ASSISTING WITH THE PRETRIAL MOTIONS

At times it seems like a trial will never get to the start of the fact determination and offence assessment stage because pretrial motions drag on month after month. Constitutional motions can especially take on a life of their own. You will not be the only one who gets frustrated with pretrial motions; the judiciary has been expressing increasing frustration like in *R. v. Moore* (1993), 27 B.C.A.C. 253; affd. *R. v. Moore*, [1995] 1 S.C.R. 756 at paras. 50-51 in the concurring reasons of Southin J.A:

> I would not wish to leave this appeal without iterating this trenchant observation made by Judge Romilly [who heard the trial] with which I agree:
>
>> Proceedings in this matter have been very lengthy. The trial has been continuing on and off over the last year and a half. The actual trial time involved was approximately four and one-half months. It is fair to say that if two words could be used to describe this lengthy trial, they would be the words, "*Charter* mania." Every possible *Charter* argument that could be raised was raised in this trial. Some may be tempted to say that this trial has made a significant contribution towards the swelling of the national debt.
>
> On the evidence, there was not the slightest shred of doubt from the outset of the trial that the appellants were guilty. I should be much surprised if the burden upon the taxpayer of this trial, quite apart from the cost of this appeal, namely, the salaries and bene-

fits of the judge, Crown counsel, the police witnesses and the court staff, and the costs of the provision and maintenance of the courtroom in which it was held, was less than $200,000. I assume that in this particular case the public did not bear the fees of defence counsel, although in many of these long conspiracy trials the public does bear that expense.

Motions may be brought before, during or at the end of a trial by either the defence or prosecution, although lawyers and judges usually prefer to get most motions out of the way at the start so as not to interrupt the flow of case facts.

Motions generally require some kind of evidentiary basis in order to be advanced or responded to, be it in an affidavit or through oral evidence, with investigators playing a crucial role because they are often in the best position to provide such evidence. As part of an adjournment application an investigator can explain why a key witness or piece of evidence is not available. In a joinder application, an investigator can articulate the interrelationship of all charges and evidence to show why it would be in the interests of justice to try the charges in a single prosecution. Investigator evidence can respond to a *Charter* application by setting out why investigators did or did not take particular actions in a case, why there were delays in bringing a case to trial, or why it would be contrary to the public interest to disclose certain information. The prosecution and defence might agree that evidence taken on a pretrial motion will also be applied as evidence in the trial proper, in which case any evidence you offer on a motion will be doubly important.

ASSISTING WITH JURY SELECTION

Jury selection can also delay the start of taking trial evidence. The procedure of a jury trial splits law and fact finding functions, with jury members being the triers of fact, and the judge the trier of law. Jury trials are guaranteed to be more complex and prone to appeal than non-jury trials, but they remain a cornerstone of the Canadian justice system with s-s. 11(f) of the *Charter* providing a limited right to jury trial "where the maximum punishment for the offence is imprisonment for five years or a more severe punishment." The important role juries play was emphasized in *R. v. Sherratt*, [1991] 1 S.C.R. 509 at 523-524:

> The jury, through its collective decision making, is an excellent fact finder; due to its representative character, it acts as the conscience of the community; the jury can act as the final bulwark against oppressive laws or their enforcement; it provides a means where-

by the public increases its knowledge of the criminal justice system and it increases, through the involvement of the public, societal trust in the system as a whole.

Investigators can provide the prosecution with valuable assistance in picking an appropriate jury.

In Canada very little can be asked of people selected for jury duty other than name, age, place of residence and occupation. There is lots of mythology out there concerning which occupations are more likely to convict or acquit for particular types of offences, or which occupations are at risk of seizing control of the jury so that it is not the decision of all 12 reasonable women and men who rule the day. There is little scientific evidence in Canada to support these myths, particularly since the passing of laws prohibiting jury members from discussing their deliberations with anyone outside of the jury. *R. v. Pan*, [2001] 2 S.C.R. 344 at paras. 50, 52-53, explained the rationale for the secrecy surrounding juries:

> The first reason supporting the need for secrecy is that confidentiality promotes candour and the kind of full and frank debate that is essential to this type of collegial decision making. While searching for unanimity, jurors should be free to explore out loud all avenues of reasoning without fear of exposure to public ridicule, contempt or hatred. This rationale is of vital importance to the potential acquittal of an unpopular accused, or one charged with a particularly repulsive crime. In my view, this rationale is sound, and does not require empirical confirmation.
>
> . . .
>
> Our system of jury selection is sensitive to the privacy interests of prospective jurors . . . and the proper functioning of the jury system, a constitutionally protected right in serious criminal charges, depends upon the willingness of jurors to discharge their functions honestly and honourably. This in turn is dependent, at the very minimum, on a system that ensures the safety of jurors, their sense of security, as well as their privacy.
>
> I am fully satisfied that a considerable measure of secrecy surrounding the deliberations of the jury is essential to the proper functioning of that important institution and that the preceding rationales serve as a useful guide to the boundaries between the competing demands of secrecy and reviewability.

In Canada most of the technique of picking jury members comes down to instinct, supported by pre-emptory challenges and challenges for cause.

Investigators can give prosecutors their personal opinions on what they think of prospective jurors, as well as possibly provide evidence in motions demanding challenges for cause. Eventually 12 suitable jurors will be found, but sometimes a massive jury pool might be called upon to get those 12. For one case in my office thousands of potential jurors were summonsed in order to get 12 people who possessed appropriate French and English language skills to hear a bilingual organized crime trial.

MARSHALLING THE WITNESSES AND EVIDENCE WHILE COMMUNICATING WITH THE PROSECUTOR

It often falls to the lead investigator to ensure all required witnesses show up at the trial court at the appointed time (which should happen automatically if subpoenas have been served) and do not subsequently wander off during courtroom delays. The lead investigator also ensures all required physical evidence, affidavits and certificates are present for trial, pretrial notices have been provided, and makes the prosecutor aware of trial readiness. Some trials end in disaster because the prosecutor believes she is missing a key witness or piece of evidence, even though the witness is in the hall or the evidence is in an investigator's briefcase.

Trial courts are very stressful places for both investigators and prosecutors, where prosecutors may be simultaneously juggling dozens of files, hoping at least one of them will be ready to proceed. A prosecutor needs a trial case to start the day, once the preliminaries of bails and adjournments have been completed. Pass the prosecutor a note to say whether or not your case is ready to go, and explain what is causing the delay if it is not ready. Impatient judges eventually start calling cases themselves, sometimes dismissing charges if there isn't a good reason why a case can't immediately proceed.

To the witnesses, the lead investigator can play the role of stage manager who ensures the correct witness walks onto the courtroom stage at just the right time, the next witness is ready to go on as soon as the current witness finishes, and who may occasionally need to find an understudy to fill in for a missing actor. To the physical evidence, the lead investigator can act as prop master, making sure each item is well cared for, put on display when required, brought back to the lockup for the night if the court has not taken custody of it, and who sometimes must find an entirely new prop in response to events in the courtroom. To the prosecutor, the lead investigator is foremost a script consultant who provides advance warning about case problems, concisely answers whispered prosecutor questions, keeps track through note-taking of what is going on at trial and who feeds prosecutor instructions back to other investigators or witnesses.

The Trial Evidence Checklist, at the end of this chapter, allows investigators to organize witnesses and exhibits in advance of trial, and then check off the various requirements as a trial progresses. For witnesses, important factors to check are whether they have been subpoenaed, are present in court, have been called for examination-in-chief, have introduced particular exhibits, have been cross-examined, may be called in rebuttal, or still need to be located. For exhibits, equally relevant factors to check are whether they are present in court, have been marked for identification purposes with a letter or number, have been formally admitted into evidence, and which witnesses have referred to them in testimony or if they still need to be obtained.

There is no question lead investigators carry a heavy trial burden. Their supervisors need to recognize that burden in balancing the workload of their other duties. The ultimate responsibility for lead investigator trial duties cannot be offloaded to anyone else, unless a new lead investigator is brought up to speed on the history of the case, but in more complex cases it is good practice for the lead investigator to employ assisting investigators to help with some of the trial administrative duties.

Ideally two investigators will be present at all but the simplest trials. One is the "inside investigator" who as lead investigator will sit beside the prosecutor to offer advice, take notes, suggest questions and produce the exhibits. The other is the "outside investigator" who will coordinate witnesses present in the courthouse, make telephone calls, visit the exhibit lock-up, and search for missing witnesses on the streets. In the biggest of cases trial assistance responsibilities should be divided among three investigators, with the additional investigator assigned to looking after the possibly thousands of exhibits, leaving inside and outside investigators free to concentrate on directly assisting the prosecutor and coordinating witnesses and outside follow-up respectively.

The Importance of Investigator Note-Taking at Trial

Q & A

Q: I'm not a secretary. Why as the lead investigator should I have to take notes of everything that goes on in the courtroom?

A: Hopefully in the not too distant future, all courtrooms will have simultaneous transcript facilities where what is said in court appears on computer screens in the courtroom right after it is said, but a system so dependant on technology will never be foolproof. In one trial I conducted, a computer recording system stopped functioning in the middle of a witness' testimony without any

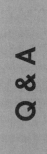

of us noticing the error until almost 30 minutes of testimony had been lost forever. At present, court transcripts often take weeks or months to obtain. In order to ensure all question angles are covered, and to be able to quote back to the court what a witness has previously testified to, good notes are imperative. It is the job of the prosecutor to take notes when possible, but simultaneously taking notes and asking questions is very difficult. The best compromise on note-taking when working as the inside investigator is to (1) write down anything said that seems important, (2) take notes when asked to do so by the prosecutor, and (3) always note down answers when the prosecutor is asking questions.

AVOIDING EXCLUSION OF ASSISTING INVESTIGATORS

R. v. Graves (1969), 9 C.R.N.S. 396 (N.S.M.C.) at paras. 3 & 14-15, explained the rationale behind the common practice of witness exclusion, and possible consequences if an exclusion order is ignored:

> The last Crown witness was a police constable who had not withdrawn from the courtroom when ordered by the Court to do so. Counsel for the accused objected to his testimony because of his presence in court contrary to the motion and during the testimony of the other witnesses.
>
> . . .
>
> It must be remembered that the basic function of sequestration of witnesses is to maintain as much as possible the purity of the evidence to be given by compelling witnesses to rely on their own memory and to prevent them from being aided or influenced in what they would say by what other witnesses have said before them. Therefore, when the Court orders sequestration of witnesses and the Crown calls a witness who has heard the preceding evidence, the burden is on the Crown to show that the testimony of that witness is not contrary to the purposes of sequestration as aforesaid. Such was not done in this particular case.
>
> In this case there is nothing to show that the police constable was not influenced in his testimony by what he heard and observed and the Court therefore cannot be certain of its accuracy. That uncertainty, coupled with the vague generalities of the other Crown witnesses as to the date of the offence, preclude me from

finding a *prima facie* case against the accused. Accordingly, I find the accused not guilty as charged and the matter is dismissed.

Where a prosecutor needs one witness to remain as inside investigator, he could ask for an exception to an exclusion order or call that witness first so she can remain in court after the completion of her testimony. The longer an investigator who is supposed to be assisting the prosecutor in court is on the stand instead, the longer that investigator will not be available to offer the prosecutor advice at crucial points in the trial.

Ideally, the inside and outside investigators should not be required witnesses at trial. In major cases it may be possible to choose from among various investigators who the inside and the outside investigators will be. If the investigator in charge of a case has refrained from making observations, seizures, arrests or taking statements in that case, then he likely will not be a required witness and thus will avoid exposure to defence cross-examination and courtroom witnesses exclusion.

Courtesy and Trial Demands

Q: The prosecutor decided in the middle of the trial of a case I was in charge of that he wanted two additional witnesses interviewed and subpoenaed by the following day. He got very upset when I told him this wasn't possible. How am I supposed to accomplish the impossible?

A: Emotions may run high during the most heated moments of a trial, but you have a right to expect common courtesy and respect at all times from the prosecutor. Sometimes there are truly unexpected developments in a trial that necessitate the calling of additional witnesses, or undertaking further investigation. It is unlikely such last minute requests are frivolous impulses on the part of the prosecutor, but you need to tell the prosecutor what can be accomplished with the resources you have to work with.

ASSISTING WITH SENTENCING SUBMISSIONS AFTER A CONVICTION

If the whole point of prosecutions is general and specific deterrence, denunciation, rehabilitation, and restoration or transformation of victim-offender relationships, then the system depends not just on offence detection and confirmation through judicial process, but also on following that confirmation through to a just sentence, well supported by the facts and law

— a sentence neither so low that the public loses confidence in the system, nor so high that an appeal court finds it to be harsh and disproportionate. The goal is a well tailored sentence, as noted in *R. v. W. (L.W.),* [2000] 1 S.C.R. 455 at para. 21:

> Even if it can be argued that harsh, unfit sentences may prove to be a powerful deterrent, and therefore still serve a valid purpose, it seems to me that sentences that are unjustly severe are more likely to inspire contempt and resentment than to foster compliance with the law. It is a well-established principle of the criminal justice system that judges must strive to impose a sentence tailored to the individual case.

Scant attention may be paid to the preparation of sentencing submissions by prosecutors and investigators who are exhausted after a contentious trial. There is a feeling of relief that the hard part is over, with the sentencing process sometimes seen as a kind of encore after the main performance has ended. Well prepared sentencing submissions are extremely important, however, because of the great degree of discretion available to trial sentencing judges, as noted in *R. v. Proulx,* [2000] 1 S.C.R. 61 at paras. 116, 123 & 125:

> There is no easy test or formula that the judge can apply in weighing these factors. Much will depend on the good judgment and wisdom of sentencing judges, whom Parliament vested with considerable discretion in making these determinations . . . . In recent years, this Court has repeatedly stated that the sentence imposed by a trial court is entitled to considerable deference from appellate courts . . . Although an appellate court might entertain a different opinion as to what objectives should be pursued and the best way to do so, that difference will generally not constitute an error of law justifying interference. . . . Again, I stress that appellate courts should not second-guess sentencing judges unless the sentence imposed is demonstrably unfit.

Investigators are the ones in the best position to know and present crucial sentencing facts that inform the exercise of that discretion. Submission of a short sentencing brief as part of the original prosecution brief will ensure prosecutors understand and have justification for investigator sentencing objectives right from the start of a case. At the point of conviction investigators might need to coordinate up-dated criminal records, check for outstanding charges, gather further victim impact statements, procure expert evidence, and even give sentencing evidence themselves. The frustrations over sentence unpredictability that investigators and prosecutors experience can be largely overcome if sentencing is jointly taken charge of long before the start of trial, and control is maintained over what sentencing evidence and precedents will be relied upon if a conviction is secured. Understanding a bit about the history of sentencing reform and currently available sentencing options will help you play an influential role in the sentencing process.

1. The Codification and Reform of Sentencing Principles

Canada has among the highest rates of incarceration among industrialized democracies. The courts have commented on alarming over-incarceration trends, with *R. v. Proulx*, [2000] 1 S.C.R. 61, finding at para. 16:

> Canada's incarceration rate of approximately 130 inmates per 100,000 population places it second or third highest among industrialized democracies . . . incarceration is costly, frequently unduly harsh and "ineffective, not only in relation to its purported rehabilitative goals, but also in relation to its broader public goals" . . . . Prison has been characterized by some as a finishing school for criminals and as ill-preparing them for reintegration into society.

R. v. Gladue, [1999] 1 S.C.R. 688 at para. 57, had earlier concluded:

> although imprisonment is intended to serve the traditional sentencing goals of separation, deterrence, denunciation, and rehabilitation, there is widespread consensus that imprisonment has not been successful in achieving some of these goals. Overincarceration is a long-standing problem that has been many times publicly acknowledged but never addressed in a systematic manner by Parliament. In recent years, compared to other countries, sentences of imprisonment in Canada have increased at an alarming rate. The 1996 sentencing reforms embodied in Part XXIII, and s. 718.2(*e*) [of the *Criminal Code*] in particular, must be understood as a reaction to the overuse of prison as a sanction, and must accordingly be given appropriate force as remedial provisions.

Faced with a growing prison population that was not commensurately diminishing with a falling crime rate, in 1996 Parliament tackled three challenges through the enactment of Part XXIII of the *Criminal Code*: reducing levels of incarceration, promoting the use of restorative justice, and codifying already established sentencing principles. *R. v. Gladue*, [1999] 1 S.C.R. 688 at para. 39, went so far as to state that "[t]he enactment of the new Part XXIII was a watershed, marking the first codification and significant reform of sentencing principles in the history of Canadian criminal law."

Expanding restorative justice initiatives was seen as the key element of the reforms, as noted in *R. v. Proulx*, [2000] 1 S.C.R. 61 at paras. 18-20:

> Restorative justice is concerned with the restoration of the parties that are affected by the commission of an offence. Crime generally affects at least three parties: the victim, the community, and the offender. A restorative justice approach seeks to remedy the adverse effects of crime in a manner that addresses the needs of all parties involved. This is accomplished, in part, through the rehabilitation of the offender, reparations to the victim and to the community, and the promotion of a sense of responsibility in the offender and acknowledgment of the harm done to victims and to the community.
>
> . . .
>
> Parliament has mandated that expanded use be made of restorative principles in sentencing as a result of the general failure of incarceration to rehabilitate offenders and reintegrate them into society. By placing a new emphasis on restorative principles, Parliament expects both to reduce the rate of incarceration and improve the effectiveness of sentencing.

The jury is still out on the long term effects of the 1996 amendments, later supplemented by the *Youth Criminal Justice Act*, S.C. 2002, c. 1, but it can certainly be said that the reforms — especially in the creation of "conditional sentences" — shook up what had been thought to be fairly well understood sentencing choices.

a. *The Six Objectives of Sentencing*

Section 718 of the *Criminal Code* now sets out the six objectives of sentencing:

> **718.** The fundamental purpose of sentencing is to contribute, along with crime prevention initiatives, to respect for the law and the maintenance of a just, peaceful and safe society by imposing just sanctions that have one or more of the following objectives:
>
> (a) to denounce unlawful conduct;
>
> (b) to deter the offender and other persons from committing offences;
>
> (c) to separate offenders from society, where necessary;

(d) to assist in rehabilitating offenders;

(e) to provide reparations for harm done to victims or to the community; and

(f) to promote a sense of responsibility in offenders, and acknowledgment of the harm done to victims and to the community

A sentence need not meet all of those objectives, but the more objectives met the better.

Denunciation, deterrence and separation (sometimes called incapacitation) are the oldest objectives, and largely follow a punitive model. Punishment affirms the power of the state, teaches the offender and others not to commit similar offences in the future, and protects society for at least as long as the offender is in jail or being closely monitored. Recognition that punishment alone was an insufficient sentencing tool led to initiatives to rehabilitate offenders to become productive members of society. Recognition that victims have legitimate rights in the justice process led to efforts to secure reparations directly through the criminal justice system, rather than forcing victims to pursue costly civil law suits against offenders of modest means. Recognition that monetary reparations cannot by themselves repair the damage offences do to victims and offenders led to broader concepts of restorative justice being increasingly promoted that urge acceptance of responsibility by offenders, acknowledgement of harm, and overall healing of victims and offenders. The provisions following s. 718 move beyond sentencing objectives to describe how trial judges are to arrive at results that meet those objectives.

b. Offences against Children

It is not yet entirely clear what the recent addition of s. 718.01 adds to the *Criminal Code*'s sentencing principles already enshrined in s. 718:

> **718.01** When a court imposes a sentence for an offence that involved the abuse of a person under the age of eighteen years, it shall give primary consideration to the objectives of denunciation and deterrence of such conduct.

Giving "primary consideration" to denunciation and deterrence will not necessarily lead to harsher sentences, as a sentence must still be appropriate for the offence and offender. It would also be surprising if Parliament intended s. 718.01 to detract from the victim-focussed principles of s-ss. 716.01(e) and

(f) of the *Code*. Since a crime being committed against a child (other than one's own) is not an explicitly enumerated aggravating factor in s. 718.2 of the *Code*, by highlighting offences against children s. 718.01 may have the effect of making it an aggravating factor.

c. *Proportionality of Sentencing to Gravity and Responsibility*

The principle of proportionality codified in s. 718.1 of the *Criminal Code* is at the root of all sentencing that must fit both the offence and the offender:

> **718.1.** A sentence must be proportionate to the gravity of the offence and the degree of responsibility of the offender.

For each offence, there is a range of available sentences stipulated in the legislation being prosecuted; determining where a sentence should fall within the range requires an intimate knowledge of the circumstances of both the offence and offender. Investigators are ideally placed to provide the prosecution and court with facts permitting an informed decision to be made about sentence proportionality in relation to gravity and responsibility, such as through providing evidence of the long-term impact of the offence on the victim and how planned or intentional the offence appeared to be on the part of the offender.

d. *Aggravating and Mitigating Factors in Sentencing*

Aggravating and mitigating factors applicable to an offence or offender can further push a sentence up or down within the available range. These factors are more specific than just the general seriousness of an offence and an offender's relative role in it. The *Criminal Code* does not directly specify mitigating factors in Part XXIII , but it does list a number of aggravating factors in s-s. 718.2 (a):

> **718.2.** A court that imposes a sentence shall also take into consideration the following principles:
>
> > (a) a sentence should be increased or reduced to account for any relevant aggravating or mitigating circumstances relating to the offence or the offender, and, without limiting the generality of the foregoing,
> >
> > > (i) evidence that the offence was motivated by bias, prejudice or hate based on race, national or ethnic ori-

gin, language, colour, religion, sex, age, mental or physical disability, sexual orientation, or any other similar
factor,

(ii) evidence that the offender, in committing the
offence, abused the offender's spouse or common-law
partner or child,

(iii) evidence that the offender, in committing the
offence, abused a position of trust or authority in relation to the victim,

(iv) evidence that the offence was committed for the
benefit of, at the direction of or in association with a
criminal organization, or

(v) evidence that the offence was a terrorism offence

shall be deemed to be aggravating circumstances;

The unlisted mitigating factors could be things like the offender being
remorseful for the offence, having compensated the victim for damage
caused, or having entered an early guilty plea that affirms the offender is
taking responsibility for his actions and saves the justice system from
expending considerable resources on a trial.

e. Comparability of Offences and Offenders

Sub-section 718.2(b) of the *Code* deals with proportionality for offences
and offenders:

> **718.2.** (b) a sentence should be similar to sentences imposed on
> similar offenders for similar offences committed in similar circum-
> stances;

Breach of this pithy principle forms the basis for a great number of appeals
that argue that the sentence imposed at trial was unfit as being outside the
proportionate range of sentences imposed in cases dealing with offenders,
offences and circumstances not particularly different from the case under
appeal. The comparability principle should, for example, result in comparable sentences after separate trials for different offenders who have no prior
criminal records and play similar roles in the sale of one gram of crack
cocaine.

For less commonly prosecuted offences, and especially for regulatory
offences, investigators should bring any known sentencing results for simi-

lar cases to the attention of prosecutors because it can be very difficult to obtain precedents from what are often unreported cases. Ideally investigators will keep useful sentencing judgments or transcripts on file, and maintain a basic computer database listing case names, dates, offences, judges and sentences. I have been successful in turning cases around where there was a risk of an insufficient sentence by relying on basic investigator-maintained sentencing records to jog the minds of judges into remembering they had previously imposed significant sentences for similar offences on similar offenders.

f. *Exercising Restraint in Consecutive Sentences*

Sub-section 718.2(c) of the *Code* addresses how consecutive sentences should be approached: "where consecutive sentences are imposed, the combined sentence should not be unduly long or harsh." This rule of restraint is also a rule of fairness. There are good public policy reasons for routinely making certain sentences run concurrently for jointly prosecuted multiple offences committed at similar times and involving similar facts. Where the seriousness of the separate offences being jointly prosecuted or the fairly loose connection among those offences dictate that resulting sentences be served consecutively, the totality principle ensures cumulative sentences imposed do not exceed overall culpability of the offender or eliminate hope in most cases of being released from jail at some point in the future.

g. *Imprisonment as a Last Resort*

Sub-sections 718.2(d) and (e) of the *Code* attempt to change the way judges, lawyers, investigators and the public think about what constitutes a suitable punishment for significant criminal offences:

> **718.2.** (d) an offender should not be deprived of liberty, if less restrictive sanctions may be appropriate in the circumstances; and
>
> (e) all available sanctions other than imprisonment that are reasonable in the circumstances should be considered for all offenders, with particular attention to the circumstances of aboriginal offenders.

Thus Parliament mandated that imprisonment can no longer be a routine sanction for a broad spectrum of offences and offenders. Prosecutors now bear a particularly heavy burden when calling for imprisonment in any case other than one where legislation specifies a mandatory minimum term of imprisonment. Investigator involvement in providing a factual basis for sentencing submissions is crucial where terms of imprisonment are sought.

The explicit instruction to take the particular circumstances of aboriginal offenders into account derives from Canada's inclination to lock up aboriginal Canadians at a rate that is dramatically disproportionate to their numbers in Canadian society, at more than six times the rate of non-aboriginal incarceration (using 1998 figures). Imprisonment especially takes many aboriginal Canadians far away from their homes and families. While a broad-based strategy that goes beyond the courts may be required to fully address aboriginal rates of incarceration, Parliament has nonetheless demanded that courts consider if something can be done to ameliorate the situation at the sentencing stage while still upholding other sentencing values.

2. Choosing among Different Types of Sentences

a. *Absolute and Conditional Discharges*

The general principles governing absolute and conditional discharges are found in s. 730 of the *Criminal Code*:

> **730.** (1) Where an accused, other than an organization, pleads guilty to or is found guilty of an offence, other than an offence for which a minimum punishment is prescribed by law or an offence punishable by imprisonment for fourteen years or for life, the court before which the accused appears may, if it considers it to be in the best interests of the accused and not contrary to the public interest, instead of convicting the accused, by order direct that the accused be discharged absolutely or on the conditions prescribed in a probation order made under subsection 731(2).
>
> . . .
>
> (3) Where a court directs under subsection (1) that an offender be discharged of an offence, the offender shall be deemed not to have been convicted of the offence . . . .

An absolute discharge is often imposed for minor first offences, takes effect immediately and registers the moral culpability of the offender, but affirms that sentencing principles do not require the offender to be punished. A conditional discharge does not take effect until its conditions have been fulfilled, which often relate to community service over the course of a few months through a probation order, in addition to keeping the peace and being of good behaviour. If a discharge seems a possibility in one of your cases, you may want to consider trying to justify why a conditional instead of absolute discharge is appropriate, such as because of the seriousness of the offence or risk the offender poses for reoffending.

b. *Suspended Sentences and Probation*

A suspended sentence does constitute a conviction, even though the imposition of punishment through a fine or imprisonment is suspended subject to the offender completing the terms of probation. Section 731 of the *Code* gives a court its general authority to impose a suspended sentence as well as authority to impose probation, either in combination with a suspended sentence or as an addition to a conditional discharge, fine or term of imprisonment:

> **731.** (1) Where a person is convicted of an offence, a court may, having regard to the age and character of the offender, the nature of the offence and the circumstances surrounding its commission,
>
> (a) if no minimum punishment is prescribed by law, suspend the passing of sentence and direct that the offender be released on the conditions prescribed in a probation order; or
>
> (b) in addition to fining or sentencing the offender to imprisonment for a term not exceeding two years, direct that the offender comply with the conditions prescribed in a probation order.
>
> (2) A court may also make a probation order where it discharges an accused under subsection 730(1).

For those on probation the primary punishment has passed and reintegration into the community is a compelling goal so conditions could be as basic as keeping the peace, being of good behaviour, attending court as required, and informing the probation supervisor of changes in address or employment. Investigators should suggest to prosecutors what sorts of probation conditions might control an offender's behaviour, protect the public, and can be effectively monitored like staying out of an area of the city, not contacting certain people, not consuming particular substances, or getting counselling for addiction, anger or other problems.

Sub-section 732.1(3)(h) of the *Code* establishes available probation conditions including: "comply with such other reasonable conditions as the court considers desirable, subject to any regulations made under subsection 738(2), for protecting society and for facilitating the offender's successful reintegration into the community." Such open-ended conditions allow for creative sentencing alternatives to be explored, like an offender giving public talks about the subject of the offence, contributing money to charities involved in research into the effects of the offence, or anything else satisfying basic sentencing principles. Let your imagination run wild.

Creativity in Sentencing

Q&A

Q: How much room for creativity is there in sentencing? It seems the only sentences I usually see being imposed are fines and imprisonment, where it all comes down to picking a number — the defence asks for a low number, the prosecution for a high number, and the judge often picks a number somewhere in between.

A: There is lots of room for creativity in sentencing, particularly for regulatory offences and less serious criminal offences. Sentencing isn't just about picking a number, although I acknowledge at times it can seem that way. Investigators can play a vital role in stimulating the creativity of all the parties by suggesting to the prosecutor creative ways to accomplish sentencing goals with dispositions other than fines or imprisonment.

c. Fines

Fines are very common sentences, but there is much more to their calculation than first meets the eye. Many Acts previously provided for modest fines within a narrow range like up to $500, so calculating an appropriate fine did not take too much effort. Newer Acts like the *Canadian Environmental Protected Act, 1999*, S.C. 1999, c. 33, now provide for fines of up to $1,000,000 per charge. Because of the very broad fine ranges now available and their possibly very onerous outcomes, determining whether a fine is appropriate at all and then determining the appropriate quantum ranging from a few dollars to a few million dollars can be a difficult task.

Fines, like any other sentence, must fit both the offence and the offender. Investigators can provide considerable assistance with fine sentencing submissions by furnishing information on fines received elsewhere for similar offences, on the amount of profit reaped from the offences subject to sentencing, on any monetarily quantifiable damage caused by those offences, and on the financial position of the offender. The offender's ability to pay is crucial to fulfilling sentencing goals, where a very small fine might suffice for a very poor individual, while a large fine might fall short for a multi-national corporation. For economic crimes, a fine may be just a cost of doing business unless the fine exceeds the total profits made not just for the offence prosecuted but for all similar offences committed by that offender which may have gone undetected in the past. Especially for regulatory offences, creative sentencing options exercisable through probation conditions may be better bets than fines.

d. *Conditional Sentences*

I recall the conditional sentence being considered by me and many of my fellow prosecutors when it arrived in 1996 as a radical innovation in the law. We asked ourselves how could there possibly be a custodial sentence that is served completely outside of prison, and how would this meet sentencing objectives? Sure, conditions were to be imposed on offenders restricting their actions while serving a conditional sentence, but it still sounded a lot like a suspended sentence with probation. The discomfort around conditional sentences took several years to abate as gaps in the new legislation governing those sentences were filled either by judicial interpretation or statutory amendment. There are still challenges posed by the way these sentences operate, but their intent of reducing prison populations while still protecting the public cannot be argued with given the high levels of incarceration in Canada.

Section 742.1 of the *Criminal Code* sets out when a conditional sentence may be imposed:

> **742.1.** Where a person is convicted of an offence, except an offence that is punishable by a minimum term of imprisonment, and the court
>
> > (a) imposes a sentence of imprisonment of less than two years, and
> >
> > (b) is satisfied that serving the sentence in the community would not endanger the safety of the community and would be consistent with the fundamental purpose and principles of sentencing set out in sections 718 to 718.2,
>
> the court may, for the purpose of supervising the offender's behaviour in the community, order that the offender serve the sentence in the community, subject to the offender's complying with the

conditions of a conditional sentence order made under section 742.3.

Very serious crimes attracting sentences of greater than two years imprisonment will be ineligible for a conditional sentence.

Section 742.3 of the *Code* lists a number of mandatory and optional conditions that accompany a conditional sentence, but s-s. 742.3(2)(f) establishes that the list is open ended:

> **732.3.** (2)(f) comply with such other reasonable conditions as the court considers desirable, subject to any regulations made under subsection 738(2), for securing the good conduct of the offender and for preventing a repetition by the offender of the same offence or the commission of other offences.

By stressing protection of the community, conditions imposed under a conditional sentence have a quite different focus than probation conditions that emphasize offender reintegration into the community. This stronger wording demonstrates these are still sentences of imprisonment, ranging anywhere up to 24-hour-a-day house arrest with random peace officer searches of residence, vehicle or person — similar to conditions imposed on an offender serving a term of closed custody in jail.

R. v. Proulx, [2000] 1 S.C.R. 61 at paras. 21-22, described the nature of conditional sentences as:

> a meaningful alternative to incarceration for less serious and non-dangerous offenders. The offenders who meet the criteria of s. 742.1 will serve a sentence under strict surveillance in the community instead of going to prison. These offenders' liberty will be constrained by conditions to be attached to the sentence, as set out in s. 742.3 of the *Code*. In case of breach of conditions, the offender will be brought back before a judge, pursuant to s. 742.6. If an offender cannot provide a reasonable excuse for breaching the conditions of his or her sentence, the judge may order him or her to serve the remainder of the sentence in jail, as it was intended by Parliament that there be a real threat of incarceration to increase compliance with the conditions of the sentence.
>
> The conditional sentence incorporates some elements of non-custodial measures and some others of incarceration. Because it is served in the community, it will generally be more effective than incarceration at achieving the restorative objectives of rehabilitation, reparations to the victim and community, and the promotion of a sense of responsibility in the offender. However, *it is also a punitive sanction capable of achieving the objectives of denuncia-*

tion and deterrence. It is this punitive aspect that distinguishes the conditional sentence from probation . . . .

As for when a conditional sentence would be appropriate the court said at para. 100:

> a conditional sentence can achieve both punitive and restorative objectives. To the extent that both punitive and restorative objectives can be achieved in a given case, a conditional sentence is likely a better sanction than incarceration. Where the need for punishment is particularly pressing, and there is little opportunity to achieve any restorative objectives, incarceration will likely be the more attractive sanction. However, even where restorative objectives cannot be readily satisfied, a conditional sentence will be preferable to incarceration in cases where a conditional sentence can achieve the objectives of denunciation and deterrence as effectively as incarceration. This follows from the principle of restraint in s. 718.2(*d*) and (*e*), which militates in favour of alternatives to incarceration where appropriate in the circumstances.

Investigators can suggest to prosecutors conditions that meet all relevant sentencing objectives and are capable of being effectively monitored to ensure the offender will not treat the conditional sentence like some kind of get out of jail free pass. Likely the greatest encouragement to conditional sentence compliance is the consequences of a judicial finding of conditional sentence breach: immediate imprisonment to serve out the remainder of the sentence.

e. *Imprisonment*

A vast array of offences in Canada have imprisonment available as a possible sentence, but the *Criminal Code* now admonishes it is a last resort to be tried only where all else has failed or is likely to fail in meeting sentencing objectives as explained in *R. v. Proulx*, [2000] 1 S.C.R. 61 at para. 107:

> The empirical evidence suggests that the deterrent effect of incarceration is uncertain . . . . Nevertheless, there may be circumstances in which the need for deterrence will warrant incarceration. This will depend in part on whether the offence is one in which the effects of incarceration are likely to have a real deterrent effect, as well as on the circumstances of the community in which the offences were committed.

Imprisonment is the most expensive kind of sentence to administer, and doubt has been cast on how effective it is at achieving sentencing objectives except for its incapacitation effect. Still, it has its place as the ultimate sanction of the Canadian justice system. My personal experience as a prosecutor has been that people will do almost anything to avoid going to jail, not just because of the way it controls actions and interrupts normal life, but also because of the stigma attached to serving a jail sentence. Investigators can play a important role in crafting terms of imprisonment by suggesting and providing factual justification for why a particular term of imprisonment is necessary.

f. *Organization Sentencing*

Although natural human beings are the most commonly prosecuted "persons" in Canada, organizations like corporations have a legal personality that can be prosecuted for regulatory or criminal offences. But the sentencing of organizations poses a great challenge because of their diverse forms, the extremes of wealth they possess, and the opacity of their operations. Organizations can range from the most minor shell company poorer in assets than the poorest individual, to major multinationals richer than the richest of people. Sometimes it is extremely difficult to figure out how an organization operates, what assets it possesses, and which human beings are behind its operations. The ultimate sanction of imprisonment is useless against an organization.

Just as the sentencing of individuals took a leap forward in 1996 with the codification and reform of universal sentencing principles, so too did organization sentencing progress in 2003 with the enactment of guiding principles in s. 718.21 of the *Criminal Code*:

> **718.21** A court that imposes a sentence on an organization shall also take into consideration the following factors:
>
> (a) any advantage realized by the organization as a result of the offence;
>
> (b) the degree of planning involved in carrying out the offence and the duration and complexity of the offence;
>
> (c) whether the organization has attempted to conceal its assets, or convert them, in order to show that it is not able to pay a fine or make restitution;

(d) the impact that the sentence would have on the economic viability of the organization and the continued employment of its employees;

(e) the cost to public authorities of the investigation and prosecution of the offence;

(f) any regulatory penalty imposed on the organization or one of its representatives in respect of the conduct that formed the basis of the offence;

(g) whether the organization was—or any of its representatives who were involved in the commission of the offence were—convicted of a similar offence or sanctioned by a regulatory body for similar conduct;

(h) any penalty imposed by the organization on a representative for their role in the commission of the offence;

(i) any restitution that the organization is ordered to make or any amount that the organization has paid to a victim of the offence; and

(j) any measures that the organization has taken to reduce the likelihood of it committing a subsequent offence.

These organization sentencing factors are not exhaustive, and only serve as a guide to add onto other applicable sentencing factors like size and wealth of the organization. Investigators can certainly come up with their own sentencing factors to suggest if there are unusual circumstances about an organization or the offences it has been convicted of committing.

Aggravating and mitigating factors for organization sentencing are mixed into s. 718.21 of the *Code*. Probably the most notable listed aggravating factor is the hiding of assets since successful hiding could significantly push down what is thought to be an appropriate fine proportionate to the wealth of an organization. It is striking just how many apparently mitigating factors are also listed in s. 718.21, since s. 718.2 does not explicitly enumerate any mitigating factors for the sentencing of individuals. Because each mitigating factor could significantly reduce the penalty to which an organization is subject, investigators should verify the truth of any claims to them. The most difficult factor to verify is probably impact on economic viability because it requires an intimate knowledge of the organization's financial affairs. Parliament appears to have mandated that a penalty must be more than just a cost of doing business, but usually less than a death sentence for an organization. Because of the lead time required, organization sentencing evidence collection and analysis must be an inherent part of the investigation.

Due to the difficulties in calculating an appropriate fine and the unavailability of imprisonment, investigators should consider creative sentencing options for organizations where possible. A number of regulatory Acts explicitly provide for creative options, like the *Canadian Environment Protection Act, 1999*, which states at s-s. 291(1):

> **291.** (1) Where an offender has been convicted of an offence under this Act, in addition to any other punishment that may be imposed under this Act, the court may, having regard to the nature of the offence and the circumstances surrounding its commission, make an order having any or all of the following effects:
>
> (a) prohibiting the offender from doing any act or engaging in any activity that may result in the continuation or repetition of the offence;
>
> (b) directing the offender to take any action that the court considers appropriate to remedy or avoid any harm to the environment that results or may result from the act or omission that constituted the offence;
>
> (c) directing the offender to prepare and implement a pollution prevention plan or an environmental emergency plan;
>
> (d) directing the offender to carry out environmental effects monitoring in the manner established by the Minister or directing the offender to pay, in the manner prescribed by the court, an amount for the purposes of environmental effects monitoring;
>
> (e) directing the offender to implement an environmental management system that meets a recognized Canadian or international standard;
>
> (f) directing the offender to have an environmental audit conducted by a person of a class and at the times specified by the court and directing the offender to remedy any deficiencies revealed during the audit;
>
> (g) directing the offender to publish, in the manner directed by the court, the facts relating to the conviction;

(h) directing the offender to notify, at the offender's own cost and in the manner directed by the court, any person aggrieved or affected by the offender's conduct of the facts relating to the conviction;

(i) directing the offender to post any bond or pay any amount of money into court that will ensure compliance with any order made under this section;

(j) directing the offender to submit to the Minister, on application by the Minister made within three years after the date of conviction, any information with respect to the offender's activities that the court considers appropriate and just in the circumstances;

(k) directing the offender to compensate the Minister, in whole or in part, for the cost of any remedial or preventive action taken by or caused to be taken on behalf of the Minister as a result of the act or omission that constituted the offence;

(l) directing the offender to perform community service, subject to any reasonable conditions that may be imposed in the order;

(m) directing that the amount of any fine or other monetary award be allocated, subject to the *Criminal Code* and any regulations that may be made under section 278, in accordance with any directions of the court that are made on the basis of the harm or risk of harm caused by the commission of the offence;

(n) directing the offender to pay, in the manner prescribed by the court, an amount for the purposes of conducting research into the ecological use and disposal of the substance in respect of which the offence was committed or research relating to the manner of carrying out environmental effects monitoring;

(o) directing the offender to pay, in the manner prescribed by the court, an amount to environmental, health or other groups to assist in their work in the community where the offence was committed;

(p) directing the offender to pay, in the manner prescribed by the court, an amount to an educational institution for scholarships for students enrolled in environmental studies; and

(q) requiring the offender to comply with any other reasonable conditions that the court considers appropriate and just in the circumstances for securing the offender's good conduct and for preventing the offender from repeating the same offence or committing other offences.

For federal Acts not explicitly setting out creative sentencing provisions, it is still possible to place an organization on probation under the *Criminal Code* using creative conditions.

Creative sentencing of organizations best upholds public confidence in the justice system, avoids seemingly random fine number picking, can directly link in victim restitution even where the victim is the Canadian public at large, and can reduce the chance of future offences. Funding research, delivering public talks, sponsoring conferences and producing publications are all examples of creative organization sentencing already imposed in Canada. If you come up with what you think would be an appropriate creative sentence, you need first to convince the prosecutor it is a good idea so the prosecutor can then convince the court and the defence. Be prepared for a series of appeals where a creative sentence is imposed by the court against the accused's wishes. The next chapter explains why in many respects a case is never really finished.

For Working with the Prosecutor at Trial

KEY POINTS

✓ Accepting that the goal is seeing that justice is done rather than securing a conviction at any cost, and learning to like surprises will help you be happy as an investigator working with a prosecutor at trial. Investigators can play key roles at all points of the trial process, including organizing witnesses and evidence for what can be a major preliminary inquiry effort, providing evidence for the prosecution on pretrial motions that frequently determine the fate of a case, and giving input during jury selection on who should be chosen.

✓ Investigators at trial can play roles of stage manager to witnesses, prop master to physical evidence, and script consultant to the prosecutor. Ideally two investigators will share these duties, one known as the inside investigator who takes notes, answers prosecutor questions and manages exhibits, and the other being the outside investigator who coordinates witnesses and conducts follow-up investigation. Ideally investigators assisting at trial will not be required witnesses.

KEY POINTS

✓ Sentencing frustrations can be largely overcome if investigators and prosecutors take charge of sentencing long before the start of the trial. Investigators can provide considerable input into the prosecution's sentencing submissions, including furnishing updates on criminal records and outstanding charges, victim impact statements, *viva voce* evidence, expert witnesses, and case sentencing precedents.

✓ According to the *Criminal Code* the six dominant objectives of sentencing are denunciation, deterrence, separation, rehabilitation, reparations, and promotion of responsibility with acknowledgement of harm. The exact sentence imposed in a case should be proportional to the gravity of the offence and the responsibility of the offender, take account of aggravating and mitigating factors, be comparable to sentences in similar cases, the combined effect of consecutive sentences cannot be unduly long or harsh, and imprisonment may only be imposed where less restrictive sanctions are inappropriate.

✓ Absolute discharges, conditional discharges, suspended sentences with probation, fines, conditional sentences of imprisonment, and imprisonment are the principal sanctions that can be imposed for an offence, but many Acts also provide latitude for creative sentences involving other sanctions that can be especially appropriate for regulatory offences or when sentencing organizations.

TRIAL EVIDENCE CHECKLIST

Accused: _____

Charges: _____

Date(s) of offence(s): _____

Lead investigator: _____

Prosecutor: _____ Defence counsel: _____

Court: _____ Judge: _____

A — EXHIBITS TO INTRODUCE

	Present in court	Marked for identification	Admitted into evidence
a. _____	❏	❏	❏
b. _____	❏	❏	❏
c. _____	❏	❏	❏
d. _____	❏	❏	❏
e. _____	❏	❏	❏
f. _____	❏	❏	❏
g. _____	❏	❏	❏
h. _____	❏	❏	❏
i. _____	❏	❏	❏

B — ADDITIONAL EXHIBITS TO OBTAIN

	Present in court	Marked for identification	Admitted into evidence
k. _____	❏	❏	❏
l. _____	❏	❏	❏
m. _____	❏	❏	❏
n. _____	❏	❏	❏

C — WITNESSES TO CALL

	Exhibits (by letter) witness will give testimony on	Subpoena served	Present in court	Called	Recalled	Potential rebutal witness
1. _____	_____	❏	❏	❏	❏	❏
2. _____	_____	❏	❏	❏	❏	❏
3. _____	_____	❏	❏	❏	❏	❏
4. _____	_____	❏	❏	❏	❏	❏
5. _____	_____	❏	❏	❏	❏	❏
6. _____	_____	❏	❏	❏	❏	❏
7. _____	_____	❏	❏	❏	❏	❏

FURTHER READING

The interpersonal relations of the trial prosecution team have not been extensively written about, nor could they be easily distilled down into fixed principles of conduct. They are foremost concerned with how people relate to each other, and bring their individual strengths and knowledge to bear through cooperation towards a common goal. Acquiring a basic understanding of criminal procedure will probably be the best way to expand your knowledge of how to work with the prosecutor at trial.

Cases

R. v. McDonnell, [1997] 1 S.C.R. 948. An appeal court cannot interfere with a sentence imposed at trial solely because it disagrees with the result of the trial judge exercising sentencing discretion.

R. v. Proulx, [2000] 1 S.C.R. 61. Trial sentencing judges have a wide discretion over the sentence to be imposed, so long as they consider and give appropriate weight to all relevant factors relating to the offence and the offender, and do not otherwise make an error in principle.

Books, Articles and Reports

N. Bala, *Youth Criminal Justice Law* (Toronto: Irwin Law, 2003). Explains the unique rules that apply at the trials of young persons.

G.S. Campbell, "Fostering a Compliance Culture through Creative Sentencing for Environmental Offences" (2004) 9 Can. Crim. L. Rev. 1.

Demographic Overview of Aboriginal Peoples in Canada and Aboriginal Offenders in Federal Corrections (Aboriginal Initiatives Branch, Correctional Services Canada,1999) [on-line: *www.csc-scc.gc.ca/text/prgrm/correctional/abissues/know/10_e.shtml*].

C. Hill et al., *McWilliams Canadian Criminal Evidence*, 4th ed., loose-leaf (Aurora, ON: Canada Law Book, 2004). A very detailed book covering all aspects of criminal evidence.

Law Reform Commission of Canada, *Studies on Sentencing* (Ottawa: Law Reform Commission of Canada, 1974). A look at alternatives to the adversarial system and the reform of punishment.

Law Reform Commission of Canada, *Working Paper No. 27 — The Jury in Criminal Trials* (Ottawa: Law Reform Commission of Canada, 1980).

A. Manson, *The Law of Sentencing* (Toronto: Irwin Law, 2001).

D.M. Paccioco, "A Voyage of Discovery: Examining the Precarious Position of Preliminary Inquiries" (2003) 48 Crim. L.Q. 151.

D. Renaud, *Speaking to Sentence: A Practical Guide* (Toronto: Thomson, 2004).

J.V. Roberts, "Victim Impact Statements and the Sentencing Process: Recent Developments and Research Findings" (2003) 47 Crim. L.Q. 365.

C. Ruby et al., *Sentencing*, 6th ed. (Toronto: LexisNexis Butterworths, 2004).

R. Salhany, *Canadian Criminal Procedure*, loose-leaf (Aurora, ON: Canada Law Book, 1993/2002).

D.M. Tanovich, D.M. Paciocco, and S. Skurka, *Jury Selection in Criminal Trials: Skills, Science and the Law* (Toronto: Irwin Law, 1997).

CHAPTER TWENTY

LOOKING AFTER POST-TRIAL PROCEDURES: WHY A CASE IS NEVER REALLY FINISHED

The function of review or, more precisely limited review and the reconciliation of disparate intermediate appellate opinions, has marked the appellate function in Canada for 140 years. In the absence of egregious error in matters of substance or practice, the trial process and its result will be maintained. The jury decides; the appellate courts review.

R. v. Robinson; R. v. Dolejs (1989),
100 A.R. 26 (C.A.) at para. 50.

In This Chapter

- Taking the long view
- Assisting with appeal preparation
- Understanding appeal procedures
- Understanding prerogative remedies
- Preserving the evidence after trial
- Updating sentencing records after conviction
- Monitoring the serving of a sentence
- Concluding thoughts

The process of investigation and prosecution is a lot like the process of climbing a mountain. In theory they can both be processes of continual progress, but sometimes there will be long periods of inactivity waiting for the legal or atmospheric weather to clear. At others times, there will be arduous courtroom or mountainside traverses where a lot of work is put into gaining not much height. Occasionally, there will be retreats down the mountain, requiring the process to be begun anew.

Figure 20-1, The Prosecution Court Process: Climbing the Mountain, illustrates the horizontal and vertical, forward and backward path that Canadian prosecutions may follow over the course of several years after charges are laid. The example shown involves an indictable offence trial in a superior court after a preliminary inquiry; a provincial court trial would eliminate the preliminary inquiry, but possibly add an additional level of summary appeal. In an increasingly litigious criminal and regulatory justice system, the trial is just one of many steps towards the ultimate conviction or acquittal of the accused. Certain aspects of a case don't even conclude after the last appeal is exhausted — trial evidence can be relevant to later proceedings as can evidence held by investigators that never made it before the trial court, sentencing records must be updated, and sentence compliance monitored.

TAKING THE LONG VIEW

It's necessary to take the long view of the process that must be followed to secure a solid conviction capable of withstanding appeal. Investigations cannot be pursued solely with the short-term goal of laying charges, and trials cannot be conducted just with the even shorter term goal of convincing the judge or jury to convict. Taking the long view means pursuing an investigation that is legally unassailable at trial, and conducting a trial that is appeal proof. Yes, the long view may make it harder to lay charges and get that initial conviction, but the long view seeks to ensure the fruits of investigation and results of trial are confirmed again and again throughout whatever circuitous path the case later follows.

The Prosecution Result Report Checklist, at the end of this chapter, provides investigators with a way to record the procedural history and ultimate outcome of that long view. Such a checklist can have particular value to investigators for purposes of accountability, statistics, offender history and sentencing precedents. It will be the place to examine every time the long view turns out to be even longer than expected because yet another legal or factual development has delayed final case resolution.

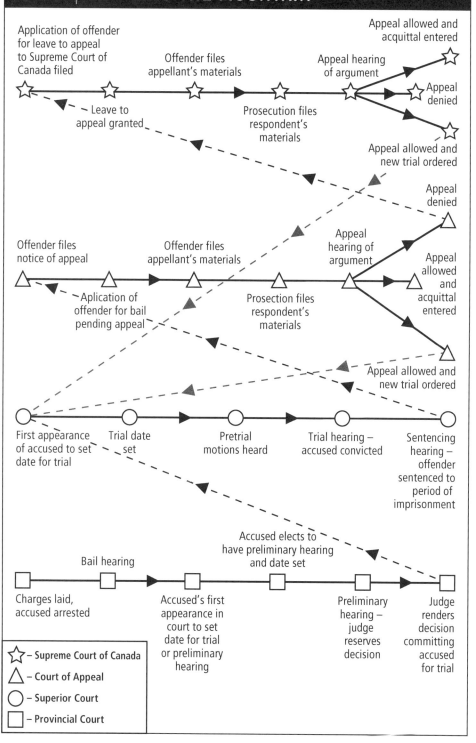

Fig 20-1

THE PROSECUTION COURT PROCESS:
CLIMBING THE MOUNTAIN

Application of offender
for leave to appeal
to Supreme Court of
Canada filed

Offender files
appellant's materials

Appeal hearing
of argument

Appeal allowed and
acquittal entered

Appeal
denied

Leave to
appeal granted

Prosecution files
respondent's
materials

Appeal allowed and
new trial ordered

Appeal
denied

Offender files
notice of appeal

Offender files
appellant's materials

Appeal
hearing of
argument

Appeal
allowed
and
acquittal
entered

Aplication of
offender for bail
pending appeal

Prosecution files
respondent's
materials

Appeal allowed and
new trial ordered

First appearance
of accused to set
date for trial

Trial date
set

Pretrial
motions heard

Trial hearing –
accused convicted

Sentencing
hearing –
offender
sentenced to
period of
imprisonment

Accused elects to
have preliminary hearing
and date set

Bail hearing

Charges laid,
accused arrested

Accused's first
appearance in
court to set
date for trial
or preliminary
hearing

Preliminary
hearing –
judge
reserves
decision

Judge
renders
decision
committing
accused
for trial

☆ – Supreme Court of Canada

△ – Court of Appeal

◯ – Superior Court

▢ – Provincial Court

ASSISTING WITH APPEAL PREPARATION

Regardless of whether there is a conviction or acquittal at trial, there will be some potential an appeal might be pursued. Sometimes a case is so serious or legally significant that there is little doubt about whether an appeal will be brought, only a question of whether it will be the defence or prosecution filing it. While trial preparation of the facts largely falls to investigators, the bulk of factual work on an appeal is usually the responsibility of the prosecutor who will be relying on transcripts and exhibits from the trial. But it can be difficult to learn solely from the cold, dry transcript what really went on at trial. Investigators who were present throughout a trial can explain the interrelationships of witness testimony, relate that testimony to the exhibits, and provide overall factual context and clarity to an otherwise legalistic appeal. Investigators could also provide the appeal prosecutor with working copies of trial exhibits if the original exhibits are difficult to access from secure court custody. Investigators who attend the argument of the appeal not only will be able to consult with prosecutors on unanticipated factual questions raised by appeal judges, but will gain a better appreciation of the long continuum of investigation and prosecution proceedings.

Investigators who continue to maintain well indexed case files, including new case information learned after trial, will be in the best position to respond to the short timelines involved in occasionally furnishing evidence for use during an appeal by way of affidavit as fresh evidence or in response to a bail pending appeal application. Investigators may also become involved in the challenging time-limited service of appeal documents, where some offenders will be difficult to track down or actively evade service. Section 678.1 of the *Criminal Code* authorizing substitutional service for indictable appeals is particularly worth knowing about:

> **678.1** Where a respondent cannot be found after reasonable efforts have been made to serve the respondent with a notice of appeal or notice of an application for leave to appeal, service of the notice of appeal or the notice of the application for leave to appeal may be effected substitutionally in the manner and within the period directed by a judge of the court of appeal.

A prosecutor will only be able to rely on s. 678.1 if an investigator can explain in an affidavit how investigators took reasonable steps to serve the respondent with the appeal notice. For Crown appeals, the cooperation of a knowledgeable prosecutor to draft the notice of appeal and a diligent investigator to serve the notice is part of the team effort needed to perfect an appeal so that a hearing date can be set.

UNDERSTANDING APPEAL PROCEDURES

Having a basic understanding of appeal procedures will help you in your job as an investigator by knowing what the options are when a trial goes bad, what timelines and costs are involved in pursuing those options, and what can be hoped to be achieved from the exercise of appeal rights. Neither an offender nor the Crown has an inherent right to appeal a conviction or acquittal, as succinctly put in *R. v. Meltzer*, [1989] 1 S.C.R. 1764 at 1773: "At common law there were no appeals. All appeals have been the creature of statute." At their most basic form, criminal and regulatory offence appeals have six features:

- they are based in legislation, so one only has to look to the *Criminal Code*, provincial or territorial Acts to figure out appeal rights and procedures;

- there are no interlocutory appeals, so a final judgment is necessary for an appeal to proceed;

- they must identify specific errors of law (or occasionally fact) made by the trial court in order to succeed;

- they proceed in an orderly fashion from lower to higher levels of court, with at most three levels of appeal being possible;

- they can result in a conviction or acquittal being overturned, and may lead to a new trial being ordered; and

- their decisions on questions of law will be binding on lower courts within the same jurisdiction.

It is the binding nature of appeal court judgments that shapes the future of investigation law throughout Canada

Just as investigators cannot allocate resources to investigate every offence believed to have taken place, prosecutors do not have the resources to pursue every appeal where a trial judge appears to have made an error that resulted in the acquittal of an accused. The public interest as well as prospects for success govern pursuit of appeals, just as they do the pursuit of prosecutions in the first place. An appeal may not be in the public interest if there were serious factual deficiencies at trial, if the offence being tried was minor in nature, or there is no compelling point of law to resolve before an appeal court.

Although appeal procedures have been modernized and rights expanded over the years, the basic structure establishing three classes of appeals — two summary and one indictable — has not changed dramatically.

Sections 674-688 and ss. 812-839 of the *Criminal Code* now authorize indictable and summary conviction appeals respectively. Each province and territory has the authority to make its own court rules concerning appeal procedures not already covered by the *Code*. Many summary and indictable appeal procedures are quite similar, but there are notable differences when it comes to court appealed to, grounds for appeal, and available remedies. Prosecutors have the final say on whether and how to proceed with an appeal, but investigators can especially contribute to the decision-making process by explaining if the facts of the case were misconstrued by the trial judge, and whether investigators believe pursuit of an appeal is in the public interest.

1. The Mostly Single Judge Summary Offence Appeal

For summary conviction offence appeals under the *Criminal Code* the appellant, be it the Crown or offender, can choose between two different tracks of procedure. The track chosen dictates the appeal grounds that may be pursued, the remedies the court can grant, and in some provinces controls whether the appeal is heard by a single superior court judge or three judges of the court of appeal. In helping prosecutors choose between the tracks, investigators can suggest whether errors of fact should be appealed, continuation of a lengthy trial or the ordering of an entirely new trial is preferable, and if this is the kind of precedent-setting appeal that will likely zoom right up to the highest courts so that skipping an appeal stage would be highly advantageous.

The most common choice for summary appeals is proceeding by way of s. 813 of the *Code* that provides the widest scope for grounds including errors of law, fact, and mixed law and fact, but leads to narrower appeal remedies mostly limited to dismissing an appeal, ordering a new trial, entering an acquittal or making a finding of guilt. Section 813 appeals proceed at a slower pace because they generally are heard by a single judge of the local superior court, and can be followed by another appeal to the court of appeal. A less common but sometimes more expeditious summary conviction appeal route is under s. 830 of the *Code,* offering narrower grounds of appeal restricted to errors of law and jurisdiction, but broader remedies including unlimited types of modification of a lower court's judgment or a continuation of the trial with benefit of an advisory opinion. In some jurisdictions local rules of practice enable s. 830 appeals to proceed directly to a three judge panel of the court of appeal that could cut a year off the time required to exhaust the appeal process and considerably reduce costs.

2. The Three Judge Indictable Offence Appeal

The main route for an indictable appeal is directly to the provincial or territorial court of appeal pursuant to ss. 675-676 of the *Criminal Code*. Indictable appeals are similar to s. 813 summary appeals in terms of what may be appealed, but an offender has broader grounds of appeal available under s. 675 (law, mixed law and fact, fact alone or any other "sufficient ground of appeal") compared to the prosecution who under s. 676 may only appeal what are effectively errors of law.

Section 686 of the *Code* gives the court hearing an indictable appeal its options for how to dispose of the appeal. It may be allowed where:

- the verdict was unreasonable or cannot be supported by the evidence;

- the trial judge made an error of law, unless there was no substantial wrong or the appellant suffered no prejudice from a procedural irregularity; or

- there was a miscarriage of justice.

Depending on the reason for allowing the appeal, and whether it is the accused or prosecution who initiated the appeal, the appeal court has power to:

- quash the verdict and enter an acquittal;

- quash the verdict, enter a conviction and impose sentence;

- order a new trial; or

- impose the correct sentence, or remit the case back to the trial court for sentencing.

3. The Nine Judge Supreme Court of Canada Appeal

Even after a trial decision has wound its way through one and possibly two stages of appeal to a provincial or territorial court of appeal, the appeal process is still not over. A further appeal can be attempted to the Supreme Court of Canada, but will usually require "leave to appeal." Sections 691 and 693 of the *Criminal Code* set out respective defence and prosecution criminal appeal rights to the Supreme Court of Canada, including "on any question of law on which a judge of the court of appeal dissents" and may appeal with leave on any other question of law. Only about 10% of cases seeking leave to appeal from the Supreme Court of Canada receive it.

The Supreme Court of Canada has a busier docket of cases than any of the United States Supreme Court, the United Kingdom's House of Lords and Privy Council, or the Australian High Court. Over 600 applications for leave to appeal are lodged with the Supreme Court of Canada every year, the court hears approximately 60 appeals as a result of those leave applications and additionally hears a little under 20 appeals per year as of right. This makes for an average of one case every 4 1/2 days, where most or all of the nine judges have to digest voluminous documentary materials and hear copious oral arguments. Several of the judges may write separate opinions in a case, and French and English translations of judgments must be checked.

a. *Assisting with Supreme Court of Canada Grounds for Leave to Appeal*

Leave to appeal will effectively only be granted for matters of national importance because of the way s. 43 of the *Supreme Court Act*, R.S.C. 1985, c. S-26, is interpreted:

> **43.** (1) . . . an application to the Supreme Court for leave to appeal shall be made to the Court in writing and the Court shall
>
> > (a) grant the application if it is clear from the written material that it does not warrant an oral hearing and that any question involved is, by reason of its public importance or the importance of any issue of law or any issue of mixed law and fact involved in the question, one that ought to be decided by the Supreme Court or is, for any other reason, of such a nature or significance as to warrant decision by it;

Investigators can contribute to leave to appeal applications or responses by thinking about whether the points of law raised truly are of national importance. There are some key questions you can ask yourself.

- Is the crime at issue prevalent throughout Canada?

- Is the legal interpretation of that crime or methods used to investigate it in question around the county?

- Will resolution of the legal questions aid the future administration of the law across Canada?

By positively answering these questions, investigators and prosecutors will be on their way to a well-founded leave to appeal application. By coming up with negative answers, a basis will be established to rebut a defence application.

b. Attending Supreme Court of Canada Hearings

Because of the ability of Attorneys General and other persons to intervene in support or opposition to appeals heard by the Supreme Court of Canada, at times dozens of lawyers will be simultaneously before the court on a single case, all putting in their two cents worth concerning how a case should be decided. The diversity of opinion possibly presented in a single case, both by the lawyers and nine justices, makes Supreme Court of Canada hearings a great show where a lot can be learned about Canada's judicial process. While the regimented nature of the short argument (one hour for parties and only 15 minutes for intervenors) means investigator assistance is generally not required during Supreme Court of Canada hearings, investigators may learn a lot from attending a hearing. Although the quality of Supreme Court of Canada oral argument is arguably not as important as the quality of written pleadings, particularly poor or good oral argument could swing the opinions of one or two crucial justices making the hearing an important event. Be sure to arrive early to get a seat in the tiny gallery whose reduced size at the back of the courtroom accommodates the space all those lawyers need up front.

4. Bail Pending Appeal Applications

Many offenders will abandon their appeals if they do not get bail because a sentence may have been served by the time a court hears the appeal, making the availability of bail pending appeal an important aspect of upholding public confidence in the justice system as noted in *R. v. Farinacci* (1993), 67 O.A.C. 197 at paras. 42-43:

> Public confidence in the administration of justice requires that judgments be enforced. The public interest may require that a person convicted of a very serious offence, particularly a repeat offender who is advancing grounds of appeal that are arguable but weak, be denied bail. In such a case, the grounds favouring enforceability need not yield to the grounds favouring reviewability.

> On the other hand, public confidence in the administration of justice requires that judgments be reviewed and that errors, if any, be

corrected. This is particularly so in the criminal field where liberty is at stake. Public confidence would be shaken, in my view, if a youthful first offender, sentenced to a few months' imprisonment for a property offence, was compelled to serve his or her entire sentence before having an opportunity to challenge the conviction on appeal. Assuming that the requirements of s. 679(3)(a) and (b) of the *Criminal Code* are met, entitlement to bail is strongest when denial of bail would render the appeal nugatory, for all practical purposes.

Because the presumption of innocence no longer applies after conviction, the prosecution is quite justified in taking a stronger line in opposing bail pending appeal than in opposing bail pending trial.

Sub-section 679(3) of the *Criminal Code* specifies the conditions that must be met for bail pending appeal to be granted:

> **679.** (3) . . .the judge of the court of appeal may order that the appellant be released pending the determination of his appeal if the appellant establishes that
>
> (a) the appeal or application for leave to appeal is not frivolous;
>
> (b) he will surrender himself into custody in accordance with the terms of the order; and
>
> (c) his detention is not necessary in the public interest.

The frivolous appeal factor exists because granting bail pending appeal for some offenders will only be putting off an inevitable custodial sentence. If the appeal is only against sentence, an applicant must meet the higher test of the appeal having sufficient merit that undue hardship would be caused by detention pending appeal. Investigators can help address the surrender and public interest questions by providing information, possibly through affidavit, on the appellant's compliance with bail conditions during the trial period, whether new outstanding charges have arisen, or if changed personal circumstances make release more risky.

Investigator Involvement in Appeals

Q: If appeals are mainly arguments about the law and not about the facts, why must I be involved in them?

A: The appeal phase is in many respects as equally an important part of the criminal and regulatory judicial system as the trial phase. It is in the appeal

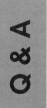

UNDERSTANDING PREROGATIVE REMEDIES

Even if there is no statutory appeal route, all is not lost for either an accused or the prosecution. The results of preliminary inquiries, the validity of search warrants, and the sufficiency of charging informations could have no appeal route if not part of a final judgment of conviction, acquittal, or finding of criminal responsibility based on mental state, but might be reviewed through prerogative remedies that are a throwback to times past when citizens directly sought the intervention of the sovereign to right the wrongs of lower officials. They are derived from the common law, not the *Criminal Code*, but are still capable of undoing, compelling or stopping an official action or securing release from state custody.

Investigators should know about prerogative remedies because their invocation can result in the overturning of investigative actions and considerably delay the start of trial. Diligent preparation of all court documents combined with patience is required for investigations to survive prerogative remedy challenges. Investigators need not, however, view these time honoured legal instruments solely in a negative way since they are equally available to the prosecution and defence. Prerogative remedies may only be granted by superior courts against inferior courts, and so are generally used against decisions of provincial court judges or justices. Prerogative remedy evolution over centuries of legal practice has led to them now only being used to fill gaps in today's laws; they are not modern and dynamic instruments capable of righting all wrongs.

There are four types of prerogative remedy still in common use relevant to the investigation and prosecution process, three of whose Latin names reveal their ancient roots: *certiorari, mandamus*, prohibition, and *habeas corpus. Taku River First Nation v. British Columbia (Project Assessment Director)*, (2002) 163 B.C.A.C. 164; 2002 BCCA 59 at para. 18, explained (in a non-prosecution context) the basis for those remedies:

the substantive law upon which the prerogative writs of *certiorari*, *mandamus*, and prohibition rested. . . . was founded upon a simple proposition: It is the duty of the Queen's judges to ensure that all those upon whom, by enactment of the Legislature . . ., powers of decision have been conferred, remain within the powers thus conferred. In other words, those persons . . . upon whom powers have been conferred, must be prevented by orders in the nature of *certiorari* and prohibition from arrogating to themselves powers which were not conferred and required by orders in the nature of *mandamus* to exercise their powers as the Legislature intended.

For any of these remedies to take effect, an error of jurisdiction must be established, not just an error of law or fact necessary in a normal appeal.

1. Quashing Decisions through *Certiorari*

Certiorari is a "quashing" remedy, meaning to disallow. A successful *certiorari* application requires convincing a superior court that an inferior official exceeded her jurisdiction by acting without a legal basis. Investigators must be on guard against introducing such serious drafting deficiencies into documents to be approved by a court or failing to provide a sufficient factual foundation to support the issuance of those documents or committal at a preliminary inquiry that court actions could later be quashed through *certiorari*. For example, care is needed in drafting charging informations as described in *R. v. Webster*, [1993] 1 S.C.R. 3 at 10-11:

> It may well be that in those rare circumstances . . . in which the charge is an absolute nullity, *certiorari* may be available. The existence of some charge of an offence known to the law, albeit very imperfectly described, is the basis of the judge's jurisdiction. There may be rare circumstances in which an information is so faulty that it fails to meet this basic requirement. There may also arise situations in which having failed to quash a defective information, a Provincial Court Judge finds himself or herself without jurisdiction. For example, if a charge does not indicate where the offence occurred and the Provincial Court Judge refused to quash or order particulars his or her decision would not be open to review through certiorari. However, if as the result of evidence adduced it is revealed that the alleged offence took place outside the court's jurisdiction, certiorari would then be available if the judge persisted in continuing exercising a jurisdiction he or she did not have.

Early investigator-prosecutor contact can shore up warrant, charging information and preliminary inquiry defences against *certiorari* attack.

2. Compelling Action through *Mandamus*

Instead of undoing what a lower official has done, the prerogative remedy of *mandamus* forces an official to perform a required duty. While *certiorari* is a remedy mostly used by the defence, *mandamus* can prove quite useful to the prosecution as well who could seek to compel a judge to make a decision like committing an accused for trial. *Mandamus* can even be used against a judge who denies he has jurisdiction to hear a prosecution, as was done in *R. v. W.(D.A.)*, [1991] 1 S.C.R. 291 at 293-94:

> The appellant . . . had been charged with offences under the *Criminal Code* and had appeared before a judge of the Provincial Magistrate's Court who was sitting as a judge of the Youth Court. Randall Prov. Ct. J. gave a ruling declining jurisdiction. By originating notice . . . the Attorney General of Nova Scotia, commenced an application to the Supreme Court of Nova Scotia in which he argued for the constitutionality of the *Young Offenders Act*, and requested an order in the nature of a mandamus. Glube C.J.T.D. found that Judge Randall had jurisdiction and authority to sit as a Youth Court Judge and issued the mandamus.

Investigator actions are unlikely to be subject to a *mandamus* application, but it remains a powerful remedy that investigators need to know about.

3. Stopping Action through Prohibition

The prerogative remedy of prohibition simply stops an action, and is usually used in the prosecution context to prevent a particular judge from hearing a case, perhaps because of alleged bias. Depending on the local rules of court, the mere filing of a prohibition application may suspend the jurisdiction of the lower court while the application is being dealt with in a higher court. Prohibition applications can therefore lead to extensive preliminary hearing and trial delays as occurred in *R. v. Tucker*, (1992) 56 O.A.C. 36 at para. 24:

> these appeals are a casebook example of how frivolous applications for prerogative remedies can be employed successfully as a vehicle for delay. The appellants have contrived to cast their applications for the prerogative relief of prohibition and *mandamus* to include totally inappropriate applications to quash. The applications to quash are in order to give the appearance of compliance with rule 4 of the Rules Respecting Criminal Proceedings so that the appellants can claim that service of the notices of the various

applications will have the effect of suspending the proceedings in the lower courts . . . In this way, the appellants have succeeded over a protracted period of time in preventing their cases from being tried on the merits in any of the lower courts.

All investigators can do when highly technical procedural defences are deployed is be patient, assist prosecutors where necessary, and preserve the evidence in anticipation of an eventual trial on the merits of the case.

4. Being Freed from Imprisonment through *Habeas Corpus*

Habeas corpus, meaning literally "you have the body," is probably the only prerogative remedy of which most Canadians have heard. The form of this remedy that is most useful in criminal proceedings is *habeas corpus ad subjiciendum* that compels a person detaining another to produce that person. *Idziak v. Canada (Minister of Justice)*, [1992] 3 S.C.R. 631 at 645-646, described this remedy's historic roots:

> The writ of *habeas corpus* is steeped in history and was one of the earliest means employed by free subjects to guarantee their liberty. It has for centuries been a weapon in the war against the tyranny of wrongful imprisonment. . . . The rules dealing with the historic writ of *habeas corpus* should always be given a generous and flexible interpretation.

The writ has now mostly fallen into disuse because of access to the s. 9 *Charter* protection against arbitrary detention or imprisonment, and the s-s. 11(e) *Charter* guarantee "not to be denied reasonable bail without just cause," coupled with the extensive bail provisions of the *Criminal Code*, which collectively provide for a right and effective procedure to secure release. But *habeas corpus* is still useful to accused who have not been successful in securing release through other means, and could be invoked against investigators wishing to detain a person without charge.

PRESERVING THE EVIDENCE AFTER TRIAL

The sometimes inevitable result of an appeal is the ordering of a new trial. Investigators must preserve all evidence, including records of continuity chains, for each piece of evidence still in their hands at the end of a trial. Just because evidence was not filed as an exhibit at the first trial does not mean it cannot be of key importance at a subsequent trial. All physical evidence, recordings and notes are included in the requirement to preserve evidence until the last appeal in a case is exhausted. A series of appeals could delay the start of a new trial until many years down the road.

Whose Job Is It to Preserve Evidence?

Q & A

Q: Don't the courts simply hang onto the evidence when a case is under appeal?

A: Often only a small portion of the available evidence is filed at trial as exhibits, with the rest remaining in the hands of investigators. Things like original investigator notebooks are almost never filed in court, but still need to be preserved for future trials. The likelihood of evidence going astray is directly proportional to the time that passes. This law of disappearing evidence holds true for people's recollections as well. Carefully categorizing evidence and placing it in a secure storage area is vital to its continued existence. It is worth considering preserving significant oral testimony for future trials through taking video statements under oath in case witnesses die or become uncooperative.

UPDATING SENTENCING RECORDS AFTER CONVICTION

The quality of prosecutor sentencing submissions and the resulting sentences imposed by trial courts depends on sentencing precedents and accurate records of prior convictions. While some precedents will exist in legal research databases, the vast majority of sentencing decisions are rendered as oral judgments where the transcript is the only record, thus investigator-maintained conviction and sentencing databases may be the primary source of precedent information for prosecutors. For individual offenders, records of past convictions are of immeasurable aid to achieving adequate future sentences, particularly where enhanced statutory penalties become available by reason of prior conviction. Investigators dealing with serious regulatory offences in areas like the environment, occupational health and safety, and taxation must be especially vigilant in maintaining their own agencies' sentencing records because of the lack of reported sentencing case law, lower frequency of prosecuting these types of offences leading to courts not always having a good sense about appropriate sentencing ranges, and need to track prior convictions that don't show up in the Canadian Police Information Centre (CPIC) databases. Be it CPIC or a local database, the more case results fed into the system, and the more detailed and correct the information provided to that system, the more accurate and persuasive will be the output when it comes time to argue for a significant sentence in a future prosecution.

The Role of CPIC

Q & A

Q: Doesn't the Canadian Police Information Centre (CPIC) look after all sentencing records?

A: Minor or regulatory offences sometimes don't get sent to CPIC for input. Even when offences are entered, the all important detailed background facts of a case that will identify its similarities to an offence now before the courts are not present, nor are the details of creative sentencing provisions. Just because someone got five years imprisonment on a first drug trafficking offence doesn't make that an appropriate sentence in all circumstances. Not only is knowing the type of drug vital, so is knowing its weight. There is a big difference between trafficking in an ounce of marihuana and trafficking in ten kilos of heroin, but both may appear on CPIC as convictions for trafficking in a narcotic contrary to s-s. 5(1) of the *CDSA*. Thus supplementary locally-maintained sentencing records are useful.

MONITORING THE SERVING OF A SENTENCE

There is no quicker way to undermine sentencing values and bring the administration of justice into disrepute than to let sentences be breached with impunity. Lack of sentence monitoring can flow both from a lack of monitoring resources and an erroneous assumption that someone else is keeping an eye on the sentence. Custodial penalties served in closed custody are the easiest though most expensive to monitor. Monetary penalties aren't particularly difficult to track, and are increasingly being pursued through various fine collection initiatives. Conditional sentences, sentences involving community service and any sentence leading to probation are more difficult to monitor because they often require field resources to verify compliance. While the courts and probation offices clearly have a role to play in sentence monitoring, in rural or remote areas investigators may be the only ones available to monitor and enforce sentence compliance. Recourse for non-compliance that could be sought in conjunction with a prosecutor include laying charges for breach of probation, or seeking to hold a conditional sentence breach or fine payment default hearing. I recognize investigators face resource challenges, but sentence compliance is the cornerstone of any justice theory advocating consequences following responsibility.

Close Sentence Monitoring

Q & A

Q: There is no way I could possibly monitor the sentences of all the people I've charged who have subsequently been convicted of offences. How is close sentence monitoring possible?

A: Close monitoring is a team effort that includes the courts, probation workers, community agencies, prosecutors and investigators. Computerization makes automatic flagging systems possible for fine due dates, or the expiry of sentence conditions. For fine recovery, while sometimes the courts initiate action for non-payment, prosecution services are increasingly pursuing offenders with civil judgment enforcement proceedings. Sentence monitoring by investigators could be blended into daily enforcement duties if those being monitored are also those being investigated for new offences or live in the area investigators patrol.

CONCLUDING THOUGHTS

All of this book's contents were guided by, and flow back to, the two themes of demystification of the law and early investigator-prosecutor contact. I firmly believe if investigators follow those two themes in the course of their daily work, they will be able to take decisive action and recognize when a brief lull before action to get legal advice will pay great dividends for case success. If you embrace a close reading of the law governing your powers and the offences you are responsible for, pay attention to detail in drafting documents for judicial approval, treat all those you contact with the greatest of respect for their rights, recognize those rights can vary according to the context of contact, keep excellent records of your actions and the evidence you collect, and take a team approach to cooperating with prosecutors, then you will maximize the chances of successful investigations leading to successful prosecutions that hold up on appeal.

You can easily incorporate the principles set out in this book into your daily investigative practices because the principles aren't weighed down by ever changing cases, although you do have to keep an eye out for evolving areas of law. The law of investigations and prosecutions is a living, breathing entity that is fed by the facts of your investigations. Good facts make good law. Ethical investigative actions taken in good faith and with full knowledge of the legal landscape will be supported by the judges who later review your actions, even if a new gloss is ultimately put on the law. Unethical investigative actions, taken in bad faith, or in ignorance of the law, will lead to the creation of bad law, with judges being keen to shut down similar future action — be it in the public interest or not — as the ends generally cannot justify the means.

Embracing demystification of the law and early investigator-prosecutor contact will lead to the creation of good law that strikes an appropriate balance between protecting the constitutionally entrenched rights of individuals and organizations being investigated, and the public from the scourge of unlawful activities that pose a threat to the physical and mental well-being of all Canadians. Investigators who appropriately position themselves within the legal landscape, after those who legislate laws and those who live under the rule of those laws, but before those who prosecute violations of the law and those who adjudicate upon the merits of alleged violations, will be most comfortable in their roles as key parts of a legal continuum, neither legally inferior nor superior to anyone else in that continuum, but occupying a distinct place. From that place, the meaning of those who legislated can be appropriately interpreted, the public can be protected, and the prosecutors and judges can be informed of the facts where legal compliance is lacking. Most importantly of all, sound investigations leading to viable prosecutions will ensure that justice is done.

On Post-Trial Procedures

KEY POINTS

✓ Taking the long view means pursuing an investigation that is legally unassailable at trial, and conducting a trial that is appeal proof. After the trial, investigators can provide appeal prosecutors with context and clarity in interpreting from the transcript what really went on at trial, discuss whether an appeal is in the public interest, serve crucial appeal documents, and furnish evidence in bail pending appeal hearings or as fresh evidence in an appeal itself.

✓ There are no inherent rights to bring appeals in the criminal courts. The *Criminal Code* plus local appeal rules must be closely examined to determine if a case can be appealed, on what basis the appeal could proceed, and to what court the appeal would proceed. Appeals involving criminal or regulatory offences will usually proceed to a single judge summary conviction appeal court, a three judge court of appeal, or on rare occasions up to a nine judge Supreme Court of Canada. The results of a bail pending appeal application can be determinative of whether the underlying appeal will proceed if a sentence will have been mostly served by the time the appeal is heard on its merits.

KEY POINTS

✓ Even a legal result in a criminal or regulatory investigation or prosecution, for which there is no statutory appeal route, may be able to be challenged by way of prerogative remedy seeking relief in a superior court from the decision of an inferior court.

✓ Regardless of the type of ongoing proceedings, investigators must preserve all evidence including records of continuity chains for each piece of evidence still in their hands until the last appeal in a case is exhausted.

✓ Updating and maintaining sentencing record databases, together with monitoring and enforcing sentence compliance, is everybody's business, as appropriate sentencing is a cornerstone of any criminal justice theory that advocates consequences following responsibility, and is crucial to maintaining public confidence in the administration of justice.

Accused: _____

Charges: _____

Dates of offences: _____

Lead investigator: _____

Prosecutor: _____ Defence counsel: _____

Level, place and name of court: _____

Judge: _____

Dates of court hearings: _____

❑ Preliminary Inquiry held

A   TRIAL EVIDENCE

Witnesses called by prosecution: _____

_____

_____

_____

Witnesses called by defence: _____

_____

_____

Exhibits introduced by prosecution: _____

_____

_____

_____

Exhibits introduced by defence: _____

_____

_____

B   LEGAL ARGUMENT AND JUDGMENT

Prosecution motions: _____ Granted ❑

_____ ❑

_____ ❑

Defence motions: _____ Granted ❑

_____ ❑

_____ ❑

Verdict: _____

Summary of reasons for judgment: _____

_____

❏ Written reasons given

    ❏ Copy of reasons obtained

❏ Transcript ordered

    ❏ Transcript preparation finished

    ❏ Copy of transcript obtained

C   **SENTENCING**

❏ Absolute Discharge   ❏ Conditional Discharge   ❏ Suspended Sentence

                                                ❏ Probation

❏ Fine   ❏ Imprisonment   ❏ Creative Sentence

                      ❏ To be served in community   Conditions

Sentence details: _____

_____

❏ Sentence complied with

D   **APPEAL**

❏ Appeal filed by prosecution   ❏ Appeal filed by defence

❏ Sentence appeal only

Court appealed to: _____

Appeal grounds summary: _____

_____

❏ Appeal allowed

    ❏ New trial ordered

    ❏ Acquittal entered

    ❏ Sentence varied

    ❏ Conviction entered

❏ Appeal rejected

Summary of reasons for judgment: _____

_____

❏ Further appeal filed to   ❏ Court of Appeal

                       ❏ Supreme Court of Canada

❏ Last appeal or time to file appeal exhausted on: _____

FURTHER READING

Books

E.G. Ewaschuk, *Criminal Pleadings and Practice in Canada*, 2nd ed., loose-leaf (Aurora, ON: Canada Law Book, 2003). See especially Chapters 23 ("Indictable Appeal from Conviction or Acquittal"), 24 ("Summary Conviction Appeals") and 25 ("Appeals Against Sentence").

B.J. Gover & V.V. Ramraj, *The Criminal Lawyers' Guide to Extraordinary Remedies* (Aurora, ON: Canada Law Book, 2000).

G. Letourneau, *The Prerogative Writs in Canadian Criminal Law and Procedure* (Toronto: Butterworths, 1976).

G.D. McKinnon, *The Criminal Lawyer's Guide to Appellate Court Practice* (Aurora, ON: Canada Law Book, 1997).

J. Sopinka and M.A. Gelowitz, *The Conduct of an Appeal*, 2nd ed. (Toronto: Butterworths, 2000).

INDEX